INSIDERS' GUIDE® TO

CHARLOTTE

HELP US KEEP THIS GUIDE UP-TO-DATE

We would love to hear from you concerning your experiences with this guide and how you feel it could be improved and kept up-to-date. Please send your comments and suggestions to:

editorial@GlobePequot.com

Thanks for your input, and happy travels!

INSIDERS' GUIDE® TO

CHARLOTTE

ELEVENTH EDITION

CRAIG DISTL

INSIDERS' GUIDE

GUILFORD, CONNECTICUT
AN IMPRINT OF GLOBE PEQUOT PRESS

All the information in this guidebook is subject to change. We recommend that you call ahead to obtain current information before traveling.

To buy books in quantity for corporate use
or incentives, call **(800) 962–0973**
or e-mail **premiums@GlobePequot.com**.

INSIDERS' GUIDE ®

Editor: Amy Lyons
Project Editor: Lynn Zelem
Text Design: Sheryl Kober
Maps: XNR Productions, Inc. © Morris Book Publishing, LLC

ISSN 1523-8334
ISBN 978-0-7627-5312-3

Printed in the United States of America
10 9 8 7 6 5 4 3 2 1

This book is dedicated to my parents—Joseph and Marian Distl—who blessed me with the writing gene, and to my high school English teachers—Alice Lawson, Beverly Russell, Betty Bates, and Tom Orr—who guided me in the "write" direction.

CONTENTS

Directory of Maps

ABOUT THE AUTHOR

Writer and publicist **Craig Distl** is a native of North Carolina, graduate of UNC Charlotte, and a long-time Charlottean. He dabbled in the hospitality industry during college—first on the log ride at Carowinds theme park and later as a bellman at a four-star hotel. His eclectic journalism career includes stints at *The Charlotte Observer, Southern Jewelry News,* and Jefferson-Pilot Communications. He's freelanced for *Charlotte Magazine, Southern Sports Journal,* and *Golfweek,* and is a member of the Society of American Travel Writers. His writing has received awards from such organizations as the North Carolina Press Association. Craig loves the Queen City for its can-do attitude and its emergence as the crown jewel of the New South. His reply to those who say Charlotte has turned its back on a rich history? "Nonsense. You just have to know where to look."

ACKNOWLEDGMENTS

A guide book with such detailed information requires the assistance of many folks. The following individuals were very generous in donating their time to provide the most updated information possible. They represent the best and brightest of a great region, and I sincerely appreciate their contributions: Chelsea Cooley Altman, Michael Applegate, Libba Barrineau, Jennifer Beasley, Bobby Black, Kevin Brafford, Gil Capps, Teresa Cody, Pam Davis, Susan Dosier, Bruce and Jill Hensley, Laura Hill, Pete Hovanec, Elizabeth Isenhour, Walt Israel, Scott Kilby, John Lineberger, Pat McCrory, Kimberly Meesters, Gary McCullough, Jim Morrill, David Newton, Mike Nixon, Sara Pitzer, Boyd Safrit, Shawna Shane, Jody Sullivan, Barbara Mason Van, Ben Vernon, and Richard Walker.

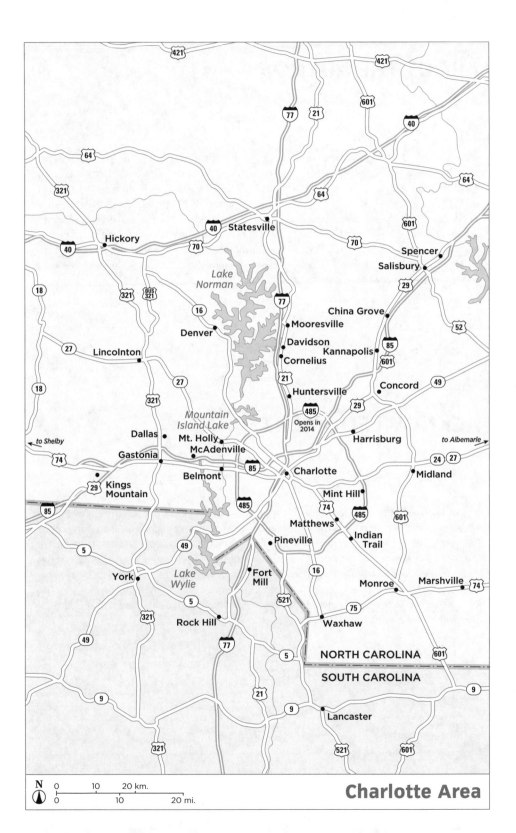

Charlotte Area

N

0   10   20 km.
0   10   20 mi.

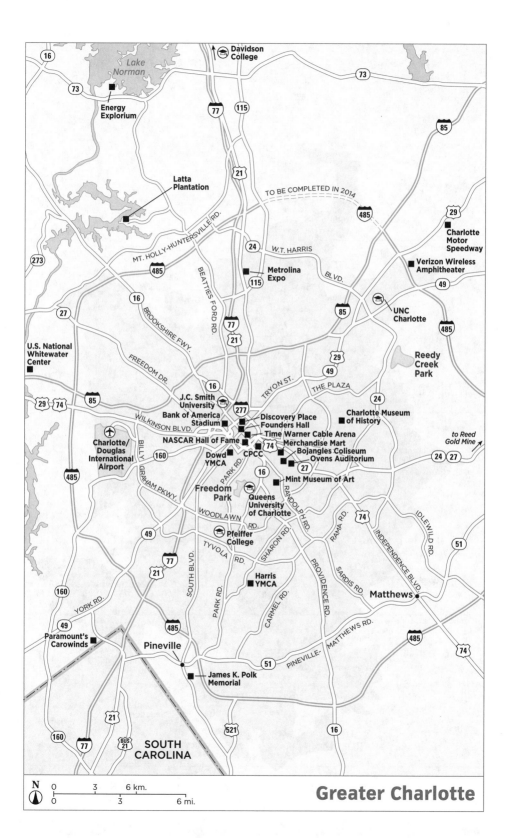

Greater Charlotte

16

73
Lake Norman

73

Davidson College

■ Energy Explorium

77 115

85

21

Latta Plantation ■

TO BE COMPLETED IN 2014

485

29

273

MT. HOLLY-HUNTERSVILLE RD.

24 W.T. HARRIS

■ Charlotte Motor Speedway

■ Verizon Wireless Amphitheater

485

■ Metrolina Expo

BLVD.

49

16

115

27

BROOKSHIRE FWY.

BEATTIES FORD RD.

77

85

🎓 UNC Charlotte

U.S. National Whitewater Center ■

FREEDOM DR.

21

29

49

Reedy Creek Park

29 74

85

16

TRYON ST.

THE PLAZA

24

to Reed Gold Mine

🎓 J.C. Smith University

277

Discovery Place
Founders Hall

■ Charlotte Museum of History

✈ Charlotte/ Douglas International Airport

WILKINSON BLVD.

Bank of America Stadium ■

Time Warner Cable Arena

24 27

NASCAR Hall of Fame ■

74 Merchandise Mart
Bojangles Coliseum

160

Dowd YMCA

CPCC

Ovens Auditorium

27

BILLY GRAHAM PKWY.

PARK RD.

16

■ Mint Museum of Art

485

🏛 Freedom Park

RANDOLPH RD.

🎓 Queens University of Charlotte

WOODLAWN RD.

RAMA RD.

74

IDLEWILD RD.

51

49

🎓 Pfeiffer College

TYVOLA RD.

SHARON RD.

PROVIDENCE RD.

77

21

SOUTH BLVD.

PARK RD.

CARMEL RD.

Harris ■ YMCA

SARDIS RD.

INDEPENDENCE BLVD.

Matthews ●

160

YORK RD.

49

■ Paramount's Carowinds

485

Pineville ●

51

PINEVILLE- MATTHEWS RD.

485

74

521

■ James K. Polk Memorial

16

21

160 77 BUS 21

SOUTH CAROLINA

N

0   3   6 km.
0   3   6 mi.

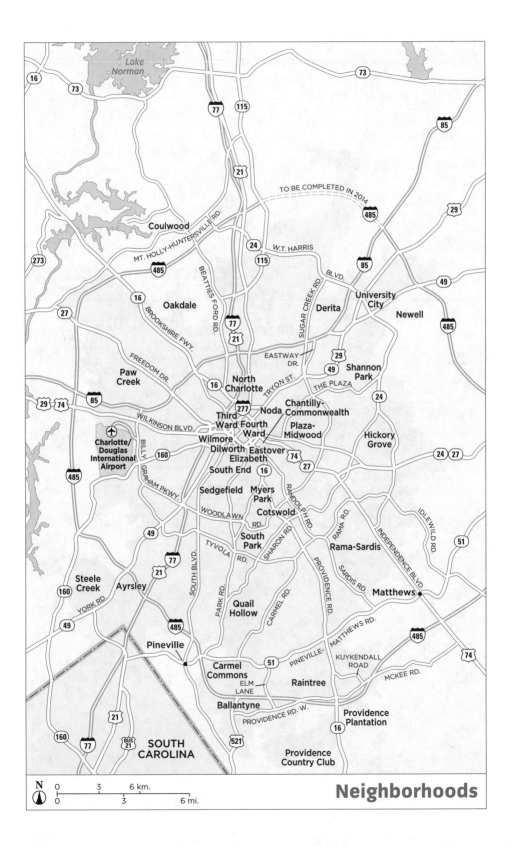

Lake Norman

16
73

73

77
115

85

21

TO BE COMPLETED IN 2014
485

29

273

Coulwood

MT. HOLLY-HUNTERSVILLE RD.

24
115

W.T. HARRIS

85

16

485

BEATTIES FORD RD.

SUGAR CREEK RD.

BLVD.

University City

49

27

Oakdale

BROOKSHIRE FWY.

77
21

Derita

Newell

485

FREEDOM DR.

EASTWAY DR.

29
49

Shannon Park

24

Paw Creek

North Charlotte

TRYON ST.

THE PLAZA

29 74
85

WILKINSON BLVD.

16

277

Noda

Chantilly-Commonwealth

Hickory Grove

Third Ward
Fourth Ward

Plaza-Midwood

24 27

Charlotte/ Douglas International Airport

BILLY GRAHAM PKWY.

160

Wilmore
Dilworth
Elizabeth

Eastover

74

27

South End

16

51

Sedgefield

Myers Park

RANDOLPH RD.

485

WOODLAWN RD.

Cotswold

RAMA RD.

49

South Park

SHARON RD.

Rama-Sardis

IDLEWILD RD.

77
21

TYVOLA RD.

SOUTH BLVD.

PROVIDENCE RD.

SARDIS RD.

INDEPENDENCE BLVD.

Matthews

51

Steele Creek

160

Ayrsley

YORK RD.

PARK RD.

Quail Hollow

CARMEL RD.

485

74

49

485

Pineville

Carmel Commons

51

PINEVILLE-

MATTHEWS RD.

KUYKENDALL ROAD

MCKEE RD.

ELM LANE

Raintree

160

21

BUS 21

SOUTH CAROLINA

77

Ballantyne

521

PROVIDENCE RD. W.

16

Providence Plantation

Providence Country Club

N

0   3   6 km.
0   3   6 mi.

Neighborhoods

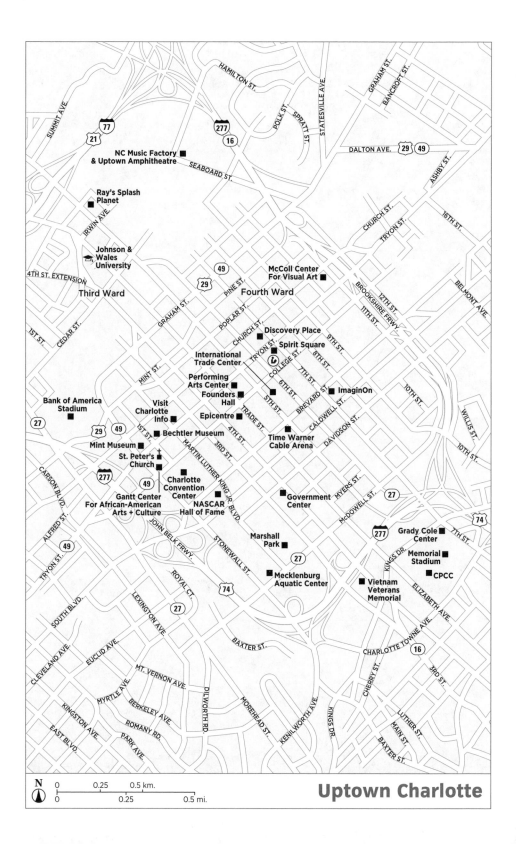

HAMILTON ST.

STATESVILLE AVE.

GRAHAM ST.

BANCROFT ST.

POLK ST.

SPRATT ST.

77

277

21

16

SUMMIT AVE.

DALTON AVE.   29   49

ASHBY ST.

NC Music Factory
& Uptown Amphitheatre ■

SEABOARD ST.

16TH ST.

Ray's Splash
Planet ■

CHURCH ST.

IRWIN AVE.

TRYON ST.

Johnson &
Wales
University

McColl Center
For Visual Art ■

BELMONT AVE.

12TH ST.

11TH ST.

4TH ST. EXTENSION

49

Third Ward

29

PINE ST.

Fourth Ward

BROOKSHIRE FRWY.

1ST ST.

CEDAR ST.

GRAHAM ST.

POPLAR ST.

CHURCH ST.

Discovery Place ■

9TH ST.

■ Spirit Square

TRYON ST.

COLLEGE ST.

8TH ST.

International
Trade Center

ⓘ

7TH ST.

MINT ST.

Performing
Arts Center ■

6TH ST.

Founders
Hall ■

5TH ST.

BREVARD ST.

■ ImaginOn

10TH ST.

Bank of America
Stadium ■

Visit
Charlotte
Info ■

Epicentre ■

TRADE ST.

CALDWELL ST.

27

29   49

1ST ST.

■ Bechtler Museum

4TH ST.

DAVIDSON ST.

WILLIS ST.

Mint Museum ■

3RD ST.

Time Warner
Cable Arena ■

St. Peter's †
Church

MARTIN LUTHER KING JR. BLVD.

277

10TH ST.

CARSON BLVD.

49

Charlotte
Convention
Center ■

Government
Center ■

MYERS ST.

McDOWELL ST.

27

74

Gantt Center
For African-American
Arts + Culture

NASCAR
Hall of Fame

ALFRED ST.

JOHN BELK FRWY.

277

Grady Cole ■
Center

7TH ST.

49

Marshall
Park

STONEWALL ST.

KINGS DR.

Memorial ■
Stadium

TRYON ST.

SOUTH BLVD.

ROYAL CT.

74

27

■ Mecklenburg
Aquatic Center

■ Vietnam
Veterans
Memorial

■ CPCC

ELIZABETH AVE.

27

LEXINGTON AVE.

CLEVELAND AVE.

EUCLID AVE.

MT. VERNON AVE.

BAXTER ST.

CHARLOTTE TOWNE AVE.

CHERRY ST.

16

3RD ST.

MYRTLE AVE.

BERKELEY AVE.

DILWORTH RD.

MOREHEAD ST.

KENILWORTH AVE.

KINGS DR.

LUTHER ST.

KINGSTON AVE.

ROMANY RD.

MAIN ST.

EAST BLVD.

PARK AVE.

BAXTER ST.

N

0   0.25   0.5 km.

0   0.25   0.5 mi.

Uptown Charlotte

PREFACE

Charlotte has changed a lot since George Washington visited in 1791 and found it to be a "trifling place." Heck, it's changed a lot since 1987, when a Sacramento sports columnist belittled the city's effort to land an NBA expansion team: "The only franchise Charlotte will receive," he wrote, "is one with golden arches."

For the record, Charlotte was awarded an NBA franchise that year by unanimous vote of the league's board of commissioners. In fact, the city later received an NFL team, plus a second NBA team when the first departed.

So, throughout its modern-day history, Charlotte has proven to be a can-do place that is growth oriented. It's also a city that arches its back in the face of criticism, whether it originates from the nation's first president or an ill-informed journalist in California.

As you read the 11th edition of the *Insiders' Guide to Charlotte,* you will learn the ins and outs of this vibrant city and what makes it tick. This book—first introduced in 1987— provides a one-stop source of information about a dynamic, growing area for newcomers, visitors, and locals alike.

Charlotte is the largest metropolitan area in North Carolina, a competitive big sister to the state's capital city of Raleigh and a crown jewel of the New South. We're one of the largest banking centers in the United States, and our superlative skyline structure—the 60-story Bank of America Corporate Center—soars higher than any building between Philadelphia and Atlanta. In recent years, *Fortune* magazine has recognized us for having the nation's No. 1 pro-business attitude, and we've won kudos for everything from livability to our public library system.

Practically every major NASCAR race team is located in the region, and the popular racing series annually holds three of its premier races at our 1.5-mile speedway. The unveiling of the NASCAR's Hall of Fame in May of 2010 solidified the Queen City's place as the true home of stock car racing. We hosted the NCAA Final Four in 1994 and nearly landed a world championship in 2004 when our Carolina Panthers battled to the wire against the New England Patriots in Super Bowl XXXVIII. Charlotte's second NBA team—the Bobcats—debuted in 2004 and is owned by Michael Jordan, a native North Carolinian and considered by many to be the greatest player in basketball history.

Meanwhile, our CROP Walk fund-raiser is among the most lucrative in the nation, and our Habitat for Humanity branch has built more houses than any other affiliate.

This buttoned-up banking town also has a quirky side—we eat more Beanie Weenies and ketchup and have the highest per capita consumption of Spam in the world. We love to tout our accomplishments and status, and we have a hang up about the term "world-class." Our civic leaders strive to build a world-class city, world-class banks, world-class culture, and a world-class business environment.

As much as we love being No. 1 in anything, we're not very fond of problems that come with being on top. We don't care too much for traffic congestion, always-under-construction roads, overcrowded schools, increased crime, or poor air quality.

In reality, Charlotte is a big small town. It's a place where home owners install water fountains for parched joggers and folks ask where you go to church before they ask where you work (it's probably a bank, anyway). We argue over issues that seem petty to other large cities, and we're always in a squabble with the school board. Yet, we're generous with our time and money for folks who need a helping hand. We can be quite stubborn, too, refusing to build a new arena for our first NBA team because no one liked the owners, then recruiting a second NBA team a few years later by building a more expensive arena.

But more than anything, Charlotte is welcoming to outsiders. Residents say "hi" to strangers they pass on the street and are happy to provide directions to a lost soul confused by what appears to be the intersection of Queens Road and Queens Road.

Newcomers do not find the city intimidating because very few people in Charlotte are actually from Charlotte. In fact, you're as likely to meet a graduate of Ohio State University as you are a graduate of UNC Charlotte. And for some unknown reason, there are a remarkable number of transplants from Buffalo, N.Y.

The region grew by leaps and bounds in the 1990s and early 2000s, as people flocked here from across the country (and world) in search of good jobs and a better quality of life. At the height of the influx, nearly 500 newcomers moved to the Queen City each week, bringing with them many different ethnic and socioeconomic backgrounds.

What they found was a warm and friendly city with an ever-changing skyline. They encountered a mostly genteel place where old money, new money, and no money come together to bolster our can-do spirit.

Now that's world-class.

HOW TO USE THIS BOOK

Imagine being on the television show *Who Wants to Be a Millionaire* and you're suddenly taken aback by a question on pop culture. You opt for a lifeline and call that one friend who's always so knowledgeable on such things. Bingo, you have the answer.

The *Insiders' Guide to Charlotte* is like that good friend. Whether you need to know just the place to take your fussy mother-in-law for a nice dinner or the best spot to enjoy live music on a Fri night, you can find it tucked into these pages. A thorough read makes you an unofficial Charlotte concierge—quickly able to locate an enjoyable round of golf or the latest museum to grace the city's arts community.

Do you know what a fish camp is? How about the queen for which Charlotte is named? It is our hope that the *Insiders' Guide to Charlotte* gives you a sense of what the Queen City is—our can-do community spirit, our silly complex about being a world-class city, our pride in banking skyscrapers and NASCAR races, even the fact that we like our iced tea sweet, our Brooks Brothers button-downs in white or blue, and our Krispy Kreme doughnuts hot.

Here's an idea of how to navigate this data-packed book to find the information you need to enjoy Charlotte, whether you're visiting, moving here, or looking for lots of information on a city you've called home for years.

The Area Overview chapter explains how Charlotte is laid out, what buildings make up the Uptown skyline, and the other towns located in Mecklenburg and surrounding counties. The Getting Here, Getting Around chapter is essential reading for some clarity on our oft-confusing streets. For a city that has experienced most of its growth in the past 50 years, Charlotte has more history than you might think. Read the History chapter to discover the rich history of the city and how past events have shaped this former trading crossroads.

Hotels and motels are in a separate chapter from bed-and-breakfast inns. Hotels are listed alphabetically, while B&Bs are listed by location. Both chapters include a helpful price code at the beginning, along with Web sites for further investigation. Restaurants, meanwhile, are divided by type of cuisine, featuring specialized categories such as Barbecue, Continental, Family-Style Dining, Southern Cuisine, Fish Camps, Local Flavor, and many ethnic varieties.

Nightlife gives you the inside scoop on an eclectic and ever-changing bar scene. It allows you to wade through the marketing clutter to find your perfect evening's destination, whether you prefer friendly neighborhood taverns, high-energy dance clubs, country line dancing, or live music. The Shopping chapter is sure to tempt your credit cards with a roundup of all area malls and major centers, popular flea markets, and recommendations by category.

Attractions are listed alphabetically and include museums, historic sites, theme parks, gardens, and popular cultural and sports venues. In Kidstuff you'll discover more things to do in Charlotte, with a special emphasis on youngsters. Here you'll find listings organized by categories such as Museums and Historic Sites; Entertainment; Science, Nature, and the Outdoors; and Camps. The book also includes chapters covering the arts as well as parks and recreation.

Golfers have their own chapter of information on the best courses to play in Charlotte and across the Carolinas. Spectator Sports covers professional, college, and club teams in the Queen City, from the NFL Carolina Panthers to UNC Charlotte 49ers basketball. Wondering what's going on in Charlotte the month you're visiting? Flip to the chapter on Annual Events for an overview of festivals, gatherings, art and sporting events, and entertainment, all listed by month. Day Trips offers ideas for great excursions to the mountains, the beach, and everywhere in between in both North and South Carolina. You'll also find Insiders' tips—look for these nuggets of information you likely won't find anywhere else.

Moving to Charlotte or already live here? Be sure to check out the blue-tabbed pages at the back of the book, where you will find the **Living Here** appendix that offers sections on relocation, real estate, education, health care, retirement, and media.

The Living Here appendix is especially helpful to folks moving to the Queen City, with a Relocation chapter that explains where to shop for a home in various parts of Charlotte, where to live while you're searching, and how to get settled once you're here. Public and private schools and child-care programs for younger children are described in their own chapter, followed by colleges and universities in the area. Health Care covers all the major hospitals and referral services when you need medical attention, while Retirement includes information for seniors from assisted-living communities to fun recreational activities for older adults. In Media you can learn more about local newspapers, magazines, radio, and television.

Don't forget the index at the back of the book that allows you to pinpoint specific places quickly and easily. Throughout the book, an updated listing of addresses, phone numbers, Web sites, and general locations help you make plans.

One helpful note: You will encounter up to three area codes in the Charlotte region. The dominant and long-standing area code is 704, so ask for it if you're relocating here. However, because of rapid growth, a second area code—980—was added a few years ago. And finally, since the Charlotte region stretches into South Carolina, the area code south of the border is 803. Don't think this is useless knowledge—dialing the area code is required to make a local call.

Use this 11th edition of the *Insiders' Guide to Charlotte* to your benefit. It is designed to provide the important things you need to know about a city we hope you enjoy.

AREA OVERVIEW

The Charlotte metro region is generally discussed in terms of Uptown (Charlotte-speak for "downtown"), the six Mecklenburg County municipalities surrounding Charlotte, and a multitude of towns and cities that make up the perimeter regions.

While these cities and towns are part of the Charlotte "umbrella," each has its own unique character. Unlike in most metropolitan regions where the suburbs popped up as a result of the growth of the largest city, many of Charlotte's "suburbs" are just as old as the Queen City. These are independent towns, many of them former mill villages, that were established not as bedroom communities for Charlotte, but as stand-alone towns and centers of commerce. It is only in the last two decades that these cities have taken on the characteristics of suburbs—often begrudgingly by some natives and long-time residents.

This chapter is divided into sections that give a general overview of each municipality.

UPTOWN CHARLOTTE

Uptown is a vibrant place—modern glass towers beside well-maintained mid-rise office buildings, high-rise condominiums overlooking heavenly church spires, green space carved from the concrete, and ever-present cranes bringing improvements to a city that always seems to be in growth mode.

The nexus of Uptown is the intersection of Trade and Tryon Streets, commonly called "The Square" and easily identified by the tall Raymond Kaskey bronze sculptures on each corner depicting industry, commerce, transportation, and the future. Trade Street was once a gathering spot for Native Americans—and later settlers—to swap wares. Tryon was a wagon road where many of the city's early homes and businesses were built. Charlotte's major businesses are still located on Tryon, the city's main street. Bank of America dominates Tryon north of The Square, while Wells Fargo (formerly Wachovia) is the main player south of The Square.

Early in its history, Charlotte was divided into four political districts, or wards. In the modern Queen City, First Ward is a growing community of condominiums and townhomes interspersed with public housing; Second Ward includes the government center, Marshall Park, and several hotels; Third Ward is home to the Carolina Panthers' Bank of America Stadium, refurbished bungalows, and a burgeoning design community; while Fourth Ward is the most established sector, known for its restored Victorian houses, restaurants, nightlife, and posh condos.

Befitting its stature as the largest city in the Carolinas, Charlotte sports an impressive skyline. The crown jewel is the 60-story Bank of America Corporate Center, the tallest building in the Carolinas. Located just north of The Square, it was designed by Cesar Pelli and completed in 1992. The ground floor and second floor of the skyscraper are combined into Founders Hall, a collection of shops and restaurants. A block northeast of the Bank of America Corporate Center is the Hearst Tower. Completed in 2002, it stretches 47 stories and has an interesting exterior architecture that gives the illusion the building is wider at the top than at the base (it's not). The art deco tower is the city's third-tallest skyscraper, and its ground level is home to an Italian restaurant, Luce; a Mediterranean bistro, Blue; and an art gallery, WDO. Upstairs, the media giant's service center shares space with Bank of America. Also on the north end of Uptown are the 32-story Interstate Tower, with Trammell

Crow Company and the Charlotte City Club; the 30-story Interstate Johnson Lane (IJL) Financial Center, where Capital Grille faces the street front; and the Bank of America–influenced Transamerica Square, a 10-story structure with a signature pyramid top and ground floor retail featuring Rock Bottom Brewery. At North Tryon and 11th Streets, the McColl Center for Visual Art is one of the nation's biggest artists' colonies. It is housed in a striking stone building erected from the shell of the burned-out First ARP Church.

Moving south from The Square, the 40-story glass-and-steel Bank of America Plaza marks the southernmost corporate influence of Bank of America on Tryon Street (although BofA does have a branch office at 400 South Tryon). Built in 1974, Bank of America Plaza was the city's tallest building for 14 years. It relinquished that title in 1988, when then-Wachovia (now Wells Fargo) built its 42-story tower a couple of blocks to the south. The 42-story Wells Fargo/Wachovia tower is often called the jukebox building for its Wurlitzer shape at the top. Two other nearby towers in the Wells Fargo stable are a 32-story modern glass skyscraper that opened in 2000 as Three Wachovia Center, and a slightly shorter 32-story building that opened in 1971 and was known for many years as Two Wachovia Center.

When the financial crisis of 2008 reached its crescendo in October of that year, Wachovia was well into the process of expanding its presence in southern Uptown with an aggressive project at Tryon and First Streets that was to be called the Wachovia Cultural Arts Campus. The campus was to include a condo tower that was never built. However, it did add to the Uptown skyline with a modernistic 48-story glass tower that is the second tallest in Charlotte. Duke Energy, also headquartered in Charlotte, bought naming rights to this tower (with its milk carton design at the top) after Wachovia was purchased by Wells Fargo. The power company is the primary tenant in what is now called the Duke Energy Center. Surrounding this unique-looking tower is the Wells Fargo Cultural Campus, which includes the Harvey B. Gantt Center for African-American Arts + Culture, the Bechtler Museum of Modern Art,

and the 1,150-seat Knight Theater. A new version of Charlotte's venerable Mint Museum debuts at the campus in late 2010.

The southern edge of Uptown is clearly defined by the postmodern 25-story Westin Hotel. Opened in 2003, the sleek Westin looks somewhat out of place with its flat design and funky cutouts near the top. Two blocks east of the Westin, the new NASCAR office tower (20 stories) and the racing-bowl shaped NASCAR Hall of Fame command quite a presence as well.

Other noteworthy Uptown structures include Time Warner Cable Arena, the 19,026-seat state-of-the-art home of the Charlotte Bobcats NBA team and Charlotte Checkers minor league hockey team. The $265 million arena debuted in late 2005 two blocks east of the Bank of America Corporate Center. Adjacent to the Bank of America tower is the N.C. Blumenthal Performing Arts Center. The Blumenthal includes the 2,100-seat Belk Theatre, a second 450-seat theater, and numerous performance halls. It's also home to many of Charlotte's arts groups, such as the Carolina Opera, the Charlotte Symphony Orchestra, North Carolina Dance Theatre, and the Community School of the Arts.

Two of the most interesting skyscrapers west of The Square are the Interstate Tower and the Carillon Building. The buildings opened in back-to-back years about a block apart. The Interstate Tower's iconic slate green dome sits 32 stories high and opened in 1990, while the Carillon's 24-story tower debuted in 1991. The Carillon is memorable for its Gothic central spire and bell-tower shape. Its architecture was inspired by the historic neo-Gothic First Presbyterian Church directly across Trade Street.

Not all of Uptown's buildings are new. Latta Arcade on South Tryon Street dates to 1915 and now includes a courtyard of shops and restaurants. The Dunhill Hotel, on the National Register of Historic Places along with Latta Arcade, opened in 1929 and still commands a presence on North Tryon. The original facade of the Ratcliffe Building has been incorporated into a condo project on South Tryon, while the old Ivey's Department Store is doing quite well in its second life as a luxury condo building. Also, the former Montaldo's Department store building, which dates to 1920, was home to a branch of the Mint Museum for a decade until 2010, when the Mint relocated and the Foundation For the Carolinas moved in. The ornate Spirit Square building on North Tryon was built in 1909, while the St. Peters Condominium building at the corner of Sixth and Poplar began life in the late 1800s as the first non-military general hospital in the state of North Carolina.

So why do Charlotteans refer to "downtown" as "Uptown"? Some say we're trying to be high-falutin', but the story is more involved. In the early part of the last century, when folks wanted to go into the city from outlying areas, they had to travel uphill. The Square at Trade and Tryon is one of the highest geographic points in the city. So, folks would take the trolley "uptown" or drive "uptown," while kids would ride their bikes "uptown." In the 1970s, marketing-savvy city leaders started branding the downtown as "Uptown," and during the phenomenal growth period in the 1990s and early 2000s, when night-life and residential life returned to the urban core, the name "Uptown" really took hold. Ironically, some highway signs still direct motorist to "downtown." And, for a while in the mid 2000s, there was a movement to re-brand it as the "Center City." Confusing, for sure, but Uptown has emerged as the term of choice for the heart of the Charlotte.

These days, Uptown is home to approximately 70,000 workers and around 12,000 residents, with a handful of additional residential towers planned or under construction.

Another boost to Uptown these days is the emergence of an economic development group called Charlotte Center City Partners. The organization works with businesses and government to lure new companies Uptown, keep existing companies there, and bring Charlotteans and tourists to the area. Center City Partners sponsors many special events, including the Green Market each Sat spring through fall and a Thurs-evening summer concert series. Center City Partners proved instrumental in bringing Johnson & Wales University to Uptown in 2004. The campus was formed by merging former Johnson & Wales locations in Charleston, S.C., and Norfolk, Va.

For a great resource on Uptown Charlotte, stop by Visit Charlotte at 330 South Tryon St., (704) 331-2700. The visitor information center has brochures on self-guided tours of Uptown and a calendar of monthly events. It also sells cool Charlotte merchandise. Go to www.visitcharlotte.com or www.charlottecentercity.org for more details.

In the new millennium, two communities have emerged that form bookends to Uptown. South End, as its name implies, is just south of Uptown (the two are separated by the I-277 loop), while NoDa is a funky community that has sprung up about two miles or so north of the center city.

South End was a former warehouse district that has seen many of its factory buildings converted to condos, apartments, artist studios, and mixed-use retail. One of the earliest examples was the conversion of the former Lance Snacks building on South Boulevard into Factory South, a mixed-use structure of loft condos with retail on the first floor. Next door to Factory South is one of the most controversial buildings in Charlotte—The Arlington. Known as the "pink building," this 22-story condo tower was the talk of the town when it opened in 2002. The talk was not because it was the tallest building outside Uptown, but because of its pink glass outer shell. The entire building is covered with glass that's the shade of Pepto-Bismol, although maverick developer Jim Gross prefers to call it "desert rose." Regardless of its official hue, The Arlington is certainly a Charlotte icon—for better or worse—and those who originally bought condos in the pink building included basketball star Emeka Okafor, Charlotte Bobcats' first-ever draft pick, and Todd Sauerbrun, an outspoken All-Pro punter for the Carolina Panthers who eventually wore out his welcome and was traded to Denver. The light rail transit line, which runs from Uptown southward all the way to the I-485 outer belt, opened in late 2007, and its path through South End spurred residential development for those wishing to live close to the center city and take the train to work instead of driving.

North of town, a run-down area of old mill houses at North Davidson and 36th Streets became an enclave for artists and musicians in the early 2000s. They began a remarkable transformation of the community away from urban blight and crime, and it eventually became known as NoDa, short for North Davidson, but pronounced "no-dah." The centerpiece of NoDa is the Neighborhood Theater. It anchors a commercial concentration of old-school storefronts that have found new life as coffee shops, restaurants, arts studios, and even a dog bar. Businesses include "Salvador Deli" and "Smelly Cat Coffee House." If you want to see the funkiest part of buttoned-down Charlotte, NoDa is the place.

i Seven of Charlotte's eight tallest towers have been built since 1988. The lone exception is the 40-story Bank of America Plaza, which opened in 1974. Meanwhile, the building known as 112 Tryon Plaza opened in 1926 with much hoopla because it was the tallest in both Carolinas. Nowadays, the 22-story tower doesn't even crack the Queen City's top 20.

MECKLENBURG TOWNS

Economic reasons inspire many Charlotte natives and newcomers to work in Charlotte. But these same folks often choose to live in one of the surrounding towns that are within reasonable commuting distance. For those who yearn for a less complicated existence, life in these suburban small towns is appealing.

Mecklenburg County has six incorporated towns: Cornelius, Davidson, Huntersville, Matthews, Mint Hill, and Pineville. Each has its own government, fire department, and library branch. Some have their own police force, while others rely on the Charlotte-Mecklenburg Police Department. Some towns get water and sewer service from Charlotte; others rely on wells and septic systems. Charlotte-Mecklenburg Schools provide public education. Charlotte-based medical conglomerates provide a good supply of doctors and dentists to towns throughout the county.

Neighbors to the north are close to Carolinas Medical Center–University (near UNC Charlotte), the Lake Norman Regional Medical Center in Mooresville, and the Presbyterian Hospital Huntersville, which opened in 2005. Several smaller hospitals and emergency-care centers are based in the Pineville-Matthews area.

A strong religious structure cements the foundation of all the towns, setting the tone for their quality of life. Social life centers around school activities, various clubs, sports, festivals, and bazaars that include barbecues with Brunswick stew or fish fries near the lake communities.

As you might have guessed, residents of the neighboring towns pay both county and town taxes, but the total amounts are less than those paid by Charlotteans (another small-town perk). The touches of modernization such as fast food, discount grocery chains, and national retailers have found their way into these once unsullied hamlets.

For most, the only downside to living in a small perimeter town but working in Charlotte is the commute. Still, when asked, most commuters feel the quality and substance of their small-town life outweighs the traffic problems, giving them the best of both worlds. Likewise, many of the neighboring towns offer attractions and shopping that Charlotteans find worthy of a short drive.

Charlotte's rampant growth in recent years has spilled over into the six small incorporated Mecklenburg towns that surround the city. The Lake Norman–area towns of Huntersville, Cornelius, and Davidson have boomed with development brought on by new interchanges for I-77. Pineville, considerably south of Charlotte near the South Carolina line, has become a focal point of retail business with malls and big-box stores. Meanwhile, the southeast Mecklenburg towns of Matthews and Mint Hill cling to their identities as Charlotte growth encroaches.

CORNELIUS

In the period of 1883 through 1888, known as the "cotton battle" time, so much cotton was

Want More Information?

Visit Charlotte
330 South Tryon St.
(704) 331-2700, (800) 231-4636
www.visitcharlotte.com
www.charlottechamber.com
A joint venture of the Charlotte Convention & Visitors Bureau and the Chamber of Commerce.

Lake Norman Chamber of Commerce & Visitors Center
19900 West Catawba Ave.,
Cornelius
(704) 987-3300
www.lakenormanchamber.org
Represents Cornelius, Davidson, Huntersville, and Lake Norman.

Belmont Town Hall
115 North Main St.
(704) 825-5586
www.ci.belmont.nc.us

Concord City Municipal Building
26 Union St. South
Customer Call Center: (704) 920-5555
Chamber of Commerce: (704) 782-4000
ww.ci.concord.nc.us

Cornelius Town Hall
21445 Catawba Ave.
(704) 892-6031
www.cornelius.org

Davidson Town Hall
216 South Main St.
(704) 892-7591
www.ci.davidson.nc.us

Fort Mill Town Hall
112 Confederate St.
(803) 547-2034
www.fortmillsc.org

Visit Gaston
620 North Main St.
Belmont
(704) 825-4044
(800) 849-9994
www.visitgaston.org
www.gastonchamber.com

Huntersville Town Hall
101 Huntersville-Concord Rd.
(704) 875-6541
www.huntersville.org

Indian Trail Town Hall
100 Navajo Trail
(704) 821-8114
www.indiantrail.org

Kannapolis Town Hall
246 Oak Ave.
(704) 920-4300
www.ci.kannapolis.nc.us

Lake Wylie Chamber of Commerce
1 Executive Court, Suite 6
(803) 831-2827
www.lakewyliesc.com

Matthews Town Hall
232 Matthews Station St.
(704) 847-4411
www.matthewsnc.com
www.matthewschamber.com

McAdenville Town Hall
125 Main St.
(704) 824-3190
www.gastonchamber.com
www.mcadenville-christmas-town.com

Mint Hill Town Hall
7151 Matthews–Mint Hill Rd.
(704) 545-9726
www.minthill.com

Monroe City Hall
300 West Crowell St.
(704) 282-4500
www.visitmonroenc.org

Mooresville Town Hall
413 North Main St.
(704) 663-3800
www.ci.mooresville.nc.us
www.racecityusa.org
www.hellomooresville.com

Mount Holly City Hall
400 East Central Ave.
(704) 827-3931
www.mtholly.us

Pineville Town Hall
200 Dover St.
(704) 889-2291
www.pinevillenc.net

Rock Hill Town Hall
155 Johnston St.
(803) 329-7000
www.ci.rock-hill.sc.us
www.rockhillrocks.com

Salisbury City Hall
217 South Main St.
(704) 638-5270
www.visitsalisburync.com
www.ci.salisbury.nc.us

Statesville City Hall
301 South Center St.
(704) 878-3550
www.ci.statesville.nc.us
www.statesvillechamber.org

Tega Cay City Hall
7000 Tega Cay Dr.
(803) 548-3512
www.tegacaysc.org

Waxhaw Town Hall
317 North Broom St.
(704) 843-2195
www.waxhaw.com

York City Hall
10 North Roosevelt St.
(803) 684-2341
www.yorkcountygov.com
www.yorkcountychamber.com

shipped from Cornelius to Liverpool, England, that this area was nicknamed "Liverpool." It was not until 1893 that the town came into existence after J. R. Stough relocated part of his Davidson cotton business outside the town limits, where he could do his own cotton weighing unhampered by Davidson's newly hired town weigher. Local farmers, rather than trudge up a muddy hill to Davidson, came to Stough in such abundance that he and associate C. J. Johnson conceived the idea of having a nearby mill to convert cotton into cloth. They didn't have the money to spare but knew a man who did—Joseph Benjamin Cornelius of Davidson. Soon the cotton mill opened, and the town took its name from the principal stockholder, incorporating as Cornelius in 1905.

The town's original cotton mill, now called Foamex Innovations, remains a strong manufacturer. But many other aspects of Cornelius have changed. In the 1990s the town's population grew from 2,581 to 11,969, a 363 percent increase. Cornelius now counts a whopping 24,060 residents. The appeal of Cornelius is its close proximity to Lake Norman. It has become an affluent suburb of lake lovers. Upscale communities such as The Peninsula have developed hundreds of homes, while retailers have followed in Jetton Village and many other shopping centers lining the town's main thoroughfare, West Catawba Avenue. That prosperity has also brought problems, such as overcrowded schools, packed roads, and strained public services. It took more than a decade of begging to get the N.C. Department of Transportation to widen West Catawba Avenue, a slow-moving project that should be completed by the middle of 2010. The long-awaited project will stretch from I-77 to Jetton Road. Cornelius also installed underground utilities along West Catawba in late 2006. The next big roads project will be the rebuilding of the outdated interchange at I-77 (exit 28). Unfortunately, a timetable has not been established. East Catawba Avenue, the gateway to the original Cornelius downtown, also is getting an overhaul. The town also has built a new fire station on the west side and a new police station on the east side and purchased 90 acres for a community park.

Cornelius serves as the hub of activity for Lake Norman. Jetton Park is one of the county's best recreation facilities with 105 acres; waterfront views; paved hiking, biking, and Rollerblade trails; playgrounds; a sunning beach; lighted tennis courts; bike rentals; picnic shelters; and a gazebo. Ramsey Creek Park also has a beach, playground, nature trails, and picnic shelters, with the added plus of boat docks. Many of Lake Norman's eateries, entertainment venues, and shops can be found along Catawba Avenue. Highlights include Fuzion Bistro in Shops on the Green and Midtown Sundries overlooking the lake.

DAVIDSON

Davidson provides the best of two worlds: life in a small college town that looks as if it came off the cover of the *Saturday Evening Post*, and easy access to Lake Norman (straight across I-77 from the town). Whoever coined the phrase "Southern hospitality" copied it from the townspeople of this quaint village. Davidson seems to cast a spell on those who come to visit, sometimes causing them to put down roots. It's a cerebral atmosphere of friendly attitudes.

Davidson College, a private 1,700-student liberal arts school, contributes heavily to the town's charm. Founded by the Presbyterians in 1837, the 100-acre campus has several buildings on the National Register of Historic Places and is designated as an arboretum with a wide variety of plant life. Several buildings have been renovated or added in the last decade, such as the $9.1-million Visual Art Center at the corner of Main and Griffith Streets. Make a point of visiting the art gallery, which is open to the public free of charge. A magnificent Auguste Rodin sculpture, commissioned by the town of Calais, France, in 1884, presides over the atrium.

Another new addition in the last decade is the Knoblauch Campus Center and its Duke Performance Hall, an elegant 600-seat proscenium theater that hosts lectures, plays, and concerts. Since 2002, the Knoblauch has partnered with England's Royal Shakespeare Company to bring the RSC to Davidson for educational and performance residencies. This has resulted in the sale of more than 20,000 tickets to RSC performances at the Duke Family Performance Hall.

The first thing you'll notice as you walk Davidson's Main Street and through the campus is a canopy of gigantic trees. The idea for this horticultural effort was born in 1869 when the faculty recommended that the campus reflect "the forest growth of the State . . . and the general botany of the region." Over the years a variety of trees and shrubs were planted. Today you can take a self-guided tree tour and identify 40 distinct varieties from their metal tags.

If you're hungry, you might try local town hangouts: the Soda Shop, Fuel Pizza, Toast, Bonsai, and Ben & Jerry's Ice Cream & Frozen Yogurt, all on Main Street; and the waterfront North Harbor Club with slips for boaters. Other restaurant options are the upscale Bucci, located at 127 Depot St. and the Brickhouse Tavern at 209 Delburg St. The Brickhouse Tavern is a refurbished 120-year-old cotton mill that's become a popular hangout for NASCAR drivers and their crews, as well Davidson alumni and sports fans. Another eatery of note is The Egg, a breakfast and lunch place on Griffith Street. If you want to spend the night or are looking for a place for out-of-town guests, a good choice is the Davidson Village Inn at 117 Depot St., which offers rooms with breakfast.

It isn't uncommon for Charlotteans and other neighbors to drive to Davidson to enjoy its many cultural amenities and sporting events. The Davidson Wildcats basketball team has a rich and storied history with coaches such as Lefty Driesell and Terry Holland, both of whom moved on to high-profile universities in the Atlantic Coast Conference, and players like All-Americans Fred Hetzel and Dick Snyder in the 1960s and All-American Stephen Curry, who was selected seventh overall in the 2009 NBA draft.

The Village Green, across from the downtown shopping area, is the site of numerous community events, including concerts and Town Day, which is held in May.

Residents have a choice of in-town housing, which includes Victorian houses, countryside liv-

ing, or homes on Lake Norman. River Run is based around a golf and country club. Other family-friendly neighborhoods such as McConnell and St. Alban's are only a mile from Main Street. A number of luxury condos have also been built on the lake, such as Davidson Landing and Harbour Place of Davidson.

Davidson, which adjoins Cornelius, is about 20 miles north of Charlotte via I-77. Incorporated in 1879, the town has a population of 9,099, not including the 1,700 students. More than half of the town's current population has located there since 1990. Davidson is governed by a mayor and five commissioners; citizens serve on a number of committees. To maintain the village's small-town charm and control development pushing north from Charlotte, Davidson officials have worked hard to develop a growth plan. The council put a moratorium on all new development to study where new utilities should go, then enacted another moratorium to draft a planning ordinance. A certain percentage of open space must be preserved in new developments, and growth must be timed with the parallel expansion of public facilities. Residents closely monitor the community and protect its small-town feel. There will likely never be a big-box retailer or a high-rise tower within the Davidson town limits.

HUNTERSVILLE

No other Lake Norman town has changed as much as Huntersville in the last decade. Closest to Charlotte at the south end of the lake, Huntersville grew from 3,023 residents in 1990 to 24,960 in 2000, an amazing 725 percent jump. Today the growing town consists of more than 40,000 residents and has won awards as a top place to live and retire. Huntersville is governed by a mayor and five commissioners.

One of Mecklenburg's oldest towns, Huntersville was originally known as Craighead for a fiery Presbyterian minister who lived in the area. In 1873 the town incorporated and was renamed for Robert B. Hunter. Several structures from Huntersville's early days remain. The Hugh Torrance House and Store has sat on Gilead

Road since 1779. The original log house and store, where neighbors bought necessities and exchanged dissenting talk of British rule, is now a museum. About 100 yards from the store is Cedar Grove, a beautifully restored 1831 brick plantation home built by Torrance's son, James. One of Huntersville's famous residents—historian and novelist LeGette Blythe—wrote about other historic sites in the area, including Latta Plantation (now a living-history museum on a nature preserve), Alexandriana, the McIntire Place, and Hopewell Presbyterian Church.

Parts of Huntersville have maintained their country charm, especially the eastern side where the original downtown sits and early growth started around the railroad line. Gilead Road, now on the "new" side of Huntersville across I-77, also offers a step back into the past with rambling old homes, beautiful magnolia trees, and stands of ancient hardwoods. But much of that is changing.

On the heels of the population growth came an explosion in retail and other commerce in Huntersville. NorthCross Shopping Center at exit 25, which includes more than 40 stores, burst onto the scene in the 1990s. Meanwhile, on the west side of I-77 at exit 25, Birkdale Village blossomed in the early to mid 2000s. Birkdale is probably Charlotte's best example of the new urbanism model: a $90 million mixed-use village spanning 52 acres. It features a walkabout town center of storefronts, restaurants, large national retailers, boutiques, apartments, a movie theater, and town park. Live bands often play outdoors on weekends, while the village square fountain is a popular spot for kids to splash and play. Birkdale Golf Club is across the street from Birkdale Village. It is a public access course designed by legendary Arnold Palmer and surrounded by upscale housing.

In recent years, Huntersville has also opened a community center, water park, high school, and hospital. Kenton Place, just around the corner from Birkdale, offers more retail stores, apartments, restaurants, and the Galway Hooker, a popular and uniquely named Irish pub. Even more growth is expected in coming years with Lake Norman's popularity and the expected widening of I-77 to four lanes in each direction.

Huntersville is also well-known for amenities and attractions, such as Blythe Landing, a 26-acre park on Lake Norman with boat launches, a playground, picnic areas, and sand volleyball courts. Latta Plantation Nature Preserve features the historic home, 10 miles of hiking trails, horseback riding, canoeing and kayaking, fishing, and an unusual raptor center for the rehabilitation and release of native hawks, owls, eagles, and other birds of prey. Bradford Park is Huntersville's newest and largest park, covering 213 acres. It was jointly developed by the Town of Huntersville and Mecklenburg County. The park is located on N.C. Hwy. 73 and includes five lighted baseball/softball fields, three soccer fields, a large picnic pavilion, and two restroom facilities. It has proved to be ideal for large sporting events and community events.

Speaking of large events, the Loch Norman Highland Games, a celebration of the area's Scottish ancestry, is held each April in nearby Rural Hill. The games include amateur athletic competitions and activities such as bagpipe music, dancing, tartan parades, and historical demonstrations.

LAKE NORMAN

Southerners love boating, fishing, NASCAR, and weekends in the sun. All of those things come together to make Lake Norman a sought-after place to live. Lake Norman is the antithesis of neatly pressed and buttoned-down Charlotte. It's the kind of place where folks do business in casual attire, NASCAR stars build multimillion dollar lakefront mansions, and a lot of pretty people live the easy life.

Ironically, despite its propensity to facilitate loafing, Lake Norman is actually a working lake, created by Duke Energy (then Duke Power) to generate hydroelectric power. Starting in 1959, Duke built the Cowans Ford Dam on the Catawba River, flooding some 32,500 acres of mostly rural pasture land to create this man-made treasure. Completed in 1963, it was named Lake Norman after Duke Power president Norman Atwater Cocke. The lake is claimed by the towns of Cornelius, Huntersville, Davidson, Mooresville, Troutman, and Denver. It touches the shores of Mecklenburg, Iredell, Lincoln, and Catawba Counties.

Slicing through the lake area, I-77 separates Cornelius, Davidson, and Mooresville to the east; Troutman to the north; and Denver to the west. Lake dwellers in each area are supplied with such services as volunteer fire departments, police departments, and separate governing bodies.

Lakeside restaurants and shopping areas, not to mention a good representation of real estate firms, are scattered about central areas of the lake, but it isn't uncommon to see cornfields and old barns sandwiched between expensive homes in this original farming community. When Duke Power began selling lake lots, summer cabins and mobile homes were the norm. Now the lake has shifted to luxury condos and sprawling mansions.

The Lake Norman Chamber of Commerce operates a visitor center on West Catawba Avenue. The center is open seven days a week except on major holidays and provides maps, brochures, real estate and recreational information, and exhibits on the towns in the area. Call (704) 892-1922 or visit www.lakenormanchamber.org.

MATTHEWS

If a movie company were searching for a quaint 19th-century country village look, it would find such a setting in Matthews. With a laid-back look and feel, the town is full of antiques stores and craft shops in turn-of-the-century buildings.

Matthews was settled in the early 1800s as Stumptown because of the stumps left from forests that covered the area. It was said that a wagon couldn't make a U-turn without running into a stump. The town later became Fullwood to honor John M. Fullwood, who operated the Stagecoach Inn and became the area's first postmaster in 1825.

When incorporated in 1879, the townspeople renamed it Matthews for Watson Matthews,

principal stockholder of the railroad. Eventually 13 trains came through Matthews daily, and the Matthews Train Depot—built in 1874—became the center of activity.

When gold was discovered in the area in the early 1800s, Matthews shared in the bounty. The Rea Gold Mine was established where Sardis Road North is today, and the Tredenic Mine was located near McAlpine Creek in the present Stonehaven area. Unfortunately, the gold found at these mines was of such fine texture that it finally became too expensive to process.

In the center of downtown on North Trade Street, you'll find Renfrow Hardware, where on any given morning in the past, the town elders gathered around the black potbellied stove to discuss politics. You can still buy seed and garden supplies, hardware items, clothing, hoop cheese, soft drinks, and pickles at this store, which has served the community since the early 1900s. Another important historic structure is the Reid House, one block from downtown. Built in the early 1900s, it is on the National Register of Historic Places and is used for Victorian teas, weddings, family gatherings, and socials.

Today Matthews is home to many prominent companies, including Family Dollar, Inc., PCA International, Conbraco Industries, Harris Teeter, and InteliCoat TechnoCom Business Systems. Sycamore Commons, a modern shopping center at Independence Boulevard and Highway 51, includes Costco, Lowe's, Michael's, Dick's Sporting Goods, Old Navy, and Pier 1. Windsor Square Shopping Center, Matthews Festival, and many other centers offer shopping, hotels, office and business spaces, plus a variety of fast-food, ethnic, seafood, and steak restaurants. The Matthews Community Farmers Market offers fresh fruits, vegetables, organic flowers, fresh baked goods, herbs, and more. The market, located on North Trade Street, is open every Sat from May to Nov.

Matthews hosts a number of events throughout the year that offer a variety of entertainment and family fun for everyone. Matthews Alive!, the town's annual Labor Day celebration since 1993, attracts visitors by the thousands. The Matthews Summer Concert and Movie Series features outdoor concerts and movies in Stumptown Park beginning in May and running through August. ArtFest of Matthews, a two-day open-air fine arts celebration, showcases juried artists. Hometown Holidays begins with the annual tree lighting and Santa making a personal appearance. Breakfast with Santa is a very popular event.

The Matthews Athletic and Recreation Association involves more than 1,000 children annually in sports programs. The Matthews Little League All Stars have won several state championships. The Matthews Playhouse of Performing Arts puts on shows and classes for both children and adults at the Matthews Community Center.

Presbyterian Hospital Matthews, opened in August 1994, adds a great deal to the town's quality of life. The 102-bed private hospital located at 1500 Matthews Township Parkway offers a full range of medical services. Central Piedmont Community College also operates a satellite campus near US 74 and I-485.

Matthews's population has grown from 91 residents in the town's first census in 1880 to nearly 27,000 today. Located about 12 miles southeast of Charlotte, the town is easily accessible to the Queen City via the I-485 outer belt. Citizens are governed by a mayor and six council members. The town has its own police force and is served by two volunteer fire departments, Matthews-Morningstar and Idlewild.

MINT HILL

Wide open spaces, neat homes in all price ranges, and a lack of strip development make Mint Hill unique from all other Mecklenburg towns. Mint Hill has maintained the most stringent zoning laws in the county and local planners adopted a forward-thinking land-use plan to steer and guide growth into the 21st century. It also has one of the lowest tax rates of municipalities in Mecklenburg County at $.275 per $100 valuation.

Settled in the mid-1700s by Scots-Irish Presbyterians, Mint Hill has a rich heritage. Philadelphia Presbyterian Church, established in 1770 in one of Mecklenburg's eight original communities, is one of the area's oldest churches. Its cha-

pel, built of handmade bricks made on the spot in 1826, may be the oldest church building in continuous use in the county. Its history and that of the once-agrarian community are chronicled in the Historical Room. The Mint Hill Historical Society operates a renovated turn-of-the-20th-century doctor's office, country store museum, and schoolhouse off Highway 51. Hours are 10 a.m. to 2 p.m. Tues through Sat, or by appointment. A farmers' market is held 9 a.m. to noon Sat, May through September. Call (704) 573-0726 for information. Nearby Bain Academy was established in 1889 as a prestigious boarding school and still serves as a public elementary school.

Mint Hill was an early military muster ground and has had several industries, including gold mining. There are a few manufacturers in the area today, but Mint Hill is primarily a residential community with several shopping centers.

Mint Hill is currently the third-largest town in Mecklenburg County with a population of approximately 21,000. The town has a number of very active civic clubs, and the Mint Hill Athletic Association provides opportunities for youth sports year-round. Residents enjoy the town's two parks, Wilgrove and Fairview; the latter is a 54-acre recreational facility. Both parks offer a variety of recreational opportunities, including soccer and softball fields, tennis and volleyball courts, nature trails, a nine-hole disc golf course, children's playgrounds, and an in-line skate path. Mint Hill Madness, an arts and crafts fall festival, is a popular annual event.

One of the highlights of Mint Hill is a cone of ice cream at Carolina Creamery in McEwen Square. You can also run into neighbors and friends at the post office and various shopping centers around town, including the Marketplace at Mint Hill, with two floors of 70 specialty and antiques shops that offer merchandise from stationery to furniture.

Residents are governed by a mayor and four commissioners. Mint Hill established its own police department in 2002 after many years of contracting the services of Charlotte-Mecklenburg. Fire and emergency services are handled by two volunteer departments. At this

Close-up

Banks Are No Longer Charlotte's "Two Rich Uncles"

Charlotte started as a trading destination before evolving into a cotton-producing town and one-time gold mining capital. However, its real growth came from banking. The one-two punch of Bank of America and Wachovia, with an assist from institutions like BB&T and First Citizens, powered the Queen City into the role of the nation's second-largest financial center behind only New York City. At the height of its financial status, Charlotte held about $2 trillion in bank resources and Bank of America and Wachovia were ranked among the top 10 banks in the United States.

But Charlotte, also home to a branch of the Federal Reserve, saw its banking stature diminish in the first decade of the new millennium. Longtime CEO Hugh McColl Jr. retired from Bank of America in 2001, and his replacement, Ken Lewis, was brought down by the prolonged recession of 2007–2009 and his controversial acquisition of Merrill Lynch. Meanwhile, a few blocks south on Tryon Street, Wachovia was being undone by the same recessionary forces and an ill-fated purchase of risky mortgage lender Golden West. Wachovia's stock plunged in the second half of 2008, causing the FDIC to step in and broker a secret weekend deal for Citigroup to purchase Wachovia. Many insiders feared the bank would go under had it opened for business as Wachovia on Mon, Sept. 29, 2008.

As it turned out, Wells Fargo Corp. swooped in with a better offer and in October 2008 Wells bought Wachovia, resulting in Charlotte's loss of Wachovia's corporate headquarters. This was a devastating blow to the pride and hubris of Charlotte, as well its corporate and charitable coffers. Meanwhile, 2009 brought much speculation on the future of Bank of America's corporate headquarters as many believed the company would benefit from a Wall Street address instead of a Tryon Street address. Finally, in the waning days of 2009, Brian Moynihan was named to replace Ken Lewis as CEO and vowed to keep a slightly humbled Bank of America headquartered here in Charlotte.

All this prompted McColl, the man widely credited for resurrecting Charlotte's Uptown, to make this statement to a group of civic leaders in 2009: "We no longer have two rich uncles we can turn to. It's time to let those days go, completely."

Without the mojo generated by the two banks, Charlotte's can-do spirit took a hit in 2009. The extrovert of the New South became an introvert. Big ideas were scaled back; caution was in vogue.

However, the Queen City is nothing if not resilient. And things began to turn around when North Carolina's newly elected governor, Bev Perdue, opened an office in Charlotte in 2009 and did something Mike Easley (her predecessor of eight years) never did. She worked diligently to bolster the Charlotte economy, knowing what's good for the biggest city in North Carolina is good for the entire state. Within a three-week flurry in late 2009 and early 2010, Charlotte and Purdue announced three major business coups for the Queen City that bode well for the coming decade.

First, Swedish home appliance manufacturer Electrolux AB agreed to establish its North America headquarters in Charlotte, bringing an $8.3 million investment in facilities and 738 much-needed jobs. Six days later, Zenta Mortgage Services was persuaded not to move across the state line to South Carolina, instead announcing the creation of 1,000 new jobs.

Power equipment manufacturer Husqvarna followed that with news that it would invest $8.25 million to establish its North American headquarters in Charlotte and bring 160 jobs to the Queen City.

Purdue had already brokered deals earlier in the year with GMAC Financial and Siemens Energy to expand into Charlotte, thus giving Queen City boosters a renewed confidence and spirit entering the second decade of the 2000s.

Charlotte will certainly miss the contributions made by its two big banking institutions in their heyday, but this commerce-driven city will continue to diversify and remain a shining star of the New South.

That you can bank on.

time, most residents rely on wells and septic tanks, but some developments have their own water and treatment systems.

PINEVILLE

Incorporated in 1873, the downtown area of Pineville still has the look of yesteryear. Hanging flower baskets adorn old-fashioned black light posts along Pineville's four-lane Main Street. Crape myrtle trees add a soft look to this town of many antiques shops—a town where you'll feel comfortable strolling down the street.

The hometown feel of Pineville's Main Street lies in sharp contrast to Carolina Place Mall and its sprawling development of retail stores, restaurants, and apartment complexes just a few miles away on Highway 51. Pineville's over-developed stretch of Highway 51 was ground zero for the beginning of Charlotte's I-485 outer belt in 1989.

While I-485 initially helped relieve congestion, it also brought new growth and, the truth be told, it is already outdated with just two lanes in each direction.

Pineville's recreation department offers many activities for all ages at Bell Johnston Center and Lake Park, including a summer camp for children. Programs range from cheerleading, self-defense, volleyball, day trips, theater, adult softball and basketball, summer camp, and an annual fall festival. Team sports are supervised by the Greater Pineville Athletic Association

Pineville's most famous native son is James Knox Polk (1795–1849), 11th president of the United States. The James K. Polk Memorial, south of town on US 521, consists of several home and barn structures of the period. Each year Polk's birthday is celebrated on the site with demonstrations of his era's weaving and cooking.

Pineville has a population of approximately 7,300 and bills itself as "the biggest small town around." It is governed by a mayor and four council members. Water and sewer service is furnished by the Charlotte-Mecklenburg Utility Department. The town's police department operates its own dispatching and 911 systems. The Pineville Volunteer Fire Department, originally the Fire Brigade organized in the 1850s, provides fire protection.

NEIGHBORING TOWNS

Belmont

Located about 15 minutes west of Charlotte in Gaston County, Belmont is a popular bedroom community with a quaint historical downtown, shorelines on Lake Wylie, an impressive botanical garden, and a magnificent Catholic cathedral and college. Belmont is also well-known for its large number of family-friendly festivals and movie and music series held in downtown's Stowe Park. Quick access to Uptown Charlotte and a small-town atmosphere make it the best of both worlds for Belmont's 8,900 residents.

Belmont was originally known as Garibaldi for John Garibaldi, the pioneer who built a railroad water tank 1 mile west of the Catawba River in the early 1870s. The tank resulted in a station stop in Belmont and opened the path for this area to become heavily industrialized with textile mills.

Belmont Abbey, which has jurisdiction over eight western North Carolina counties, has been a part of Belmont since 1876. Its cathedral at Belmont Abbey College is one of only a few abbey cathedrals in the country. Be sure to see the painted glass windows, which came from Myers Brothers Studios in Bavaria and received four gold medals at the Chicago World's Fair in 1892. The college is also the site of a massive block of granite that was once a Native American altar and later an auction block for slaves. Today it is used as a baptismal font. The Sisters of Mercy convent is also a major presence in Belmont. Members of the order direct Holy Angels, a facility for mentally and physically disabled children, and live in a huge stone building at the former Sacred Heart College campus in town.

Closer to Lake Wylie, Daniel Stowe Botanical Garden is an all-season attraction with acres of perennials, day lilies, annuals, herbs, and trees in themed gardens. Surrounded by rolling meadows, the garden also includes a dozen beautiful fountains, a woodland trail, a beautiful light-filled Visitor Pavilion with gift shop, and space for special events. Outdoor symphony concerts, plant sales, and gardening symposia are held at the garden, which also offers classes and workshops for children and adults. A glass-enclosed conservatory with orchids and live butterfly releases are also popular. HGTV has named the garden among the nation's 20 best botanical attractions. For details, call (704) 825-4490 or visit www.dsbg.org.

A Wal-Mart Super Center and waterfront communities overlooking Lake Wylie are part of continued growth in this neat town, where everyone recognizes the importance of preserving Belmont's downtown. A revitalization continues downtown with interesting shops, businesses, restaurants, bars, and new condominiums built in old Main Street stores.

Concord

Concord's claims to fame include gold mines, Revolutionary patriots, race cars, and an upscale outlet mall that has become the state's most popular tourist site. Additionally, Concord was bestowed the honor of All-America City in 2004.

This city of 71,071 is located in Cabarrus County, which was once a part of Mecklenburg County until the two split in 1792. In starting a town in the new county, settlers disagreed over its location. But when they reached a compromise, they chose the name Concord, which means harmony.

In 1771 nine young men from the area captured and destroyed munitions of war being transported through North Carolina by royal-supported Governor William Tryon. The brave feat contributed to the independence movement in the area. Concord's next major event occurred in 1799 when 12-year-old Conrad Reed found a piece of gold the size of an iron. Hundreds of gold miners would later scour the Piedmont section of the Carolinas, including what is now Uptown Charlotte, looking for treasure. Visitors can still pan for gold and tour the historical site.

In a sign of changing times, Concord recently lost its largest employer, cigarette manufacturer Philip Morris USA. However, it has become a hub for NASCAR race teams and NASCAR suppliers. Charlotte Motor Speedway is located in Concord and is home to three major events on the NASCAR schedule. On back-to-back weekends in May, the speedway hosts the NASCAR All-Star race and the Coca-Cola 600. The Coca-Cola 600 is the longest race on the circuit. In October the speedway is the site of a 500-mile race that's a key part of NASCAR's 10-race playoff system, known as the Chase for the Championship. The Coca-Cola 600 is always held Memorial Day weekend and is among the world's largest sporting events with attendance exceeding 200,000 people.

Concord Mills Mall, located off I-85 at exit 49, has become a huge drawing card with hundreds of outlet stores, restaurants, a movie theater, Best Buy, Bass Pro Shops Outdoor World, and NASCAR theme park.

i Visitors and newcomers often mispronounce "Concord." The correct pronunciation is "con-cord," just like it is spelled. If you pronounce it "con-kurd," you might be labeled a "Yankee," and everyone will know you "ain't from around here."

While Concord Mills anchors the west side of exit 49, a growing number of hotels, restaurants, and shops have popped up on the east side of exit 49. The exit is the primary route to Charlotte Motor Speedway and has become a destination in its own right with 12 hotels and 50 restaurants. The highest profile hotel at exit 49 is the Embassy Suites Golf Resort & Spa. The resort, which opened in 2007, is a public-private partnership between the City of Concord and hotelier John Q. Hammons. It includes an 11-story 308-suite tower, the Concord Convention Center, a fine dining restaurant, and a full-service spa. The Embassy Suites also took over management of the adjacent, city-owned Rocky River Golf Club, making it a complete resort. And, all this is located just a half-mile from the speedway.

Concord isn't solely the area around the speedway, however. Residents and visitors enjoy the McEachern Greenway and community events such as Union Street Live, Dog Days Out Pet Festival, and the annual Christmas parade. Medical needs are served by the 457-bed NorthEast Medical Center, the 12th-largest hospital in the state. The downtown area has a nice mix of shops and restaurants.

Fort Mill, South Carolina

Like so many small towns that emerged because the railroad made a stop there or someone put in a cotton gin, Fort Mill was so named for two separate occurrences—a fort and a mill. The fort was built in the late 1750s by South Carolina's governor to protect the area's friendly Catawba Indians from attacks by the Shawnee and Cherokee tribes. In 1775 a gristmill was erected on Steele Creek.

In addition to its Native American heritage, Fort Mill has an interesting colonial past that can be traced through its remaining historic sites. These include the Spratt family graveyard; Spratt's Spring, where General Cornwallis camped during the American Revolution; Confederate Park; Springfield Plantation; and White Homestead.

A crescent of land to the north of town was purchased by textile manufacturer Elliott Springs during Revolutionary times. It remains with the Close family (Springs's descendants), who have placed 2,200 acres in a land trust, creating the Anne S. Close Greenway, and have planned for careful development of the remaining property.

Fort Mill has 10,835 residents in its town limits and thousands more in outlying areas. Residents enjoy being close enough to commute to Rock Hill or Charlotte, but appreciate the quiet, slower pace of life. Even more residents are choosing Fort Mill thanks to two new developments. Baxter, at I-77's exit 85, is a planned community with townhomes, houses, a town center, restaurants, shops, a public library, an elementary school, parks, trails, and a recreation center. Springfield, next to the Anne Springs Close Greenway, is built around an 18-hole golf course. Amenities include a five-acre park, tennis, pools, a family activity center, and playgrounds.

Fort Mill also is home to the LeRoy Springs Recreation Complex and Knights Stadium and is close to Paramount's Carowinds, Lake Wylie, and the Museum of York County.

Gastonia

Built on what was once a large dairy farm, Gastonia grew into a textile giant when two railroad lines intersected at the town. Today Gaston County, west of Mecklenburg, is a major manufacturing county in North Carolina, with textile businesses such as Pharr Yarns, American & Efird, and Parkdale Mills; tractor-trailer truck maker Freightliner; Wix Corp., a division of Dana that makes auto filters; Christmas ornament company Rauch Industries; and Buckeye Technologies, a recent arrival in Gaston County, making absorbent materials. Incorporated in 1877, Gastonia was once called the Spindle Capital of the World. During World War I mills here operated 24/7 to supply materials for the war effort, and by the end of the war, the county had more mills than any other place in the country. Loray Mill, built in 1900, was the largest in the United States in its day; in 1929 it was the site of a violent labor strike in which the chief of police and a union supporter were killed.

Gastonia has lived in Charlotte's shadow for many years, but the 2000 All-America City has many worthy attributes of its own. The Schiele Museum of Natural History draws thousands of visitors each year for its planetarium and living-history settlements depicting the life of Native Americans and backcountry settlers who once lived here. Home decorators throughout the Carolinas flock to Mary Jo's Cloth Store for a wide selection of upholstery and drapery fabric at good prices. Martha Rivers Park, a city greenway, and a recently refurbished vintage kids' train are other Gastonia attractions.

On the Gaston-Cleveland county line west of Gastonia, Crowders Mountain State Park has two pinnacles popular with rock climbers, hiking trails, canoe rentals, and special programs such as nighttime owl prowls. This area also is home to Kings Mountain National Military Park, where

Americans damaged Britain's southern campaign and captured 1,100 Tories. In Dallas, the county's original town seat, the Gaston County Museum of Art & History gives great insight into what life was like in the agricultural and textile environment of the 19th century. It also features the largest public collection of horse-drawn vehicles in North Carolina.

Back in Gastonia, military buffs enjoy the American Military Museum with uniforms and artifacts from every war from the Civil War to Desert Storm, plus a diorama of Pearl Harbor under Japanese attack. Just down Franklin Boulevard from the museum is Tony's Ice Cream, a popular year-round treat since 1915. Fish camps, scattered around the county, are unique to the region with fried fish, hush puppies, sugar-water tea, and a family-friendly atmosphere.

Gaston County has increased its emphasis on art in the past few years. Theater groups include the Gastonia Little Theatre, Belmont Playmakers, and Gaston Children's Theatre. A community-wide school of the arts is located in Gastonia, along with a small chamber orchestra and choral society. Business boosters sponsor summer concerts and festivals downtown, and the United Arts Council hosts Pops in the Park with the Charlotte Symphony Orchestra at Gaston County Park. More than 68,500 people now call Gastonia home.

Indian Trail

Indian Trail was so named for the Native American trading path that ran straight through it from Petersburg, Virginia, to Waxhaw, the Indian settlement established in the 1800s. It's east of Charlotte about 1 mile off US 74 (Independence Boulevard) on Indian Trail Road. When the town incorporated in 1907, it was designed as a circle extending a half-mile in all directions from the center of the railroad tracks at the intersection of the main street. Today the town stretches for miles. Like so many tiny towns, Indian Trail was just a place to stop along the road until the railroad came through in 1874, connecting it with Charlotte and Monroe. Cotton bales lined the

railway platforms for many years, and the town had a fine gin. Stores, churches, a sawmill, and a brickyard made this a thriving community until the Great Depression of 1929. Then times were lean until World War II.

Indian Trail still retains its rural beauty, and many dedicated citizens are the third or fourth generation in the community. Although Indian Trail is considered a Charlotte bedroom community, it's actually located in Union County. Union is the fastest-growing county in the Carolinas, and Indian Trail hasn't escaped the influx. In the 1990s Indian Trail gained nearly 10,000 people for a total of nearly 12,000 residents, a 513 percent increase. Today the town, governed by a mayor and a five-member city council, has continued to grow to 15,000 residents.

Wal-Mart and Union West Medical Plaza have opened in the last decade, and the 87,000-square-foot Extreme Ice Center, built in 2006 with three rinks, has been a big plus for the town. It includes the Center Ice Tavern and even hosted Charlotte Checkers playoff games in 2009 when the team's home venue, Time Warner Cable Arena, was unavailable.

Kannapolis

This town of 40,000 residents in both Cabarrus and Rowan Counties northeast of Mecklenburg was mostly farmland with a half-dozen churches, schools, and businesses until the early 1900s. In 1906 James W. Cannon bought a large farm, built Cannon Mills, and developed the town around the mill. His son, Charles, brought the mill to prominence as the world's largest producer of household textiles—towels, sheets, and bedding. A village of mill workers rented homes at low rates from the Cannon family and enjoyed amenities such as a YMCA, a hospital, police, community services, low-cost utilities, home maintenance, and free garbage collection while paying no taxes.

But things started to change in 1982 when Cannon Mills was sold. It merged with Fieldcrest Mills to become Fieldcrest Cannon in 1985, and was bought by Pillowtex in 1997. By 2003, the company went bankrupt and folded, laying off around 4,800 workers. Today, Kannapolis is embracing a new industry—biotechnology. The massive former Cannon Mills/Pillowtex complex is being redeveloped into the NC Research Campus, a joint venture between Dole Foods, Duke University, and the UNC system. Plans include institutes for nutrition and fruit and vegetable science, an incubator for start-up firms, and extensive laboratories. Billionaire David Murdock, who owns Dole Foods and once owned a stake in Fieldcrest Cannon, is the driving force behind the unbelievable renaissance that will transform Kannapolis into a $1.5 billion research campus. When completed, the N.C. Research Campus will attract an influx of white-collar workers and executives, and, it is hoped, replace the thousands of jobs lost when the mill shut down.

Other recent improvements in Kannapolis include a $4 million YMCA, a senior center, a public library, an industrial business park on Highway 73, and a pro baseball stadium for the Class A Kannapolis Intimidators.

Lake Wylie, South Carolina

Lake Wylie is named for Dr. W. Gill Wylie, who convinced Ben and Buck Duke to invest in a hydroelectric power operation on the Catawba River. In 1904 Wylie brought in his engineer, William S. Lee, to design the $8 million project that would convert water power into energy from the proposed 12,455-acre lake. The lake's waters were mud red in those early days, when lots were leased to power company employees for $45 a year.

Today some 25,000 residents make their homes in modest cabins, middle-class houses, and million-dollar mansions lining the lake. Restaurants and marinas also dot the shores, and boaters can cruise past the banks of the Daniel Stowe Botanical Garden. Several shopping centers with more restaurants and service businesses for nearby residents also are near the lake.

Lake Wylie really began to develop residentially in the 1970s when two major developments,

River Hills Plantation and Tega Cay, opened with lake recreation, tennis, golf, and a fairly short commute. In the late 1980s several Charlotte Hornets professional basketball players built huge mansions in Riverpoint, on the Charlotte banks of the lake. Today development is sprouting up all along the shoreline. Woodland Bay, Misty Waters, and Reflection Pointe are newer neighborhoods on the lesser developed Gaston County side. The Palisades and The Sanctuary, both in Mecklenburg County, have hosted the prestigious HomeArama home tour of multimillion-dollar homes. The Sanctuary, in particular, has been nationally recognized for its environmental building and development practices.

Now that Highway 49 from Charlotte has been widened, retail development is following residential growth. RiverGate, at Highways 49 and 160, offers restaurants and major stores such as a SuperTarget, Best Buy, and Marshall's.

Neighbors and visitors use Lake Wylie's beautiful 325 miles of shoreline to sail, water-ski, swim, fish, and participate in boat races and sailing regattas. You'll find that marinas are a good source of information on activities in the area and offer a full range of services and storage facilities for your boat. There are several public-access boat ramps around the lake, where you can take out your boat, drop anchor in a quiet cove, and enjoy a picnic lunch.

McAdenville

Nearly two million people come to see the lights at McAdenville every Christmas. This tradition began over 50 years ago when the Men's Club of McAdenville and the owners of Stowe-Pharr Mill came up with the idea of generating Christmas spirit by decorating a few trees around town. Both Mr. Stowe and Mr. Pharr not only supported the idea but offered to pay for the decorations and electricity. Those nine decorated trees have grown every year to now include almost every tree in McAdenville, making this tiny town of 615 people "Christmastown USA." During the holidays the town is transformed by thousands of lights—a sight you shouldn't miss. You'll find the reflection of red, blue, green, and white lights upon the little pond near the town's center especially beautiful.

Like many aging textile towns, this small community is beginning to grow after years of no change at all. Old mill homes are being replaced, and several hundred new residents are moving in. The city enacted its first property tax in 2004.

But the Christmas lights tradition? That will never change.

Monroe

Monroe is the county seat and hub of commerce for Union County, one of the fastest-growing counties in the state. Union County draws newcomers with peaceful farms, bucolic countryside, and friendly people. Monroe, a charming southern small town, is located about 25 miles from the border of south Mecklenburg County. Monroe has undergone a successful downtown revitalization. The 1888 redbrick county courthouse on the town square has been refurbished, along with several shops and homes in the downtown area. Mixed-use residential and commercial areas are under construction downtown and visitors have access to free Wi-Fi in the downtown business district. Downtown Monroe also hosts movie nights and outdoor concerts throughout the spring and summer. The Beach, Blues and BBQ Festival takes place the first Sat in May.

The earliest inhabitants of the area were Native Americans of the Waxhaw tribe, part of the Catawba Nation. German, English, and Scots-Irish settlers moved here in the 1800s. Union County was carved out of Anson and Mecklenburg Counties in 1842; the city of Monroe was incorporated in 1844. In the 1990s Monroe's population jumped by 63 percent, and since 2000 it has continued to rise to a total of 37,500. Dealing with the immense growth has been challenging, as longtime locals and newcomers fight to keep their small town small.

The area has many diverse industries, including manufacturing facilities for heat-treated metal alloys, door closers, aircraft and automobile parts, and textiles. Monroe has become a popular choice for various businesses in the aerospace industry and has gained national attention for its ability to recruit and retain these suppliers.

In keeping with its aerospace connections, Monroe is home to the annual Warriors and Warbirds Air Show the first weekend in November at the Charlotte-Monroe Executive Airport. The event features several dozen flying World War II aircraft, pyrotechnic displays, information booths, and children's activities. It's a family-friendly educational event that draws upwards of 75,000 people and pays tribute to the men and women who serve the country in the armed forces.

Cotton was Union's cash crop for many years, and you'll still find family-operated farms—some of them more than a century old. Dairy farms dot the northeast end of Union; horse farms make up the south. Poultry, soybeans, corn, beef, swine, and other agricultural products are also produced here. Wingate University, a four-year institution with a unique approach to education, is located in nearby Wingate. The Jesse Helms Center, a 26,000-square-foot tribute to the Monroe native and U.S. senator, displays the longtime Republican leader's memorabilia in Wingate. Cane Creek Park in southern Union has more than 1,000 acres with playgrounds, hiking trails, picnic areas, fishing, swimming, horseback riding, camping, and mini-golf for kids. Theater, music, and the visual arts also flourish in Monroe.

Mooresville

Mooresville is named for John Moore, a wealthy farmer and merchant who donated land for a railroad depot and cotton-weighing platform in 1857. The only catch? Moore insisted that the proposed 60-foot-wide streets be changed to 40-foot widths so they wouldn't cut into his cotton fields, and that Main Street curve away from the railroad tracks so that he could sit on his front porch after lunch to see if passing wagons were stopping at his store across from the depot.

Except for the absence of wagons and the addition of utility poles, nothing much has changed the architecture or the atmosphere of downtown Mooresville since those early days. The same color awnings and glass front have remained at D. E. Turner Hardware since it moved to its "new location" across from the depot on Main Street in 1902. Inside, the original now-sagging wood floor, same wooden counters, and a rolling 20-foot wood ladder make you feel like time has stood still—and that's the way people like it. A frozen treat from Mooresville Ice Cream Company completes this tradition.

What has changed have been improvements for the Iredell County town of around 28,000 residents. The railroad depot was recycled into an arts center, and a Citizen Center was built with an auditorium, exercise pool, and banquet facilities for 500 people. New shops, including a cooking store and an upscale bakery, now share the street with longtime businesses like D. E. Turner Hardware and Landmark Galleries, home of watercolorist and Mooresville native Cotton Ketchie.

Mooresville's real growth—a 102 percent population jump in the last decade—has occurred closer to I-77 and Lake Norman, west of the old downtown. One example is The Point Lake & Golf Club, which has million-dollar Nantucket-architecture homes set on the lake and around an 18-hole golf course designed by Greg Norman. Family farms are giving way to new subdivisions and shopping centers such as the massive Morrison Plantation at Brawley School and Williamson Roads.

After many years as a cotton, textile, and farming town, Mooresville experienced two major changes in the last century. First came the creation of Lake Norman in the early 1960s, bringing new residents and scores of weekenders in search of fun on the water. Next came the influx of more than 50 NASCAR race teams in the 1980s and 1990s. Nowadays, the town bills itself as "Race City USA" and includes the N.C. Auto Racing Hall of Fame. Many of the race shops are open to the public and the NASCAR Technical Institute provides training in all facets of the automotive industry and offers NASCAR–specific courses.

But the biggest change to Mooresville's economy came when home-improvement retailer Lowe's relocated its corporate headquarters from Wilkesboro, N.C., in 2003. Lowe's built a massive 400,000-square-foot corporate campus on 165 acres near I-77's exit 33. The campus currently employs 1,500 and that number could swell to 8,000 employees in more than two million square feet of space when the campus is complete. Meanwhile, as many as 400 companies who act as vendors to Lowe's could set up shop in Mooresville.

Popular annual events in Race City USA include the Lake Norman Downtown Fest in May and the Greater Charlotte Antique and Classic Boat Festival in September. Attractions include the *Catawba Queen,* a Mississippi-style riverboat that cruises the lake, and the Lazy 5 Ranch, with drive-through or hayride safaris to see more than 400 animals.

Many race fans enjoy stopping at Dale Earnhardt Inc. to see memorabilia, cars, and trophies of the late seven-time NASCAR champion and to learn more about the team's current drivers. Meanwhile, Dale Earnhardt Jr.'s JR Motorsports team is based in Mooresville and has signed Indy Car sensation Danica Patrick to drive in the Nationwide Series, one step below Sprint Cup, the highest level in NASCAR racing. Penske Racing and Red Bull Racing are two more Sprint Cup teams headquartered in Mooresville.

Mount Holly

Located on the eastern end of Gaston County about 15 minutes from Charlotte, Mount Holly is where Gaston's textile empire began. However, like many cities in the North Carolina piedmont, most of the textile facilities have closed and the ones that remain are much smaller operations.

Today this city of 9,618 residents is transitioning from its rich textile history to developing the downtown and corridors into the city. Most recently, Mount Holly redeveloped its oldest textile mill into the Mount Holly Citizen's Center, exhibiting both an appreciation of the past and a promise for the future. The city's parks and recreation department operates six parks, along with two gymnasiums/fitness centers. Tuckaseegee Park has become the city's crown jewel with a series of renovations and upgrades. Located next to the Catawba River, Tuck Park has multiple athletic fields, picnic shelters, a dog park, walking trails, and a kayak launch.

In the last decade Mount Holly has begun to embrace its largest natural resource, the Catawba River. A couple of residential communities have been built near the water, and the city contributed $1 million to help construct the U.S. National Whitewater Center, which is located directly across the river in Mecklenburg County. North Carolina Flatwater Outfitters recently relocated to Mount Holly and offers kayaking on the tranquil waters of the Catawba from the Tailrace Marina.

Mount Holly appears poised for a future of continued commercial and residential growth.

Rock Hill, South Carolina

Just 20 minutes south of Charlotte is Rock Hill. It is the fourth-largest city in South Carolina with a population of 67,339, and an active business climate and educational opportunities. Rock Hill has four industrial parks and the busiest general aviation airport in the area. The city has more than 200 manufacturing businesses, producing everything from pneumatic hand tools to egg rolls to textiles. York Technical College provides training for many area industries. The city is also home to Winthrop University, a four-year institution with undergraduate and graduate programs.

Settled in the 1800s and now a part of South Carolina's Olde English District (see Day Trips chapter), Rock Hill is rich in history. Glencairn Garden was once the private garden of Dr. and Mrs. David A. Bigger. Opened to the public in 1960, it is also a popular site during the annual Come-See-Me Festival, an 11-day spring event that features exhibits, concerts, gourmet gardens, crafts, road and bicycle races, children's events, a parade, and fireworks. Vernon Grant, the creator of Kellogg's Rice Krispies' Snap, Crackle, and Pop, designed the frog that serves as the festival's emblem.

The Museum of York County's wild animal collection is one of the most comprehensive any-

where. Featured are animals from Africa, North America, and South America. The museum also devotes space to exhibits on York County, Indian tribes of the area, photography, and traveling shows. The Settlemyre Planetarium and the Rock Hill Telephone Company Museum are also popular with visitors. The Rock Hill Transportation Exhibit, located downtown, features an Anderson 640 touring car made by the Anderson Motor Company in 1915. The Catawba Cultural Center preserves the rich heritage of the Catawba Indian Nation through art, literature, jewelry, pottery, and an annual November festival.

Residents also enjoy Cherry Park, a 68-acre recreational facility with five softball fields, multipurpose fields, picnic areas, and paved paths, as well as River Park with 70 environmentally sensitive acres overlooking the Catawba River. River Park's nearly 2 miles of trails are wheelchair accessible .

Insider Top 10: What We Google

According to statistics released by the popular search engine, here are the 10 most "Googled" things in Charlotte:

1. Charlotte-Mecklenburg Schools (CMS) Parent Assistant
2. Charlotte Restaurant Week
3. Mez (Uptown movie theater/restaurant)
4. EpiCentre Charlotte
5. CMS Schools
6. CMS Intranet
7. Mecklenburg County Sheriff mug shots
8. YMCA Charlotte
9. Charmeck.org
10. Birkdale Movies

Salisbury

Two and a half centuries ago, Salisbury was the jumping-off point for pioneers, visionaries, and even a few scoundrels and fugitives on their way to the American frontier. When Revolutionary War Gen. Nathanael Greene rode into Salisbury in 1781, he stopped off at Elizabeth Maxwell Steele's tavern. After Mrs. Steele heard of the pitiful conditions of Greene's troops, she gave him two small sacks of money for provisions. As he accepted the gift, the general saw portraits of King George III and Queen Charlotte on the tavern wall. He turned the picture of the king to the wall and wrote on the back with a piece of chalk: "O George! Hide thy face and mourne." Today you can find those portraits, with the inscription still legible, hanging at Thyatira Presbyterian Church. In the church cemetery, a monument marks the grave of Mrs. Steele.

A century ago Salisbury and nearby Spencer were important stops on Southern Railway's line. The city's historic train depot, designed with a Spanish mission motif by Frank Pierce Milburn in 1907, has been beautifully restored and now serves as the home of the Historic Salisbury Foundation, Inc. Trains are also the focus of the N.C. Transportation Museum in Spencer, once the largest steam locomotive repair facility between Washington, D.C., and Atlanta.

Salisbury is a city with both a rich history and a progressive attitude. It has three colleges: Catawba, Livingstone, and Rowan Cabarrus Community College, and is the birthplace and corporate headquarters of supermarket giant Food Lion. The National Sportscasters & Sportswriters Hall of Fame is located in Salisbury, and each year many of the biggest names in sports broadcasting and sports writing descend upon Salisbury for the Hall's induction ceremony and awards program.

In recent years, Salisbury has revived its historic downtown in a vibrant area where people actually come for commerce and leisure. There are two coffeehouses, two wine shops, an expanded independent book store (with an entire floor devoted to children's books), and a variety of quality arts and crafts studios.

During the growing season, Salisbury holds a farmers' market on Wed and Sat at the corner of Main and Bank Streets where shoppers can buy local produce, beef, pork, chicken, eggs, baked goods, and crafts.

If you visit on a weekend, tour the home of Dr. Josephus Hall, who served as surgeon general for the nearby Confederate prison. The home was requisitioned in the closing days of the Civil War by Union Gen. George Stoneman, during his infamous "Stoneman's Raid" on North Carolina. Mrs. Hall, who etched her name in a window glass to prove ownership of this lovely mansion, instructed Stoneman to keep his soldiers' horses off her boxwood path borders. The boxwoods, as well as the home's interior, remain intact.

Thirty blocks make up the National Register Historic District, whose character has been saved by the Historic Salisbury Foundation, Inc. Several historic buildings are open to the public year-round, and you can get a look at many of the private homes during the annual Historic Salisbury tour in October. Crafts are also demonstrated at this time. Another good time to visit the city is during the Christmas season, when some of the historic buildings are decorated for the holidays. Historic Salisbury trolley tours are offered on Sat April through Oct.

This active community of about 28,000 residents always has something going on, such as Mayfest and the Autumn Jubilee. The Waterworks Art Gallery is a must-see, as is 1905 Meroney Theater, one of the oldest community theaters in the state. You'll also find historic buildings such as the 1819 Rowan Museum, the CLDL Stone House built in 1766, and the 1839 Salisbury Female Academy. Rowan County has some fine parks and recreational areas. One worth the drive from Charlotte is Dan Nicholas Park.

The Salisbury Visitors Center, 204 East Innes St., is open Mon through Sat from 10 a.m. to 4 p.m. Here you'll find brochures on self-guided walking and dining tours featuring Salisbury's heritage, Civil War sites, and African-American history. While in town, plan to see the 127-by-48.5-foot mural painted on the side of Wachovia Bank & Trust—the largest mural in the state—

which depicts Salisbury's heritage at the turn of the 20th century. Downtown also features an 1892 church bell tower, fountains at the entrance of the historic district, and a 1909 Confederate monument of an angel holding a dying soldier.

Statesville

Pioneer John Edwards purchased a land grant from the Earl of Granville in 1751 for what is today the seat of Iredell County, located due north of Charlotte at the intersection of I-77 and I-40. At first, settlers described their new community as Fourth Creek, meaning the fourth creek west of Salisbury. The center of the settlement was a log cabin where the Presbyterians worshipped and where First Presbyterian Church is located today. The original cemetery where many pioneers are buried is adjacent. In 1755 Governor Arthur Dobbs chose the area for a fort to safeguard settlers from French and Indian attacks. The fort, named after Dobbs, successfully repelled a Cherokee attack but was later abandoned and fell into ruin. Nowadays you can see artifacts on display at the fort's visitor center and get a feel for what life was like at a time when Statesville was on the edge of the western frontier. Plans are under way to reconstruct Fort Dobbs to further enhance the trip back to pre-Colonial America.

In 1789 the town was incorporated as Statesville. Town leaders began pushing for a railroad as early as 1833, but when it finally arrived in 1858, the town was still struggling from a devastating fire. Located at the end of the rail line and later the home of two railroads, Statesville grew quickly. The town took another blow four days after Confederate troops surrendered in the Civil War. Yankee invaders burned the two railroad depots, freight houses, and the local newspaper's building, and stole everything of value. Once larger than Charlotte, Statesville began to rebuild.

Today the town of 23,500 prides itself on four residential historic districts and the historic downtown business district, which is centered at the square. The only original building still standing downtown is the Statesville Drug Company with its signature clock on top. The clock, costing $500 in 1890, was renovated in 1990, and its chime can be heard on the hour and half hour. Statesville has many homes and buildings listed on the National Register of Historic Places and is undergoing a Main Street transformation that has already made great progress in returning much of the city's original design. Mitchell Community College is located in the heart of one historic district that features 170 buildings.

The Zebulon Vance Home, where Governor Vance lived and practiced law, is here. This 1832 house, open to the public, served as his headquarters during his exile from the state capital in Raleigh during the last months of the Civil War.

Although Statesville is historic, it doesn't live in the past. The old textile plants have been replaced by German machinery manufacturers, Japanese engine manufacturers, and a plastic recycling plant, and movie film production companies have utilized the area for a variety of feature and made-for-television movies. Statesville's Fire Fly Balloons is a major manufacturer of hot-air balloons. What started out as a small pig pickin' for eight balloonists and 300 spectators in 1973 has become the nationally recognized Carolina BalloonFest, the second oldest balloon rally in the nation. It draws 50 balloonists and a crowd exceeding 30,000 every year—an event you don't want to miss.

Statesville has been named an All-America City by the National Civic League two times. In 1997 Statesville embraced three community projects to win this special designation: Save the Depot, a restoration project; CommuniCare, an after-school tutoring program for minority children; and the Open Door Clinic, built and paid for by volunteers and located at the shelter that provides free medical care to the homeless. In 2009 the featured projects were Mi Familia Institute, which helps Statesville's Hispanic community navigate the difficult assimilation process; Fifth Street Ministries, which provides services to those with the most need, including a new overnight and emergency shelter, and a shelter and programs for victims of domestic violence; and the Boys and Girls Club of the Piedmont, a comprehensive community effort to help a generation of disadvantaged youth.

On top of all that, Statesville is a nice place to live and educate children.

Tega Cay, South Carolina

With excellent schools and strong community spirit, Tega Cay is a wonderful place to raise a family or even retire. The town of more than 4,000 is located on the east side of Lake Wylie just 15 miles south of Charlotte. The name "Tega Cay" means "beautiful peninsula" in Polynesian, and the South Seas theme was carried out in the street names and in the architecture of this picturesque area. Incorporated on July 4, 1982, the city has 13 miles of shoreline and a rugged topography and is densely wooded with tall pines and hardwoods. Each Fourth of July, the city celebrates its birthday with ceremonies, parades, fireworks, and the cutting of a birthday cake made in honor of our country's birthday.

The city's extensive recreational amenities include 27 holes of golf; 4 waterfront parks, with 2 new ones being planned; 8 lighted tennis courts; walking trails; inland parks; a marina; and 3 boat-launching areas.

Waxhaw

Waxhaw has rapidly grown from a town of about 1,500 people in the mid 1990s to a residential Charlotte suburb of about 7,000 today.

Most visitors come to this quaint area of south Union County near the South Carolina border for the antiques. More than a dozen antiques shops are open just about every day year-round, and more are open on weekends. If you tire of looking for treasures, consider some of the other sites. Six miles to the east is the Mexico-Cardenas Museum at JAARS (Jungle Aviation and Radio Service). It honors Lázaro Cárdenas, Mexico's former president, who was a close associate of JAARS founder Cameron Townsend. The museum offers a glimpse into the work of this unique world organization that has about 250 specialists translating the Bible into languages all over the world. Or you might head to Cane Creek Park, a 1,000-acre recreation facility surrounding a large lake. It offers camping, boating, fishing, and picnicking. The Andrew Jackson Museum has a large display of historic artifacts. An annual military reenactment is staged with the museum's assistance.

Some folks take regular trips to Waxhaw to eat lunch at the Bridge and Rail Restaurant, 112 East South Main St. If you like country food, this is the place to visit. The helpings are large, and the atmosphere with photographs of Waxhaw's past highlights this historic setting.

A number of special events are also worth a visit: the Downtown Waxhaw Antique Festival, held each Memorial Day weekend; Listen and Remember, an outdoor drama that tells the story of President Andrew Jackson and the Waxhaw Native Americans, performed each weekend in June; and the Waxhaw Scottish Highland Games in Cane Creek Park in October, featuring bagpipes and traditional Scottish competitions. Be sure to wear your plaid!

One of the area's newer annual events is the Queen's Cup Charlotte Steeplechase, an all-day affair that features horse races, equestrian events, a lawn tailgate party, and a hat parade. In recent years more than 25,000 people have attended the April steeplechase on a farm just outside of downtown Waxhaw.

Charlotte Vital Statistics

Mayor: Anthony Foxx, Democrat

North Carolina governor: Beverly "Bev" Perdue, Democrat

Population: 716,874 city, 935,304 county, 1,725,759 greater Charlotte region

Area (square miles): 268 city, 527 city and county

County: Mecklenburg

Nickname: The Queen City

Time zone: Eastern Time

Founded: 1762 county, 1768 city

Major area employers: Bank of America, Charlotte-Mecklenburg Schools, , Carolinas Healthcare System, City of Charlotte, Duke Energy, Lowe's Home Improvement, State of North Carolina, Mecklenburg County, Presbyterian Healthcare/Novant Health, Ruddick/Harris Teeter, U.S. Government, US Airways, Wells Fargo/Wachovia.

Famous sons and daughters: Rev. Billy Graham, evangelist; Charles Kuralt, journalist; Andrew Jackson (Waxhaw), 7th U.S. President; James K. Polk (Pineville), 11th U.S. President; Romare Bearden, artist; Randolph Scott, movie cowboy; Davis Love III, PGA golfer; Charles Sifford, retired PGA golfer; James B. Duke, industrialist and philanthropist; Carson McCullers, author; Elizabeth Dole (Salisbury), former U.S. Senator and Red Cross president; Erskine Bowles, former White House chief of staff; Dale Earnhardt Sr. (Kannapolis), race car driver; Jim and Tammy Faye Bakker, fallen televangelists; James Worthy (Gastonia), Hall of Fame basketball player; Chelsea Cooley Altman, Miss USA 2005; Dale Earnhardt Jr. (Kannapolis), race car driver; Bobby Jones, pro basketball player; Randy Travis (Marshville), country singer; Brooklyn Decker, swimsuit model; Jim Beatty, first runner to break the four-minute mile indoors; Fred Durst (Gastonia) singer and director; Ray Durham, pro baseball player

Average temperatures: January (high/low) 49/29, July (high/low) 88/69

Average annual precipitation: 43 inches

State/city holidays: New Year's Day, Martin Luther King Day, Presidents Day, Easter, Memorial Day, Independence Day, Labor Day, Thanksgiving Day, Christmas Day

Chamber of commerce:
Charlotte Chamber of Commerce
330 South Tryon St.
Charlotte, NC 28232
(704) 378-1300
www.charlottechamber.org

Major airport: Charlotte/Douglas International Airport

Major roads: Interstates 77, 85, 485 (outer belt), 277 (inner belt); U.S. Highways 74, 29; North Carolina Highways 49, 16

Public transportation: Charlotte Area Transit System (CATS); LYNX Blue Line light rail

Driving laws:
Seat belts must be worn by all passengers.
Texting is prohibited while operating a motor vehicle.
Children under age 12 are not permitted to ride in the front seat in vehicles with airbags.

Right turns permitted on red, unless otherwise marked.

Pedestrians have the right-of-way in crosswalks.

New residents must get a North Carolina driver's license within 60 days of establishing residence. Written, skills, sign-recognition, and vision tests are required, along with a current out-of-state license or two other forms of identification, your Social Security card, proof of liability insurance, and proof of residency. New residents with a valid license are exempt from a road-skills test.

Alcohol laws:

You must be 21 to purchase or consume alcoholic beverages legally.

Legally, you are presumed to be intoxicated if your blood alcohol concentration is .08 percent.

Bars can serve alcohol until 2 a.m.

Many counties in South Carolina do not sell alcohol in stores, restaurants, or bars on Sun.

Daily newspaper: *The Charlotte Observer*

Sales tax: 8.25 percent city/state taxes on all retail sales

GETTING HERE, GETTING AROUND

Transportation has always been integral to Charlotte. In its earliest days, Charlotte was a trading crossroads for settlers and Native Americans. Later, it developed into a railroad hub for the South's burgeoning textile industry. In the 1920s, Wilkinson Boulevard became the state's first four-lane paved highway. A few decades later, construction of Interstates 77 and 85, which intersect just northwest of the center city, made the Queen City a hub for trucking companies like Roadway, Overnight, Yellow Freight and Thurston Motor Lines. In the 1980s, Charlotte/Douglas Airport evolved into a major player for air travelers, thanks in large part to the hub established by homegrown Piedmont Airlines, later purchased by US Airways.

Getting around in Charlotte was somewhat of a struggle in the 1980s and 1990s as the city's growth outpaced its ability to provide transportation infrastructure. However, Queen City leaders and state leaders have rallied in the last two decades to balance the scales. Both Interstates have been widened and I-77 features the state's first High Occupancy Vehicle (HOV) lanes. A third runway was recently added to Charlotte/Douglas Airport, which is among the top 15 in the nation in terms of air passengers. Our first light rail line emerged in late 2007, the I-485 loop is more than three-fourths complete and a recent Federal grant promises to bring a third daily Amtrak route between Charlotte and Raleigh.

For visitors and newcomers, transportation options are many and there is an ample supply of roads, although they're admittedly a bit confusing. With the exception of Uptown, Charlotte's street system is not designed in the traditional grid manner. Roads meander, make sharp turns, change names and often don't run directly east-west or north-south.

A thorough read of this chapter will get you up to speed on Queen City transportation.

AIR TRANSPORTATION

Charlotte/Douglas International

Charlotte/Douglas is the nation's 14th-busiest airport in number of passengers, handling about 35 million passengers per year. The airport has 614 flights departing daily with nonstop service to 130 cities. More than half the population of the United States lives within a two-hour flight of the city.

In addition, the airport offers nonstop international flights to and from: Antigua; Aruba; Bridgetown, Barbados; Belize; Bermuda; Cancun, Mexico; Cozumel, Mexico; Frankfurt, Germany; Freeport, Bahamas; Grand Cayman Islands; Liberia, Costa Rica; London, England; Mexico City; Montego Bay, Jamaica; Munich, Germany; Montreal, Canada; Nassau, Bahamas; Paris, France; Providenciales, Turks & Caicos; Punta Cana, Dominican Republic; Rio de Janeiro, Brazil; San Jose, Costa Rica; San Juan, Puerto Rico; St. Croix, U.S. Virgin Islands; St. Lucia; St. Maarten, Netherland Antilles; St. Kitts; St. Thomas, U.S. Virgin Islands; Toronto, Canada; Rome, Italy; and Sao Paulo, Brazil.

Ten major carriers serve the airport: Air Canada, AirTran, American, Continental, Delta, JetBlue, Lufthansa, Northwest, United, and US Airways, which calls Charlotte its super hub. US Airways Express serves a fast-growing commuter and regional base, shuttling passengers to Charlotte for jet service to all points of the United States and abroad.

Unfortunately, Charlotte is one of the country's more expensive markets from which to fly. Because US Airways has a hub at Charlotte/

Douglas and controls most of the gates, it has a monopoly on the number of flights and can charge higher prices without having to worry about competition, especially on direct flights. Business travelers frequently complain about the higher rates, particularly when they can save several hundred dollars by driving 90 minutes northeast to Greensboro to catch the same US Airways flight when it stops at Charlotte/Douglas. Other travelers drive two and a half hours to Raleigh to catch low-fare Southwest flights. One positive of being a hub for US Airways is that the Charlotte airport offers a nice array of nonstop flights. If you are traveling to another major city in the United States, it is likely you can fly there nonstop from the Queen City.

Charlotte/Douglas International encompasses five concourses with 91 total gates. The airport now has four runways in use and a 1.7-million-square-foot terminal. With a total work force of more than 18,000, Charlotte/Douglas is one of the largest employers in the county.

Under the guidance of director Jerry Orr, the airport has focused on more than just moving people. It gives many visitors their first impression of the Queen City. As Charlotte's "front door," the airport goes to great lengths to welcome visitors to the region. Expertly landscaped, the airport greets travelers with green grass, colorful flowers, and Southern camellias. A bronze sculpture of Queen Charlotte, crafted by artist Raymond Kaskey and given to the city by a group of anonymous benefactors called the Queen's Table, rises nearly three stories at the main entrance of the terminal.

Built in a wheel-and-spoke design with concourses meeting at a central hub, the airport features a range of amenities for passengers. Boutiques and restaurants fill the shopping mall center. You'll find Chili's, Stock Car Cafe, Brookwood Farms Barbecue, Fox Skybox, Speedway Grill & Cafe, California Pizza Kitchen, Sbarro, KFC Express, TCBY Yogurt, Cinnabon, Burger King, Pizza Hut Express, Manchu Wok, Mrs. Fields Cookies, Starbucks Gourmet Coffee, Candy Express, Carolina Sports Bar, Charlotte Bistro, and Great American Bagel. Shoppers can load up at Simply Books, Erwin Pearl jewelry, Mind Works, Johnston & Murphy, Brookstone, Body Shop, Sunglass by Design, and Time to Write.

One of most popular additions in recent years is the Yadkin Valley Wine Bar, featuring a large selection of wines from North Carolina's fast-growing Yadkin Valley wine region.

i Due to heightened security measures, only ticket-holding passengers are allowed past the security stations at Charlotte/Douglas International Airport. The mall area with restaurants and shops is within the secured zone, so nonpassengers cannot access these areas.

Travelers are also welcomed to Charlotte/Douglas International with an unusual twist—rocking chairs. Passengers waiting for a flight in the glass-enclosed atrium can rock and relax in the chairs, a trend that started in the Queen City and has spread to other airports around the country. The atrium, surrounded by shops and restaurants, also includes the circular First in Flight Bar with an interesting art mobile and a quiet zone for business travelers who want to use desks, phones, and dataports. Outside, the Queen Charlotte courtyard under the Kaskey statue features a fountain, landscaping, and park benches. US Airways operates club-level areas on Concourses B, C, and D.

Although growing, Charlotte/Douglas International is still compact enough that getting to and from the boarding gates is not a long journey. And, the airport is a mere 15 to 20 minutes from the center of the city. Billy Graham Parkway and Wilkinson Boulevard offer easy access to the airport's 6,000-acre complex, along with direct access from Interstates 85 and 77.

In addition to increased passenger traffic, cargo traffic is brisk. The airport handles 132,000 tons of cargo each year.

Nearby, off Morris Field Drive, Signature Flight Support (704-359-8415, www.signature flight.com) is a fixed-base operator offering charter and private flight service. Many of the region's corporate jets and planes are stationed at this facility.

Frequently Called Numbers

If you need information on Charlotte/Douglas International Airport, call the following numbers or go to www.charlotteairport.com. Here are a few of the most frequently called numbers for Charlotte/Douglas International.

- Emergency Medical: (704) 359-4012
- Lost and Found: (704) 359-8765
- Main Switchboard: (704) 359-4000
- Paging Service: (704) 359-4013
- Public Parking: (704) 359-4038
- Taxi Dispatch: (704) 359-4085
- Transportation Security Administration (TSA): (704) 916-2200
- Welcome Center/Visitor Information: (704) 359-4027

Major Carriers

AIR CANADA
(888) 247-2262
www.aircanada.com

AIRTRAN
(800) 247-8726
www.airtran.com

AMERICAN
(800) 433-7300
www.aa.com

CONTINENTAL
(800) 525-0280
www.continental.com

DELTA
(800) 221-1212
www.delta.com

JETBLUE
(800) 538-2583
www.jetblue.com

LUFTHANSA
(800) 399-5838
www.lufthansa.com

NORTHWEST
(800) 225-2525
www.nwa.com

UNITED
(800) 241-6522
www.united.com

US AIRWAYS
(800) 428-4322
www.usairways.com

Ticketing

The major carriers operating at Charlotte/ Douglas offer ticket desks on the upper departure level.

Parking

More than 23,000 parking spaces serve the airport, thanks to the recent additions of two modern parking decks.

The airport provides several options for parking. The remote and long-term lots cost $4 for each 24-hour period. Closer to the terminal, the daily lots cost $6 for each 24-hour period. Both are serviced by shuttles to the main terminal. Covered hourly parking, adjacent to the terminal, is $1 per half hour up to a maximum of $16 a day.

Picking someone up? Hourly parking is free for the first 30 minutes. Drivers also can wait in the Cell Phone Lot. Designed to prevent drivers from circling the airport or parking outside the baggage claim area, the Cell Phone Lot is free all the time, however you cannot leave your car unattended at the Cell Phone Lot.

Curbside valet parking is available at the end of the departures/ticketing level for $4 the first half hour, $1 each additional half hour, and $19 maximum. To retrieve your car, stop by the valet booth or call (704) 359-VALET.

For current parking conditions, call (704) 359-5555.

Airport Transportation Services

All ground transportation is located on the lower level of the main terminal, with the exception of city buses operated by Charlotte Area Transit System (CATS). Buses pick up at the east end of the upper level. Service is available between the airport and Uptown daily, via Highway 5.

Taxi service is available on the lower level outside baggage claim. An attendant is on duty from 6:45 a.m. until 12:15 a.m. daily. Base rate for taxi service is $2.50, plus 50 cents per each one-fifth mile. Additional charges are incurred for travel outside city limits and for handling more than three bags. Count on a $25 fare from the airport to Uptown and a $13 minimum fare within a 3-mile radius of the airport.

Eight rental car agencies man service counters at the airport: Alamo, National, Avis, Budget, Dollar, Enterprise, Hertz, and Thrifty. All are located on the lower level, near baggage claim.

Many Charlotte–area hotels offer shuttle service to and from the airport, picking up outside of baggage claim on the lower level. Hotels and motels may be contacted through one of four Traveler Information Centers on the baggage claim level. Limousine service, which charges according to the number of people in your party, also is available.

i Charlotte/Douglas International Airport offers complimentary motorist assistance for passengers and visitors who have dead batteries, are locked out of their vehicles, or cannot find their cars. For help, contact any member of the parking staff, including shuttle drivers, or call on emergency phones located throughout the parking deck. Assistance is given on a first-come, first-served basis, but calls are typically answered within 15 minutes.

Airport Services

Charlotte/Douglas offers several conveniences to airport passengers and visitors.

General airport information and paging services are available at the Welcome Center on the baggage (lower) level from 7:30 a.m. until 11 p.m. daily and at the information counter on the ticketing (upper) level from 7 a.m. until 9 p.m. daily. The Welcome Center also has a wide range of Charlotte and North Carolina tourism information. Call (704) 359-4027 for details.

Full-service banking, including currency exchange, is available at First Citizens Bank in the lobby of the ticketing level. A foreign currency ATM is located at the Ticketing C Checkpoint. Regular ATMs are located in Concourse A and the Concourse D connector with First Citizens, Wells Fargo/Wachovia, and Bank of America.

Computer and high-speed Internet access, faxing and copying services, and conferencing capabilities are available in the Business Center located in the Atrium; call (704) 359-4320 for details.

To help with transporting luggage, baggage cart rentals are available on stands throughout the airport. The cost is $2, payable in coins, bills, or by credit card.

First Aid is located near Security Checkpoint A on the ticketing level. A 24-hour chapel and meditation room is open near Security Checkpoint B on the upper level.

Concord Regional Airport

Located about 25 minutes northeast of Charlotte's central business district, the City of Concord Regional Airport is another option for private and corporate flights. The airport is in close proximity to I-85 and has convenient access to Charlotte Motor Speedway, the new zMax Dragway, Concord Mills Mall, premier golf courses, local business parks, and restaurants. It is open 24/7 and offers a secure ramp area and control tower, as well as on-site fire and rescue personnel. Call (704) 920-5900 for more information.

Wilgrove Airport

Located east of Charlotte off Albemarle Road at 10525 Parkton Rd. (704-545-1875), Wilgrove Airport has served private and commercial flights since the early 1970s. The facility has one runway totaling 3,200 feet, compared to Charlotte/Douglas's 26,345 feet. It offers hangars and tie-down services, maintenance, fuel, flying lessons, and scenic tours. The Metrolina Flying Club, based there, has a staff of professional instructors and offers qualifying for all pilot ratings, from private through ATP.

GROUND TRANSPORTATION

Highway

Instead of a crown, some say the Queen City's symbol ought to be an orange traffic cone. Growth came to Charlotte faster than its roads could handle, and officials and planners are diligently working to catch up.

First, the basics: I-85 passes just north of the urban core on basically an east-west route through the county. It has several exits that will bring you to Uptown or other points south. I-77 runs due north and south, skirting the western edge of Uptown and intersecting with I-85 just northwest of the center city. From the southeast, you can enter Charlotte via US 74. I-485, the outer belt, will eventually form a loop completely around the entire Charlotte area.

The city's biggest road construction project at the moment is I-485, an outer belt loop that bypasses the congested core of Charlotte and connects I-85 and I-77. The 67-mile project is just five miles from being complete and the hope is that it will be completely finished in 2014.

If you think of it as a clock, the outer belt now stretches from 2 o'clock around University City and moves clockwise through south Charlotte, on to 9 o'clock at I-85 west of Charlotte, and back around to just after 12 o'clock near Huntersville.

Eventually the outer belt will include 32 interchanges, shortening commute times for drivers in outlying counties and helping out-of-town drivers avoid the congested 77–85 interchange north of Uptown. While some drivers are elated with the outer belt, others are already frustrated that it's packed. The state designed the road as a rural bypass with only two lanes in each direction and badly underestimated how many Charlotte

drivers would use the road. The oldest stretch of I-485, its southern leg, is now one of the state's most heavily traveled highway, carrying more than 120,000 vehicles a day—nearly as much as I-85 in nearby Gastonia. Backups during rush hour sometimes stretch for miles. In newer legs of the outer belt, the road was built with three or four lanes in each direction.

HOV Lanes

North Carolina's first High Occupancy Vehicle (HOV) lanes opened in Charlotte in fall 2004. Located on I-77 North, HOV lanes are open to vehicles with two or more passengers. HOV lanes are designed to encourage carpooling and offer a faster and more convenient route for vehicles carrying more than one person. The far left lanes are marked with a diamond symbol on the pavement, overhead signs, and double white solid lines at the access and exit points. HOV lane violations can result in a $100 fine, court costs, and two points on your driving record.

Other major road projects have recently been completed. I-77 North moving toward Lake Norman is now six to eight lanes wide with High-Occupancy Vehicle (HOV) commuter lanes in some places. The interstate reduces back to two lanes in each direction at Huntersville.

I-85 is four lanes in each direction throughout most of Mecklenburg County, and the next step is to widen the road from exit 49 near the speedway to the Highway 73 interchange in Concord.

Just outside of Uptown, East Independence Boulevard has been widened to a limited access freeway out to Sharon Amity Road, with a bus lane in the median and a major redesign of the interchange with Albemarle Road.

In the southwest section of Mecklenburg County, Highway 49 has now been widened from the Buster Boyd Bridge over Lake Wylie to the I-485 outer belt.

In town, driving is not always an enviable task. The largest city in the Carolinas, Charlotte has a reputation for fast drivers and significant rush-hour traffic.

Driving in Charlotte can be a bit confusing for folks unfamiliar with its unusual road system. Uptown Charlotte, surrounded by I-77, I-277 (John Belk Freeway and Brookshire Freeway), uses a grid system. Trade and Tryon, former Native American trading paths, are the main streets. Look for four bronze statues at their intersection known as The Square. East-west streets are numbered in Uptown, with the exception of Second Street, which was recently renamed Martin Luther King Jr. Boulevard. Also, Trade Street is located between Fourth and Fifth. Cross streets are Church, Poplar, Mint, and Graham Streets west of Tryon; College, Brevard, Caldwell, Davidson, and McDowell Streets east of Tryon.

Charlotte's main arteries extend from Uptown like the spokes of a wheel. South Boulevard winds through South End and leads down to Pineville. I-77 runs south from the center city to Fort Mill, South Carolina. Providence Road (Highway 16), Park Road, and Monroe Road are other routes headed south/southeast. Independence Boulevard (US 74) takes you southeast to Matthews and eventually eastward to the coast near Wilmington. Albemarle Road, Central Avenue, and The Plaza lead to east Charlotte. To the north, Tryon Street (US 29/Highway 49) heads northeast to the University area, while I-77 goes due north to Lake Norman. Brookshire Freeway (Highway 16) moves northwest to Mountain Island Lake. Points west—including the airport and Gaston County—are accessible via Wilkinson Boulevard (US 74 West). I-85 runs parallel with Wilkinson beginning a few miles outside of Uptown.

Driving through town requires navigation by landmark, not street name. Charlotte is notorious for its name-switching streets. One major thoroughfare, for example, starts as Mulberry Church Road before becoming Billy Graham Parkway. The Billy Graham Parkway eventually changes names to Woodlawn Road, which later becomes Runnymede Lane. Tyvola Road, another major artery, also has stretches called Fairview, Sardis, Rama, and Idlewild. Eastway Drive turns into Wendover Road and then becomes Sharon Road. Meanwhile, Sharon Amity Road (not to be confused with Sharon Road) changes names to Sharon Lane. One intersection in Myers Park has intersecting streets that share the same name. Take a right off Queens and you're still on Queens; left off Providence and you're still on Providence. The system may confuse newcomers and visitors, but eventually becomes part of the city's quirky charm.

Charlotte Road Conditions & Traffic

A wide range of information on issues concerning Charlotte roads is available. For questions on street maintenance, call (704) 336-2930 or go to www.charmeck.org/departments/transportation. Drivers can dial 511 to get traffic news and winter road conditions. Real-time travel info, traffic cameras, and information on North Carolina transportation is at www.ncsmartlink.org. The *Charlotte Observer* regularly covers traffic and transportation issues. Visit www.charlotte.com.

Car Rental Agencies
- **Alamo** (800) 327-9633
- **Avis** (800) 831-2847
- **Budget** (800) 527-0700
- **Dollar** (800) 800-4000
- **Enterprise** (800) 325-8007
- **Hertz** (800) 654-3131
- **National** (800) 227-7368
- **Thrifty** (800) 643-7368

Bus Service

CHARLOTTE AREA TRANSIT SYSTEM (CATS)
901 North Davidson St.
(704) 336-RIDE (7433)
www.charmeck.org
The Charlotte Transportation Center at 310 East Trade St. is the center of activity for CATS. A covered drive-through bus station with retail and service businesses, the center was the first of its kind in the nation. Passengers can buy bus passes, get schedule information, stop by the bank, grab lunch, buy sundries and souvenirs, and even seek medical care all in one place. More than 40 routes currently serve Charlotte and six Mecklenburg County towns (Davidson, Huntersville, Cornelius, Matthews, Pineville, and Mint Hill), as well as Concord in Cabarrus County, Gastonia in Gaston County, Mooresville in Iredell County, Rock Hill in York County, Monroe in Union County, and Denver in Lincoln County.

CATS also offers a neighborhood-based van service that takes passengers to main bus routes; door-to-door service within the city limits for disabled passengers; vanpool/carpool matching services; 56 Park 'N' Ride lots with free parking; bike racks on buses; guaranteed rides home for vanpool and Express riders; e-mail notification service; and a newspaper for commuters.

CHARLOTTE TROLLEY
2104 South Blvd. at Atherton Mill
(704) 375-0850
www.charlottetrolley.org
On weekends the historic Charlotte Trolley runs from Atherton Mill in South End, through a tunnel inside the Charlotte Convention Center in Uptown, and all the way up to Ninth Street. Fees for the trolley are $3 round-trip for adults and $1.50 for seniors and students. There is also a museum at the trolley barn.

GOLD RUSH CIRCULATOR
(704) 336-RIDE (7433)
www.charlottecentercity.org
These red trolleys on wheels offer free rides throughout the center city from 6:45 a.m. to 10 p.m. weekdays, usually at seven-minute intervals. The Gold Rush, which takes its name from the Charlotte region's late-1700s gold discovery and mining rush, has three lines—red, blue, and orange—with numerous stops around Uptown.

Bright Future for Charlotte Rail Service

Charlotte and North Carolina recently received more than $600 million for improvements in passenger rail service. A federal grant of $545 million went to the state to get Amtrak trains running faster and more frequently between Charlotte and Raleigh. The money will go for track improvements to bring the trains' top speed from 79 mph to 90 mph by 2015. That money will also fund a third daily round-trip Amtrak train between Charlotte and Raleigh. Meanwhile, Charlotte officials have received $100 million in stimulus funds to help create a railroad superhighway through the Queen City. That money will build a bridge and relocate tracks in a congested area on the northern edge of Uptown. Charlotte will also use its funds to buy land for a future high-speed rail maintenance facility behind Bank of America Stadium.

GREYHOUND BUS LINES
601 West Trade St.
(704) 375-3332
www.greyhound.com
Greyhound offers passenger service from an aging building on West Trade Street between the heart of Uptown and the Johnson & Wales campus.

Trains

LYNX LIGHT RAIL
www.charmeck.org

The LYNX Blue Line, which runs southward from Seventh Street in the city to I-485 in Pineville, made its long-awaited debut in November of 2007. It marked the first high-speed mass transportation in Charlotte history. The 92-foot-long trains run at a top speed of about 50 mph and carry up to 236 passengers. Modern and aerodynamic with a silver-and-blue paint scheme, the Charlotte Area Transit System (CATS) trains also feature bike racks and wheelchair accessibility.

The 9.6-mile South Corridor serves 15 stations from 5:30 a.m. to 1 a.m. daily, arriving every 7.5 minutes during rush hour and every 15 minutes during non-peak times. Ticket prices are $3 round-trip for adults and $1.50 round-trip for students and seniors. One-way tickets are half of those prices.

Other planned lines include the North, running 30 miles from Uptown toward Mooresville along the Norfolk Southern rail line paralleling Graham Street and Old Statesville Road, and a Northeast line following North Tryon Street to the University area.

Other plans call for a Center City streetcar system connecting the Beatties Ford Road area near Johnson C. Smith University with the Eastland Mall area near Central Avenue. Also on the wish list is a Charlotte Gateway Station at Graham, Fourth, and West Trade Streets in Uptown. The station would be a central hub for light rail, Amtrak, Greyhound, and the streetcar system. It would also house shops, restaurants, and parking decks.

Charlotte's light rail project is funded by a half-cent sales tax increase approved by voters. Months before light rail carried its first passengers, its economic impact was already being felt through condominiums, apartments, and shops going up in South End along the new line.

AMTRAK
1914 North Tryon St.
(704) 376-4416
www.amtrak.com

Amtrak offers passenger service north and south from its station off North Tryon, about a mile outside of Uptown. Two trains of special interest to Charlotte businesspeople are the Carolinian and the Piedmont, which offer daily service to Raleigh. The Carolinian proceeds north through Washington, D.C., to New York, and offers extra pampering and entertainment in Business Class, as well as sandwiches, snacks, and drinks in the Dinette Car. The Crescent also provides daily service from New Orleans to New York and back via Charlotte.

HISTORY

The prevailing image of Charlotte is that of New South dynamo—a commerce-driven city comprised of glass, steel, concrete and new construction. At first glance this image seems perfectly correct. A look at the Queen City skyline leads people to believe Charlotte has little to offer in the way of history. Also, many current residents are transplants who haven't taken the time to learn the city's significance in the annals of history, so it becomes a prevailing attitude amongst residents that Charlotte is historically lacking.

Yet, a closer inspection reveals a city that was the site of the first gold rush in the United States; a city that hosted the final meetings of the cabinet of the Confederate States of America; a city that built Camp Greene to house tens of thousands of troops during World War I; and a city that can lay claim to officially declaring its independence from England more than a year before the rest of the original 13 colonies created the Declaration of Independence. Most people don't realize our 11th President—James K. Polk—was born and raised in Pineville and his homestead is a state historic site just beyond the shadows of Carolina Place Mall and the area's shopping centers.

This chapter serves as an eye-opening study of Charlotte's background. It shows how past events molded the city into what it is today, and how our Scots-Irish roots fostered a collectively strong personality that still exists in the Queen City.

CHARLOTTE'S FOUNDING FATHERS

The Scots-Irish Presbyterians, a devout religious group, began to settle here in the 1730s. A century and a half earlier, these settlers had immigrated from Scotland and England to Ulster in Ireland, then to the Piedmont of North Carolina from Pennsylvania. Since they differed in background and religion from the Irish, there had been little blending. Set in their ways, they were strongly determined to have both freedom of religion and government, along with freedom of the one from the other. Native Catawba Indians were friendly, establishing trade with the settlers and sharing trading routes to Charleston, South Carolina.

Mecklenburg County was carved from Anson County in 1762. In an attempt to win favor from King George III, citizens named the county "Mecklenburg" in honor of Queen Charlotte's birthplace, the German principality of Mecklenburg-Strelitz. The town of Charlotte, established in 1768, was named for the queen herself, which is why locals often call Charlotte the "Queen City" and why the Bank of America tower wears a crown. Tryon Street, the major thoroughfare running through Uptown, was so named to honor the 1769 visit of Royal Governor William Tryon.

But it wasn't long before Mecklenburgers were at odds with British rule. The settlers had been extremely loyal, but already facing serious financial problems, they suffered from the continuing sting of escalating British taxes and an increasingly corrupt government.

EARLY REVOLUTIONISTS

The Crown steadfastly refused to listen to the colonists' economic plight. This provoked the commander of the county militia, Thomas Polk, to call citizens to elect two representatives from each militia district to meet in the Charlotte Town Courthouse on May 19, 1775. The story goes that these men framed the first document "declaring the citizens of Mecklenburg free and independent of the Crown of Great Britain." More than a year before the Declaration of Independence in Philadelphia, they read the Mecklenburg Declaration of Independence to the assembled town at noon the following day. Unfortunately, they didn't have time to present it to the congress, and worse still, the document burned in a fire. Although some historians are skeptical, Charlotteans believe that the declaration existed. They celebrate that first demand for freedom each May 20th at the Hezekiah Alexander house, the oldest standing house in Charlotte. Several years ago the kickoff speaker for the event was none other than Senator Elizabeth Dole, a Salisbury native and descendant of Hezekiah Alexander's sister, Elizabeth. The date May 20, 1775, on the North Carolina state flag recalls the controversial story of the Mecklenburg Declaration of Independence.

The determination and tenacity of Mecklenburg citizens was further proven on Sept. 26, 1780, when British Gen. Earl Cornwallis invaded the town. In a mere 18 days, the general racked up humiliating losses. Owing this to the "obstinate integrity" of those cantankerous early Mecklenburgers, he unwittingly coined the phrase "this rebellious country, the hornet's nest of America." You can find the term "hornets" or "hornet's nest" on our county seal, as well as part of the name of an elementary school, a park, Charlotte's former NBA team, and the trophy that is annually presented to the winner of the Davidson-UNC Charlotte basketball rivalry.

CHARLOTTE'S GROWTH BEGINS

Unlike the Scots-Irish, the Germans wanted freedom to establish independent communities on a religious basis (such as the Moravians in Winston-Salem). The Germans also wanted to do missionary work among the Native Americans. The German sects, predominantly Lutheran and German Reformed (now part of the United Church of Christ), moved into the eastern section of then-Mecklenburg County. That section of Mecklenburg split off in 1792 to become Cabarrus and Rowan Counties. Since the predominant spo-

ken language was English, the German minority struggled with the new language and customs, and many chose to anglicize their names. In the 1800s French Huguenots, Swiss, Highland Scots, and a large migration of Germans left Europe for many of the same reasons as the Scots-Irish, and traveled from Pennsylvania along the same route. Although Charlotte has a rich diversification of religious denominations, a strong Scots-Irish Presbyterian influence still remains.

The first recorded discovery of gold occurred next door to Charlotte in Cabarrus County in 1799. A boy by the name of Conrad Reed found a 17-pound nugget in a creek and his family, not knowing its significance, used the huge nugget as a doorstop until 1802, when it was sold to a jeweler for $3.50. Eventually word got out about the true worth of this doorstop, creating the nation's first gold rush (Georgia's gold rush did not start until 1828). Gold made Mecklenburg the mining capital of the United States, and the discovery became the first building block in constructing the city as a financial center.

In 1837 city fathers built a United States Mint on West Trade Street to process gold instead of sending it to Rutherfordton for private coinage. The 1800s blossomed into a prosperous era for Charlotte but the invention of the cotton gin soon overtook gold, which was difficult to mine. "King Cotton" transformed Mecklenburg into a textile hotbed, bringing money, warehouses, traders, farm workers, and development. But nothing changed the way Charlotte did business as much as the arrival of the railroad. Its ideal location, connected by rail between Columbia and Greensboro, eventually turned Charlotte into a distribution hub.

THE CIVIL WAR YEARS

The Civil War curtailed steady development in the 1800s. Although the city never saw military action, Charlotte families suffered huge casualties, and the city hospitalized many wounded soldiers at the Charlotte Military Academy.

More than 2,700 men from Mecklenburg County fought for the Confederacy, nine of whom are buried in Settlers' Cemetery in Uptown. The city also played other roles in the war effort. The United States Mint was taken over as Confederate headquarters. In 1862 the Confederate Navy Yard moved from Norfolk, Virginia, to Charlotte to protect it from Union forces. Many naval weapons were produced here, but on Jan. 7, 1864, fire and an explosion at the navy yard destroyed more than $10 million worth of munitions and supplies. The Mecklenburg Courthouse stored the State Department of the Confederacy records in 1865.

As the Civil War waned in April of 1865, Charlotte briefly served as headquarters of the Confederacy. The city could stake a claim to being the "last capital of the Confederacy," however, Danville, VA, is recognized as such and Charlotte has never been interested in the title. But as Confederate president Jefferson Davis and his cabinet retreated southward via the railroad after the fall of Richmond, it turned out the last official meetings of the Confederate cabinet took place not in Danville, which was to be the new capital, but in Charlotte. Danville's stint as the capital lasted only eight days, forcing Jefferson and his entourage to flee southward into North Carolina, first to Greensboro, then to Charlotte. On April 18, shortly after his arrival in Charlotte, Davis addressed a crowd that had gathered on Tryon Street. While talking, he was handed a telegram informing him that his political adversary, President Abraham Lincoln, had been assassinated. Today, a plaque at the corner of Tryon and Fourth Streets marks the place Davis stood when he learned the news. The Confederate cabinet held official meetings from April 22–25 in the Bank of North Carolina branch on Tryon Street and the last official meeting of the cabinet took place at the Phifer House on North Tryon on April 26, 1865. Later that day, the group fled southward again, with Davis eventually captured by Union troops in Georgia in early May.

An interesting local legend from this time period dealt with the mysterious disappearance of the Confederate treasury during a fateful wagon caravan trip through North Carolina. As the story (documented by historian Burke Davis and others) goes, the treasury, accompanied by Jefferson Davis, Confederate cabinet members, and naval cadets, arrived in Charlotte, where it picked up additional protection from Confederate cavalry and naval yard workers. As the caravan traveled along, some of the money was used to pay disillusioned and mutinous soldiers who demanded their share of back wages. When a Union attack on the caravan appeared imminent, some of the money was secretly buried or hidden on Southern plantations. Some of it was placed in a bank, and some of it was confiscated by Union soldiers. Large sums were entrusted to two Confederate officers (to take out of the country) to use for continuing the war when reinforcements were received from the west. A sizable sum has never been accounted for. Don't go digging up your backyard, though; historians believe the treasury was intact when the caravan left Charlotte.

Charlotte was spared the worst of Reconstruction nightmares and eventually recovered to become a major production center in the 1900s. The city advanced economically in the early part of the century, although some historians feel that the Mecklenburg area did not regain its earlier momentum until after World War II.

TEXTILES BUILD A TOWN

Charlotte's way of doing business evolved when visionary Daniel Augustus Tompkins came on the scene in 1883. This aristocratic South Carolinian duly noted that Charlotte was "an extremely dull place . . . but a town disposed to improve." He did a great deal to promote Charlotte's improvement with his Southern Cotton Oil Manufacturing Company, which made cooking oil and other products from cotton seeds and stimulated growth for the entire Southern textile region. Tompkins outlined a way for communities to build their textile mills in his book, *A Plan to Raise Capital*. He spawned the idea of stock subscription to guarantee local ownership instead of English and Northern industrialist ownership. Some of the history of this important era is preserved in the renovated Atherton Mill on South Boulevard.

Tompkins saw textiles as the engine that would drive the New South. It did, bringing

(Q) Close-up

Top 10 Events in Charlotte History

Local history buff Gary L. McCullough, author of *North Carolina's State Historic Sites* and docent at the Charlotte Museum of History, provides his list of the Top 10 events in Charlotte history:

1. By act of the N.C. colonial legislature, Mecklenburg County is created Dec. 11, 1762, named in honor of Queen Charlotte of Mecklenburg, Germany, who recently wed King George III of England. Act takes effect Feb. 1, 1763.

2. The town of Charlotte, likewise named in the Queen's honor, has its beginnings in 1766, when town commissioners map out plots at the intersection of two ancient Indian trading paths. Charlotte is incorporated Dec. 7, 1768.

3. The Mecklenburg Declaration of Independence of May 20, 1775 (a document questioned by some) and the Mecklenburg Resolves of May 31, 1775 (accepted by all), demonstrate that the mostly Scots-Irish population of Charlotte-Mecklenburg County favors separation from Great Britain. They regard themselves "a free and independent people."

4. In 1799, gold is discovered on a family farm in nearby Cabarrus County. Gold is subsequently found in Mecklenburg and other neighboring counties in the Piedmont. Soon North Carolina earns the nickname "The Gold State." On Oct. 19, 1837, a branch of the U. S. Mint opens in Charlotte at the corner of Mint and Trade Streets.

5. Local merchants and planters help build the first railroad. The Charlotte & South Carolina Railroad (from Columbia) opens in 1852. The North Carolina Rail Road (from Raleigh) arrives in 1854. Connections to Goldsboro are completed in 1856. Charlotte becomes the Carolinas' first important rail crossroad and sees first significant growth in population.

6. In the Civil War's aftermath, cotton becomes king and is sent from Southern farms to Northern cities for processing. In the 1880s, local businessmen build their own cotton mills in Mecklenburg and surrounding counties. Charlotte becomes the center of textile production. By the turn of the 20th century, Charlotte is the "Industrial Center of the New South."

7. Cotton creates cash, and Charlotte becomes home to many banks, including Commercial National Bank and Union National Bank. The former (founded in 1874 by William Holt of Burlington's Glencoe Mills) experiences several mergers and acquisitions to eventually become Bank of America. The latter, through mergers and acquisitions of its own, becomes Wachovia (recently acquired by Wells Fargo). By the 1990s, Charlotte is the second leading banking center in the nation.

8. When the United States enters World War I in 1917, the Charlotte Chamber of Commerce convinces the Army to build Camp Greene on the city's west side. During its two years, 60,000 soldiers pass through the camp, leading to another major burst in population.

9. In the early 1920s, with the determined leadership of governor and Mecklenburg native Cameron Morrison, North Carolina becomes the leading builder of paved roads in the South; the first four-lane paved highway in the state is Wilkinson Boulevard, leading west from Charlotte to the mills in Gastonia. North Carolina earns the nickname "The Good Roads State."

10. In as much as major sports define a city's social ranking, the arrival of the NBA's Charlotte Hornets (1988) and the NFL's Carolina Panthers (1995) underscores the Queen City's slow-but-steady transition into one of the nation's foremost metropolitan areas.

men, women, and children out of the fields and into the mills. The mills breathed spirit and independence into an impoverished economy, giving families a mill home and a somewhat better economic life with regular pay and easier work. Textile manufacturing hummed along, then cranked to full throttle when tobacco giant James B. "Buck" Duke had the Catawba River dammed to build his hydroelectric plant in the early 1900s. With the advantage of good roads, the railroad, electricity, and stable government, Charlotte began to prosper.

SCHOOLS AND THE NEW SOUTH

The early pioneers had only private education, usually taught by ministers or teachers who traveled from home to home. Instruction involved strictly practical ideas about learning. Schooling in religion, rudimentary skills, and the learning of a trade constituted the curriculum. Something akin to public education didn't begin until 1839, when $750,000 was appropriated for North Carolina schools.

In 1969 Charlotte was the center of a landmark desegregation case in which a federal judge ordered Charlotte-Mecklenburg Schools (CMS) to use all methods of desegregation, including busing. The issue surfaced again in 1997, this time from white parents who claimed CMS race-based policies denied their children access to neighborhood schools and subject-specific magnet schools because a designated number of spots were held for minorities. The case went to trial in 1999 and was finally resolved in spring 2001 when the courts ruled CMS had achieved unified status and that race-based policies were no longer needed. The school system later introduced a unique choice plan that allowed families to have a voice in where their children attended school. Today, families are guaranteed a spot at their neighborhood school or may make limited choices among magnet schools and schools in other areas of the city.

However, the future of local schools continues to be a hot-button topic in Charlotte.

Parents, politicians, and administrators constantly argue over issues such as neighborhood schools versus busing, crowded suburban schools versus outdated older buildings in the center city, and conflicting needs and limited funds.

In our higher education system, you'll find a number of excellent schools such as Davidson College (1837), Queens University at Charlotte (1857), Johnson C. Smith University (1867), and UNC Charlotte (1946). Other academic institutions include Central Piedmont Community College, established in 1963, and Johnson & Wales University, a prestigious culinary school that opened a campus in Uptown in 2004. The for-profit Charlotte School of Law moved to a new facility just west of Uptown in 2008.

A BANKING BOOM

Banking began in the Mecklenburg area with the early settlers but stayed a private business until 1865, when it became nationalized. During the Civil War a branch of the Bank of Charlotte transported 3,000 pounds of gold bullion 18 miles to Grasshopper Springs, where it remained buried until the war's end.

It was not until 1927 that a branch of the Federal Reserve Bank of Richmond was established in Charlotte, another step toward making the city an important financial center. After the Second World War, two Charlotte banks, American Trust Company and Commercial National Bank, merged. The result of this merger eventually became NCNB, and later NationsBank. In April 1998 NationsBank merged with San Francisco-based BankAmerica in a $66-billion stock swap to create the country's largest consumer bank, now called Bank of America. In 2001, Charlotte's First Union bank bought Wachovia, which was based in Winston-Salem. The resulting bank was named Wachovia and headquartered in Charlotte, with the distinction of being the nation's fourth-largest bank. However, Wachovia fell on tough times during the financial crisis of 2008 and was bought by Wells Fargo, resulting in the loss of the Wachovia name and Charlotte's loss of the banking headquarters.

Close-up

Insider Top 5: Local Historic Sites

Here is a list of five key historic sites in the Charlotte area:

1. **The Charlotte Museum of History**—Showcases interesting artifacts within its galleries, but its true attraction is the restored 1774 home of Hezekiah Alexander, which houses the museum. This "rock" house is the oldest surviving structure in Mecklenburg County. Interpreters dressed in period clothing conduct tours of the main house, replica kitchen, and reconstructed springhouse. The site is home to the American Freedom Bell, seven times the size of the Liberty Bell and the largest bell at ground level in the world.

2. **Kings Mountain National Military Park**—Located just south of the state line off I-85. The battle on Oct. 7, 1780, between an army of Loyalists and a unified gathering of so-called "Over-the-Mountain Men" was one of the most significant engagements of the Revolutionary War, and one of the battles that helped the colonies win their independence. The site includes a museum and annotated walking trail to the summit.

3. **The James K. Polk Memorial**—A state historic site in Pineville to honor the birthplace of the nation's 11th president. The farmhouse is not the actual Polk homestead, but closely resembles the original and is representative of the typical Mecklenburg County farmhouse at the turn of the 19th century. James Knox Polk served but one four-year term (1845-1849), yet was an accomplished president, fulfilling almost all of his major campaign promises.

4. **The Reed Gold Mine**—Located in neighboring Cabarrus County, this is the site of the first documented discovery of gold in the United States (1799). Until the gold rush in California, North Carolina was the leading gold-producing state. Visitors tour an underground mine and try their hand at panning for the precious yellow metal.

5. **Latta Plantation**—A 62-acre farm and the only Catawba River plantation open to the public. Listed on the National Register of Historic Sites, it consists of the original two-story, Federal-style plantation home, circa 1800, and numerous outbuildings and dependencies, including smokehouse, barn, slave cabin, and replica kitchen. Costumed interpreters provide tours, and a visitor center and museum enhance the visit.

At the height of its banking glory, around 2005–2006, Charlotte was home to 20 different banks and holding companies and controlled more than $1.8 trillion in bank resources, second only to New York City.

CENTER CITY COMES BACK TO LIFE

It was during the late 1970s and early 1980s that Uptown's Fourth Ward, an area of quaint and charming Victorian homes, was rehabilitated. This brought people back to city living at a time when most had fled to the suburbs. Lake Norman emerged from weekend cabin status to a burgeoning community of year-round luxury homes and condominiums. Lake Wylie, southwest of Charlotte on the South Carolina line, followed the same trend.

Charlotte did not begin to grow in earnest until the 1980s, following IBM's 1978 arrival, which insiders say caused the city to perk up and residential property prices to edge upward. Charlotte became an international city in the late '80s when US Airways won the London route. Charlotte/Douglas International Airport is now the nation's 14th-busiest airport and a US Airways hub with international flights to London, Munich, and Frankfurt in Europe; Toronto, Canada; Mexico City, Cozumel, and Cancun; four Central American cities; and 16 destinations in the Caribbean.

Today Charlotte is at the center of the largest consolidated rail system in the nation, offering two major rail systems—Norfolk Southern Railway and CSX Transportation—that link 27,000 miles of rail systems between Charlotte and 22 states in the eastern United States. To Amtrak officials, trains aren't passenger transportation of the past. The Carolinian, which runs between Charlotte and Raleigh, has been so successful that a second train, the Piedmont, now also offers service between the two cities. The Crescent is still running from New Orleans to New York and back via Charlotte.

The arts community is strong in Charlotte, due to enthusiastic and generous individual and corporate arts supporters. The Charlotte Arts & Science Council gives annual operating grants to 28 affiliates in the arts, sciences, history, and heritage, ranging from the Charlotte Symphony to Wing Haven Gardens & Bird Sanctuary. With community donations, endowments, and city and county funds, the Arts & Science Council distributed $12.8 million in 2006.

Charlotte's "Cultural District" includes North Carolina Blumenthal Performing Arts Center, Spirit Square, ImaginOn, Levine Museum of the New South, Discovery Place, Harvey B. Gantt Center for African-American Arts + Culture, and Bechtler Museum of Modern Art. Outside of Uptown, the Mint Museum, Ovens Auditorium, and facilities at the area's universities also provide cultural entertainment options. Several years ago Discovery Place, a hands-on science museum, was named the top tourist attraction in the Southeast by the Southeast Tourism Society. The museum continues to provide exciting programs and films in its OMNIMAX Theatre.

In addition, local business and arts leaders are working on the 2020 Vision Plan, a growth and urban design plan to make Charlotte a "great and memorable" city.

Charlotte may be poised to become the arts center of North Carolina, but the sports industry runs a close second. Uptown Charlotte has Bank of America Stadium, a state-of-the-art facility built for $187 million in the mid-1990s. The 73,778-seat open-air stadium routinely draws capacity crowds for the NFL's Carolina Panthers. In late 2005, the $200 million Charlotte Bobcats Arena opened on Trade Street in Uptown. It is home to the NBA's Charlotte Bobcats, the Charlotte Checkers minor-league hockey team, and a host of college basketball tournaments and nationally touring concerts. The much-anticipated $195 million NASCAR Hall of Fame opened in Uptown in May of 2010. The impressive oval-shaped hall encompasses 150,000 square feet and is connected to the Charlotte Convention Center. It is conservatively estimated to attract 800,000 visitors a year with an annual economic impact of $60 million.

In addition, the minor-league Charlotte Knights baseball team, now located down I-77 in Fort Mill, South Carolina, is lobbying to build a 10,000-seat baseball stadium in Uptown.

Charlotte Motor Speedway, just across the Mecklenburg County line east of Charlotte, hosts three of NASCAR's more popular events. Combined, those three events draw approximately half a million fans each year, while tens of thousands more come for smaller races, NASCAR-related driving schools, and tours of area race shops. The Charlotte region is home to the vast majority of all NASCAR race teams, plus the N.C. Auto Racing Hall of Fame is located in Mooresville.

In south Charlotte, one of the PGA Tour's best events takes place each May. The Quail Hollow Championship, held annually since 2003 at Quail Hollow Club off Gleneagles Road, has been won by Tiger Woods, Vijah Singh, and Jim Furyk, and rivals the Players Championship as the best non-major on the Tour schedule. Strong rumors persist that Johnny Harris, president of the club, will pull the necessary strings to bring a major tournament, likely the PGA Championship, to Quail Hollow this decade.

Charlotte's latest sports venue is the U.S. National Whitewater Center, a 307-acre outdoor recreation facility that opened on the banks of the Catawba River, west of the city, in 2006. The centerpiece of the $32-million facility is a man-made whitewater river designated by the U.S. Olympic Committee as an official Olympic training site.

i Hopewell Presbyterian Church, located in Huntersville, is the town's oldest church and a Who's Who of local history. The stately brick church, which dates to the late 1740s, features original glass panes, a slave entrance, a massive earthquake protection beam, and a hand-carved pulpit. A well-kept cemetery includes the graves of Revolutionary War hero General William Lee Davidson and Captain James Knox, grandfather and namesake of President James K. Polk.

FUTURE GROWTH

Many businesses are attracted to Charlotte's mild weather, healthy business climate, and low tax base. In the past two decades, Charlotte has become home (or second home) to industries such as microelectronics, aerospace manufacturing, computer software, metal working and vehicle assembly, research and development, and high-tech and service-oriented international and domestic firms. The Charlotte area is home to nine *Fortune* 500 headquarters, with 310 *Fortune* 500 firms represented. Pundits have named Charlotte the third best metro area for business location, the seventh best for business development, and the eighth best for entrepreneurship.

Uptown also keeps moving forward—and upward—with new projects and buildings. Just outside of Uptown, Mecklenburg County's first mall (built in 1959) has been redeveloped into the Metropolitan: a mixed-use center with shops, restaurants, and condos overlooking a long, shady plaza, fountain, and city greenway.

The city's two major interstates—I-77 and I-85—are both slated for additional widening projects, and work continues until 2014 on the final leg of the I-485 outer belt. Developers have positioned themselves at strategic interchanges, building new communities, shopping centers, and office parks at nearly every road off the beltline. A prime example is the Ballantyne area, which has rapidly grown and includes a country club community, resort and public golf course, office parks, townhome complexes, and several retail centers.

One of the biggest changes on the horizon is the continued development of light rail. Passenger service began in 2007 on the south corridor running from Uptown to I-485 in Pineville, and next up are rail lines northward to Mooresville and a corridor running northeast to the University City area. Also planned is a streetcar line in the center city region and a major Uptown transit station.

In the past few years, Charlotte has been blessed with a great deal of positive publicity. It has been featured in publications such as *Southern Living, Sports Illustrated, Financial World, Newsweek,* the *Wall Street Journal,* the *New York Times,* and *National Geographic,* to name a few.

When you drive through this beautiful town, designated "the city of trees," think of those early ancestors who, throughout the centuries, refused to knuckle under to failure. Their character built a foundation that was able to change—change not only for the sake of prosperity, but change for a better quality of life. You'll find that can-do flexibility in Charlotte. It's a great place to live and raise a family.

HOTELS AND MOTELS

Charlotte's popularity as a business and travel destination is evident in the steady increase in hotel rooms constructed in the area. From budget motels to luxury hotels, Charlotte offers its overnight guests numerous choices.

If you are a first-time visitor, keep in mind that during special events, race weeks, football weekends, and large conventions, the availability of rooms in certain areas may be limited or nonexistent. So plan ahead and make your reservations as soon as you know when you'll be visiting the Queen City.

Since bed-and-breakfasts are in demand, they have been given their own chapter (see Bed-and-Breakfast Inns). If you intend to stay more than a week, you may enjoy residing at an extended-stay facility (see our Relocation chapter).

In this chapter hotels and motels are arranged alphabetically. All are in Charlotte unless otherwise noted.

Price Code

For the purposes of comparing prices, we have categorized accommodations with one to five dollar signs ($) based on the typical daily rate charged for a standard room with two double beds. Weekend rates may vary, and in some case are lower. Keep in mind these rates are subject to change; however, to give you a rough idea of what to expect, we offer the following guide:

$	Under $76
$$	$76 to $99
$$$	$100 to $150
$$$$	$151 to $199
$$$$$	$200 and up

HOTELS AND MOTELS

aloft CHARLOTTE UPTOWN $$$$
210 East Trade St.
(704) 333-1999
www.aloftCharlotteUptown.com
Part of the EpiCentre entertainment complex, this modern European-style loft hotel has made a big splash in Uptown. There is nothing quite like this colorful, art deco–inspired facility in the center city. Headboards are part of a large center

console in the middle of the room. Guests enjoy 9-foot ceilings and extra-large windows. Each room is equipped with a recharging station for personal electronic devices and a 42-inch LCD flat screen TV. Spa products come standard in each room, as do free wired and wireless high-speed Internet access. This hotel has a total of 175 guest rooms and an indoor pool.

BALLANTYNE HOTEL &
LODGE $$$$–$$$$$
10000 Ballantyne Commons Pkwy.
(704) 248-4000, (866) 248-4824
www.ballantyneresort.com
Charlotte has its share of fine hotels, but only one luxury resort. Opened in late 2001 in the booming Ballantyne area south of town, the Ballantyne Hotel features 214 deluxe guest rooms, including parlor suites and palatial presidential suites. Marble baths with oval soaking tubs and separate showers, original artwork and antiques, 10-foot ceilings with crown moldings, fine linens, plush robes, and nightly turndown with chocolates are just a few of the indulgent details that make you feel miles away from Charlotte. Business travelers appreciate the spacious work desks, two telephones with dual phone lines, free local calls,

and complimentary high-speed Internet access. Ballantyne guests also enjoy an indoor grotto pool, two continuous-wave lap pools, his and her saunas, a whirlpool, full-service health club, and an outdoor patio for sunbathing.

For an extra treat, choose from among 60 treatments at the Ballantyne Resort Spa. On-site dining options include the relaxed Grill Room for breakfast and lunch, and Traditions, an intimate and upscale fine-dining restaurant, for dinner. Enjoy a drink in the Lobby Bar, with its veranda and sweeping golf course view, or at the 19th Hole Lounge in the clubhouse. If you're in town for a meeting or special celebration, the resort offers 20,000 square feet of meeting space on two levels, including a 6,500-square-foot ballroom with 16-foot ceilings and elegant chandeliers.

A separate facility called the Lodge is perfect for corporate retreats with 35 custom-furnished guest rooms, tennis courts, a basketball court, a business center, and conference facilities in a tranquil golf course setting. Ballantyne guests also get privileges at the resort's 18-hole golf course, voted the best new course in North Carolina in 2001. In addition, the course is home to the nationally known Dana Rader Golf School, a state-of-the-art instruction facility with a variety of clinics for golfers who want to improve their game. Popular with visiting celebrities, professional athletes, politicians, and CEOs, the Ballantyne is a AAA Four-Diamond Award winner and a member of Starwood Hotels' Luxury Collection.

THE BLAKE HOTEL $$$
555 South McDowell St.
(704) 372-4100
www.blakehotelnc.com
Longtime Charlotte visitors will remember this as the Adam's Mark, which was the city's largest hotel for many years. The hotel was purchased and rebranded as the Blake Hotel in 2006. Contemporary and trendy, the Blake has the feel of a New York boutique hotel with sleek furniture, clean lines, and a decor of black, white, and red animal-print accents. The 613 rooms of the

Adam's Mark were converted to 308 larger rooms at the Blake, with wireless Internet, flat-screen televisions, and stereos with iPod docking stations. The hotel's restaurant and lounge also have undergone renovation. Other amenities include an onsite business center, conference room, and exhibit space; seasonal pool; health club; Egyptian linens; and designer toiletries. Overlooking Marshall Park and the Mecklenburg Aquatic Center, the Blake is 3 blocks from the Charlotte Convention Center, 7 blocks from Bank of America Stadium, and within walking distance of Uptown's financial and cultural districts.

i For more information on places to stay in Charlotte, call the Charlotte Convention & Visitors Bureau at (800) 231-4636 or log on to www.visitcharlotte.com.

CHARLOTTE MARRIOTT
CITY CENTER $$$$–$$$$$
100 West Trade St.
(704) 333-9000
www.marriott.com
The Marriott City Center sits on the corner of Trade and Tryon Streets in the heart of the city on the spot once occupied by North Carolina's first skyscraper. With 434 guest rooms and 4 suites on 19 floors, the hotel caters to both business travelers and tourists with a concierge level and lounge, complimentary 24-hour health club with indoor pool, a 24-hour business center, and meeting space to accommodate 10 to 1,450 guests. High-speed Internet access is available in all rooms for $12.95, and high-speed wireless access is in all public areas. Parking is $12 per day. Guests can dine at a breakfast buffet, Champions sports bar, Cutter's cigar bar, and the exclusive dinner-only Savannah Red, which serves Southern-twist dishes such as corn-fried oyster salad, pecan-crusted grouper, and Krispy Kreme bread pudding with bourbon sauce. Starbucks coffee and Krispy Kreme doughnuts also are available on-site. Overlooking The Square, this is one of the most convenient locations Uptown.

CHARLOTTE MARRIOTT AT EXECUTIVE PARK $$$–$$$$
I-77 and Tyvola Road
(704) 527-9650
www.marriott.com

Designed with both large and small meetings in mind, the Charlotte Marriott at Executive Park has 297 guest rooms, 3 hospitality suites, a presidential suite, 19 meeting rooms, and a 6,600-square-foot grand ballroom. Amenities at the 18-floor hotel renovated in 2006 include an indoor/outdoor pool, an exercise room, tennis courts, volleyball, and basketball. Gratzi's and Gratzi's Bar serve breakfast, lunch, and dinner. In warm weather, cool refreshments are popular at the pool bar. Room service, high-speed Internet access ($9.95 per day), complimentary parking, and free airport shuttle also are available. With a location overlooking I-77, this hotel is busy with more business people than tourists.

CHARLOTTE MARRIOTT SOUTHPARK $$$$
2200 Rexford Rd.
(704) 364-8220
www.marriott.com

This was Charlotte's first true luxury hotel, operating for many years as the city's only four-star option as The Park Hotel. Now owned by Marriott, the hotel still exudes grace, elegance, and exquisite taste in the refined SouthPark community. Guests arrive at the tucked-away hotel to see a beautiful three-tiered fountain in a circular drive. Uniformed bellmen handle bags and a valet parks the car, while visitors check in and relax. The six-story hotel has 194 rooms and space for small meetings, and there's an intimacy here you won't find in a regular hotel. The recently renovated guest rooms are decorated in beautiful combinations of color and fabric with 18th-century pieces and original lithography. Formal and elegant with dark wood and soothing colors, the oversized guest quarters give the feel of a private residence. Guests dine in The Grill or enjoy a drink a Smoky's Lounge, both of which are adjacent to several other restaurants, shops, and a spa at Specialty Shops on the Park. A nice holdover from its days as The Park is the 1,100-sqaure-foot Presidential Suite, with its dining room table, chandelier, separate living quarters, and floor-to-ceiling windows.

The hotel also features 24-hour concierge and room service, a full-service fitness center, an outdoor swimming pool, complimentary daily newspapers, high-speed Internet access, airport limousine service, and turndown service with chocolates left on the down pillows. You could get used to this kind of treatment.

COMFORT INN & SUITES— LAKE NORMAN $$–$$$
19521 Liverpool Parkway, Cornelius
(704) 896-7622
www.choicehotels.com

This recently built hotel at I-77's exit 28 features 60 rooms and several suites with whirlpools. Located 2 miles from Lake Norman and from Davidson College, the property also has a 24-hour business center with free Internet access, an outdoor pool with hot tub, and a 30-item deluxe breakfast buffet. Other area Comfort Inn locations are University City, Westpark, Carowinds, Matthews Rock Hill, Monroe, Kings Mountain, Statesville, and Lincolnton. Comfort Suites, part of the same national chain, are at the airport, University City, Pineville, Concord, Gastonia, and West Harris Boulevard. Most locations allow pets.

CROWN PLAZA HOTEL $$$
201 South McDowell St.
(704) 372-7550
www.CrownPlaza.com

This recently renovated full-service hotel is located on the edge of Uptown, a short walk from the Charlotte Convention Center, Mecklenburg County Government Center, Time Warner Cable Arena, and most financial institutions. The hotel offers 191 rooms and 2 suites on 11 floors. Ask for a room overlooking the city, rather than the busy I-277 freeway. Full-service amenities include a 24-hour business center, 24-hour on-site fitness center, outdoor pool, free high-speed Internet access, and bell service.

DOUBLETREE HOTEL CHARLOTTE—
GATEWAY VILLAGE $$$—$$$$
895 West Trade St.
(704) 347-0070
www.doubletree.hilton.com

Located in western Uptown this hotel is unique because it is owned and operated by the adjacent Johnson & Wales University. The university is a culinary and hospitality school, and students earn valuable real-life experience while working in this three-diamond property. Another neat aspect of this hotel is that it has a Hertz rental location on-site.

The DoubleTree includes 187 rooms, plus a full-service health club, outdoor pool, meeting rooms, and free Uptown shuttle. Casual dining is available in Orchards Restaurant, drinks in the Exchange Lounge. But the best perk? All guests receive free DoubleTree chocolate chip cookies. Located close to Bank of America Stadium.

DOUBLETREE GUEST SUITES
CHARLOTTE—SOUTHPARK $$$-$$$$
6300 Morrison Blvd.
(704) 364-2400
www.doubletree.hilton.com

Formerly SouthPark Suite Hotel, this 208-luxury-suite hotel is now a DoubleTree in the Hilton chain. A recent $3.5-million renovation freshened up all of the hotel's public areas and one- or two-bedroom suites, which come with a living room, dining area, and fully equipped kitchen. Guests can dine in, buy grocery items at the Market Cafe, or choose from one of many upscale restaurants in the SouthPark area. The hotel also has a health center, an outdoor pool with cascading waterfall, flexible meeting space, high-speed Internet access, a lovely garden courtyard, and special weekend packages. If you're visiting on a Sun evening in June, request a room with a balcony overlooking Symphony Park. Thousands of Charlotteans pack picnics to enjoy classical music in an open-air setting. Located next door to upscale South Park Mall, it's also a great place to drop after you shop.

DRURY INN & SUITES $$-$$$
6920 Northlake Mall Dr.
(704) 599-8882
www.DruryHotels.com

New and located next to Northlake Mall, this hotel makes for a great location in the north part of town. There are plenty of dining and shopping options within walking distance, and you're adjacent to I-77, so the convenience factor is strong. The hotel itself is seven stories with 180 rooms and suites. All rooms have microwave and refrigerator, iron and board, free wireless high-speed Internet access, HBO and—get this—they give you 60 minutes of free long distance on the phone! More free stuff includes full breakfast (including Belgian waffles) and a 5:30 p.m. kick-back reception with complimentary food and drinks, including beer, wine, and mixed libations.

There is also a Drury Inn & Suites on W.T. Harris Boulevard in the University area.

DUNHILL HOTEL $$$-$$$$
237 North Tryon St.
(704) 332-4141
www.dunhillhotel.com

The Dunhill is the city's only Historic Landmark Hotel and only member of Historic Hotels of America. Step back to the era when grand hotels occupied the city. The Dunhill opened in 1929 as the Mayfair Manor and wowed the city with its unheard-of 10 stories featuring private baths, telephones, and radios. After the Depression and a series of owner mismanagements, the hotel closed in 1981. Preservationists later returned the hotel to its original elegance and it reopened in 1988. Located two blocks from the Square on North Tryon Street, the Dunhill is a quick walk from financial institutions, top-notch restaurants, and cultural sites such as the Blumenthal Performing Arts Center, Spirit Square, Levine Museum of the New South, and Discovery Place. The 60 guest rooms in this Gilded Age hotel are elegantly furnished in 18th-century decor and feature original art, four-poster beds, custom draperies, and sitting areas. Other nice touches include turndown service, valet parking, limousine service, health club privileges , and a complimentary continental breakfast. Splurging? Request the penthouse suite, which includes a dining area, fireplace, step-down whirlpool, Oriental rugs, original marble floors, and a double balcony with incredible views of the city. Casual pub fare and more formal dining are offered in the hotel, along with 24-hour room service. Other amenities include a refrigerator stocked with complimentary beverages; and bathrobes and slippers.

Charlotte-area hotels, motels, and bed-and-breakfasts charge an occupancy tax of 8 percent and a sales tax of 7.5 percent on all rooms. For a $150 room, for example, the tax would be an additional $23.25. A 2 percent increase in the occupancy tax took effect in May 2006 to help fund the NASCAR Hall of Fame.

ECONOLODGE INN & SUITES $-$$
3000 East Independence Blvd.
(704) 377-1501
www.econolodge.com
Located beside Bojangles' Coliseum, Ovens Auditorium, and The Park merchandise mart, the Econolodge Inn & Suites is an affordable option about two miles outside of Uptown. This is an older property, dating back to its days as the Coliseum Inn, and the neighborhood is not the best. However, it's a nice, clean place to rest your head. The property was purchased in 2008 by local businessman B.V. Belk, who grew up not far away and didn't want to see the hotel fall by the wayside. Belk redecorated and upgraded the rooms, picking up quality furnishings made available during a renovation of the luxury Hampton Inn & Suites at tony Phillips Place. There are 124 total guest rooms, and the inn provides complimentary continental breakfast, daily paper, and high-speed wireless Internet access. Rooms are in several buildings, so request one close to the main office.

EMBASSY SUITES $$$-$$$$
4800 South Tryon St.
(704) 527-8400
www.embassy-charlotte.com
Embassy Suites, located a few miles from the airport and about 5 miles from Uptown, has 274 two-room suites and 10,000 square feet of meeting space. The hotel features the Omaha Steakhouse restaurant and lounge, a nice indoor pool, whirlpool, sauna, and exercise facility. Guest suites have two TVs, two telephones, a coffeemaker with coffee, a microwave, and a minirefrigerator. Guests receive a complimentary cooked-to-order breakfast, manager's reception each evening, and complimentary airport shuttle service.

EMBASSY SUITES GOLF RESORT & SPA
CHARLOTTE—CONCORD $$$-$$$$
5400 John Q. Hammons Dr. NW
(704) 455-8200
www.embassysuitesconcord.com
Opened in January 2007, this $65-million 308-suite hotel joined forces with the adjacent Rocky River Golf Club to become a destination golf resort and spa just a half-mile from Charlotte Motor Speedway. In addition to its luxury rooms and golf course, the hotel has a full-service spa and a fine dining restaurant and includes the Concord Convention Center, with space for conventions of up to 2,500 people.

In-room amenities include high-speed Internet access, two flat-screen televisions, microwave, leather designer furniture, and refrigerator. Guests receive complimentary made-to-order breakfasts and evening reception daily. There's a fitness center, indoor pool and whirlpool, and wireless access in the atrium.

HAMPTON INN CHARLOTTE—
UPTOWN $$$-$$$$
530 Martin Luther King Blvd.
(704) 373-0917
www.charlotteuptown.hamptoninn.com
Just 1 block from the Charlotte Convention Center and NASCAR Hall of Fame, the Hampton Inn Charlotte-Uptown offers a great location, and is also convenient to Bank of America Stadium. A newer Uptown hotel, the Hampton Inn has 149 guest rooms and suites, including specialty suites with a separate bedroom and living room with full kitchen. Guests enjoy a free continental breakfast,

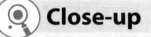

Close-up

Great Wolf Lodge Splashes Down

The new Great Wolf Lodge in Concord is not just a hotel. It's a destination.

With a massive indoor waterpark that's home to 11 slides, plus several other water fun areas, this is one place not to be missed. The best thing, or worst thing, about Great Wolf Lodge is you have to be a registered guest to use the play areas. So if you live in Charlotte, it means paying an expensive room night to turn the kids—or yourself—loose in the waterpark. But by limiting the waterpark to just hotel guests, it ensures that it will never be overcrowded with long lines, like at most waterparks.

The features of the waterpark include a four-story interactive water fort with 12 levels of super-soaker surprises, a huge water slide that's so big you ride a whitewater raft on it, a six-story funnel that makes you feel like one of those TV commercial scrubbing bubbles getting sucked down the drain, a multi-lane slide for racing, and an oversized wave pool.

There's also something called MagiQuest, a high-tech adventure game in which you take a wand and go through the resort solving challenges and earning points.

By the way, guest rooms are pretty cool, too. They have a lodge motif, and you can even book suites that have a cave for the children to sleep in.

Rates start at around $190 a night for a standard room that sleeps four, and go up to about $475 for the fancy suites.

For information, call (704) 549-8206 or visit www.greatwolf.com

USA Today, a fitness center, indoor pool, business center, and free parking, a rarity in Uptown.

HAMPTON INN & SUITES
CHARLOTTE/SOUTHPARK AT
PHILLIPS PLACE   **$$$–$$$$$**
Fairview Road at Phillips Place
(704) 319-5700
www.hamptoninn.hilton.com
This south Charlotte hotel with spacious rooms and suites is clearly a step above most Hampton Inn locations popular with budget travelers. Set in Phillips Place, the city's most upscale shopping center, this Hampton Inn feels more like a quiet and elegant European manor. The cream stucco facade has a circular drive highlighted by a fountain with large white lions. Great restaurants—including The Palm, P.F. Chang's China Bistro, Upstream, and Dean & Deluca—are steps away, as are the city's best boutiques and specialty stores. A stadium-seat movie theater is on the opposite end of the pedestrian-friendly center set around a Main Street with iron lamp-posts, park benches, and fountains. The Phillips Place Hampton Inn also features an outdoor pool, 24-hour business center, fitness center, and complimentary breakfast. Other deluxe hotel amenities include room service, refrigerators, laundry and valet services, garden bathtubs, and fax machines.

HILTON CHARLOTTE—
CENTER CITY   **$$$–$$$$**
222 East Third St.
(704) 377-1500
www.charlotte.hilton.com
One of two Hilton hotels in Uptown Charlotte, this AAA Four-Diamond facility in the heart of Charlotte's bustling financial district is the city's fifth-largest hotel and one of its most striking. The 22-floor Hilton Towers (not to be confused with the Hilton Garden Inn a few blocks away) was built in 1990; just four years later, new owners spent $5 million refurbishing the hotel's 407

spacious, well-appointed rooms. Executive-level rooms are even more luxurious with private floor access, in-room fax machines, complimentary continental breakfast, evening hors d'oeuvres, robes, turndown service, bottled water, and a separate lounge and concierge. In executive-level rooms, guests also enjoy English Penhaligon bath amenities, Hilton's new pillow-top beds, and CD players. The hotel is located steps away from the Charlotte Convention Center and Uptown shops, restaurants, culture, and nightlife. Guests can use the Uptown YMCA adjacent to the hotel, work at a state-of-the-art business center, or order from room service 24/7. High-speed Internet access is complimentary.

**HILTON CHARLOTTE AT
UNIVERSITY PLACE** $$$
8629 J. M. Keynes Dr.
(704) 547-7444
www.charlotteuniversity.hilton.com
This modern property nestled along a picturesque lake in Charlotte's bustling University City area is surrounded by a village of shops, restaurants, jogging trails, and nightlife. It offers 393 rooms in a high-rise tower, including 4 executive suites on a private floor with a concierge lounge. Meeting facilities can accommodate up to 2,000 people in over 20,000 square feet of flexible banquet space. Other amenities include a 24-hour business center, free copies of *USA Today*, complimentary parking, a fitness facility or in-room fitness equipment, a lakeside jogging trail, and an outdoor pool and sundeck. The University location is close to Verizon Wireless Amphitheater, Charlotte Motor Speedway, Concord Mills Mall, and UNC Charlotte, IBM, as well as TIAA-CREF. Wireless Internet is now complimentary in all guest rooms and common areas.

HOLIDAY INN CHARLOTTE—AIRPORT $–$$
2707 Little Rock Rd.
(704) 394-4301
www.ichotelsgroup.com
Formerly a Best Western hotel, the Holiday Inn Charlotte–Airport caters to budget-minded business travelers flying in and out of Charlotte/

Douglas International Airport. The hotel has 212 rooms, 24-hour free airport shuttle service, a sports bar and lounge, a heated outdoor pool, a fitness room, billiards, and 8 meeting rooms. Pets are welcome. High-speed Internet access is complimentary.

**HOLIDAY INN CHARLOTTE—
CENTER CITY** $$$–$$$$
230 North College St.
(704) 335-5400
www.holidayinn.com
Located on the corner of College and Sixth Streets, this Holiday Inn has 296 guest rooms and 26 suites just steps away from Charlotte's cultural attractions and pulsating nightlife. The fitness center and jogging track are complimentary, and the rooftop pool and spa with incredible views of the city will make you dread checking out to go home. Last renovated in 2004, the hotel serves upscale Italian fare in a warm, comfortable environment at Cafe Siena, or you can relax in the pub. Other amenities include 24-hour fax and copy service, airport shuttle, and a "kids eat free" program. Parking is $10 daily.

HOMEWOOD SUITES $$$
Davidson
125 Harbour Place Dr.
(704) 987-1818

University
8340 North Tryon St.
(704) 549-8800

Airport
2770 Yorkmont Rd.
(704) 357-0500
www.homewoodsuites1.hilton.com
These spacious, apartment-style suite hotels, part of the Hilton chain, are comfortably furnished with all the features and amenities you expect and some that may surprise you. Separate sleeping and living areas, two remote-controlled color TVs, and complimentary high-speed Internet access are standard. A free deluxe breakfast buffet is served daily, plus there's a complimentary evening social hour Mon through Thurs that

includes a light meal. You can work off stress at the exercise center, sports/activity court, swimming pool, or whirlpool.

The new Davidson location is particularly nice. It is in an urban village environment just west of the town and convenient to I-77.

LA QUINTA INN & SUITES $-$$$
Charlotte Airport South
4900 South Tryon St.
(704) 523-5599
www.lq.com

With upscale amenities at an economy price, the La Quinta offers a central location, free, unlimited local calls, satellite TV, continental breakfast, 24-hour coffee in the lobby, and airport shuttle service. Other features include a 24-hour fitness center, seasonal pool and hot tub, free high-speed Internet service, and meeting space that opens to a patio, courtyard, and gazebo. King rooms have a microwave, refrigerator, and two-line speaker phone.

OMNI CHARLOTTE HOTEL $$$$-$$$$$
132 East Trade St.
(704) 377-0400
www.omnihotels.com

This 374-room Uptown hotel overlooking the Square at Trade and Tryon Streets offers many outstanding features. The 15-story sharp-angled hotel is covered with smoked glass and features a second-level marble lobby. Junior suites in the building's point have odd-shaped dimensions, vaulted ceilings, and great views. Two penthouse parlors cover 1,200 square feet, while the presidential parlor is the hotel's most lavish digs, with a formal dining room table, large wet bar, marble bath, and connecting rooms on the top floor. The hotel restaurant, Illumé Mediterranean Bistro, serves breakfast, lunch, and dinner, plus a luncheon buffet. A short walk from the escalator is the entrance to the Overstreet Mall, an indoor mall featuring 30 shops and restaurants. Omni guests may use the hotel's exercise facility or the adjoining Charlotte Athletic Club, or request a Get Fit room with portable treadmill and healthy snacks in the minibar. A rooftop pool and sun-

deck are open seasonally. A full-service business center is open 24/7.

RENAISSANCE CHARLOTTE
SUITES HOTEL $$$-$$$$
2800 Coliseum Centre Dr.
(704) 357-1414
www.marriott.com

This upscale hotel was built next to the Charlotte Coliseum. Unfortunately, the city built a new arena in Uptown and tore down the old one. Nonetheless, this remains a very nice hotel in close proximity to Charlotte/Douglas International Airport and the Billy Graham Library. The Renaissance Charlotte has 275 suites in a full-service, deluxe hotel setting. The nine-story hotel, part of the Marriott chain, also has a restaurant, lounge, and room service, as well as banquet facilities and catering service. Other amenities include a business center with high-speed Internet access, pool, health club, and free airport shuttle.

i International visitors who need a tour guide fluent in a specific language or need to exchange money can contact the Charlotte Convention & Visitors Bureau at (704) 331-2700. The CVB can help locate a guide and provide a list of banks that have foreign currency available.

RENAISSANCE CHARLOTTE—
SOUTHPARK $$$-$$$$
5501 Carnegie Blvd.
(704) 554-1234
www.charlotte.hyatt.com

Formerly the Hyatt SouthPark, this 262-room property is beautifully appointed and has a stately exterior befitting its location across from North Carolina's most exclusive mall. The hotel has an indoor pool, sauna, fitness center, 24-hour room service, free valet parking, full-service business center, wireless Internet access, and complimentary airport shuttle service. The Fountain Grill offers dining to the soothing sounds of the atrium fountain. This is an elegant place to stay, and you'll appreciate the helpful and friendly staff.

RITZ-CARLTON CHARLOTTE $$$$$
201 East Trade St.
(704) 547-2244
www.ritzcarlton.com
The Ritz-Carlton Charlotte created a lot of firsts. It's the first Ritz-Carlton in the Queen City. It's the first Ritz-Carlton in North Carolina. And, it's the first LEED Gold certified Ritz-Carlton in the world.

This landmark addition to the Charlotte business and leisure travel scene debuted in 2009. It features outstanding dining choices, dramatic skyline views, a penthouse wellness center/spa, and the eco-friendly designation.

The building itself is 18 stories and contains 146 guest rooms. Each of those luxurious rooms includes iPod docking station, last-minute office supplies, 10-foot ceilings and floor-to-ceiling windows, 400-thread count linens, dual vanities and separate tub and shower, two Ritz-Carlton signature terry bathrobes, and 24-hour in-room dining.

SHERATON CHARLOTTE
AIRPORT HOTEL $$$–$$$$
I-85 at Billy Graham Parkway
(704) 392-1200
www.sheraton.com
This bright, well-appointed hotel is close to the airport and about 5 miles from Uptown. It offers 222 rooms, executive suites, and a presidential suite; a number of meeting rooms; complimentary airport shuttle; fitness center; and indoor/outdoor pool. A daily copy of *USA Today* and a fruit bar are complimentary from 6:30 to 9:30 a.m. Mon through Fri. You can dine at Oscar's Restaurant.

STAYBRIDGE SUITES $$$
Arrowood, 7924 Forest Pine Dr.
(704) 527-6767

Ballantyne, 15735 John J. Delaney Dr.
(704) 248-5000
www.staybridge.com
When business travel requires remaining away from home for an extended period, hotels such as Staybridge Suites combine a residential feel with the amenities of an office. But you may never want to leave, thanks to the on-site laundry, complimentary breakfast bar, Tues through Thurs beverage reception, 24-hour sweet shop and business center, library stocked with books and games, health club, pool, whirlpool, barbecue grill, and putting green. Preferred privileges for golf and spa treatments at nearby Ballantyne Resort are an added special touch.

Staybridge has two Charlotte locations: Ballantyne, near I-485 in south Charlotte, and Arrowood, off I-77 near Carowinds. Both offer just under 120 suites with full kitchens.

Largest Area Hotels

1. The Westin Charlotte, 700 rooms
2. Charlotte Marriott City Center, 438 rooms
3. Hilton Charlotte Center City, 407 rooms
4. Hilton Charlotte University Place, 393 rooms
5. Omni Charlotte Hotel, 374 rooms
6. The Blake Hotel, 308 rooms (tie)
7. Embassy Suites Golf Resort & Spa (Concord), 308 rooms (tie)
8. Charlotte Marriott at Executive Park, 297 rooms
9. Holiday Inn Charlotte Center City, 296 rooms
10. Renaissance Charlotte Suites Hotel, 275 rooms
11. Embassy Suites Charlotte, 274 rooms

SUMMERFIELD SUITES $$–$$$
4920 South Tryon St.
(704) 525-2600
www.hyatt.com

Convenient to the airport and I-77 South, this 135-room hotel has one- and two-bedroom suites with full kitchens and separate living areas. Breakfast is complimentary, as are the airport shuttle and in-room high-speed Internet access. Guests also can take advantage of the free grocery shopping service, or dine at one of many nearby restaurants. A business center, laundry, outdoor pool, shuttle service, and social hour are added perks.

THE WESTIN CHARLOTTE $$$–$$$$
601 South College St.
(704) 375-2600
(800) WESTIN-1 (937-8461)
www.westin.com

Opened in 2003, the Westin Charlotte is the city's largest hotel with 700 guest rooms, including 20 executive suites and a luxurious presidential suite. City leaders chipped in $16 million of the $134-million price tag, believing it would benefit the Charlotte Convention Center, which reportedly lost meetings every year because of the lack of Uptown hotel rooms. The modern high-rise with a smoked-glass facade is across the street from the Charlotte Convention Center and steps away from the trolley and light rail lines leading to exciting galleries, shops, restaurants, Uptown cultural sites, and Time Warner Arena. The Westin can easily accommodate big crowds with more than 46,000 square feet of convention facilities, including just over 38,000 square feet of meeting space and a 16,300-square-foot ballroom where up to 1,220 people can hold a banquet.

Guest rooms and suites feature the Westin's signature Heavenly Bed line, dual-line telephones with voice mail, a large work desk, in-room dataport, complimentary Starbucks coffee, movies on command, a safe, and a minibar. When it's time to relax, guests can enjoy an indoor swimming pool with sauna, on-site health club, massage, and spa treatments. The gourmet Ember Grille restaurant serves breakfast, lunch, and dinner; and a cafe, Charlotte's Treats & Eats, offers casual all-day dining. The Westin also has a lounge called Bar 10, 24-hour room service, and catering for upscale events. Other amenities include a concierge, gift shop, business center, valet and self-parking for 1,650 vehicles, express check-out service, and guest office rooms.

WYNDHAM GARDEN HOTEL $$
2600 Yorkmont Rd.
(704) 357-9100
www.wyndham.com

Close to the airport, the Charlotte farmers' market, and Lake Pointe Business Park, this 173-room hotel caters to individual, corporate, and motor coach travelers. Guests may take advantage of the in-room movies, coffeemaker, and a complimentary copy of *USA Today*. The hotel has a heated lap pool, whirlpool, and exercise room. The Garden Cafe provides meals.

BED-AND-BREAKFAST INNS

Charlotte, although known as a destination for business travel, has a surprising amount of bed-and-breakfast inns. These lodging options provide a much different experience than the standard hotel/motel setup. Visitors who choose our B&Bs encounter a more genteel atmosphere that's slower in pace, harkening back to simpler times when Charlotte was just a mid-sized Southern burg.

Two of the most popular—the Duke Mansion and Morehead Inn—are conveniently located just outside of Uptown, with three more nice options available slightly further outside the urban core.

Folks wishing to escape the bustle of the city can find an array of B&Bs in permiter towns like Davidson, Mount Holly, Huntersville, Matthews and Rock Hill.

Each place has its own charm and character.

Price Code

For the purposes of comparing prices, we have categorized accommodations with two to four dollar signs ($), based on the typical daily rates charged for a standard room with two double beds. Keep in mind that these rates are subject to change; however, to give you a rough idea of what to expect, we offer the following guide:

$$ .... $50 to $95
$$$ .... $96 to $124
$$$$ ....$125 and up

CHARLOTTE

THE DUKE MANSION $$$$
400 Hermitage Rd.
(704) 714-4400, (888) 202-1009
www.dukemansion.com
The United States may not have royalty, but the entrepreneurs of the Gilded Age—the Dukes, Astors, and Vanderbilts, for instance—come pretty close. At the Duke Mansion, guests live like original owner James Buchanan "Buck" Duke and his famous daughter, Doris Duke, when the family bought the Colonial Revival home in 1919. The mansion was completely refurbished and opened as a historic inn and meeting center in

1998. Guests may choose from 20 rooms, some with sleeping porches and treetop views overlooking four and a half acres of gardens. All rooms have private baths, exquisite linens, luxurious robes, fine toiletries, and gourmet treats by the bed. Restaurants, shops, and parks are within easy walking distance, and when business calls you back to reality, Uptown is a mere two minutes away. Breakfast is served daily; room service for beer, wine, and cocktails is available, along with a 24-hour guest pantry. Lunch and dinner are available with advance arrangements. The Duke Mansion also hosts many meetings and special events, from CEO retirement parties to anniversary celebrations.

THE MOREHEAD INN $$$$
1122 East Morehead St.
(704) 376-3357
(888) MOREHEAD (667–3432)
www.moreheadinn.com
Just minutes from Uptown Charlotte and Bank of America Stadium, the Morehead Inn is an elegant Southern estate endowed with quiet elegance and fine antiques. This historic Dilworth home features spacious public areas with intimate fireplaces, luxurious private rooms, and a lovely four-bedroom carriage house. Built in 1917 and

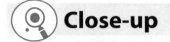 **Close-up**

The Duke Mansion

Wrapped in Southern splendor, the Duke Mansion may be the best-known and most admired home in Charlotte. But like many other Queen City historical jewels, the home was nearly lost forever.

Built in 1919, the Colonial Revival–style home was purchased the same year by James Buchanan "Buck" Duke, founder of Duke Energy, Duke University, and the Duke Endowment. Duke wanted a gracious home that would introduce his daughter, Doris, to life in the South and to serve as a base for his growing businesses. Duke tripled the size of the home and lived there until 1929.

The Duke Mansion was purchased by Martin Cannon in 1929 and renamed White Oaks. His daughter, Frances, married there in front of guests including John F. Kennedy, one of her former beaus. The Cannons owned White Oaks until 1957, when it was left to Myers Park Presbyterian Church.

Henry and Clayton Lineberger, members of a textile family in Belmont who had mansions of their own, bought the mansion in 1957 and restored it to its original splendor. A dining room chandelier still used in the home was a Christmas gift from Mr. to Mrs. Lineberger. In 1966 a fire gutted the third floor, and the home was near destruction. But the Linebergers stepped in again to rescue and restore White Oaks. The couple left the home to the Duke Endowment in 1976.

In the late '70s many Charlotteans were beginning to lament the city's destruction of historic sites in favor of new banks, businesses, and neighborhoods. The Junior League led an effort to create a new life for the mansion, and the home was divided into several condominiums. Fortunately, Rick and Dee Ray of Raycom, a sports media company, bought all of the condominium units and adjoining land to keep White Oaks intact. In 1989 the nonprofit Lynnwood Foundation was created to preserve the Duke Mansion in years to come. The Rays sold the house to the foundation in 1996, and two years later it was opened as a meeting center and inn.

Today guests can relax in the lush gardens of surrounding Myers Park, walk to quaint restaurants and boutiques, and dream of life in the era of the Dukes.

renovated in 1995, the Morehead has earned a first-class reputation as one of the finest inns in the South with numerous awards for renovation, cuisine, and service. In addition to overnight accommodations and a full Southern breakfast, the inn provides a gracious setting for seminars, business luncheons, executive meetings, and some of the city's grandest weddings and social events.

Features include 13 elegantly appointed guest rooms, all with private baths, and high-speed Internet, 5 indoor meeting areas, a complete business center, and a secluded outdoor courtyard. Corporate and special package rates are available.

MS. ELSIE'S CARIBBEAN BED & BREAKFAST INN $$$$
334 North Sharon Amity Rd.
(704) 365-5189
www.mselsies.com

Featured in *Southern Living* magazine and on Turner South, Ms. Elsie's is an unexpected and delightful find. Most B&Bs in Charlotte and in the South go with traditional decor, from colonial to Victorian, but innkeepers Cheryl and Trevor Watkins pay homage to Cheryl's beloved grandmother, Ms. Elsie, and to their own roots in Aruba and Barbados. The three-room B&B in the Cotswold area embraces a Caribbean theme, but not in a garish way. You'll find soothing pastels, rattan furniture, tropical fabrics, mosquito netting, and ceiling fans in the Mango Suite, Peach Suite, Bamboo King Suite, and the Aloe Vera Sun Room. Serene with a quaint, intimate feel, Ms. Elsie's welcomes businesspeople, couples, even the prime minister of Barbados, but cuts loose, too, by inviting people to have fun dancing to steel drum music or doing the limbo. A three-course breakfast features recipes handed down from five generations of Creoles—seafood entrees such as St. Maarten creole shrimp and pan-fried salmon, fresh fruit, and desserts such as banana with rum glaze and bread pudding. Children 14 and older welcome; no pets.

ROSWELL INN $$
2320 Roswell Ave.
(704) 332-4915
You can wake up to the appetizing smell of homemade biscuits and rolls or maybe coffee cake being prepared by effervescent innkeeper Lea Harrison from her own special recipes (passed down from generations). During the warmer season you can dine on the terrace in one of Charlotte's loveliest gardens, then walk beneath towering trees through Myers Park, one of the city's oldest neighborhoods. This beautifully decorated, family heirloom–filled home is an inviting place to relax over afternoon Russian tea or old-fashioned lemonade with warm-from-the-oven cookies. It's a short drive to Uptown and the airport.

VANLANDINGHAM ESTATE $$$$
2010 The Plaza
(704) 334-8909, (888) 524-2020
www.vanlandinghamestate.com
A sister property to the elegant Morehead Inn, this 1913 California bungalow-style home built for a wealthy cotton broker and his family is equally impressive. The inn is located 3 miles from Uptown in the historic Plaza-Midwood neighborhood and offers nine private guest rooms with names that reflect Charlotte notables from the literary (Charles Kuralt) to the kitschy (Betty Feezor, Fred Kirby). All feature private baths and high-speed Internet. A full Southern breakfast is

included. Nearly five acres of gardens include a French orangery greenhouse and a historic lily pond. Special events are big business here, including corporate meetings for up to 90 people, wedding receptions for up to 500 people, and other celebrations for as many as 700. The estate's Web site offers virtual views of all guest rooms.

DAVIDSON

DAVIDSON VILLAGE INN $$$–$$$$
117 Depot St.
(704) 892-8044, (800) 892-0796
www.davidsoninn.com
Located across from Davidson College, this inn was built in 1993 on the site of the original Maxwell Chambers Hotel. The inn includes 18 rooms and suites, 2 corporate relocation apartments, and an attached conference room. A full continental breakfast and an afternoon tea are served daily; room service is provided by neighboring restaurant Jasper's and Joel's Asian Grill. Business travelers may use the conference room, photocopier, fax, and other services. Business functions and corporate meetings are well suited for this inn located in the heart of Davidson. Custom-bottled toiletries, terry robes, and fitness center access are nice perks. Children welcome.

HUNTERSVILLE

GARDEN GATE BED & BREAKFAST $$
108 Gilead Rd.
(704) 947-7700
www.bedandbreakfast.com
This two-story Federal home in the old downtown section of Huntersville at Lake Norman dates to 1895. Jerry and Rachel Ingalls completely gutted the home nine years ago, and after a year of construction, opened with three guest rooms. The B&B features a huge yard with gardens on about two-thirds of the land, and a city park with seven tennis courts and a playground sits behind the property. Rooms are large, with high ceilings and antiques, and a deep front porch is a perfect place to rock and catch the breeze. The traditional country breakfast includes eggs, pota-

toes, meats, breads, fruit, and pastries. Davidson College visitors, businesspeople, and locals with visiting family frequent the inn.

LAKE WYLIE

**VICTORIAN VILLA ON
LAKE WYLIE**   **$$$–$$$$**
10925 Windy Grove Rd., Charlotte
(704) 394-5545
www.victorianvillainn.com
This lakefront home, built in the 1920s, has been painstakingly restored and renovated into a blue-and-white gingerbread-trimmed Victorian with rooftop ornaments from Charlotte churches. Opened in 1997, the inn serves a full breakfast to guests in the sun room that overlooks the lake. Guests may relax and fish off the dock, take a day cruise or moonlit midnight cruise of the lake on their boat, or arrange a water arrival at local waterfront restaurants. The villa has over 2,500 feet of deck to enjoy the views of the lake. Five rooms are furnished with antiques; some even come with wet bars and sitting areas. The villa is located close to the airport and is only a short ride to Uptown attractions.

LANCASTER, SC

THE HOMEPLACE BED & BREAKFAST   **$$**
7096 Pageland Hwy.
(803) 285-7773, (800) 249-7773
www.yancylou-homeplace.com
A colonial-style home built around a circa 1800s log house, the HomePlace has five guest rooms, each with a private bath and two with whirlpools. The countryside setting is restful and relaxing, with walks around a pond and leisurely Southern breakfasts. Opened in 1994 by innkeepers Roy and Dianne Catoe, the HomePlace is popular with businesspeople, church missionaries, couples, and families gathering for reunions.

KILBURNIE—THE INN AT CRAIG FARM $$$$
1824 Craig Farm Rd.
(803) 416-8420
www.kilburnie.com

Located 45 minutes south of Charlotte's airport, Kilburnie is Lancaster's oldest surviving residence, dating to circa 1827. The antebellum home was saved from demolition in 1998 and moved to the historic Craig Farm, the homestead of Scots-Irish John Craig, who immigrated here in 1772 and fought in local Revolutionary War battles. Kilburnie was lovingly restored, from intricate carved plaster ceilings and moldings to original heart pine mantels on 11 fireplaces. Four guest rooms and one suite are available, all with private baths and massage tubs. The winner of the S.C. Heritage Tourism Award, Kilburnie blends antiques and antebellum charm with modern conveniences such as high-speed wireless service. Golf, state parks, historical sites, and even an air-gliding school are nearby. For special events, the 20-column Palladium Pavilion set in an English boxwood garden makes for lovely outdoor entertaining.

MATTHEWS

803 ELIZABETH BED & BREAKFAST $$–$$$
803 Elizabeth Lane
(704) 841-8900, (800) 327-4843
www.803elizabeth.com
Slip off your shoes and sit a spell on the porch of this cozy home with innkeepers Martha and Will Krauss. The 803 Elizabeth sits on five acres of woods and gardens 12 miles southeast of Uptown. Three guest rooms, all with private baths, offer queen, double, or twin beds, as well as family antiques, pretty linens, and flowers cut from the garden. Two rooms open onto a porch. Continental breakfast includes homemade muffins, fresh fruit, juice, tea, coffee, and cereal in the dining room or on the porch.

MATTHEWS MANOR   **$$$–$$$$**
1726 Spring Stone Dr.
(704) 708-5560, (800) 536-1728, ext. 2552
www.charlottebedandbreakfast.com
This 7,000-square-foot manor home in the quiet suburb of Matthews sits 12 miles south of Uptown. Built in 1973, the home was transformed into an inn by current owners Linda and George Megee, Philadelphia natives who lived in South

Close-up

The Morehead Inn

The Morehead Inn in Dilworth, one of Charlotte's best-known and respected properties, was the first private home in the city to have electricity, gas, and air-conditioning. Built in 1917 for Marjorie and Charles Campbell Coddington, the home was appropriately lavish and modern for the man who made a fortune as the exclusive Buick dealer in the Carolinas. British-born architect William Peeps designed the Coddingtons' home to reflect their entertaining lifestyle. The couple became social and civic players in the Charlotte community, but died tragically in separate incidents three years apart.

The Old Coddington House, as it was known to locals for years, was selected by local members of the American Society of Interior Designers as a designer house in 1976. In 1984 the 14,000-square-foot home was converted into a country inn. One year later the Morehead Inn earned an official Charlotte Historic Landmark designation from the Mecklenburg Historic Properties Commission. Today the two-story white clapboard home featured in *Southern Living* and many other top-notch magazines greets guests with a green tile roof, ivy climbing up double chimneys, and rooms full of history and memories.

Florida for 20 years. The four guest rooms offer all the amenities of home—cable TV with HBO, desks, phones, wireless Internet, and window seats. Guests also have access to a large living room and private kitchen with microwave, refrigerator, dishwasher, washer/dryer, and television. Downstairs, visitors can take a swim, stroll through the gardens, watch birds on the veranda or play billiards in the sunroom. A 29-acre park with fishing lake, picnic areas, trails, and a playground is across the street. Continental breakfast includes fruit, pastries, and coffee. Traveling with a pet? Boarding is available 1 mile away.

MOUNT HOLLY

ROBIN'S NEST BED & BREAKFAST $$–$$$
156 North Main St.
(704) 827-2420
www.robinsnestbb.com
This 1914 Classical Revival home just off I-85 in Gaston County is convenient to the Charlotte airport, Daniel Stowe Botanical Garden in Belmont, and the west side of Lake Norman. Opened by Robin and Jerry Williams nearly eight years ago, the Robin's Nest has four guest rooms with pri-

vate baths, each named for a Carolina bird such as Cardinal, Blue Bird, Blue Jay, and Hummingbird. Bird-watchers and nature lovers enjoy the natural theme, as well as the character of clawfoot tubs, fresh baked goods set out for guests, and a goldfish pond on the grounds. Full breakfast includes specialty pancakes, eggs, baked fruits, quiche, and banana bread. Children age 14 and up welcome. No pets. No smoking.

ROCK HILL, SC

THE BOOK & THE SPINDLE $$–$$$
626 Oakland Ave.
(803) 328-1913
Directly across from Winthrop University, a selection of restaurants, art galleries, and performance centers, this historic brick Georgian home takes its name from the town's trademarks—academics and cotton.

Each of the four guest rooms is decorated in a different South Carolina theme and has a private bath, cable TV, and coffeemaker. Two are suites with separate full kitchens and sitting areas. Children and small pets accepted; limited smoking areas.

EAST MAIN GUEST HOUSE $$–$$$
600 East Main St.
(803) 366-1161
www.eastmainsc.com

Conveniently located in the Historic District, the East Main Guest House was built in 1916 and completely renovated in the 1990s by owners Melba and Jerry Peterson. The three guest rooms have private baths and cable TV; one is a honeymoon suite with hot tub, and two have working fireplaces. Other amenities include full gourmet breakfast, backyard gardens, a sitting area with television and VCR, and a fax machine. The inn, which won a historic preservation award for its renovation, draws Winthrop University parents and snowbirds traveling to Florida.

PARK AVENUE INN $$
347 Park Ave.
(803) 325-1764, (877) 422-0127
www.bedandbreakfast.com

A large front porch with rocking chairs and twin parlors add charm to this inn, built in 1916 and completely restored in 1991.

Like going to grandmother's house, the inn features three guest rooms furnished with antiques. All have private baths. Small pets are welcome.

RESTAURANTS

Charlotte's culinary offerings have expanded dramatically in recent years, spurred by the city's emergence as a national and international commerce hub, the influx of tens of thousands of new residents, and the addition of Johnson & Wales University.

What was once a predictable southern town of down-home diners and run-of-the-mill chain eateries has greatly evolved. Twenty-first century Charlotte blends the best of the old—slow-cooked vegetables, stick-to-the-ribs meat and potatoes, Southern barbecue, and ultra-sweet tea—with sophisticated new menus featuring international cuisine, upscale presentations, and inspired recipes.

Not only do we have chefs trained in Europe and across the United States, we now celebrate the culinary delights of chefs trained right here in the Queen City at Johnson & Wales, which opened in Uptown in 2004. Restaurants are arranged alphabetically by type of cuisine. Listings are located in Charlotte unless otherwise noted.

Price Code

We have included a price code that gives you a general idea of how much a dinner for two, excluding appetizers, desserts, or alcoholic beverages, will cost. Daily specials are offered at many restaurants. Some restaurants offer senior citizen discounts, children's menus, and early evening dining discounts. Prices do not reflect sales tax or gratuities, which should be 15 to 20 percent for good service.

Although menu suggestions and days open are included, keep in mind that these, as well as restaurant ownership and food prices, may change. Call ahead for more specific information.

$..................... Under $21
$$ .... $21 to $35
$$$ .... $36 to $50
$$$$ ....$51 and up

AMERICAN

FENWICK'S ON PROVIDENCE $$
511 Providence Rd.
(704) 333-2750
It's often said that no one who lives in Charlotte is from Charlotte. But they do exist, and many of them frequent Fenwick's in the heart of Myers Park, the city's first suburb and one of its best old-money addresses. During the day ladies who lunch nibble on homemade muffins, croissant sandwiches, quiche, casseroles, and salad plates. But at night the tiny restaurant takes an upscale, yet casual, turn with fresh seafood and salads, grilled chicken, steaks, and other standard not-too-nouveau cuisine. Take a break from low carb here—the bread, muffins, and desserts are well worth it. Reservations are not accepted. Fenwick's is open for lunch and dinner Mon through Sat.

FIREBIRDS WOOD FIRED GRILL $$–$$$
7716 Rea Rd.
Stonecrest Shopping Center
(704) 752-7979

6801 Northlake Mall Dr.
Northlake Mall
(704) 295-1919

3920 Sharon Rd.
SouthPark
(704) 366-3655
www.firebirdsrestaurants.com
Firebirds is a true Charlotte success story. The first location was established in 2000 at Stonecrest in

South Charlotte. That restaurant, set in a contemporary rustic lodge with a roaring fire, vaulted ceilings, exposed beams, massive stone fireplace, leather sofas, and columns made of aspen, set the tone for future growth. There are now 17 Firebirds locations in seven states. Firebirds has a large menu. You'll find steaks, chops, seafood, pasta, salads, and sandwiches with bold sauces and, at times, a bit of a Southwestern kick. The open-air kitchen teases diners with the aroma and sizzle of rotisseries and pizza straight out of the wood-fired oven. Portions are huge. Suggested wine pairings on the featured menu is a nice touch. The Rea Road location is a favorite spot on weekends, so expect a waiting period before being seated. Hours are 11 a.m. to 10 p.m. Mon through Thurs; 11 a.m. to 11 p.m. Fri and Sat; and 10:30 a.m. to 10 p.m. Sun.

HARPER'S $$
6518 Fairview Rd., Sharon Corners
(704) 366-6688

11059 Carolina Place Parkway, Pineville
(704) 541-5255
www.harpersrestaurants.com
Is there somebody in your group who's hard to please? Head to Harper's, a straightforward, traditional American restaurant with a little bit of everything and no strange combinations or skimpy portions. The menu includes California-style wood-fired pizzas and grilled items; standard but good sandwiches; and fresh salads, steak, pasta, chicken, and fish. A couple of the more unique items are the roasted salmon wrap and the pimento macaroni and cheese. Overall, both restaurants are comfortable and casual places in a somewhat upscale setting. The booths at the Sharon Corners location are particularly large and roomy. Both locations offer lunch and dinner daily.

HOTEL CHARLOTTE $$
705 South Sharon Amity Rd.
(704) 364-8755
www.hotelcharlotterestaurant.com
The furnishings and decor of the original Hotel Charlotte were transported from the city to the suburbs and serve as a backdrop for this traditional Charlotte eatery. The menu is American, with a New Orleans flair. For lunch, try burgers or po'boys with "add-ons" of your choice. For dinner, try the shrimp creole, steak Diane, crawfish étouffée, jumbo gumbo, live Maine lobster, or New England clam chowder. The restaurant's wine and beer clubs are just the thing for sampling a wide variety of beverages (it boasts more than 100 varieties of beer). Hotel Charlotte is open for lunch and dinner Mon through Fri, and open only for dinner on Sat. Sun is brunch only, from 11 a.m. to 3 p.m.

MACADO'S $-$$
9111 Concord Mills Blvd., Concord
(704) 979-3700
www.macados.net
If you've ever spent time in the Blue Ridge Mountains of North Carolina, Tennessee, and Virginia, you've probably run across this hometown chain of eateries based in Roanoke, Va. Tucked into Concord Mills Mall, Macado's has probably the largest sandwich menu in the Charlotte area, and all the sandwiches are tasty. If you've ever had an unusual sandwich combination that you really loved, chances are Macado's has it, or something similar. There are also flavorful entrées and appetizers. Best of all, you get a lot of good food without spending a lot of dough.

MICKEY & MOOCH $$-$$$
8128 Providence Rd., Arboretum
(704) 752-8080

9723 Sam Furr Rd., Huntersville
(704) 895-6654
www.mickeyandmooch.com
Both locations of Mickey & Mooch are considered among the top restaurants in Charlotte. They have been recognized by *Zagat, Wine Spectator*, and several local publications. Mickey, the owner, is an Italian from New Jersey who knows his cuts of beef. You can't go wrong with the aged center-cut beef and chops. The rest of the menu is highly regarded, too, including pastas and risotto, fresh boiled and sautéed fish, baby-back ribs, lobster,

crab cakes, and shrimp and grits. The décor is upscale, yet the dress code is fairly casual. Mickey & Mooch is a great place to take a date, with live music a couple nights a week. Outside dining is available seasonally. Dinner nightly; reservations recommended.

SONOMA MODERN
AMERICAN CUISINE $$–$$$
100 North Tryon St.
(704) 377-1333
www.sonomarestaurants.net
Sonoma features the hottest trends in New American cuisine. This local favorite, a *Wine Spectator* Award of Excellence winner, has more than 300 varieties of wine to accompany its fresh, healthy, and uniquely combined cuisine. Sonoma is located in the same building as the Blumenthal Performing Arts Center. So, if you're going to a Broadway play or to the symphony or opera at the Blumenthal, take advantage of Sonoma's show special: a three-course dinner for $30 from 5 to 7:30 p.m. show nights. Lunch is served weekdays; dinner, Mon through Sat. Patio seating is available; reservations recommended.

TRIO $–$$
10709 McMullen Creek Parkway, Pineville
(704) 541-8000
www.trio-charlotte.com
With all the chain restaurants in Pineville, it's easy to overlook Trio. Make sure you don't, however, because this versatile eatery offers good food and good service at a great price. Trio is the place to bring your hard-to-please mother-in-law because the menu offers something for every taste. From brick-oven pizzas to crab cakes, from filet mignon to three cheese tortellini to fried North Carolina flounder, it's all there, and served in an open floor plan illuminated with ceiling lights. Trio's Sun brunch is one of the best-kept secrets in the Queen City. Open for lunch and dinner seven days a week.

ZINK $$–$$$
201 North Tryon St.
(704) 444-9001
www.harpersgroup.com/zink
Zink is a great option if you're looking for American fare in an atmosphere that's a bit more formal. The menu puts a new twist on our traditional comfort foods. For example, you can dine on American wagyu meat loaf or lobster mac 'n' cheese. Other options include crab-stuffed mountain trout and buttermilk fried chicken sliders. Zink has a prime location on Tryon Street, just north of The Square. Its outdoor patio is a great option because it's set back from the bustle and slightly above street level. The wine list is derived exclusively from U.S. vineyards, and the extensive beer selection is also all-American. The bar at Zink is a popular spot after work and on weekends. Open daily for lunch and dinner; reservations accepted.

ASIAN

BAODING $$–$$$
4722 Sharon Rd.
Sharon Corners Shopping Center
(704) 552-8899
www.baodingsouthpark.com
This SouthPark restaurant's design looks more like an upscale New York eatery than the typical Asian restaurant. The northern Chinese food is chic, matching the decor. You'll know it's Asian, but modern preparation techniques make dining here exceptional. Open for lunch and dinner seven days a week. Takeout is available.

P. F. CHANG'S CHINA BISTRO $$
Fairview Road at Phillips Place
(704) 552-6644

10325 Perimeter Parkway, Northlake
(704) 598-1927
www.pfchangs.com
This Chinese bistro chain opened its first Charlotte location in Phillips Place, Charlotte's most upscale shopping center. The restaurant was received so well, often with a wait, that P.F. Chang's opened a second location at Northlake Mall. Both locations offer many wines by the glass and great appetizers such as lettuce wraps, but don't fill up before you try the signature spicy chicken, honey shrimp, fried rice, and lo mein. Lunch and dinner served daily.

SHUN LEE PALACE $-$$
4340 Colwick Rd.
(704) 366-2025
This is a favorite Chinese restaurant for many Charlotteans. It offers a wide variety of entrees to choose from, serving Mandarin, Szechuan, Hunan, and Cantonese cuisine. Lunch is served Mon through Fri plus Sun; dinner is served seven days a week.

THAI HOUSE $$
3210 North Sharon Amity Rd.
(704) 532-6868

8706 Pineville-Matthews Rd., Pineville
(704) 542-6300

230 East W. T. Harris Blvd., University
(704) 717-8006
Thai House has been voted Best Thai food in the Queen City by *Charlotte Magazine*. The restaurants feature a classic menu with more than 70 traditional recipes—seafood, chicken, duck, pork, and beef, served with hot rice and spicy sauces (mild, medium, or hot). Try the King and I, prepared with grilled Thai whole shrimp seasoned with fresh garlic, tomatoes, chili pepper, onion, and carrots and garnished with broccoli, or the Gulf of Siam, featuring a choice of shrimp, baby clams, squid, or seafood combination cooked in a clay pot and served with vegetables and spices. It is open seven days a week for lunch and dinner.

THAI TASTE $$
324 East Blvd.
(704) 332-0001

2025 East Arbors Dr., University
(704) 688-9179

131 Matthews Station St., Matthews
(704) 841-4455
www.thaitastecharlotte.com
Thai Taste was the first Thai restaurant in the Queen City and operated as a single restaurant for many years on East Boulevard, where it catered to the many "foodies" who live in Dilworth and dine there. *Creating Loafing* has twice recognized it as the best Thai food in Charlotte. In recent years, it has added locations in shopping centers in the University City

area and in Matthews. The curry dishes at Thai Taste are excellent—just let the waitperson know how "hot and spicy" you like it. Lunch is served Mon through Fri, and dinner is served every night.

i Taste of Charlotte, held in Uptown the first weekend in June, is a great way to sample popular dishes of many area restaurants. Patrons buy tokens at the festival and use them to purchase samples from restaurant booths lining Tryon Street. Admission is free.

BARBECUE

First off, here in North Carolina the term "barbecue" is a noun. It refers to a food dish of chopped or pulled pork basted in either an Eastern North Carolina or a Western North Carolina barbecue sauce. The correct verb to describe the act of putting some type of meat on a grill is "grilling" or "grilling out." Therefore, you should never confuse the food "barbecue" with the act of "grilling." If you invite somebody over for "barbecue," you'd better be serving "barbecue" pork.

Second, there are only two kinds of barbecue that true Charlotteans will eat: Eastern North Carolina barbecue, which uses the whole hog and is basted with a vinegar-based sauce, and Western North Carolina barbecue, which uses the fattier shoulder portion of the hog and is basted in a tomato/ketchup-based sauce.

Finally, in barbecue terms, Western North Carolina refers to the portion of the state starting at Lexington and heading westward. So, Lexington's famous barbecue joints actually serve Western North Carolina barbecue, although they're located east of Charlotte. Got it?

To be completely forthright, the Queen City is not known as a barbecue hotbed. The best stuff is in Lexington (about an hour to the northeast) or in Shelby (about 45 minutes west). If you choose to stay closer to home, the best bets are listed below.

BILL SPOON'S BARBECUE $
5524 South Blvd.
(704) 525-8865

Bill Spoon began serving eastern-style barbecue in Charlotte in 1963. Although he has since passed away, his family carries on the tradition of this popular eatery. Spoon's is a Charlotte landmark so well known for its vinegar-based barbecue that it has been the subject of television shows and culinary documentaries. Everyone from construction workers to the richest men in the city eat here. And, if you find yourself short of cash, the owners have been known to let folks mail in a check. Open 10:30 a.m. to 3 p.m. Mon through Sat.

BUBBA'S BARBECUE $
4400 Sunset Rd.
(Exit 16B from I-77 North)
(704) 393-2000
www.bubbasbarbecue.com
Bubba's cooks the whole pig Eastern North Carolina style, using peppers and spices in a vinegar base in a 33-hour process. You can also order barbecue chicken, barbecue beans, barbecue ribs, barbecue french fries, Brunswick stew, meat loaf, and, of course, hush puppies. In true Southern tradition, Bubba's offers sweet potato pie and pecan pie.

If you choose takeout, remember to purchase a bottle of Bubba's sauce—it's not included with a regular take-home order. Join the Bubba's Birthday Club, and you can eat free on your special day. Open for lunch and dinner daily.

HILLBILLY'S BBQ & STEAKS $
720 McAdenville Rd., Lowell
(704) 824-8838

930 East Garrison Blvd., Gastonia
(704) 861-8787

838 Tyvola Rd.
(704) 525-2799
www.hillbillysbbqsteaks.com
Western-style barbecue cooked over an open flame using mesquite wood. This is about as good as it gets in the Charlotte area. Hillbilly's is probably so tasty because it originated next door in Gaston County, where folks know their 'cue. Gerald Duncan opened the first Hillbilly's in 1989

at the Lowell-McAdenville exit off I-85, and added a second location two years later in Gastonia. Hillbilly's came to Charlotte in recent years, taking over the old Carolina Country Barbecue location on Tyvola Road near I-77. The large or small pork plates come with baked potato, slaw, and the best hushpuppies around. They also have steaks, turkey, and a great salad bar, but you should be coming here for the barbecue. Open for lunch and dinner Mon through Sat, and lunch on Sun.

HOG HEAVEN BARBECUE $
1600 Purser Dr.
(704) 535-0154
This is one of those hole-in-the-wall joints that you could pass by, but shouldn't. The small building, with just six tables, produces great Lexington-style (Western North Carolina) barbecue. In fact, Southern food connoisseur Bob Garner praises Hog Heaven's barbecue in his book, *Bob Garner's Guide to North Carolina Barbecue,* by calling it the "best Lexington-style barbecue in Charlotte." Owner Sonny Lyon also makes a mean homemade Brunswick stew, and his wife makes a tasty coconut pie for dessert. Hog Heaven is open Mon through Sat for lunch and dinner.

OLD HICKORY HOUSE $
6538 North Tryon St.
(704) 596-8014
There are people who swear the Brunswick stew is the best in the state. The pit-cooked barbecue is pretty good, too. You don't get a lot of ambience at Old Hickory House, just great food and friendly service. Takeout and catering are available. Open for lunch and dinner Mon through Sat.

OLE SMOKEHOUSE #1 $
1513 Montford Dr.
(704) 523-7222
This landmark serves great barbecue—ribs, chicken, beef, and pork—but it also has steaks and fresh seafood for the non–barbecue lovers in your crowd. Be sure to inquire about the daily specials. It's open for lunch and dinner Mon through Sat.

BISTROS, BARS, AND GRILLS

ALEXANDER MICHAEL'S $$
401 West Ninth St.
(704) 332-6789
www.almikestavern.com

Housed in a late 1800s Victorian building once occupied by Charlotte's general store, this is one of Fourth Ward's favorite spots. Drop by for lunch or for dinner and a drink after work to enjoy the friendly neighborhood atmosphere. Don't miss the "What It Is" house specialty—blackened chicken tenders over rotini with Cajun cream sauce, or the famous fried pickles. Women should be careful to avoid the pole that's right in the way as you enter the bathroom. Open for lunch and dinner Mon through Sat.

BLACKFINN AMERICAN SALOON $–$$
210 East Trade St., EpiCentre
(704) 971-4440
www.blackfinncharlotte.com

Although it is popular as a nightspot, BlackFinn is also a very good spot to grab lunch or enjoy a nice meal. The dining room is on the first floor and completely separate from the downstairs bar area. The décor and furnishings are classy, and the menu features more than just bar fare. General manager Gregg McConnell, who played college football at Duke, says the most popular dinner entrees are the filet mignon and sautéed lemon chicken cutlets. The shaved prime rib sandwich is a big seller on the lunch menu, along with the ahi tuna salad and seared ahi tuna appetizers. Beef, pork, and chicken sliders are also in demand. Open for lunch and dinner seven days a week.

CHARLEYS RESTAURANT $$
274 South Sharon Amity Rd.
Cotswold Village Shops
(704) 364-7475
www.charleys-charlotte.com

Not to be confused with the chain restaurant O'Charley's, this popular eatery has been a Charlotte favorite for more than 20 years. Charleys serves tasty soups, specialty salads, and panini sandwiches, plus create-your-own pizzas and quesadillas. Customers may order brunch anytime, with quiche, crepes, or eggs Benedict. More upscale options include pastas such as lobster ravioli and three-cheese tortellini. Grilled baby back ribs are also a favorite, and low-carb choices are available. Sunday brunch includes items such as stuffed French toast, grilled salmon with raspberry-almond beurre blanc, crab cakes Benedict, and quiche. Desserts at Charleys are stellar. If you can't decide, try the Dessert Trio with samples of chocolate Oreo pie, Key lime pie, and crème brûlée cheesecake. Charleys is tucked away in a courtyard area of Cotswold Shops, providing a pleasant atmosphere in which to unwind after shopping. Live music is available on the patio during the summer. The restaurant is open for lunch and dinner daily.

CITY TAVERN $$–$$$
7828 Rea Rd.
Stonecrest Shopping Center
(704) 543-8587

14142 Rivergate Parkway
(704) 504-8888
www.city-tavern.com

City Tavern has been a restless stalwart of the Charlotte restaurant scene. It began with a location on East Boulevard that was the Thurs night spot for the "in crowd" and expanded into Uptown (twice), north to Lake Norman, and south to Stonecrest and Rivergate. The latter two make up its current configuration. Both locations are comfortable and offer an extensive wine list and an extensive martini list. The menu provides a nice array of appetizers, including fried oysters Rockefeller, sesame-encrusted ahi tuna, lollipop lamb chops, and firecracker popcorn shrimp. Dinner offers smothered Cajun Carolina trout, chicken panzanilla, twin-tail lobster, gourmet meat loaf, several steak combinations, lobster ravioli, and overstuffed sandwiches from burgers to roasted veggies. Lunch has a wider variety of sandwiches and salads, and many of the same dinner menu items. A special musical treat takes place each Fri at the Rivergate location. Local singer Tommy Joy plays the piano and croons the songs of classic American greats like Frank Sinatra, Tony Bennett, Louis Armstrong, and more. Lunch and dinner daily; Sun brunch features various omelets, eggs Benedict, steak and eggs, and French toast made with cinnamon raisin bread.

COMMON HOUSE $$
1101 Central Ave.
(704) 332-1010
www.charlottecommonhouse.com
Common House, a neighborhood restaurant & bar, is one of the new hot spots in the artsy Plaza-Midwood district. Although located in an older building, the restaurant is modern, casual, and as comfortable as the food. The reasonably priced menu tempts the palate with such items as the fried green tomato BLT, shrimp burger, chicken pot pie, and pan-seared mountain trout. Common House opened in 2009 to glowing reviews from the foremost food critics in the city, with particular praise for chef Emily Hahn. Open for lunch and dinner seven days a week.

DILWORTH NEIGHBORHOOD GRILLE $-$$
911 East Morehead St.
(704) 377-3808
www.neighborhoodgrille.com
Southern Living profiled this bar and grill in November 2008. A writer happened to be in Charlotte, stopped in for lunch, and was struck by the ambience, quality food, and great customer service. Owner Norm Randall opened Dilworth Neighborhood Grille in 2004 after serving as sales manager for Carolina Beer Company. He keeps the menu updated and has connected with alumni groups from many colleges, who faithfully turn out to watch their teams. Dilworth Neighborhood Grille recently expanded into an area next door that was previously a bookstore, and now provides private meeting rooms and banquet facilities. Open for lunch and dinner seven days a week.

FRENCH QUARTER $
321 South Church St.
(704) 377-7415

This restaurant began as a little lunch place in the heart of Uptown serving good food at reasonable prices. The salads (taco, chef's, and Greek) are delicious, or you might want to try a chicken sandwich, burger, or pasta. As the Uptown population has grown, the French Quarter has seen its evening bar business pick up. Lunch and dinner are served 11 a.m. to 8 p.m. Mon through Fri. Closed weekends, but does open on days when the Carolina Panthers play home games.

LAVA BISTRO & BAR $$-$$$
8708 J. W. Clay Blvd.
(704) 549-0050
www.lavabistro.com
Lava Bistro is one of the few upscale, locally owned restaurants in chain-filled University City. You'll find several seafood dishes, steak, pasta, lamb, veal, lobster, and eggplant. Appetizers are heavily seafood influenced, ranging from seafood meritage to lobster gnocchi to lava gumbo. Lava also makes a great place for a light meal and glass of wine enjoyed on the lakeside patio. Four private dining rooms can handle special events. Open for lunch and dinner Mon to Sat. Closed on Sun.

PEWTER ROSE BISTRO $$-$$$
1820 South Blvd.
(704) 332-8149
www.pewterrose.com
This bistro offers a quiet, expertly prepared lunch or dinner that exemplifies creative cuisine at its best. Try the almond baked Brie with bourbon and brown sugar, the Low Country shrimp and grits; seafood paella; Chesapeake crabcakes; flat iron steak; or xim-xim, a Brazilian stew of chicken and shrimp. A 17-year tradition in Charlotte, the Pewter Rose occupies a turn-of-the-20th-century textile warehouse with exposed brick walls, 30-foot ceilings, massive wood beams, French paned glass, and treasures from attics and flea markets. Live music is offered occasionally. Late-night appetizers and desserts are served in the bar on weekends. Lunch and dinner are served daily.

PROVIDENCE CAFE $$–$$$
110 Perrin Place
(704) 376-2008
www.providencecafe.com

At this popular Myers Park hangout, you'll find everyone from regulars to special-occasion diners. The eclectic menu includes great salads and a range of beef, chicken, fresh seafood, and pork. The appetizer menu goes beyond the standards, with pan handle crab cakes topped with cucumber-tomato salad, crab-stuffed mushrooms, and mini brie baked in puff pastry.

For dinner, you can go heavy with such favorites as filet mignon, prime rib, pork loin, and pastas, or try the "lighter fare" section of the menu with items like lowcountry crab cake salad and the petit filet sandwich.

Both the patio and high-ceiling, open dining room make a nice setting for a relaxing glass of wine or late-night dessert. There's live jazz every Wed and Thurs. Open for lunch and dinner daily, with Sun brunch.

PROVIDENCE ROAD SUNDRIES $–$$
1522 Providence Rd.
(704) 366-4467

Known simply as "Sundries," this is the place to go for great burgers and sandwiches. It's also the place to go to see or be seen by the local "in" crowd. Opened in 1933, Sundries serves lunch and dinner seven days a week.

RED ROCKS CAFE & BAKERY $$–$$$
4223–B Providence Rd., Strawberry Hill
(704) 364-0402

Birkdale Village, Huntersville
8712 Lindholm Dr.
(704) 892-9999
www.redrockscafe.com

Red Rocks successfully debuted in 1992 near the intersection of Providence and Fairview, and added a second location in 2003 in Huntersville's Birkdale Village. Both restaurants cater to an upscale clientele, with the Birkdale location a popular spot for NASCAR drivers and Carolina Panthers players. Trendy yet relaxed, Red Rocks offers a good mix of casual and upscale American entrees, many named for local celebrities who frequent Red Rocks. At the Birkdale location, racing fans enjoy such dishes as Kasey Kahne's lobster tail dinner, Jeff Gordon's ribs, and A.J. Allmendinger's blackened grouper, while NFL fans can sample Jason Baker's lobster ravioli. The Providence Road location features dishes named more for civic leaders and politicos, although former Charlotte Hornet Dell Curry, now a local broadcaster, has a tasty chicken penne pasta entree. At either place, leave room for dessert, with cheesecake, tiramisu, and the signature three-layer chocolate cake on the menu. Lunch and dinner daily; brunch on Sun.

THE ROASTING COMPANY $
1601 Montford Dr.
(704) 521-8188
www.roastingco.com

This casual hangout specializes in rotisserie chicken and roasted pork topped with jaco sauce. The sauce is like a Caribbean-style au jus, and the staff will gladly provide extra to cover everything on your plate. Soft tacos are popular, with a serve-yourself condiment bar. The vegetables are fresh and rotate daily. Don't miss the stewed okra and tomatoes on Fri. An outdoor patio overlooks Montford Drive, a nice little byway of restaurants and pubs. Open for lunch and dinner daily.

ROCK BOTTOM BREWERY $$
401 North Tryon St.
(704) 334-2739
www.rockbottomsouth.com

Right across the street from Uptown's big banks, Rock Bottom is a popular after-work hangout that offers a lively bar with pool tables, booths, and TVs on one side and a quieter restaurant on the opposite end. The menu features classics with a twist, such as lowcountry shrimp and grits (with its own thimble-size bottle of Tabasco) and gourmet grilled cheese on focaccia bread, as well as piled-high nachos, salads, burgers, steaks, pizza, pasta, and sandwiches. Rock Bottom has a nice selection of German beers brewed on site, several of which have won medals at beer festivals.

Lunch and dinner daily; bar menu available late. Patio seating is available.

300 EAST $$
300 East Blvd.
(704) 332-6507
www.300east.com

Whether you have a large group or just want a cozy corner for two, this Dilworth mainstay is carved out of an old house with lots of nooks and crannies, as well as a great patio overlooking East Boulevard. The New American menu has it all—from pizzas to grinders—including a good chunky chicken salad. It's a great place to start Sun morning off with a relaxed brunch in informal surroundings. Open for lunch and dinner daily.

VILLAGE TAVERN $$-$$$
4201 Congress St.
(704) 552-9983
www.villagetavern.com

Located near SouthPark Mall, the Tavern's huge outdoor patio is a fun place to meet with friends for a drink when the weather is nice. Many Charlotteans enjoy going for jazz music on Wed and Thurs evenings spring through fall, or to sit above the crowd at symphony concerts on Sun nights in June. It will take you a while to get through the large menu known for its thin-crust pizzas, nice salads, piled-high sandwiches, and pastas in rich sauces. Sun brunch offers several different omelets and a variety of eggs Benedict. For a change of pace, try the crab cake Benedict or the Belgian waffles. Open daily for lunch and dinner.

CAJUN & CREOLE

BOUDREAUX'S LOUISIANA KITCHEN $$
501 East 36th St., NoDa
(704) 331-9898
www.boudreauxs.com

In the middle of a funky arts district full of cool galleries and shops, Boudreaux's goes beyond Bourbon Street with authentic Cajun cuisine in a casual setting. You'll find real-deal Bayou fare, including fried alligator, gumbo, red beans and rice, po'boys, muffaletta, étouffée, shrimp and grits, and blackened dishes cooked in a cast-iron skillet. For dessert, try the Chocolate Bomb, an individual warm chocolate cake filled with creamy fudge and topped with Chantilly cream. Open 11:30 a.m. to 10 p.m. Mon through Thurs and Sun; 11:30 a.m. to 11 p.m. Fri and Sat.

CAJUN QUEEN $$-$$$
1800 East Seventh St.
(704) 377-9017
www.cajunqueen.net

Cajun Queen's bayou-inspired kitchen turns out authentic Cajun food. It specializes in blackened fish and steaks, but also offers crawfish, shrimp, étouffée, and its own homemade Oreo cheesecake and bourbon bread pudding. Nightly live Dixieland jazz entertainment adds spice to your dining enjoyment. The restaurant is located in a charming old home. Dinner is served every day.

CAJUN YARD DOG $$
8036 Providence Rd., Arboretum
(704) 752-1750
www.cajunyarddog.com

This is a fun Cajun bar and grill with live entertainment on weekends. The menu covers the requisite entrees, from chicken jambalaya to crawfish creole to a variety of po'boys on crispy baguettes. An interesting selection on the appetizer menu is jalapeno deviled eggs, followed by this disclaimer: "not your grandma's deviled eggs." Open for lunch and dinner Mon through Sat and closed on Sun.

CARIBBEAN

ANNTONY'S CARIBBEAN CAFE $$
2001 East Seventh St.
(704) 342-0749
www.anntonys.com

Anntony's offers a variety of Caribbean cuisine, the most popular being the rotisserie-style Caribbean chicken served with your choice of greens, rice, or potato salad. Takeout is available, and the popular seasonings and sauces are bottled for purchase as well. Open for lunch and dinner Mon through Sat. Live entertainment is featured on Fri and Sat nights.

CONTINENTAL

BARRINGTON'S $$$
7822 Fairview Rd.
(704) 364-5755
www.barringtonsrestaurant.com

Cozy and romantic, this small candlelit restaurant prepares beautifully presented dishes such as rope-grown Prince Edward Island mussels with crushed tomatoes, white wine, and garlic; hand-made Parmesan gnocchi with braised organic veal and Italian porcinis; and pecan marinated lamb with roasted sweet potatoes, french beans, and a chipotle barbecue sauce. Owner/chef Bruce Moffett is a Culinary Institute of America graduate; about 70 percent of the customers order his wonderful specials. Open 5:30 to 10 p.m. Mon through Thurs; 5:30 to 11 p.m. Fri and Sat.

BONTERRA $$$–$$$$
1829 Cleveland Ave.
(704) 333-9463
www.bonterradining.com

Built in a turn-of-the-20th-century Dilworth church that has been masterfully restored, Bonterra is an immensely popular fine-dining choice with a seasonally changing menu and influences from Asia, France, and Italy. Bonterra is also well known for its wide range of wines by the glass—about 200 at last count. The wine bar has its own appetizer menu and wine flights. Dinner is served Mon through Sat.

CARPE DIEM $$–$$$
1535 Elizabeth Ave.
(704) 377-7976
www.carpediemrestaurant.com

Despite moving multiple times, Carpe Diem has a loyal following of fans who seek it out again and again. The quiet surroundings make this fabulous little restaurant a comfortable place to enjoy a superb meal of American food with ethnic influences. The eclectic menu includes every-thing from grilled Asian barbecue duck breast to

pistachio-crusted snapper. The large, cozy bar—dubbed the Living Room—is an intimate spot for drinks. Dinner only Mon through Sat.

MCNINCH HOUSE $$$$
511 North Church St.
(704) 332-6159
www.mcninchhouserestaurant.com

It's reservations required at the McNinch House, which has received AAA's Four-Diamond Award for 10 consecutive years and has been named an "extraordinary" restaurant by *Zagat's Dining Guide*. The McNinch House is the place you go to pop the question, close the deal of your career, and drop about $150 per person in the process. But the six-course gourmet meal served with antique china, crystal, silver, and linen in the owner's 1892 Fourth Ward Victorian home is worth it. Reservations are typically made 10 days in advance, but up to a year for the holidays. Before arriving, diners select an entree such as lamb, fowl, seafood, salmon, lobster, veal, venison, or beef tenderloin. Chef/owner Ellen Davis handles the rest. The opening course is shellfish, often a Carolina favorite such as crab cakes. One of 30 varieties of soup follows, from potato and apple bisque to shiitake mushrooms and wild rice. A small Victorian-style salad is third, then a sorbet to cleanse the palate. Fifth in line is the entree—many people choose the house specialty, rack of lamb with a rosemary-mustard crust. Finally, desserts such as white chocolate mousse laced with roasted macadamia nuts and raspberry sauce finish the often four-hour meal. The McNinch House also has more than 100 bottles of wine in its cellar. Dinner Tues through Sat.

THE MELTING POT $$$
901 South Kings Dr.
Kings Court Plaza
(704) 334-4400

230 East W. T. Harris Blvd.
(704) 548-2432
www.meltingpot.com

The Melting Pot offers a variety of fondue in a relaxed atmosphere. Choose from beef, chicken,

Charlotte Restaurant Week

Foodies and non-foodies alike have embraced Charlotte Restaurant Week, making it the hottest thing in Queen City culinary circles. Restaurant Week, which actually lasts 10 days, started in summer 2008 and has grown to become a twice-yearly event in late January and the middle of July.

The concept is simple: participating restaurants offer a three-course meal at a fixed price of $30, before tax and gratuity. At $30, the meal has to provide a discount from its regular menu price, while the restaurant is free to sweeten the deal with a fourth course and/or beverage offering.

So, just how popular is Charlotte Restaurant Week? Consider this: the July 2009 event generated approximately 63,000 meals and $2.92 million in revenue for 70 participating eateries.

Furthermore, Charlotte Restaurant Week's Web site attracted 14,317 unique visitors on the first day of the January 2010 event, and "Charlotte Restaurant Week" is the second-most searched for item in the Queen City via Google.

Charlotte Restaurant Week, also known as Queen's Feast, covers much of the metro region, including Lake Norman, Concord, Belmont, and Fort Mill, S.C.

For information on the next Queen's Feast, visit www.charlotte restaurantweek.com.

or seafood, or select a cheddar or Swiss cheese fondue served with fruit and fresh breads. For dessert? Chocolate fondue, of course. The Melting Pot is open for dinner seven days a week. Reservations are recommended, especially on weekends.

NOBLE'S $$$–$$$$
6801 Morrison Blvd.
(704) 367-9463
www.noblesrestaurants.com
Located in the Morrocroft area of SouthPark, Noble's is the only Charlotte location of this popular family-owned chain based in the Triad. Farm-to-table freshness is emphasized in French- and Italian-inspired Mediterranean dishes that use local ingredients and rely on a family history of gardening and cooking to make them unique. Many folks think of this as a high-priced splurge, but Noble's shoots for a relaxed, friendly, unpretentious atmosphere that's like a fun French brasserie. The restaurant tweaks its menu almost daily but always offers a wide range of meats, such as beef, veal, lamb, duck, rabbit, venison, ostrich, and free-range chicken; several seafood dishes; pasta; and wood-fired pizza. The Noble's signature is the oyster salad of baby spinach and Asian greens tossed with balsamic vinaigrette and topped with smoked bacon, eggs, roasted red peppers, and fried oysters. The Angus filet pan-seared in a cast-iron skillet is another favorite. Two private dining rooms are available. Lunch weekdays; dinner Mon through Sat. Reservations recommended.

DELI

THE BAGEL BIN $
9815 Sam Furr Rd., Huntersville
(704) 895-1455
The Bagel Bin is owned by former New Yorkers, giving this place a New York feel even though it is located in a Target shopping center. The bagels are authentic, with a number of flavors to choose from. Come hungry, because they pile on the deli meats and cheeses. This is also one of the few places in the area where you can buy Tastykakes,

just like the kind they have up north. Open for lunch Mon through Sat.

JASON'S DELI $–$$
210 East Trade St., EpiCentre
(704) 688-1004

1600 East Woodlawn Rd.
(704) 676-5858

16639 Birkdale Commons, Huntersville
(704) 895-2505

10610 Centrum Parkway, Pineville
(704) 541-1228

3509 David Cox Rd., University
(704) 921-1545
www.jasonsdeli.com
Yes, this is a national chain, but it is an insider favorite. The extensive menu offers everything from soups and salads to wraps, sandwiches, po'boys, pasta, and baked potatoes. Jason's is health conscious, listing the fat content and calories of many items, as well as offering vegetarian items and organic choices. There is a large choice of soups daily, and the salad bar goes on and on and on. After your meal, take advantage of the free low-fat soft-serve ice cream. Did we mention it is free?

RUSTY'S DELI & GRILLE $
8512 Park Rd.
(704) 554-9012
(704) 553-7084 fax
www.rustysdeli.com
Rusty's has been a favorite for locals since 1983. Located in the Quail Corners Shopping Center, the deli is long and thin, although mirrored walls make it appear twice its size. Guests order at a window and go through a self-serve drink line before picking up their order at the register. Soups are quite good, and there is a great selection of tasty sandwiches. Rusty's is open until 9 p.m. Mon through Sat, although most of the activity comes at lunchtime. You'll often encounter a line, but it moves quickly. Still accepts fax orders.

FAMILY-STYLE DINING

BEAUREGARD'S $–$$
3030 Freedom Dr.
(704) 399-5155
www.beauregards.biz
While Charlotte has grown in other directions and Freedom Drive has experienced its ups and downs, Beauregard's has remained a constant since 1974.

It just keeps providing good food at reasonable prices. Lunch is especially popular at this Westside eatery and you can't wrong with the French dip hoagie. The cheese sticks are a good choice, too. For dinner, Mom and Dad can bring the family and get a lot, but not spend a lot (dessert items are less than $4). Picky kids are no match for Beauregard's menu because there's something for everybody. Open for lunch and dinner daily.

CHARLOTTE CAFE $
Park Road Shopping Center
4127 Park Rd.
(704) 523-0431
Charlotte Cafe is one of the best moderately priced places to go for breakfast. The extensive menu includes everything from deli items to steaks, seafood, a variety of Italian dishes, and 25 different home-cooked vegetables daily. A family favorite in south Charlotte, the cafe is open for breakfast, lunch, and dinner Mon through Sat.

GUS' SIR BEEF RESTAURANT $
4101 Monroe Rd.
(704) 377-3210
It's not unusual to see a line of people all the way to the parking lot of this family-style restaurant. It's been serving vegetables fresh from the garden for over 30 years. No fats are used to cook the delicious squash, greens, and other vegetables. You'll also appreciate the lean roast beef. Banana pudding is a popular dessert choice. Lunch and dinner are served Mon through Sat.

LUPIE'S CAFE $
2718 Monroe Rd.
(704) 374-1232

101-A Old Statesville Rd., Huntersville
(704) 948-3959
www.lupiescafe.com
The hot, super-hot, and smoking-hot chili selections are this cafe's drawing card, along with chicken and dumplings, burgers, old-fashioned vegetables, and meat loaf that tastes as good as mom's. This original location is a folksy place off Monroe Road in Elizabeth. It has wooden booths and bar stools, neon bar signs, black-and-white photos of past and present employees, a huge wire rooster in the yard, and Gumby in the tip jar. You'll rub elbows with politicians and mill workers, and you'll keep coming back. In 2002, a second location was added off Old Statesville Road. Lunch and dinner are served Mon through Sat.

PIKE'S SODA SHOP $
1930 Camden Rd.
(704) 372-0092
www.pikesrestaurant.com
Kids—and young-at-heart adults—love this old-fashioned soda shop with hearty breakfasts, straightforward sandwiches like grilled cheese, Kahn's hot dogs, thick milk shakes, fresh-squeezed lemonade, and fountain Cokes. Dinner includes steaks, pasta, and seafood, along with beer, wine, and mixed drinks. Sunday brunch is also popular at this "finer diner." Sit on the patio in good weather and wave at the kids as the trolley goes by, clanging its bell on the way to Uptown. Lunch and dinner Mon through Sat; Sun brunch.

FISH CAMPS

A North Carolina tradition, fish camps are informal, inexpensive, family-friendly eateries where everything is fried, the tea is like sugar water, and the waitresses call you "honey." Fish camps built their reputation for years on generous portions of fresh fried fish, served piping hot, with french fries, cole slaw, and hush puppies. Some have since broadened their menus to include healthier choices.

These indigenous restaurants are found in out-of-the-way places—down country roads, beside riverbanks, and in small communities nearby. Only a few of these venerable establishments remain in the Charlotte area, and they continue to pack in crowds of hungry diners. The greatest concentration of the old-fashioned fish camps (and the most authentic) is found near the Catawba River, where it forms the county line for Mecklenburg and Gaston Counties.

Charlotte

CAPTAIN STEVE'S $-$$
8517 Monroe Rd.
(704) 535-1400
www.captainsteves.net
Captain Steve's menu is a "treasure map for your appetite." Founded in 1996, the restaurant is usually packed for dinner. Its best advertising is the full parking lot that people see as they drive by on Monroe Road. The fare includes such high falutin' items as surf 'n' turf and filet mignon, but most people come for the fried fish, hush puppies, and friendly service. Very popular are the large fried platters featuring either perch, catfish, flounder, or shrimp.

RIVERVIEW INN $-$$
10012 Moores Chapel Loop
(704) 399-3385
www.the-riverview-inn.com
Located on a knob jutting into the Catawba River, this historic fish camp is reachable by car or boat. The Riverview Inn was founded in 1946 by Irwen Burns Sr. His sons—Jon and Irwen Jr.—now operate the family business. Famous visitors over the years include Randy Travis, Clint Black, Johnny Cash, and The Platters. The original building was struck by lightning on New Year's Eve 1973 and burned to the ground. The current restaurant, built later that year, has a weathered gray exterior and resembles a pirate fort.

The menu features fried perch, catfish, bass, flounder, oysters, and Calabash shrimp. The all-you-can-eat buffet contains more than 20 items, including Alaskan white fish and pickled onions (a special in-house recipe). It is billed as "the South's most famous seafood buffet." Kids menu is available for ages 10 and younger. Open for dinner Wed through Sun, and reservations are accepted.

THE SEAFARER $
9306 Albemarle Rd.
(704) 536-7540
www.south21seafarer.com
For folks in east Charlotte and eastern Mecklenburg County, the Seafarer is a long-standing favorite. It is well-known for its large billboard overlooking Albemarle Road with a whale that moves up and down. The restaurant's slogan is "For a whale of a meal." They offer fried and broiled white fish and tilapia, as well as fried calamari and hush puppies. Open for lunch Thurs and Fri, and for dinner Tues through Sat.

Gaston County

CATFISH COVE $
1401 Armstrong Ford Rd., Belmont
(704) 825-3332
Probably the most famous fish camp remaining in Gaston County, Catfish Cove is located on a secluded stretch of the Catawba River. The all-you-can-eat buffet is most popular, and the modest salad bar is fresh and tasty. The service is good and everybody seems to know everybody. Dinner Tues through Sat; lunch buffet Sun.

GRAHAM'S FISH FRY $
4539 South New Hope Rd., Gastonia
(704) 825-8391
Full orders are all-you-can-eat, and free salad bar comes with meals. Saturday's special is the five-item combo, so come hungry. Graham's is located across the road from Twin Tops. Open for lunch Wed through Fri, and open for dinner Tues through Sat. Country and seafood buffet is available 11 a.m. to 3 p.m. Sun.

TWIN TOPS FISH CAMP $
4574 South New Hope Rd., Gastonia
(704) 825-2490
One of those places where the plates are piled high and the waitresses never let your glass get empty. Hush puppies are brought to the table with your drinks, and the menu is, as expected, heavy on fried fish. Kids love the Ms. Pac Man machine and the old-time candies lining the wall. Open for dinner Tues through Sat.

FRENCH

CAFÉ MONTE FRENCH
BAKERY & BISTRO $$–$$$
6700 Fairview Rd., SouthPark
(704) 552-1116
www.cafemonte.net
Reasonably priced and not stuffy, Café Monte serves classic French country favorites from breakfast through dinner. The eatery has a Parisian feel with French artwork throughout, cobblestone marble flooring in the serving area, and heart of pine flooring in the dining area. There is also a large farm table for families and parties. All breads, croissants, and crepes are baked fresh daily, and the café also features tasty pastry from Amelie's, a local French bakery located in NoDa. Open for breakfast, lunch and dinner Mon through Sat, and for brunch on Sun. Online reservations available.

GLOBAL RESTAURANT $$$–$$$$
3520 Toringdon Way, Ballantyne
(704) 248-0866
www.global-restaurant.com
Technically, Global features international cuisine. However, founder and chef Bernard Brunet is French and the menu is heavily French influenced. For example, the pork tenderloin is created in the French style of sealing the meat in bags and submerging it in hot, but not boiling, water for a slow-cooked treat. Meanwhile, *Creative Loafing* has called the duck with French lentils one of the best dishes in the city. Brunet is careful to use local products whenever possible. Hours are 6 to 11 p.m. Mon through Sat. Reservations accepted.

ZEBRA $$$–$$$$
4521 Sharon Rd.
(704) 442-9525
www.zebrarestaurant.net

Insider Top 5: Restaurants

Here's an insider list of five great places to eat in the Queen City, courtesy of Susan Dosier, former executive foods editor for *Southern Living* magazine. Dosier now resides in Charlotte and promotes culinary tourism statewide as PR director for Loeffler Ketchum Mountjoy:

1. **Mert's Heart and Soul in Uptown**—Great Southern food and a great Southern staff. I go for fried chicken, collard greens, red beans and rice, and homemade desserts such as red velvet cake. I could make a meal alone out of the sweet cornbread loaves that come hot out of the oven after you sit down.

2. **Upstream in SouthPark**—Perhaps my favorite fine dining restaurant in the city. The ceiling looks like the bottom of a stream with swirling leaves; it's gorgeous. Great execution here with fresh seafood and quality ingredients, plus a great atmosphere.

3. **Mac's Speed Shop in South End (original location)**—This biker bar is known for its barbecue, and some serious Mexican food, too. At lunchtime during the week, it's packed with guys in white shirts and a business crowd. The weekends are more laid back with bikers showing up and enjoying outdoor dining in warm weather. Used to be a car wash and you can still see that original architecture.

4. **Pewter Rose in South End**—My favorite spot for Sun brunch. Decadent French toast, scones, and wonderful hash combinations. On warm days, dine outside on the porch. The interior is cozy and warm with big fat sofas in the bar.

5. **Vitner Wine Market in south Charlotte**—Located at the Arboretum, this classy wine and beer shop has some of the best food in town. Specials such as egg rolls made with slow-simmered short ribs, or goat cheese truffles made with Bosky Acres cheese from Waxhaw, make this a perfect place to relax after a long day or a good place for date night with the spouse. The sandwiches are great, too, especially the killer grilled cheese. The staff is enthusiastic and the chef is just plain darling.

This contemporary French restaurant, one of the hottest places in Charlotte's culinary scene, keeps a menu that is both interesting and approachable. Servers begin the meal by bringing a complimentary tidbit to the table, and when a companion is the only one to order an appetizer or soup, the other diner receives a tiny cup of soup or a small salad to join in. Entrees include a lamb tenderloin au poivre, surf and turf with a basket of angel hair pasta, butter-braised lobster, roasted beef tenderloin and sautéed shrimps and scallops, and a lobster salad with bits of shellfish tucked inside a paper-thin casing of pear and topped with two shelled claws. Color, height, and even Dover sole bones linked together roller coaster style are part of the dramatic presentation. And don't forget the wine—you can choose from nearly 1,000 selections on the wine list and 10,000 bottles in the cellar at this *Wine Spectator* award winner. Co-owners are Culinary Institute of America graduate and former Myers Park Country Club chef Jim Alexander and Pete Pappas, who worked at his family's Epicurean restaurant in Charlotte for many years. The decor is minimalist African. Breakfast, lunch, and dinner weekdays; dinner only on Sat.

ITALIAN

ARIA TUSCAN GRILL $$–$$$
100 North Tryon St.
(704) 376-8880
www.ariacharlotte.com

Aria brought Uptown a much-needed infusion of Italian fare with its opening in January 2010. The restaurant is located in the Bank of America Corporate Center, nestled in a step-down location on the Trade Street side, across from the Omni Charlotte and easily accessible to the EpiCentre and Ritz-Carlton. The décor is contemporary and comfortable, and the food is straightforward Tuscan of high quality. Lots of good pasta dishes, including Grandma A's lasagna and five types of pizza. Interesting dishes include roasted butternut squash ravioli, braised duck ragu, and potato gnocchi. Open for lunch Mon through Fri; dinner Mon through Sat.

FIAMMA $$–$$$
2418 Park Rd.
(704) 333-3062

Located in the heart of Dilworth, Fiamma is a media darling. One food critic proclaimed the risotto the best she's had outside of Florence. A big plus is the menu's emphasis on freshness. Pasta and pizza dough are made twice a day, and the fish is flown in daily from Europe. Where else in Charlotte can you get roasted Norwegian salmon? The open layout and open kitchen are inviting as well. Dinner seven days a week; lunch Mon through Sat.

LUCE RISTORANTE $$$–$$$$
214 North Tryon St.
(704) 344-9222
www.luceristorante.net

Luce is an upscale dining experience located in the Hearst Tower in Uptown. The restaurant is decorated in fine Italian marble with sandstone fixtures and Murano sconces. The artwork is from famed local fresco artist Ben Long. As for the food, it's considered Northern Italian, featuring house-made pastas, fresh seafood, and prime meats. The desserts, including torta di cioccolato

and Italian custard, are tempting. Open for lunch Mon to Fri and dinner Mon to Sat. Closed on Sun.

MAMA RICOTTA'S $$–$$$
601 South Kings Dr.
(704) 343-0148
www.mamaricottasrestaurant.com

Want international flair coupled with dynamite Italian food and wine? This is a great place for Italian cuisine in the Myers Park area. Dinner begins with fresh-baked Italian bread served with olive oil for dipping. The pasta dishes are all delicious—the pasta with prosciutto is beyond imagination. Lunch and dinner are served seven days a week, with brunch on Sun. Online reservations available.

THE OPEN KITCHEN $–$$
1318 West Morehead St.
(704) 375-7449
www.theopenkitchen.net

In business since 1952, this is the kind of place to bring the kids and let them feast on spaghetti while Mom and Dad savor the finer subtleties of Italian cooking. Specialties include scaloppine, parmigiana, cacciatore, and gourmet pasta dishes. Pizza, which the Open Kitchen introduced to many Charlotteans in the '50s and '60s, is also available. It's open for lunch Mon through Fri and for dinner seven days a week.

> **i** Too busy to cook, or need a quick meal for house guests? Pasta & Provisions at 1528 Providence Rd. is a great place for takeout. There are more than 20 types of pasta, with all pasta and sauces made fresh daily. You can also purchase fresh-baked bread and Italian specialty items such as olive oil and wine. Open Mon through Sat. For more information call (704) 364-2622.

PHIL & TONY'S ITALIAN
CUISINE & SPORTS BAR $–$$
2225 Matthews Township Parkway, Matthews
(704) 541-3111
www.philandtonys.com

After many years in the Arboretum shopping center, Phil & Tony's recently moved to Sycamore Commons in Matthews. The restaurant also dropped "pizza" from its name to emphasize Italian fare. The menu offers a wide range of items, including pizzas, pastas, strombolis, salads, and soups. There are also Italian classics like chicken parmesan and chicken marsala. Live music in the bar area also makes this a popular choice when you want a go-as-you-are neighborhood place. Lunch and dinner daily. Kids eat free on Wed, with the purchase of adult entrée.

PORTOFINO'S RISTORANTE $$
5126 Park Rd.
(704) 527-0702

3124 Eastway Dr.
(704) 568-7933

3736 East Franklin Blvd., Gastonia
(704) 824-2144

2127 Ayrsley, Ayrsley Town Centre
(980) 297-7090

591 River Hwy., Mooresville
(704) 660-9855
www.portofinos.us
Portofino's is a hidden jewel in the Charlotte restaurant scene. The homemade house dressing is awesome, well worth the trip by itself. It's not your typical oil-based Italian dressing. Instead, it is tomato influenced with a light, creamy texture. Make sure to order extra for dipping the soft, Italian house bread. The chicken cacciatore is the insider's favorite, and you can't go wrong with the spaghetti Bolognese. The pizzas are pretty special, too. Open for lunch and dinner seven days a week.

ROMANO'S MACARONI GRILL $$
10706 Providence Rd.
(704) 841-2511
www.macaronigrill.com
This is a great option for Italian fare located at the Intersection of I-485 and Providence Road. The food has always been excellent, and the restaurant is newly remodeled after a fire in 2008.

Romano's has a cozy feel with stone work and mahogany throughout, plus an open kitchen. The "create your own pasta" option is great when you just want something comfortable and familiar, without all the extras that a lot of chef-inspired dishes include.

VILLA ANTONIO ITALIAN
RESTAURANT $$$–$$$$
4707 South Blvd.
(704) 523-1594

14825 John J. Delaney Dr., Ballantyne
(704) 369-5060
www.villaantonio.com
The restaurant's authentically prepared Italian cuisine is simply delicious, and the quiet, romantic atmosphere will create a very special evening. The Villa Antonio experience is formal, from white linen tablecloths to the impeccably clad maître d'. There's also nightly entertainment with a pianist tickling the ivories of a baby grand. Villa Antonio regularly hosts wine tastings, martini tastings, and sorbet tastings.

Lunch is served Mon through Fri; dinner every night.

LOCAL FLAVOR

Some restaurants are unique to Charlotte, giving the city character and history with several generations served. Most of them are locals-in-the-know eateries, places visitors aren't likely to venture to on their own.

GREEN'S LUNCH $
309 West Fourth St.
(704) 332-1786
www.greenslunch.com
Hot dogs smothered in secret-recipe chili since 1936, plus breakfasts of eggs, bacon, sausage, biscuits, grits, home fries, and pancakes. Breakfast weekdays; lunch Mon through Sat.

MR. K'S $
2107 South Blvd.
(704) 375-4318

This tiny South End restaurant has served burgers (try the Big K), homemade onion rings, shaved ice sodas, thick shakes, and soft-serve ice cream since 1967. Fight your way in—it's worth the wait. Lunch and dinner weekdays only.

PENGUIN $
1921 Commonwealth Ave.
(704) 375-6959
A Charlotte institution where bluebloods and blue collars have mixed since 1954, the Penguin is an ice-cream shop turned drive-in turned colorful landmark in Plaza-Midwood. A must-see. Open 11 a.m. to midnight Mon through Sat; noon to 11 p.m. Sun. Bar is open until 2 a.m. nightly.

PRICE'S CHICKEN COOP $
1614 Camden Rd.
(704) 333-9866
www.priceschickencoop.com
For the best Southern fried chicken, insiders flock to Price's Chicken Coop. The old brick building is not very attractive and the food (takeout only) is served in brown paper bags and cardboard boxes. But that doesn't seem to matter to folks who line up out the door for this greasy Queen City delicacy. Family-owned, Price's started as a fresh poultry market in the late 1930s. Customers selected a live chicken and left with a plucked bird. In 1962, frying replaced the do-it-yourself method. The main event is fried chicken. Also on the menu are fried fish, golden brown shrimp, Eastern North Carolina barbecue, chicken gizzards, and burgers. All dinners come with cole slaw, 'tater rounds, hush puppies, and roll.

    Important note: Bring cash. Price's doesn't accept credit cards, debit cards, or checks. ATM is available. Lunch and early dinner offered Tues through Sat.

SHOWMARS $
25+ locations in metro Charlotte
www.showmars.com
George Couchell, son of Greek immigrants, founded Showmars in the early 1980s on the idea that Charlotte needed something to fill the void between fast food and full service. His concept has been wildly successful with constant growth through good times and bad. At Showmars, you order at the counter and are served at the table. Employees have the opportunity to work their way up to become managing partner in each restaurant. Billed as the home of the famous pita burger, Showmars also offers a variety of fried fish and seafood items and goes through 500 gallons of tartar sauce per week. Greek dishes, like souvlaki and gyros, are big sellers, along with milkshakes. So just how well-liked is Showmars in the Queen City? Years ago, a Kenny Rogers Roasters opened in Elizabeth against the wishes of neighborhood residents. It was a disaster and quickly closed. It reopened as Showmars and has been in business ever since.

SIMMONS FOURTH WARD $
516 North Graham St.
(704) 334-6640
Down-home meats and vegetables are offered at Simmons, where you'll see pro athletes and power suits at the table together. It's the favorite Charlotte eatery of singer Patti Labelle. Expect a soulful Southern feast with meat loaf, barbecue ribs, fried chicken, smothered pork chops, macaroni and cheese, squash, Southern green beans, pintos, cabbage, collards, potato salad, peach cobbler, and banana pudding, to name a few. Lunch and dinner daily.

UNITED HOUSE OF PRAYER CAFETERIA $
1019 South Mint St.
(704) 377-1835
Uptown business people and in-the-know locals flock to this rotunda cafeteria with its partial views of Bank of America Stadium. At the height of his influence over Charlotte as CEO of Bank of America, Hugh McColl was a regular here. The cafeteria provides southern cookin' and comfort food. Most popular are the squash casserole and collards. Pick an entrée item, such as chicken 'n' dumplings, meat loaf, or baked chicken, and then add some tasty vegetables and a sweet tea. Doesn't get much better than this! Open weekdays, 11 a.m. to 2:30 p.m.

MEDITERRANEAN

BLUE $$$–$$$$
Corner of Fifth and College
Hearst Tower
(704) 927-2583
www.bluecharlotte.com

Owner Alex Myrick, son of congresswoman and former Charlotte mayor Sue Myrick, hit on a winning combination when he opened Blue in the Hearst Tower in 2003. Fantastic Mediterranean food and a sophisticated lounge make this one of the premier restaurants in Uptown. The restaurant has received awards from *Wine Spectator* and *Zagat's,* and was named best restaurant in Uptown in 2009 by *Charlotte Magazine.* The Mediterranean sea bass is a top-seller, as well as the vegetarian mushroom Bolognese. Open for dinner Mon through Sat. Reservations recommended.

MEXICAN/SPANISH/LATIN

CABO FISH TACO $
3201 North Davidson St., NoDa
(704) 332-8868
www.cabofishtaco.com

Dubbed a "Baja seagrill," Cabo Fish Taco in Charlotte's lively NoDa arts community features a fresh, eclectic menu in a relaxed, untuck-your-shirt-and-unwind atmosphere. You'll find vegetarian, chicken, and seafood tacos and entrees, along with homemade margaritas. Show your big-city visitors some of Charlotte's funky flavor here. Open for lunch and dinner daily.

CANTINA FIFTEEN ELEVEN $$
1511 East Blvd.
(704) 331-9222

7708 Rea Rd., Stonecrest
(704) 752-9797
www.cantina1511restaurant.com

Cantina Fifteen Eleven started in Dilworth and its popularity led to a second location in Stonecrest in south Charlotte. The Dilworth restaurant has an authentic Mexican feel with rattan furnishings and a very popular patio overlooking East Boulevard. The Stonecrest location is a bit more upscale. Both offer authentic, chef-driven Mexican food and are evening hot spots. Everybody seems to love the homemade guacamole. Open daily for lunch and dinner.

EL PULGARCITO DE AMERICA $
4816-A Central Ave.
(704) 563-6500

Pupusas, tender little corn cakes stuffed with white cheese, a pork-and-cheese paste, or beans and cheese, are the staple of this cuisine from El Salvador. For $1.50 each, you can't beat the price or the authenticity. Open for breakfast, lunch, and dinner daily.

LA PAZ $$
1910 South Blvd.
(704) 372-4168
www.lapaz.com

Located in South End, this is probably Charlotte's most popular Mexican restaurant, serving traditional Mexican and regional Southwestern cuisine. The food is excellent, and the margaritas are dynamite. There's also a patio for alfresco dining. Takeout is available. Lunch is served weekdays; dinner, nightly.

LAS RAMBLAS $$
2400 Park Rd.
(704) 335-8444
www.lasramblascafe.com

Las Ramblas is a Spanish café and tapas bar in Dilworth. The restaurant is tastefully decorated and offers a large selection of modern and traditional tapas. There is also an extensive selection of Spanish wines, and bottles of wine are half price on Mon and Wed. Online reservations available. Open for dinner Mon through Sat.

PHAT BURRITO $
1537 Camden Rd.
(704) 332-7428
www.phatburrito.com

As its name implies, this funky SouthEnd eatery serves up large burritos, Southwestern style. Steak, chicken, fish, bean, and veggie burritos are available, along with tacos, quesos, and tortilla salads. Located on the light rail line, Phat Burrito has picnic tables outside, while the inside is basic, with lime, blue, and yellow walls. Plans are to expand into the vacant building next door. Serving lunch and dinner seven days a week.

SOLE SPANISH GRILLE $$
1608 East Blvd., Dilworth
(704) 343-9890

MIRO SPANISH GRILL $$
7804 Rea Rd., Stonecrest
(704) 540-7374
http://solespanishgrille.com

Owned by the Luong brothers, these two Spanish/Mediterranean/Latin bistros are interesting and upscale, with everything from tapas dishes to paella. Sole is on Dilworth's hopping East Boulevard; Miro is located in the Stonecrest Shopping Center off I-485 in south Charlotte. Both have outdoor seating. Lunch weekdays; dinner nightly at both.

ZAPATA'S CANTINA
MEXICAN RESTAURANT $$
8927 J. M. Keynes Blvd., University
(704) 503-1979

15105 John J. Delaney Dr., Ballantyne
(704) 752-6869

1990 South Hwy. 73, Lake Norman
(704) 987-8890
www.zapatascantina.com

This menu of quality Mexican dishes is quite extensive—appetizers, soups, sides, salads, burritos, tostadas, enchiladas, tacos, meats, chicken, seafood, sandwiches, and the house specialty, fajitas. Small and large combinations are also offered, along with a kids' menu and a few American items for picky eaters. Atmosphere is Old Mexico, not the fake sombreros and adobe walls of some chain places. Open for lunch and dinner daily.

PIZZA

BRIXX WOOD-FIRED PIZZA $$
1801 Scott Ave., Dilworth
(704) 376-1000

225 East Sixth St., Uptown
(704) 347-2749

7814 Fairview Rd., Foxcroft Village
(704) 295-0707

16915 Birkdale Commons Parkway, Huntersville
(704) 894-0044

9820 Rea Rd.
(704) 940-2011
www.brixxpizza.com

California-style thin-crust pizzas cooked in wood-fired ovens are the draw here, but these popular restaurants in lively areas also offer delicious salads, pastas, and other Italian fare. Selections range from traditional pepperoni to goat cheese and shrimp pizza. The barbecue chicken pizza is good and the pear and gorgonzola pizza is unique. Plus there's a wide selection of beers on tap. All five locations are open for lunch and dinner daily.

BROOKLYN SOUTH $-$$
19400 Jetton Rd., Cornelius
(704) 896-2928
www.brooklynsouthpizzeria.com

If you're missing authentic New York pizzerias, you'll appreciate this Lake Norman gem operated by a Brooklyn family. Order at the counter, where you can watch the dough for your pie being tossed into the air, caught, and spun before marinara sauce and delicious toppings are piled on. Tempt the taste buds with unusual combinations (try the buffalo wing pizza), cheese-less styles, traditional pies, and square thin-crust topped with basil, olive oil, tomatoes, and mozzarella. Calzones, pasta, and heroes are also available. Lunch and dinner daily.

FUEL PIZZA CAFÉ $
1501 Central Ave., Midwood
(704) 376-3835

214 North Tryon St., Hearst Tower
(704) 350-1680

500 South College St., Shops on the Green
(704) 370-2755

1801 South Blvd., South End
(704) 335-7375

4267 Park Rd.
(704) 525-3220

14145 Rivergate Parkway
(704) 588-5333
www.fuelpizza.com

Fuel Pizza has taken Charlotte by storm since opening its first location in an old Central Avenue gas station about a decade ago. There are now six Fuel Pizzas in Charlotte (listed above), plus three more locations in Davidson, Gastonia, and Rock Hill. Over the years, Fuel has been named Charlotte's Best Pizza by *Creative Loafing*, *Charlotte Magazine* and *City Search*. Folks order at the counter—by the pie or the slice—choosing from unusual varieties and fresh toppings. Strombolis, calzones, salads, wings, and tasty garlic-knot mini-sandwiches complete the menu. Open for lunch and dinner daily. The Hearst Tower location in Uptown stays open into the wee hours of the morning on weekends to accommodate the bar crowd.

QUEEN CITY PIZZA DEPOT $
2212 Park Rd.
(704) 334-3884
www.qcpizzadepot.com

It's takeout only at the Queen City Pizza Depot, located beside Ed's Tavern near the corner of Park Road and Ideal Way. Many locals say the pizza is ideal, hand-tossed with great flavor. And, most important for takeout, this pizza travels well. You don't have to worry about soggy crust or failed expectations once you get the pies home. Calzones, subs, and salads are available as well. Ask about the lunch specials.

WOLFMAN PIZZA & PASTA $
1039 Providence Rd., Myers Park
(704) 377-4695

106-B South Sharon Amity Rd.
(704) 366-3666

10620 Providence Rd.
(704) 845-9888

8418 Park Rd.
(704) 552-4979
www.wolfman.com

Charlotte's original pizza success story; Wolfman was the first to do California-style pies in the Queen City and the first to open multiple locations, growing like crazy in the 1990s. These days, Wolfman has scaled back to four locations and focuses on what it does best—making yummy pizzas for dine-in, carry-out or take-and-bake. Wolfman uses all fresh ingredients and puts them together in unique ways. Toppings include everything from the standards, to capers and scallions to broccoli florets and artichoke hearts. Homemade sauces are as unusual as marinated black bean. Strombolis, salads, and pastas are also available, but pizza is the big draw. Lunch and dinner Mon through Sat; dinner Sun.

SEAFOOD

AQUAVINA $$$–$$$$
435 South Tryon St.
(704) 377-9911
www.aquavina.com

An innovative and contemporary seafood restaurant in Ratcliffe on the Green in Uptown, Aquavina is one of Charlotte's hottest new establishments. Fresh seafood from around the world is flown in daily and used in colorful and dramatic culinary presentations. Signature dishes include snow crab cobbler and hush puppy dusted shrimp starters, entrees that range from lobster to surf and turf, and, for dessert, roasted banana crème brûlée. Aquavina also offers 40 wines by the glass and specialty martinis. Lunch weekdays; dinner Mon through Sat.

LAVECCHIA'S SEAFOOD GRILLE $$$
225 East Sixth St.
(704) 370-6776
www.lavecchias.com

High-profile and trendy, this upscale seafood restaurant features a funky decor and hip atmosphere with aquariums, fish sculptures, and mosaics. The focus, of course, is seafood, with lobster, blackened mahi mahi, and the house specialty, a three-coast oyster sampler, but there are also several choices, including steak, for land-lubbers. Open 5:30 to 10 p.m. Mon through Thurs; 5:30 to 11 p.m. Fri and Sat.

MCCORMICK & SCHMICK'S $$-$$$
200 South Tryon St.
(704) 377-0201

4335 Barclay Downs, SouthPark
(704) 442-5522
www.mccormickandschmicks.com

This national chain has settled nicely into the Charlotte market. It debuted in Uptown and added a second location in SouthPark. Both offer menus prepared twice daily, showcasing the fresh seafood arriving each day. The menu provides the location of its latest catches, such as Atlantic salmon from the Bay of Fundy in Canada, ahi tuna from Cona, Hawaii, and cod from Massachusetts. The Uptown location has patio seating on Tryon Street, overlooking the spot where Confederate president Jefferson Davis was standing when given the news that Abraham Lincoln had been assassinated. McCormick & Schmick's also has a famously low-priced happy hour menu that includes $1.95 fish tacos and $2.95 half-pound cheeseburgers. Weekdays, the restaurants are open for lunch and dinner. It's dinner only on weekends.

UPSTREAM $$$-$$$$
Fairview Rd. at Phillips Place
(704) 556-7730
www.upstreamit.com

One of the hottest restaurants in town, Upstream is operated by the same folks who own Mimosa Grill and Harper's. Executive chef and part-owner Tom Condron trained at Johnson & Wales University in Charleston and has worked in New York, Washington, San Francisco, Paris, and London. Long before Charlotte diners were as adventurous as they are now, Condron pushed the culinary envelope with shrimp and grits dishes and hollowed-out hush puppies stuffed with shrimp, crawfish, and Creole seasoning. Mimosa and Harper's are upscale casual, but Upstream takes Charlotte dining up a notch with the freshest ingredients combined in unique ways. Condron is known to drive three hours to Charleston to handpick fresh seafood for the restaurant, so it's no surprise that awards are piling up for this eatery often said to be one of the nicest in Charlotte. Menu highlights include wood oven–roasted scallops, sake-marinated Chilean sea bass, and crispy fried calamari in a sweet-and-sour glaze. The Phillips Place atmosphere, with chic boutiques, a wine bar, and upscale retailers, doesn't hurt either. Open for lunch and dinner daily and Sun brunch.

VINNIE'S SARDINE GRILL & RAW BAR $$
1714 South Blvd., SouthEnd
(704) 332-0006

10619 Black Dog Lane, Mt. Island Lake
(704) 393-2203

142 East John St., Matthews
(704) 849-0202

643 Williamson Rd., Mooresville
(704) 799-2090
www.vinniesrawbar.com

Everyone from bankers to bikers hangs out at these casual watering holes for raw oysters and other seafood, along with cold beer for a buck. Open for lunch and dinner daily.

SOUTHERN

MERT'S HEART & SOUL $-$$
214 North College St.
(704) 342-4222
www.mertsuptown.com

Southern food is still Southern food at this funky, locally owned Uptown restaurant filled with vibrant art. Lunch and dinner offer homemade chicken soup, blackened pork chops, salmon cakes, chopped steak with mushroom sauce, veggie plates, and sandwiches from homemade pimento cheese to BLTs. Lowcountry specials include soft-shell crab, shrimp po'boys, fried catfish, shrimp and grits, and red beans and rice. Desserts are homemade. Lunch and dinner daily; open late weekends.

MIMOSA GRILL $$–$$$
327 South Tryon St.
(704) 343-0700
www.mimosagrill.com
Located at the bottom of Two Wachovia Center overlooking the large fountain plaza, Mimosa Grill features gleaming wood, columns of rock quarried from North Carolina, and comfortable booths and tables in an atmosphere that's both rustic and elegant. The Southern regional cuisine served here isn't your typical Southern veggies, fried chicken, and carb fare—Mimosa Grill adds sophistication to fresh fish, steak, handmade pizzas, and pasta dishes. You'll also find interesting combinations, such as Asian shrimp spring rolls with Georgia peanut sauce and papaya slaw or pulled barbecue pork in a martini glass piled with buttermilk corn bread. Lunch weekdays and dinner nightly.

NEW SOUTH KITCHEN & BAR $$–$$$
8140 Providence Rd., Arboretum
(704) 541-9990
www.newsouthkitchen.com
Chef/owner Chris Edwards, from Shelby, N.C., mixes old South heritage with a few modern twists at New South Kitchen & Bar, which opened in late 2007. The menu has such Dixie standbys as fried green tomatoes, fried chicken, fried okra, and Pabst Blue Ribbon beer. An interesting appetizer is the redneck cheese board, which is pimento cheese with flatbread. The "new" South can be found in dishes like pork ravioli, pesto chicken salad, and duck sausage with buttered cabbage. Open seven days a week for lunch and dinner.

STEAK HOUSES

BEEF 'N BOTTLE $$–$$$
4538 South Blvd.
(704) 523-9977
If you're looking for an old-time Charlotte steak house with a romantic touch, try this one. Famous for its superb steaks, it also offers excellent seafood dishes and has an extensive wine list. Don't let the plain exterior fool you. This locals-in-the-know joint is just as good as the high-dollar steak houses Uptown. Best-selling author Patricia Cornwell, a former *Charlotte Observer* reporter, even mentioned it in her novel *The Hornet's Nest*. The restaurant is open for dinner Mon through Sat.

BLT STEAK $$$$
110 North College St.
(704) 972-4380
www.bltsteak.com
The first Ritz-Carlton in North Carolina brought with it a unique steakhouse. BLT doesn't stand for bacon, lettuce, and tomato. It stands for Bistro Laurent Tourondel, the boutique chain of steak houses from celebrity chef Laurent Tourondel.

Voted the best steakhouse in New York City, BLT provides a twist on the typical steakhouse concept. It blends a traditional American steakhouse with a stylish French bistro. Expect prime cuts of beef and seafood, with a tempting array of side dishes. Breakfast, lunch, and dinner served daily. Reservations recommended and available online.

THE CAPITAL GRILLE $$$–$$$$
201 North Tryon St.
(704) 348-1400
www.thecapitalgrille.com
This national chain has locations in many cities, but in Charlotte, it's the place where bigwig bankers sip scotch and broker deals. Prime aged beef, seafood, vegetables, and libations steps away from the Square in Uptown. Open for lunch weekdays, dinner nightly.

DEL FRISCO'S CHARLOTTE $$$$+
4725 Piedmont Row, SouthPark
(704) 859-5057
www.delfriscos.com

"Opulence" comes to mind as you walk into 16,000 square feet of two-story luxury. This restaurant, which cost millions to build, has everything from floor-to-ceiling windows to its own elevator and escalator. It definitely exudes the "wow" factor.

The pricey menu provides a top selection of meats and seafood, headlined by the prime beef. It's the ideal place to celebrate a major business deal or impress the heck out of a special lady. The staff reserves certain "power" tables for Charlotte's elite. Open for dinner seven days a week. Reservations suggested.

MORTON'S OF CHICAGO $$$-$$$$
227 West Trade St., Uptown
(704) 333-2602
www.mortons.com

You can't call yourself a big city until you have a branch of this big-daddy chain with monster steaks in a power-broker atmosphere. The Charlotte location doesn't disappoint. Open 5:30 to 11 p.m. Mon through Sat; 5 to 10 p.m. Sun.

OLD STONE STEAKHOUSE $$$
23 South Main St., Belmont
(704) 825-9995
www.oldstonesteakhouse.com

A shining example of the redevelopment of downtown Belmont, Old Stone Steakhouse took over the old police department and turned it into an upscale steak house with a mountain lodge feel. Stone accents and exposed wooden beams make it warm and inviting. For fun, the owners left the words "Belmont Police Department" on the back wall.

Successful Charlotte restaurateur Nick LaVecchia is a partner in Old Stone, which serves choice USDA steaks and a few interesting items like black and bleu Cajun sirloin, Tuscan chicken penne, and salmon and poached pear salad. Open for lunch and dinner Mon through Sat.

THE PALM $$$-$$$$
6705 Phillips Place Court
Phillips Place Shopping Center
(704) 552-7256
www.thepalm.com

The Manhattan-based Palm is a classic American steak house that has served huge cuts of prime beef and jumbo lobsters since 1926. A see-and-be-seen restaurant, the Palm blends celebrity caricatures with mahogany, leather, an upscale bar, and a private cigar bar and dining room. Charlotte's location is especially well-known for Palm Night, an annual charity dinner and auction that raises hundreds of thousands of dollars. Dinner is served seven days a week, and lunch is served Mon through Fri.

RANCH HOUSE OF CHARLOTTE $$-$$$
5614 Wilkinson Blvd.
(704) 399-5411
www.ranchhouseofcharlotte.com

If you enjoy good steaks in the company of regular, down-home folks, put this restaurant on your to-do list. Serving Charlotteans since 1951, the Ranch House offers the finest cuts of aged USDA charbroiled steaks and fresh fish nightly. Ranch House has the atmosphere of an old-fashioned supper club with a Western motif unchanged for decades. The menu is straightforward with items like the 22-ounce bone-in ribeye and the 18-ounce black angus T-bone. Add a skewer of shrimp to any entrée and make sure to try their famous (and spicy) cocktail sauce. Not a frilly place, just fulfilling. Located on the west side near the airport, this restaurant is open Mon through Sat for dinner.

SULLIVAN'S STEAKHOUSE $$$-$$$$
1928 South Blvd.
(704) 335-8228
www.sullivansteakhouse.com

Perfectly grilled steaks, side dishes meant for sharing, an extensive wine list, and great martinis are the draw at this high-energy steak house decorated with hand-painted murals from the swing era. Live jazz in the bar nightly. Open for lunch weekdays, for dinner seven days a week.

SUSHI

ENSO ASIAN BISTRO & SUSHI BAR $$–$$$
210 East Trade St., EpiCentre
(704) 716-3676
www.ensocharlotte.com
Not only the newest sushi hotspot in Charlotte, but considered by many foodies as the best sushi in Charlotte. You basically can't go wrong with anything on an extensive menu of sushi, seafood, and wagyu Japanese beef. A favorite is the sexy salmon roll, consisting of spicy salmon topped with apple sauce and black tobiko. Open for lunch Mon through Fri, and dinner daily. Reservations available online.

NIKKO $$–$$$
1300-F South Blvd.
(704) 370-0100

15105 John J. Delaney Dr., Ballantyne
(704) 341-5550
www.nikkosushibar.net

Nikko has probably been Charlotte's most popular spot for sushi and Japanese food since it opened in South End in 1998. It recently moved next door to upscale digs in the ground floor of the Arlington, a.k.a. the Big Pink Building, and added a second location in Ballantyne. Nikko is known for having fresh and interesting rolls, along with a free-spirited female owner who wears funky cowboy hats and greets customers loudly as they enter. If you need a suggestion, try the yellowtail sashimi. Also, there is a diverse sake selection. Open for lunch on weekdays and dinner seven days a week.

RU SAN'S $$
2440 Park Rd.
(704) 374-0008
www.rusans.com
If you want good sushi without all the fancy accoutrements, Ru San's is the place. This small, non-descript place is always crowded and bustling with activity. Employees yell greetings as you enter, and it's all about having a good time.

NIGHTLIFE

olks who lived in the Queen City a couple decades ago are usually shocked upon return. Their somewhat sleepy Southern city blossomed in a big way, and nowhere is that more apparent than the nightlife scene.

It wasn't too long ago that the most popular bars, nightclubs, theaters, and music venues were scattered willy-nilly throughout the suburbs. The downtown area was a pristine business center that rolled up the sidewalks at 6 p.m. But those days are no more. Uptown has developed a critical mass of cultural and nightlife options, with more likely to spring up by the time you read this. Meanwhile, villages in the new urbanism style emerged in places like Ballantyne, Fort Mill, Ayresly, Birkdale, and Lake Norman to offer after-dark fun, suburban style.

If there is one holdover aspect from the sleepier times, it's that Charlotte is not a happening place seven nights a week. Sun through Tues is particularly slow, while Wed nights are hit-or-miss. It seems our buttoned-down banker mentality and Protestant work ethic still keeps us subdued early in the week. However, we get more playful as the week progresses. To wit, Sat nights in Uptown are becoming legendary throughout the Carolinas.

An interesting facet of our nightlife involves liquor laws. Charlotte is located in the heart of the Bible Belt and many folks remember that not-so-distant time in the past when we didn't have liquor by the drink. In September 1978, Queen City voters overwhelmingly approved a referendum on liquor by the drink, and two months later, 23-year-old waiter Hank Stoppelbein ordered the first legal cocktail in 70 years in the state of North Carolina. This took place at 8:04 a.m. in front of a crowd of people and media in the old Benedictine's Restaurant on Fairview Road. Stopplebein enjoyed a bloody Mary, and, according to *Time Magazine,* proclaimed the occasion "history, right there along with George Washington crossing the Delaware."

In the three decades since that historic drink, Charlotte and North Carolina have accumulated a confusing patchwork of alcohol laws. One law that sometimes comes into play is that a bar or nightclub must derive at least 30 percent of its sales from food to be able to serve liquor. Otherwise it has to become a "private" club. However, don't be misled by the term "private." Most "private" clubs will allow entrance for a nominal membership fee, usually about $10. And, if they restrict entrance to members only, hang around outside and find a member to sign you in as his or her guest. Other laws limit the time when bars must stop serving (2 a.m.) and when alcohol sales can resume on Sun (noon). Also, happy hours are illegal in North Carolina. If an establishment wants to offer a drink special, it must be available the whole day, not just during happy hour, although some bars have developed clever ways to sidestep this regulation. All of this is to say that sometimes a little patience is required to enjoy a night of revelry in the Queen City.

Below is an inside look at Charlotte nightlife. Nightspots are divided into several categories, such as: bars, pubs, and taverns; beach; comedy; cosmopolitan; country; dance clubs; jazz; music venues; sports bars; and wine bars.

At the end of the chapter you will find information on concerts, special events, and cinemas. Listings are located in Charlotte unless otherwise noted.

BARS, PUBS, AND TAVERNS

ALEXANDER MICHAEL'S
401 West Ninth St.
(704) 332-6789
www.almikestavern.com
Tucked away in an old house in the historic Fourth Ward in the Uptown area, Alexander Michael's is known for its long wooden bar, neighborhood atmosphere, cold beer, and fried pickles. A great lunch or dinner spot, it's well loved by residents and neighbors.

BLACKFINN AMERICAN SALOON
210 East Trade St., EpiCentre
(704) 971-4440
www.blackfinncharlotte.com
BlackFinn was one of the first bars to open in Epi-Centre and is probably the most popular. There are good crowds at this two-story speakeasy from Wed through Sat, and on Sun during football season. BlackFinn provides a nice atmosphere with solid wood furnishings, brass accents, and hardwood floors. It's a classic bar done right. You can enter on either level, although the main entrance is downstairs. The lower level features a separate dining room, and a bar area that is more laid back than the upstairs bar. The crowd is generally a little older downstairs and the music is not as loud. Upstairs is where the action is on Thurs, Fri, and Sat nights. The bar is in the middle with access on all sides, and the tables in the back area are cleared to make way for a dance floor as the evening wears on. There's a DJ booth overlooking the dance area, and there's also a private room available, which has its own fully stocked bar.

BRAZWELLS PREMIUM PUB
1627 Montford Dr.
(704) 523-3500
www.brazwellspub.com
Guys, make note of Brazwell's. It opened in the spring of 2009 and quickly became a gathering spot for attractive, single women. The interior is nice, nothing too fancy, while the bar's calling card is a large back patio that actually holds more

people than the bar. Fri night is the busiest night at Brazwell's, although a good crowd can be found on Thurs and Sat, too, especially in warm weather. Lead bartender Christy is considered by many regulars to be one of the best in Charlotte. The food is quite good, too, with tasty burgers and sandwiches and a few gourmet-esque entrées. Brazwell's replaced The Press Box, a Queen City classic that was a sports bar before anybody ever used the term "sports bar."

BRICKHOUSE TAVERN
209 Delburg St., Davidson
(704) 987-2022
www.brickhousetavern.com
Surprisingly enough, a happening time can be had at this refurbished cotton mill in Davidson. Yep, conservative and low-key Davidson now has an "it" place for non-students. A typical evening at Brickhouse Tavern reveals a nicely dressed crowd of 30- and 40-somethings enjoying a selection of 50 beers on tap, with live music to boot. Weekends are great, as well as any night of a Davidson College home basketball game. The restaurant is good, too.

BUCKHEAD SALOON
201 East Fifth St.
(704) 370-0687
A transplant from Atlanta's trendy Buckhead neighborhood, this Uptown modern-day honky-tonk is popular with the 20-something crowd for its great drink prices, lively atmosphere, and weekend music. Buckhead Saloon is especially known for its two guitarists, who play everything from originals to requests to cover tunes with hilarious new lyrics. A large patio is a nice spot for a break, and there's a Beer Pong area in the back section of the bar. Expect a line out the door on Sat.

COMMON HOUSE
1101 Central Ave.
(704) 332-1010
www.charlottecommonhouse.com
In addition to its great food, Common House is popular for its bar atmosphere. The scene is

lower-key and more relaxed than Uptown. This is a great spot for an after-work drink or a fun, but not too crazy, weekend night. The crowd is more mature, both in age and conduct.

CONNOLLY'S ON 5TH
115 East Fifth St.
(704) 358-9070
www.connollysirishpub.com
Uptown's neighborhood Irish pub, this local hangout is the perfect place to kick back with a pint of Guinness. The Charlotte Guinness Club meets the first Wed of every month from 7 to 9 p.m. Live music is available regularly, and Connolly's is the unofficial headquarters of the two-day Charlotte Irish Festival, held each August.

DIXIE'S TAVERN
301 East Seventh St.
(704) 374-1700
www.dixiescharlotte.com
Dixie's is a Louisiana-style tavern with a great outdoor patio and lots of weekly specials. It's a popular place to start an evening of revelry because there's rarely a cover and you can munch on pub food. Late night on Fri and Sat, tables are cleared near the DJ booth creating a makeshift dance floor that usually attracts an enthusiastic crowd. Dixie's occasionally schedules big, parking-lot concerts with performers such as Liz Phair, Fountains of Wayne, Josh Kelley, Billy Idol, and Cowboy Mouth.

THE FLYING SAUCER DRAUGHT EMPORIUM
9605 North Tryon St., University
(704) 568-7253
www.beerknurd.com
This chain offers hundreds of beers on tap and in bottles, plus a limited bar menu. But what's particularly cool is the UFO Club. Members pay $18 to join and receive a T-shirt and membership card. Each time you drink a brand of beer, the card is swiped. Once you've enjoyed 200 different beers, you are immortalized with a personal saucer on the wall, including a personal inscription.

Smoking Ban

As of January 2, 2010, smoking was prohibited in all bars and restaurants in North Carolina, except for cigar bars and nonprofit private clubs. The passing of this law marked a change of epic proportions for a state that was largely built on the cash crop of tobacco and has long been considered "Tobacco Road." Folks in Charlotte had a hand in getting the law passed. A progressive movement to ban smoking in public places in the Queen City produced a petition of many thousands of names, which helped create momentum for a statewide law in the General Assembly. North Carolina was one of the first 30 states to enact such a ban.

GIN MILL
1411 South Tryon St.
(704) 373-0782
www.ginmill.biz
The Gin Mill is the quintessential tavern for the average guy (and gal). Everybody seems to be on a first-name basis with the bartender, and there are plenty of tables and booths for people to scatter throughout the place. The shuffleboard table is popular, while team trivia draws a crowd on Tues nights. The latest addition is a rooftop patio, which offers nice views of the Charlotte skyline. There's live music on a regular basis and if you happen to catch the right night, you can enjoy $2.50 drafts and $2 Pabst Blue Ribbon tallboys.

HICKORY TAVERN
8 locations in greater Charlotte
www.thehickorytavern.com
Hickory Tavern is currently the biggest success story on the Charlotte bar scene. Continued

expansion has brought the number of taverns to eight in the Charlotte metro, with three additional locations across the Carolinas. Hickory Taverns offer good food in a sports bar atmosphere. Drinks specials are plenty, UFC bouts are always televised, and live music is a staple. Wed is shrimp night, Thur is oyster night, and the fifth of every month is Cinco de Drinco.

JACKALOPE JACK'S
1936 East Seventh St.
(704) 347-1918
www.jackalopejacks.com
Jackalope Jack's is play time for adults located in an early 1900s house along a neat stretch of Seventh Street east of Uptown. A regular crowd of locals enjoys pool, skee ball, corn-hole tournaments, trivia, karaoke, beer bingo, and a surprisingly varied menu. Our European transplants love it because the bar gets satellite feeds of international soccer and rugby matches. And for those who need to feel connected to Jackalope Jack's at all times, the Web site has a live cam so they can see what's going on when they're not there. To view the Web cam, you'll need the username (cold) and the password (beer).

MIDTOWN SUNDRIES
3425 David Cox Rd., University
(704) 597-7413

18665 Harborside Dr., Lake Norman
(704) 896-9013

7296 Hwy. 73, Denver
(704) 822-1380
www.midtownsundries.com
The original Midtown Sundries, just off Uptown on Kenilworth, was closed to make way for the Little Sugar Creek Greenway. Prior to that, this popular watering hole had branched out to the northern suburbs and it continues to thrive there with locations in University City, Denver, and on Lake Norman. Midtown caters to the 30-and-up crowd that prefers a neighborhood bar. Loyal patrons enjoy trivia nights, karaoke, live music, and shooting pool. The Lake Norman location is very popular with many partiers arriving by boat.

PEWTER ROSE BISTRO
1820 South Blvd.
(704) 332-8149
www.pewterrose.com
Situated on the second floor of a turn-of-the-20th-century textile warehouse in South End, the Pewter Rose Bistro is a favorite of tony Charlotteans. Not only does it have one of the most complete wine lists in the city with 500 selections, it offers live music in the bar and patio area on weekends.

PROVIDENCE CAFE
110 Perrin Place
(704) 376-2008
www.providencecafe.com
Providence Cafe is a delightful place for lunch or dinner, but it has also become a local hangout for the Myers Park and professional crowd. Look for the 20- to 40-something well-dressed set, some of whom call this place "Divorcee Cafe." Live jazz on Wed and Thurs is lively, along with weekends. Many couples also enjoy late-night desserts or relaxing with a glass of wine on the patio.

SELWYN AVENUE PUB
2801 Selwyn Ave.
(704) 333-3443
Founded by a professor at nearby Queens University, Selwyn Pub is one of Charlotte's great neighborhood hangouts. The place is usually packed on Wed evenings and after Panthers games. This low-key, no-frills bar is built in an old home on the edge of Myers Park, and its large front porch is a favorite place for 20- and 30-something professionals to people watch and relax without a meat-market scene. Think Carolina and Wake grads a few years out of school. Great pizza, too.

THOMAS STREET TAVERN
1228 Thomas Ave.
(704) 376-1622
www.thomas-street-tavern.com
The place to go in Plaza-Midwood, this local hangout has a well-stocked jukebox, pool tables, and a laid-back vibe where construction work-

Bar Crawlin'

Bar crawls are big-time in Charlotte. Most are centered in Uptown, although a few cover places like Ballantyne and Lake Norman. www .LazyDay.com, a local nightlife Web site, hosts several throughout the year, often renting party buses to ferry crawlers to and from participating bars and clubs. LazyDay's most popular crawl is the Santa Bar Crawl, an Uptown walking crawl that began in 2000 and draws 350–400 people, many dressed like Old St. Nick. Other LazyDay crawls are themed-based, such as the Rock Star Bar Crawl and the 80s Bar Crawl. Local entrepreneurs Rich Saner and Jeff Bennett of RockHouse Events host the uber-popular Rich & Bennett's St. Patrick's Day Pub Crawl. This 13-hour crawl began in 2001 and set a world record by attracting 4,987 participants in 2009. The 2009 event was also featured on an episode of The Travel Channel's "Extreme Wild Parties." For crawl info, visit www .LazyDay.com and www.RockHouse Events.com.

easy in 2009. The new owners put in a second entrance on the Fifth Street side of the building and turned the downstairs dance area into a room for private parties, reunions, and alumni events. Upstairs, there are new plasma TVs to attract the sports crowd, and sing-along party music to keep the atmosphere lively. Town Tavern is also an official bar of the Buffalo Bills Backers (see, we told you there are a lot of Buffalo natives in Charlotte!).

TYBER CREEK PUB
1933 South Blvd.
(704) 343-2727
www.tybercreek.com
A pioneering South End neighborhood hangout, this bar has a great patio for summer evenings and a lively St. Paddy's Day celebration. Entertainment often includes area bands and traditional Irish music. Home of $3 pints of Guinness—all day, every day.

VILLAGE TAVERN
4201 Congress St.
Rotunda Building, SouthPark
(704) 552-9983
www.villagetavern.com
Terrific food and a fabulous patio make this a popular after-work hangout for young and middle-aged professionals. The tavern offers live jazz music on Wed and Thurs evenings spring through fall.

VINNIE'S SARDINE GRILL & RAW BAR
1714 South Blvd., SouthEnd
(704) 332-0006

10619 Black Dog Lane, Mt. Island Lake
(704) 393-2203

142 East John St., Matthews
(704) 849-0202

643 Williamson Rd., Mooresville
(704) 799-2090
www.vinniesrawbar.com
As casual and laid-back as it gets, Vinnie's is a fun, raucous joint known for its oysters, crab legs,

ers, CPAs, and the artsy crowd chill in harmony. Pooches can even hang out on the front patio. Thomas Street Tavern has been named the Best Neighborhood Bar in the city by the readers and editors of *Creative Loafing*.

TOWN TAVERN
200 North Tryon St.
(704) 334-3324
www.towntaverncharlotte.com
This tavern has become a hopping spot since it was converted from the Brick & Barrel Speak-

shrimp, fiery wings, and $1 beers. Bankers and bikers alike hang out at the often-crowded South Boulevard location in SouthEnd. The Lake Norman Vinnie's in Mooresville overlooks the water and brings in droves of boaters and partiers from the lake.

BEACH CLUBS

BOPPER'S BAR AND BOOGIE
5237 Albemarle Rd.
(704) 537-3323
Located near the corner of Albemarle and Sharon Amity, Bopper's features swing and hustle dancing on Wed and beach music and shag dancing Thurs and Sun. Beginner through advanced shag dance lessons are offered on Thurs and Sun. Fri is ladies' night with no cover charge, and Sat includes dance tunes from the '70s to today's Top 40.

O'HARA'S BEACH CLUB
212 West Woodlawn Rd.
Ramada Woodlawn
(704) 525-8350
One of Charlotte's longtime venues for beach music and shag dancing, O'Hara's in the Ramada Woodlawn offers live music Wed, Fri, and Sat nights. Popular with baby boomers who remember shagging at Ocean Drive in Myrtle Beach.

COMEDY

ALIVE NODA
2909 North Davidson St.
(704) 930-2200
www.alivenoda.com
Alive is a combination comedy club and live music venue. It's new on the scene in Charlotte and includes some of the key personnel from the old Comedy Zone in Matthews.

COMEDY ZONE LAKE NORMAN
17044 Kenton Dr.
(704) 895-1782
www.lkncomedyzone.com
Hot comedians on the national circuit—Carrot Top, Tim Wilson, Pauly Shore, James Gregory, and others—perform at this comedy club, located in the top floor of the Galway Hooker Pub in Cornelius. Shows and times vary. Call for reservations; it's often sold out.

COSMOPOLITAN

BAR 10
601 South College St., The Westin
(704) 375-2600
www.westin.com/charlotte
Off the lobby in the sleek, modern Westin hotel in Uptown, Bar 10 is a sophisticated setting for drinks and conversation. A rock fountain running along the perimeter gives the feeling of sitting outdoors.

BLUE
Corner of Fifth and College
Hearst Tower
(704) 927-2583
www.bluecharlotte.com
Original art, mosaic tile floors, and subdued blue accents in this modern restaurant and bar will leave you wondering if you're really in Charlotte. Slick and sophisticated, it combines Mediterranean-style dining with live jazz and a crowd of lookers. Enjoy the wine bar next to the original bar. Mr. Big may walk in at any moment.

MADISON'S
115 East Fifth St.
(704) 358-4244
www.madisonsbar.com
This bar is swanky and dark, with lots of wood, granite, and stone, not to mention two over-sized leather Victorian couches. Madison's always shows pay-per-view boxing and UFC bouts, so it's the perfect place for pugilistic fans to enjoy the sweet science on large HD screens. It's also a good place to unwind in style with an after-work drink, but if you stay too late, Madison's typically gets crowded (especially on Fri and Sat). However, if it gets too crowded, you can always slip next door to The Attic, an adjoining bar that allows free passage between the two.

THE SUNSET CLUB
1820 South Blvd.
(704) 373-9900
www.sunsetclubcharlotte.com
The Sunset Club is still trying to determine what it wants to be when it grows up. It burst on the scene in the late 1990s as an exclusive, private club with personalized cigar lockers for heavy hitters in Charlotte business circles. Many Carolina Panthers hung out there, including former team president Mark Richardson. After several years, the attraction of the private club atmosphere waned, and it morphed into a less-restrictive private club for the younger, up-and-coming set. Recently, the club was remodeled into an "ultra lounge," with DJs playing pulsating dance music for a diverse crowd amid a high-energy light show and hip furnishings. Memberships are back in vogue, with people paying anywhere from $250 a year for general memberships with a few perks to $5,000 per year for diamond memberships that include, among other things, complimentary car service, four nights at a local hotel, preferential line treatment, VIP seating, and a house account.

THERAPY CAFE
401 North Tryon St.
(704) 333-1353
www.therapycafe.net
Therapy will always get props from the insider for being the first bar in Uptown to go smoke-free, years before it became a law. Located on the first floor of Transamerica Square beside Rock Bottom Brewery, Therapy Cafe sells sandwiches, salads, and organic coffee by day. But at night, the cafe becomes a cool lounge with a huge selection of martinis, acoustic tunes, and drink specials. Martinis are half-price on Wed nights, which is a great night to check out Therapy. Listen to live music Fri and Sat.

TUTTO MONDO
1820 South Blvd.
(704) 332-8149
www.tuttomondo.net
A sister establishment of Pewter Rose Bistro, Tutto Mondo caters to the 30-something profes-sional crowd who come after work and late night for top-notch martinis, cigars, and apps from the bistro menu. Trendy with a Manhattan vibe, the swanky lounge features velvet drapes, antique leather chairs, and subdued, loftlike lighting in this renovated textile mill warehouse. The feel is relaxed early in the evening, then takes on an energetic tempo when a DJ starts spinning house tunes.

COUNTRY

COYOTE JOE'S
4621 Wilkinson Blvd.
(704) 399-4946
www.coyote-joes.com
Charlotte's most popular country nightclub, Coyote Joe's sports a large dance floor that's usually full of fun-loving people doing the Texas two-step. Not sure of the steps? No problem. On Wed you can take line-dancing lessons. Big-name acts such as Travis Tritt, SheDaisy, Keith Urban, Trace Adkins, Tracy Lawrence, Charlie Daniels, Tracy Byrd, and Hank Williams III also appear here. Open Wed, Fri, and Sat.

PUCKETT'S FARM EQUIPMENT
2740 West Sugar Creek Rd.
(704) 597-8230
www.puckettsfarm.com
Puckett's began life as a farm equipment store when that area of town—Derita—was still rural. Over the years, as the city encroached and the farms disappeared, the owners realized they were selling more beer than farm equipment. So, Puckett's Farm Equipment became what they like to call a "21st century honky-tonk" with sawdust floors and a great music stage showcasing authentic Americana, country, and bluegrass music. This is definitely one of the places that gives buttoned-down Charlotte some character. Stop in to hear great bands with names like Loose Lugnuts, South 85, Rockabilly Junkies, Notorious Gringos, Tater Family Traveling Circus, and New Dixie Pharaohs. Thurs is open-mic night and there's a modest cover charge on weekends. Also a great place to watch NASCAR racing.

DANCE CLUBS

BAR CHARLOTTE
300 North College St.
(704) 342-2557
www.barcharlotte.com
If you're old enough to remember when Ronald Reagan was president and Russia was the Soviet Union, this is not the place for you. Bar Charlotte caters to college students and 20-somethings who are into chugging beers and dancing on bars. Bar Charlotte was actually a pioneer in Uptown nightlife way back in the mid 1990s, and it has prospered with a simple formula—scantily-clad beer tub girls serving cold beers to rowdy young guns, while rowdy young gals ride the mechanical bull and dance with each other on top of the main bar. Oh yeah, most everybody eventually makes it to the dance floor. The Bar Yard is a 36-ounce shot of brew—try it if you dare. Ages 18 and up welcome. Open Wed through Sat.

BREAKFAST CLUB
225 North Caldwell St.
(704) 374-1982
www.that80sclub.com
For a totally awesome 1980s experience, check out Breakfast Club in Uptown. Owner/DJ Jody Sullivan opened this three-level dance venue in 2003. It offers a fun trip back to the decade of parachute pants, break dancing, and new wave synth-pop. The décor has a distinct 80s feel. There are neon colors, Pac Man machines, album covers on the walls, and a giant Rubik's Cube above the dance floor. The crowd, ranging from mid-20s to early 40s, dances to blockbuster hits from the retro era, while Sullivan mixes in a few old-school hip-hop tunes like "Electric Kingdom," "Apache" and "Let the Music Play." Adding to the atmosphere is a continuous loop of movie clips from *The Breakfast Club* and *Fast Times at Ridgemont High*. The drink menu features such concoctions as Purple Rain, Top Gun, and Super Freak, plus plenty of Bartles and Jaymes wine coolers. There's even a Billy Idol impersonator on weekends. Breakfast Club is a choice spot for girls' night out. It's common to see groups of women dressed in neon stripes, black tights, hoop earrings, and big hair. They're usually having a ball on the dance floor.

Insider Top 5: Most Requested at Breakfast Club

Breakfast Club owner/DJ Jody Sullivan shares the five most requested artists at his Uptown dance club:

1. Michael Jackson
2. Madonna
3. Prince
4. Duran Duran
5. Run-DMC

CLOSET
1202 Charlottetowne Ave.
(704) 375-1777
www.closetnightclub.com
Closet is the newest addition to Charlotte's gay and lesbian club scene. It opened in January 2010 and is divided in two. One half is a retro video lounge and the other half is a dance club. The retro lounge shows a variety of music videos from the 1970s and 80s, while the dance portion plays a high-energy mix of today's dance music bathed in an extravagant light show. Two balconies overlook the dance floor, each with its own bar.

CLUB ICE
300 East Stonewall St.
(704) 334-8700
www.clubicenc.com
Rock out to the latest hip-hop and R&B jams at Club Ice, which bills itself as the "hottest urban nightclub in North Carolina." Celebrity acts have included Young Jeezy, Lil' Kim, and Three 6 Mafia. You might even see a celebrity guest like NBA star Lebron James or boxer Floyd Mayweather. Fri is ladies night.

COSMOS CAFÉ
8420 Rea Rd., Ballantyne
(704) 544-5268
www.comoscafe.com
When folks in Ballantyne (and south Charlotte) want a nightclub experience without driving into the city, they head over to Cosmos Café. An upscale tapas restaurant by day, Comos transforms into Ballantyne's hottest dance venue on weekend nights. The place has a nice feel, with a custom-made circular bar and décor with an international flair.

i Uptown parking can be expensive, especially when there's an NBA basketball game or major concert. However, here's the insider scoop on how to park free any night of the week. All metered spaces in Uptown have to be empty between 4 and 6 p.m. to facilitate rush-hour traffic. But once the clock hits 6 p.m. the spaces can be used again, and the city doesn't charge parking fees after 6 p.m. So for free parking all night, simply arrive for your evening in Uptown just before 6 p.m. Pull into a metered space and sit there with the engine running. Once the clock strikes six, turn the car off and you're in the clear!

THE EXCELSIOR CLUB
921 Beatties Ford Rd.
(704) 334-5709
For more than 60 years, the historic Excelsior Club has been a prominent institution in Charlotte's African-American community. It has hosted such legendary performers as Nat King Cole and was designated a historic landmark in 1986. The Excelsior caters to an older crowd. Patrons must be 30 or older and show ID. The club features disco and old-school R&B.

HALO
820 Hamilton St.
(704) 246-1755
www.haloclt.com
Uptown got its Halo in the summer of 2009 when this dance club opened in the N.C. Music Factory complex. The club is hard to find, separated from Uptown proper by railroad tracks and a weird street configuration. However, once you locate Halo, it's like discovering something new. Halo sets itself apart from other Uptown venues by offering free parking, no lines, no pretension, and no stairs. Customer-friendly service too—now there's a novel idea in Queen City nightlife. The clientele is mostly 20-somethings, especially on Fri nights, which are '90s rewind nights. They also have pre-concert parties from 4 to 8 p.m. prior to shows next door at the Music Factory's 5,000-capacity Uptown Amphitheatre.

SUITE
210 East Trade St., EpiCentre
(704) 999-7934
www.suitecharlotte.com
Suite brings all the big city trappings to Charlotte. There are four private suites, appearances by celebrity models and personalities, waiting in line behind the ropes, and an ultra-sleek interior with a great sound system and light show. It's the place where pretty people in their 20s and early 30s go to see and be seen. One side of the club is glass walls and provides nice views of the Uptown skyline. The dance floor is situated in the center of the club, which gets everybody involved. Suite has a stricter dress code than most Charlotte nightspots—no T-shirts, hats, sneakers, shorts or baggy clothing.

WHISKY RIVER
210 East Trade St., EpiCentre
(704) 749-1097
www.whiskyrivercharlotte.com
In the early years of his career, NASCAR driver Dale Earnhardt Jr. transformed his basement into a makeshift nightclub. "Club E," as it was called, became the inspiration for Whisky River. When Earnhardt debuted Whisky River in early 2008, it was one of the EpiCentre's first businesses and set the tone for how popular the entertainment complex would be. Whisky River is a hybrid. It takes a back-woods honky-tonk and blends it with a big-city dance club. Much like Earnhardt himself, it appeals to a wide audience, not just

EpiCentre is the Epicenter

The EpiCentre, Charlotte's new Uptown entertainment and nightlife megaplex, has become the hot spot of the city's social scene. This exciting mix of bars, clubs, restaurants, attractions, and shops was designed to be Charlotte's version of Times Square. Through early 2010, it was 90 percent occupied and drawing folks like crazy, especially on weekends.

The nightlife lineup includes BlackFinn American Saloon, Whisky River (dance club), Howl at the Moon (piano bar), Suite Lounge (dance club), Buffalo Wild Wings, Mez (movie theater/restaurant), and Strike City, the hippest, wildest bowling alley in town.

There's also a Fleming's Steakhouse, Enso Asian Bistro, Jason's Deli, Five Guys Burgers, Bruegger's Bagels, Libretto's Pizza, and a Cold Stone Creamery. The luxury hotel, aloft, is also in the complex.

The EpiCentre has not experienced total smooth sailing. A planned condo tower never made it past the second floor because of a legal battle between the developer and the general contractor, while many businesses were granted waivers by the state of North Carolina to stay open after their temporary occupancy permits expired. But, overall, the EpiCentre has delivered on its promise to be the defining centerpiece of Charlotte nightlife.

More on the complex is available at www.epicentrenc.com.

NASCAR fans. The music ranges from Lynyrd Skynyrd to Lady Gaga to Kanye West, sometimes in the same set. There's usually a line out the door on weekends, although it tends to move quickly. Earnhardt makes occasional appearances, staying strictly in the limited-access VIP area. The beers are cold and the vibe is hot. One tip: If you have to go to the bathroom, start your trek early. The restrooms are in the back corner of the club and only accessible via a crowded area that often becomes part of the dance floor.

JAZZ

CAJUN QUEEN
1800 East Seventh St.
(704) 377-9017
www.cajunqueen.net
If you're looking for Dixieland jazz at its best, plan on a visit to Cajun Queen, which serves up live music seven nights a week. A visit provides fabulous 'Nawlins-style food mixed with great conversation and music for a genuine Cajun experience in Charlotte. Don't miss a Dixie beer, the brew that made New Orleans famous.

MUSIC VENUES

AMOS' SOUTHEND
1423 South Tryon St.
(704) 377-6874
www.amossouthend.com
Amos', in the heart of the SouthEnd, recently expanded into larger surroundings. While it lost some intimacy, the larger venue attracts bigger and better-name acts. The playbill runs the gamut from rock and heavy metal to rap and hip-hop to alternative, indie, and bluegrass. Amos' has hit on a niche with a regular lineup of tribute bands that pay homage to such iconic acts as KISS, Journey, Led Zepplin, Dave Matthews Band, Elton John, Bruce Springsteen, and Michael Jackson. The godfathers of Carolina beach music, General Johnson and the Chairmen of the Board, appear on a regular basis, and other national acts known to drop by include Jackyl, Goodie Mob, Doug E. Fresh, Bowling for Soup, Ratt, Mother's Finest, and Firehouse.

The venue is a two-level music hall, with a long, deep floor on the main area and a small balcony ringing the upper level. There are multiple bars and bathrooms, which is nice. Some shows are for ages 16 and up, allowing local high-schoolers to catch the bands as well.

DOUBLE DOOR INN
1218 Charlottetowne Ave.
(704) 376-1446
www.doubledoorinn.com
Since 1973, the Double Door has brought quality blues music to the Queen City. This historic venue has a bevy of autographed photos on the walls and is a cornerstone of Charlotte's music scene. From Buddy Guy and Delbert McClinton to Eric Clapton and Stevie Ray Vaughn, many a big name has played here early on, and often returned after making it big. (Ironically, Vaughn drew only six people to his first Double Door gig.) Great music is always guaranteed at this no-frills, jeans kind of place with cold beer and hot licks. Mon night features an all-star jam of local musicians, and Tues is an open jam session. Local, regional, and national acts take the stage Wed through Sat. The Double Door claims the title of "oldest blues club in the United States under original ownership." Although this little white house on the corner hasn't moved since opening, it has changed addresses. The street out front was known as East Independence Boulevard until recently changing names to Charlottetowne Avenue. So if your map or GPS unit doesn't recognize 1218 Charlotte-towne Ave., try 218 East Independence Blvd. It's still there, we promise!

THE FILLMORE CHARLOTTE
820 Hamilton St.
(704) 549-5555
The Fillmore is a new venue in the Queen City, part of the N.C. Music Factory complex on the northwest corner of Uptown. The Fillmore occupies a former textile mill and is patterned after the famous Fillmore in San Francisco. The place is owned by national concert promoter Live Nation and therefore has leverage with top name bands. Some of the performers from its first year include

Alice in Chains, David Allan Coe, Train, Uncle Kracker, Megadeth, Roger Daltrey, Foreigner, Wolfmother, Blues Traveler, The Black Crowes, Indigo Girls, Collective Soul, and The B-52s.

MILESTONE CLUB
3400 Tuckaseegee Rd.
(704) 398-0472
www.themilestoneclub.com
The Milestone is a real dive and proud of it, too. It features up-and-coming bands from the rock/punk/metal/indie and underground scene, 30 of which have gone on to grace the cover of *Rolling Stone* (R.E.M. and Natalie Merchant, for example). The walls are covered with graffiti, but it has an eclectic charm that attracts punks, yuppies, matrons, and even some brave mainstreamers—throwing them all together for a great time. The Milestone, which proudly serves beer and colas in cans, has been open since 1969. It's now owned by people who watched bands there during their youth. Shows are for age 18 and up, and the club is open Wed through Sat nights.

NEIGHBORHOOD THEATRE
511 East 36th St.
(704) 358-9298
www.neighborhoodtheatre.com
A renovated movie theater in Charlotte's hip NoDa district, the Neighborhood Theatre books a truly eclectic mix of music—American jug bands, folk guitarists such as Doc Watson, Louisiana smokin' slide guitar, bluegrass, acoustic string, funk fusion, ethereal rock, projection art set to live music and country acts from David Allan Coe to the Nitty Gritty Dirt Band. South Carolina native Edwin McCain makes an appearance or two yearly. The setting is intimate, with a capacity of 956, including the bar area. Open only when concerts are scheduled.

SMOKEY JOE'S CAFÉ
510 Briar Creek Rd.
(704) 338-9380
www.myspace.com/smokeyjoemymusic
A hardscrabble shack on the corner of Monroe Road and Briar Creek, Smokey Joe's attracts a T-shirt and flip-flip crowd for live music several nights a

week. Smokey Joe's is a Charlotte institution with a sandy-beach patio that includes a Ping-Pong table and fire pit. There's no food, even though it is called a café, and everyone is on a first-name basis. Beers are cold and cheap. The bands play hard, chasing their dreams and hoping to win fans.

SYLVIA THEATER
27 North Congress St., York, SC
(704) 609-6149
www.sylviatheater.com
This vintage small-town movie theater has been brought back to life as a music hall for local and regional acts. The Sylvia hosts an eclectic mix of musical genres, from rock to country to Celtic to bluegrass. There's even a clean hip-hop night. Movies have returned to the Sylvia as well, featuring timeless classics and children's films.

TREMONT MUSIC HALL
400 West Tremont Ave.
(704) 343-9494
www.tremontmusichall.com
One of Charlotte's best places to see live music that's far from mainstream. All kinds of bands are booked here, from Rob Zombie to the Rollins Band. They describe the genres as "modern rock, indie rock, punk, hardcore, metal, SKA, and roots rock." A former warehouse with no frills and no plans to change, Tremont is a place where people actually listen to the music—not consider it background for their conversations. No seats, hot temperatures, and beer that tends to get warm, but still a big draw with younger music fans, especially those dabbling on the dark side of musical expression. Open dodge ball games are held every other Mon at 8 p.m.

VISULITE THEATRE
1615 Elizabeth Ave.
(704) 358-9200
www.visulite.com
A cinema from the late 1930s, this is a multipurpose entertainment venue with concerts, film screenings, poetry readings, and theme parties. The adventurous music schedule books everything from alternative country to Southern

redneck rock, with performers such as Lucinda Williams, Col. Bruce Hampton, Bellglide, Dillon Fence, Bob Schneider, Southern Culture on the Skids, the Rev. Horton Heat, and Los Lonely Boys.

SPORTS BARS

CHAMPIONS SPORTS BAR
100 West Trade St.
Marriott City Center
(704) 358-6562
www.marriottcitycenter.com
Located in the Marriott City Center overlooking The Square, Champions is not your typical hotel bar. There is autographed memorabilia on the walls and 18 televisions and video projectors. Thirsty fans find 25 types of beer and a menu with appetizers, salads, sandwiches, and burgers.

DILWORTH NEIGHBORHOOD GRILLE
911 East Morehead St.
(704) 377-3808
www.neighborhoodgrille.com
A great place to catch a game with five separate viewing areas, eight 120-inch high-def screens and another 20 smaller flat-screen TVs. DNG is home to alumni groups from Auburn, Georgia, Michigan State, North Carolina, Tennessee, Texas, and West Virginia. Also a popular spot for fans of the New York Yankees, Pittsburgh Steelers, and the hometown Carolina Panthers and Bobcats.

JILLIAN'S
200 East Bland St.
(704) 376-4386
www.jillians.com
Simulator rides, driving games, hoops, air hockey, virtual reality, and video games are the draw at this arcade and bar. When all the noise starts getting to you, head over to the Sports Cafe with big-screen TVs and a casual menu, or sit down for a hibachi-style meal.

JOCKS & JILLS
4109 South Stream Blvd.
(704) 423-0001
www.jocksandjills.com

Close-up

What's New? Olde Mecklenburg Brewery

Charlotte's most authentic beer experience is the Olde Mecklenburg Brewery, located in a warehouse district off South Boulevard about 15 minutes from Uptown. Brewmaster John Marrino and a partner opened the microbrewery in March 2009. Marrino is a water purification expert who often traveled on business to Germany. He fell in love with the German style of making—and enjoying—beer, and that was the impetus for Olde Mecklenburg Brewery (OMB). The brewery's main room is patterned after a traditional German beer hall. It has high ceilings, mahogany walls, and long tables. In warm weather, the front patio transforms into a "biergarten," often with live music and a food vendor serving bratwurst.

At OMB, it's all about the beer. There are no pool tables, video games, or cornhole tournaments. There is a hi-def flat-screen television, reluctantly installed after many requests. Instead of the usual distractions, patrons focus on enjoying the brews. All ingredients (except for water) are imported from Germany. OMB features two signature beers, along with a rotation of seasonal ales. The signature brews are OMB Copper and OMB Kölsner. Copper is an authentic Düsseldorf style "altbier" lager made from Bavarian hops. The Kölsner is a tasty blending of the kölsch and pilsner styles of beer. So far, the most popular seasonal is the Mecktoberfest, which goes quickly!

The brewery has modest hours of operation. It is open Wed and Thurs from 4 to 8 p.m. Hours are 4 to 10 p.m. Fri, and noon to 6 p.m. Sat. OMB hosts two brewery tours each Sat, one at 2 p.m. and one at 4 p.m. The tours are becoming quite popular.

If you wish to enjoy OMB brews away from the brewery, they offer German-style take-home growlers in sizes of 37 and 74 ounces. The beers are also available on tap at approximately 100 locations in the Charlotte area.

For more information, call (704) 525-5644 or visit www.OldeMeckBrew.com.

This upscale sports bar chain headquartered in Atlanta is well designed, with two distinct dining areas, hardwood floors, big booths, and every inch of wall space crammed with signed and framed sports memorabilia. More restaurant than smoky sports bar, you'll be surprised at the quality of food.

PICASSO'S SPORTS CAFE
1301 East Blvd.
(704) 331-0133
Packed with the young professionals who live in Dilworth, South End, and Myers Park neighborhoods nearby, Picasso's has been a staple of Charlotte's sports bar scene for several years. The cafe offers 14 types of pizza, 16 beers on tap, and 19 TVs (2 wide-screen).

STRIKE CITY
210 East Trade St., EpiCentre
(704) 716-9300
www.strikecitycharlotte.com
The best sports bar in Uptown is actually a bowling alley. But don't fret, this ain't your father's bowling alley. Strike City is a state-of-the-art palace of bowling with as much emphasis on the sports bar as the lanes. There are 75 high-def televisions, including big screens, and an awesome, easy-to-read sports ticker running continuously along one wall. Strike City subscribes to all the major satellite packages; therefore, chances are they're showing your game. If you love Ohio State University, this is the place to be on a fall Sat when the Buckeyes have a big matchup.

NIGHTLIFE

WINE BARS

AROOJI'S WINE ROOM & RISTORANTE
5349 Ballantyne Commons Parkway
(704) 845-5244

720 Governor Morrison St., SouthPark
(704) 366-6610
www.aroojis.com
A large selection of wine and live entertainment make Aroojis a great place to enjoy a glass, or bottle, of your favorite vino. Both locations also have an extensive Italian menu and are open for lunch and dinner seven days a week.

D'VINE WINE CAFÉ
14815 John J. Delaney Dr., Ballantyne
(704) 369-5050
www.dvinewinecafe.com
This has become a hot spot in Ballantyne with 35 wines by the glass and about the same number of specialty beers. Live music is available several nights a week, including light jazz during wine dinners. The patio offers the only outdoor cushy couch seating in Ballantyne. A great place to meet Mr. Right.

DOLCE VITA
3205 North Davidson St., NoDa
www.dolcevitawines.com
Located in the artsy NoDa district, Dolce Vita is a wine bar in the truest sense, with the emphasis on enjoying wine by the glass, not purchasing it by the bottle. Wine and beer tastings take place monthly in a fun, relaxed atmosphere. Bet you can't name another wine bar that hosts Ping-Pong tournaments.

DOLCETTO WINE ROOM
4625 Piedmont Row, SouthPark
(704) 295-1111
www.dolcettowineroom.com
Dolcetto is upscale and elegant in every way. This trendy SouthPark spot offers 40 wines by the glass and more than 300 by the bottle. Enjoy the modern interior while watching the game on 42-inch plasma televisions, or relax on the patio and enjoy live music on weekends.

THE WINE SHOP
7824 Fairview Rd., Foxcroft
(704) 365-6550
www.thewineshopatfoxcroft.com

14142 Rivergate Parkway, Rivergate
(704) 831-9000
www.thewineshopatrivergate.com
Not the most exciting name, but The Wine Shop is the top choice for Charlotte wine aficionados. The Foxcroft location came first, then the Rivergate shop was added to serve the growing region around Lake Wylie in southwest Charlotte. Both have impressive selections of wines by the bottle and glass. The Rivergate location has more of a bar atmosphere, and also has a tasting room that can be rented for private parties. A nice touch: Both Web sites feature blogs on which the owners disperse their expertise on all things vino.

CONCERTS

For big-name and up-and-coming concert performances, there are several venues in the Charlotte area.

BANK OF AMERICA STADIUM
(704) 358-7407
www.panthers.com

BOJANGLES' COLISEUM
(704) 372-3600
www.bojanglescoliseum.com

NEIGHBORHOOD THEATRE
(704) 358-9298
www.neighborhoodtheatre.com

OAKBORO MUSIC HALL
Oakboro
(704) 485-2221
www.oakboromusichall.com

97

OVENS AUDITORIUM
(704) 372-3600
www.ovensauditorium.com

**PALADIUM AMPHITHEATRE AT
PARAMOUNT'S CAROWINDS**
(704) 522-6500
www.carowinds.com

SYLVIA THEATER
York, SC
(803) 684-5590
www.sylviatheater.com

TIME WARNER CABLE ARENA
(704) 688-9000
www.timewarnercablearena.com

TREMONT MUSIC HALL
(704) 343-9494
www.tremontmusichall.com

**UPTOWN AMPHITHEATRE AT
NC MUSIC FACTORY**
(704) 987-0612
www.ncmusicfactory.com

VERIZON WIRELESS AMPHITHEATER
(704) 549-5555
www.verizonwirelessamphitheater.com

VISULITE THEATRE
(704) 358-9200
www.visulite.com

SPECIAL EVENTS

Outdoor concerts and special events are a big part of Charlotte's social scene, especially from spring through fall.

Alive After Five, held Uptown on Thurs evenings from May through early Sept, entertains several thousand Uptown workers with a free after-work concert series.

Also on Thurs evenings, groups of friends and families gather below the Ratcliffe condo tower on South Tryon Street for the Center City Partners' Movies on the Green. Admission is free, and you can buy a hot dog for dinner at Matt's Chicago Dog.

Ballantyne has its own weekly summer after-work concert series, Mix at Six, on Wed at Ballantyne Village.

Sun evenings in June draw thousands for the Charlotte Symphony Orchestra's free Summer Pops concerts at Symphony Park next to SouthPark Mall.

Insider Top 5: Charlotte Parties

John Lineberger has been czar of Charlotte parties for as long as anyone can remember. He started alerting folks to the best events long before e-mail, by sending postcards via the United States Postal Service. These days it's e-mail only. Below are his five best annual parties. To sign up for Lineberger's e-blasts, send a request to: partyczar@yahoo.com.

1. **Alive After 5**—EpiCentre party deck, Thurs evenings Apr through late summer.

2. **Ronnie Stephen's Lake Bash**—Most people don't know who Ronnie is, but they know about this huge party each June at Lake Norman.

3. **Second String Santas**—Charlotte's largest Christmas party in early December. So big it was moved to Time Warner Cable Arena.

4. **Red Hot Turkey Trot**—A Queen City tradition, usually two days before Thanksgiving at the Wachovia Atrium.

5. **Toys for Tots**—Another holiday tradition. This dress-up party is held in Uptown and benefits the U.S. Marine Corps Toys for Tots Foundation.

The Mint Museum of Art also sponsors several outdoor events. Derby Days, held on the lawn of the Mint, is a day of mint juleps and live music leading up to the Kentucky Derby, always the first Sat in May. In the NoDa arts district, gallery crawls are held the first and third Fri of each month.

SPECIALTY THEATERS

BELMONT DRIVE-IN THEATER
314 McAdenville Rd., Belmont
(704) 825-6044
www.belmontdriven.20megsfree.com
Take a trip back to the '50s at this drive-in. Located in nearby Belmont, this theater offers first-run movies as well as some second-run, and for only $4 per person.

BESSEMER CITY–KINGS MOUNTAIN
DRIVE-IN THEATER
1365 Bessemer City Rd.
Kings Mountain
(704) 739-2150

About 45 minutes west of Charlotte in the small town of Kings Mountain, this family-friendly drive-in typically shows three recently released movies each weekend night.

IMAX DOME THEATRE
Discovery Place
301 North Tryon St.
(704) 372-6261
www.discoveryplace.org
This state-of-the-art facility features a five-story, 79-foot-diameter tilted dome theater. Surround yourself with sight, sound, and motion!

SUNSET DRIVE-IN
3935 West Dixon Blvd., Shelby
(704) 434-7782
Pile the kids in the car for first-run family comedies and action films that are often still out in regular theaters. At $7 per car, it's cheaper than one adult admission at the multiplex.

SHOPPING

Shoppers will discover an abundance of choices waiting in the Queen City. Visit outlet centers for name-brand clothing and shoes at discount prices. Browse specialty shops, upscale boutiques, and galleries for that one-of-a-kind item. Enjoy the best national retail stores at regional mega-malls. Choose fresh fruits and vegetables at Charlotte Regional Farmers Market or the Center City Green Market. Explore small towns for great buys on a variety of antiques. Find funky little shops, galleries, and restaurants in converted textile mills from South End to NoDa. There's something to suit every taste here.

Entries in this chapter are arranged alphabetically according to the size of the shopping experience, starting with the big malls and ending with small specialty shops. Listings are located in Charlotte unless otherwise noted.

SHOPPING MALLS

CAROLINA PLACE MALL
11025 Carolina Place Parkway, Pineville
(704) 542-4111
www.carolinaplace.com
Conveniently located near the I-485 outer belt, Carolina Place Mall is anchored by Dillard's, Macy's, Belk, JCPenney, and Sears. The mall's 130+ specialty stores fit its suburban surroundings, and while they aren't as uptown and high-profile as those at SouthPark Mall, they offer practicality rather than fantasy window-shopping. Notables include Buckle, Pacific Sunwear, Gap, Victoria's Secret, Abercrombie & Fitch, American Eagle, Hot Topic, Gymboree, the Disney Store, Cache, Express, Wet Seal, Kirkland's, and Sharon Luggage. When you tire of shopping, head to the food court or the children's play area on the lower level outside Sears. Free to the public, it includes a jungle gym, tunnels, climbing nets, and a ball chamber. The mall has plentiful parking, though traffic can be bad getting in and out. One fun perk: nightly indoor "snowfalls" in December.

CONCORD MILLS MALL
8111 Concord Mills Blvd., Concord
(704) 979-5000
www.concordmills.com

Located off I-85 at exit 49, and two miles from Charlotte Motor Speedway, Concord Mills features more than 200 manufacturer outlets, off-price retailers, and unique specialty shops designed in an oval racetrack layout. Since opening, it has surpassed even the Blue Ridge Parkway as the No. 1 tourist destination in the state.

Concord Mills has something for every interest. Deposit Dad at the mammoth Bass Pro Shops Outdoor World, where everything from boats to golf clubs are sold. Kids and preteens enjoy the Build-A-Bear Workshop store, where youngsters pick out a bear, help stuff it, choose its clothes and accessories, and register their new friend on the computer. Older teens can head to the 24-screen theater, large food court, or the very cool NASCAR SpeedPark, a racing theme park with several souped-up go-kart tracks and an arcade.

Wear your walking shoes and start early. There's a lot of ground to cover here: Off 5th Saks Fifth Avenue; Bed, Bath & Beyond; Burlington Coat Factory; TJ Maxx; and Books-A-Million for starters. Clotheshorses will enjoy Ann Taylor Loft, Gap Outlet, Polo Ralph Lauren, Tommy Hilfiger, Nautica, Brooks Brothers, Old Navy, Jones New York, the Limited, and Lane Bryant. Popular children's outlets include Carter's, Gymboree, The Children's Place, and Osh Kosh B'Gosh. Teens and 'tweens have Aeropostale, No Fear, and American Eagle Outfitters. Restaurants include Macado's, Chili's, California Pizza Kitchen, and more.

The success of Concord Mills and nearby Charlotte Motor Speedway has created a cluster of other retailers, restaurants, and hotels on both sides of I-85's exit 49, so there are plenty of places to stay and eat while you recharge your batteries and prepare for another round of shopping.

NORTHLAKE MALL
6801 Northlake Mall Dr.
I-77 at Exit 18
(704) 921-2000
www.shopnorthlake.com

Opened in September 2005, Northlake Mall includes 150 shops and a 14-screen movie theater at I-77 and Harris Boulevard, just north of Charlotte. The 1.1-million-square-foot shopping center, just under the size of Carolina Place in Pineville, caters to residents of northern Mecklenburg County. Many stores are major ones found at other Charlotte malls, but for folks who live in this area it saves a drive into the city or across the other side of Charlotte. Anchors include Belk, Dillard's, Macy's, Dick's Sporting Goods, and AMC Theatres. Teens will love Abercrombie & Fitch, Guess, PacSun, Express, and Hollister Co., while soccer moms can indulge at Coldwater Creek, Ann Taylor, Crabtree & Evelyn, Brighton Collectibles, Cache, Casual Corner, and Victoria's Secret. More unique offerings include L'Occitane en Provence, which carries bath, body, and fragrance products, and Z Gallerie, a more exotic version of Pottery Barn (there's one of those here, too). Valet parking, stroller rental, free wheelchair use, and a kids' indoor play area also are featured at Northlake. Another nice touch is free Wi-Fi in the center court and food court.

SOUTHPARK MALL
4400 Sharon Rd.
(704) 364-4411
www.southpark.com

SouthPark Mall, at the corner of Sharon and Fairview Roads about 15 minutes south of Uptown, has long been Charlotte's best-known and most upscale shopping experience. But when the city's first Nordstrom opened in 2004 in a new wing and Neiman Marcus followed in another new wing in 2006, it took SouthPark to another level, attracting other new upscale retailers and inspiring existing ones to get a facelift.

Nordstrom, known for its great customer service, top designer lines, and incredible shoe department, inspired 30 new retailers to move in, more than 40 percent of which are exclusive to the area. You'll now find Louis Vuitton, Burberry, Kate Spade, L'Occitane, Sur la Table, Tommy Bahama, Frontgate, Tumi, Apple Store, Pottery Barn Kids, Ann Taylor Loft, Anthropologie, Puma, Urban Outfitters, Teavana, Lindt Chocolate, Origins, and Coach. Several shops, including St. John, Carlyle & Co., Jessica McClintock, Chico's, and Rangoni of Florence, moved from other parts of the mall to the Nordie's wing.

Anchor stores at SouthPark also underwent massive renovations in anticipation of Nordstrom's arrival. Belk completed a $34-million expansion, including the addition of a parking deck. Macy's expanded its store by 60,000 square feet and added a furniture department in a $22-million renovation. Dillard's also underwent an expansion.

In addition, a new Sharon Road entrance to the mall was unveiled, with a 12,000-square-foot Cheesecake Factory and an equally big Italian family-style restaurant called Maggiano's Little Italy. Even SouthPark's food court got an overhaul.

In the Neiman Marcus wing, Ralph Lauren, BCBG Max Azria, Juicy Couture, Hermès, and Billy Reid set up shop. The city's first Crate & Barrel opened in the Village at SouthPark in late 2006.

Throughout SouthPark there's a mix of luxury and low-key. You'll find fine jewelry at Tiffany & Co. and Fink's; and everyday items at J. Jill, Coldwater Creek, White House/ Black Market, Guess, J. Crew, Abercrombie & Fitch, bebe, Brookstone, Pottery Barn, Banana Republic, Ann Taylor, the Limited, Express, Caswell Massey, Bath & Body Works, and Nine West.

Mall customers also enjoy concierge services, including executive services, gift wrap, local information, delivery, and special requests, along with valet service during the holidays. On Sun evenings in June, thousands of Charlotteans pack Symphony Park beside the mall for the Charlotte Symphony Orchestra's Summer Pops series.

Overstreet Mall

In the 1970s, Charlotte Chamber officials toured Minneapolis and liked that city's downtown "mall," created by using skywalks to connect second-floor retail areas of several major buildings. They copied that concept in Charlotte with the Overstreet Mall. This is Charlotte's "hidden" mall, spanning the second floors of buildings along Tryon and College Streets. Overstreet Mall has its fans and detractors. Downtown workers like it because they can get lunch or shop without having to go outside when it is cold, hot, or raining. Urban planners and Uptown boosters hate it because it reduces pedestrian traffic on sidewalks and is not visible to visitors. Overstreet Mall has fewer stores now than its heyday in the 1980s, and many of its businesses are eateries. However, it is a neat escape when in Uptown.

SHOPPING CENTERS

THE ARBORETUM
Providence Road at Highway 51
www.shoparboretum.com
South Charlotte's Arboretum is one of the busiest shopping centers in town with Wal-Mart; Michael's Arts & Crafts; Bed, Bath & Beyond; Gap; Stride Rite; Birkenstock; and a Harris Teeter grocery store. Boutiques such as Hand Picked, with

sterling silver and beaded jewelry; two children's clothing stores; and a nice lamp shop create a more interesting atmosphere than the standard chain offerings. On weekends this suburban center is an entertainment hub, with couples, families, and groups of friends headed to eat at Mickey & Mooch, New South Kitchen & Bar, and a breakfast joint called Le Peep. The Arboretum also has a 12-screen multiplex movie theater.

BIRKDALE VILLAGE
I-77 at Exit 25, Huntersville, Lake Norman
(704) 895-8744
www.birkdalevillage.net
A 52-acre pedestrian-friendly shopping center north of the city, Birkdale Village combines an old-fashioned Main Street design with modern, mixed-use aspects such as offices and apartments over the shops. The Nantucket-style village includes national chains such as Gap and Gap Kids, Dick's Sporting Goods, Chico's, Pier 1 Imports, Barnes & Noble, Williams Sonoma, White House/Black Market, Lane Bryant, Jones New York, Liz Claiborne Shoes, Ann Taylor Loft, Banana Republic, Talbot's, Bath and Body Works, Victoria's Secret, and Starbucks. Locally owned boutiques make an interesting mix. Poppies carries great stationery and gifts, while Belle Ville sells women's and men's European clothing. Madison's carries fine shoes, and Payton's Closet is a children's boutique. Maddi's Gallery, a great art and craft gallery in Dilworth, has a branch here.

A hub of weekend entertainment at the lake, Birkdale Village also has several good restaurants. You'll find steak and seafood at Dressler's, casual pub fare at Fox and Hound, quick Mexican at Qdoba, and frozen treats at Cold Stone Creamery. Red Rocks Cafe & Bakery, a great American restaurant serving lunch and dinner, often draws NASCAR drivers who live nearby. After dinner enjoy a glass of wine at Corkscrew wine bar or Total Wine & More, or head to the village movie theater. In the middle of the village square, kids can splash in the fountain, take in an outdoor concert, buy a Halloween pumpkin, or visit Santa.

CAROLINA PAVILION
South Boulevard at I-485, Pineville
Carolina Pavilion opened in 1997 on the northern edge of Pineville's retail development sprawl. Located at the intersection of I-485 and North Polk Street, it has remained popular even as other centers popped up at nearby Carolina Place Mall. Tenants include such discount giants as Target, Office Max, Marshall's, Best Buy, Michaels, Sports Authority, Babies 'R Us, hhgreg, Kohl's, Designer Shoe Warehouse, Old Navy, and Bed, Bath & Beyond, plus several fast-food restaurants.

COLONY PLACE
Colony Road and Rea Road
South Charlotte
This is a neighborhood-oriented shopping center with great restaurants, service businesses, and several unique stores. Harris Teeter and Walgreen's anchor the center, with restaurants such as Tomi and Caribou Coffee scattered throughout. The Mole Hole is a longtime Queen City gift shop that moved from the SouthPark area. Social Butterflies is a great place for party invitations, place cards, and other stationery.

COTSWOLD VILLAGE SHOPS
224 South Sharon Amity Rd.
(704) 364-5840
www.shopcotswold.com
Cotswold was built in 1963 as an enclosed mall with several large tenants. In the late 1990s a major renovation created a lovely courtyard with nice architecture, unique shops, outdoor dining, benches, and awnings. Cotswold is a great example of how an aging shopping center can be redeveloped into a vibrant place with a mix of chain retailers, service businesses, and locally owned shops. The center houses Stein Mart, Bath and Body Works, Old Navy, ULTA, Marshall's, David's Ltd., Rack Room Shoes, Merle Norman, Blockbuster Video, and Harris Teeter. Carmen Carmen Salon e' Spa, originally an upscale hair salon that expanded into a full-fledged day spa, is also located here. You can find unusual gifts at several unique shops, including Skillbeck Gallery, featuring handmade pottery and other art objects, and Ten Thousand Villages, with wares from around the world.

For a meal or a snack, try Atlanta Bread Company, Dairy Queen, Wolfman Pizza, Salsarita's, Mama Fu's, Bruegger's Bagels, Starbucks, or Charley's, a popular locally owned restaurant. Outdoor concerts, art demonstrations, and other cultural events are scheduled Fri evenings, May through Sept.

METROPOLITAN
1224 Metropolitan Ave.
(704) 295-7638
www.metmidtown.com
Metropolitan provides the best shopping option near Uptown. This mixed-use project combines retail, condos, lofts, and office space on the site of the old Midtown Square Mall, which was Charlotte's first enclosed mall. Shopping options include Target, Best Buy, Marshall's, Staples, West Elm, Trader Joe's, and Modern Salon & Spa. Developer Peter Pappas received a blow in 2009 when the Home Depot Design Center closed. It was one of the original anchors and had not been replaced as of early 2010. However, the Met has been a blessing for center city residents who have needed more retail for years. A neat aspect of this project is the involvement with the Little Sugar Creek Greenway. The greenway flows alongside the Metropolitan.

MORROCROFT VILLAGE
Colony Road at Sharon Road, SouthPark
Just a block away from SouthPark Mall, Morrocroft Village's redbrick exterior, domed architecture, Palladian windows, and nearby lake continue the area's upscale shopping atmosphere. Its Harris Teeter grocery store, which caters to owners of million-dollar homes in a gated community across the street, is known as the "Taj Ma Teeter" for its extensive wine collection, in-house florist, gourmet items, and self-serve restaurant. The village is full of fancy and clever boutiques and specialty stores such as Papitre, which has stationery and gifts; Jos. A. Banks Clothiers and Paul Simon for men's clothing; Lynda Reid for women's clothing; and Monkee's, which has a great selection of shoes and fun, funky purses. A two-story Borders Books & Music, with a gourmet coffee bar, and

Ruby Tuesday, a chain restaurant known for its wonderful salad bar, also are located here.

i There are people who say Charlotte's retail landscape forever changed when IKEA opened in 2008. This Swedish home furnishings chain has a cult-like following, and the Charlotte location is the only one in the Carolinas. IKEA's mammoth stores sell sleek and stylish furniture at reasonable prices. They are so big they have their own restaurant. Charlotte's location is off I-85 at exit 43. Just look for the line of cars.

NORTHCROSS
I-77 at Exit 25, Huntersville, Lake Norman

Often voted the best shopping center by readers of *Lake Norman Magazine*, NorthCross features more than 50 stores. Anchors include Target, Lowe's, Rack Room Shoes, Kohl's, Old Navy, and Omega Sports, but you'll also find more unusual offerings such as imported pottery and garden accessories at Uncommon Scents, and a pottery-painting studio called Meg-art. Mickey & Mooch is a popular restaurant for both Lake Norman residents and Charlotteans. After shopping, relax at the outdoor fountains, where musicians perform from 7 to 9 p.m. Fri and Sat from early May to early July.

PARK ROAD
4201 Park Rd.
(704) 523-2640
www.parkroadshoppingcenter.com

Charlotte's oldest shopping center is also one of its favorites, with a variety of food, service, and specialty shops. Harris Teeter, Rite Aid, Great Outdoor Provision Company, Michaels Crafts, Omega Sports, GNC, and a branch of the post office are located here. Catherine's Plus Sizes, Recycle Boutique, and Julie's offer women's clothing; Rack Room Shoes and Brownlee Jewelers may help complete the outfit. McCranie's Pipe Shop, Corners Framing, a Hallmark shop, toy store, bike shop, ski store, local music store, and musical instrument shop are a few of the other stores at

Park Road. Indie bookstore Park Road Books is an excellent source on a variety of subjects. At Blackhawk Hardware friendly handymen help with everything from cutting keys to choosing cabinet hardware. Park Road also has several restaurants, including casual fare at Charlotte Cafe and the Soda Shoppe, English pub food at Sir Edmond Halley's, bagels at Bruegger's, and Indian food at Situl.

PHILLIPS PLACE
Fairview Road, SouthPark
www.phillipsplace.info

The most upscale shopping center in Charlotte, Phillips Place on Fairview Road (down the street from SouthPark Mall) offers an eclectic mix of boutiques, high-end retail, restaurants, and entertainment. Plant your guy at noted clothier Taylor, Richards and Conger, then head across the way to Coplon's and Luna for designer clothing and accessories by Armani, Dolce & Gabbana, Thierry Mugler, Trish McElvoy, and Lulu Guinness. The Poole Shop and Civilian skew younger and a bit less pricey. Restoration Hardware carries furniture, accessories, and everything from drawer pulls to cool party CDs, while Bedside Manor offers fine European linens. The city's first Dean & Deluca is located here, along with a Dean & Deluca Wine Room and other top-notch restaurants such as Upstream, Palm, and P.F. Chang's. Orvis offers everything for today's outdoor adventurers, while Old Dog offers traditional clothing for men and women. Some of the city's biggest selections of Jimmy Choos, Manolos, and other top designer labels can be found at Bob Ellis (inside Coplon's) and at Via Veneto. Magic Windows offers special treats in children's clothing and accessories. A 10-screen stadium-seat movie theater and posh Hampton Inn & Suites also make their home at Phillips Place. In a new annex adjacent to Phillips Place, don't miss designer lines for special occasions at Nitsa's Apparel and fine art and crafts at Red Sky Gallery.

PROMENADE ON PROVIDENCE
Providence Road at I-485
www.promenadeonprovidence.com

One of south Charlotte's newer shopping centers, the Promenade's stores are designed with parking on both sides and pedestrian-friendly sidewalks in the inner courtyard. Stein Mart, Home Depot, Staples, and Ann Taylor Loft are the bigger chain stores. Boutiques include Belly Guru, with pre- and post-maternity wear; women's clothing and accessories at Ecco Couture; unique gifts and home furnishings at Go Fish; eclectic home and women's accessories at Sedona; and art at Stillwater Galleries. Arooji's Wine Room, Café Carolina & Bakery, Cold Stone Creamery, Sushi 101, and Wolfgang Puck Express are good places for a post-shopping snack or meal.

SHARON CORNERS
Fairview Road at Sharon Road, SouthPark
www.shopsharoncorners.com
Opposite SouthPark Mall, this shopping center has been redesigned into a two-story architectural blend of Georgian and Colonial Williamsburg with open walkways, plantation moldings, and cupolas. There are clothing options for the entire family, including women's boutique Chocolate Soup, Men's Wearhouse, Scarlett Plus-Size Boutique, Destination Maternity, and Shower Me With Love. For those who love the outdoors, you'll find a great selection at Jesse Brown's Outdoors, which carries first-rate equipment for fly fishing, camping, backpacking, and climbing. Footwear aficionados love Mephisto, a high-end European shoe store. After shopping grab a bite at the Original Pancake House, Harper's Restaurant, Baoding, or Moe's Southwest Grill.

SPECIALTY SHOPS ON THE PARK
6401 Morrison Blvd., SouthPark
Located directly across from SouthPark Mall, this unique shopping plaza offers an unusual blend of national and locally owned specialty shops. Here you'll find Talbot's, Mack and Mack, and Oilily for the latest in fashion apparel. Elizabeth Bruns offers exquisite jewelry and china, and Williams-Sonoma has a wonderful gourmet kitchenware selection. Nesting sells everything you need to create the baby room of your dreams. Specialty Shops also has a great day spa, Charles Grayson.

Fine dining choices include Café' Monte French Bakery & Bistro; Frank Manzetti's, a classic American grill; BrickTops, a sophisticated American bistro; and Toscana Ristorante Italiano.

STONECREST AT PIPER GLEN
I-485 and Rea Road
www.shopstonecrest.com
Located near the growing Ballantyne area and Piper Glen Country Club in south Charlotte, Stonecrest features the same style as Phillips Place near SouthPark and Birkdale Village at Lake Norman: a community gathering spot with fountains, live music, and a wide range of interesting boutiques and eateries. At Finee and Claire's you'll find cute casual clothing for women, while Reign Fine Apparel focuses on prom and evening gowns. Other great shops include Dewoolfsen Down for fine linens; Dilly Dally for children's furniture, linens, and gifts; educational toys at Learning Express; and Alcoves, a home-accessories market with many different vendors under one roof. Target, Regal Cinemas, and several upscale restaurants, from Spanish and Asian to American and Rocky Mountain fare, are also at Stonecrest.

UNIVERSITY PLACE
US 29 at W. T. Harris Boulevard
University Place near UNC Charlotte has been the nexus for retail and commercial development in the northeast area. Patterned after European villages, even down to the red tile roofs on the buildings, this shopping center is built around a small man-made lake. More than 80 stores are housed here, including Old Navy, Best Buy, TJ Maxx, OfficeMax, Michaels, Gap/Gap Kids, Pier 1, and Sam's Club. You can even ride a paddleboat on the 11-acre lake.

NEIGHBORHOOD RETAIL CENTERS

BALLANTYNE
South Charlotte used to mean SouthPark, but this growing planned community near the Union County line in southern Mecklenburg has recreated the definition. Twenty-five minutes from

Uptown, Ballantyne is a straight shot down Johnston Road, and also easily accessed via I-485. Ballantyne Hotel & Lodge and Ballantyne Country Club are anchors here, and the main shopping centers are Ballantyne Commons and Ballantyne Village. Restaurants include Providence Bistro, McAlister's Deli, Fox and Hound, Planet Noodle, Villa Antonio, Zappata's Mexican Cantina, the Wok, and Maggie Moo's ice cream. The centers offer mostly service businesses, such as Harris Teeter, Modern Nails, Blockbuster, and Wolf Camera, but there are a few shops such as Ballantyne Jewelers, the Crystal Shoppe, Miss Priss, and Ballantyne Silver & Gifts.

DILWORTH

Stretching from South Boulevard to Queens Road, the section of East Boulevard in the Dilworth neighborhood offers a varied shopping experience.

Near South Boulevard you'll find antiques and consignments shops, home accessories, a bakery, and several restaurants. Don't miss Paper Skyscraper, with its one-of-a-kind gifts, quirky cards, and interesting books.

Cottage Chic on East Boulevard has Kate Spade, Maine Cottage Furniture, Paper Denim, James Perse, Little Giraffe, SheShe Me, Lulu Guinness, Bella Notte, and BedHead.

At the intersection of Scott Avenue and East Boulevard is Dilworth Gardens, with a variety of specialty shops, Matrix Nails, and Outback Steakhouse. Across East Boulevard the Shops at Twin Oaks has fashion-forward clothing at Sloan and designer shoes at sister store Step by Sloan, beautiful lingerie at I.C. London, cosmetics at Potion, and fashionable eyewear at Sally's Optical Secrets. Stop for a salad or sandwich at Dikadee's Deli. Around the corner on Kenilworth Avenue, Hand Picked specializes in silver and beaded jewelry.

Newer additions to East Boulevard are Maddi's Gallery, which carries art and fine crafts by American artists from across the country. One of the best places to find a gift or to treat yourself, Maddi's has a friendly, helpful staff and a wide variety of price points and styles. Busbin Lamps next door is another locally owned place where you can purchase a lamp off the floor or bring in your own favorite object for a one-of-a-kind style.

Don't miss T. Reid and Company, a funky and fun salon set up in an old cozy home on East Boulevard. Take a minute before or after your hair or spa treatment to browse their delicate jewelry, tapestry travel bags, whimsical purses, precious baby clothes, and addictive beauty products.

MYERS PARK

Myers Park has always been a mecca of specialty shopping. Located along Providence Road are a number of specialty shops, services, and restaurants. Colony and Mecklenburg Furniture offer fine home furnishings; John Dabbs Ltd. and Details in Design have great gifts for friends or for yourself; the Golden Goose offers wonderful maternity and children's apparel; and The Buttercup is one of the best places in town to buy invitations and special gifts. Allen's Jewelers and Morrison Smith are top-notch jewelers on Providence Road. Fresh and Shelagh have hip, fashion-forward styles. Fancy Pants fills a niche with fine children's clothing from newborns to teens.

NODA

If suburbs, SUVs, and soccer moms make you cringe, try NoDa, one of the few funky enclaves in Charlotte and full of local shops, restaurants, and art galleries. Running along North Davidson Street at 36th Street, NoDa is built from an old textile-mill village, with shops in old homes and warehouses. Sunshine Daydreams is the place for vintage clothes, concert T-shirts, and funky jewelry. Lark & Key carries the works of independent artists and designers in a warm space, with pottery as well. Meow & Fetch caters to dog and cat lovers. Fabric Art prints original artwork or photography on silk scarves to upholstery. Herbal bath products, lotions, and handmade soaps are available at Everyday Essentials. The Boulevard at NoDa is a renovated century-old building that showcases a variety of independent retailers in a marketplace setting. The Boulevard includes such neat options as Primpy Princess Accessories and Black Dachshund Pottery. After shopping grab a bite at Revolution Pizza & Ale House, Cabo Fish

Taco, Boudreaux's Louisiana Kitchen, Crepe Cellar Kitchen & Pub, Salvador Deli, , Smelly Cat Coffee House, or Dog Bar, a pup-friendly pub. For details, visit www.noda.org.

CONSIGNMENT SHOPPING

CLASSIC ATTIC
Back Court, Park Road Shopping Center
(704) 521-3750
www.classicattic.biz
Bargain shop for consigned furniture, then rehab your discovery with new upholstery, bedding, and pillows from the Classic Attic's store-within-a-store called the Linen Closet.

CLEARING HOUSE
701 Central Ave.
(704) 375-7708
www.clearinghousesouth.com
Home furnishings and accessories, antiques, silver, and crystal are highlighted at this shop with an ever-changing inventory. Located in Charlotte's funky Plaza-Midwood neighborhood.

A CLOSET FULL
1729 Garden Terrace
(704) 372-5522
Located just off East Boulevard in Dilworth, A Closet Full is a consignment shop for plus-size women. The store carries only gently-used, upscale clothing, sizes 14W through 32W. It is a great place to find good quality dresses for social occasions.

CONSIGNMENT 1ST
10916 Independence Pointe Parkway, Matthews
(704) 847-2620
www.consignment1st.com
Since 1986, Consignment 1st has offered clothing for the entire family, baby equipment, furniture, and household items. In recent years, Consignment 1st has expanded to include 10 locations across the Southeast, including five in the greater Charlotte market. Other locations are Pineville, University City, Lake Norman, and Gastonia.

FINDERS' KEEPERS
10416 East Independent Blvd., Matthews
(704) 847-1672
Here you will find top-quality designer labels for ladies, including jeans, sportswear, career dresses, and suits, as well as manufacturers' samples and below-wholesale jewelry. You can also find a good selection of cocktail/evening wear and maternity clothes.

JLC WEARHOUSE
1117 Pecan Ave.
(704) 377-1854
www.jlcharlotte.org
This shop, which sells consignment, donated, and overstocked new items, is operated by the Junior League of Charlotte. The Junior League is a non-profit volunteer organization of women, many of whom are from the city's upper social circles. The JLC Wearhouse dates to 1936, and recently moved from its longtime location on Fourth Street to a nicer, larger facility on Pecan Avenue between the Chantilly and Plaza-Midwood neighborhoods. The store offers clothes and shoes for the entire family, as well as accessories and housewares.

RECYCLE BOUTIQUE
4301 Park Rd.
(704) 527-2211
www.recycle-boutique.com
Located in the Park Road Shopping Center, this is a great upscale option for consignment shoppers. The store specializes in brands from boutiques and better department stores. Recycle Boutique only accepts clothes that have been purchased in the last two years and are in like-new condition from a smoke-free environment.

SWEET REPEATS
300 East Blvd.
(704) 372-0002
www.sweetrepeatsboutique.com
This consignment shop features expensive designer clothing, such as Carlisle, Escada, Dana Buchman, and Doncaster. Shoes and accessories are also available.

VERY TERRY CONTEMPORARY CONSIGNMENTS

310 East Blvd.
(704) 375-0655
www.shopveryterry.com
Organized by color, this hip Dilworth shop carries only natural fibers such as silk, cotton, linen, and wool—nothing from the sisters Poly and Ester. Very Terry has been named the Best Bargain Shopping in the city by two Charlotte magazines.

OUTLET SHOPPING

J-R CIGAR
1515 East Broad St., Statesville
(704) 872-5300
www.jrstatesville.com
You can get more than just cigars at J-R, although it bills itself as "the world's largest cigar store." There are cigars from every corner of the world, and most every manufacturer known to man. However, if you're not interested in tobacco, this massive place also serves as an outlet for apparel, beauty and fragrance, books, household items, shoes, and toys. J-R is located just off I-77 and you won't miss it because they have more billboards per mile than probably any other business in North Carolina.

ANTIQUES

Antiques abound in Charlotte and in the surrounding areas. You can search the Internet, check the local Yellow Pages, or pick up a copy of the *Antique and Gift Guide for North Carolina,* (336) 292–5870, available at most antiques shops.

ANTIQUES SHOPS OF MYERS PARK
Selwyn Avenue and Providence Road
Charlotte's first suburb naturally has some of its best antiques. Start on Selwyn Avenue near Runnymeade at the Plantation Shop, Heritage Antiques, Sterling Manor, and Antiques on Selwyn, the last of which features a great inventory with great prices. When Selwyn turns into Providence Road past Queen's University, look for Windwood Antiques, with its great selection

of majolica and wide range of price points, and for Circa, which has a full-service design division and to-the-trade lines such as Nina Campbell. Acquisitions, close to CPCC, carries French country designs, upholstery and leather, and many home accessories.

ANTIQUES SHOPS OF PINEVILLE
Main Street, Pineville
South of Charlotte, a variety of antiques shops offer early American, English, and continental furniture; old books; antique linens; Persian rugs; and much more.

ANTIQUES SHOPS OF SOUTH END
South Boulevard
Hidden in old cotton mills and exposed-brick warehouses along South Boulevard just off Uptown are several antiques shops. Wander through Crossland in the heart of South End for old fireplaces, doors, iron gates, and other architectural antiques. Interiors Marketplace has 80 vendors selling antiques and home accessories in individually stocked rooms. On Worthington Avenue off South Boulevard, Dilworth Antique Lighting carries beautiful old fixtures that add character and grace to homes of any age. Englishman's, moving along South Boulevard away from Uptown, features a huge selection of antiques, reproductions, and estate pieces.

i Saturday mornings are the busiest times in the Charlotte region for garage and attic clearances local folks call "yard sales." The *Charlotte Observer* lists yard sales a few days prior and on Sat; many families also tack up signs. Most sales begin around 7 a.m., but expect to see early birds with flashlights rooting through the merchandise before the sun comes up.

ANTIQUES SHOPS OF WAXHAW
Providence Road, Highway 16
This turn-of-the-20th-century town is an antiques lover's paradise, with numerous shops filled with antiques and collectibles.

BY-GONE DAYS ANTIQUES
114-T Freeland Lane
(704) 527-8717
If you are considering remodeling, this shop, a block off South Boulevard near South End, specializes in architectural antiques.

CHARLOTTE ANTIQUES & COLLECTIBLES SHOW
7100 North Statesville Rd.
Metrolina Expo
(704) 596-4643
www.dmgantiqueshows.com
One of the largest collections of furniture, home accessories, estate jewelry, vintage clothing, and other collectibles are for sale the first weekend of each month at the Metrolina Expo. Special shows are held at various times throughout the year. Call for show dates.

BOOKSTORES

Yes, we have those ubiquitous mega-stores like Barnes & Noble, Books-A-Million, Borders, and Waldenbooks, but you don't need a guide to find those. Instead, we focus on niche places and off-the-beaten-path stores that provide a more fulfilling experience.

AUDIO BOOKS OF THE CAROLINAS
Rea Road at I-485, Stonecrest
(704) 341-0794
www.audiobooksnc.com
This store rents and sells audio books on a wide range of topics. Customers can visit the store or go online to browse among 10,000+ titles. Categories include mystery, classics, history, personal growth, humor, business, sports, biography, and kids' books. You can pick up or drop off books at conveniently located centers across the city.

BLACK FOREST BOOKS & TOYS
115 Cherokee Rd.
(704) 332-4838
www.blackforestbooksandtoys.com

Personalized attention and a good selection of both books and toys for children are hallmarks of this family-owned shop opened in 1978.

THE BOOK RACK
8326 Pineville-Matthews Rd.
(704) 544-8006
www.thebookrack.com
The Book Rack has thousands of used paperbacks at half price, and used hardcovers at paperback prices. It also sells new paperbacks for 20 percent off and rents new hardcovers for two weeks for $3. Trade your gently used paperbacks for credit. Additional location in Gastonia.

THE BOOKMARK
Uptown in Founders Hall
(704) 377-2565
www.thebookmark.biz
Uptown's only bookstore, the Bookmark offers best sellers, hardbacks, paperbacks, and audio books and will search for out-of-print or hard-to-find titles. Special orders and gift certificates are available. The Bookmark has been in business for nearly two decades and carries more than 20,000 titles. The store is located in Founder's Hall in the Bank of America Corporate Center. Park in the building's parking deck and they will validate your parking ticket for up to two free hours.

GRAY'S COLLEGE BOOKSTORES
9430 University City Blvd.
(704) 548-8100
www.graysbooks.com
Gray's specializes in college, medical, nursing, and allied health publications.

JOSEPH-BETH BOOKSELLERS
4345 Barclay Downs, SouthPark
(704) 602-9800
www.josephbeth.com
Joseph-Beth is a small chain of large bookstores. The Charlotte location at SouthPark is one of five in a chain based in Lexington, Ky. The stores are upscale and a bit pricy, but worth it. The children's section is a real treat. Best sellers and staff picks are listed on the Web site, and there's a discount for teachers.

LIFEWAY CHRISTIAN STORES
3 locations in the Charlotte area
www.lifewaystores.com
LifeWay carries religious books, Bibles, and reading material for children at three area locations: 10412 Centrum Parkway across from Carolina Place Mall in Pineville, (704) 541-5033; 8821 J. W. Clay Blvd. in the University area, (704) 503-5012; and Franklin Square in Gastonia, (704) 823-8200.

PARK ROAD BOOKS
Park Road Shopping Center
(704) 525-9239
www.parkroadbooks.com
An independent bookstore, Park Road has been a favorite among local bookworms for years, thanks in large part to its helpful service, special orders, convenient location, and book signings with top authors.

UNITY BOOKSTORE
401 East Arrowood Rd.
(704) 523-0062
www.unityofcharlotte.org.
For those with a metaphysical and/or turn of mind, check out Unity Bookstore.

WHITE RABBIT BOOKS & THINGS
920 Central Ave.
(704) 377-4067
www.whiterabbitbooks.com
White Rabbit is Charlotte's main gay and lesbian bookstore, with cards, magazines, music, videos, and gifts.

CLOTHING AND SHOES

We can hardly scratch the surface of great specialty shops and boutiques around town, so we will have to settle for mentioning those that are either institutions in Charlotte or special places we are admittedly subjective about.

B NATURAL
5341 Ballantyne Commons Parkway
(704) 847-3557
www.bnaturalclothing.com

Need relief from Charlotte's hot, humid summers? Head to B Natural, with its casual, contemporary, and comfortable clothing made from natural fibers such as cotton and linen. You'll find a wide selection of embroidered T-shirts, cute beach dresses, washable linen, and fun accessories.

BEAUX BELLY
6401 Morrison Blvd., SouthPark
(704) 366-9007
www.beauxbelly.com
Clothes so cute, you'll wish you were pregnant. This trendy maternity store stocks fashionable frocks that will keep you looking stylish throughout your pregnancy. Cool halter tops and slip dresses, flared-leg jeans, and great bags in a style similar to Kate Hudson and Courteney Cox.

BELLE VILLE
Birkdale Village, Huntersville
(704) 655-9506

EpiCentre, Uptown
(704) 971-7413

The Promenade, Ballantyne
(704) 847-5352
www.lovemybelleville.com
Cutting-edge and contemporary designer T-shirts and jeans, with lines mostly from Paris, Milan, and Belgium. Flirty, fun, and affordable, these European styles cater to the slim and trim, but great handbags, jewelry, and accessories offer something for every figure. The best part? You don't have to drive to the other side of town to find one near you.

COPLON'S
6800 Phillips Place Court
(704) 643-1113
www.coplons.com
Coplon's is known for carrying luxurious designer labels such as Alice + Olivia, Burberry, Valentino, Dolce & Gabbana, Pucci, and Roberto Cavalli, as well as accessories such as Trish McEvoy makeup and Lulu Guinness handbags. Go in for friendly service, or admire through the window while waiting for dinner at Phillips Place.

Insider Top 5: Queen City Shops

Charlotte native and Miss USA 2005 Chelsea Cooley Altman knows about shopping and style. So we asked the Independence High grad and Charlotte Insider to rate her top five Queen City shopping options. Although she's busy these days running StandOut Productions, a premier image consulting and life coaching company (www.standoutproductions.net), and has a burgeoning family, she graciously took time to divulge her fab five:

1. **Lotus**—This is a great place to shop with a lot of fun pieces. You can always find something to wear at Lotus.

2. **Nordstrom's shoe department**— The selection is fabulous. As every woman will attest, you can find what you are looking for, and even what you're not looking for.

3. **WinkBaby.net**—This online boutique is based in Charlotte and has the cutest accessories for moms and babies. You can buy everything you need as a new mom, and it's a great source when you need a gift for a new mom.

4. **Luna**—Located at Phillips Place, Luna offers a lot of fun dresses, my favorite designer jeans, and all the classic staples for your wardrobe.

5. **T.J. Maxx**—I am a T.J. Maxx junkie! You have to be in the mood for a good one to two hours of shopping, but you can find everything from Calvin Klein to Michael Kors. Discover things at every price point to develop your own sense of style.

FAIRCLOUGH & CO. INC.
102 Middleton Dr.
(704) 331-0001
www.faircloughonline.com
One of the finest men's clothing stores in the city, Fairclough offers tailored classics and exquisite styles and fabrics, from formal to casual. Service is its special strength, from helpful advice to coordinating an entire wardrobe.

JORDANO'S
Stonecrest Shopping Center
8440 Rea Rd. at I-485
(704) 543-8800
www.shopjordanos.com
A surprisingly hip find in the suburban world of SUVs and soccer games, this cool boutique carries women's and men's funky styles by Betsey Johnson, Kenneth Cole, Paper Denim, Cloth, and Policy.

LEBO'S
7300 East Independence Blvd.
(704) 563-0500
www.lebos.com
The flagship store is located on Independence Boulevard, and there are also locations in Pineville, Concord, Monroe, Gastonia, and Rock Hill. Lebo's has been a purveyor of country and western wear since 1923. It also offers all types of dance wear, fitness clothing, English and Western riding wear, and footwear in hard-to-find sizes. The place to go to find a great Texas two-stepping outfit, buy cool boots, or purchase a cowboy hat. No time to visit? Check out Lebo's extensive Web site.

LUNA
Phillips Place, Fairview Road
(704) 554-6000
www.shopluna.com
Fun, yet sophisticated, with lines such as Theory, BCBG, Nanette Lepore, Seven Jeans, Ruth and Robin Jordan, and Rhonda Colley jewelry. The boutique is located in Phillips Place, which makes a great girls'-day outing with unique shops, lunch at the Palm, a glass of wine at Dean & DeLuca, and a chick flick at the movies.

MONKEE'S
3900 Colony Rd., Morrocroft Village
(704) 442-7337
www.shopmonkees.com
One of the hottest shoe stores in town, Monkee's carries trendy footwear by designers such as Donald Pliner, Kate Spade, Stuart Weitzman, Armand Basi, Isaac Mizrahi, Anne Klein, Via Spiga, and Cole Haan. Funky handbags in beaded styles and unusual fabrics are also sold, along with hats, gifts, and accessories. Did we mention they have designer clothing, too? A second location has been added in Davidson.

NITSA'S
4705 Savings Place, Phillips Place
(704) 940-1999
Located in Phillips Place in the SouthPark area, Nitsa's is the place to go for the perfect party dress, whether it's a garden-soiree sundress or a couture wedding gown. One of the few places in town to find lines such as Vera Wang and Amsale.

OFF BROADWAY SHOE WAREHOUSE
2408 South Blvd.
(704) 523-4480
www.offbroadwayshoes.com
Off Broadway Shoes started as a three-day-a-week warehouse in 1989 in Nashville, Tenn. Charlotte's location debuted a couple of years later on South Boulevard in South End with a huge selection of more than 25,000 pairs of women's and men's designer shoes at discount prices. Its popularity has led to three more locations in Charlotte, and another store at Concord Mills, plus more than 50 stores nationwide.

OUR PLACE
4732 Sharon Rd.
Sharon Corners
(704) 554-7748
www.our-place.us
While the salespeople put together a stunning outfit, including accessories and jewelry, you can have a cup of coffee or a glass of wine and a snack. You'll feel pampered and have fun with the experience. Located in the Allen Tate Building at Phillips Place.

PAUL SIMON FOR MEN
1027 Providence Rd.
(704) 372-6842

4300 Sharon Rd., SouthPark
(704) 366-4523
www.paulsimonco.com
Superior service and fine clothing have made Paul Simon the go-to shop for custom clothing and shirts, formalwear, and fashion by Burberry, Ermenegildo Zegna, Hickey Freeman, and Zanella. Quiet and comfortable with a helpful, knowledgeable staff.

PAUL SIMON FOR WOMEN
1033 Providence Rd.
(704) 333-6139
www.paulsimonco.com
For classic women's clothing and fabulous accessories, from casual day wear to professional, this shop has it all—and in lots of sizes. Free basic alterations.

THE POOLE SHOP
4010 Sharon Rd.
(704) 366-0388
www.pooleshop.com
Owned by local fashionista and Capitol owner Laura Vinroot Poole, this boutique offers designer duds in a more moderate price range. Look for lines such as Marc by Marc Jacobs, Milly, and Swimsuits by Shoshanna.

RAHE LYNNE CLOTHIER
2116 Hawkins St., Ste. 650, South End
(704) 334-5180
www.rahelynne.com
No time to shop? This by-appointment-only boutique will work around your schedule, with one-on-one service and classic lines such as Trixi Schober, Lafayette 148, Annette Gortz, and Raffinalla.

SLOAN & STEP BY SLOAN
Twin Oaks, 1419 East Blvd.
(704) 338-1400
www.shopatsloan.com
www.stepbysloan.com

These sister boutiques—one for clothing and one for shoes and bags—overlook Dilworth's trendy East Boulevard. Sloan was the first to arrive, with lines such as Vivienne Tam, Betsey Johnson, ABS, Nanette Lepore, Theory, Cambio, Jill Stuart Jeans, and Spanx hosiery. Step by Sloan, where Daniel "Shoe Man Dan" Mauney is the go-to guy, is a great in-town find, with designer shoes by Michael Kors, Marc Jacobs, Claudia Cuitti, and Christian Lacroix.

TAYLOR RICHARDS & CONGER
Phillips Place, SouthPark
(704) 366-9092
www.trcstyle.com
Often voted the best men's clothing store in Charlotte, this shop offers elegant lines and classic European cuts. From jackets and fun wear to heavenly ties, formal wear, and suits, this store is a treat. It also features an intimate shoe salon, cherry-paneled study for customized clothing, a rustic sportswear shop, and a coffee bar. TRC-W, a new division, carries high-end women's clothing.

VIA VENETO
Phillips Place, Fairview Road
(704) 556-0710
Named for the most fashionable boutique-lined street in Rome, Via Veneto is known for its fine Italian shoes and accessories for men and women. The Phillips Place corner store carries designer brands such as Jimmy Choo and Guiseppe Zanotti. A great place to window-shop, it also features friendly service and surprisingly affordable sales. Via Veneto recently added men's and women's clothing as well.

Children's Clothing
CHOCOLATE SOUP
Sharon Corners
(704) 556-0889
This private-label clothing handmade in Missouri is known for its colorful, vibrant, and whimsical designs, and you won't find it anywhere else in Charlotte but at the SouthPark-area store. Choco-

late Soup carries girls' styles from infant to size 14 and boys' styles from infant to size 7.

FANCY PANTS
1025 Providence Rd.
(704) 344-0333
www.fancypantschildren.com
This children's boutique has full lines of fine children's clothing from newborn to teen, including an extensive boys' department. You can buy everything from classy to casual from more than 200 of the top American and European designers.

OILILY
Specialty Shops on The Park
6401 Morrison Blvd.
(704) 366-6111
www.oililyusa.com
The only Oilily shop in the Carolinas, this Netherlands-based boutique carries high-end clothing and accessories from newborn to size 12, as well as styles for women. Bright, fun, and funky, Oilily designs incorporate interesting pattern combinations, vibrant colors, and a lot of texture through beads, sequins, and felt appliqués. The SouthPark-area shop also is known for its scents, lip balms, and other cosmetics that have been featured in *Cosmopolitan, Vogue,* and *Elle*.

PAYTON'S CLOSET
16835 Birkdale Commons Parkway
(704) 987-2100
www.paytonscloset.com
This children's boutique carries designer girls' and boys' apparel, as well as baby items and monogramming services.

Fabric
MARY JO'S CLOTH STORE
401 Cox Rd., Gastonia
(704) 861-9100
www.maryjos.com
Located in the Gaston Mall, Mary Jo's has fabric for all your sewing needs, but is especially well-known for upholstery and drapery fabric. For more than 50 years, the cavernous store with a

helpful staff has sold items to brides, designers, pageant contestants, athletes' tailors, and performers from around the world.

FOOD SHOPS AND FARMERS' MARKETS

ARTHUR'S
Belk, SouthPark Mall
(704) 366-8610
www.arthurs-wine.com
This gourmet food shop with gifts, coffees, teas, baskets, chocolates, candies, and baked goods also has an award-winning wine selection and a great restaurant. Founded in 1972, the shop is neatly tucked away on Belk's first level and features a complete selection of California and imported wines, along with one of Charlotte's largest wine bars.

CENTER CITY GREEN MARKET
Trade and Tryon, The Square
(704) 332-2227
www.charlottecentercity.org
Started in 1998 to generate weekend traffic Uptown, the Center City Green Market has been a huge success with folks from all over the city. The open-air market is held from 8 a.m. to 1 p.m. Sat from mid-May through late Oct. A scaled-down version of the market is available weekdays during that same time period. Stroll through Uptown's skyscrapers and cultural attractions to buy fresh fruit and vegetables, just-out-of-the-oven bread, pastries, seafood, cut flowers and garden plants, ready-to-eat meals, and local arts and crafts.

CHARLOTTE REGIONAL FARMERS MARKET
1715 Yorkmont Rd.
(704) 357-1269
www.ncagr.com
Open year round, this is the largest farmers' market in the county, and most Saturdays it takes on the atmosphere of a friendly country fair. In the past few years, savvy farmers have branched out to include many items you'd find in the grocery store, such as bananas and pineapples, and the

bouquets of farm-grown flowers have almost been nosed out by local area nurseries that bring truckloads of plants and shrubs. On the whole, shopping at farmers' markets is a bit less expensive and a lot more fun. You'll get to know regular craftspeople, plus find a revolving number of new ones each time you visit. This market, operated by the N.C. Department of Agriculture, is open from 8 a.m. until 6 p.m. Tues through Sat from March through Sept, and 8 a.m. until 5 p.m. Oct through Feb. It's also open Sun, May through Aug from 12:30 to 6 p.m.

DEAN & DELUCA
Phillips Place, Fairview Road
(704) 643-6868

Phillips Place Wine Room
(704) 552-5283

201 South Tryon St., Uptown
(704) 377-0037

7804 Rea Rd., Stonecrest
(704) 541-7123
www.deananddeluca.com
Grab coffee and a danish; take lunch to go; relax on the outdoor patio with wine, cheese, and baguettes; or pick up an after-dinner dessert at this gourmet market with three locations, plus a wine room. Hot take-out meals, specialty meats, a salad bar, made-to-order sandwiches, and hard-to-find items from French soda to Italian gelato are also available.

FRESH MARKET
Strawberry Hill Shopping Center
4223 Providence Rd.
(704) 365-6659

7625 Pineville-Matthews Rd.
(704) 541-1882

20623 Torrence Chapel Rd., Cornelius
(704) 892-8802
www.thefreshmarket.net
A neighborhood specialty grocer, each store is filled with the sights and aromas of fresh vegetables, freshly ground coffee, cheeses, an

old-fashioned butcher's shop, fresh seafood, a bakery, wine, and all sorts of unusual items for the gourmet. Customers also can shop online or through a catalog.

HEALTHY HOME MARKET
5410 East Independence Blvd.
(704) 536-4663

2707 South Blvd.
(704) 522-8123

261 Griffith St., Davidson
(704) 892-6191
www.hemarket.com
This store has hundreds of foods that you can buy by the ounce or by the pound. It also sells natural foods, natural personal-care products, vitamins, wines, herbal teas, gourmet coffees, baking supplies, and more. The store offers a full-service deli featuring homemade soups, sandwiches, and salads.

KINGS DRIVE FARMERS MARKET
Corner of Kings Drive and Morehead
(704) 392-5948
Open Tues, Fri, and Sat from 7 a.m. to 3 p.m. This is a great option just outside the downtown area. Farmers and produce companies, mostly from nearby Union County, offer big fresh tomatoes, corn on the cob still in the husks, cucumbers, squash, zucchini, and other vegetables, as well as apples, grapes, blueberries, strawberries, and watermelons. A great place to pick up a fall pumpkin, too.

REID'S FINE FOODS
225 East Sixth St., Uptown
(704) 377-1312
www.reids.com
Since 1928 Reid's Fine Foods has offered gourmet groceries, the freshest cuts of meat, fine wine, and gifts in Charlotte. After many years in Myers Park, Reid's moved Uptown to Seventh Street Station and closed its original location. You'll find a butcher shop, bakery, coffee shop, hot lunch station, sushi bar, Boar's Head deli, cheeses from

around the world, and impressive gift baskets. Take-home meals and dine-in tables also are available, along with cooking classes, a wine club, and catering services. Reid's Wine Bar offers tastings from 5:30 to 7:30 p.m. each Wed. Online ordering and delivery and UPS shipping are other convenient services, but the quality inventory and helpful staff warrant merit on their own.

TRADER JOE'S
1133 Metropolitan Ave.
(704) 334-0737

1820 East Arbors Dr.
(704) 688-9578

6418 Rea Rd.
(704) 543-5249
www.traderjoes.com
People in Charlotte were all a dither over Trader Joe's coming to the Queen City. The stores are kind of weird, not really designed in a typical fashion and the selection of products is all over the map, but that's part of the charm. Don't expect to do all your food shopping here, but it's a great place to pick up organics and unique items, and the prices are reasonable.

GIFTS AND STATIONERY

E-mail may have made longhand letter-writing more rare, but fine stationery will always be popular with the fashionable crowd. Here's a look at the Queen City's wonderful paper stores, many of which also carry an outstanding gift selection.

THE BUTTERCUP
343 Providence Rd.
(704) 332-5329
This shop offers a wonderful selection of all types of paper goods and distinctive gifts. You'll find unique items for entertaining; for birthday, baby, anniversary, or graduation gifts; and for those little touches that make a house a home. The entire upstairs is devoted to stationery supplies, with hundreds of invitations and announcements for all occasions.

Specialty Food Stores

International specialty food stores have become very popular. Check out the following:

- **Parthenon Gift and Gourmet Shop,** 4328 Central Ave., (704) 568-5262
- **Oriental Foods,** 4816-B Central Ave., (704) 537-4281
- **Middle East Deli,** 4508 East Independence Blvd., (704) 536-9847
- **Las Dos Rosas Mexican Food Market,** 7015 South Blvd., (704) 554-9902
- **Payal Indian Groceries & Spices,** 6400 Old Pineville Rd., (704) 521-9680
- **Ferrucci's Old Tyme Italian Market,** exit 28 off I-77, Cornelius, (704) 896-3190, www.ferruccis.com
- **Pasta & Provisions,** 1528 Providence Rd., (704) 364-2622, www.pastaprovisions.com.
- **World Market,** 9557 South Blvd. in Carolina Pavilion, (704) 554-1692; 8104 University City Blvd. in Target Plaza, (704) 597-7717; Sycamore Commons, Matthews, (704) 849-2004; www.WorldMarket.com

PAPER SKYSCRAPER
330 East Blvd.
(704) 333-7130
www.paperskyscraper.com
Stop in on your way to a party for everything from the card to the hostess gift to the wrapping paper at this eclectic shop in Dilworth. A longtime favorite of hip Charlotteans, Paper Skyscraper carries a great selection of irreverent, laugh-out-loud, and alternative cards. It has stationery, journals, notebooks, and calendars, but it isn't your mother's Hallmark. There's also a noteworthy book section with many coffee-table editions on photography, art, and architecture, as well as funky candles, bath products, frames, toys, home accessories, and gag gifts.

PAPITRE AT MORROCROFT VILLAGE
3908 Colony Rd.
(704) 364-4567
This south Charlotte stationery store carries a wide variety of in-stock invitations and can even perform the miracle of 24-hour turnaround when needed.

HARDWARE

BLACKHAWK HARDWARE
4225 Park Rd.

Park Road Shopping Center
(704) 525-2682
www.blackhawkhardware.com
One of Charlotte's true treasures lies within Blackhawk Hardware, an old-fashioned hardware store crammed with quality tools, household items, gardening supplies, kitchen wares, paint, laugh-out-loud greeting cards, birdhouses, planters, and home accessories. If you're remodeling, building a home, or looking for a quick project, Blackhawk also has one of the biggest selections of cabinet hardware, house numbers, and door hardware in town. Plenty of helpful, friendly handymen offer grandfatherly advice, and the first thing you smell as you enter is freshly popped corn in the machine at the registers. This has been a Charlotte institution since 1977, and don't miss the garden center just a few doors down from the hardware store.

HOME FURNISHINGS

North Carolina is home to just about every major furniture manufacturer in the country. Here are just a few of the large variety of home furnishings and accessories stores and numerous professionals to help you put it all together.

BLACKLION
10605 Park Rd.
(704) 541-1148

9751 Sam Furr Rd., Huntersville
(704) 892-9011
www.blacklion.com
Individually stocked and decorated show spaces at BlackLion's two locations feature antiques, artwork, lamps, rugs, furniture, home accessories, gifts, and Christmas ornaments. Consider this your central location for home furnishings and gifts. A great rainy-day retreat.

BOYLES FURNITURE
11410 Carolina Place Parkway, Pineville
(704) 542-4770
www.boyles.com
Boyles offers discounts of 40 to 50 percent below retail on famous-name manufacturers. The store showcases premier furniture lines such as Henkel Harris and Lexington Home Brands.

BY DESIGN
2130 South Blvd.
(704) 342-4600

11501 Carolina Place Parkway, Pineville
(704) 542-8803
www.bydesignfurniture.com
Thinking about updating your furnishings or bedroom set? By Design is a worthy choice. The stores offer sensible, contemporary furniture with an emphasis on European design. Neat furniture options are available for every room in the house, including the home office, which is important in the age of telecommuting.

COLONY FURNITURE
811 Providence Rd.
(704) 333-8871
www.shopcolonyfurniture.com
The area's oldest complete interior design show-room features distinctive furnishings, period antiques, and handmade rugs. Located in the heart of Myers Park, the store was open week-days only for several years before finally adding Sat hours from 11 a.m. to 3 p.m. Also open by

special appointment. Interior design by ASID-level designers and white-glove delivery are complimentary.

LEE LIGHTING
11600 Carolina Place Parkway, Pineville
(704) 540-5878
www.leelighting.com
Lee Lighting offers a wide selection of lighting fixtures and other related products. Trained con-sultants are available to assist in the showroom or at your home.

METRO
911 East Morehead St.
(704) 375-4563
www.metroformodern.com
Contemporary and unusual home furnishings and accessories, including Versace and Calvin Klein china, ultracool lighting, and hundreds of hard-to-find fabrics. Free gift wrapping.

PERSIAN RUG HOUSE
312 Main St., Pineville
(704) 889-2454
www.persianrughouse.com
The Persian Rug House has the largest selection of Persian rugs in the area. In business since 1986, it buys and trades old rugs and provides professional cleaning, repair, appraisal, pickup, and delivery.

POST & GRAY
2139 South Tryon St.
(704) 332-2252
www.postandgray.com
Located in South End, Post & Gray features over 35 merchants in 8,000 square feet of space. Shop-pers can browse most anything home-related, including art, antiques, fine linens, furniture, light-ing, and accessories from around the world.

JEWELRY

Southern women love their jewelry, and Charlotte doesn't disappoint when it comes to upscale jewelers. Many jewelers are concentrated around

SouthPark Mall, where some of the Queen City's most affluent residents live and shop.

DONALD HAACK DIAMONDS
4611 Sharon Rd.
(704) 365-4400
www.donaldhaack.com

Owner Donald Haack once managed a diamond mining company in South America and has been involved in all phases of cutting, design, and jewelry manufacturing since 1954. His store maintains one of the largest diamond inventories in the Southeast and has an international reputation for dealing in quality gems. When looking for that perfect stone, this is the place to go.

FINK'S JEWELERS
SouthPark Mall
(704) 366-3120

Northlake Mall
(704) 927-4888
www.finks.com

Formerly Garibaldi & Bruns, Fink's is a longtime favorite of many Charlotteans. Fink's has two Charlotte locations and carries famous names such as Rolex, David Yurman, John Hardy, Di Modolo, Breitling, Cartier, and Tag Heuer. As a member of the American Gem Society, Fink's is required to meet strict guidelines on quality, customer service, and business ethics. It shows through helpful and courteous salespeople, who never forget the names of their repeat customers.

PERRY'S AT SOUTHPARK
SouthPark Mall
(704) 364-1391
www.perrysjewelry.com

Perry's is one of Charlotte's finest and most unusual jewelry stores. A specialist in fine, antique, and estate jewelry, it can buy, sell on consignment, trade, or repair your family treasures. Jewelry ranges from modern David Yurman to 1800s estate pieces.

TIFFANY AND CO.
SouthPark Mall
(704) 365-7773
www.tiffany.com

Simply wrapped in a little light blue box, gifts from Tiffany and Co. seem extra-special. The famous New York City–based jeweler opened in Charlotte a few years ago, and for shopping fanatics, the debut catapulted the Queen City's reputation as an upscale destination. Tiffany does have jaw-dropping jewels, but in truth, you can also find reasonably priced gifts, china, and other baubles. The SouthPark location is the jeweler's only North Carolina store.

ATTRACTIONS

Like any large metropolitan region, Charlotte offers its fair share of attractions. For years, folks from around the region have flocked to Paramount's Carowinds, the 112-acre theme park that straddles the state line just south of town. Discovery Place, a hands-on science and nature museum, has been a popular draw in Uptown, and a recent renovation only added to its luster. Most school children who grew up within a 100-mile radius of the Queen City took a field trip to Discovery Place at one time or another. Nowadays, Discovery Place has been joined in the center city by the Bechtler Museum of Modern Art, the new Mint Museum Uptown, Harvey B. Gantt Center for African-American Arts + Culture and the city's 19,000-seat multi-purpose arena—Time Warner Cable Arena.

NASCAR fans have made pilgrimages to Charlotte for decades for races at Charlotte Motor Speedway and to visit race team shops in the northern suburbs. Now, the $195 million NASCAR Hall of Fame gives fans another reason to come to the Queen City, while giving Uptown a signature attraction.

History buffs like to check out such spots as the Reed Gold Mine in nearby Cabarrus County, the James K. Polk birthplace in Pineville and the Charlotte Museum of History/Hezekiah Alexander Homesite.

Three newer attractions that are unique are the Billy Graham Library, honoring the longtime evangelist; the U.S. National Whitewater Center, the largest man-made whitewater river in the world; and the Daniel Stowe Botanical Garden in Belmont, named one of the nation's Top 20 gardens by HGTV.

With such a wide variety of year-round and seasonal attractions, all you have to do is decide whether you want to be a participant or a spectator. Additional suggestions on things to do and places to visit in the Metrolina area are given in our chapters on Annual Events, Kidstuff, Parks and Recreation, and Day Trips. In this chapter entries are arranged alphabetically and are located in Charlotte unless otherwise noted.

BANK OF AMERICA STADIUM
800 South Mint St.
(704) 358-7538
www.panthers.com
Take a one-hour tour of this $187-million facility, the home of the Carolina Panthers and among the more high-tech stadiums in the NFL. You'll see private suites overlooking the 50-yard line, check out the "nosebleed" section, and learn more than you ever imagined about the 73,778-seat open-air stadium that has also hosted major concerts such as the Rolling Stones. Public tours, with no reservations required, are given at 10 a.m. Wed, and Fri at 10:30 a.m. and noon. Meet at the ticket office between the East and South gates on Mint Street. Tickets are $5 adults, $4 senior citizens (age 55 and up), $3 ages 5 to 15, and free for children under 5. Group tours of 11 or more people are available weekdays by appointment. Cost is $75 per 30 people.

BECHTLER MUSEUM OF MODERN ART
420 South Tryon St.
(704) 353-9200
www.bechtler.org
The Charlotte arts scene took a quantum leap forward with the opening of the Bechtler Museum of Modern Art in January 2010. The Bechtler is a

key component of the Wells Fargo Cultural Campus in Uptown. More important, it gives Charlotte the type of museum usually reserved for larger cities like Chicago or New York. Furthermore, it is the only 20th-century modern art museum in the Southeast.

So how did the Queen City land this crown jewel? In a way, it can thank its textiles heritage. Hans and Bessie Bechtler were Swiss collectors of art who also owned stock in a textile machine company that had a plant in Charlotte. The Bechtlers were intrigued by modern art, mostly European, which made sense because they lived there. That love of modern art was passed to their son, Andreas, who moved to Charlotte in 1979. Eventually Andreas inherited the family's 1,400-piece collection and was interested in displaying this treasure trove in some fashion. Local arts leaders convinced Bechtler to base his collection in a museum at the Uptown cultural campus and he agreed, as long as his friend—noted Swiss architect Mario Botta—designed the building.

The result of Botta's vision is a distinct building with a striking earth tone exterior of terra cotta tiles. At street level, visitors are struck by its cantilevered gallery that hangs over a terrace anchored by a swelling column set in the middle. A glass-and-mirror Phoenix statue on the terrace is quickly becoming a Charlotte icon.

Once inside, visitors take the elevator (or stairs) to galleries on the second, third, and fourth floors that are pierced by a soaring, light-filled atrium. Exhibits from the massive collection rotate at various points throughout the year. Artists include Jean Tinguely, Alberto Giacometti, Joan Miro, Edgar Degas, Georges Rouault, Max Ernst, Barbara Hepworth, Andy Warhol, and Pablo Picasso. Many of the works were produced by artists associated with the School of Paris, a loosely connected group who lived and worked in Paris after World War II.

Adding to the aura of the Bechtler is the fact that very few of these works had been seen in the United States prior to the opening of this $20-million museum.

The Bechtler is closed on Tues, and is open 10 a.m. to 5 p.m. every other day of the week, except Sun, when it is open noon to 5 p.m. Admission fee is $8 for adults, $6 for seniors, educators and college students, and $4 for ages 11-18. There is no charge for children age 10 and under.

BILLY GRAHAM LIBRARY & GRAHAM FAMILY HOMEPLACE
4330 Westmont Dr.
(704) 401-3200
www.billygraham.org
The Billy Graham Library is a 40,000-square-foot facility that takes visitors through the life and legacy of this Charlotte native who's been called America's Pastor. Graham is a South Baptist evangelist who grew up on a farm not far from this site. He has met with every U.S. President since Harry Truman, and personally counseled Dwight Eisenhower, Lyndon Johnson, Richard Nixon, Gerald Ford, Jimmy Carter, Ronald Reagan, George H.W. Bush, Bill Clinton, and George W. Bush.

The Graham Library is a barn-shaped structure that documents Graham's journey from humble farm boy to one of the most recognizable religious figures in the world. Learn about this legend through multimedia presentations, interactive kiosks, photos, and memorabilia.

Also available for touring is Graham's boyhood home, which was relocated and restored. Admission is free. Hours of operation are 9:30 a.m. to 5 p.m. Mon through Sat.

CARL J. MCEWAN HISTORIC VILLAGE
4311 Hillside Dr., Mint Hill
(704) 573-0726
www.minthillhistory.com
Get a glimpse of Mecklenburg County life more than a century ago at the Carl J. McEwan Historic Village off Matthews-Mint Hill Road. The Mint Hill Historical Society has brought together original buildings of historical value to re-create the Mint Hill of a bygone era. The Mint Hill Country Doctor's Museum is the restored building of Dr. Ayer Whitley, one of the last country doctors in Mecklenburg County. Also on site are the Ira V. Ferguson Country Store, circa 1921, and the Ashcroft One Room Schoolhouse, built in the late 1800s when the county mandated a school

be built every five miles so that children could walk to their studies. There are also several other outbuildings, and the assay office of Mint Hill's old Surface Hill Gold Mine, which was part of the first gold rush in the United States.

Hours are 10 a.m. to 2 p.m. Tues to Sat or by appointment. A farmers' market also is held 9 a.m. to noon Sat, May through Sept. Admission is $5 for adults, $1 for children, students, and seniors.

CAROLINA RAPTOR CENTER
Latta Plantation Nature Preserve
6000 Sample Rd., Huntersville
(704) 875-6521
www.carolinaraptorcenter.org
Hundreds of injured and orphaned birds of prey—hawks, owls, falcons, eagles, vultures, and ospreys—are brought to this educational conservation and rehabilitation facility each year. Half are nursed back to health and released into the wild; the rest become permanent residents and teaching tools for 90,000 visitors who walk through exhibits and along a wooded nature trail. Most of the raptors live in large cages; others are part of up-close demonstrations in a fenced-in ring or in a 40-foot-tall, 100-foot-wide, tree-filled aviary where guests can see the birds in flight. One of the center's most popular residents is Cinnamon, an American kestrel. Presentations with live birds take place three times on Sat (11 a.m., 1 and 3 p.m.) and twice on Sun (1 and 3 p.m.), weather permitting. Hours of operation are 10 a.m. until 5 p.m. Mon through Sat, noon to 5 p.m. Sun. The center is closed Mon and Tues during winter. Admission is $8 adults, $7 seniors, $6 students, free under age 5. Group rates also available.

CAROLINAS AVIATION MUSEUM
4108 Minuteman Way, Charlotte/Douglas
International Airport
(704) 359-8442
www.carolinasaviation.org
Built in the original hangar of Charlotte's airport, this museum is manned by retired pilots and Air National Guardsmen who love to show off "birds" from various eras of history. You'll find a replica of the Wright Brothers' glider, Huey helicopters, a Piedmont DC-3, and several military planes, including a T-28 Trojan, A-4 Skyhawk, A-7 Corsair II with Desert Storm markings, an F-4 plane, and a "Top Gun" F-14 Super Tomcat. Flight simulators, airplane engines, and other memorabilia are also displayed. Hours are 10 a.m. until 4 p.m. Tues through Fri, 10 a.m. until 5 p.m. Sat, and 1 until 5 p.m. Sun. Admission is $8 adults, $5 seniors and children, free for kids 5 and under.

CHARLOTTE MOTOR SPEEDWAY
5555 Concord Parkway South, Concord
(704) 455-3200
www.charlottemotorspeedway.com
Charlotte Motor Speedway ranks high among America's premier NASCAR facilities. This 1.5-mile oval draws huge crowds with 140,000 permanent seats and room for approximately 50,000 more in the infield. Located northeast of Charlotte, just across the Cabarrus County line in Concord, the speedway hosts three of the top events on the NASCAR Sprint Cup schedule.

May's speedweeks include NASCAR's longest race—the Coca-Cola 600—always held the Sun evening prior to Memorial Day. Eight days prior to the 600 is the exciting NASCAR All-Star Race, a Sat night shootout with $1 million going to the winner. In the fall, the circuit returns to Charlotte Motor Speedway for an October 500-miler that is part of the sport's 10-race Chase for the Championship, which is essentially NASCAR's playoffs. The track also hosts races in NASCAR's junior divisions, the Nationwide Series, and the Camping World Truck Series.

Attending a race at Charlotte Motor Speedway is a unique experience, quite different from most major sports events. First of all, fans are allowed to bring in their own coolers, packed with fried chicken, snacks, soft drinks, and, yes, alcoholic beverages. There are only two rules: one, the cooler can be no wider or taller than 14 inches (ushers have 14-inch sticks used to measure every cooler), and two, your alcohol and soft drinks must be in cans. No glass allowed. Folks camp out for days around the track and in the infield, and start the festivities pretty early on race day. If you've never attended a race before, here's a word to the wise: front-row seats are not desirable. If you sit in the first few rows, you can't see all the way around the track, you get blasted with dirt and rubber from the track, and there's a good possibility you'll get hit by a chicken bone or beer can (fans throw both down to the walkway just inside the safety fence). If this doesn't sound like your cup of tea, Charlotte Motor Speedway also offers luxury suites and five-star dining in the Speedway Club, and it was the first (and only) sports facility to offer year-round living accommodations when it built the Turn One Condominiums in 1984.

Folks looking for a first-hand racing experience can get behind the wheel of a real stock car via one of the many professional driving schools that operate at the track. The most popular is the Richard Petty Driving Experience. The rookie experience starts at $449 and includes a few laps by yourself on the speedway, or you can do a ride-along with a professional driver for $109.

For a tamer experience, the track offers "Feel the Thrill" tours that give you a close-up look at the garage area, pit road, and victory lane, as well as a lap around the track in a passenger van. Tours offered hourly on non-event days 9:30 a.m. until 3:30 p.m. Mon through Sat and 1:30 until 3:30 p.m. Sun. Cost is $5 per person.

CHARLOTTE MUSEUM OF HISTORY AND HEZEKIAH ALEXANDER HOMESITE
3500 Shamrock Dr.
(704) 568-1774
www.charlottemuseum.org
Charlotte's oldest surviving structure, this 1774 rock house was the home of Hezekiah and Mary Alexander and their 10 children. Alexander was a blacksmith and planter by trade and assumed a leadership role in the new community called Charlotte. He eventually became a signer of the Mecklenburg Declaration of Independence.

Visitors can tour the homesite, a replicated kitchen, and reconstructed springhouse, learning about 18th-century life from costumed docents. The adjacent Museum of History, which was completely renovated in the late 1990s, takes

guests through the area's beginnings, from the 1700s to today. Changing exhibits focus on local, regional, and state history as well as on special collections.

Newer additions to the museum grounds include the American Freedom Bell, a bronze backcountry patriot statue, and many beautiful plants, flowers, and wooded trails. The Freedom Bell, funded in large part by the Belk Foundation of former Charlotte mayor John Belk, is the largest bell at ground level in the world. It is nearly seven feet wide and weighs seven tons.

The average visit lasts three to four hours, allowing one to two hours in the museum and an hour or so for the homesite tour. Hours are 10 a.m. until 5 p.m. Wed through Sat, and 1 until 5 p.m. Sun. Homesite tours at 1:15 and 3:15 p.m. daily. Admission is $6 adults, $5 seniors and students, $3 children age 6-12. Under 6, free.

CHARLOTTE NATURE MUSEUM
1658 Sterling Rd.
(704) 372-6261
www.charlottenaturemuseum.org
The Charlotte Nature Museum is adjacent to Freedom Park, one of the city's most popular parks. Renovated and expanded over the years, it allows visitors to experience wildlife through live exhibits and interactive programs. Here you will find animals and plants of the Piedmont, including birds, snakes, and mammals such as groundhogs. In the Butterfly Pavilion, hundreds of the winged beauties flit around while others go through their amazing transformation. There are indoor and outdoor exhibits year round, with a special emphasis on puppet shows, workshops, summer camps, and nature trails. Open 9 a.m. until 5 p.m. Tues through Fri, 10 a.m. until 5 p.m. Sat, and noon to 5 p.m. Sun. Admission is $6 for ages 2 and up, free for children under 2 and members.

CHARLOTTE TROLLEY AND MUSEUM
2104 South Blvd. at Atherton Mill
(704) 375-0850
www.charlottetrolley.org
Learn about Charlotte's history and the streetcars that once carried residents between Uptown and

the city's first suburbs by taking a 20-minute trip aboard the restored No. 85 streetcar, the last in its fleet to be retired. Interesting landmarks include old factories and mills that are now shops and condominiums, Charlotte's first grocery, and the site of underground mines that drew thousands of gold miners long before California's gold rush. Full of nostalgia and local color, the museum that houses the trolley provides a glimpse into Charlotte's past before buses and automobiles were a common sight.

The trolley runs on weekends from Atherton Mill in South End through a glass tunnel inside the Charlotte Convention Center on Stonewall Street and up to Ninth Street. Trolley hours are 10 a.m. to 5 p.m. Sat and 10:30 a.m. to 5:30 p.m. Sun. Cost is $1.50 one way or $3 round trip for adults. Seniors and youth pay half price. The museum is open 9:30 a.m. to 5 p.m. weekdays.

ℹ️ Groundhog Day is special at Charlotte Nature Museum thanks to its famous resident, Queen Charlotte. This cute, furry groundhog is thrust into the local limelight each Feb 2 to find out if she sees her shadow, which, of course, we hope she doesn't because that means six more weeks of winter weather. Queen Charlotte can sometimes be cantankerous, like the time a few years ago when she tried to bite then-mayor Pat McCrory. "Queen Charlotte was an assertive person with King George, and she was that day as well," quipped the popular McCrory, who served seven terms as mayor.

DANIEL STOWE BOTANICAL GARDEN
6500 South New Hope Rd., Belmont
(704) 825-4490
www.dsbg.org
Named one of the Nation's 20 Great Gardens by HGTV, Daniel Stowe Botanical Garden is among the most significant visitor attractions to open in the Charlotte region in the last two decades. This superb destination is located just south of Belmont along the banks of Lake Wylie, and convenient to Charlotte.

Its features include a spectacular 13,500-square-foot Visitor Pavilion and the 8,000-square-foot Orchid Conservatory. The conservatory is the only glasshouse in the Carolinas dedicated to the display of orchids and tropical plants. The Daniel Stowe Botanical Garden's nearly 400 acres also include themed gardens, a dozen sparkling fountains, a woodland trail, unique gift shop, and a grassy outdoor amphitheater for special events. The garden offers educational classes for all ages, summer camps for kids, semiannual plant sales, and Holiday Lights at the Garden, a Christmas celebration that features more than 600,000 lights and live entertainment throughout the month of December. Because of its beauty, the garden has become a popular place for weddings.

The garden was born in 1991 when local textile magnate Daniel J. Stowe set aside this large parcel of family land with the vision that it develop into one of the world's best botanical gardens. The master plan for the site calls for expansion in phases over the coming decades to include such aspects as an English walled garden, children's garden and learning center, home demonstration garden, restaurant, and gardens and docks on Lake Wylie.

Open daily from 9 a.m. until 5 p.m. except Thanksgiving, Christmas, and New Year's Day. Admission is $10 adults, $9 seniors, $5 children ages 4 through 12, free to members and children under age 4. Group rates available.

DISCOVERY PLACE
301 North Tryon St.
(704) 372-6261
www.discoveryplace.org
Now's a great time to visit Discovery Place because this hands-on science and technology museum is born again after a $31.6-million renovation. Discovery Place, which opened in 1981 on Tryon Street in Uptown, was in need of a face-lift, and a multi-stage upgrade was completed in mid 2010.

The first of the new exhibits to open was Cool Stuff, which allows families to discover the strangeness and beauty of physics. Launch objects into the air, rest on a bed a nails, or crush a garbage can. It's an eccentric world of physical phenomena right in your hands.

Other new exhibits include a digital 3-D the-ater, a large, diverse aquarium, and new lab stations for investigating with real science. The renovation also features improved infrastructure and the abil-ity to rotate exhibitions more frequently.

Longtime fans of Discovery Place can still enjoy their favorites, like the three-story rain for-est, five moving dinosaurs, and the IMAX theater, a 79-foot domed planetarium.

The IMAX boasts one of the largest movie screens in the Carolinas and shows films days and weekend evenings. The Planetarium projects more than 10,000 stars, along with planets and special effects.

Discovery Place has built a reputation as one of the top science and technology museums in the country, and it is a field trip staple for children throughout the Carolinas. The museum draws more than half a million visitors annually and is regularly ranked in the top 10 most visited muse-ums and attractions in North Carolina.

Discovery Place KIDS, a spin-off community-based children's museum will open in late 2010 in the Huntersville Town Center.

Discovery Place hours are: 9 a.m. to 4 p.m. Mon through Fri; 10 a.m. to 6 p.m. Sat; and noon until 5 p.m. Sun. Museum admission is $10 adults and $8 children and seniors. Combo tickets that include an IMAX showing range from $16-$19 for adults, and $13-$15 for children and seniors. Sep-arate rates for the IMAX theater are also available.

ENERGYEXPLORIUM
13339 Hagers Ferry Rd., Huntersville
(704) 875-5600
www.duke-energy.com
Operated by Duke Energy and located at the McGuire Nuclear Station on Lake Norman, this energy information center offers hands-on exhib-its of model nuclear and coal-fired power plants and a film entitled *Lake Norman—the Great Inland Sea*. You can walk through the wildflower garden, travel the 1-mile nature trail, and enjoy a picnic lunch. EnergyExplorium is accessible via boat

and car and is open six days a week year round, except for New Year's Day, Easter, Thanksgiving, Christmas Eve, and Christmas. Hours are 9 a.m. until 5 p.m. Mon through Fri, and noon until 5 p.m. Sat. Inquire about tours for McGuire's Con-trol Room Simulator. Free.

EXTREME ICE CENTER
4705 Indian Trail–Fairview Road, Indian Trail
(704) 882-1830
www.xicenter.com
Extreme Ice is the biggest thing to ever hit Charlotte's ice skating and hockey scene. This 87,000-square-foot facility opened in 2006 with two regulation-sized hockey rinks and a smaller rink nicknamed "the puddle." Extreme Ice was co-founded by Tom Logano, father of NASCAR driver Joey Logano, and is the official practice facility of the Charlotte Checkers minor league hockey squad. Figure skaters can take lessons from Paul Wylie, a free style medalist in the 1992 Winter Olympics.

Away from the ice, Extreme offers a fitness center, pro shop, arcade, locker rooms, snack bar, multi-purpose room and the Center Ice Tavern, serving food and drinks.

FEDERAL RESERVE BANK
530 East Trade St.
(704) 358-2100
www.richmondfed.org
Pre-arranged group tours are available at this nondescript Uptown building that ships more than $75 million a day to banks around the Caro-linas. See how checks are processed, how surplus currency is handled and stored in a three-story vault guarded by two 15-ton doors, and how 4.5 million notes are inspected for counterfeits. Millions of dollars of worn-out bills are shredded on the spot, and you can take home a free bag of money shredded as finely as new spring grass.

FOURTH WARD
Bordered by Tryon, Fifth, Graham,
and Tenth Streets, Uptown
(704) 331-2700
www.fofw.org

Close-up

Touring the Queen City

Riding and walking tours are a great way for visitors and newcomers to Charlotte to learn the history and sites of the city.

Charlotte's longest-running daily city tour is **Queen City Tours,** a minibus excursion that visits 50 sites, including the Trolley Museum, Duke Mansion, Marshall Park, Uptown Square, Dilworth, Myers Park, the Queen Charlotte statue, and Old Settler's Cemetery. The two-hour tours are offered at 9:30 a.m. and 1:30 p.m. Mon through Sat and 1:30 p.m. Sun. A Black Heritage Tour also is offered daily. Queen City picks up from all major hotels, as well as several sites around Charlotte. Advance tickets are $22 adults, $20 seniors, and $13 children. Day-of-tour tickets are $27, $25, and $18. Call (704) 566-0104 or visit www.queencitytours.com.

Several different tours for groups of 10 or more are available through **Charlotte Arrangements,** including the overview that visits Uptown, the Mint Museum, SouthPark, the elegant homes of Myers Park and Dilworth, performing and visual arts, and banks. Others focus on the trolley line, gardens, shopping, African-American heritage, arts and culture, the NASCAR scene, and Fourth Ward. Day excursions take visitors to the Yadkin Valley wine area. Call (704) 332-8445 or visit www.charlottearrangements.com.

A **horse-drawn carriage** tour is one of the most unique ways to learn about Uptown. Clip-clop through the streets of historic Fourth Ward on tours ranging from 20 minutes to a half hour. Southern Breezes Farm in Union County conducts the tours from 6:30 until 11 p.m. Fri and Sat, April through May and Sept through Dec. Summer hours are 6:30 until 11 p.m. Wed through Fri and 2 until 11 p.m. Sat. Tours pick up on Tryon Street in front of Discovery Place. Rates are $20 for two adults, $5 additional adults, $3 children ages 4 through 10 for 15-minute tours; $30, $7, and $5 for half-hour tours. Call (704) 301-5111 or visit www.southernbreezes.com.

On a budget? Sign up for a **free narrated walking tour** of Uptown with Russ Ford, a Charlotte historian and former journalist who volunteers at Visit Charlotte, 330 South Tryon St. Tours are available at 10 a.m. and 1 p.m. Fri or by appointment for groups. To sign up, call Ford at (704) 847-3302 or visit www.CharlotteTour.org. Visit Charlotte also has free brochures with do-it-yourself walking itineraries focusing on Fourth Ward, Center City, and public art. See www.visitcharlotte.org for details.

In the mid-1800s Charlotte was divided into four political wards. The northwest quadrant, called Fourth Ward, was a prosperous area containing the homes of merchants, ministers, physicians, and others. In the early 1900s the trolley expanded travel throughout Charlotte, and Dilworth and Myers Park became the prestigious places to live. By the '50s, Fourth Ward was becoming an undesirable area with abandoned or substandard housing, scattered businesses, and crime.

But in 1970, when many homes had been destroyed by fire, vandals, and neglect, the Junior League, UNC Charlotte, and a few other civic-minded people had a dream. It was of interest to the city, banks, and, most important, the residents to save Fourth Ward and make it a desirable area once again. By 1978 most of the homes had been bought by adventurous, modern-day pioneers. The restoration was strictly governed by the homeowners association, and this is now a beautiful, active community that has increased the tax revenue to the city tenfold. This turn-of-the-20th-century Victorian neighborhood, in the heart of Uptown, is a nice spot for strolling during the day or for taking the tour of homes at Christmastime. Pick up a detailed guide from Visit Charlotte at Main Street, 330 South Tryon St.

GASTON COUNTY MUSEUM OF ART & HISTORY

131 West Main St., Dallas
(704) 922-7681
www.gastoncountymuseum.org

Located in the historic Dallas court square in the restored 1852 Hoffman Hotel, this museum features Victorian period rooms with exhibits on American art and history. Permanent exhibits focus on Carolina textiles, Gaston County's place in the center of the nationwide business, and how the industry shaped people and their way of life. The largest public collection of carriages and sleighs in the state is displayed in the Stowe Carriage House. Hours are 10 a.m. until 5 p.m. Tues through Fri; noon to 5 p.m. Sat; and 2 to 5 p.m. the first Sun of each month. Free.

HARVEY B. GANTT CENTER FOR AFRICAN-AMERICAN ARTS + CULTURE

551 South Tryon St.
(704) 547-3700
www.ganttcenter.org

The Gantt Center opened in October 2009 as one of the key components of the Wells Fargo Cultural Campus at South Tryon and First Streets. It replaced the Afro-American Cultural Center, located in First Ward in the restored former Little Rock AME Zion Church, as the city's preeminent facility to showcase and preserve African-American art, culture, and history. The center was named for Harvey Gantt, a South Carolina native who built a thriving architectural firm in Charlotte in the 1970s and 80s and was the Queen City's first black mayor. Gantt served a pair of two-year terms from 1983-87, and has been deeply involved in other civic, business, and cultural endeavors in Charlotte.

The 46,500-square-foot, four-story building is among the most unique in Uptown. Its narrow exterior incorporates designs reminiscent of woven textile patterns from West Africa, as well as quilt patterns from the Underground Railroad era. Stairs and escalators are central to the design theme of the Gantt Center, which has its main lobby on the second floor. The stairs are an architectural nod to the old Myers Street School,

located nearby in the predominately black Brooklyn neighborhood, which was razed in the 1960s. The school had a notable exterior stair configuration and was often called "Jacob's Ladder."

The centerpiece of the $18.6-million Gantt Center is a permanent 58-piece collection of works from 20th-century African-American artists. It was cobbled together by New York City residents Vivian and John Hewitt. The Hewitts weren't wealthy—he was a writer and she a librarian—but they bought each other works of art for Christmas presents and even took out loans over the years to add to their collection. Vivian Hewitt's parents were from Statesville and Kings Mountain, and her cousin is local U.S. Representative Mel Watt. The Hewitts sold the collection to Bank of America in 1998 under the agreement that it would be displayed when Charlotte built a new African-American cultural center. It includes such noted black artists as Henry O. Tanner, Ann Tanksley, John Biggers, and Romare Bearden, a native of Charlotte.

The first two rotating exhibits at the center featured the works of Atlanta-based mixed-media artist Radcliffe Bailey and Tennessee native Juan Logan, who lives just outside Charlotte in the town of Belmont.

Hours are 10 a.m. until 5 p.m. Tues through Sat, and 1 to 5 p.m. on Sun. Admission is $8 per person, and $5 per person for seniors and groups.

HISTORIC BRATTONSVILLE

1444 Brattonsville Rd., McConnells, SC
(803) 684-2327
www.chmuseums.org

Like historic homes? Then you'll love this village of more than 30 restored structures from the 18th and 19th centuries. Start with the pre–Revolutionary War backwoods cabin and end with the elegant Bratton Plantation Home. Farm animals, crops, gardens, and orchards are part of the 775-acre living-history museum, as are costumed docents and demonstrations. Many visitors are interested in *The Patriot*, portions of which were filmed here. Don't miss the annual Candlelight Tour, when Brattonsville is filled with the sights, sounds, and smells of an old-fashioned Christmas, or the Battle of Huck's Defeat, a two-day Revolutionary War battle reenactment held each July. Hours are 10 a.m. until 5 p.m. Mon through Sat and 1 until 5 p.m. Sun. Admission is $6 adults, $5 seniors, $3 students, free for ages 3 and under.

HISTORIC ROSEDALE
3247 North Tryon St.
(704) 335-0325
www.historicrosedale.org
Rosedale, the 1815 private home of Archibald Frew, was part of a 911-acre plantation. It showcases classic Federal architecture with early-1800s faux finishes made to look like exotic woods such as rosewood and mahogany. Outlandish in its day, the home was dubbed "Frew's Folly" by conservative locals, although it is now considered one of North Carolina's finest examples of architecture from the Federal period.

You'll see Frew's taste in carved Adams mantels, elaborate cornices, detailed moldings, a classic porch, dormers, and French wallpaper. Opened to the public in late 1993, the restored home is largely unfurnished to showcase the decorative elements.

You can also tour the restored boxwood garden where you'll see seven "treasure trees," some thought to have been planted by Archibald Frew and three of which are considered to be the largest known of their species in this area. Guided tours are at 1:30 and 3 p.m. Thurs through Sun. Admission is $5 adults, $4 seniors and students. Children under 3 and members of Historic Rosedale are admitted free. Group rates are $4 per person (15 or more).

HISTORIC RURAL HILL FARM
4431 Neck Rd., Huntersville
(704) 875-3113
www.ruralhillfarm.org
Historic Rural Hill Farm was the home of Major John and Violet Davidson and six generations of the Davidson family before Mecklenburg County bought the 265-acre farm for preservation purposes in 1989. The county leases the former plantation to the Catawba Valley Scottish Society, which provides guided tours, educational programs, walking trails, hay rides by reservation, and a range of special events. Visitors can see a reproduction of the first Davidson home, which dates from the Revolutionary War era, as well as plantation ruins, the family cemetery, a smokehouse, ash house, well house, barn, chicken shed, and granary. Two one-room schoolhouses serve as interpretive centers of early American education.

Among the special events held at Rural Hill Farm are the Loch Norman Highland Games in April and the Sheep Dog Trials in November. Every other year, from late August through mid-October, the farm challenges visitors to work their way through the Rural Hill Amazing Maize Maze. Open Mon through Fri by appointment only. Admission is $6 adults, $4 children 5 to 12, free for children 4 and under.

HUGH TORANCE HOUSE AND STORE
8231 Gilead Rd., Huntersville
(704) 875-3271
The oldest standing store in the state, this restored 18th-century Federal house and log store is open the second Sun of the month June through Sept. Tours are offered from 2 to 5 p.m. Group tours by appointment. Cost is $3 for adults, and $2 for children (age 6–13).

IMAGINON
300 East Seventh St.
(704) 416-4600
www.imaginon.org
A multimedia playground and the home of the children's public library and Children's Theatre of Charlotte, ImaginOn opened in fall 2005. Its massive tilting roof, glass exterior, colorful and playful interiors, and recycled materials also make ImaginOn Charlotte's most architecturally adventuresome public building and the city's first "green" public building.

The 102,000-square-foot building provides a variety of experiences for young people and their families, all around the common theme of storytelling. Children can read a story, see a story performed, or even film their own story.

From the lobby, a recycled-rubber ramp stretches high above to give visitors a view of most of the building without traditional walls and levels. In the Children's Library, preschoolers and elementary-school-age kids can read with parents, play at the pretend library desk, or move the puzzle-piece ottomans to create their own storytelling area. The Round provides storytelling space with a puppet theater, while the adjacent courtyard offers outdoor space for story time, creative play, and reading.

Tech Central is a light-filled area for school-age kids and teenagers with 35 flat-screen computers for homework, writing, or editing animations or films made on site. A five-person support staff is there to help. Inspiration comes from the Story Jar, an interactive feature that lights up and provides instant feedback. Hanging from a 30-foot spiral sprouting from the jar are hundreds of everyday objects meant to become potential story elements.

For teenagers, The Loft serves as a place to do homework or projects, read books or magazines, check out audiovisual materials, surf on computers, or plug in a laptop. In nearby studio i, kids can use animation and video to tell their own stories.

ImaginOn also includes a 580-seat main theater. Here the Children's Theatre of Charlotte puts on family-friendly productions such as *Junie B. Jones, Billy Jonas,* and *The Magician's Nephew.* More intimate productions are staged at the 250-seat Playhouse. Other creative spaces include the glass-lined art studio, the dance studio, and the computer training lab.

The best feature of all? Exploring the building and using the library are free. (Shows require a ticket.)

Underground parking accessible via Sixth Street is free for the first 90 minutes with validated ticket. Three hours of free parking are available in the Seventh Street Station parking deck after 5 p.m. weekdays and anytime on weekends.

Open 9 a.m. to 9 p.m. Mon to Thurs, 9 a.m. to 6 p.m. Fri and Sat, 1 to 6 p.m. Sun.

JAMES K. POLK STATE HISTORIC SITE
12031 Lancaster Hwy., Pineville
(704) 889-7145
www.nchistoricsites.org/polk

James K. Polk, 11th president of the United States, was born in a log cabin on a cotton and grain farm in Pineville in 1795. His homestead has been reconstructed and is now a state historic site. No original buildings or articles remain from Polk's childhood, but the memorial depicts how the future president's family would have lived at the time. A log house, separate kitchen, and barn are each authentically furnished.

A museum details Polk's family and political career. It covers the significant events that occurred during his administration from 1844 to 1848, including the Mexican-American War, the annexation of California, and the settlement of the Oregon boundary dispute. In fact, it was Polk's stance on the occupation of Oregon that helped sweep him into the White House as the first dark horse candidate in American politics. His campaign slogan was "Fifty-Four Forty or Fight," which referred to the northern boundary of the Oregon territory.

Guided tours of the buildings are available anytime but are especially beautiful when the candles are lit at the annual Christmas celebration, and during July and August, the Polk Historic Site hosts a series of one-day history camps for children. Regular hours are 9 a.m. until 5 p.m. Tues through Sat. Free.

KNIGHTS STADIUM
2280 Deerfield Dr., Fort Mill
(I-77 at Exit 88)
(704) 357-8071 (NC)
(803) 548-8050 (SC)
www.charlotteknights.com

Known locally as "Knights Castle," this 10,002-seat stadium is home to the Charlotte Knights, the top minor-league farm team of the Chicago White Sox. Families, college kids, and the after-work crowd enjoy baseball games, two picnic areas, a playground, restaurant, mini-golf, beer garden, speed-pitch machine, and the humorous Knights mascot, Homer the Dragon.

Knights Stadium draws its biggest crowds on evenings when a fireworks show is presented after the game. These occur frequently on Sat during the season, which runs from mid-April through early September. The largest crowd to ever watch a game at the castle was July 4, 2008, when 15,591 showed up for a game and fireworks. There are grass banks down the left field and right field sides of the stadium that accommodate overflow crowds.

The Home Run Café, located on the second level behind home plate, is a great spot to watch a game while enjoying a meal and beverage, and it can be rented throughout the year for special functions. The Knights have also launched a new initiative called "Field of Dreams," which allows groups to rent the field and hold their own softball game on the diamond.

Game tickets range from $6 to $10.

LATTA PLANTATION
5225 Sample Rd., Huntersville
(704) 875-2312
www.lattaplantation.org
This early-1800s river plantation was owned by James Latta, a prosperous traveling merchant who bought wares in Charleston and Philadelphia and peddled them to his Carolina Piedmont neighbors. Costumed guides give tours of the two-story house, which is on the National Register of Historic Places, and demonstrate weaving, spinning, sewing, woodworking, and open-hearth cooking. The plantation comes complete with farm animals and a unique equestrian center.

Open 10 a.m. until 5 p.m. Tues through Sat and 1 until 5 p.m. Sun. Call for guided tour times. Admission is $6 adults, $5 seniors and students ages 6 and older, children under 6 free. For details on Latta Plantation Nature Preserve, check our chapter on Parks and Recreation.

LEVINE MUSEUM OF THE NEW SOUTH
200 East Seventh St.
(704) 333-1887
www.museumofthenewsouth.org
Located in Uptown's cultural district, this social-history museum depicts the post–Civil War Southern history of Charlotte told from the perspective of the people who lived it. An 8,000-square-foot permanent exhibit, Cotton Fields to Skyscrap-

ers, is the centerpiece, using more than 1,000 artifacts, images, video clips, and oral histories to show the economic transformation of Charlotte from a region of small farms after the Civil War to America's main textile factory region in the 1920s to one of the country's largest banking centers today. Quilts, civil rights photography, Carolina pottery, Victorian architecture, Charlotte neighborhoods, Southern music traditions, and political cartoons have been temporary exhibits. Lectures, panel discussions, book signings, workshops, walking tours, and youth activities are regular programs.

Hours are 10 a.m. to 5 p.m. Tues through Sat, noon to 5 p.m. Sun. Admission is $6 adults, $5 seniors and children ages 6 to 18, $4 per person for groups, free for children under 6, and $17 for families. Free two-hour parking at the adjacent Seventh Street Station parking deck.

MINT MUSEUM RANDOLPH
2730 Randolph Rd.
(704) 337-2000
www.mintmuseum.org
The building housing the Mint Museum served the region as the first branch of the Philadelphia Mint, coining $5 million in gold from 1836 until the outbreak of the Civil War. A grassroots effort during the Depression saved the original Federal-style building from demolition and moved it to its present Randolph Road site where, in 1936, it opened as the Mint Museum of Art, the state's first art museum. The Mint has since grown and is now one of the Southeast's leading art museums.

In 2010, the museum was renamed the Mint Museum Randolph to distinguish it from the new Mint Museum Uptown, and is scheduled to celebrate its 75th anniversary in 2011. Collections at the Mint Museum Randolph include pre-Columbian, African, and Spanish colonial art; historic costumes and fashionable dress; art of the ancient Americas; Asian art; ceramics; and coins and currency. Local-interest pieces include a portrait of Queen Charlotte, paintings by Mecklenburg County native Romare Bearden, and gold coins made at Charlotte's U.S. Mint. The permanent collection is enhanced by special changing exhibitions.

In conjunction with opening the new Uptown location, the Randolph museum was renovated and upgraded. When some collections moved Uptown, that created more display space at Randolph and allowed the staff to bring more items out of storage and on display.

Throughout the year lectures, seminars, films, festivals, and other activities supplement the exhibitions. Also, the Mint Museum Randolph has a gorgeous front lawn that is used for outdoor events like the annual Derby Days celebration, a popular social event sponsored by the Young Affiliates of the Mint that includes a showing of the Kentucky Derby on a projection screen.

The Mint Randolph is open 10 a.m. until 9 p.m. on Tues, and 10 a.m. until 5 p.m. Wed through Sat. Admission is $10 for adults, $8 for seniors and college students, and $5 for ages 5 to 17. Children under 5 admitted free, and everyone is in for free on Tues from 5 until 9 p.m. Tickets are also good at the Uptown location on the same day.

MINT MUSEUM UPTOWN
500 South Tryon St.
(704) 337-2000
www.mintmuseum.org
The Mint expands its Uptown presence in October 2010 with the completion of a $56-million five-story facility on South Tryon Street in the Wells Fargo Cultural Campus. The Mint Museum Uptown encompasses 145,000 square feet and gives the museum a signature, modern structure in the center city. The new museum includes the collections of the Mint Museum of Craft + Design, which closed after 10 years on North Tryon Street in the former Montaldo's Department Store.

The Mint Museum Uptown features a grand entry facing Tryon Street. Suspended above the entry and visible from the street is Dale Chihuly's Royal Blue Mint Chandelier, a welcoming beacon for visitors as they access a multi-story atrium that will serve as the central hub of activity. A 60-foot by 60-foot glass curtain wall overlooks First Street. Just off the atrium sits a 240-seat auditorium for public programs, symposiums, performances,

and films. A special events pavilion is the highlight of the fifth floor. The pavilion includes a 4,000-square-foot special events room available for rental, and a 4,000-square-foot rooftop terrace with superb views of the Charlotte skyline.

The third and fourth levels offer two full floors of galleries, one dedicated to craft and design and one to American art, contemporary art, and a selection of European art. Each floor has 12,000 square feet of permanent exhibits and 6,000 square feet of changing exhibits. Relocating from the Mint Museum Randolph are important American and European paintings and sculpture; regional crafts; and one of America's premiere collections of pottery and porcelain.

A family gallery on the second floor brings adults and children together for hands-on art activities, while the Romare Bearden House provides playful introductions to the collections.

Back at ground level, a museum café serves up indoor and outdoor dining, while the museum's expanded gift shop showcases pottery and glass made by local artists.

Admission price to the new Mint Museum Uptown will be $10 for adults, $8 for seniors and college students, and $5 for ages 5 to 17. Children under 5 admitted free. For days and hours of operation, call (704) 337-2000 or visit the Web site.

MUSEUM OF THE WAXHAWS ANDREW JACKSON MEMORIAL
8215 Hwy. 75, Waxhaw
(704) 843-1832
www.museumofthewaxhaws.com
Discover the backcountry and pioneering lifestyle of the Scots-Irish who settled in this area, including Waxhaw native Andrew Jackson, seventh president of the United States. Historic artifacts document the area, from the Waxhaw Indians and early European settlers to the American Revolution, Jackson's presidency, and the Civil War. Open Fri and Sat from 10 a.m. to 5 p.m. and Sun from 2 until 5 p.m. Admission is $5 adults, $4 seniors (60+), and $2 for children ages 6 to 12. Children under 6 admitted free.

MUSEUM OF YORK COUNTY
4621 Mount Gallant Rd., Rock Hill, SC
(803) 329-2121
www.chmuseums.org
This museum is a true find for children and adults as well. With more than 200 fully mounted animals of Africa, the largest collection in the Southeast, the museum's phenomenal animal exhibits are reminiscent, though on a smaller scale, of New York's Natural History Museum. The museum also features a planetarium, astronomy exhibits, the artwork of Kellogg's Rice Krispies "Snap, Crackle, Pop" creator and area native Vernon Grant, and curriculum-based school programs. It offers an excellent gift shop, nature trail, and picnic facilities. Hours are 10 a.m. until 5 p.m. Mon through Sat and from 1 until 5 p.m. on Sun. Admission is $5 adults, $4 seniors, $3 students, free for children younger than 4.

NASCAR HALL OF FAME
400 E. Martin Luther King Blvd.
(704) 654-4400
www.nascarhall.com
Charlotte beat out major cities across the country—including Atlanta, Kansas City, and Daytona—to become home of this shrine to stock car racing's finest. The NASCAR Hall of Fame's $195-million complex is first-class in all facets, from its oval-shaped 150,000-square-foot hall to a massive 2,500-seat ballroom to the 19-story NASCAR Plaza office tower.

Fans begin their tour in the High-Octane Theater, where they view a short video introduction to the history and heritage of NASCAR racing. This cutting-edge theater features 275 seats and a 64-foot wide curved projection screen with surround sound. Built-in air vents create a surge of air as cars race across the screen.

Next up is a move to the Great Hall for a trip around Glory Road. Glory Road is the Hall's centerpiece. It is a sweeping road that begins with 0-degree banking and eventually reaches 33 degrees of banking as it curves along the building's perimeter. Along Glory Road fans see 18 actual race cars, starting from the early years and graduating to modern-day speedsters. As the road increases in banking, fans are permitted to walk the surface and experience the amount of banking at each track on the NASCAR circuit. Meanwhile, a huge video billboard displays images, messages, and videos about the sport.

At the end of Glory Road comes the Hall of Honor, the place where NASCAR legends are enshrined. In keeping with the oval theme, the Hall of Honor is round and offers a 360-degree video experience. Instead of using busts of its inductees like other halls, each honoree has a permanent "spire" along the wall. This spire features a portrait of the inductee and incorporates multiple media to present his or her accomplishments and contributions to the sport. The center of the Hall of Honor is home to an exhibit focusing on members of the most recent class of inductees. The Hall plans to induct five members per year initially, but will probably reduce that number in future years.

Fans then move to the Race Week and Heritage Speedway exhibits. Race Week is like being at the track for a NASCAR event. There's a race shop, 18-wheeled transporter, pit road area, inspection station, display on qualifying, followed by the race day experience, media experience, and victory lane. Heritage Speedway tells the story of NASCAR's history in three stages: 1948–1971, 1972–1999, and the 2000s. It includes the Greatest Finishes Theater, which shows videos of the closest and most exciting finishes ever experienced in NASCAR.

Merchandise is available in a 5,800-square-foot gift shop, and there's a Buffalo Wild Wings sports restaurant to ensure nobody goes home hungry.

The NASCAR Hall of Fame is open every day of the year except Easter, Thanksgiving, and Christmas. Hours are 10 a.m. to 6 p.m. Mon through Sat, and noon to 6 p.m. Sun. Admission is $19.95 for adults, $17.95 for seniors and military personnel, and $12.95 for children.

NASCAR SPEEDPARK
Concord Mills, I-85 at Exit 49
(704) 979-6770
www.nascarspeedpark.com

Close-up

A Hall of Fame City

With the opening of the NASCAR Hall of Fame, Charlotte became part of a small and elite group of cities that offer a hall of fame to one of America's major sports. Cooperstown is synonymous with baseball's best, Canton is home to the all-time football greats, Springfield and hoops go together, and now Charlotte and stock car racing are forever intertwined.

It made sense for NASCAR's Hall of Fame to be in the Queen City. After all, more than 90 percent of the sport's race teams are located within a 35-mile radius of the city, and shortly after it formed in 1949, NASCAR held its first official race on a speedway that was located off Little Rock Road. Local leaders and fans used the slogan "Racing was built here, racing belongs here" as a rallying cry during the process to determine where NASCAR would locate its shrine.

There were some detractors during the wooing process, especially when it was announced that a two percent increase in the hotel/motel occupancy tax would provide the bulk of funding for the $195-million project, which also includes a 19-story NASCAR office tower.

However, the vast popularity of racing in Charlotte and the prospect of making the Queen City a year-round tourism destination were overriding reasons to pursue this national attraction. Conservative estimates call for around 800,000 visitors per year to the NASCAR Hall of Fame, with a projected annual economic impact of $60 million. If those figures are even close to the actual amounts, the Hall is a year-round trip to victory lane for Charlotte.

A clever aspect of the Hall is its location adjoining the Charlotte Convention Center. The two facilities are connected by a wide, enclosed skywalk over Brevard Street, so anybody in town for a convention can enjoy a tour of the Hall without having to hail a cab, ask directions, or even walk outside.

Interestingly, the NASCAR Hall of Fame has direct ties to the internationally renowned Louvre in Paris. Its sleek and modern design was created by Pei Cobb Freed & Partners, the New York City architects who designed two additions to the Louvre museum. Now there's a wake-up call to folks who think NASCAR is just a Southern good-old-boy sport.

And here's an Insider tidbit for you: don't underestimate the significance of the Hall's massive ballroom. It is by far the largest ballroom in Charlotte, seating 2,500 comfortably in 40,000 square feet with a prominent stage. It wasn't built to such extravagance by happenstance. The ballroom could very well assist the convention center in luring a major event, such as the national convention of a political party, and don't be surprised if some day it hosts NASCAR's prestigious end-of-the-season awards banquet. You can bet money that the first truly red-carpet event in Charlotte history will take place in that ballroom.

One of six NASCAR SpeedParks in North America, this seven-acre racing amusement park features five tracks, including a quarter-mile oval with 5/8-scale Nextel Cup–style cars, a slip-and-slide with twists and turns, an indoor two-story figure-8 track, and a 200-foot starter track for kids. Several area NASCAR pros have made appearances, and it's a popular place for children's birthday parties and for adults to cut up and have fun. Other amusements include speed bumper boats, an 18-hole mini-golf course, an arcade with 50-plus games, a rock-climbing wall, an indoor playground, laser tag arena, and kids' rides. Height requirements for tracks range from 40 to 60 inches. Individual track tickets are $3.50, or you can buy packages of seven tickets for $18 or 12 tickets for $25. Annual passes are also available. Open at 10 a.m. Mon through Sat, and 11 a.m. Sun. Closing times vary. Located at Concord Mills Entry 7.

NORTH CAROLINA FLATWATER OUTFITTERS
1000 Marina Village Dr., Mount Holly
(704) 827-0000
www.ncflatwateroutfitters.com

Just west of Charlotte in Mount Holly, enjoy paddling on the calm waters of the Catawba River as it slowly flows into Lake Wylie. North Carolina Flatwater Outfitters rents one-person and two-person kayaks, as well as canoes. Rates are $10 per hour or $40 for six hours in the single-person kayaks, and $15 per hour or $50 for six hours in the two-person kayaks and canoes. Excursions depart from the Tailrace Marina, directly across the Catawba River from the U.S. National Whitewater Center. Hours are 2 p.m. to sunset Wed through Fri, and 9 a.m. to sunset on weekends.

NORTH CAROLINA TRANSPORTATION MUSEUM AT SPENCER SHOPS
411 South Salisbury Ave., Spencer
(704) 636-2889
www.nctrans.org

This former repair shop for Southern Railway Company features transportation displays and train rides on specified days. The authentic train depot houses 25 locomotives and dozens of rail cars, as well as antique automobiles, including North Carolina's first Highway Patrol car. The site has a terrific gift shop with railroad items not found elsewhere. Part of the facility's mission is to restore and preserve artifacts from North Carolina's transportation history.

Meanwhile, special "Thomas the Tank Engine" days and other seasonal train rides are held periodically. Regular hours (May-Oct) are 9 a.m. to 5 p.m. Mon through Sat, and 1 to 5 p.m. Sun. Winter hours (Nov-April) are 9 a.m. until 5 p.m. Tues through Sat, and 1 to 5 p.m. Sun. To get to Spencer Shops from Charlotte, take I-85 North to exit 79. Free admission to museum; train rides $6 adults, $5 ages 3 to 12 and seniors. Ride in the cab with the engineer for $10.

OUR TOWN CINEMAS
227 Griffith St., Davidson
(704) 237-3235
www.ourtowncinemas.com

Davidson received a cool present Christmas day 2009 with the opening of Our Town Cinemas. This "movie theater" is more an old-school cinema. Two 90-seat theaters and two 40-seat theaters show first-run movies in a comfortable setting. The seats are oversized office chairs, complete with rollers, and clustered around small tables. Concession stand items include hamburgers from White Castle and hotdogs from Nathan's, plus pizzas from nearby Brick House Tavern. Say "no" to big-box mega-theaters and "yes" to this hometown movie house. Tickets are $9 adults, $8 students, and $7 seniors and kids 3 to 12. Matinees are $7 for everybody.

PARAMOUNT'S CAROWINDS
Avenue of the Carolinas
I-77 South at Exit 90
(800) 888-4386
www.carowinds.com

Paramount's Carowinds, a world-class 112-acre theme and water park, features more than 50 thrill rides, shows, and movie-theme experiences for all ages, as well as numerous shops and restaurants. The park straddles the North Carolina–South Carolina state line and that location inspired its unusual name.

The park's main draw is a heart-pounding collection of 12 roller coasters, including the Intimidator, the most-anticipated ride in the park's 38-year history when it debuted in 2010. The super-speed coaster is named for local NASCAR legend Dale Earnhardt Sr., whose brash driving style earned him the "Intimidator" nickname. It reaches speeds in excess of 75 miles per hour, making it the fastest roller coaster in the Southeast.

Another great ride is the BORG Assimilator, a unique flying coaster that suspends riders below the track in a horizontal superhero-like position. This Star Trek–theme coaster travels up to 50 mph in twists and sweeping turns, most of which are taken face first in the flying position. The 11-story coaster also boasts eight inversions, the most of any theme park in the Southeast. Another popular scream-your-head-off ride is the Top Gun Jet Coaster. The Top Gun climbs

113 feet, races at 62 mph, and shoots through six inversions in a suspended car hanging from a track above. On hot, humid days check out the Flying Super Saturator, the world's first high-flying water ride and suspended swing coaster surrounded by spray stations, water cannons, geysers, and water curtains. Guests waiting in line can douse riders from 22 spray stations. But beware: Each car is equipped with 16 gallons of water for riders to drop on the crowd below.

Other coasters include the Vortex, in which riders stand up for loops and drops at 50 mph; the Hurler, a "most excellent" 50-mph attraction in Wayne's World; the Carolina Cyclone, with four consecutive 360-degree loops and an uphill helix; and Thunder Road, a traditional favorite with twin racers and a stomach-dropping hill plunge. Carolina Goldrusher has been around for decades, but is fun for younger kids and adults who've chickened-out of the thrill rides.

Two other don't-miss thrill rides for adrenaline junkies: Drop Zone (shoot up a 16-story tower in seconds, then free-fall at 56 mph) and Xtreme Sky Flyer (harnessed and hoisted 153 feet in the air, riders pull a rip cord and experience a 50-foot free fall at 60 mph).

There's plenty for younger kids, too, such as the Animation Station section with train rides; an antique carousel; and characters such as Scooby Doo, Dora the Explorer, and Boy Genius Jimmy Neutron. Children also enjoy the Taxi Jam coaster, the high-flying Chopper Chase, and the Road Rally. Families can climb aboard the Mystery Machine for an interactive ghost hunt in the Scooby Doo Haunted Mansion, navigate a rugged river with the Wild Thornberrys, or plunge down 45-foot waterfalls on WhiteWater Falls. When it's time for a break, shows include Meet the Nicktoons Live, Nickelodeon Celebration Parade, and Paramount's Magic of the Movies Live with a behind-the-scenes look at special effects in blockbuster films.

In 2006 Carowinds introduced Boomerang Bay, an adjacent Aussie-themed 15-acre water playground. It has more than 25 water activities, including more than a dozen water slides, a tropical lagoon, a 1,000-foot lazy river, a wave pool, and two play areas for families. Boomerang Bay is open to all Carowinds ticket holders. Headlining Boomerang Bay are the Koobaburra Bay and Platypus Plunge. Kookaburra Bay is a 125,000-gallon heated lagoon, where swimmers wade in and splash under mushroom-shaped fountains. Platypus Plunge, a double water slide with a two-person tube, sends kids and families twisting, curving, and slipping through 100 feet of turns before splashing into a pool.

Other highlights include the Great Barrier Reef, a 25,000-square-foot pool with surfing waves; Pipeline Peak, a cluster of four enclosed slides; and Awesome Aussie Twister, a black-hole tube ride in total darkness. Down Under Thunder lets four people raft down a slide four stories tall. For the less adventurous, Crocodile Run offers a leisurely float down a lazy river.

Carowinds also schedules concerts and special events at its 13,000-seat Palladium Amphitheater. Shows run mid-April to mid-September and require a separate ticket.

Open weekends spring and fall, daily during summer, Paramount's Carowinds has a popular one-price ticket covering all rides and park shows. General admission is $49.99 adults, $22.99 children and seniors. Season passes begin at $59.99, with a $79.99 option that includes free parking and admission to Scarowinds Halloween Haunt in October. Parking is $10. Carowinds is located 10 miles south of Uptown.

QUEEN'S LANDING
CATAWBA QUEEN AND *LADY OF THE LAKE*
1459 River Hwy., Mooresville
(704) 663-2628
www.queenslanding.com
The main attractions at this family entertainment center overlooking Lake Norman are the *Catawba Queen,* a replica of a Mississippi paddlewheel boat; and *Lady of the Lake,* a 90-foot luxury yacht. Sit back, relax, and enjoy a cruise on scenic Lake Norman. There are sightseeing cruises, lunch cruises, and dinner cruises. Queen's Landing also features mini-golf, a deli/grill, a dueling piano bar, and Lake Norman's only floating dock bar.

Close-up

The Intimidator Cometh!

The tallest, fastest, and longest roller coaster in the Southeast.

Got your attention? That's what Carowinds was hoping when it created the **Intimidator.** Named after NASCAR legend Dale Earnhardt Sr., this coaster is some kind of fast. It reaches speeds in excess of 75 miles per hour and has a heart-swallowing first drop of 211 feet at a 74-degree angle. Overall, the Intimidator covers 5,316 feet of track—more than a mile—and each ride lasts three minutes and 33 seconds.

As daring as the late Earnhardt was in his Hall of Fame racing career, he never drove a "side-less" car. However, that's exactly what riders experience when locked into the coaster's open-air cars patterned after Earnhardt's legendary No. 3 Chevrolet Monte Carlo.

Although much emphasis is placed on the gigantic first hill, this super coaster is no one-trick pony. There are seven remaining hills, including three that are 178 feet, 151 feet, and 105 feet. Designed by Swiss engineers, the $23-million Intimidator has several turns banked higher than Talladega or Daytona. And for all you non-NASCAR fans out there, yes, the roller coaster does turn right.

Carowinds' Intimidator is one of two unveiled in 2010 by parent company Cedar Fair Entertainment. Sister park Kings Dominion in Richmond, Va., is home to the other Intimidator. The coasters received the blessing of Dale Earnhardt Inc. and the Dale Earnhardt Foundation, and the first rides in at both parks were auctioned off, with the proceeds going to benefit local charities via the foundation.

"We are delighted to partner with Cedar Fair Entertainment to commemorate Dale's legacy with the Intimidator roller coaster," said Teresa Earnhardt, Dale's wife and CEO of Dale Earnhardt Inc.

If you can't wait to experience the Intimidator in person, take an amazing (and somewhat scary) simulated ride online at: http://intimidator.carowinds.com.

Sightseeing cruises aboard the *Catawba Queen* leave at 11 a.m. and 1 p.m. daily. The *Catawba Queen* dinner cruises are at 7 p.m. daily. Tickets are $12.50, $19.50 including lunch, and $46.95 including dinner. *Lady of the Lake* dinner cruises depart at 7:30 p.m. nightly and cost $56.95 per person. Reservations required for dinner and for groups of six or more.

REED GOLD MINE
9621 Reed Mine Rd., Midland
(704) 721-4653
www.nchistoricsites.org/reed
California's 1849 gold rush may be better known, but Reed Gold Mine 25 miles east of Charlotte is actually the site of the first authenticated gold find in the United States. Young Conrad Reed discovered a 17-pound nugget in 1799, and for three years the family used what they thought was just a yellow rock as a doorstop. After a Fayetteville jeweler identified the rock as gold and bought it for a measly $3.50, the gold rush began.

Today visitors flock to this remote Cabarrus County spot where they can tour the underground mine, walk the nature trails, enjoy a picnic, visit the gift shop, or learn more about gold mining in the museum. There is no charge to tour the museum or mine, but it does cost $2 to pan for gold. Hours are 9 a.m. to 5 p.m. Tues through Sat. Be sure to visit in late October for the annual haunted mine Halloween thriller and hayride.

SCHIELE MUSEUM OF NATURAL HISTORY & PLANETARIUM
1500 East Garrison Blvd., Gastonia
(704) 866-6900
www.schielemuseum.org

One of the most visited museums in North Carolina, the 60,000-square-foot Schiele features an outstanding exhibit of the state's natural history, an extensive collection of North American land mammals, informative prehistoric exhibits, plus a 50-foot domed planetarium. Both children and adults enjoy the nature trail and 18th-century backcountry farm, a pioneer site where living-history demonstrations are staged throughout the year. Also on the nature trail, the Catawba Indian Village includes a prehistoric bark-covered reproduction house, a large council house, and two log cabins, all depicting the way of life of local Native Americans.

Hours are 9 a.m. to 5 p.m. Mon through Sat and 1 to 5 p.m. Sun. Entry is $7 for adults, $6 for seniors and students, and free for children 3 and under. City of Gastonia residents receive discounted rates, and there are additional fees for planetarium and special exhibits. From Charlotte, take I-85 South to Gastonia's New Hope Road exit. Follow New Hope Road southward to Garrison Boulevard, and turn right on Garrison. The museum will be on your right.

TIME WARNER CABLE ARENA
333 East Trade St.
(704) 688-9000
www.timewarnercablearena.com

Time Warner Cable Arena was built to house Charlotte's second NBA basketball franchise, the Bobcats. It seats 19,026. This $265-million state-of-the-art facility is owned by the city of Charlotte and operated by the Bobcats, but it is important to note this is not just a basketball arena. Since its inception in October 2005, Time Warner Cable Arena has hosted major national music acts like U2, The Police, Bruce Springsteen & the E Street Band, Van Halen, Bob Seger, Beyonce, Lil' Wayne, Miley Cyrus, Tim McGraw, Taylor Swift, and many others. Other events include Disney on Ice, Ringling Brothers Circus, monster truck rallies, and home games of the Charlotte Checkers minor league hockey team.

Insider Top 5: Off the Beaten Path

Local writer Sara Pitzer, author of *Off the Beaten Path North Carolina* (Globe Pequot Press, 2009) shares her Top 5 off the beaten path attractions in the Charlotte area:

1. **Ben Long Fresco at Bank of America Corporate Center in Charlotte**—This three-panel fresco is Long's largest work to date, depicting work and commerce in a blend of abstract and realism.

2. **Orchid Conservatory at Daniel Stowe Botanical Garden in Belmont**—The only glasshouse for orchids in the Carolinas, and an 8,000-square-foot escape to tropical paradise.

3. **Every/Smith Galleries at Davidson College**—These excellent galleries put you in the heart of Davidson, and the Belk Visual Arts Center is next door.

4. **UNC Charlotte Botanical Gardens**—A great escape hidden on the campus of UNCC, and I especially like the outdoor garden with its emphasis on native North Carolina plants.

5. **The Lazy 5 Ranch outside of Mooresville**—A drive-through park with 3.5 miles of animals from across the globe. View water buffalo, zebras, and giraffes from the safety of your car, or ride in their horse-drawn wagons.

The high-tech arena features one of the largest indoor scoreboards in the nation, and the largest video screen in the NBA. Other interesting elements include Rock the Rooftop, a fan zone in the upper concourse that is open to the arena bowl below. Adults enjoy indoor tailgating while kids play in an interactive area. Public art, a range of food and beverage options, and a team store also are part of the arena.

In addition to hosting Bobcats games, Time Warner Cable Arena has hosted a number of college basketball conference tournaments and opening round games of the NCAA tournament. Each December, thousands of young professionals flock to the arena for the Second String Santa Christmas party, which provides school supplies to children in need.

Tours of the arena are available by appointment for groups up to 20. Requests must be made between 14 to 90 days prior to the date of the tour by calling (704) 688-TOUR.

UNC CHARLOTTE BOTANICAL GARDENS
Highway 49, UNC Charlotte
(704) 687-2364
http://gardens.uncc.edu
Less promoted than other local gardens, UNC Charlotte's Botanical Gardens offer a quiet oasis in the middle of the northern Charlotte suburbs, shopping centers, and research parks. Three unusual gardens await: (1) the two-level McMillan Greenhouse, which includes orchids, desert plants, carnivorous plants, spice and fruit plants, and a kaleidoscope of tropical ferns, vines, and flowers; (2) the seven-acre VanLandingham Glen, with more than 3,000 hybrid rhododendrons and 1,000 trees; and (3) the Susie Harwood Garden featuring exotic ornamentals and Oriental architecture.

The McMillian Greenhouse was the center of national attention in July 2007 when Bella, a rare titan arum, bloomed. The titan arum is known as the "corpse flower" because it smells like rotting flesh when it blooms. Bella was the first titan arum to ever bloom in the Carolinas and only the 20th to do so in North America. The staff reported attendance of 4,000 that week, and tens of thousands more watched it online via a greenhouse Webcam.

The outdoor gardens are open seven days a week during daylight hours, and the McMillan Greenhouse is open 10 a.m. to 3 p.m. Mon through Sat, and on Sun from 1 to 4 p.m. Free.

> **i** The largest city between Washington, D.C., and Atlanta, Charlotte is the No. 1 travel destination in the Carolinas with 18 million visitors a year. The travel and tourism industry generates more than $3.5 billion a year in the Charlotte area.

U.S. NATIONAL WHITEWATER CENTER
5000 Whitewater Center Parkway
(704) 391-3900
www.usnwc.org
The world's largest man-made whitewater river is the main attraction at the U.S. National Whitewater Center, which opened in August 2006 on the banks of the Catawba River, just west of Charlotte. The county-owned 307-acre center also includes a 22,000-square-foot lodge and conference center, a rock-climbing tower, zip lines, and mountain-biking trails. Visitors can watch Olympic-caliber paddlers kayak the Class III and IV rapids or can pay $49 for an AllSport day pass, which includes a 90-minute run in a raft. The $35-million center, the idea of two paddlers who jotted the initial design on a napkin, features four adjustable channels that control the flow of water and size of the rapids. While North Carolina's mountains have several appealing natural whitewater runs, Charlotte's Whitewater Center offers the convenience of paddling within 20 minutes of Uptown.

The park and trails are open, weather permitting, 365 days a year from dawn to dusk.

VERIZON WIRELESS AMPHITHEATER
707 Pavilion Blvd.
(704) 549-5555
www.livenation.com
Located 11 miles from Uptown on US 29 North near UNC Charlotte, Verizon Wireless Amphitheater attracts some of North Carolina's biggest

concerts and music festivals during its warm-weather season, which runs from April through October. Guests can bring a blanket and relax outside with refreshments from the concession areas (sorry, you can't bring your own). Performers have included Sting, Rod Stewart, Dave Matthews Band, Alan Jackson, Blink 182, Fleetwood Mac, Rush, and John Mayer.

WING HAVEN GARDENS & BIRD SANCTUARY
248 Ridgewood Ave.
(704) 331-0664
www.winghavengardens.com

Wing Haven was only a bare three-acre patch of land in 1927 when Edwin and Elizabeth Clarkson built their home and began working on their garden in this quiet pocket of Myers Park. Now, more than 75 years later, the fruits of their labor include formal gardens, wooded areas, pools, and fountains in a peaceful city retreat.

The gardens are now the responsibility of the Wing Haven Foundation, a nonprofit corporation. Membership is open to anyone. The gardens are open 3 until 5 p.m. Tues, 10 a.m. to noon Wed, and 10 a.m. to 5 p.m. Sat. Guided tours may be arranged Tues, Thurs, and Fri mornings. Admission is $5 per person.

KIDSTUFF

Although it's sometimes okay to take the kids along on activities geared toward mom and dad, most of the time parents need activities and attractions that specialize in kid-friendly fun. Fortunately, Charlotte has a well-rounded offering of "kidstuff" that will keep the little ones engaged and entertained.

The possibilities seem endless—from a safari at Lazy 5 Ranch to panning for gold at Reed Gold Mine to clanging the bell on the historic Charlotte Trolley, kids will have a ball in the Queen City. There are waterparks, museums, ice-skating rinks, laser-tag arenas and more.

Here's a smattering of what insiders in the Queen City recommend to newcomers and visitors with kids in tow. For more ideas, check out our Attractions, Day Trips, and Parks and Recreation chapters. Local newspapers and free specialty publications (see *Charlotte Parent* magazine) are good sources for information on upcoming family events and activities.

Entries in this chapter are arranged alphabetically under type of activity. Listings are located in Charlotte unless otherwise noted.

MUSEUMS AND HISTORIC SITES

CHARLOTTE MUSEUM OF HISTORY AND HEZEKIAH ALEXANDER HOMESITE
3500 Shamrock Dr.
(704) 568-1774
www.charlottemuseum.org

The Charlotte Museum of History gives you a "slice of life" of the North Carolina Piedmont region with a special focus on the history of Charlotte and Mecklenburg County. The museum offers exhibits, classes, arts and crafts demonstrations, and occasional special events.

The Hezekiah Alexander homesite, home to a signer of the 1775 Mecklenburg Declaration of Independence, was built in 1774 of stone quarried nearby. The oldest original dwelling still standing in Mecklenburg County, it is listed in the National Register of Historic Places. Learn how the Alexanders lived through costumed docents who demonstrate gardening, cooking, and other backcountry pioneer skills. A reconstructed barn, a kitchen, and a springhouse are also on the property.

Guided tours ($6 adults, $5 seniors and students, $3 children) are given Tues through Sun afternoons. The homesite hosts several events of

interest to children throughout the year, including the Rites of Spring (where sheep shearing is a popular spectator sport), a Summer Sampler, and a Colonial Christmas program.

CHARLOTTE TROLLEY AND MUSEUM
2104 South Blvd. at Atherton Mill
(704) 375-0850
www.charlottetrolley.org

The Charlotte Trolley makes for a fun history lesson for kids, who quickly become enamored of the clanging bell and rattling streetcar running between the restored mills and factories of South End and the glistening skyscrapers of Uptown. Conductors share the history of the trolley, which carried Charlotteans between Uptown and the city's first suburbs from 1887 until 1938, and passers-by wave to folks who've hopped aboard.

The trolley runs on weekends from Atherton Mill in South End through a glass tunnel inside the Charlotte Convention Center on Stonewall Street and up to Ninth Street. Trolley hours are 10 a.m. to 5 p.m. Sat and 10:30 a.m. to 5:30 p.m. Sun. Cost is $1.50 one way or $3 round trip for adults. Seniors and youth pay half price. The museum is open 9:30 a.m. to 5 p.m. weekdays.

ℹ New moms (and new-to-Charlotte moms) trade tips, receive encouragement, plan play dates, share recipes, and arrange nights out without the kids at http://charlottemommies.com. This free, members-only online community lets mothers connect with fellow moms in various parts of the city. Women can ask advice about raising children, find play groups with children of similar ages, share stories, and get referrals from their peers. Sponsored by *Charlotte Parent* magazine, http://charlottemommies.com has more than 3,000 members.

DISCOVERY PLACE
301 North Tryon St.
(704) 372-6261
www.discoveryplace.org

Discovery Place is one of the largest and most exciting science and nature museums in the country. It contains the OMNIMAX Theater, a planetarium, a replica of a tropical rain forest, aquariums, computer labs, discovery areas for young children, and much more. It's easy to spend a day or two inside the sprawling complex in Uptown Charlotte. The museum offers classes, workshops, and day camp activities for children of all ages.

Discovery Place hours are 9 a.m. to 4 p.m. Mon through Fri; 10 a.m. to 6 p.m. Sat; and noon until 5 p.m. Sun. Museum admission is $10 adults and $8 children and seniors. Combo tickets that include an IMAX showing range from $16–$19 for adults, and $13–$15 for children and seniors. Separate rates for the IMAX theater are also available.

HARVEY B. GANTT CENTER FOR AFRICAN-AMERICAN ARTS + CULTURE
551 South Tryon St.
(704) 547-3700
www.ganttcenter.org

Children of diverse backgrounds explore African-American history and heritage at this fabulous museum in the Wells Fargo Cultural Campus in Uptown. The center includes an art gallery with changing exhibits, theater and musical productions, and a wide range of classes and programs

for all ages. Subjects include African-American role models, literature, art, jazz history, folk crafts, and music.

Hours are 10 a.m. until 5 p.m. Tues through Sat, and 1 to 5 p.m. on Sun. Admission is $8 per person, and $5 per person for seniors and groups.

IMAGINON
300 East Seventh St.
(704) 416-4600
www.limaginon.org

One of the coolest kids' attractions in Charlotte, ImaginOn opened in fall 2005 as a multimedia playground jointly created by the public library and Children's Theatre of Charlotte. Designed around the common theme of storytelling, the 102,000-square-foot building lets children read stories, see stories performed, and even film a story they created.

Drama fans will enjoy professional productions by the Children's Theatre of Charlotte in a 580-seat main theater, where shows such as *Junie B. Jones, Billy Jonas,* and *The Magician's Nephew* are held. A 250-seat Playhouse Theatre houses smaller productions.

In The Round, kids can attend storytelling events and watch puppet theaters or go outside in the adjacent courtyard for creative play and reading.

Older kids enjoy Tech Central, a light-filled area with 35 flat-screen computers for homework, writing, or editing animations or films made on site. Teenagers head to The Loft to work on projects, read books or magazines, check out audiovisual materials, surf the Web, or plug in a laptop. Nearby studio i challenges kids to use animation and video to tell their own stories.

Other educational spaces at ImaginOn include the Children's Library, a computer lab, and studios for art and dance. Best of all, the only thing you'll pay for is admission to shows. Exploring the building and using the library are free, as is 90 minutes worth of parking in ImaginOn's underground parking deck. Three hours of free parking are available in the Seventh Street Station parking deck after 5 p.m. weekdays and anytime on weekends.

Open 9 a.m. to 9 p.m. Mon through Thurs, 9 a.m. to 6 p.m. Fri and Sat, and 1 to 6 p.m. Sun.

LATTA PLANTATION
5225 Sample Rd., Huntersville
(704) 875-2312
www.lattaplantation.org
Latta Plantation is the restored and furnished house (circa 1800) of James Latta, a merchant and planter in the Catawba River region. Guided tours are available of the house, which is listed on the National Register of Historic Places. There are outbuildings and gardens to explore, and farm animals graze nearby.

The Carolina Raptor Center (see the Science, Nature, and the Outdoors section of this chapter) and the Latta Plantation Equestrian Center are also on the grounds of the 700-acre nature preserve overlooking Mountain Island Lake just northwest of Charlotte. During the summer the park operates one-week day camps and offers riding instruction and classes on equestrian care.

Plan to bring a picnic and spend a sunny afternoon hiking, canoeing, or riding horses through the old plantation grounds. See the Attractions chapter for hours and prices, or call for information.

MINT MUSEUM RANDOLPH
2730 Randolph Rd.
(704) 337-2000
www.mintmuseum.org
The Mint was originally built as the first branch of the United States Mint in 1836. Among other uses, the building later served as a headquarters for the Confederacy and as a hospital. The Mint building was moved to its present location in 1933 and opened as North Carolina's first art museum in 1936.

The museum includes fine collections of pre-Columbian art, American and European paintings, decorative arts, and special collections such as North Carolina and African galleries.

The Mint Randolph is open 10 a.m. until 9 p.m. on Tues, and 10 a.m. until 5 p.m. Wed through Sat. Admission is $10 for adults, $8 for seniors and college students, and $5 for ages 5 to 17. Children

under 5 admitted free, and everyone is in for free on Tues from 5 until 9 p.m. Tickets are also good at the Uptown location on the same day.

NORTH CAROLINA TRANSPORTATION MUSEUM AT HISTORIC SPENCER SHOPS
411 South Salisbury Ave., Spencer
(704) 636-2889
www.nctrans.org
Take a train ride and see antique cars, engines, and railway cars at this former locomotive repair facility. The state transportation museum also sponsors special events for kids, including "Thomas the Tank Engine" days. Free museum admission; train rides $6 adults, $5 ages 3 to 12 and seniors. Ride in the cab with an engineer for $10.

PUBLIC LIBRARY OF CHARLOTTE AND MECKLENBURG COUNTY
310 North Tryon St.
(704) 416-0100
www.plcmc.org
The main library and its 24 branches offer a wealth of activities for children throughout the year—storytimes, educational programs, films and videos, family-day programs, and special exhibitions and events. Its facilities offer traditional services and the latest in computer technology. The library has been named Library of the Year and Library of the Future and has received awards for its youth coordinator. Kids can also visit the Bookhive page on the library Web site for children's literature, books, and reading.

REED GOLD MINE
9621 Reed Mine Rd., Midland
(704) 721-4653
www.reedmine.com
Pan for real gold at the site of the first documented discovery of gold in the United States. The Reed Gold Mine includes a museum, guided tours of the old mine, nature trails, picnic area, and gift shop. Admission is free; gold panning is $2 per pan.

If the kids are brave enough, visit the Reed Gold Mine in October for the annual haunted mine Halloween thriller and hayride.

ENTERTAINMENT

BIRKDALE VILLAGE
I-77 at Exit 25, Huntersville
(704) 895-8744
www.birkdalevillage.net

A popular pedestrian-friendly shopping center at Lake Norman, Birkdale Village features a center fountain that's often packed with frolicking youngsters on hot summer days. Treat the kids to a wood-fired pizza at Brixx, a matinee movie, a stop at the ice-cream shop, and a splash in the fountain, or return for outdoor concerts, a Fourth of July parade, an autumn pumpkin patch, trick-or-treating, and visits with Santa Claus and the Easter Bunny. Free.

BUILD-A-BEAR WORKSHOP
Carolina Place Mall
11025 Carolina Place Parkway, Pineville
(704) 543-9800

Concord Mills, I-85 at Exit 49
8111 Concord Mills Blvd.
(704) 979-0328

Northlake Mall
I-77 at Exit 18
6801 Northlake Mall Dr.
(704) 494-4403
www.buildabear.com

Build-A-Bear Workshops let youngsters create a personalized stuffed animal from among 30 styles and hundreds of outfits and accessories. Kids choose a stuffed animal, watch workers put in its heart, help stuff the bear, and choose clothes for it before filling out a computerized birth certificate and storybook. Everything from sunglasses and hats to T-shirts are available, along with recorded sounds, personalized embroidered clothing, and cub condos to carry them home. Animals start at $10, not including clothes. Birthday parties also are big here. Pineville location open 10 a.m. until 9 p.m. Mon through Sat, noon until 6 p.m. Sun. Concord location open 10 a.m. until 9 p.m. Mon through Sat, noon until 7 p.m. Sun. Northlake location open 10 a.m. until 9 p.m. Mon through Sat, noon until 6 p.m. Sun.

CHILDREN'S THEATRE OF CHARLOTTE
300 East Seventh St. at ImaginOn
(704) 973-2800
(704) 973-2828 (box office)
www.ctcharlotte.org

The Children's Theatre of Charlotte has produced professional performances by and for kids ages 3 to 18 since 1948. The Theatre's Mainstage productions are for the whole family and include shows such as Madeline, Hansel and Gretel, and The Littlest Angel. Ensemble shows are performed by kids in grades 8 and up. The Theatre also hosts other productions by well-known local and touring performers such as the Grey Seal Puppets and Billy Jonas.

Educational programs at the theater teach drama, acting, and musical theater to thespians from ages 3 through high school.

ICE HOUSE
400 Towne Centre Blvd., Pineville
(704) 889-9000
www.icehouserinks.com

Though ice-skating has never been the South's biggest sport, it's grown in popularity in recent years. And, thanks to the Ice House, anyone can enjoy skating year-round here in Dixie. Adults and children can take lessons or just skate for the pure pleasure of it. It's also a great place for birthday parties, and for children to learn how to play hockey. There is a youth hockey academy and youth hockey leagues. Public skate sessions are offered daily. Call or visit the Web site for details.

i Want to go ice skating Rockefeller Center-style without flying to New York City? Each year, from late November through early January, radio station WBT sponsors the Holiday on Ice skating rink in Uptown Charlotte. The outdoor ice skating rink is built at The Green, a park adjacent to The Ratcliffe condominium building on South Tryon Street. For details visit www.wbtholidayonice.com.

INNER PEAKS CLIMBING CENTER
9535 Monroe Rd.
(704) 844-6677
www.innerpeaks.com
The largest indoor climbing gym in the Charlotte area, Inner Peaks has 8,000 square feet of sculptured climbing walls and 40 top rope stations. Beginning, moderate, and advanced terrain is offered, and beginners can learn in a separate teaching area. Tall, challenging lead climbs, long traverses, and obstacles such as arches, roofs, and cracks give climbers practice for many climbing situations. Open noon until 10 p.m. Mon through Fri; 10 a.m. to 7 p.m. Sat; and noon until 7 p.m. Sun. Individual day passes $14, equipment rental $8. Memberships, monthly discounts for children 12 and under, and birthday parties available. Located in rear of Greylyn Business Park.

LASER QUEST CHARLOTTE
5323-A East Independence Blvd.
(704) 567-6707
www.laserquest.com
Step inside an obstacle-filled room illuminated with black lights for the ultimate game of tag. Birthday parties and special all-night sessions also available. Open Wed through Sun, and available for private events on Mon and Tues. Cost is $8 per person for a 20-minute game. Memberships available.

MECKLENBURG AQUATIC CENTER
800 E. Martin Luther King Blvd.
(704) 336-3483
www.charmeck.org
Among the most under-utilized facilities in the city, the Mecklenburg Aquatic Center is a great place to take the kids. There is lane swimming available in a 50-meter competition pool and a 25-yard instructional warm pool. The center also has relics from your childhood that your kids may have never seen in person—diving boards.

Birthday parties are available and the center even offers kayaking classes for children. Daily admission is $8 for non-resident adults and $4 for non-resident children. Resident rates are $5 and $3. Open daily with varying hours of operation.

NASCAR SPEEDPARK
Concord Mills, I-85 at Exit 49
(704) 979-6770
www.nascarspeedpark.com
One of six NASCAR SpeedParks in North America, this seven-acre racing amusement park features five tracks, including a quarter-mile oval with 5/8-scale Nextel Cup–style cars, a slip-and-slide with twists and turns, an indoor two-story figure-8 track, and a 200-foot starter track for kids. Several area NASCAR drivers have made appearances, and it's a popular place for children's birthday parties.

Height requirements are 40 inches for The Qualifier track, 48 inches for The Rookie track, and 54 inches for the SlideWayz and Champions tracks.

Other kid fun includes speed bumper boats, an 18-hole mini-golf course, an arcade with 50-plus games, a rock-climbing wall, an indoor playground, laser tag arena, and kids' rides. Individual track tickets are $3.50, or you can buy packages of seven tickets for $18 or 12 tickets for $25. Annual passes also available. Open at 10 a.m. Mon through Sat, and 11 a.m. Sun. Closing times vary. Located at Concord Mills Entry 7.

ℹ️ The Charlotte Knights minor league baseball team has a Junior Knights Kids Club that's a real bargain. For about $25, kids receive a membership card good for admission to 10 home games, Junior Knights T-shirt, set of Knights baseball cards, monthly newsletter, and discounts in the team store and on birthday parties at Knights Stadium. Charlotte is the Triple-A affiliate of the Chicago White Sox.

OUTDOOR FAMILY FUN POOL
11725 Verhoeff Dr., Huntersville
(704) 766-2222
www.hffa.com
One of the most popular places in town to cool off is this $8.5-million facility at Huntersville Family Fitness & Aquatics. Standard swimming pools seem boring after kids dive into the Fun Pool's interactive water activities—spraying

water spouts, a playground in the middle of the shallow pool, waterfalls, tubes, slides, and, best of all, water cannons that douse those who dare to step too close. Indoor swimming lessons also available for kids. Hours and days vary based on the season.

PARAMOUNT'S CAROWINDS
Avenue of the Carolinas
I-77 South at Exit 90
(800) 888-4386
www.carowinds.com
What better way to fulfill a child's fantasy than a day with Scooby Doo, Dora the Explorer, and Boy Genius Jimmy Neutron? Paramount's Carowinds has big fun for little visitors at Boomerang Bay water park, Zoom Zone with three diving rides, and Animation Station, a special area of more than 15 attractions and shows for families with young children. For the older child, the Southeast's best selection of roller coasters and adrenaline-packed water-park rides provide a day of fun and excitement. For more information on Paramount's Carowinds, see our Attractions chapter.

RAY'S SPLASH PLANET
215 North Sycamore St.
(704) 432-4729
www.charmeck.org
A joint venture between the Mecklenburg County Park and Recreation Department and Charlotte-Mecklenburg Schools, Ray's Splash Planet is an indoor water park adjacent to Irwin Avenue Open Elementary School in the Fourth Ward section of Uptown. Open year-round, Ray's has all the features of an outdoor water park without the worry of rain or cool temperatures. The Blue Comet is a three-story giant slide in the form of double figure eights, and Saturation Station has four slides, interactive water play, and tumble buckets. The Vortex is a circular pool with a quick current, while the Orbiter winds tube riders around the Blue Comet slide on a slow, relaxing journey. Fill-and-spill buckets, squirters, a gradual-entry pool, water basketball, water volleyball, and lap swimming complete the fun. Birthday parties can be

held in private rooms, and there's a playground and concession stand. There's also a fitness center where mom and dad can get in a workout while the children play.

Open daily, with varying hours of operation depending on the season. Daily rates are $6 for county residents up to age 17 and $8 for adult county residents. Non-resident rates are $8 youth, $11 adults. Bring your own towel.

> **i** Pike's Soda Shop at 1930 Camden Rd. in South End is a great place to take kids for lunch. The old-fashioned soda shop serves kid-friendly sandwiches like grilled cheese, Kahn's hot dogs, thick milk shakes, fresh-squeezed lemonade, and fountain Cokes. After lunch take a ride on the historic Charlotte Trolley, clanging the bell and waving at folks on Pike's patio nearby.

SPIRIT SQUARE CENTER FOR THE ARTS
345 North College St.
(704) 348-5750
www.performingartsctr.org
There's just about everything associated with the arts here: seven art galleries with a variety of changing exhibits, three theaters for dramatic and musical productions, and classes galore for adults and children. Spirit Square is located in a renovated church building, creating a unique setting for artistic expression.

ZUMA FUN CENTER
10400 Cadillac St., Pineville
(704) 552-7888
www.zumafuncenter.com
Formerly Celebration Station, this popular spot for birthday parties and family outings has miniature golf, bumper boats, go-kart rides, batting cages, a video arcade, and a huge indoor play station with a monstrous two-story slide. When you're tired from all the activity, there's plenty to eat and drink while you rest up for the next go-round. All-day pass is $18.99; attractions also priced individually. Open noon to 8 p.m. Mon through Thurs; noon to 11 p.m. Fri; 10 a.m. until 11 p.m. Sat; and noon to 9 p.m. Sun.

SCIENCE, NATURE, AND THE OUTDOORS

BIRDBRAIN OSTRICH RANCH
6691 Little Mountain Rd., Sherrills Ford
(704) 483-1620
www.birdbrainranch.com

The first thing to note about BirdBrain Ostrich Ranch is this is a commercial operation that raises ostriches as a source of meat. So, make sure the kids are okay with the notion that these cute and quirky birds will end up on someone's kitchen table.

BirdBrain provides an in-depth look in the ostrich industry, past and present. You get the historical perspective with postcards and memorabilia from farms in the late 1800s and early 1900s. You also learn the products that are obtained from ostriches, including meat, leather, feathers, eggs, and oils used in household products. The most popular part of the tour is the up-close opportunity to feed these unique animals their "dinosaur" food. Open Sat and Sun by appointment only; $5 per person. After the tour, stop for an ostrich burger at The Landing, a nearby restaurant.

CAROLINA RAPTOR CENTER
Latta Plantation Nature Preserve
6000 Sample Rd., Huntersville
(704) 875-6521
www.carolinaraptorcenter.org

This unusual educational conservation and rehabilitation facility north of Charlotte fascinates children with close-up encounters with hawks, owls, eagles, falcons, ospreys, and vultures. The birds come to the center injured or orphaned, and are released back to the wild if possible. Others live here as teaching tools for youngsters to learn about habitats and hunting methods, adaptations, life in the wild, endangerment, and the respect birds of prey have in different cultures. Programs include behind-the-scenes tours, wildlife photography, and festivals with hay rides, science shows, crafts, and storytelling.

Presentations with live birds take place three times on Sat (11 a.m., 1 and 3 p.m.) and twice on Sun (1 and 3 p.m.), weather permitting. Hours of operation are 10 a.m. until 5 p.m. Mon through Sat, noon to 5 p.m. Sun. The center is closed Mon and Tues during winter. Admission is $8 adults, $7 seniors, $6 students, free under age 5. Group rates also available.

i Visiting families, or local families in search of an easy getaway, should check out the Great Wolf Lodge in Concord. Children love Great Wolf because of its massive indoor waterpark, which has everything from a four-story treehouse water fort to tube slide races on mats. Don't forget to check out the wet and wild Howlin' Tornado, a six-story funnel drop. As with other Great Wolf Lodges, access to the waterpark is included in the room rate and you have to stay on property to experience the fun.

ENERGYEXPLORIUM
13339 Hagers Ferry Rd., Huntersville
(704) 875-5600
www.duke-energy.com

EnergyExplorium, operated by Duke Energy at the McGuire Nuclear Station on Lake Norman, makes learning fun. It offers hands-on exhibits of model nuclear and coal-fired power plants and a film entitled *Lake Norman—the Great Inland Sea*. Kids love the 1-mile nature trail and lakeside picnic lunches. EnergyExplorium is accessible via boat and car and is open six days a week year round, except for New Year's Day, Easter, Thanksgiving, Christmas Eve, and Christmas. Hours are 9 a.m. until 5 p.m. Mon through Fri, and noon until 5 p.m. Sat. Admission is free.

LAZY 5 RANCH
15100 Mooresville Rd., Mooresville
(704) 663-5100
www.lazy5ranch.com

Not your typical ranch, the Lazy 5 is more like a zoo that stretches over 180 acres of rolling farmland. Visitors can take a leisurely ride along the gravel road in their own vehicles and view the animals or opt for a horse-drawn wagon ride. More than 750 species of animals, many of which come from different continents, roam freely and are not at all shy. They know the routine and will cautiously approach your vehicle—probably hoping that you stocked up on the feed available for purchase at the Welcome Center.

You and your children will be amazed by the beauty of the ranch and the peaceful nature of its inhabitants. The most popular animals are the giraffes, kangaroos, zebras, and water buffaloes. Younger children love the petting area where they can get close to a variety of small and large critters, from baby goats to lambs to camels. There's also a playground, picnic area, trading post, and snack shop. The Lazy 5 Ranch opens daily at 9 a.m., except for Sun, when it opens at 1 p.m. The ranch always closes one hour before sunset. Make sure you bring cash, because Lazy 5 Ranch does not accept debit or credit cards! Admission is $8.50 for adults and $5.50 for ages 2 through 11 and over 60. Wagon rides are an additional $5 for adults and $3 for kids and seniors. Feed is $3 a bucket.

MCDOWELL NATURE CENTER & PRESERVE
15222 York Rd.
(704) 588-5224
www.charmeck.org
McDowell Nature Center serves as the gateway to the 1115-acre McDowell Nature Preserve and is the source for educational programs and information on the preserve's natural communities, flora, and fauna. The preserve, the oldest in Mecklenburg County, is 90 percent undeveloped and covers forested, rolling terrain along the banks of Lake Wylie.

Activities at the nature center include camping, fishing, miles of nature trails, and the indoor nature center. The park sponsors special programs throughout the year: evening campfires and storytelling, moonlight hikes, and nature classes for young and old. No admission charged.

MECKLENBURG COUNTY PARK AND RECREATION'S ECOLOGY PROGRAMS
(704) 598-8857
www.charmeck.org
A number of ecology programs geared to children and adults are offered at various parks in the county. Explore bogs, ponds, and wildlife; join an ecology club; take a canoe ride or hike; or learn about Mecklenburg's unique habitats in Eco-Explorers Camp.

REEDY CREEK NATURE CENTER AND PRESERVE
2900 Rocky River Rd.
(704) 598-8857
www.charmeck.org
Most of this 700-acre nature preserve in northeast Charlotte is in its natural wooded state. There are several fishing lakes on the property, nature trails, picnic sites, ball fields, and a playground. The Environmental Center has exhibits and hands-on activities to enjoy and explore. For Fido, there's a four-acre fenced dog park. Free.

i *For younger children not ready for a full-fledged round of golf, check out The Golf Village on North Polk Street in Pineville. It has a very short, 9-hole course that's perfect for youngsters and beginners. The longest hole is about 100 yards. The Golf Village also has Race Mountain minigolf, a lighted driving range, and a snack bar. Details? Call (704) 889-5086.*

U.S. NATIONAL WHITEWATER CENTER
5000 Whitewater Center Parkway
(704) 391-3900
www.usnwc.org
This 307-acre county-owned play land includes a man-made whitewater river right here in the Piedmont. The center is great for children because they can receive quality instruction in rafting, kayaking, and rock climbing. They can also hike, bike, or zip line. The park and trails are open, weather permitting, 365 days a year from dawn to dusk. For more information, see the Attractions section of this book.

WING HAVEN GARDENS & BIRD SANCTUARY
248 Ridgewood Ave.
(704) 331-0664
www.winghavengardens.com

(Q) Close-up

Rainy-Day Fun

Rain and extreme temperatures don't have to ruin the fun for kids in Charlotte. When the weather's bad, there are various indoor entertainment options in addition to those listed in this chapter. Here's a list of places to get you started.

ARCADES

• **Dave & Buster's,** Concord Mills Mall, I-85 North at exit 49, (704) 979-1700, www.daveand busters.com.

• **Jillian's,** 200 East Bland St. in South End, (704) 376-4386, www.jilliansbilliards.com.

ART

• **Meg-art,** Northcross Shopping Center, I-77 North at exit 25, (704) 896-5211, www.painta-plate.com. Popular paint-your-own pottery shop offering birthday parties, summer camps, and drop-off art sessions.

• **Noah's Art: Park Selwyn Terrace,** 5110 Park Rd., (704) 521-6657, and Stonecrest Shopping Center in Ballantyne, 9852 Rea Rd., (704) 542-2388; www.noahs-art.com. Theme-based art classes, birthday parties, summer classes, and camps for ages 2–10. Free trial class.

EXTREME BOWLING

• **Northcross Lanes at the Lake,** 16317 Statesville Rd., Huntersville, (704) 892-7117, www .northcrosslanes.com. Forty lanes, food court, birthday rooms, video center, laser tag, and billiards.

FITNESS

• **Gymboree Play & Music,** 3419 Toringdon Way in Ballantyne, (704) 759-8521, and 20619 Tor-rence Chapel Rd., Cornelius, (704) 655-9650, www.gymboreeclasses.com. Fun fitness classes, music, art, baby signs, yoga, mom-and-me classes, and more for infants to age 5.

• **The Little Gym,** 9810 Gilead Rd. in Huntersville, (704) 948-7665 and 8700 Pineville-Matthews Rd. in south Charlotte, (704) 541-2940, www.thelittlegym.com. Incorporates music, movement, gymnastics, sports, exercise, listening, and teamwork.

• **My Gym,** 5110 Park Rd. in Park Selwyn Terrace, (704) 522-6966 and 9852 Read Rd., (704) 543-0682, www.my-gym.com. Children's fitness center with open play, scheduled gymnastics-based classes, and birthday parties.

SKATING RINKS

• **Kate's Skating Rink,** 14500 East Independence Blvd., Indian Trail, (704) 821-7645; plus three Gastonia locations and one Rock Hill location. www.katesskating.com or www.kates online.com.

• **Starlight Roller Rink,** 8830 East W.T. Harris Blvd., (704) 568-5700, www.starlightrollerrink .com.

SWIMMING

• **Charlotte Swim Academy,** 9315-A Monroe Rd., (704) 845-8377, www.charlotteswimacademy .com. Kids ages 9 months and up can take swimming lessons or parent-and-tot classes in a 90-degree indoor pool.

• **Little Otter Swim School,** 8200 Tower Point Dr., (704) 846-7946, www.littleotterswim.com. Swim instructors use a gentle, fun approach to teach kids swimming and water safety in this 90-degree indoor pool. Flexible schedule available.

Wing Haven is a beautiful garden and bird sanctuary in the middle of Charlotte, the former home and grounds of Elizabeth and Edwin Clarkson. More than four acres are filled with woods, formal gardens, and lovely walks, and the home, designed to bring the outdoors in and highlight the garden, is also open. There is a garden shop, tours of the home and grounds, and special children's programs throughout the year. The gardens are now the responsibility of the Wing Haven Foundation, a nonprofit corporation. Membership is open to anyone. The gardens are open 3 until 5 p.m. Tues, 10 a.m. to noon Wed, and 10 a.m. to 5 p.m. Sat. Guided tours may be arranged Tues, Thurs, and Fri mornings. Admission is $5 per person.

i Three ski resorts are located less than three hours away in the North Carolina High Country. Appalachian Ski Mountain, between Boone and Blowing Rock, is the most kid friendly. The resort is alcohol free and parents can easily watch their children on the 27-acre ski area from several vantage points in the lodge. App Ski Mountain is also home to the French-Swiss Ski College, which has given more than one million ski lessons. Other skiing options in the High Country are Sugar Mountain Resort in Banner Elk and Beech Mountain Resort in the town of Beech Mountain. Sugar and Beech have more slopes, more advanced runs, and steeper vertical drops. Sugar and Beech also have tubing parks, which are popular with kids. For information go to www.skithehighcountry.com.

CAMPS

Mecklenburg County Park and Recreation offers extensive day camps and playground programs during the summer. Day camps with structured activities are available at more than 20 recreation centers, including Recreation On The Move, which is a mobile recreational unit, fully staffed and equipped to provide supervised experiences in athletics, arts and crafts, music, dance, and special events. The cost varies depending on the program.

Playground programs for which there is no charge are given at several sites and feature planned activities as well as free time. A number of citywide special events, such as the Junior Tennis Tournament, are planned each summer at Renaissance Park.

Mecklenburg County Park and Recreation holds one-week day camps at different sites, featuring special programs, field trips, games, athletics, and arts and crafts. Visit www.parkandrec.com for more information.

Many local YMCA branches schedule camps suited to a range of interests and located at convenient sites around the country.

One of the finest coed boarding camps in the Southeast is YMCA-affiliated Camp Thunderbird on Lake Wylie, where kids learn to water ski, sail, swim, and participate in competitive sports and other activities. (The camp is also a center for the YMCA's extensive Y-Indian Guide program.) Most YMCA camps offer counselor-in-training programs for teens. Since the YMCA camps are very popular, it's a good idea to register early. Some scholarships are available. See www.charlotteymca.org.

The Jewish Community Center's day camp is Camp Maccabee, which is open to everyone, regardless of religious faith. A number of daycare centers and learning/tutoring centers in the Charlotte area also offer summer programs. Call local facilities for more information.

THE ARTS

The Queen City's vibrant arts community is backed by the Arts & Science Council (ASC), a proactive nonprofit organization that provides planning, oversight, and funding to dozens of affiliates in art, science, history, and heritage. Organized in 1958, the ASC operates one of the nation's most successful united arts fund drives, raising between $7 million and $10 million annually.

Charlotte is full of visual and performing arts opportunities. A variety of art graces our buildings, thanks to a city law that requires 1 percent of all new public building costs be allocated to artistic expression. The Queens Table, an anonymous group of arts patrons, has also donated art throughout the city, most notably the statues at Trade and Tryon Streets and Queen Charlotte at the airport. Corporations also add to the artistic landscape, with beautiful pieces such as the Ben Long frescoes in the Bank of America Corporate Center and the Transamerica Square Building. For more information on public art, see the sidebar in this chapter.

Performing arts also are important to Charlotteans. Events range from symphony pops shows at SouthPark and after-work Uptown concerts on Thurs evenings to the Charlotte Sunset Jazz Festival. Holiday traditions include *The Nutcracker* and the Singing Christmas Tree.

On a weekly basis, one of the best ways to find out what's happening in the arts is through the *Charlotte Observer*'s Sunday Arts section. The CLT section, available in Friday's paper, will let you know what's going on around town and in the Carolinas. The ASC (227 West Trade St., Suite 250 in the Carillon Building, 704-372-9667, www.artsandscience.org) is a good place to start if you are interested in becoming involved in the community's arts programs.

The following is a guide to the Charlotte arts community broken down into sections on dance, music, theater, visual arts, and writing. Entries are alphabetical and are located in Charlotte unless otherwise noted.

DANCE

ALLEGRO FOUNDATION
6600 Kirkstall Court
(704) 412-5229
www.allegrofoundation.net
The Allegro Foundation combines movement instruction with education and medical expertise to teach disabled children and enhance their quality of life.

The program serves children who are mentally disabled, have Down syndrome, cerebral palsy, learning delays, emotional problems from abuse or neglect, and orthopedic challenges.

CHARLOTTE YOUTH BALLET
(980) 322-5522
www.charlotteyouthballet.com
Founded in 1980, the Charlotte Youth Ballet provides performance opportunities of the highest artistic level to young dancers, offers a chance to perform with guest talent of national and international acclaim, and performs for a wide variety of audience ranges. Full-length classical ballets such as *Alice in Wonderland* are presented each spring, and *The Nutcracker* is performed each holiday season. Both are held at Halton Theater at Central Piedmont Community College. Charlotte Youth Ballet is the performing division of the Charlotte School of Ballet, led by Gay Porter.

KINETIC WORKS
1609 Nassau Blvd.
(704) 338-1533
www.mckineticworks.org

Founded by contemporary choreographer Martha Connerton in 2000, Kinetic Works offers winter and summer professional concerts at the Harvey B. Gantt Center for African-American Arts + Culture, preprofessional training through intensive workshops, and open classes for intermediate-level teens and adults at Spirit Square. Dance ensembles also perform in local schools.

MOVING POETS THEATER OF DANCE
8116 South Tryon St., Suite B3-209
(704) 527-6683
www.movingpoets.org

This innovative professional performing arts company uniquely merges contemporary dance and theater with visual arts, music, and video to bring great works of literature to life.

N.C. DANCE THEATRE (NCDT)
622 E. 28th St., Ste. 113
(704) 372-0101
www.ncdance.org

The granddaddy of dance companies in the Queen City, the N.C. Dance Theatre is a fully professional dance company performing in Charlotte and around the world. Founded in 1970, NCDT has undergone several European tours and performed at venues such as Charleston's Spoleto, the American Dance Festival in Durham, and DanceAspen in Colorado. Led by artistic director Jean-Pierre Bonnefoux, the troupe's versatile repertoire ranges from full-length classical ballets to bold, witty, contemporary works. The *New York Times* called NCDT "unstinting in range and thunder . . . a pleasure to behold." Each holiday season, NCDT stages an elaborate production of *The Nutcracker* at the N.C. Blumenthal Performing Arts Center, a production involving more than 100 artists. DancePlace, the official school of NCDT, offers classes to dance enthusiasts of all ages and levels, but particularly focuses on training aspiring young professionals.

Dance Instruction

There are many opportunities for young people and adults who wish to study dance in the Queen City. Dance studios and schools for children abound.

BARBARA MORGAN'S RHYTHM DANCE STUDIO, LTD.
120 West Matthews St., Matthews
(704) 845-5260
www.dancerhythm.com

CENTRAL PIEDMONT COMMUNITY COLLEGE (CPCC)
1201 Elizabeth Ave.
(704) 330-2722
www.cpcc.edu

CHARLOTTE SCHOOL OF BALLET
627 South Sharon Amity Rd.
(704) 366-9675
www.charlotteballet.com

COMMUNITY SCHOOL OF THE ARTS
Dance Program
9517-D Monroe Rd.
(704) 377-4187
www.csarts.org

DANCE PRODUCTIONS
5945-C Orr Rd.
(704) 598-8288
www.danceproductionsstudio.com

QUEENS UNIVERSITY OF CHARLOTTE
1900 Selwyn Ave.
(704) 337-2537
www.queens.edu

SCHOOL OF NORTH CAROLINA DANCE THEATRE
622 E. 28th St., Ste. 113
(704) 372-3900
www.ncdance.org

🔍 Close-up

Wachovia's Parting Gift to the Arts

Wachovia and its predecessor, First Union, were always good corporate citizens who supported hometown causes. Because of that nobody realized when Wachovia entered talks for a new cultural arts campus, back in 2002, that the campus would wind up being the bank's parting gift to the Queen City.

But that's exactly what happened. The financial crisis of 2008 sent Wachovia into a tailspin and led to its purchase by Wells Fargo. The purchase meant Charlotte lost the corporate headquarters of Wachovia, the nation's fourth largest bank, and it ensured Wachovia's last major civic contribution would be the **Wells Fargo Cultural Campus.**

The cultural campus is part of an $880-million redevelopment of a parcel of land between Tryon and Church Streets in the southern part of Uptown. It includes the 54-story Duke Energy Center (originally to be named for Wachovia), plus the Mint Museum Uptown, Bechtler Museum of Modern Art, Harvey B. Gantt Center for African-American Arts + Culture, and the Knight Theater. The project's working title was Wachovia Cultural Campus, but by the time buildings began opening in late 2009, it was rebranded the Wells Fargo Cultural Campus.

As an aside, the Wachovia name will remain in Charlotte through 2010 and parts of 2011 as Wells Fargo systematically completes the takeover, starting in the western-most reaches of the Wachovia empire and working eastward to the Carolinas.

Regardless of its title, the Wells Fargo Cultural Campus is a spectacular addition to the Charlotte arts scene. It gives us a world-class concentration of arts to be enjoyed by locals and visitors alike. The end result of Wachovia's forward thinking in the early years of the new millennium is a combined 291,100 square feet of cultural goodies for the Queen City.

Wachovia's name may disappear from Charlotte, but it will not be forgotten.

UNC CHARLOTTE
Department of Dance & Theatre
(704) 687-2482
www.dancetheatre.uncc.edu

WEIR DANCIN'
855 Sam Newell Rd., Matthews
(704) 841-7762
www.weirdancin.net

MUSIC

Music is everywhere in Charlotte—in church sanctuary concerts, formal orchestra performances, summer symphony Pops in the Park shows, dramatic opera presentations, and outdoor concerts at a variety of locations.

If it's musical instruction you want, check out Community School of the Arts, Central Piedmont Community College, UNC Charlotte, Queen's University of Charlotte, and other music clubs. A diverse collection of the city's musical groups is noted below.

AMERICAN GUILD OF ORGANISTS
(704) 759-3479
www.charlotteago.org
The American Guild of Organists promotes the organ in its historic and evolving roles, with weekly summer Sun-night concerts at churches around the city. In winter monthly meetings are open to the public. The guild also offers workshops on choral techniques and classes on subjects of interest to church members.

AMERICAN HARP SOCIETY
(704) 821-3657
www.charlotteharps.org
The objectives of the Charlotte Harp Society are to develop among its members and the public an

appreciation of the harp as a musical instrument, to offer a variety of presentations about the harp through concerts and school programs, and to support the arts in our city. Each spring, student auditions with a well-known harpist clinician are held, culminating in a student recital. Periodically, members perform in large harp ensemble concerts.

BARBERSHOP HARMONY SOCIETY
10107 Thomas Payne Court
(704) 400-0945
www.goldstandardchorus.com
Chartered in 1950, the Charlotte chapter includes the Gold Standard Chorus and several quartets, which produce an annual show and a Singing Valentines program. The group participates in civic functions, performs for numerous audiences around the Metrolina region, and competes internationally. Men of all ages are welcome to join. Meetings are held at 7 p.m. Mon in the Fellowship Hall at Aldersgate retirement community.

CAROLINA CROWN DRUM AND BUGLE CORPS
227-A Main St., Fort Mill, SC
(803) 547-2270
www.carolinacrown.org
This outstanding group comprises 135 young people, who come from all over the world each summer for a seven-week tour of the United States and Canada. This all-volunteer organization rehearses and performs with the drum corps relying solely on brass and percussion instruments. The color guard unit (descendant of the units formed by veterans' groups after World War I) is not what you'd expect, and the music isn't of the John Philip Sousa variety either. You'll hear musical selections that run the gamut from jazzy show-business numbers to light classical. The corps travels 15,000 miles a year to compete throughout the United States. Each summer the group presents Nightbeat, a Charlotte show with 8 to 10 nationally ranked groups taking the field.

CAROLINA PRO MUSICA
(704) 334-3468
www.carolinapromusica.org

Established in 1977, this ensemble offers concerts featuring pre-1800 music with historic instruments and period dress in a concert series at Covenant Presbyterian Church, Saint Mary's Chapel, and Saint Martin's Episcopal Church, as well as throughout the community and the Carolinas.

CAROLINA VOICES
1900 Queens Rd.
(704) 374-1564
www.carolinavoices.org
This umbrella organization supports fiver different choral groups—MainStage Choir, IMPROMPTU!, Festival Singers, Noteability, and VOX. MainStage includes 80 singers and swells to 100 voices at Christmas when it presents the Singing Christmas Tree, a 50-year holiday tradition performed at Ovens Auditorium. IMPROMPTU! performs jazz pieces with 10 voices, and the Festival Singers, with two dozen members, performs short-form classical works, often a cappella. Noteability is an outreach group that sings for churches, schools, and nursing homes and at community festivals. VOX is a collaborative choral venture between Carolina Voices and Central Piedmont Community College. This 24- to 32-member ensemble presents cutting-edge performances and music, often in collaboration with some of the region's finest artists from all disciplines.

CHAMBER MUSIC AT ST. PETER'S
115 West Seventh St.
(704) 335-0009
www.cmsp.wordpress.com
Based at St. Peter's Episcopal Church in Uptown, this program presents chamber music including string quartets and pianists in free sanctuary concerts. Concerts run the first Tues of the month, Sept through May, with 45-minute programs offered at noon and at 5:30 p.m. Benefit concerts often feature bigger-name performers such as Jon Nakamatsu, a Gold Medal winner of the Van Cliburn International Piano Competition. A free wine-and-cheese reception follows the 5:30 p.m. performances at Hodges Taylor art gallery.

CHAMBER MUSIC OF CHARLOTTE
(704) 535-3024
This musical group is a nonprofit organization of approximately 85 musicians who play early and modern instruments. The group includes string quartets, Baroque ensembles, dance bands, jazz groups, and other combinations of instruments—music professionals who play for weddings, parties, and other private and public events for a fee. The organization also assists musicians of all levels in finding places to play in the Charlotte area.

CHARLOTTE CHILDREN'S CHOIR
Holy Trinity Lutheran Church
1900 The Plaza
(704) 374-1892
www.charlottechildrenschoir.org
Founded in 1986 in conjunction with the Queens University of Charlotte Music Department, the Charlotte Children's Choir is one of the area's premier arts organizations for young people. The group is made up of six choirs involving more than 240 children from six counties and two states. Participants study and perform a variety of music, sing in many languages, and receive music education and Kodaly and basic rhythm training. Membership is open to children ages 8 to 18.

There are several major group concerts during the year, with the December and May concerts being the most popular. The choir also participates in competitions and provides special performances.

CHARLOTTE CIVIC ORCHESTRA
P.O. Box 11334, Charlotte, NC 28220-1334
(704) 334-0098
www.charlottecivicorchestra.org
Charlotte's only all-volunteer civic symphony strives to make classical music accessible to everyone by performing for a diverse audience and offering affordable concert prices.

CHARLOTTE CONCERTS
122 West Woodlawn Rd.
(704) 527-6680
www.charlotteconcerts.org
Charlotte Concerts, formerly Carolinas Concert Association, was founded in 1930. This group is Charlotte's oldest concert organization. Each year the association offers a season of classical music, the Crown Jewel Series, by outstanding orchestras, dance companies, soloists, and instrumentalists from around the world. Past performers have included such internationally renowned artists as violinist Itzhak Perlman, pianist Van Cliburn, soprano Kathleen Battle, the Vienna Boys Choir, Academy of St. Martins in the Field, the London Symphony Orchestra, and the New York Philharmonic Orchestra. Season memberships are available.

CHARLOTTE FLUTE ASSOCIATION
9620 Twin Falls Court, Mint Hill
(704) 893-2835
www.charlotteflutes.com
This group sponsors the Charlotte Flute Choir and brings to Charlotte some of the world's finest flutists for concert performances and master classes.

CHARLOTTE FOLK MUSIC SOCIETY
P.O. Box 36864, Charlotte, NC 28236
(704) 372-3655
www.folksociety.org
The Charlotte Folk Music Society was formed to preserve traditional mountain music but has expanded to include other elements of mountain life. The society sponsors and/or participates in many area festivals, including the annual Folk Frolic at CPCC each April. This celebration honors the best of Appalachian, bluegrass, Celtic, black string, minstrel, children's folk, and blues musicians in a fun setting. Workshops in informal settings allow fans to listen and see playing styles and instruments up close. A dance stage with Hispanic, African, Filipino, Irish, Appalachian clogging, and Eastern Indian steps also is included.

The 500-member organization has monthly meetings at 7:30 p.m. Fri at CPCC, where anyone can bring an instrument and join the jam. Classes in a variety of folk instruments also are held at CPCC, 1220 Elizabeth Ave. The society publishes a magazine for its members, listing workshops, classes, and concerts.

CHARLOTTE PHILHARMONIC ORCHESTRA
P.O. Box 470987, Charlotte, NC 28247
(704) 846-2788

The 75 members of the Charlotte Philharmonic Orchestra perform a full season of Boston Pops–style shows, mostly at Belk Theater and Ovens Auditorium. In recent years the orchestra has branched out to perform patriotic and other themed pops shows at community events in Matthews, Belmont, and Dallas. Reasonable ticket prices and unique programming of classics, Broadway, and show tunes have made the orchestra popular. Guest artists have included community choral groups, solo vocalists, ballet dancers, and world-class instrumentalists.

The Philharmonic has performed in concert with recording artists Natalie Cole, John Tesh, Linda Ronstadt, and Yanni, among others. The orchestra also has recorded CDs, performed for television commercials, and has contracted with the Motion Picture Company of Los Angeles to make motion-picture soundtracks.

CHARLOTTE SYMPHONY ORCHESTRA
1300 Baxter St., Ste. 300
(704) 972-2003
(704) 972-2000 (box office)
www.charlottesymphony.org

The Charlotte Symphony Orchestra was founded in 1932 by Guillermo South De Roxlo and today is under the baton of internationally acclaimed music director Christof Perick. The orchestra is made up of more than 100 musicians and each year entertains more than 250,000 people.

The 40-week season is highlighted by the orchestra's Classical Series featuring world-renowned guest artists and conductors and a Winter Pops season. The orchestra also performs free summer Pops in the Park concerts at SouthPark Mall and in neighboring towns. All regular-season concerts are performed in the Belk Theater of the North Carolina Blumenthal Performing Arts Center.

The Symphony also manages the Oratorio Singers of Charlotte, the youth Oratorio, and two youth orchestras.

> **i** Sometimes art shows up in places you least expect it. Bank of America Stadium, home of the Carolina Panthers NFL team, features two cast-bronze panther statues outside each of its four entrances. The growling, ready-to-pounce cats are each 7 feet tall, 20 feet long, 2,800 pounds, and worth $75,000.

COMMUNITY SCHOOL OF THE ARTS (CSA)
345 North College St., Ste. 413
(704) 377-4187
www.csarts.org

In his work as church organist and choir director at First Presbyterian Church, Henry Bridges realized that the vacant Sunday-school rooms and idle pianos could be put to good use. In 1969 he organized what would later become Community School of the Arts, a flourishing school that now reaches thousands of students of all ages throughout the Charlotte-Mecklenburg area. The school—which offers courses in music, dance, visual arts, and drama—is the only arts organization that is 100 percent educational. The school has a satellite location at 4949 Albemarle Rd. and an outreach program free to all participants. Scholarships for classes are available.

Some of CSA's main programs include a private music academy with classes in instruments from piano and strings to folk and rock, a cutting-edge preschool arts program and arts lab, a music program for children from newborns to age 4, a beginning orchestra and band for fourth- and fifth-graders, summer camps, and family workshops.

ONE VOICE CHORUS
P.O. Box 9241, Charlotte, NC 28229
(704) 716-1129
www.onevoicechorus.com

Founded in 1989, this community chorus includes gay, lesbian, transgender, and gay-supportive singers who gather for friendship, fellowship, and the love of song. The group performs two concerts a year, sponsors a summer camp, and competes internationally.

OPERA CAROLINA
301 South Tryon St.
(704) 332-7177
www.operacarolina.org
Opera Carolina is the oldest and largest professional opera company in the state. The company's productions feature singers and artistic personnel of national and international stature, alongside local and regional singers and technicians of exceptional ability. Four shows per season are presented at the Belk Theatre in the North Carolina Blumenthal Performing Arts Center. Recent productions have included *Macbeth, Samson & Delilah, Tosca,* and *The Magic Flute.* Opera Carolina's education division presents fully staged operas/musicals and curriculum-based activities to schools and community groups throughout the state. The community programs department creates opportunities in collaboration with the region's minority communities.

QUEENS COMMUNITY ORCHESTRA
1019 Circlewood Dr.
(704) 364-4917
www.queensorchestra.org
This string orchestra of professional and amateur musicians, founded in 1969, presents two free concerts a year at Dana Auditorium at Queens University of Charlotte. Each spring Painting With Music invites local artists to paint, draw, or sculpt during rehearsals, then show their music-inspired works at the concert.

SWEET ADELINES INTERNATIONAL QUEEN CHARLOTTE CHORUS
(704) 556-0690
www.queencharlottechorus.com
Sweet Adelines trains its members in musical harmony, barbershop style, without instrumental accompaniment. The Queen Charlotte Chorus presents an annual show at Ovens Auditorium and performs for private groups, civic and community groups, and others. Call for audition information.

THEATER

ABBEY PLAYERS
Belmont Abbey College
Performing Arts Theater, Belmont
(704) 461-6787
www.belmontabbeycollege.edu
Often overlooked in the Charlotte area, this volunteer troupe of Belmont Abbey students, faculty, and local residents produces six very good shows a year, ranging from dramas to comedies to musicals. The Abbey Players of Belmont Abbey College were founded in 1883, serving the arts in eastern Gaston County for more than 125 years.

Recent productions include *Copenhagen, Long Day's Journey into Night, Of Mice and Men, Assassins,* and *The Importance of Being Earnest.* In addition, the troupe presents The Abbey Shakespeare Series, an ongoing project to produce each of William Shakespeare's plays.

ACTOR'S THEATRE OF CHARLOTTE
650 East Stonewall St.
(704) 342-2251
www.actorstheatrecharlotte.org
This contemporary professional theater company produces works by new and thought-provoking playwrights. The schedule includes five to six shows a season in a diverse and challenging collection of comedy and drama.

BROADWAY LIGHTS SERIES
130 North Tryon St.
(704) 372-1000 (box office)
(704) 333-4686 (administration)
www.blumenthalcenter.org
Charlotteans who go to the theater only a few times a year typically opt for this wildly popular series of Broadway hits presented by the North Carolina Blumenthal Performing Arts Center. The high-profile traveling shows are held in Belk Theater and at Ovens Auditorium. Past shows have included *West Side Story, Mamma Mia!, Aida, Greater Tuna, Seussical The Musical, Jesus Christ Superstar, The Lion King, The Producers, The King & I, Movin' Out, On the Record, Oklahoma!, Hairspray,* and *Joseph & The Amazing Technicolor Dreamcoat.* Series sub-

scriber and single-show tickets are available, but the big-name Broadway hits often sell out.

CENTRAL PIEDMONT COMMUNITY COLLEGE
1201 Elizabeth Ave.
(704) 330-6534 (box office)
www.cpcc.edu
Performances of Broadway-style shows in the opulent 1,020-seat Halton Theater on campus are a treat for locals and visitors alike. The popular, professionally staged productions feature both professional actors and students, and include musicals and comedies such as *Anything Goes, Chicago, The Foreigner,* and *West Side Story.* Each summer a show is included for children.

CHILDREN'S THEATRE OF CHARLOTTE
300 East Seventh St.
ImaginOn, Joe & Joan Martin Center
(704) 973-2800
www.ctcharlotte.org
With both a production and education program, the Children's Theatre is the place for burgeoning Sarah Bernhardts and Laurence Oliviers. The production program has four components— MainStage, productions geared for the entire family; Ensemble Company, a series of plays performed by and for young actors and audiences in high school; Tarradiddle Players, the touring component of the theater; and Special Events, productions not produced by the theater. All MainStage productions include at least one signed performance for the hearing impaired. Special events include productions by the Grey Seal Puppets, Omimeo Mime Theatre, and touring groups such as West African drummers and dancers. The education program offers children ages 3 to 18 classes and workshops in theater arts, creative drama, and dance. Founded in 1948 by the Junior League, the Children's Theatre became independent in 1952.

DAVIDSON COLLEGE
THEATER DEPARTMENT
P.O. Box 340, Davidson, NC 28036
(704) 894-2361
www.davidson.edu

The Davidson Theater Department presents four full-length plays and several one-acts each year. Performances are held at Hodson Hall in the John Cunningham Fine Arts Building and the adjacent Studio Theatre.

DAVIDSON COMMUNITY PLAYERS
107 North Main St., Davidson
(704) 892-7953
www.davidsoncommunityplayers.org
Founded in 1965, this community theater for the North Mecklenburg area presents two major summer productions, a winter children's play, "fireside" readings, dinner theater productions, and receptions.

THE ENSEMBLE COMPANY
1017 East Morehead St.
(704) 973-2800
www.ctcharlotte.org
This company is cosponsored by the Children's Theatre and Charlotte-Mecklenburg Schools, and students receive school credit for their work. The company is cast only by audition and is open to all high-schoolers, but it is intended for the very serious drama student. Students engage in intense study and acting techniques throughout the eight-month session with professional theater teachers and directors. Two productions are staged each year in the Children's Theatre's downstairs Black Box Theatre. The Ensemble Company is Charlotte's only preprofessional training program for young actors.

GREY SEAL PUPPETS
231 Foster Ave.
(704) 521-2878
www.greysealpuppets.com
The internationally acclaimed Grey Seal Puppets make their home in Charlotte but travel across the country to perform in theaters and on television. The company writes, designs, builds, and performs unique shows, most of which cater to children but a few of which are aimed at mature audiences. Performances often focus on Hans Christian Andersen stories and other well-known writers and familiar tales. Local shows run at the

Children's Theatre of Charlotte and other community venues.

KNIGHT THEATER
430 South Tryon St.
(704) 372-1000
www.blumenthalcenter.org
This warm and modern $32-million theater was unveiled in the fall of 2009. Knight Theater adjoins the Bechtler Museum of Modern Art in the Uptown complex known as the Wells Fargo Cultural Campus. The theater includes deep orange carpet and upholstery to complement the earth-toned exterior of the Bechtler.

Guests to the Knight Theater find this 1,200-seat showplace to be cozier than the Belk Theater at the Blumenthal. There is one large balcony and a modern, open-air lobby that's connected to the Bechtler, but also has a large portion of glass walls facing Tryon Street.

Performances at the Knight range from plays to dance groups to intimate musical performances. The facility was christened by the bluegrass band Steep Canyon Rangers, which features famous comedian and movie actor Steve Martin. Booking and operations for the Knight Theater are handled by the Blumenthal Performing Arts Center.

LISTEN AND REMEMBER
Museum of the Waxhaws, Waxhaw
(704) 843-1832
www.discoverwaxhaw.com
Performed annually each Fri and Sat evening in June, the historical outdoor drama *Listen and Remember* portrays American history lived by early pioneers of the Old Waxhaw Settlement, among them the family of young Andrew Jackson. A reenactment of the Revolutionary War depicts the thirst for freedom that motivated those early settlers.

JOHNSON C. SMITH UNIVERSITY
100 Beatties Ford Rd.
(704) 378-1069
www.jcsu.edu
Performing in historic Biddle Hall, JCSU puts on two plays a year, plus a Christmas program. The productions are diverse, ranging from Neil Simon comedies to ancient Greek tragedies.

MATTHEWS PLAYHOUSE
100 McDowell St., Matthews
(704) 846-8343
www.matthewsplayhouse.com
Started in 1995, the Matthews Playhouse has two divisions: Theatre Matthews, with two adult productions a season, and Theatre for Young People, with two children's shows per season. All are presented at the Matthews Community Center, which features a refurbished 362-seat theater. Shows in both segments of the Playhouse lean to the traditional, with musicals such as *Oklahoma!* and *Grease* for adults, and *Peter Pan, Winnie the Pooh, Heidi, Beauty and the Beast, Cinderella,* and *The Lion, The Witch and the Wardrobe* for kids. Matthews Playhouse also offers creative classes for children and summer camps in drama, music, art, and dance.

NORTH CAROLINA BLUMENTHAL PERFORMING ARTS CENTER
130 North Tryon St.
(704) 372-1000
www.blumenthalcenter.org
The crème de la crème of art buildings, the dazzling Blumenthal Center is part of the Bank of America Corporate Center in Uptown. This impressive five-level building with its dramatic marble and mosaic tile interior includes the 2,100-seat Belk Theatre performance hall for the symphony and opera; the 434-seat Booth Playhouse for local and regional theatrical productions; and the 150-seat Stage Door Theater. For convenience, a glass walkway connects the center to a guarded parking garage. Charlotte residents especially flock to see Broadway Lights series productions such as *The Lion King, Jersey Boys,* and *Phantom of the Opera.*

The Blumenthal is home to the Charlotte Symphony Orchestra, Opera Carolina, North Carolina Dance Theatre, Carolina Voices, the Carolinas Concert Association, ArtsTeach, Community School of the Arts, and the Light Factory.

OMIMEO MIME THEATRE
P.O. Box 221267, Charlotte, NC 28222
(704) 375-4012
www.hardinminor.com/omimeo.html
Founded in 1978 by Hardin Minor and Eddie
Williams, this performance troupe presents eclectic, unpredictable, often hilarious vignettes that
integrate traditional and street-style mime, mask,
dance, clowning, circus arts, and improvisation
into a unique movement theater experience.
Omimeo Mime has created a number of original
productions and collaborated with a wide variety
of guest artists. The repertory includes *Mime
Time, Satire and Slapstick, Close Encounters of the
Invisible Mind, The Whiz Bang Circus,* and other
hits. Omimeo Mime also offers residencies and
workshops in mime and clowning.

OVENS AUDITORIUM
2700 East Independence Blvd.
(704) 372-3600
www.ovensauditorium.com
Ovens Auditorium, formerly the city's main performing arts center with 2,603 seats, books arts-
oriented productions locally but also offers touring
Broadway plays as well as musical productions,
concerts, and comedy shows. In addition, Ovens
Auditorium provides space for such community
events as dance recitals and graduations.

TARRADIDDLE PLAYERS
1017 East Morehead St.
(704) 973-2808
www.ctcharlotte.org
Since 1971 the Tarradiddle Players have provided the experience of quality theater to young
people throughout the Carolinas. The troupe,
now the touring arm of the Children's Theatre,
performs at its theater and at other Charlotte
facilities, as well as at schools, community halls,
and festivals. It also offers children's theater workshops for groups.

THEATRE CHARLOTTE
501 Queens Rd.
(704) 372-1000 (box office)
www.theatrecharlotte.org

Theatre Charlotte, founded in 1927 as the Little
Theatre of Charlotte, is the grande dame of theater
in Charlotte—and North Carolina—as the oldest
community theater in the state. Over the years it
has performed hundreds of main-stage productions to more than 500,000 people. The company
produces five main-stage plays a year, plus a special
production of Charles Dickens' *A Christmas Carol.*
   Theater Charlotte offers a "second stage"
series known as Stage 501. Stage 501 is dedicated
to presenting works by classic contemporary
writers, such as Beckett, Pinter, and Albee, and
writers from diverse ethnic backgrounds. This
series also showcases the original work of local
playwrights.
   Hundreds of volunteers work at this nonpro-
fessional theater company.

UNC CHARLOTTE DEPARTMENT OF DANCE AND THEATRE
9201 University City Blvd.
(704) 687-2482
www.dancetheatre.uncc.edu/season.htm
The department produces four or five major productions during the school year, as well as occasional student productions. Held at Belk Theater
or Robinson Hall, they include contemporary and
classical plays and musicals, dance concerts, and
original theater and dance productions.

VISUAL ARTS

Probably none of the arts is as free to see or as
approachable as the visual arts. You can even get
in free at the Mint Museum Randolph on certain
days. Around Charlotte, and especially in Uptown,
you can take in a wide range of visual arts, both
public and private ventures. In the funky NoDa
arts district, take advantage of the gallery crawl
on the first and third Fri of the month.
   In this section, we've outlined many of the
outlets for visual arts in the Queen City.

CENTER OF THE EARTH
3204 North Davidson St.
(704) 375-5756
www.centeroftheearth.com

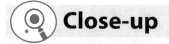
Close-up

Charlotte's Public Art

You don't have to look very hard to find great examples of unusual and inspiring public art in Charlotte. Here are a few examples of public art to scout out:

- **Raymond Kaskey statues** on the four corners of the Square at Trade and Tryon. The bronze sculptures depict Charlotte's industry, commerce, transportation, and vision for the future.

- **Frescoes** by North Carolina native Ben Long. You'll find them at Uptown's Bank of America Corporate Center, at the Charlotte-Mecklenburg Law Enforcement Center, and on the domed lobby ceiling of the Transamerica Square Building beside Rock Bottom Brewery on North Tryon Street.

- *Queen Charlotte,* an illuminated fountain and 1990 sculpture by Raymond Kaskey, extends her crown to welcome visitors to the Charlotte/Douglas International Airport. Locals joke that Queen Charlotte looks as if she has just been punched in the stomach. *Queen Charlotte* can also be seen at the International Trade Center on College Street in Uptown. This sculpture is regal and adorned with jewels.

- The **bronze 49er** panning for gold at UNC Charlotte's Main Administration Building represents Charlotte as the site of the country's first gold rush in 1799.

- *Cascade,* a kinetic hanging sculpture by world-famous artist Jean Tinguely, incorporates colored lightbulbs, wheels, wrought iron, and a cow's skull, among other objects, inside the Carillon Building on Trade Street, Uptown.

- Beside the Carillon, you'll find **Jerry Peart's large-scale aluminum sculpture** in bright shades of green, yellow, purple, and red. It symbolizes Charlotte's changing seasons.

- Charlotte's latest Uptown park, called **The Green,** features three giant fish with water spouts that form a beautiful fountain, stone walkways that look like hopscotch games, Miss Muffet's tuffet–style seating, a huge stack of bronze books, a signpost with directions related to literature, and even sound effects triggered by folks walking by. The Green is on South Tryon between St. Peter's Catholic Church and the new Ratcliffe condominiums.

- Best viewed from a distance at night is *Quadrille,* a dancing holographic neon-light sculpture by California artist Michael Hayden. It's on the side of the Duke Energy Building Uptown and is also visible during the day.

- More than just a parking garage, the Seventh Street Station deck features *Touch My Building* by Christopher Janney, a nationally known artist. The interactive artwork combines neon, glass, paint, and sound to create a game. Solve the riddle, and the parking deck artwork plays music.

- At Wachovia Plaza four **bronze sculptures** of children are perched amid the splashing fountains and are so lifelike, you expect them to emerge from the water, laughing and smiling. During the holidays giant red Christmas ornaments are added to the Plaza.

- *Il Grande Disco* by Arnolodo Pomodero at The Square outside the Omni Charlotte Hotel is a copper-colored disc balancing perfectly on its edge as a monument to industry.

- **Hugh McManaway,** a local character who directed traffic at a busy Myers Park intersection, is remembered with an Elsie Shaw statue at the corner of Queens and Providence Road. Nearby Queens University students often dress him up with scarves, hats, and umbrellas.

Center of the Earth, the first art gallery in the historic north Charlotte area called NoDa, opened in 1989. Owner/sculptor J. Paul Sires and owner/artist Ruth Ava Lyons have the largest offering of contemporary sculpture and art work in Charlotte, representing more than 50 emerging and mature artists. A few figurative pieces stand among abstract works of stone, steel, and wood. Many narrative pieces convey simple to complex messages. This gallery differs from the usual mainstream commercial galleries in that it became an outgrowth of the owners' search for an interesting place to work, educate the community, and showcase the work of local, regional, and national artists. The distinctive difference in their approach focuses on the work's integrity, not its marketability. Always a favorite on the gallery art crawls and a recipient of the Governor's Business Award, the center is open 11 a.m. to 5 p.m. Tues through Fri, noon to 7 p.m. Sat, and by appointment.

i Visit Charlotte at 330 South Tryon St. offers several interesting and informative brochures about Charlotte's arts community. Look for guides on the Charlotte Public Art Walking Tour, Art of Gateway Village, and Historic North Charlotte's Art District. For more information, call the CVB at (800) 231-4636 or go to www.visit charlotte.org.

COFFEY AND THOMPSON
1412 East Fourth St.
(704) 375-7232
www.coffeyandthompson.com
Open since 1946, this gallery features original art by artists from around the country, from contemporary to traditional, plus it has a wide selection of signed limited-edition prints. The gallery is an authority on sporting art, and also features bronze sculptures and wood carvings. Coffey and Thompson is well known for its high-quality framing. Open 9 a.m. to 5:30 p.m. weekdays, 10 a.m. to 2 p.m. Sat.

HARVEY B. GANTT CENTER FOR AFRICAN-AMERICAN ARTS + CULTURE
551 South Tryon St.
(704) 547-3700
www.ganttcenter.org
The Gantt Center recently replaced the Afro-American Cultural Center as the city's preeminent facility to showcase and preserve African-American art, culture, and history. The centerpiece of the center is a permanent 58-piece collection of works from 20th-century African-American artists. It includes such noted black artists as Henry O. Tanner, Ann Tanksley, John Biggers, and Romare Bearden, a Charlotte native.

The first two rotating exhibits at the center featured the works of Atlanta-based mixed-media artist Radcliffe Bailey and Tennessee native Juan Logan, who lives just outside Charlotte in the town of Belmont.

Hours are 10 a.m. until 5 p.m. Tues through Sat, and 1 to 5 p.m. on Sun. Admission is $8 per person, and $5 per person for seniors and groups.

HODGES TAYLOR GALLERY
401 North Tryon St.
(704) 334-3799
www.hodgestaylor.com
Founded in 1981 by Dot Hodges and Christie Taylor, Hodges Taylor Gallery was Charlotte's first Uptown gallery. Since its inception the gallery has represented professional artists from throughout the Southeast. An active exhibition schedule from September through May features these award-winning artists working in a variety of media. Hodges Taylor also is the only gallery in the area with a professional fine-print curator on staff and with a photography room presenting the region's finest black-and-white photography. Open 11 a.m. to 3 p.m. Tues through Sat, and by appointment.

JERALD MELBERG GALLERY
625 South Sharon Amity Rd.
(704) 365-3000
www.jeraldmelberg.com
Owner Jerald Melberg, the former curator of the Mint Museum of Art, opened this well-respected

gallery in 1983. The gallery presents a continuing series of individual artist exhibitions and theme and invitational shows, with artists represented from Alaska to Argentina. Paintings, drawings, prints, and sculptures are showcased, many times by big-name artists such as Charlotte native Romare Bearden, the master collagist of the 20th century; Dale Chihuly, the world's preeminent glass artist; and Wolf Kahn, often considered America's premier living landscape painter. The gallery also has a private presentation room so clients can view its extensive inventory at any time. Open 10 a.m. to 6 p.m. Mon through Sat.

JOIE LASSITER GALLERY
1430 South Mint St., South End
(704) 373-1464
www.lassitergallery.com
This original gallery and art-consulting service opened in 1997 to bring together great artists from New York and the Southern states. Billed as a cutting-edge gallery in the New South, Lassiter also supplies the dozen large-scale contemporary sculptures for Bank of America Plaza, all of which are by artists living and working in the South or from the South. Open 10 a.m. to 5:30 p.m. Tues through Fri and 11 a.m. to 4 p.m. Sat.

THE LIGHT FACTORY
345 North College St., Spirit Square
(704) 333-9755
www.lightfactory.org
Formed in 1972 as a nonprofit arts organization, the Light Factory Photographic Arts Center has evolved into the foremost photographic resource facility in the Southeast. Its unique gallery has exhibited fine-art and documentary photography by many outstanding artists, and its Web site has received national acclaim. The center sponsors exhibitions, classes, lectures, workshops, art auctions, member shows, independent-film screenings, and community outreach programs. An annual shoot-out event brings the area's best photographers and hair and makeup artists together for public portraits from formal to wacky. It's your chance to be a supermodel, but be warned—appointments often sell out. Hours are from 9 a.m. to 6 p.m. Mon to Sat, and from 1 to 6 p.m. Sun.

MADDI'S GALLERY
1530 East Blvd.
(704) 332-0007

16925 Birkdale Commons Parkway
(704) 987-7777
www.maddisgallery.com
This fun, eclectic gallery in the middle of hip restaurants and shops on Dilworth's lively East Boulevard presents diverse and unique work by American artists. It opened in 2006 and was named Best New Gallery in America by the Niche Top Retailer Awards. On the heels of its successful launch in Dilworth, Maddi's recently expanded to a second location in Birkdale Village.

Maddi's is known for its wide range of prices and as a great place to find a gift for a friend or for yourself. While some galleries come off as snobbish, these places are laid-back and friendly. The galleries carry ceramics, glass, folk art, jewelry, furniture, fiber, gifts, garden accessories, practical kitchen items, and artwork related to children. Each category includes a number of price points, a range of styles, and artists from across the country, but you'll always find the Carolinas represented. Dilworth location is open 10 a.m. to 6 p.m. Mon through Sat and 1 to 5 p.m. Sun. Birkdale location stays open until 8 p.m. Mon through Sat.

MCCOLL CENTER FOR VISUAL ART
721 North Tryon St.
(704) 332-5535
www.mccollcenter.org
Once a burned-out, dilapidated eyesore on the edge of Uptown, this former First A.R.P. Church was converted into a gleaming stone and glass artists' colony—one of the largest in the country. Much of the funding for the center was provided by Bank of America; the center is named in honor of the bank's former chairman, Hugh McColl Jr.

Artists-in-residence have work space at McColl Center and put on occasional showings, including one that involved burning hundreds of chairs in a huge pyre. Five new exhibitions are presented each year, along with several open houses. Open 11 a.m. to 4 p.m. Tues through Sat.

MINT MUSEUM RANDOLPH
2730 Randolph Rd.
(704) 337-2000
www.mintmuseum.org
Built in 1836 on West Trade Street, this building originally processed gold that came from 75 to 100 gold mines discovered around Charlotte in the early 1800s. In 1933 the building was moved to its current location in Eastover. Reconstructed, the classic structure opened in 1936 as the first art museum in North Carolina.

The American Museum Association and the National Endowment for the Arts have both hailed Charlotte's Mint Museum as a national model for regional and mid-size museums. The museum hosts major national touring exhibits, organizes traveling exhibits from its own collections, works with computers and online to expand arts education, and schedules diversified programming to reach a wide audience.

The Mint has undergone a series of changes and moves in recent times. Once things settle out in late 2010, the Mint's Randolph Road location will focus on its particularly strong collections of pre-Columbian art and traditional European and American ceramics.

By moving a portion of its collection of 27,000-plus pieces to the new Mint Museum Uptown, this location will have more space than ever to showcase its visual arts, such as Alan Ramsay's 1762 *Queen Charlotte* portrait of the German-born English queen for which the city is named.

Under the new configuration, the following categories will be featured in the 73,000-square-foot Mint Museum Randolph: African art, art of the ancient Americas, Asian Art, ceramics, coins and currency, decorative arts, historic costume and fashionable dress, Native American art, and Spanish colonial art.

For more information on the Mint Museum Randolph, see the Attractions chapter.

MINT MUSEUM UPTOWN
500 South Tryon St.
(704) 337-2000
www.mintmuseum.org
The Mint Museum Uptown will complete the Wells Fargo Cultural Campus when it opens in October 2010. Although this $56-million, five-story facility will be multifaceted, there will be plenty of exhibit space dedicated to the visual arts.

The third and fourth levels provide two full floors of galleries, one dedicated to craft and design and one to American art, contemporary art, and a selection of European art. Each floor has 12,000 square feet of permanent exhibits and 6,000 square feet of changing exhibits. Relocating from the Mint Museum Randolph are important American and European paintings and sculpture; regional crafts; and one of America's premier collections of pottery and porcelain. Meanwhile, the gift shop on the first level will showcase pottery and glass from local artists.

The Mint's famous royal blue mint chandelier, created by Dale Chihuly, will capture everyone's attention as they access the grand entry off of Tryon Street.

Admission price to the new Mint Museum Uptown will be $10 for adults, $8 for seniors and college students, and $5 for ages 5 to 17. Children under 5 admitted free. For days and hours of operation, call (704) 337-2000 or visit the Web site.

RED SKY GALLERY
1244 East Blvd.
(704) 377-6400

9848 Rea Rd.
(704) 542-0995

210 East Trade St.
(704) 971-7552
www.redskygallery.com
An expanding player in Charlotte's arts scene, Red Sky has grown to three locations, including its latest gallery in the EpiCentre in Uptown. Red Sky showcases more than 500 local, regional, and national artists in its fine-art and crafts gal-

leries. Owner Kellie Scott features contemporary paintings and two-dimensional art, as well as exceptional fine crafts in glass, metal, ceramics, wood, and basketry. You'll find functional and decorative home accessories, tableware, lighting, garden art, furniture, sculpture, and jewelry. Red Sky also offers art consultation and corporate gift services. Open 10 a.m. to 6 p.m. Mon through Sat, except for the EpiCentre location, which is closed on Mon and opens at 11 a.m. daily. The EpiCentre gallery is open until 7 p.m. each evening.

SPIRIT SQUARE CENTER FOR ARTS & EDUCATION
345 North College St.
(704) 372-1000
www.performingartsctr.org
Spirit Square is a multi-arts complex providing classrooms, studios, art galleries, performance centers, and office space for small arts organizations. The center, now affiliated with North Carolina Blumenthal Performing Arts Center, opened in 1975 in the renovated First Baptist Church and has added two adjoining buildings. Adults and children can take classes in clay, fiber arts, drawing, printmaking, and theater. Spirit Square has two theaters: the 720-seat McGlohon Theatre in the former church sanctuary and the 180-seat Duke Power Theatre.

Art Instruction
CENTRAL PIEDMONT COMMUNITY COLLEGE
1201 Elizabeth Ave.
(704) 330-2722
www.cpcc.edu

COMMUNITY SCHOOL OF THE ARTS
345 North College St.
(704) 377-4187
www.csarts.org

QUEENS UNIVERSITY OF CHARLOTTE
1900 Selwyn Ave.
(704) 337-2537
www.queens.edu

WRITING

Charlotte boasts its share of literati throughout the years — the unforgettable Harry Golden, creator of *The Carolina Israelite* and author of *Only in America,* and Carson McCullers, who wrote *The Heart Is a Lonely Hunter.* Newsman and native son Charles Kuralt will always be remembered for his *On the Road* series on CBS, while crime-thriller novelist Patricia Cornwell was inspired to write her first best-seller during her reporter days at *The Charlotte Observer.*

Former WBTV news anchor Bob Inman wrote the acclaimed *Home Fires Burning,* which later became a Hallmark Hall of Fame film, and he continues to write from his retirement getaway on Beech Mountain. Frye Gaillard and Ruth Moose also received national attention for their works. Noteworthy poets include Irene Honeycutt, Judy Goldman, Rebecca McClanahan, and North Carolina Poet Laureate Cathy Smith Bowers, who teaches at Queens University.

Legendary newspaper columnist and golf writer Ron Green Sr. went straight from the old Central High School to the *Charlotte News* and banged at the typewriter for five awarding-winning decades until retiring from *The Charlotte Observer* and passing the mantle to his son, Ron Jr., a talented and award-winning writer himself. Meanwhile, UNC Charlotte has produced a number of accomplished sports journalists, including Joe Posnanski, senior writer for *Sports Illustrated.*

Charlotte is kind to writers and has quite a colony of them, producing everything from travel stories to science fiction to romances to mainstream novels. If you want to enjoy the company of other scribes, there are many opportunities for doing so through writing classes offered at local colleges and workshops sponsored by writers' groups.

CAROLINA ROMANCE WRITERS
P.O. Box 620353, Charlotte 28262
www.carolinaromancewriters.com
Affiliated with Romance Writers of America, Carolina Romance Writers meets at 11:30 a.m. the first Sat of the month at Hickory Tavern, 9010 Harris

Corners Parkway. Open to published and nonpublished writers since 1984, this active group sponsors conferences and weekend workshops with professional guest-speaker writers and editors.

Gallery crawls—one part street festival, one part exhibit opening, and one part block party with art, musicians, drum circles, tarot card readers, and street vendors thrown in—are held the first and third Fri evenings of each month from 6 to 9:30 p.m. in the NoDa arts district on North Davidson Street between 35th and 36th Streets. Uptown gallery crawls are on first Fridays. For details, visit www.noda.org or www.charlottecentercity.org.

CHARLOTTE WRITERS' CLUB
P.O. Box 220954
Charlotte 28222-0954
www.charlottewritersclub.org

Since 1922 this group has welcomed professional and amateur writers for programs, annual workshops, and contests in poetry, fiction, short stories, and nonfiction. The goal has always been to provide the encouragement and support to elicit the creative best from members. Meetings are held at 7 p.m. the third Tues of each month from Sept through May at Joseph-Beth Booksellers in the SouthPark Mall and are followed by an open-mike session and light refreshments. All activities, including regular meetings, are open to both members and nonmembers. The Charlotte Writers' Club has added a branch club in recent years, CWC-North in Davidson.

NORTH CAROLINA WRITERS' NETWORK
P.O. Box 954, Carrboro 27510
(919) 967-9540
www.ncwriters.org

This nonprofit statewide organization publishes a bimonthly newsletter, sponsors an annual conference, and offers a wide variety of information and support for fiction and nonfiction writers and poets.

NOVELLO FESTIVAL OF READING
Charlotte-Mecklenburg Public Library
310 North Tryon St.
(704) 416-0100
www.plcmc.org/novello

Charlotte Public Library's Novello is a weeklong festival held each year in mid-October with top-name authors such as Pat Conroy, Kurt Vonnegut, Toni Morrison, Patricia Cornwell, Maurice Sendak, Dr. Cornel West, and Mitch Albom. In addition to nationally renowned writers, Novello also encourages local and regional writers to give workshops and speak at other functions.

PARKS AND RECREATION

Charlotte and Mecklenburg County have 210 parks and facilities covering more than 17,600 acres. Included in that total are 27 public recreational centers offering numerous programs. Three major lakes are within easy driving distance: Lake Norman to the north with over 520 miles of shoreline; Lake Wylie to the southwest with 325 miles of shared shoreline between North and South Carolina; and Mountain Island Lake, a smaller and less developed body of water northwest of the city.

The Mecklenburg County Park and Recreation Department maintains the parks, recreational centers, swimming pools, greenways, golf courses, and historic sites and provides a variety of activities and educational programs. You can find out about registering for team sports such as basketball and football by calling the Park and Recreation Department at (704) 336-7600, but you should also watch for notices in your neighborhood announcing sign-ups. If you or someone in your family has a disability, you'll be pleased to know that the Park and Recreation Department offers equal access to all recreation programs for persons with special needs. To reserve county facilities, call the individual park. For additional information, visit www.charmeck.org.

Not every park in the city and county is listed in this guide. We offer a sampling and invite you to explore the many other parks scattered throughout the county. After parks we list other outdoor facilities and activities. Entries are alphabetical and located in Charlotte unless otherwise noted.

PARKS

FREEDOM PARK
1900 East Blvd.
(704) 432-4280
This 98-acre park between Dilworth and Myers Park is one of the most popular recreation destinations in town, whether it be coworkers walking on their lunch break, moms and children at the playground, Little Leaguers playing on the baseball diamond, or nearby families walking on the trails and paths. Freedom Park is located adjacent to the Charlotte Nature Museum. Park features include softball fields, basketball courts, playgrounds, lighted tennis courts, and paved walkways. Activities are centered around a 7-acre lake, which serves as the official residence of the local duck population. Festival in the Park, one of Freedom's most popular events, is a four-day festival held every September.

HORNET'S NEST PARK
6301 Beatties Ford Rd.
(704) 336-8096
A 102-acre park in northwest Charlotte, Hornet's Nest boasts the area's only BMX bicycle track. Monitored practice sessions, Sat races, and teaching clinics are held in conjunction with the track. The park also offers softball, fishing, hiking, picnic shelters, a multipurpose trail, 10 playgrounds, tennis courts, horseshoes, a concession stand, and an 18-hole disc golf course.

IDLEWILD ROAD PARK
10512 Idlewild Rd.
(704) 336-3586
Idlewild Road Park covers 55 acres and serves residents in the Mint Hill/Matthews area. It offers a playground, softball field, picnic shelters, horseshoes, an outdoor fitness center, and a 1.5-mile nature trail.

Mecklenburg County Park and Recreation publishes a full-color *Get Going Guide* to help you enjoy its many facilities and programs. It includes detailed information on bikeways and greenways, nature preserves, county parks, and sports recreation centers. Call (704) 336-3586 or download it online at www.charmeck.org.

JETTON PARK
19000 Jetton Rd., Cornelius
(704) 896-9808

Lake Norman is the centerpiece of this 105-acre park, which is located on a peninsula with inviting coves on two sides and a broad stretch of water at its toe. A loop road winds through the oblong-shaped park, and there are 1.5 miles of asphalt bike and in-line skate paths, plus another mile of gravel trails that dip in and out of the shoreline. Tennis courts are scattered among gazebos and picnic tables. Although there is a sunning beach, no swimming is allowed, and the park has no boat-launching ramps. Admission is charged weekends and holidays: $3 per car for county residents, $5 per car for nonresidents, and $2 per car for senior citizens.

LATTA PLANTATION NATURE PRESERVE
6211 Sample Rd., Huntersville
(704) 875-1391

This 1,343-acre nature preserve on Mountain Island Lake is centered around the restored 1800 river plantation home of James Latta, a traveling merchant who first purchased the land in 1799. The park contains the Carolina Raptor Center, where injured birds of prey are cared for; a canoe access area; and a nature center with live native animals and an outdoor amphitheater. The Equestrian Center features two horse arenas, 80 permanent stalls, and 16 miles of bridle trails. Individuals may use the trails or school in the Equestrian Center free of charge. The park sponsors special events such as photo safaris, night fishing, sunset canoeing, summer hayrides, and hunter-safety courses. At the new boat-rental harbor, canoes and johnboats are available for a small fee on weekends beginning in mid-March and daily beginning in June.

MALLARD CREEK COMMUNITY PARK
3001 Johnston-Oehler Rd.
(704) 336-3586

Located in northeast Charlotte, Mallard Creek is one of the county's newer parks, covering 515 acres. Softball leagues flock here for its four lighted softball fields, softball pavilion, and nearby concession stands and restrooms. The park serves the soccer community with eight full-size fields, plus a volleyball court, picnic shelter, and one of the county's best playgrounds, with slides, swings, tubes, and climbing stations. In the recreation center, there's fitness equipment, a gym, a computer room, a game room, and a kitchen. A synthetic turf multiuse field at adjacent Mallard Creek High School can be reserved through a joint-use agreement with Charlotte Mecklenburg Schools.

MCALPINE CREEK PARK
8711 Monroe Rd.
(704) 568-4044

A 462-acre park in east Charlotte, McAlpine features a 3-acre lake, 2-mile bike trail, 1.5-mile nature path, and popular 5K championship cross-country course. McAlpine Creek Greenway is an adjacent 3-mile stretch of trails with picnic areas, a boardwalk, and a gazebo. Ray's Fetching Meadow is a "bark park" within McAlpine.

MCDOWELL PARK AND NATURE PRESERVE
15222 York Rd.
(704) 588-5224

One of the county's largest, this nature preserve encompasses 1,115 acres on Lake Wylie, 90 percent of which has been left undeveloped. It offers a 56-site campground, hiking, fishing, picnicking, and other activities. There are playgrounds as well. Visitors can launch boats free of charge or rent a paddleboat or canoe during the summer months. There are 7 miles of nature trails and a nature center with hands-on exhibits.

NEVIN PARK
6000 Statesville Rd.
(704) 336-3586

Nevin Park in northeast Charlotte offers 340 acres with five bocce ball courts, four lighted softball fields, three soccer fields, three lighted picnic shelters, a walking trail, playground, horseshoe pits, shuffleboard, and 18-hole disc golf course. Multipurpose asphalt trails are used for walking, jogging, biking, and in-line skating. A "spray-ground" is popular with kids.

PARK ROAD PARK
6220 Park Rd.
(704) 643-5725

This 122-acre park's main focus is an 11-acre lake where visitors can walk along gravel trails, cook on lakeside grills, feed the ducks, or simply sit by the banks. The lake was drained in 2009 for repairs, effectively eliminating fishing, which had been a popular option. The six lighted softball fields bustle with league play from early spring through late fall. Playgrounds and pickup basketball games are also favorites here, along with bike trails, tennis, volleyball, and picnic shelters. Clever Charlotteans sometimes joke that the road running through this park should be called Park Road Park Road. Get it?

RAMSEY CREEK PARK
18441 Nantz Rd., Cornelius
(704) 336-3586

Ramsey Creek, overlooking Lake Norman, is a 44-acre park with free boat ramps, a beach area (no swimming), a fishing pier, horseshoes, volleyball, umbrella rentals, picnic tables, nature trails, and a play area for small children. Special programs and live performances feature local musicians and jugglers. There's also a 3-acre dog park.

REEDY CREEK NATURE CENTER
AND PRESERVE
Reedy Creek Park
2900 Rocky River Rd.
(704) 598-8857

There's plenty to do at this 727-acre nature preserve and adjacent 116-acre park in northeast Charlotte. At the preserve, where Native Americans and early Charlotte settlers once lived, head to the award-winning Environmental Education Center for nature-trail studies, or take a walk on 10 miles of winding paths. One of the most popular routes leads to the ruins of the Robinson Rockhouse, built circa 1790. The nature center features live native animals, an exhibit hall, a classroom, and a gift shop. Outside there are bird-feeding stations and butterfly gardens. A total of 109 species of birds are known to inhabit the preserve. The park features fields for softball and soccer, volleyball and basketball courts, picnic shelters, playgrounds, a walking path, a disc golf course, and a lake for fishing. Barkingham Park, a leash-free park for dogs, is a recent addition.

RENAISSANCE PARK
1200 West Tyvola Rd.
(704) 353-1244

Located near the Charlotte Coliseum, Renaissance covers 140 acres and is part of a recreation complex with an 18-hole golf course, tennis center, soccer fields, volleyball courts, a championship-level disc golf course, softball fields, and bike trails. The golf course is built on the site of a former county landfill.

The Jeff Adams Tennis Center, one of the area's premier facilities, has 13 lighted courts with private lessons, clinics, and open-to-the-public play. An unusual aspect of this park is that it is bisected by a six-lane byway, Tyvola Road, which was constructed to provide access to the Charlotte Coliseum, a 23,000-seat arena that served the region for two decades before it was imploded in June of 2007.

THOMPSON PARK
1129 East Third St.
(704) 432-4280

Just east of town, on the other side of the I-277 loop is this charming, 3.3-acre park. Thousands drive by it every day because it is nestled between Third and Fourth Streets, but few take advantage of this urban oasis. Its biggest draw is a powerful one—the Charlotte-Mecklenburg Vietnam Veterans' War Memorial. The memorial, built entirely by private donations, honors the 105 Mecklenburg County soldiers lost in the war, and the thousands more who served. This tree-shaded park with gazebo is also known for its historic St. Mary's Chapel, which is available for weddings and memorial services. The park is open dawn to dusk.

St. Mary's Chapel

Picturesque St. Mary's Chapel, just off Uptown in Thompson Park, is one of the most popular places in town to get married. The chapel was designated a historic landmark in 1975 and the parks department rents it for weddings for the reasonable price of $400 to county residents and $500 to nonresidents. Rental includes full use of the 100-person chapel, including one dressing room, for two hours and 45 minutes. Renters are responsible for providing the minister, music, and decorations. A word of caution: The chapel's often booked up months in advance, particularly if you're interested in a Sat wedding. For info and reservations, call (704) 333-1235.

VETERANS PARK
2136 Central Ave.
(704) 432-4280
Built to honor Lt. Budd Harris Andrews, who crashed his airplane in 1945 to avoid hitting a Charlotte neighborhood, this 19-acre park serves the Plaza-Midwood area. It has ball fields, lighted tennis courts, a playground, an indoor shelter, and a popular summer treat, a "sprayground."

WILLIAM R. DAVIE PARK
4635 Pineville-Matthews Rd.
(704) 554-0402

A park for the fast-growing southeast area of the city, Davie Park covers 106 acres with basketball courts, four softball fields, two soccer fields, a volleyball court, horseshoe pits, hopscotch courses, picnic shelters, a lake, a playground, and walking trails. The Davie Dog Park is a 5-acre, fenced-in, off-leash area for canines. There are two separate fenced-in sections—one for dogs 20 pounds and up, and another for dogs less than 20 pounds.

FLORA AND FAUNA

DANIEL STOWE BOTANICAL GARDEN
6500 South New Hope Rd., Belmont
(704) 825-4490
www.dsbg.org
Named one of the Nation's 20 Great Gardens by HGTV, Daniel Stowe Botanical Garden is among the most significant visitor attractions to open in the Charlotte region in the last two decades. This superb destination is located just south of Belmont along the banks of Lake Wylie, and convenient to Charlotte.

Its features include a spectacular 13,500-square-foot Visitor Pavilion and the 8,000-square-foot Orchid Conservatory. The conservatory is the only glasshouse in the Carolinas dedicated to the display of orchids and tropical plants. The Daniel Stowe Botanical Garden's nearly 400 acres also include themed gardens, a dozen sparkling fountains, a woodland trail, a unique gift shop, and a grassy outdoor amphitheater for special events. The garden offers educational classes for all ages, summer camps for kids, semiannual plant sales, and Holiday Lights at the Garden, a Christmas celebration that features more than 600,000 lights and live entertainment throughout the month of December. Because of its beauty, the Daniel Stowe Botanical Garden has become a popular place for weddings.

The garden was born in 1991 when local textile magnate Daniel J. Stowe set aside this large parcel of family land with the vision that it develop into one of the world's best botanical gardens. The master plan for the site calls for expansion in phases over the coming decades to include such aspects as an English walled garden, children's garden and learning center, home demonstration garden, restaurant, and gardens and docks on Lake Wylie.

Open daily from 9 a.m. until 5 p.m. except Thanksgiving, Christmas, and New Year's Day. Admission is $10 adults, $9 seniors, $5 children ages 4 through 12, free to members and children under age 4. Group rates available.

GLENCAIRN GARDEN
725 Crest St., Rock Hill, SC
(803) 329-5620
www.ci.rock-hill.sc.us
The gift of a few azaleas to Dr. David and Hazel Bigger in 1928 grew into 400 profuse and colorful bushes 30 years later. The private garden was later donated to the city of Rock Hill, which has transformed Glencairn into a botanical jewel with 3,000 azaleas, a three-tiered fountain, a Japanese arched bridge, and six acres of beauty. Trails wind under canopies of dogwood, oak, cherry, wisteria, and crape myrtle, and past camellias, day lilies, lily ponds, and sweeps of bulbs. Plants grow and bloom year-round, but the peak is during Rock Hill's annual Come See Me Festival each April, when azaleas, rhododendrons, and dogwoods explode in color. Hostas, ferns, lilies, and annuals are also showcased. A multistage renovation has added more features to the garden in recent years. Open dawn to dusk daily; free.

i Charlotte is famous for its towering native trees known as willow oaks, which line hundreds of residential streets. There are around 120,000 trees. In 2004 Charlotte officials committed to spending more than $1 million to add 2,700 trees along nearly 300 streets and medians. A good place to see the tree canopy is in Myers Park, along Queens Road, Selwyn Road, and Queens Road West.

MCGILL ROSE GARDEN
940 North Davidson St.
(704) 333-6497
This petaled paradise on an industrialized edge of Uptown Charlotte started with a few roses to brighten a drab coal yard and has grown to more than 1,000 rose bushes, 200 varieties, and an AARS Rose Garden designation. Owner Henry McGill no longer enjoys the garden. He passed away in 2007 at the age of 103, but he did live long enough to see the renovation in 2002. The McGill Rose Garden's 1.3-acre urban enclave has been featured in *Southern Living* and several regional magazines. Roses peak for the garden's annual Mother's Day celebration, when thousands of Charlotteans stroll through in their Sun finest. Open 10 a.m. to 4 p.m. Tues through Fri year-round; free.

UNC CHARLOTTE BOTANICAL GARDENS
9201 University City Blvd.
(704) 687-2364
http://gardens.uncc.edu
Impressive and eclectic, the UNC Charlotte Botanical Gardens has three parts. McMillan Greenhouse features one of the largest orchid collections of any public garden in the South, as well as carnivorous plants, pitcher plants, desert cacti, and a two-level tropical rain forest. Peak season for the unusual and delicate orchid blooms is February through April, and a large plant sale is held each spring. Native plantings including more than 3,000 hybrid rhododendrons and 1,000 trees fill seven acres in Van-Landingham Glen. The Susie Harwood Garden highlights the exotic with unusual ornamental plants from around the world and an Asian atmosphere of pagodas, arched bridges, and Japanese maples, as well as gardens designed to attract butterflies and hummingbirds. Gardens open daylight hours daily. Greenhouse open 10 a.m. to 3 p.m. Mon through Sat. Free.

RECREATION AREAS

CROWDERS MOUNTAIN STATE PARK
I-85, Exit 13, Kings Mountain
(704) 853-5375
www.ncparks.gov
For those who love the adventures of hiking, bird-watching, and rock climbing, this accessible getaway in Gaston County includes more than

5,000 acres. The park's two peaks (Kings Pinnacle at 1,705 feet and Crowders Mountain at 1,624 feet) are joined with 15 miles of trails, picnic areas, and a 9-acre lake. On a clear day, Crowders' peak provides awesome views of Charlotte's skyline. Boat rentals available. Free.

KINGS MOUNTAIN NATIONAL MILITARY PARK
I-85, Exit 2, Blacksburg, SC
(864) 936-7921
www.nps.gov/kimo

The Revolutionary War battle on Oct. 7, 1780, at this site was called the "turn of the tide of success" in the war by Thomas Jefferson. Kings Mountain National Military Park covers 3,945 acres, including a popular 1.5-mile Battle Trail that begins at the visitor center and circles around to points of interest and up to the ridgetop. Special events are held around October 7 each year to commemorate the battle. Free.

Dog Day Afternoon

Bark in the Park is a fun-filled day for dogs and the people they own. This event is run by the Mecklenburg County Park and Recreation Department and takes place every April at the Metrolina Expo, 7100 Statesville Rd. It began a few years ago at the county's Davie Dog Park, but with an attendance of more than 10,000 dogs (and people) it outgrew the park and moved to Metrolina Expo. The day includes a pooch parade, pet/owner look-alike contest, and contests for best bark, largest dog, smallest dog, and best trick. Admission and parking are free; dogs must be on a leash. For details call (704) 336-3854 or visit www.charmeck.org.

KINGS MOUNTAIN STATE PARK
1227 Park Rd. (I-85, S.C. Exit 8)
Blacksburg, SC
(803) 222-3209
www.southcarolinaparks.com

Sprawling across 6,885 acres adjacent to the National Military Park, Kings Mountain State Park offers two lakes with swimming, trails, fishing, boat rentals, a bridle trail and stable, miniature golf, and campgrounds. A mid-1800s upcountry farm features historical interpretations and demonstrations of pioneer life. Admission is $2 for adults, $1.25 seniors, free for ages 15 and younger.

LAKE NORMAN STATE PARK
159 Inland Sea Lane, Troutman
(704) 528-6350
www.ncparks.gov

Lake Norman State Park features 13 miles of shoreline overlooking the largest man-made lake in the state and is a great family destination for hiking, fishing, boating, camping, nature programs, and lazy-day picnics. A beach, with swimming access, draws many visitors. Open year-round, the park also has its own 33-acre lake, nature programs, and trails for walking and biking. Free.

UWHARRIE NATIONAL FOREST
789 NC Hwy. 24/27 East, Troy
(910) 576-6391
www.cs.unca.edu/nfsnc

John F. Kennedy approved the Uwharrie National Forest in 1961, the last major national forest created in America. This 50,189-acre undisturbed forest is an outdoor destination for folks in the Charlotte area. Plenty of hiking, biking, camping, fishing, and other opportunities abound. Most people are unaware there is a chain of mountains east of Charlotte, but the Uwharrie Mountains do exist. They are small peaks today, with elevations of about 1,000 feet, but archaeologists say these ancient mountains were created by volcanoes and were once 20,000 feet high.

RECREATION CENTERS

**YMCA OF GREATER CHARLOTTE
METROPOLITAN OFFICE**
(Administrative Office)
500 East Morehead St.
(704) 716-6200
www.ymcacharlotte.org
The YMCA operates a variety of popular programs in Charlotte, including after-school care, summer camp, and a summer resident camp. Seventeen locations throughout the area offer different classes and programs, including aerobics, aquatics, babysitting, baseball, basketball, canoeing, corporate wellness, dance classes from ballet to jazz, gymnastics, fitness instruction, martial arts with an emphasis on self-defense, sailing, swimming, tennis, waterskiing, yoga, and many more. Call for more information on a specific location's facilities and programs.

YWCA
3420 Park Rd.
(704) 525-5770
www.ywcacentralcarolinas.org
A separate entity from the YMCA chain, the YWCA has one central Charlotte location with a full-service fitness center and exercise classes, an indoor pool, tennis courts, a gym, after-school programs, and summer camps. The YWCA's workout facilities were overhauled in 2001—you'll find it less crowded but equally equipped compared to most of the popular YMCA branches.

SPORTS

Baseball

You can play baseball through a number of different avenues. Neighborhood athletic groups, nationally sanctioned leagues, the Park and Recreation Department, and the YMCAs have programs for all ages. There's even a chapter of the National Adult Baseball Association for older sluggers.

The county offers organized league play for ages 5 through 18. Participants are placed in compatible age divisions to provide proper training and skill development through organized practices and games. T-Ball and Coach Pitch programs are geared to children ages 5 to 8, while Player Pitch baseball and girls' softball programs offer organized league play. For more information, call (704) 336-3854.

Basketball

Future Atlantic Coast Conference hoopsters can get a head start at any of the many basketball programs available through city recreation centers, neighborhood athletic associations, YMCA programs, or Salvation Army Boys Clubs. Sign-ups for organized Park and Recreation leagues for youths ages 7 to 17 begin in October at participating recreation centers. Team registration is held during October and November, with practice and exhibition games in December and regular-season games in January. Qualifying teams participate in citywide, regional, and state tournaments. For more information, call (704) 336-3854.

UNC Charlotte conducts summer camps for boys and girls. For details, call (704) 687-4939 or visit www.charlotte49ers.com. The YMCA sponsors a basketball league for players 18 and older, and the county offers organized league play for adult men and women as well as industrial teams. Registration for summer games (June through August) is held in May; for winter games (December through April), in October. Call (704) 336-2884. Many local players also participate in church leagues.

Blades and Boards

Rollerbladers and skateboarders often head to the concrete and asphalt trails of Freedom Park, Jetton Park, and Nevin Park to escape traffic and get back to nature. Others zip through neighborhoods including Dilworth, Myers Park, Elizabeth, and Plaza-Midwood; or after hours, use the wide selection of concrete structures Uptown to jump and ride.

The Methodist Home SkatePark in east Charlotte (704-568-3363, www.charmeck.org) features a 6-foot vertical half-pipe, 6-foot bank ramps, a pyramid ramp, and other street-course challenges.

Boating

Boating is very popular in the region because of easy access to Lake Norman, Mountain Island Lake, and Lake Wylie. Lake Norman has over 520 miles of shoreline; Lake Wylie has 325 miles. Residents enjoy sailing, waterskiing, fishing, and other water-associated activities, including boat races and sailing regattas. To find out where and when, check with one of the numerous marinas surrounding both lakes.

Most of the marinas provide the full range of services for boat owners, including storage, supplies, and repairs. On Lake Wylie, the Buster Boyd Bridge marks the North Carolina/South Carolina state line and divides the lake in north/south sections. Within a half-mile of the bridge are Lake Wylie Marina (803-831-2101) and River Hills Marina (803-831-1802).

Terry's Marina (704-588-0418) is 14 miles from Uptown on the Charlotte side of the lake, while Harbortowne Marina (704-825-5050) is in Belmont on the Gaston County shore. On the lake's southern end are Tega Cay Marina (704-543-1899) and Lake Club Marina (803-324-2232).

Lake Norman's marinas are typically divided into north and south at the Highway 150 bridge. In the north try Long Island Marina (828-241-4877), North Bridge Marina (704-663-4600), River City Marina (704-663-6600), or Morningstar Marina/Skippers (704-528-3328). At the Highway 150 bridge, head to Midway Marina (828-478-2333). Mountain Creek Marina (704-483-0077), Lake Norman Marina (704-483-5546), the Boat Rack (828-478-2118), and The Landing Restaurant Bar & Marina at the Lake Norman Motel (828-478-2817) are in Catawba County. In Denver on the western shore of Lake Norman, there's Westport Marina (704-483-5172). Mooresville is served by Inland Sea Marina (704-664-4414), Stutts Marina II (704-664-3106), and All Seasons Marina (704-892-3478). On the southern end of the lake, try King's Point (704-892-3223) and Holiday Marina (704-892-0561).

Public boat ramps are available at McDowell Park, Copperhead Island, the Buster Boyd Bridge, and the South Point, Nivens Creek, Ebenezer, Fort Mill, and Allen access areas on Lake Wylie. On Lake Norman ramps are at Blythe Landing, Ramsey Creek Park, Jetton Park, Stumpy Creek Park, Lake Norman State Park, and the Hager Creek, Long Creek, Pinnacle, McCrary Creek, Little Creek, and Beatties Ford access areas.

Bowling

Bowlers will find plenty of competition at the four AMF Bowling Centers locations: South Boulevard (704-527-0333), Matthews (704-841-7606), University area (704-596-4736), and Gastonia (704-867-7243). Park Lanes (704-523-7633) in south Charlotte-is owned by George Pappas, a Professional Bowling Association Hall of Famer; it is known for attracting some of the best scratch bowlers in the city. In the northern suburbs, check out Northcross Lanes (704-892-7177), located in Huntersville. In addition to 40 lanes, it includes a lounge, billiards, karaoke, arcade, laser tag, bumper bowling, food court, and party room.

Charlotte's newest "bowling alley" is more of an entertainment/nightlife experience. Strike City (704-716-9300) is part of the Uptown EpiCentre complex and is part bowling alley, part sports bar, and part nightclub. Not for serious bowlers; more for serious fun.

Camping

You can't pitch a tent just anywhere in Charlotte-Mecklenburg, but it's perfectly fine to do so at McDowell Park and Nature Preserve (704-588-5224). Camping is also permitted at Lake Norman State Park (704-528-6350), Morrow Mountain State Park (704-982-4402) near Albemarle, and Kings Mountain State Park (803-222-3209) in South Carolina. A few of the marinas around Lake Wylie and Lake Norman also offer camping sites.

Cycling

The Charlotte area is rich in cycling opportunities for riders of all abilities. The gently rolling countryside offers pleasant routes for the recreational road rider, while occasional longer climbs challenge the fitter cyclists. Although Dilworth began hosting a criterium around Latta Park long ago, cycling has become even more popular since the 1996 Tour Du Pont came through Charlotte. In August 2004, a new race, the Presbyterian Hospital Invitational Criterium, was introduced. The professional bicycle race pits the country's top USCF riders in a competitive, invitation-only twilight race over 60 miles in Uptown. Amateurs can race the previous weekend in 24 Hours of Booty, a fun 24-hour event that takes its name from the "Booty Loop," a popular cycling/exercise area around Myers Park and Queens University at Charlotte.

A permanent bike route, designated by oval signs with a bike symbol, makes a 10-mile loop between southeast Charlotte and Uptown. Bike racks are stationed at most public buildings, and bike lockers are located beside Charlotte Transit shelters along Central Avenue. There is also a great biking opportunity at McAlpine Creek Park on a pit gravel trail.

Groups of colorfully clad riders are a common sight along the back roads in the Waxhaw, Monroe, and Huntersville areas on weekends. Off-road riders new to the area will be pleasantly surprised to learn that trail riding is available within a short distance from Charlotte. Cane Creek Park, near Waxhaw, has many miles of highly prized "single track" trails ranging from fairly easy for the new rider to fairly challenging for more adventurous souls. Check with local bike shops for additional information on trails and activities.

Disc Golf

Many newcomers are surprised to learn that Charlotte has six disc golf courses at area parks—five 18-hole tracks and one 9-hole layout. Courses vary in difficulty from beginner to professional, but all are free. The inexpensive sport that involves throwing discs at targets can be played with a standard Frisbee, but specialized equipment may improve your score. For details on local disc golf, call Dave Marchant at (704) 905-4070 or Alan Beaver at (704) 643-5725.

Fishing

There are plenty of lakes and streams in the Charlotte-Mecklenburg area. If you use live bait, you can fish for free in your home county. Using lures requires a $15 annual state license in North Carolina and a $30 license in South Carolina, available at local bait-and-tackle shops. A number of parks—Latta Plantation, Hornet's Nest, McAlpine, McDowell, Ramsey Creek, Freedom, and Pineville Parke—offer excellent fishing (catfish, bream, bass, and crappie). The county park fishing fee is $1 per day.

Flying

Several schools on the outskirts of the city will teach you the basics of how to fly an airplane as well as provide the proper training for a private, instrument, commercial, or instructor license. To get a private airline pilot's license, you must have at least 40 hours of instruction and be 17 years of age (you can start training and even do your solo at age 16). Try Carolina Flight Academy (704-400-0945, www.flycarolina.com), Long Aviation at Goose Creek Airport near Weddington (704-882-1102), or Statesville Flying Service (704-873-1111) north of town.

Football

Friday night high school football is a huge attraction in Charlotte and surrounding small towns, and the sport has become even more popular with the success of 2004 Super Bowl contenders, the NFL Carolina Panthers. Even the peewee set starts training early through neighborhood athletic associations. Late-starters can get good experience through the Charlotte-Mecklenburg junior and senior high schools or through private school programs. Visit www.popwarnerlittlepanthers.org for information about the Pop Warner League, sanctioned by the NFL.

Golf

The Charlotte metro area is home to nearly 100 golf courses and more than 15 driving ranges. Because of fairly mild winters, many golfers play year-round. Serious golfers often join private clubs that range from an initiation fee of a few thousand dollars to the "if-you-have-to-ask, you-can't-afford-it" variety. In the past two decades, though, several new semi-private and top-quality public courses have opened. Mecklenburg County Park and Recreation operates three 18-hole courses, one 18-hole par-3 course, and one 9-hole course. See the Golf chapter for in-depth details on local places to play.

Gymnastics

The city has several gymnastic schools. Clemmer's in Pineville (704-583-9998) is the oldest, having been in business since 1935. Others are International Sports Center (704-841-8407) in the Matthews area, Carolina Stars Gymnastics Academy (803-548-3441) in Fort Mill, Southeastern Gymnastics (704-847-0785) in Weddington, and Charlotte Gymnastics Academy (704-714-3547) off South Boulevard. Weyandt's Gymnastics (704-568-1277) on Monroe Road offers instruction by world-class Russian coaches. A number of dance studios also teach gymnastics. The Harris, Lake Norman, and Siskey YMCA branches also offer instruction; the Dowd YMCA offers a summer gymnastics camp. The Mecklenburg County Park and Recreation Department has classes, gym meets, and competitions.

Horseback Riding

Latta Equestrian Center is located in historic Latta Plantation Nature Preserve, 6201 Sample Rd., Huntersville, (704) 992-1550. First built by the county Park and Recreation Department as a horse-show facility, Latta Equestrian Center has 194 stalls, 2 show rings, 2 practice rings, and 10 miles of scenic trails, all available to the public for shows or use with privately owned horses. Horses are available at the center for guided trail rides and for group or private lessons. Latta Equestrian Center offers pig pickin's and hayrides for private parties, along with horse shows and other activities that are open to the public. Check the Internet or local phone book or places to board your horse or take horseback riding lessons.

Ice Hockey

Hockey players in Charlotte have two primary options for competitive games. The Ice House in Pineville offers a recreational league for boys and girls ages 4 to 18 with games held at the rink September through March, plus pickup games and clinics in the off-season. The Ice House also has an adult league with four divisions for beginner through advanced players.

Extreme Ice Center in Indian Trail is the official practice facility of the Charlotte Checkers minor league squad, and offers a variety of hockey leagues for youths to adults.

For information on joining a hockey league, call Ice House at (704) 889-9000 or Extreme Ice Center at (704) 882-1830.

Ice Skating

Ice-skaters, whether those strapping on blades for the first time or experienced competitors, can choose from the same two options as hockey players—the Ice House in Pineville and Extreme Ice Center in Indian Trail. Both offer public skating sessions daily as well as figure-skating lessons from beginner to advanced levels. Summer "cool" camps and birthday parties also are available.

Paul Wylie, 1992 Olympic skating silver medalist, teaches at Extreme Ice. For information on ice skating, call Ice House at (704) 889-9000 or Extreme Ice Center at (704) 882-1830.

Jogging, Running, and Walking

Charlotte's mild climate makes it ideal for jogging, running, and walking out of doors most of the year. You'll find trails and tracks in county parks, including a popular path around the lake at Freedom Park in central Charlotte and a 2-mile biking/jogging path and 5K cross-country running course at McAlpine Creek Park. Many folks also enjoy walking along sidewalks in tree-lined neighborhoods or hitting outdoor tracks at public junior and senior high schools. Many commercial health clubs and YMCAs have indoor tracks that become quite appealing during 20-degree or 100-degree days.

◉ Close-up

A Greenway Renews Little Sugar Creek

For decades, Charlotte considered Little Sugar Creek more a nuisance than asset. The stream was unwanted and oft-polluted as it flowed from north of the city to the South Carolina line. We thought so little of this stream that it was capped with concrete in the 1950s to facilitate a parking lot for the new Midtown Square Mall and other nearby business interests. In fact, there was a time not long ago when Little Sugar Creek had the worst water quality of any stream in North Carolina and was considered unhealthy for human contact.

Fortunately, the Queen City's ugly duckling is being transformed into a beautiful swam via the Little Sugar Creek Greenway project. This multi-stage project will eventually produce a 12.5-mile greenway trail stretching from Cordelia Park just north of Charlotte's urban core to the southern end of Mecklenburg County near the South Carolina border. Along the way, it will forever link Uptown, Central Piedmont Community College, the Metropolitan urban village, Carolinas Medical Center, Park Road Shopping Center, and Carolina Place Mall.

This massive—and carefully designed—greenway includes paved paths, gathering areas, park land, rich landscaping, fountains, and public art. The development of the Little Sugar Creek Greenway responds to the vital need for a more livable and sustainable community. It encourages alternate forms of transportation such as walking and biking, and will be easily accessible by crosswalks and well-marked entrances. Buffer zones of native vegetation will line the creek. Although these buffer zones won't be manicured for aesthetics, they will provide nature's intended protection for the creek and greatly enhance its water quality.

Local runners train year-round for Charlotte's Thunder Road Marathon, a December event that attracts participants from all over the Southeast. In late November the annual Charlotte SouthPark Turkey Trot 8K takes place. A Thanksgiving Day tradition, this 8K road race benefits local charities. Call the hotline, (704) 377-8786, or visit www.charlotterunning.com for more details.

John Linberger, a longtime Charlotte runner, offers a local training program to help runners complete their first marathon, half marathon, or 10K race. This "almost free" program is open to runners of all ages. For info, e-mail Lineberger at bridgeruntraining@yahoo.com.

Martial Arts

There are many schools in the Charlotte area that teach the martial arts and self-defense. Instruction is also available at some of the YMCAs. Unless you already know the specific sort of instruction you want, check at several of the studios and ask questions before you sign up. Many studios will let you observe a class.

Skydiving

Learn to perform aerial tricks and safe jumps with Skydive Carolina, an advanced parachute center operating at the airport in Chester, South Carolina. The professionally licensed staff offers instruction for first-time to advanced participants. Tandem jumps and group rates are available. For details on this daring sport, call Skydive Carolina at (803) 581-5867 or go to www.skydivecarolina.com.

Soccer

A number of athletic associations offer soccer programs. One of the top three is sponsored by the Harris YMCA, with approximately 1,100 participants. Groups such as Charlotte Junior Soccer, North Mecklenburg Youth Soccer, and the American Youth Soccer Organization (AYSO) also sponsor programs of similar size. Programs are also available through the Mecklenburg County Park and Recreation Department and the YMCAs. The county offers organized league play for youths ages 7 through 18. The fall program is played outdoors and is geared to recreational teams in the 7 through 15 age group. The winter program is played indoors for recreational and selected teams in the 7 through 18 age group. Leagues also have been organized through recreation centers and neighborhood associations. Sign-ups are usually held at participating recreation centers.

Softball

Programs are offered by neighborhood athletic associations, the Mecklenburg County Park and Recreation Department, and various churches. The county offers organized league play for adult men and women through industrial and co-recreational teams. Registration for the spring/summer program is in Jan and Feb, with league play occurring from mid-April through early Aug. Registration for the fall program is during July and Aug, with games scheduled from early Sept through Nov. For more information, call (704) 336-3854.

Special-Populations Programs

The Mecklenburg County Park and Recreation Department offers recreational programs for all Mecklenburg citizens, but places a special emphasis on programs for the physically, mentally, and emotionally challenged at the Marion Diehl Recreation Center (704-527-0237). The center, among the few of its type in the nation, is fully accessible, with a playground for the developmentally challenged, a therapeutic playground, and wheelchair fitness course. The center operates Camp Spirit on summer days.

Swimming

The Mecklenburg County Aquatic Center (MAC) opened its doors to the public in 1991. Located on East Second Street in Uptown, MAC is a full-service swimming, diving, and fitness center offering a wide variety of instructional, recreational, and competitive aquatic programs. The center is outfitted with an eight-lane 50-meter competitive pool and a state-of-the-art timing system. Diving enthusiasts have access to two 3-meter diving boards and two 1-meter boards. The facility also offers a 25-yard hydrotherapy pool, 16-foot in-ground spa, exercise/fitness room, sunning deck, and meeting rooms, all for minimal daily or annual fees. Call (704) 336-DIVE or go to www.justswimmac.org for more information.

In addition to the nationally known MAC, Mecklenburg County Park and Recreation operates a six-lane 25-meter indoor pool, a 1-meter springboard, and a wading pool with beach entry at the Marion Diehl Recreation Center. Water temperatures are kept several degrees warmer than at other pools, and the center offers specialized instruction for the disabled. Daily and 12-visit passes are available. For details, call (704) 527-3175.

County-owned outdoor pools include Cordelia, Double Oaks, and Revolution, all open Memorial Day through Labor Day. Swimming lessons are offered at all county pool sites in June. There is a citywide two-week session, cosponsored by the American Red Cross, at Revolution Pool. The YMCAs and YWCA have pools and swimming classes year-round, including life-saving classes. The Jewish Community Center also offers a full aquatic program.

The latest addition to Charlotte's swimming scene is Ray's Splash Planet, an indoor water park adjacent to Irwin Avenue Open Elementary School in Uptown. The year-round park, operated by Park and Recreation and the local school system, has a three-story giant slide shaped like double figure eights, interactive water play stations, a quick-current pool, and slow-moving inner tube cruises. Water basketball and water volleyball are available, along with mischievous fun with fill-and-spill buckets and squirt guns. Lap swimming also is available. Call (704) 432-4729 or visit www.charmeck.org.

Tennis

Tennis took Charlotte by storm over a decade ago, and it's still going strong. Thirty-three city and county parks have tennis courts free to the public. The Jeff Adams Tennis Center on Tyvola Road is one of the area's best, with 13 lighted courts, a grandstand, private lessons, and clinics. Country clubs and private swim/tennis clubs require membership. Olde Providence Racquet Club (704-366-9817) is the best-known tennis club in town; another is Charlotte Indoor Tennis Club (704-554-7777). Most tennis clubs, including the Y's, belong to leagues. For more information, visit www.nctennis.com/charlotte.

Volleyball

This team sport is one of the hottest activities in town, particularly with singles. You can play at several locations, including Myers Park United Methodist Church, the Jewish Community Center, and St. John's Baptist Church. Mecklenburg County Park and Recreation has courts at 27 area parks and offers leagues based on various ability levels. Leagues are divided into high, moderate, and novice levels for team competition. There are three seasonal leagues—spring, fall, and winter. The winter program is for co-recreational teams only. To find out more, call the Mecklenburg County Park and Recreation Department at (704) 336-3854.

Water Sports

The Charlotte area's three lakes—Norman and Mountain Island to the north, Wylie to the west—offer a range of water sports options from traditional skiing to adrenaline-pumped wake-boarding and hydrofoiling. Several local board shops, water-ski centers, and YMCA branches offer instruction in water sports, while area marinas hold periodic test-drive days to give potential customers a chance to try out boats and Jet Skis. Youths under 16 are required to take a safety course before driving personal watercraft on local lakes.

GOLF

S ay the word around here and ears perk up. With all due respect to basketball and football, golf is Charlotte's passion, not to mention the unofficial sport of the Carolinas. In fact, many consider golf a religion in the Charlotte area. That's little wonder, considering our temperate climate and proximity to some of the best courses in the world. Don't label golf a "pastime." Upwards of 11 percent of all Carolinians play, and the Carolinas are among the top three travel destinations for golfers in the United States. All this means big business and a big boost to the regional economy.

While not necessarily a golfing destination, Charlotte has a rich history with golf. Charlotte's first golf course, Charlotte Country Club, dates to 1910 and was designed by renowned course architect Donald Ross. Legendary Gene Sarazen was once an assistant pro at the club, and Davis Love Jr. was the club's head pro when his son, future PGA Tour superstar Davis Love III, was born in 1964. The private club is filled with Charlotte's elite and continues to rank as one of the finest courses in the state and the country, especially after a $10-million restoration project that set it up nicely to host the prestigious 2010 U.S. Women's Amateur.

Speaking of prestige tournaments, Charlotte has long been a host for the best of the best. The PGA Tour stopped at Myers Park Country Club in the 1930s and '40s for the Charlotte Open. In 1945, Bryon Nelson's win at Myers Park was part of his Tour-record 11 straight victories that year. Charlotte Country Club hosted the U.S. Amateur in 1972, while the PGA Tour's Kemper Open was played at Quail Hollow Club from 1969 through 1979. When the Senior Tour (now the Champions Tour) cranked up in the early 1980s, a fellow by the name of Arnold Palmer, who had long-standing ties to the Queen City, made sure the tour had a tourney in Charlotte, first at Quail Hollow and later at the TPC at Piper Glen. The LPGA also spent time in Charlotte, when the Fieldcrest Cannon Classic was played in the 1990s at the Peninsula Club on Lake Norman.

In 2003, the PGA Tour returned to Charlotte in a big way with an annual event that started as the Wachovia Championship and is currently known as the Quail Hollow Championship. Quail Hollow Club president Johnny Harris, a local developer and prominent member of the golf world, put together this first-class tournament for the first week of May. The tournament is played on a great Quail Hollow layout that has been renovated over the years by noted golf architect Tom Fazio, and it is considered by many PGA Tour pros as the fifth-best tournament on the PGA schedule, behind the four majors. There is always an elite field and the list of winners includes Vijay Singh, Tiger Woods, Jim Furyk, David Toms, and Anthony Kim. Meanwhile, strong rumors persist that Harris will bring a major championship to Quail Hollow this decade, probably the PGA Championship, but possibly a U.S. Open.

Charlotte has contributed to the ranks of the PGA over the years. Clayton Heafner was a PGA Tour star in the 1940s and '50s. He played on two Ryder Cup teams and twice finished second in the U.S. Open. Clayton's son, Vance, also spent time on the PGA Tour. In 1961 Charlie Sifford became the first African-American golfer to play on the PGA Tour full time, and a couple of years later, James Black, another Charlotte-born African American, competed on the circuit. Sifford was inducted into the World Golf Hall of Fame in November 2004. As mentioned, superstar Davis Love III was born in the Queen City, although he moved to Atlanta at a young age.

For golfers in the Queen City, there are tremendous opportunities to play the sport on a variety of layouts. In fact, within a 50-mile radius of Uptown you can locate nearly 100 golf courses, Financially, it's a good time to be a golfer in the area because prices are reasonable due to a saturated market.

Entries in this chapter are listed under public and semiprivate, and private courses in the Charlotte area, then courses farther afield in the Carolinas. Listings are located in Charlotte unless otherwise noted.

PUBLIC AND SEMIPRIVATE GOLF COURSES

BALLANTYNE GOLF CLUB
10000 Ballantyne Commons Parkway
(704) 248-4383
www.theballantynehotel.com
The Golf Club at Ballantyne is an 18-hole resort course located 25 minutes from Uptown off I-485 in upscale south Charlotte. This rolling, tree-lined daily-fee course does not have a "name" architect. It was a collaboration design between owner Smoky Bissell and the course construction firm. It opened in 1998 to much fanfare and was named the Best New Course in North Carolina by the North Carolina Golf Panel. The course is not overly long, 6,710 yards from the back tees and a par of 71. The original design had several wonderful holes and a couple of clunkers. A renovation project in 2008 addressed those issues and converted the greens from bent grass to the latest hybrid Bermuda grass. The closing hole is particularly memorable as golfers hit their tee shots on this dogleg left straight for the grand hotel, being careful not to reach the pond just below the edifice.

Ballantyne Golf Club is also home to the Dana Rader Golf School. Both Dana and her school are nationally ranked for instruction. After the round relax in a 30,000-square-foot clubhouse filled with antiques, locker rooms, golf shop, lounge, and grill. Non-golfers can enjoy the resort's luxurious spa and nearby shopping. Tee times may be made seven days in advance.

BIRKDALE GOLF CLUB
16500 Birkdale Commons Parkway,
Huntersville
(704) 895-8038
www.birkdale.com
Legendary Hall of Fame golfer Arnold Palmer designed this well-respected public course that opened in late 1996 across the street from Birkdale Village in Huntersville. The 18-hole championship course earned four stars from *Golf Digest* and has hosted numerous collegiate tournaments on its 7,013-yard layout. The course has generous fairways and greens, but plenty of water hazards, wetlands, and deep bunkers to prove challenging. The 18th is Birkdale's signature hole, a par-4 that requires a second shot over water to an extremely difficult green to access. All the amenities of a private course are available—a lighted driving range; a complete short game practice area; Cape Cod–style clubhouse with golf shop, restaurant, and locker rooms; and an all-season special events pavilion with an oversize stone fireplace and an antique bar. Birkdale was purchased a few years ago by the San Diego–based IRI Golf Group, which operates a number of Charlotte-area courses under the umbrella of the "Carolina Trail."

> **i** Many Charlotte-area golf courses offer discounted off-season rates, as well as twilight rates for late afternoon and evening play. Charlotte courses also stay open year-round, while many courses two hours away in the North Carolina mountains close due to frost and freezing temperatures.

HIGHLAND CREEK GOLF CLUB
7001 Highland Creek Parkway
(704) 875-9000
www.carolinatrail.com
Highland Creek was one of the first top-notch public courses that came online in Charlotte during the 1990s. It set the standard for daily-

fee golf with a modern, well-designed layout, manicured greens, full-fledged practice area, and upscale clubhouse. The course offers a variety of challenges, with four sets of tees measuring 5,080 to 7,000-plus yards, 72 bunkers, five lakes, and water features on 13 holes. It has one of the highest slope ratings of any area public facility at 138. Not to worry. You'll vividly remember each hole of this par-72 course that is often considered among the best and the toughest public course in Charlotte. Located northeast of the city in the Mallard Creek area, Highland Creek is also a gigantic residential community with more than 4,000 homes stretching from Mecklenburg into Cabarrus County.

LINCOLN COUNTRY CLUB
2052 Country Club Rd., Lincolnton
(704) 735-1382
www.lincolncountryclub.net
Lincoln Country Club is often overlooked, which it shouldn't be, and often thought to be private, which it isn't. What this semi-private course is, is a very enjoyable golf experience on two different nines from distinctly different eras. The course opened as a nine-hole layout back in 1946. It remained that way until 1992, when a new nine was added. The new nine became the front nine, while the old nine became the back nine. The front nine is a meandering trip around farmland and a few houses, and it happens be bisected by a four-lane highway, US 321. Golfers access the holes on the other side of the road by riding (or walking) though a tunnel burrowed under the highway. Some of the best holes on the course are on the other side of the road, designed with creativity and ingenuity.

The back nine is more traditional and what you'd expect of a World War II-era course. It wasn't set up for the advances of modern-day equipment, so if you can hit some long drives there are excellent chances for birdies.

The clubhouse at Lincoln Country Club was rebuilt several years ago and is very functional, with a fully-stocked pro shop, locker room facilities, and a friendly 19th hole for enjoying a cold beverage or three.

OLDE SYCAMORE GOLF PLANTATION
7500 Olde Sycamore Dr., Charlotte
(704) 573-1000
www.oldesycamoregolf.com
A golfing treat nestled among a mature forest of hardwoods in Mint Hill, Olde Sycamore Golf Plantation is only a few minutes from I-485. This semi-private course was sculpted by architect Tom Jackson, who's built many high-profile courses in the Carolinas. Jackson routed Olde Sycamore through a hilly, forested tract of land ideal for golf. Houses in the community have 100-foot setbacks to keep the golf experience pure. Fairways are hybrid Bermuda and the undulating bent grass greens are usually among the best in the Charlotte region.

The course plays to a par of 72 and measures 6,965 yards from the back tees. Three additional sets of tees make it playable for all skill levels. The front nine is tighter than the back nine and has several doglegs, placing a premium on driving accuracy. The ninth hole, however, is all about distance. This 442-yard par-4 is considered the signature hole. It requires a long drive to reach the top of a hill, followed by a fairly long second shot over water to a well-protected green. The clubhouse frames the hole perfectly. The back nine is more open than the front, but is also longer. The par-5 12th is the longest hole on the course at 601 yards, and several of the finishing holes play uphill. Overall, Jackson did an excellent job of incorporating variety and challenge into the course architecture.

"You have strategic holes, and also holes where you can bomb it. There is a nice mix," says general manager Ted Staats. "There are also a few short holes, but those are not necessarily easy holes."

RED BRIDGE GOLF CLUB
6291 Albemarle Rd., Locust
(704) 781-5231
www.redbridgegolfclub.com
The newest course in the Charlotte region, Red Bridge opened on the Fourth of July in 2009. It is located just off Hwy. 24/27, about 30 minutes east of Charlotte. Architect David Postlethwait,

a former protégé of Pete Dye, designed a very playable course that has some bite from the back tees. This semi-private layout has a lot of rolling hills and is bordered by several creeks. The signature design element is—you guessed it—a covered red bridge beside the ninth green.

REGENT PARK GOLF CLUB
5055 Regent Parkway, Fort Mill, SC
(704) 547-1300
www.regentparkgolfclub.com
This 18-hole public course straddles the North Carolina–South Carolina border. It was designed by Florida architect Ron Garl in 1995 and drew high praise and rave reviews in its early years. The course had its struggles and changed ownership a couple of times in the last decade, and seems to be headed in the right direction these days. Garl did a fine job designing the par-71, 6,785-yard layout, and the par-3 17th hole is one of the prettiest and best one-shotters in the region. An interesting side note, the course was built on property that was once part of the PTL ministry of televangelists Jim and Tammy Faye Bakker.

RENAISSANCE PARK GOLF COURSE
1525 West Tyvola Rd.
(704) 357-3373
www.charlottepublicgolf.com
The most convenient public course in Charlotte with a central location between Uptown and the airport, Renaissance Park was built on top of a landfill in 1987. It's a solid and affordable course without the fluff and frills, making it one of the city's most-played courses. Just don't confuse popular and affordable with easy. Renaissance Park can be a formidable challenge. The front nine of this par-72, 6,880-yard course is similar to a links style, while the back nine plays more like a Carolina mountains course with fairways lined with mature hardwoods. No. 13 is Renaissance Park's signature hole—a 235-yard par-3 with an elevated tee of 70 feet. The course is owned by Mecklenburg County and managed by Ratcliffe Golf Services.

ROCKY RIVER GOLF CLUB
6900 Speedway Blvd., Concord
(704) 455-1200
www.rockyrivergolf.com
Another wonderful daily-fee course perfect for locals and tourists is Rocky River Golf Club at Concord. Rocky River began life in 1997 as a stand-alone municipal course owned by the City of Concord and designed by noted architect Dan Maples of Pinehurst. The course became part of something bigger in 2007 when the city added an 11-story, $65-million Embassy Suites hotel and spa adjacent to the course, creating the Embassy Suites Golf Resort & Spa.

Despite the fancy connotation, the golf course remains open to locals, and flows through a picturesque tract of land near Charlotte Motor Speedway. Although the course features great views of the NASCAR speedway, it remains in a mostly undisturbed enclave surrounded by woods, streams and marshes, and the hotel. Rocky River's front nine has a links style to it, while the back nine weaves its way through a more wooded portion of the property.

SPRINGFIELD GOLF CLUB
990 Springfield Parkway, Fort Mill, SC
(803) 548-3318
www.playspringfield.com
Springfield has been well-received since it opened in 2001 south of Charlotte in Fort Mill, South Carolina. This par-72 course is hilly and wooded, with a lot of cresting fairways and well-protected greens. The par-3 fourth hole catches the eye. The green is farther away than you would like it and set up on a ridge with a stone wall protecting the front of the green. Clyde Johnston, another well-known Carolinas architect, is the creator of this 6,906-yard gem. Enjoy most of your round in seclusion, even though the course is part of a housing community.

VERDICT RIDGE
7332 Kidville Rd., Denver
(704) 489-1206
www.verdictridge.com

Close-up

Local Tour Lets You Play Just Like the Pros

Charlotte is home to the eGolf Amateur Golf Tour, which takes the PGA Tour concept and turns it into a local circuit for amateurs of all skill levels.

Beginning in late February and running through early October, the tour holds tournaments on top-notch courses in the greater Charlotte area. Tournaments are on Sat and occur roughly every other week. Golfers submit their handicap when joining the tour and it is used to place them in one of four flights. However, handicaps are not used in scoring. Everybody plays straight-up golf against their peers, just like the pros.

Prizes, in the form of gift certificates, are awarded to the top finishers in each flight at every tournament. Meanwhile, all golfers earn points toward a season-long point championship in their flight that's akin to the PGA Tour's FedEx Cup standings.

The tour was founded in Charlotte in 1995 by Dennis McCormac. The concept became so popular that he branched out to other cities after a couple years. Tours now operate in more than three dozen cities nationwide, with the best players from each city coming together for a national championship each October on Hilton Head Island.

The eGolf Amateur Tour is open all golfers, male or female, plus there's a Senior Amateur Golf Tour specifically for ages 50 and up. Local courses on the schedule typically include a number of private clubs.

For more info, call (704) 844-8264 or visit www.amateurgolftour.net or www.senioramateur golftour.net.

Located on the quiet west side of Lake Norman about 35 minutes north of Uptown, Verdict Ridge was intended to be a private club, but has settled into the role of semi-private and will likely remain that way for several years. Former Charlotte mayor Eddie Knox created Verdict Ridge, and the name is a nod to his profession as a lawyer. Knox is an avid golfer and designed much of the course himself. Most golfers judge it to be enjoyable and scenic, but also a bit challenging. One prominent feature is a series of wetlands that traverse the course. There are several times when you must carry a shot over the wetlands or else. The hills at Verdict Ridge are not just "rolling." A few are downright steep. The 18th hole is a tough, downhill par-5 that crosses a couple of creeks, including one just in front of the green.

Amenities include a 15,000-square-foot clubhouse, restaurant, lounge, locker room, full-service practice area, and a recreation complex with three lighted tennis courts, a pool, and cabana.

THE WARRIOR

890 Lake Wright Rd., China Grove

(877) 999-8337

www.warriorgolf.com

Average players flock to this course, located in rural China Grove, about 40 minutes northeast of Charlotte. The course circumnavigates Lake Wright, the municipal water supply for the nearby town of Landis. The reason for Warrior's popularity is that , despite its ferocious name, the course is geared to average golfers with everyday skills. It is not overly long, the fairways are fairly wide, and the greens are reasonably flat. Those same bent grass greens are known for their great condition, even in the heat of summer. Lined with thick groves of hardwoods and only a few homes, the course layout is refreshing. Holes No. 7, 16, and 17 are especially stunning.

i The Internet has become a great avenue for purchasing discount rounds of golf. Several Web sites offer this service, including two based in the Charlotte area. If you're looking for bargain golf in or near the Queen City, check out www.clickitgolf.com or www.golfholes.com. Click It Golf is the larger of the two. It has more bells and whistles, and offers discount rates at more than 40 courses. Golf Holes provides discount rates at more than 20 courses, usually for foursomes. Although not overly fancy, Golf Holes has hole-by-hole photos of each course, so you see it before you play it.

Other Public Courses

CHARLES T. MYERS GOLF COURSE
7817 Harrisburg Rd., Charlotte
(704) 536-1692
www.charlestmyersgolfcourse.com

CHARLOTTE GOLF LINKS
11500 Providence Rd.
(704) 846-7990
www.charlottegolf.com

CHARLOTTE NATIONAL GOLF CLUB
6920 Howey Bottoms Rd., Indian Trail
(704) 882-8282
www.golfholes.com

CRESCENT GOLF CLUB
220 Laurel Valley Way, Salisbury
(704) 647-0025
www.crescentgolfclub.com

DEER BROOK GOLF CLUB
201 Deer Brook Dr., Shelby
(704) 482-4653
www.deerbrookgolfclub.com

THE DIVIDE
6803 Stevens Mill Rd., Matthews
(704) 882-8088
www.charlottegolf.com

EAGLE CHASE GOLF CLUB
3215 Brantley Rd., Marshville
(704) 385-9000
www.eaglechasegolf.com

EMERALD LAKE GOLF CLUB
9750 Tournament Dr., Matthews
(704) 882-7888
www.emeraldlakegolfclub.com

FORT MILL GOLF CLUB
101 Country Club Dr., Fort Mill, SC
(803) 547-2044
www.leroysprings.com

FOX DEN COUNTRY CLUB
170 Clubhouse Dr., Statesville
(704) 872-9990
www.foxdencc.com

GASTONIA MUNICIPAL GOLF COURSE
530 Niblick Dr., Gastonia
(704) 866-6945
www.cityofgastonia.com

LARKHAVEN GOLF CLUB
4801 Camp Stewart Rd., Charlotte
(704) 545-4653
www.thegolfcourses.net

MALLARD HEAD GOLF CLUB
Brawley School Road, Mooresville
(704) 664-7031

MOORESVILLE MUNICIPAL GOLF CLUB
West Wilson Avenue, Mooresvillle
(704) 663-2539
www.golfmooresville.com

PEBBLE CREEK PAR-3
6207 Hwy. 74, Indian Trail
(704) 821-7276

REVOLUTION PARK (NINE HOLES)
2661 Barringer Dr., Charlotte
(704) 342-1946
www.revolutionparkgolf.com

RIVER BEND GOLF CLUB
Highway 150, Shelby
(704) 825-2651

SPRING LAKE COUNTRY CLUB
1375 Spring Lake Rd., York, SC
(803) 684-4898

STONEBRIDGE GOLF CLUB
2721 Swilcan Burn Dr., Monroe
(704) 283-8998
www.stonebridgegolfclub.com

SUNSET HILLS GOLF COURSE
800 Radio Rd., Charlotte
(704) 399-0980
www.charlottepublicgolf.com

TEGA CAY GOLF CLUB
1 Molokai Dr., Tega Cay, SC
(803) 548-2918
www.tegacaygolfclub.com

THE TRADITION
3800 Prosperity Church Rd., Charlotte
(704) 503-7529
www.charlottegolf.com

WATERFORD GOLF CLUB
1900 Clubhouse Rd., Rock Hill, SC
(803) 324-0300
www.charlottegolf.com

PRIVATE CLUB COURSES

The Charlotte regional area is blessed with many top-notch private golf clubs, with memberships ranging from a few thousand dollars to more than $50,000. Prospective members can choose from clubs that are more golf-centric, to traditional, family-oriented country clubs with a significant emphasis on non-golf amenities such as swimming pools, tennis centers, fine dining, and social events.

If you want to play a private course in Charlotte, inquire about the guest policy or ask your home club's professional about reciprocal agreements. Most private clubs allow members to bring guests and invite prospective members to play.

Venerable private courses include Charlotte Country Club, consistently ranked among the Top 10 courses in North Carolina and also nationally recognized, and Quail Hollow Club, a five-star course where Charlotte's PGA event is held each May. Myers Park Country Club, which recently underwent a fantastic renovation by architect Kris Spence of Greensboro, and Carmel Country Club are two more that round out the quartet of venerable private clubs in Charlotte.

Newer clubs with plenty of prestige include TPC at Piper Glen, Providence Country Club, the Club at Longview, Ballantyne Country Club, The

Gil Capps: NBC's Golf Guru

Ever wonder how television golf announcers are able to spout off so many interesting facts about pro golfers as they prepare to hit a shot? Do you question how they know Phil Mickelson is exactly 169 yards from the pin and holding an 8-iron? The answer, at least on NBC telecasts, lies right here in Mecklenburg County. Gil Capps is a producer for NBC and the guru of golf knowledge for the network's announcing crews. Though never seen or heard on the air, Capps sits between Johnny Miller and Dan Hicks in the tower at the 18th green and feeds them timely bits of info about the pros on the course. Capps is a student of the game who studies players intently. During a tourney, he's in constant contact with spotters on the course and stealthily provides yardages and other details to the on-air talent.

Peninsula Club, The Point Lake & Golf Club, and the Club at Irish Creek in Kannapolis. For a more affordable option, Raintree, River Run, Cedarwood, River Hills, Cowans Ford, NorthStone, and Carolina Golf Club offer memberships ranging from $2,000 to $10,000.

Some of the newer private courses serve as centerpieces of suburban residential developments. Many were designed by golf professionals and famous course architects. Jack Nicklaus sculpted one of his signature courses at the Club at Longview, a beautiful design set on rolling hills behind Old English–inspired rock walls and wrought-iron gates in the Union County town of Weddington.

At Lake Norman, private golf clubs line the water and are dotted with million-dollar homes. There you'll find the Peninsula Club designed by Rees Jones, River Run Golf & Country Club by Raymond Floyd, and The Point Lake & Golf Club by Greg Norman. NorthStone Country Club, located in a more moderate neighborhood in Huntersville, features a P. B. Dye signature course and expansive clubhouse.

i The Quail Hollow Championship, a PGA Tour golf tournament that began in 2003 at Charlotte's Quail Hollow Country Club, is one of the hottest tickets in town each spring. The tournament draws the likes of Tiger Woods, Phil Mickelson, Davis Love III, Vijay Singh, and Mike Weir with a $6-million purse. For a one-day visit, try a $10 Mulligan Ticket, a grounds ticket donated back to the tournament by someone unable to stay for the entire day. Call (800) 945-0777 or visit www.quailhollowchampionship.com.

CAROLINA COURSES

Because Charlotte's smack in the middle of the Carolinas, area golfers have access to some of the best golfing facilities in the world. By car, it's two hours to the mountains, two hours to Pinehurst, less than four hours to Myrtle Beach, and four hours to Hilton Head Island.

MOUNT MITCHELL GOLF CLUB
1184 State Hwy. 80 South
Burnsville, NC
(828) 675-5454
www.mountmitchellgolfresort.com
The mountains of North Carolina provide the challenge of dramatic elevation changes and wildlife-filled forests along with the pleasures of scenic beauty and cool temperatures. Patrons of Mount Mitchell Golf Club can take advantage of all those things. Nestled at the base of the highest peak east of the Rockies, the course is actually relatively flat and features bentgrass from tee to green. The natural hazards of streams and forests have been wonderfully incorporated into the course to form another major distraction—breathtaking scenery. Beware especially of the picturesque 10th and 14th holes. Course-side rental villas and condos are available.

BOONE GOLF CLUB
433 Fairway Dr., Boone, NC
(828) 264-8760
www.boonegolfclub.com
From Mount Mitchell, golfers can travel the Blue Ridge Parkway northeastward to Boone, where the Boone Golf Club is waiting. Designed by the late Ellis Maples, a legendary designer from Pinehurst, Boone Golf Club is a wonderful public course with plenty of mountain scenery and straightforward golf architecture. Portions of the course are on some of the flattest land in the Boone area, and the 3,333-foot elevation of Boone makes for lush bent grass greens and fairways.

JEFFERSON LANDING
(800) 292-6274
www.visitjeffersonlanding.com
Further up the Blue Ride Parkway, in the northwest corner of the state, Jefferson Landing opened in 1991 along the New River. Former U.S. Open and PGA champion Larry Nelson designed this 7,111-yard layout. Its gently rolling, open terrain would allow golfers a greater margin for error if it weren't for the creeks and ponds, which are in play on 15 holes. Golfers must stay on property

to play the course, which is okay, because the accommodations are quite nice.

MAGGIE VALLEY CLUB
1819 Country Club Dr.
Maggie Valley, NC
(800) 438-3861
www.maggievalleyclub.com

SPRINGDALE COUNTRY CLUB
200 Golfwatch Rd., Canton, NC
(800) 553-3027
www.springdalegolf.com

WAYNESVILLE INN GOLF RESORT & SPA
176 Country Club Dr., Waynesville, NC
(800) 627-6250
www.wccinn.com

GROVE PARK INN AND RESORT
290 Macon Ave., Asheville, NC
(800) 438-5800
www.groveparkinn.com
Farther west in the North Carolina mountains, back down the Parkway to the other side of Asheville, there are several neat golfing getaways that sometimes go unnoticed. The recently renovated Maggie Valley Club, along with venerable Springdale Country Club and Waynesville Inn Golf Resort & Spa, all offer on-site accommodations and enjoyable golf in the Great Smoky Mountains. If you happen to find yourself in Asheville with clubs in hand, pay a visit to the historic Grove Park Inn and Resort. The inn's century-old Donald Ross course was restored and renovated in 2002, giving an authentic old-school Donald Ross golf experience right in the heart of trendy Asheville.

i Most area golf courses require players to wear nonmetal "soft" spikes to protect fairways and greens. Appropriate attire includes a collared shirt and Bermuda-length shorts. At most courses, jeans, cutoffs, T-shirts, and halter tops are prohibited, along with personal coolers.

PINEHURST RESORT
80 Carolina Vista Dr.
Village of Pinehurst, NC
(800) 487-4653
www.pinehurst.com
Every avid golfer who visits Charlotte, or moves to Charlotte, asks one important question: How far is it to Pinehurst? The answer is two hours by car or 20 minutes by plane to this golfing mecca in the North Carolina Sandhills. Whatever you do, make sure to make this short trip to experience a brand of golf like no other. The centerpiece is Pinehurst. This golfing utopia was established in 1895 by Boston soda-fountain magnate James Walker Tufts, and has grown to eight courses over the years. In 1900 Scottish-born architect Donald Ross moved to Pinehurst and redesigned Pinehurst No. 1, then created course Nos. 2, 3, and 4. Pinehurst No. 2, which he tweaked over the years until his death in 1948, is the crown jewel of golf in North Carolina and ranked among the top 10 courses in the world. It hosted the U.S. Open Championship in 1999 and 2005, and will do so again in 2014. Pinehurst No. 4 has gained quite a bit of notoriety since its renovation by Tom Fazio back in 2000. There are five courses at the core of the resort, plus three courses—Nos. 6, 7, and 8—in locations just outside the Village of Pinehurst.

Guests at the resort's grand old Carolina Hotel, which now includes a luxurious spa, can choose from all eight courses, but there is a premium added to the rounds on No. 2.

The Pinehurst region, which includes neighboring Southern Pines, is home to more than 40 golf courses, providing golfers a wealth of options. Generally speaking, the golf becomes less expensive the farther you get away from the Village of Pinehurst.

NATIONAL GOLF CLUB
One Royal Troon Dr.
Village of Pinehurst, NC
(800) 471-4339
www.nationalgolfclub.com
Just down Midland Road from Pinehurst Resort is the Jack Nicklaus–designed National Golf Club, which celebrated its 20th anniversary in 2009.

Nicklaus built a beautiful course on one of the most scenic tracts of land in the Sandhills. It features significant elevation changes, streams, ponds, and a lake interspersed among the sand and longleaf pines.

PINE NEEDLES LODGE & GOLF CLUB
1005 Midland Rd., Souther Pines, NC
(800) 747-7272
www.pineneedles-midpines.com
Another stellar Pinehurst-area course is Pine Needles Lodge & Golf Club, which has hosted three U.S. Women's Open Championships. Pine Needles and its sister course, Mid Pines, are Donald Ross classics situated across Midland Road from each other.

THE PIT GOLF LINKS
410 Pit Links Lane, Aberdeen, NC
(800) 574-4653
www.pitgolf.com
A few miles south of Pinehurst in Aberdeen is The Pit Golf Links, a unique course because it was built on the site of an old sand quarry. Architect Dan Maples creatively routed holes over and around mounds from the mine, which produced sand in the 1930s to make concrete for the Blue Ridge Parkway. About 15 miles northeast of Pinehurst is Tobacco Road, another interesting course on the site of a former sand quarry. Maverick architect Mike Strantz took much creative license with this layout, which has been described as "The Pit on steroids," and was voted the 10th hardest course in America by *Golf Digest* magazine.

LEGACY GOLF LINKS
12615 US 15, Aberdeen, NC
(800) 314-7560
www.legacygolfnc.com
Jack Nicklaus' son, Jack Nicklaus II, added a second Pinehurst-area design to the family portfolio by creating Legacy Golf Links. The label "challenging, yet enjoyable" fits this course perfectly. Picturesque par-3s, reachable par-5s, and testy par-4s flow naturally among longleaf pines in a pastoral setting.

OCEAN RIDGE PLANTATION
351 Ocean Ridge Parkway, SW
Ocean Isle Beach, NC
(800) 233-1801
www.big-cats.com

THISTLE GOLF CLUB
1815 Olde Thistle Club Rd.
Sunset Beach, NC
(800) 571-6710
www.thistlegolf.com

TIDEWATER GOLF CLUB
1400 Tidewater Dr.
North Myrtle Beach, SC
(843) 913-2424
www.tidewatergolf.com
While the Pinehurst area considers itself the home of American golf, the brasher and bolder Myrtle Beach bills itself as the "golf capital of the world." Myrtle Beach's Grand Strand, which includes Brunswick County in North Carolina, peaked at 120 golf courses in the early 2000s. Nowadays, that number is around 100, still an awesome amount of golf concentrated in one place. The Grand Strand is more commercialized than Pinehurst, so keep that in mind if you're a golf purist.

Starting at the north end of the strand in Sunset Beach, North Carolina, the feline-themed Ocean Ridge Plantation offers four excellent courses—Leopard's Chase, Lion's Paw, Panther's Run, and Tiger's Eye—with a Jaguar-inspired fifth course on the way for 2011. Local architect Tim Cate handled the lion's share of design work at Ocean Ridge, and his courses are a treat, especially Leopard's Chase. It's one of the finest courses on the Grand Strand. Cate also designed the 27 holes at nearby Thistle Golf Club, a Scottish links design that is a real hidden treasure and well worth a visit. Migrating southward across the state line, Tidewater Golf Club in North Myrtle Beach is a stand-alone course that stands out. It is located along the salt water marshes of the Intracoastal Waterway and was named Best New Public Course in America in 1990.

North Carolina's Top 50: Courses

The North Carolina Golf Panel, founded by Charlotte publicist Bill Hensley, annually ranks the top 100 golf courses in the state. The rankings include all courses—public and private—and are published in the March issue of *Business North Carolina* magazine. The panel consists of roughly 140 golf executives, media, golf professionals, coaches, and notable amateurs. Listed below are North Carolina's Top 50, with location, from the 2010 rankings:

1. Pinehurst No. 2, Pinehurst
2. Grandfather Golf & Country Club, Linville
3. Old North State Club, New London
4. Quail Hollow Club, Charlotte
5. Pine Needles, Southern Pines
6. Country Club of NC (Dogwood), Pinehurst
7. Charlotte Country Club, Charlotte
8. Forest Creek Golf Club (South), Pinehurst
9. Elk River Club, Banner Elk
10. Pinehurst No. 4, Pinehurst
11. Linville Golf Club, Linville
12. Pinehurst No. 8, Pinehurst
13. Cape Fear Country Club, Wilmington
14. Eagle Point Golf Club, Wilmington
15. Biltmore Forest Country Club, Asheville
16. Forest Creek Golf Club (North), Pinehurst
17. Rock Barn Golf & Spa (Jones), Conover
18. Sedgefield Country Club, Greensboro
19. Wade Hampton Golf Club, Cashiers
20. Country Club of NC (Cardinal)
21. National Golf Club, Pinehurst
22. Bright's Creek Golf Club, Mill Spring
23. Raleigh Country Club, Raleigh
24. Old Town Club, Winston-Salem
25. River Landing (River), Wallace
26. Balsam Mountain Preserve, Sylva
27. Myers Park Country Club, Charlotte
28. Willow Creek Country Club, High Point
29. The Club at Longview, Weddington
30. Treyburn Country Club, Durham
31. The Hasentree Club, Wake Forest
32. Duke University Golf Club, Durham
33. The Cliffs at Walnut Cove, Asheville
34. The Club at Irish Creek, Kannapolis
35. Leopard's Chase, Sunset Beach
36. Linville Ridge Country Club, Linville
37. Tiger's Eye Golf Links, Sunset Beach
38. Finley Golf Course, Chapel Hill
39. Pinehurst No. 7, Pinehurst
40. St. James Plantation (Reserve), Southport
41. Governors Club, Chapel Hill
42. Forsyth Country Club, Winston-Salem
43. Gaston Country Club, Gastonia
44. Bald Head Island Club, Bald Head Island
45. Innsbrook Golf & Boat Club, Merry Hill
46. Alamance Country Club, Burlington
47. Grandover (East), Greensboro
48. River Landing (Landing), Wallace
49. Pinewild Country Club (Magnolia), Pinehurst
50. Old Chatham Golf Club, Durham

BAREFOOT RESORT
4980 Barefoot Resort Bridge Rd.
North Myrtle Beach, SC
(800) 320-6536
www.barefootgolf.com
Just south of Tidewater in the heart of North Myrtle Beach is a grand slam of great golf at Barefoot Resort. This luxury getaway is home to superb courses designed by Greg Norman, Tom Fazio, Davis Love III, and Pete Dye. Norman's course might just be the best; its minimalist approach follows the lay of the land and incorporates stunning views of the Intracoastal Waterway.

MYRTLE BEACH NATIONAL
www.mbn.com
Moving to the south end of the Grand Strand, Myrtle Beach National features three courses: King's North, Southcreek, and the West Course. King's North is the standout of the trio, designed by Arnold Palmer. It features a par-5 hole called "the gambler" where you can cut distance on the hole by hitting to an island in the middle of a lake. The 18th hole at King's North is known for its 42 bunkers, believed to be the most on any hole in America.

CALEDONIA GOLF AND FISH CLUB
369 Caledonia Dr.
Pawley's Island, SC
(843) 237-3675
In the quieter southern Strand, golf courses lined with live oaks have been carved from former rice plantations. Caledonia Golf and Fish Club in Pawley's Island is a shining example and has been rated among America's best modern courses by *Golfweek*.

WILD DUNES
5757 Palm Blvd.
Isle of Palms, SC
(888) 778-1876
www.wilddunes.com

Farther down the coast in the Charleston region, Wild Dunes was one of the original island resorts to be built in the lowcountry. Wild Dunes has two courses designed by Tom Fazio, with the Links Course garnering the most attention. The 17th and 18th hole play along the Atlantic Ocean, so close that coastline erosion forced a redesign of the 18th hole a few years ago.

KIAWAH ISLAND GOLF RESORT
Kiawah Island, SC
(800) 654-2924
www.kiawahresort.com
On the southern side of Charleston, Kiawah Island offers four top-drawer courses. The most famous is the Ocean Course, designed by Pete Dye and host to the memorable 1991 Ryder Cup. The Ocean Course has been called the "Pebble Beach of the East" because so many holes play along the sea. The Atlantic lurks in the distance on the front nine—you hear it but can't see it until the ninth hole. However, the backside sweeps closer to the water, providing spectacular seascape views from multiple vantage points among the dunes.

HARBOUR TOWN GOLF LINKS
11 Lighthouse Lane, Hilton Head Island, SC
(843) 842-8484
www.seapines.com
A bit farther down the South Carolina coast is Hilton Head Island, a posh enclave known for its outstanding collection of courses. The best of which is generally considered to be Harbour Town Golf Links. When it opened in 1969, the course's small greens, railroad tie–supported bunkers, and tight fairways were considered radical. Today, professionals rave about the course at the Heritage Classic held here each spring, especially the approach shot to the 18th green, a forced-carry over a marsh with the famed lighthouse in the backdrop.

SPECTATOR SPORTS

Charlotte offers more professional sports than any other city from Washington, D.C., to Atlanta. We're home to the NFL Carolina Panthers, the NBA Charlotte Bobcats, a premier PGA Tour event, NHRA Championship Drag Racing, and three NASCAR races, including the circuit's All-Star race and the Coca-Cola 600, a Memorial Day weekend tradition that's among the largest single sporting events in the world.

Outside the major leagues, the Queen City is home to minor league baseball, minor league hockey, USL professional soccer, a Champions Series pro tennis tourney, a professional golf mini tour, and two prominent NCAA Division I basketball teams—the Charlotte 49ers and Davidson Wildcats.

The Queen City has been a sports-crazy town to varying degrees over the years. Flirtations with upstart pro football leagues never took hold, but the Panthers have been widely popular, selling out the vast majority of games since settling into their 73,778-seat palace in 1996. The city's first big-time sports franchise—the Charlotte Hornets—was the hottest ticket in the NBA for several years. The Hornets set league records for attendance and consecutive sellouts at the now-demolished Charlotte Coliseum and were given a ticker-tape parade and treated as royalty until the ownership group committed a series of blunders and moved the team in the face of waning support. The Bobcats marked the NBA's return to Charlotte in 2004, but our once-innocent sports psyche was damaged by the Hornets and the city has been slower to warm up to the Bobcats.

Our passion for NASCAR has always run high thanks to annual races at Charlotte Motor Speedway and the migration of most NASCAR team headquarters to areas north and northeast of the city. Given our long and devoted love affair with stock car racing, it was only natural that NASCAR chose Charlotte for the location of its Hall of Fame.

College basketball is another passion in these parts. Alumni and fans of Atlantic Coast Conference schools North Carolina, North Carolina State, Duke, and Wake Forest are everywhere, supporting the nation's best basketball conference that's held so many of its tournaments in the Queen City. Before the NCAA Final Four was required to play in domed stadiums, Charlotte hosted the 1994 Final Four, won by Arkansas in an exciting game against Duke. Charlotteans have special traditions for March Madness—televisions are rolled into classrooms and employers often look the other way when office workers are absent during the ACC tournament, and when they fill out their NCAA brackets. While ACC hoops are most prominent, our local teams have plenty of fans and have grabbed their share of the limelight. UNC Charlotte's unheralded squad made a Cinderella run to the Final Four in 1977, led by future NBA All-Star Cornbread Maxwell, while Davidson embarked upon a storybook run of its own in 2008, reaching the Elite Eight in the NCAA tournament behind the exploits of future NBA lottery pick Stephen Curry.

So, you can say that sports are part of the fabric of life in the Queen City. And that's something in which we take great pride.

In this chapter you'll find information for the spectator—from professional and collegiate sports teams to the most popular sporting events in the area. For recreational activities and participant sports, see our Parks and Recreation chapter. Entries are arranged alphabetically by sport. Listings are located in Charlotte unless otherwise noted.

BASEBALL

CHARLOTTE KNIGHTS

Knights Stadium
2280 Deerfield Dr., Fort Mill
(704) 357-8071 (NC)
(803) 548–8050 (SC)
www.charlotteknights.com

Minor-league baseball has been a Charlotte tradition for more than a century, bringing us numerous all-star selections, postseason berths, championships, and one trip to Las Vegas for the Triple-A World Series. The city's history with hometown baseball dates to 1901 with the Charlotte Hornets, and includes such notable players as Cal Ripken Jr., Eddie Murray, Ken Singleton, Manny Ramirez, Jim Thome, and Brian Giles. The best name is Charlotte baseball history belongs to Drungo La Rue Hazewood, an outfielder for the Double-A Charlotte O's in the late 1970s and early 1980s.

The Charlotte Knights, the Triple-A affiliate of the Chicago White Sox, have played at Knights Castle in Fort Mill since 1990. Though team officials hope to move to a new Uptown stadium, for now it's a 12-mile drive down I-77 to exit 88. Knights Castle features 10,000 seats, the 250-seat Home Run Cafe overlooking the field, a 75-seat meeting room, and a Family Fun Zone with a carousel, minigolf, speed-pitch machine, rock-climbing wall, and playground. Adults can kick back in Lancelot Lounge; youngsters 12 and under can join the Knights Kids' Club for T-shirts, autograph books, game tickets, birthday cards, and player meet-and-greets. The team's season in the International League runs mid-April through early September, with 72 home games.

The Knights hold many promotions, the most popular of which being fireworks shows after Sat home games. There are also Thirsty Thursdays, an annual train ride to play the Durham Bulls, and discounted tickets through Harris Teeter and Time Warner Cable. Kids love to chase foul balls and hug Homer the Dragon.

Game time is generally 7 p.m. Mon through Sat and 2 p.m. Sun. There are occasional "business day specials" that provide early afternoon starts on weekdays.

KANNAPOLIS INTIMIDATORS

FieldCrest Cannon Stadium
I-85 at Exit 63, Kannapolis
(704) 932-3267
www.intimidatorsbaseball.com

Named for Kannapolis' most famous son, racing legend Dale "The Intimidator" Earnhardt, this team is a Single-A affiliate of the Chicago White Sox and features many players just starting out in professional baseball. Kannapolis is one of 16 teams in the long-standing South Atlantic League, playing such nearby teams as the Hickory Crawdads and the Asheville Tourists.

The Intimidators began play in 1995 in 4,700-seat FieldCrest Cannon Stadium, a nice venue for baseball and conveniently located of I-85 just north of Concord. The home season consists of 70 games between early April and early September. Regular promotions include fireworks, cornhole tournaments, bring your dog nights, and Family Fun Days on Sunday, when kids 12 and under are allowed on the field after the game to run the bases.

BASKETBALL

CHARLOTTE BOBCATS

Time Warner Cable Arena
333 East Trade St.
(704) 688-9000
www.bobcats.com

The Carolinas have long been basketball country, and in 2004 the city's new NBA team, the Charlotte Bobcats, brought big-league play back to town. The Bobcats have had their ups and downs since this franchise debuted in the wake of the Charlotte Hornets departure to New Orleans. Original Bobcats owner, Bob Johnson, founder of BET and the first African-American team owner in NBA history, didn't spend much time in Charlotte and alienated many fans and members of the business community. Johnson, who paid $300 million for the franchise, grew tired of ownership after losing tens of millions each year, and sold the team to a group led by North Carolina native Michael Jordan in the spring of 2010. Jordan had been a minority owner and director of basketball operations for the Bobcats, and he's now the second African-American team owner in league history.

The good news for Jordan—and the city—is the Bobcats have a solid base for the future with legendary coach Larry Brown at the helm and a reasonably young nucleus of talent in Gerald Wallace, Stephen Jackson, Raymond Felton, and D. J. Augustin. Season tickets are readily available for games at Time Warner Arena, while single-game seats are normally available as well. Sellouts are usually only against big-name teams like the Los Angeles Lakers and Cleveland Cavaliers. Ticket prices range from $10 to $300. The arena is a great venue for watching basketball, with a huge scoreboard and video screen suspended over the floor and all the modern amenities fans come to expect these days. The team mascot, Rufus, does a good job with his routines and the cheerleaders are quite popular, especially with male fans. Concessions are a little pricey.

If you can't attend the games in person, many are televised locally on Fox Sports Carolinas and Fox Sports South.

FOOTBALL

ACC FOOTBALL CHAMPIONSHIP GAME
Bank of America Stadium
800 South Mint St.
www.accfootballcharlotte.com

Looking to find a suitable home for its football championship game, the Atlantic Coast Conference is shifting the matchup to Charlotte for the 2010 and 2011 seasons. The ACC title game was created in 2005 when the league expanded to 12 teams, but it did not sell out during three years in Jacksonville and two in Tampa, and the atmosphere at either location was not what conference officials envisioned. So, Charlotte put together a strong bid to host the title affair for two years, a bid backed by local politicos and business leaders. Hopes are the game will find a permanent place on the Queen City's sports landscape.

Bank of America Stadium will be the venue for the games, slated for Dec. 4, 2010, and Dec. 3,

---

Bojangles' Coliseum

Bojangles' Coliseum on Independence Boulevard began life in 1955 as the 11,666-seat Charlotte Coliseum. It was the largest unsupported steel dome in the world. Over the years, it hosted ACC men's and women's basketball tournaments, NCAA tournament opening rounds, UNC Charlotte home games, and a variety of other spectator sports, such as ice hockey, arena football, lacrosse, professional wrestling, roller derby, and rodeos. These days its primary sports use is high school and college basketball tourneys and UFC bouts.

This landmark arena has also hosted concerts by such legends as Elvis Presley, Bob Dylan, Bruce Springsteen, and the Rolling Stones. Future NBA Hall-of-Fame David Robinson played his last collegiate game at the arena on March 13, 1987, when he scored 50 points for Navy in a 97-82 loss to Michigan in the NCAA tournament.

2011. Events surrounding the game will include an ACC coaches and awards luncheon; the ACC Night of Legends, which will honor great football players in league history; an ACC FanFest; a commissioner's brunch; and a pre-game pep rally. Ticket prices are $25 and $40 for upper level seats and $70 and $90 for lower level seats. Club Level tickets are $150 and $175 and only available through ticket packages.

CAROLINA PANTHERS
Bank of America Stadium
800 South Mint St.
(704) 358-7000
(704) 522-6500 (tickets)
www.panthers.com

On Oct 26, 1993, the Carolina Panthers became the 29th NFL team, the first expansion team in the league since 1976 and the only one to win the bid by total owner acclamation. The Panthers played at Clemson University's Death Valley their first season, 1995, before taking the proper place in Charlotte the next year in Ericsson Stadium, now called Bank of America Stadium. Nestled on a 33-acre site in Uptown Charlotte, the open-air natural-grass facility was financed through a public-private venture that included the sale of Permanent Seat Licenses. PSLs give buyers the ability to permanently control and purchase season tickets for all Panthers home games. More than 62,500 PSLs were sold before the Panthers ever played their first game.

In their first season the Panthers established an NFL mark for the most wins by an expansion team, finishing 7–9. The team improved dramatically in their first season in Charlotte, winning the NFC West in 1996. In the franchise's first-ever playoff game, the Panthers defeated the Super Bowl champion Dallas Cowboys 26–17 at home and advanced to the NFC Championship Game before losing to Green Bay.

The Panthers had some up and down years after that, including a woeful 1–15 in 2001, but current coach John Fox came to Carolina in 2002 and turned the team into a Super Bowl contender. Fox believes in an aggressive defense; a conservative, run-oriented offense; and avoiding turnovers. In the 2003 season that took the Panthers to the Super Bowl, the Panthers dropped a 32–29 heartbreaker to the New England Patriots.

Since then the Panthers have stayed the course with Fox and developed one of the NFL's most potent rushing attacks by drafting Deangelo Williams and Jonathan Stewart. In 2009, Carolina became the first team in NFL history to have two backs rush for more than 1,100 yards. Kicker John Kasay has been a constant over the years, and is the only player from the original 1995 squad who is still on the roster.

Game days in Charlotte are a special event. Tailgating takes place at numerous locations across Uptown and along Morehead Street, starting early in the morning for Sunday games. Fans are loud, but for the most part respectful, and the club has a long-standing policy of not allowing fans to take off their shirts. Concessions are pricey and it takes a lot longer to enter the stadium nowadays because of elevated terrorism-related security measures.

A limited number of single-game tickets are sold each season to the Panthers' eight home games, and two home preseason games. Carolina's average ticket price of $63.32 is among the lowest in the NFL. Tickets are available online at www.panthers.com, via charge-by-phone at (704) 522-6500, or at the Bank of America Stadium box office on the southeast side of the stadium. Box office hours are 8:30 a.m. to 5:30 p.m. weekdays.

MEINEKE CAR CARE BOWL
Bank of America Stadium
(800) 618-8149
www.meinekecarcarebowl.com
A team from the Atlantic Coast Conference battles a team from the Big East in this college football bowl game held in late December at Bank of America Stadium. The game began in 2002 as the Continental Tire Bowl and has achieved surprising success in a short period of time. Average attendance is more than 62,000 with three sellouts. Participating teams have included North Carolina, Pittsburgh, Virginia, N.C. State, South Florida, and West Virginia. The game is televised live by ESPN and pays out a minimum of $1 million per school.

An Uptown Street Festival and Pep Rally add to the fun and bring out Charlotteans hungry for big-time college games in the city.

GOLF

QUAIL HOLLOW CHAMPIONSHIP
Quail Hollow Country Club
(800) 945-0777
www.quailhollowchampionship.com
When Charlotte decided to get back into hosting a regular PGA Tour event in 2003, everything was thought out in advance to make this a special event on the Tour's schedule. The key compo-

nents were an excellent golf course (Quail Hollow), a big-time sponsor (Wachovia/Wells Fargo), great spot on the calendar (late April to early May), and a highly-respected television partner (CBS). Tournament chairman Johnny Harris also did a lot of little things right, like providing every player a Mercedes courtesy car and making sure caddies and wives are treated as well as the players.

The result is the Wachovia Championship turned Quail Hollow Championship, which has featured an elite field every year. Many golfers have said that, outside of golf's four majors, the Charlotte event is the best on tour, or among the best. Just look at the list of champions and you see names like Tiger Woods, Vijay Singh, David Toms, Jim Furyk, and rising superstar Anthony Kim.

Tickets are hard to come buy as golf-crazy Charlotteans gobble them up weeks before the tournament, and even show up in droves at practice rounds to get a glimpse of major players.

Tickets for the championship are $40–$50 for individual days, or a weekly pass for $140.

ICE HOCKEY

CHARLOTTE CHECKERS
Time Warner Cable Arena
333 East Trade St.
(704) 342-4423
www.gocheckers.com
In 1993, after a 16-year hiatus, professional hockey returned to the Queen City in the form of the Charlotte Checkers minor league hockey team. The team played in the East Coast Hockey League through the 2009-2010 season, and regularly qualified for the ECHL playoffs. Big news was made in early 2010, however, as the Checkers announced they would switch leagues from the ECHL to the higher-level American Hockey League. The AHL is the last step before the NHL, so expect to see a stronger caliber of play and a roster dotted with talented young players on their way to the big leagues. As part of the move, the Checkers changed affiliation and signed a multi-year deal to be the top minor league team

of the Carolina Hurricanes. The Hurricanes, who play in Raleigh, are the only NHL team in the Carolinas and captured the Stanley Cup in 2006.

The Checkers are one of 29 teams in the AHL and will face off against teams from Texas to Canada. Owner Michael Kahn promises big things from the upgraded Checkers franchise, while still keeping ticket prices affordable.

The Checkers' regular season in the AHL runs from October to mid April and features 40 home games at Time Warner Cable Arena in Uptown, where portions of the upper deck are curtained off to make it more intimate for minor league hockey. Crowds averaged around 5,500 per game the last couple of years the team played in the ECHL and those numbers will likely increase in the AHL.

RACING

Auto

CHARLOTTE MOTOR SPEEDWAY
(704) 455-3200
www.charlottemotorspeedway.com
The racing fervor that fills the Queen City anytime NASCAR races are taking place is something that must be experienced by anyone who visits Charlotte. The city is a hotbed for racing enthusiasts, often drawing crowds in excess of 200,000 to Charlotte Motor Speedway when the big races come to town.

Located 12 miles northeast of Charlotte, the 2,010-acre Charlotte Motor Speedway hosts many races and shows year-round. However, the main attractions are its three NASCAR Sprint Cup dates—the Sprint All-Star Race, the Coca-Cola 600, and the Bank of America 500. Other noted races are the Nationwide Series 300-miler and the Truck Series 200-miler.

Stock-car racing started as summer fun on Carolina red-clay tracks, a sport that grew out of the days when moonshiners tried to outrun the law on backcountry roads. But as the sport has grown into a multibillion-dollar industry and fans have scattered across the country, NASCAR officials have moved a lot of races out of the Carolinas. Fortunately for Charlotteans, the owners of Charlotte Motor Speedway keep the 1.5-mile track updated with the latest amenities, so Charlotte remains the epicenter of NASCAR racing. Many of the sport's superstars—including Dale Earnhardt Jr., Jeff Gordon, Jimmie Johnson, Ryan Newman, and Matt Kenseth—live here, and most of the race teams are based just north of town around Lake Norman. The Coca-Cola 600 is one of the best-attended sporting events in the world. An entire tourism industry has been built around our track, shops, and races. And the addition of the NASCAR Hall of Fame only solidifies our place in the sport.

If you're new to the sport and planning a trip to Charlotte Motor Speedway, here are several key points to keep in mind before heading to the track. Since many events are sold out in advance, get your tickets early. The best seats are higher up in the stands on the front stretch. Leave for the track very early and allow plenty of time for parking. Bring a cooler packed with refreshments, as this will save time waiting in line at the concession stands, but make sure your cooler is not larger or taller than 14 inches and you don't bring any glass containers. You may also want to bring a seat cushion, as well as earplugs to protect against the loud noise.

Part of the May race festivities take place Uptown with Speed Street, a three-day street festival with driver appearances and autograph signings, interactive exhibits, food vendors, family-friendly activities, racing souvenirs, and live music ranging from rock and roll to country to urban and alternative.

If you're not visiting during race weeks in May and Oct, you can still check out the Speedway with on-track tours open to the public. Tours are offered Mon through Sat from 9 a.m. until 4 p.m. and Sun from 1 until 4 p.m. Call the track office for more information.

ZMAX DRAGWAY
5555 Concord Parkway South, Concord
(704) 455-3205
www.charlottemotorspeedway.com/dragway
Charlotte Motor Speedway owner Bruton Smith built the zMax Dragway in 2008 and it is the Taj Mahal of dragstrips. This state-of-the-art facility seats 30,000 and is the only four-lane quarter-mile concrete dragway in the world. There are also 28 luxury suites.

The dragstrip debuted in September of 2008 with the NHRA Nationals. In 2009, it hosted the NHRA Carolina Nationals, and it is slated to begin hosting two major events annually in 2010. Daily tickets vary in price from $10 to $55.

Bicycle
PRESBYTERIAN HOSPITAL INVITATIONAL CRITERIUM
Uptown
(704) 386-3043
www.charlottecriterium.org
Introduced in August 2004, the criterium is part of the USA Cycling's National Racing Calendar (NRC) and attracts pro cyclists from around the world for a competitive, invitation-only twilight race over 50 miles. Uptown streets offer plenty of places to watch the race for free, or you can pay to party in the hospitality tent. Proceeds benefit the Brain Tumor Fund for the Carolinas. For those who want to ride rather than watch, 24 Hours of Booty is an around-the-clock amateur bike ride for all skill levels held the weekend prior to the criterium. Run on a 3-mile route around Queens University that locals call the "Booty Loop," the community event takes its name from the area known for attracting lots of shapely bikers, runners, and walkers. The amateur event benefits the Brain Tumor Fund for the Carolinas and the Lance Armstrong Foundation.

Road
CHARLOTTE RACEFEST
SouthPark
(704) 377-8786
www.charlotteracefest.com
A spring event organized by the same folks who put on the Charlotte SouthPark Turkey Trot 8K each Thanksgiving, Charlotte RaceFest occurs in April and includes a half marathon and 10K. The race winds through SouthPark; proceeds benefit the American Red Cross.

Insider Top 5: Race Shops

David Newton, NASCAR writer for ESPN.com, ranks the race shops in the Charlotte region that provide the best visitor experience:

1. **Michael Waltrip Racing**—Located in Sherrills Ford, this shop has lots of character because of its former life. Prior to becoming Michael Waltrip Racing, it was a movie theater and skate park. A catwalk allows fans to watch crews work on cars from high above.

2. **Penske Racing**—You can land a 747 jetliner in this shop, a former Panasonic warehouse in Mooresville. The size of it is overwhelming, and fans can check out the Indy Car operation, too.

3. **Richard Childress Racing**—It's worth the longer drive to Welcome, N.C., to see the museum of cars from Richard Childress Racing's most popular driver of all time, the late Dale Earnhardt Sr. There's a neat fan deck overlooking the shop, and a showroom displaying animals from Richard Childress's hunting trips. Also, the elegant Childress Winery is nearby.

4. **Hendrick Motorsports**—The cream of the crop in NASCAR racing, with 9 of the last 15 Sprint Cup championship trophies. Also home of NASCAR's most popular driver, Dale Earnhardt Jr., and located in Concord, close to Charlotte Motor Speedway.

5. **Joe Gibbs Racing**—Located in Huntersville, the only race shop in the world where you can see NASCAR championship trophies displayed alongside Super Bowl trophies. Gibbs won three Super Bowls as coach of the Washington Redskins and three NASCAR titles as owner of Gibbs Racing.

CHARLOTTE SOUTHPARK TURKEY TROT 8K
SouthPark
(704) 377-8786
www.charlotterunning.com

Before bellying up for a huge Thanksgiving Day meal of turkey, dressing, and all the trimmings, hundreds of Charlotteans run the annual Charlotte 8K Turkey Trot. The 8K road race begins and ends on Morrison Boulevard beside SouthPark Mall and winds past homes and offices around SouthPark Mall. All funds raised go to the Leukemia Society and the Sharon United Methodist Church Youth Ministry.

SOCCER

CHARLOTTE EAGLES & LADY EAGLES
1020 Crews Rd., Ste. N, Matthews
(704) 841-8644
www.charlotteeagles.com

As soccer participation grows in the surrounding area, so has support of the Charlotte Eagles and Lady Eagles, professional soccer teams with rising stars who could go on to play in the MLS or abroad.

The Charlotte Eagles are a men's professional soccer franchise that competes in the Second Division of the United Soccer Leagues. The USL Second Division consists of 10 teams across the East Coast and the Caribbean. The Charlotte Eagles are a member of the USL Hall of Fame for their history of success on and off the field. They have made the playoffs 15 of the last 17 seasons, with seven trips to the national championship resulting in two USL-2 National Championships in 2000 and 2005. The team has also had three MVP performances over the years—Jacob Coggins (2004 and 2005) and Dustin Swinehart (2008).

The Charlotte Lady Eagles are a women's elite soccer team that competes in the W-League of the United Soccer League. The W-League is a national pro-am women's league with teams across the United States and Canada. The Lady Eagles were formed in 2000 and made the playoffs nine times in the first 10 seasons.

The Eagles and Lady Eagles play all home games in south Charlotte at Charlotte Christian School. Fans have the opportunity to see professional soccer in a family-friendly environment at affordable prices. Advance tickets start at $8 for adults and $5 for students.

SWIMMING

CHARLOTTE ULTRASWIM
Mecklenburg Aquatic Center
800 East Martin Luther King Blvd.
(704) 336-3483
www.charlotteultraswim.com
Each June the Mecklenburg Aquatic Center in Uptown hosts UltraSwim, a nationally recognized meet with some of the world's best swimmers. Past and future Olympians can be seen competing at this event, a Charlotte tradition for more than 20 years. In 2009, the swimming world's attention was focused on this event as it marked the first competition for American Michael Phelps after he captured a record eight gold medals in the Beijing Olympics.

COLLEGIATE SPORTS

DAVIDSON COLLEGE
Davidson
(800) 768-2287 (tickets)
www.davidsonwildcats.com
Davidson College is one of the smallest NCAA Division I institutions in the nation with 1,700 students, but it fields 21 varsity teams. Around 25 percent of students at the school participate in varsity sports. Davidson, located a half hour north of Charlotte, is known for producing teams that are fiercely competitive and draw much game-day support.

The Davidson football team is a Division III member of the Pioneer Football League. Nearly all other Wildcats teams are NCAA Division I and compete in the Southern Conference. Davidson has consistently provided competitive basketball

teams and men's and women's tennis teams. The 2008 men's basketball team became the darling of the NCAA tournament with a magical run to the Elite Eight, and narrowly losing to Kansas in a bid to make the Final Four. That team was led by Stephen Curry, son of former Charlotte Hornet Dell Curry and now a member of the Golden State Warriors. Davidson's rich basketball legacy dates to the 1960s, when Lefty Dreisell was coach and the team was ranked in the Top 20 nationally.

Men's sports include football, basketball, baseball, soccer, cross-country, golf, swimming, diving, track and field, tennis, and wrestling. Women's sports are field hockey, basketball, cross-country, lacrosse, soccer, swimming, diving, tennis, track and field, and volleyball.

JOHNSON C. SMITH UNIVERSITY
100 Beatties Ford Rd.
(704) 378-1091 (tickets)
www.goldenbullsports.cstv.com
Year after year, students cheer their Golden Bulls to victory in six men's sports and seven women's sports. Johnson C. Smith University, a NCAA Division II school, is a member of the Central Intercollegiate Athletic Association (CIAA) and a historically black university located in west Charlotte, just across I-77 from Uptown.

The basketball program at Smith dates to 1929 and has produced such notable stars and longtime Harlem Globetrotters star Curly Neal. The Golden Bulls often play to capacity crowds at cozy Brayboy Gymnasium, the team's on-campus facility. The court at Brayboy is named for longtime men's coach Stephen Joyner. The Golden Bulls also have the luxury of playing their CIAA tournament games in their home city, as Time Warner Cable Arena hosts this annual hoops showcase.

Johnson C. Smith fields the city's only collegiate football team, which plays at the modern, $4.5-million Irwin Belk Complex. This 4,500-seat venue is situated such that is provides great views of the Uptown skyline. The large bronze bull statue overlooking the stadium is one of the nicest pieces of public art in the Queen City.

If you go to a home football game, be sure to catch JCSU's entertaining marching band.

i If coming from outside the city, the easiest and most efficient way to attend a sporting event in Uptown is via the Lynx light rail system. Park in one of the free lots at stations along the rail line's southern end and take the train into the heart of the city. This avoids the hassle (and expense) of parking in Uptown. Get off at the Stonewall Station for football games at Bank of America Stadium, and get off at the Arena Station for sporting events in Time Warner Arena. Cost is $3 round-trip for adults and $1.50 round-trip for youths and seniors.

QUEENS UNIVERSITY OF CHARLOTTE
1900 Selwyn Ave.
(704) 332-2509
www.queensathletics.com

Queens University of Charlotte developed a full athletic program in 1989, two years after becoming coeducational. The school participates in 16 sports as part of Conference Carolinas at the NCAA Division II level. Both men and women participate in basketball, golf, cross-country, soccer, tennis, lacrosse, and track; women also participate in softball and volleyball.

Basketball is the primary spectator sport. The Royals men's and women's teams play in Ovens Athletic Center, a tiny gymnasium nicknamed "the Oven." The biggest rival for Queens is nearby Belmont Abbey. Often, home games against the Abbey are moved to a larger location in Charlotte, such as the Grady Cole Center.

UNC CHARLOTTE
9201 University City Blvd.
(704) 687-4949 (tickets)
www.charlotte49ers.com

UNC Charlotte, whose athletic teams are called the Charlotte 49ers, has the most visible athletic department in the city. The 49ers compete at the NCAA Division I level in 14 men's and women's sports. That number could grow in coming years as Charlotte is seriously considering adding a football program, which would force the university to add several women's sports to meet feder-

ally mandated ratios for male and female athletes.

UNC Charlotte has been a member of the Atlantic 10 Conference since 2005. Prior to that, the 49ers spent time in the Sun Belt Conference, Metro Conference, and Conference USA. Membership in the Atlantic 10 pits the 49ers against such notable schools as Xavier, Dayton, Richmond, Temple, St. Louis, Rhode Island, UMass, and St. Joseph's.

The men's basketball program has been the flagship of UNCC athletics over the years. The 1977 team, led by Cornbread Maxwell and Melvin Watkins, reached the Final Four, while the 1976 squad advanced to the championship game of the NIT. Since moving into their 9,105-seat on-campus arena in 1996, the 49ers have been to the NCAA tournament seven times. In particular, Charlotte has a knack of playing well against teams ranked No. 1 in the nation. In 1977, they upset top-ranked Michigan 75-68 en route to the Final Four. In 1987, they traveled to Kentucky to take on the No. 1-ranked Wildcats in a holiday tournament at Rupp Arena. The 49ers were even with Kentucky until the final seconds, when a controversial call went in Kentucky's favor and allowed the Wildcats to eke out an 84-81 victory. In 1998, after waiting 33 years for the chance to play North Carolina, the 49ers met the No. 1-ranked Tar Heels in the second round of the NCAA tournament in Hartford, Conn. The 49ers put a scare in the Heels, taking the game to overtime before falling 93-83.

In addition to basketball, the 49ers field teams in men's and women's soccer, cross-country, track and field, and tennis; men's baseball and golf; and women's volleyball and softball. All but golf and cross-country are played on campus, which has seen the addition of $40 million in athletic facilities since 1994.

The men's soccer team reached that sport's final four in 1996, and the men's golf team became the first sports team in school history to be ranked No. 1 in the country when it ascended to the top spot in the fall of 2007. The golf team concluded that season in the spring by placing eighth in the country.

ANNUAL EVENTS

Charlotte is a can-do city with an appetite for fun, so it's only natural that the Queen City supports a full calendar of special events. From galas to garden tours, from small-town festivals to big-city extravaganzas, there's an annual event for everyone. Some of the major events are listed below, while more detailed calendars are available upon request from Visit Charlotte, 330 South Tryon St., Charlotte, NC 28202, (704) 331-2700, or visit www.visitcharlotte.com. For Uptown events, check out www.findyourcenter.com.

Additionally, the state's annual "Calendar of Events" is a handy reference. It's available by calling the N.C. Division of Travel and Tourism, (800) VISIT NC (847-4862), or online at www.visit nc.com. Local newspapers provide another good way to keep informed on specific dates and events. Events in this chapter are listed in alphabetical order within each month.

JANUARY

CHARLOTTE FLY FISHING SHOW
The Park (formerly Charlotte Merchandise Mart)
2500 East Independence Blvd.
(866) 481-2393
www.flyfishingshow.com
When it's too icy to fish the trout streams in the mountains, anglers from all over the Carolinas descend on The Park for two days of fly fishing demonstrations, seminars, and clinics. Anglers also shop for the latest in fly rods and equipment, and learn about popular fishing destinations, such as the Western North Carolina Fly Fishing Trail.

CHARLOTTE RESTAURANT WEEK
Various locations
www.charlotterestaurantweek.com
Charlotte Restaurant Week, also known as Queen's Feast, is a 10-day culinary extravaganza. Participating upscale restaurants offer a delicious three-course selection of meals at a reduced price of $30 per person (not including tax and gratuity).

FIGHT NIGHT FOR KIDS
Charlotte Convention Center
501 South College St.
(704) 688-8520
www.charlottesports.org
The black-tie charity extravaganza starts with a reception, followed by gourmet dining and live entertainment from a big-name performer. Next is a live auction leading into the evening's main event: professional boxing and mixed martial arts sanctioned by the World Boxing Council. When the bell sounds, ringside is where you'll want to be. Best of all, the proceeds benefit children's charities throughout Mecklenburg County.

MARTIN LUTHER KING DAY
Various locations
(704) 332-2227
www.findyourcenter.com
Charlotte honors Dr. Martin Luther King Jr. on the third Mon of each January with a breakfast and march, an Uptown parade, children's activities, programs at the Harvey B. Gantt Center for African-American Arts + Culture, and inspirational concerts.

TWELFTH NIGHT
Charlotte Museum of History and Hezekiah Alexander Homesite
3500 Shamrock Dr.
(704) 568-1774
www.charlottemuseum.org
Instead of the ubiquitous colonial Christmas celebration that most museums do, the Charlotte Museum of History celebrates Twelfth Night as many Scots-Irish who settled in the Carolinas did. The end of the 12-day Christmas season marks the arrival of Epiphany, the day when wise men brought gifts to baby Jesus in the manger. To Scots-Irish, Christmas was a day of reverence, and Twelfth Night was the day to celebrate with presents and treats. The first Sat in Jan, the museum celebrates with open-hearth cooking, cake, colonial dancing, storytelling, and a candlelight tour of the 1774 home. Cost is $6 per person.

FEBRUARY

CHARLOTTE COIN CLUB SHOW
7100 Statesville Rd., Metrolina Expo Center
(704) 641-2959
www.charlottecoinclub.org
Coin collectors across the Carolinas have flocked to this three-day mid-February event every year since 1970. It is a utopia for coin aficionados with nearly 150 exhibitors.

CHARLOTTE HEART BALL
Charlotte Convention Center
501 South College St.
(704) 208-5585
www.americanheart.org
Sponsored by the American Heart Association, this black-tie gala held every February for more than 50 years features a silent auction, seated dinner, and dancing to live music. Reservations are required. The oldest and largest black-tie event in the Charlotte area.

MID-ATLANTIC BOAT SHOW
Charlotte Convention Center
501 South College St
(704) 339-6000
www.ncboatshows.com

Since 1972, this has been the place for Charlotteans to start the boating season. It may still be chilly in February, but about 12,000 people attend this four-day event that highlights top-of-the-line boats, personal watercrafts, boating accessories, and water-sports gear. Tickets are $8 for adults, $7 for seniors, $5 children age 6–12. Under 6 free.

PALM NIGHT AT THE PALM
Phillips Place
(704) 376-7180 extension 215
This annual black-tie event held at the Palm restaurant draws Charlotte's business, civic, and social elite, from the owners of the NFL Carolinas Panthers to banking bigwigs to Mercedes dealers. The evening includes a five-course dinner, dancing, and a silent and live auction with items such as a new Mercedes-Benz, a limited-edition Harley-Davidson motorcycle, Super Bowl tickets, and a diamond necklace and earrings from Tiffany & Co. Sponsorships with two tickets start at $1,500 and sell out months in advance to benefit the Family Center, a nonprofit devoted to the prevention and treatment of child abuse and neglect in Mecklenburg County. Previous events have raised more than $750,000.

RINGLING BROTHERS BARNUM & BAILEY CIRCUS
333 East Trade St.
(704) 688-9000
www.timewarnercablearena.com
Step right up! In late February or early March, elephants and other circus creatures lead an Animal Walk through Uptown to kick off the Big Top show with clowns, acrobats, daredevils, and exotic animals.

MARCH

CABARRUS ANTIQUE DESIGNER SHOWCASE
Cabarrus Arena & Events Center
4751 Hwy. 49 North, Concord
(704) 596-4643
www.cabarrusantiqueshowcase.com

Antiques dealers and shoppers from all over the Southeast attend this event, which recently moved from the Metrolina Expo in Charlotte. This is a three-day show, held Fri through Sun.

RICH & BENNETT'S ST. PATRICK'S DAY PUB CRAWL
Uptown Charlotte
(704) 376-4441
www.rockhouseevents.com

Join in the merriment of the world's largest pub crawl. Two buddies—Rich and Bennett—started this event in 2001 and it grew so large it was featured on the Travel Channel in 2009, when 4,987 crawlers turned out for this all-afternoon and into-the-night crawl. Event starts at 1 p.m. the Sat before St. Patrick's Day (or St. Patrick's Day if it falls on Sat). The crawl includes more than 20 pubs and bars, and every crawler gets a green T-shirt.

ST. PATRICK'S DAY PARADE AND IRISH FESTIVAL
Uptown Charlotte
(803) 802-1678
www.charlottestpatsday.com

Not to worry if you aren't Irish—lots of people in Charlotte celebrate St. Patrick's Day with the city's annual parade and family-friendly festival held Uptown. Grab something green to wear and join the fun. Free.

SOUTHERN SPRING HOME & GARDEN SHOW
The Park (formerly known as Charlotte Merchandise Mart)
2500 East Independence Blvd.
(704) 376-6594
(800) 849-0248
www.southernshows.com

Southern Shows, founded by Robert and Joan Zimmerman in 1959, is Charlotte's homegrown producer of consumer and trade shows held throughout the Southeast. One of Charlotte's most popular events, the Spring Show draws thousands of visitors to see the latest in home improvement, remodeling, gardening, outdoor living, craft, and travel exhibits and merchandise. The Spring Show is usually held in early March.

APRIL

ALIVE AFTER FIVE AT EPICENTRE
Rooftop Terrace
210 East Trade St.
(704) 609-4010
www.aliveafterfiveatepicentre.com

Bankers and other young professionals roll up their Brooks Brothers shirt sleeves to enjoy Thurs evening outdoor concerts from late Apr to late Aug. Performers include popular beach bands, college-party crooners, regional rock 'n' roll groups, and tribute bands. Beer, wine, and food are sold. Free admission.

CHARLOTTE WINE & FOOD WEEKEND
Uptown Charlotte
(704) 332-2227
www.findyourcenter.com

This two-day series of events started in 1989 and raises money for charity. The goal of the weekend is to create an educational and fun series of food- and wine-related activities. Over time the event has grown in stature and notoriety, attracting guest winemakers from around the world.

COME-SEE-ME FESTIVAL
Rock Hill, SC
(800) 681-7635
www.comeseeme.rockhill.net

Approximately 125,000 people converge on Rock Hill during this 10-day event, which features a street dance, a charity ball, a car show, exhibits, concerts, crafts, hot-air balloons, road and bicycle races, a soap box derby, children's events, a parade, and fireworks. The festival also includes a wide range of athletic competitions. To get to Cherry Park, take exit 82B off I-77 and go a half mile west.

FOOD LION AUTOFAIR
Charlotte Motor Speedway, Concord
(704) 455-3200
www.charlottemotorspeedway.com

More than 2,000 cars are displayed, with another 1,500 collector cars for sale, and thousands of vendors sell automotive accessories and memorabilia at this four-day event held every April and September. $10 admission, children 12 and under free.

KITCHEN INGREDIENTS TOUR
Various locations
(704) 372-7961
www.cfcrights.org
A different twist on the traditional home tour, Kitchen Ingredients invites Charlotteans into the gourmet areas of eight private homes in the city's top neighborhoods. Area designers, florists, and gift and kitchen shops adorn the kitchens with fine china and tableware, accessories, and fresh flowers. Mini-seminars on lighting, tile, and top-of-the-line appliances are held, along with cooking classes led by local chefs, wine tastings, and appetizer sampling. Held in early April over one weekend. Proceeds benefit the Council for Children's Rights. Admission is $20, advance; $25 weekend of event.

LOCH NORMAN HIGHLAND GAMES
Rural Hill Farm, Lake Norman
(704) 875-3113
www.ruralhillfarm.org
Many early settlers in the Carolinas were Scots or Scots-Irish, and their tradition of testing strength against one another through athletic competition still endures. Charlotte's mid-April games have been held near Lake Norman for nearly 15 years and are one of several on a nationwide circuit. Participants compete in the hammer and battle-ax throw, sheaf and weight toss, longbow, climbing wall, Highland wrestling, triathlon, and kilted races. Nearly 100 clans attend, as well as many people with no Scottish roots, for living-history demonstrations, bagpipe playing, dancing, Celtic music, and food.

MINT MUSEUM HOME & GARDEN TOUR
Various locations
(704) 337-2000
www.mintmuseum.org
Taking this 53-year-old tour provides an opportunity to see some of Charlotte's most beautiful homes in Myers Park, Eastover, SouthPark,

and Plaza-Midwood. The four-day tour, which includes nine gardens and four homes, takes place in April. The tour week also includes a decorative arts seminar and a black-tie gala.

QUEEN'S CUP STEEPLECHASE
Hwy. 75, near Waxhaw
(704) 843-7070
www.queenscup.org
Spend a day in the country partying among elaborate tailgate spreads and watching silk-clad horses and jockeys soar over hedges. About 18,000 people—many donning outlandish equestrian-themed hats—attend the annual event on the 260-acre Brooklandwood Farm. Recent additions include a guided course walk with former steeplechase jockeys and an infield exhibit area. General admission tickets are $20. Reserved-space packages range from $150 in the party village to $6,000 for a lifetime seat at the finish line.

TASTE OF THE NATION
Wachovia Atrium
401 South Tryon St.
(704) 375-9715
www.charlottetasteofthenation.com
Enjoy signature dishes from more than two dozen Charlotte restaurants, wine, live entertainment, and a silent auction at this long-standing community gala. Restaurants, culinary schools, and gourmet groceries take part in competitions based on taste and presentation. Proceeds benefit Second Harvest Foodbank, Community Food Rescue, and Community Culinary School of Charlotte. Gala tickets are $85 for the preview, $60 general admission. Demonstrations free.

MAY

CENTER CITY GREEN MARKET
The Square at Trade & Tryon
(704) 332-2227
www.charlottecentercity.org
A favorite warm-weather weekend hangout, this city market is held 8 a.m. to 1 p.m. Sat from early May through late Sept in Uptown. Fresh fruits and

vegetables, specialty foods, flowers and plants, art, crafts, and live entertainment are the focus of this city market with a cosmopolitan feel. Free.

DAVIDSON TOWN DAY
Village Green, Davidson
(704) 892-3349
www.ci.davidson.nc.us
Davidson celebrates its annual festival the first Sat in May on the Village Green with entertainment, games and demonstrations, and lots of good food. Take an old-fashioned carriage ride around town, participate in the merchant-sponsored Treasure Trek, or sign up for the 45-minute stroll to raise money for Habitat for Humanity. To get there, take the Davidson exit (exit 30) off I-77.

DERBY DAYS
Mint Museum Randolph
2730 Randolph Rd.
(704) 337-2093
www.youngaffiliates.org
Charlotte celebrates the festivities of Churchhill Downs the first Sat in May on the lush lawn of the Mint Museum. Put on a party hat, sip mint juleps, and cheer for horses in the Kentucky Derby, which is shown on large screens. Sponsored by the Young Affiliates of the Mint, Derby Daze is especially popular with 20- and 30-something Charlotteans.

GARIBALDIFEST
Stowe Park, Belmont
(704) 825-8191
www.belmontparksandrec.com
Named for original town founder John Garibaldi, this spring festival includes live performers, children's rides and games, food vendors, and art-lined sidewalks. The family-friendly festival is held the third Sat. Take I-85 South to the Belmont exit. Free.

MARCH OF DIMES SHOWHOUSE
Location varies
(704) 377-2009
Interior designers furnish and decorate a new house each spring to showcase their talent and benefit the March of Dimes. Runs early May to early June. Admission charge.

MOTHER'S DAY AT MCGILL ROSE GARDEN
940 North Davidson St.
(704) 333-6497
A Queen City tradition since 1967, Mother's Day at the McGill Rose Garden draws thousands of Charlotteans in their Sunday finest. This 1.3-acre petaled paradise was the pride and joy of Henry and Helen McGill, who bought this drab coal yard in 1950 and began planting a wonderful rose garden. Henry McGill passed away in 2007 at the age of 103, but his spirit lives on in the 1,000-plus rose bushes from more than 200 varieties.

NASCAR RACE WEEKS
Charlotte Motor Speedway, Concord
(704) 455-3200
www.charlottemotorspeedway.com
Each year during the two weeks before Memorial Day, tens of thousands of race fans flock to Charlotte for the Queen City's Race Weeks, which include several track events, a street festival, and a hogs and hot rods show. The NASCAR Sprint Cup All-Star Challenge features an exclusive field of the season's race winners and past champions vying for a $1-million top prize. The following weekend features the longest race on the NASCAR circuit—the Coca-Cola 600, always held the Sun before Memorial Day.

OLE TIME FIDDLER'S AND BLUEGRASS FESTIVAL
Union Grove
(828) 478-3735
www.fiddlersgrove.com
Started in 1924, this three-day celebration of traditional American music and dance is held Memorial Day weekend. You can join competitions or workshops for autoharp, hammered dulcimer, bass fiddle, dobro, harmonica, banjo, and guitar, or participate in clogging and storytelling programs. The regulars swap jokes as they eat homemade barbecue and ice cream. The spacious site, Fiddlers Grove Campground, 1819 West Memorial Hwy., north of Statesville, is

equipped with electricity and hookups for RVs. Tickets are $15 to $60 for the weekend.

QUAIL HOLLOW CHAMPIONSHIP
Quail Hollow Country Club
3700 Glen Eagles Dr.
(800) 945-0777
www.quailhollowchampionship.com
Introduced in 2003, this PGA Tour golf tournament features top-notch players such as Phil Mickelson, Tiger Woods, Jim Furyk, Fred Couples, Vijay Singh, David Toms, Charles Howell III, and Anthony Kim; draws sell-out crowds; and offers a hefty purse. Many golfers on Tour consider it the premier event outside of golf's four majors.

RACE CITY FESTIVAL
Main Street, Mooresville
(704) 664-3898
www.mooresvillenc.org
Held the Sat after Mother's Day, this family-friendly festival is a 25-year tradition in Mooresville, the Charlotte area's capital of NASCAR racing about 30 minutes north of the city.

Live entertainment, arts and crafts, food vendors, children's activities, and a wide range of performers fill Main Street, which is shut down for the day. Take I-77 north to Mooresville's exit 36. Free.

SPEED STREET
Tryon Street, between
Seventh and Stonewall
(704) 455-6814
www.600festival.com
A NASCAR street festival, Speed Street is held Thurs through Sat prior to Memorial Day during Charlotte's annual Race Weeks.

Events include driver appearances and autograph signings, interactive exhibits, food vendors, kids' activities, racing memorabilia, and live performers in country, urban, alternative, and oldies genres. Past headliners include George Jones, Keith Urban, REO Speedwagon, Three Doors Down, Styx, Herman's Hermits, and Cameo. Free.

JUNE

CHARLOTTE SYMPHONY ORCHESTRA
Pops in the Park Concerts
Morrison Blvd. at Barclay Downs SouthPark
(704) 972-2000
www.charlottesymphony.org
Thousands of Charlotteans pack a picnic for free Sunday-night concerts under the stars at the Symphony Park in SouthPark. The symphony also plays free summer concerts in surrounding towns; see Web site for dates and details.

DRAGON BOAT FESTIVAL/ASIAN FESTIVAL
Ramsey Creek Park
(704) 540-6808
www.charlottedragonboat.com
Members of the Carolina Asian American Chamber of Commerce representing 14 countries have sponsored this unique event for eight years. The festival includes cultural programs, stage performances, exhibits, merchandise, Asian food booths, and several races of the beautiful dragon boats with ornate heads and tails. A team of 22 people races in each boat, with 20 people paddling in synchronization, a drummer in an ornate headdress in the front, and a steer man in the back. Free admission.

LISTEN AND REMEMBER
Waxhaw Amphitheatre
(704) 843-2877
This outdoor drama, presented for more than 40 years, recalls the days of Waxhaw's Indians and early pioneers, including Andrew Jackson's family. Beginning with events in 1670, the play culminates with Jackson's presidency. Shows run at 8:30 p.m. Fri and Sat in June.

TASTE OF CHARLOTTE
North Tryon Street, between
Trade and Seventh
(704) 947-6590
www.tasteofcharlotte.com
Sample more than 100 tasty treats from Charlotte's top restaurants at this three-day event held the first weekend in June in Uptown Charlotte. A

beer and wine garden, live entertainment, children's activities, and more than 100 artists from across the nation add culture to this culinary festival. Entertainment and art show are free.

JULY

REENACTMENT OF THE BATTLE OF HUCK'S DEFEAT IN 1780
Historic Brattonsville, SC
(803) 684-2327
www.chmuseums.org
This exciting two-day drama of a local American Revolution battle is held on the second weekend in July. Historic Brattonsville, a 775-acre living-history village, is near McConnells, S.C., 9 miles south of York. Take exit 82B off I-77 South. Follow the historic markers.

24 HOURS OF BOOTY
Myers Park
(704) 839-6103
www.24hoursofbooty.com
Held in late July the weekend prior to Charlotte's Invitational Criterium, this amateur bike ride for all skill levels is an around-the-clock endurance test. The quirky name comes from the popular three-mile bike route around Queens University known for its attractive bikers, runners, and walkers that is often called the "Booty Loop." Proceeds benefit the Brain Tumor Fund for the Carolinas and the Lance Armstrong Foundation.

WBT SKYSHOW
Knights Stadium
(704) 374-3558
www.wbtskyshow.com
This Fourth of July fireworks extravaganza mixes baseball, hot dogs, apple pie, and fireworks. Nothing could be more American on a warm July evening!

AUGUST

CHARLOTTE IRISH SUMMER FESTIVAL
Uptown Charlotte
(704) 358-9070
www.charlotteirishsummerfestival.com

This annual family-friendly event features Irish music, dancing, drinks, and food, as well as crafts and games (for adults and kids). Dogs are welcome, too, as long as they are on a leash.

PRESBYTERIAN HOSPITAL INVITATIONAL CRITERIUM
Uptown
(704) 386-3043
www.charlottecriterium.org
First held in 2004, this professional bicycle race pits the country's top USCF riders in a competitive, invitation-only twilight race over 50 miles. Uptown streets offer plenty of places to watch the race for free, or you can pay to party in the hospitality tent. Proceeds benefit the Brain Tumor Fund for the Carolinas.

SEPTEMBER

ARTFEST OF MATTHEWS
Downtown Matthews
(704) 847-3649
www.matthewschamber.com
This annual juried fine arts and crafts festival held in late September attracts thousands of locals with 75 painters, potters, sculptors, and other artists. Free.

BLUES, BREWS, & BBQ
Uptown Charlotte
(704) 332-2227
www.findyourcenter.com
Approximately 60 teams compete for more than $20,000 in prizes and supreme bragging rights in the BBQ competition. Teams decorate their areas with elaborate decorations, but the cooking battle is just part of the fun. Be on the lookout for blues music, an array of beer samples, and some of the best barbecue around.

FESTIVAL IN THE PARK
Freedom Park
(704) 338-1060
www.festivalinthepark.org
One of the largest and longest-running festivals in Charlotte, this volunteer-operated festival

features arts and crafts, live music, food, clowns, games, and performances by various organizations. Free since 1964.

INTERNATIONAL FESTIVAL
UNC Charlotte
(704) 687-2521
http://ifest.uncc.edu
Explore the culture, art, crafts, food, and entertainment of more than 50 nations at this late-Sept festival set up as a colorful marketplace. Free.

LINCOLN COUNTY APPLE FESTIVAL
Downtown Lincolnton
(704) 736-8458
http://lincoln.ces.ncsu.edu
Held the third Sat in Sept in the Courthouse Square downtown, this popular festival draws 50,000 spectators with arts and crafts, children's activities, a farmers' market, quilt show, food booths, and a cooking contest for every apple creation you can imagine. Proceeds benefit local nonprofits. Free.

MATTHEWS ALIVE!
Downtown Matthews
(704) 814-9779
www.matthewsalive.org
This outdoor family arts and crafts festival is held on Labor Day weekend with a parade, children's activities, food vendors, close to 200 craftsmen, and live entertainment. Free.

MINT MUSEUM POTTERS MARKET INVITATIONAL
Mint Museum Randolph
2730 Randolph Rd.
(704) 337-2000
www.mintmuseum.org
Introduced in 2005, this pottery festival featuring the work of more than 40 regional artists drew 2,000 buyers its first year. See and buy pieces by potters from North Carolina's talented regions and rich traditions while supporting the museum's decorative arts collection.

SOUTHERN WOMEN'S SHOW
The Park (formerly known as Charlotte Merchandise Mart)
2500 East Independence Blvd.
(704) 376-6594, (800) 849-0248
www.southernshows.com
This late-September event features fashion shows, makeovers, cooking demonstrations, home decor, and information of special interest to women. Admission is $8 at the door, $7 in advance.

SUNSET JAZZ FESTIVAL
Uptown, various locations
(704) 375-9553
www.charlottesunsetjazzfestival.com
Sponsored by *Pride* magazine and Charlotte Center City Partners, this free three-day festival features local and regional jazz bands, jazz workshops, and an exhibit at the Harvey B. Gantt Center for African-American Arts + Culture on the festival's history.

SYMPHONY GUILD OF CHARLOTTE ASID SHOWHOUSE
Location varies
(704) 525-0522
www.symphonyguildcharlotte.org
Charlotte designers show off their talents, offering the latest in decorating trends during this three-week event in late September. A black-tie preview party with dinner, silent auction, and dancing often sells out. Lectures, a meet-the-designers party, neighborhood reception, and champagne brunch and preview also are planned.

YIASOU GREEK FESTIVAL
Holy Trinity Greek Orthodox Cathedral
600 East Blvd.
(704) 334-4771
www.holytrinityclt.org
Greek food, music, dancing, and arts and crafts are featured at this authentic event sponsored by Charlotte's large Greek community.

OCTOBER

BANK OF AMERICA 500
Charlotte Motor Speedway, Concord
(704) 455-3200
www.charlottemotorspeedway.com
Charlotte's fall race week in mid-October includes Pole Night, the Nationwide series Charlotte 300 on Fri, and the Bank of America 500 Sprint Cup race on Sat night. The Bank of America 500 plays a pivotal role in NASCAR's 10-race Chase for the Championship. Cost is $49 to $135, or $99 weekend packages.

CAROLINA BALLOONFEST
Statesville Airport
(704) 873-2892
www.carolinaballoonfest.com
This two-day hot-air balloon event in late October paints the sky with colorful expressions of beauty and whimsy, and is the second oldest balloon rally in the nation. Carolina BalloonFest features balloon rides, contests, arts and crafts, military displays, activities for children, food, and wine tastings. Admission is $10 for adults, $5 for ages 6-12, and free for 5 and under. Tickets can be purchased online or at the gate. Note: bring cash as credit cards are not accepted at the festival.

CAROLINA RENAISSANCE FESTIVAL
Highway 73, north of Charlotte
(704) 896-5555
www.royalfaires.com/carolina
Hear ye! Hear ye! Medieval merriment abounds at this re-created European Market Faire from the 16th century. Hundreds of elaborately costumed performers fill the village, which is set up on 10 acres of beautiful woods and meadows for seven weekends. Watch a jousting tournament (don't worry, the blood's fake), defend a castle with medieval weaponry, and nibble on a turkey leg like Henry VIII.

CHRISTMAS MADE IN THE SOUTH
Cabarrus Arena and Event Center
Concord
(704) 847-9480
www.carolinashows.com
Get into the holiday spirit early at this annual juried arts and crafts show highlighting more than 400 artists and craftsmen. The three-day event has taken place for three decades.

CLEVELAND COUNTY FAIR
1751 East Marion St., Shelby
(704) 487-0651
www.clevelandcountyfair.com
Enjoy a slice of vanishing Americana at one of the oldest remaining county fairs in North Carolina. Since 1924, the Cleveland County Fair has been an autumn staple in the western Piedmont. The fair includes games, rides, live music, food vendors, arts and crafts, livestock judging, garden club presentations, pie baking contest, and a good old-fashioned demolition derby. This alcohol-free event takes place over 10 days in early October.

DILWORTH JUBILEE
Latta Park
www.dilworthonline.org
Held at Dilworth's quaint, home-lined Latta Park the first Sat in Oct, this neighborhood get-together has grown in popularity and draws visitors from all over the city. The oldest neighborhood festival in Charlotte, this 35-year tradition includes children's activities, art, a road race, and a home tour. Tour tickets $20 in advance at Harris Teeter, $25 day of tour.

HAUNTED HOMESITE TOUR
Charlotte Museum of History and Hezekiah Alexander Homesite
3500 Shamrock Dr.
(704) 568-1774
www.charlottemuseum.org

Close-up

Celebrating Charlotte's Diversity

As Charlotte continues to become more multicultural, so do its festivals. A number of ethnic celebrations are now part of the city's annual lineup. Here's a look at several to consider.

MARCH

St. Patrick's Day Parade and Irish Festival (Uptown Charlotte; 803-802-1678; www .charlottestpatsday.com). Uptown parade and family-friendly festival. Free.

APRIL

Festival of India (Location varies; 704-343-0026; www.festivalindia.org). Folk dances, art, artifacts, fashion, and food. Free.

Loch Norman Highland Games (Rural Hill Farm, Huntersville; 704-875-3113; www .ruralhillfarm.org). Scots and Scots-Irish descendants participate in authentic athletic competitions. Living history demonstrations, bagpipe performances, dancing, Celtic music, and food also included. Admission is $10 to $15 adults, $5 children ages 10–17.

MAY

Native American Powwow (Pearl Street Park on Kenilworth Avenue; 704-926-1524). Dancing, arts and crafts, heritage demonstrations; sponsored by the Metrolina Native American Association. Free.

JUNE

Dragon Boat Festival/Asian Festival (Ramsey Creek Park; 704-540-6808; www .charlottedragonboat.com). Cultural programs representing 14 Asian nations, stage performances, exhibits, food, and dragon boat races. Sponsored by the Carolina Asian American Chamber of Commerce. Free.

AUGUST

Bon Odori Festival (Location and admission varies; 704-333-2775). Celebration of Japanese culture.

SEPTEMBER

International Festival (UNC-Charlotte; 704-687-2521; http://ifest.uncc.edu). Culture, art, crafts, food, and entertainment of more than 50 nations in a colorful marketplace atmosphere. Free.

Yiasou Greek Festival (Holy Trinity Greek Orthodox Cathedral, 600 East Blvd.; 704-334-4771 www.holytrinityclt.org). Four days of Greek food, music, dancing, arts, and crafts. Admission is $2.

OCTOBER

Latin American Festival (Mint Museum of Art, 2730 Randolph Rd; 704-531-3848). Live music and traditional folkloric dance performances. Admission is $5 adults, $3 children.

Oktoberfest (Waldhorn Restaurant, Pineville; 704-540-7047; www.waldhorn.us). Three weekends of German beer, food, and music. Admission is $3 adults and children over 12.

Oktoberfest Beer Festival (NoDa; www .charlotteoktoberfest.com). Beer from around the world, food, music. Admission is $25.

Waxhaw Scottish Games and Festival (Cane Creek Park, Waxhaw; 704-243-0855; www.wshg.org). Celtic music, bagpipes, Highland dancing, and traditional athletic competitions. Admission is $11 for adults.

DECEMBER

Kwanzaa (Harvey B. Gantt Center for African-American Art + Culture, Uptown; 704-374-1565; www.ganttcenter.org). Religious and cultural celebration of African heritage and the family.

Pumpkin decorating, bobbing for apples, candlelight tours of homes, and scary stories around a campfire are part of this Saturday-before-Halloween event.

KOMEN CHARLOTTE RACE FOR THE CURE
Uptown Charlotte
(704) 347-8181
www.komencharlotte.org
This charitable event draws thousands of runners (and walkers) to Uptown to raise money for Susan G. Komen for the Cure, a foundation to defeat breast cancer. There is a competitive 5K run, non-competitive 5K, and one-mile fun run/walk. The event begins with a survivor recognition photo.

NOVELLO FESTIVAL OF READING
Charlotte-Mecklenburg Public Library
(704) 336-2725
www.novellofestival.net
Started in 1991, this celebration of reading and books features programs by best-selling authors and regional writers from creative nonfiction to kids' books. Past headliners include Tom Clancy, Pat Conroy, John Grisham, Frank McCourt, John Berendt, Sue Grafton, Norman Mailer, and Mary Higgins Clark. WordPlay Saturday, held the first Sat of the festival, is a family-friendly street celebration with storytelling, music, stage acts, and author appearances. Admission charge varies.

WAXHAW SCOTTISH GAMES AND FESTIVAL
Cane Creek Park, Waxhaw
(704) 243-0855
www.wshg.org
A long-standing tradition, these Scottish games draw more than 3,500 spectators with Celtic music, bagpipes, Highland dancing, and traditional athletic competitions on the last Saturday of October.

NOVEMBER

CAROLINAS' CARROUSEL PARADE
Uptown Charlotte
(704) 525-0250
www.carrouselparade.org
This Thanksgiving Day event, one of North Carolina's most extravagant Christmas parades, marks the beginning of the Christmas season. Free.

CHARLOTTE SOUTHPARK TURKEY TROT 8K
SouthPark
(704) 377-8786
www.charlotterunning.com
This annual 8K road race is run on Thanksgiving morning. All proceeds go to charity. The event begins at the Marriott SouthPark Hotel and is preceded by a Sports Expo. A 1-mile fun run, 8K wheelchair race, family relay, and tot trot also are included.

RURAL HILL SHEEP DOG TRIALS
Rural Hill Farm, Huntersville
(704) 875-3113
www.ruralhillfarm.org
Up to 4,000 spectators come to Rural Hill Farm at Lake Norman in early November to watch 75 border collies from around the country participate in sheepdog trials. The event also includes exhibitions, veterinary examinations, merchandise booths, arts and crafts, and farm tours.

SOUTHERN CHRISTMAS SHOW
Charlotte Merchandise Mart
2500 East Independence Blvd.
(704) 376-6594
www.southernshows.com/scs
A winter wonderland of crafts, gifts, food, and anything remotely connected with the Christmas season, this mid-November show is a Charlotte tradition. The show includes cooking clinics,

crafts demonstrations, and a food pavilion. Thousands of visitors come to get a head start on their Christmas shopping.

SOUTHPARK HOLIDAY TREE LIGHTING
SouthPark Mall
(704) 364-4411
www.simon.com
Tens of thousands gather after Thanksgiving dinner to hear music and watch Santa light the 60-foot tree. Free.

WARRIORS AND WARBIRDS AIR SHOW
Charlotte-Monroe Executive Airport
(704) 282-4542
www.warriorsandwarbirds.com
Held the first weekend of November, this show features several dozen WWII aircraft and pyrotechnic displays. It's a family-friendly educational event, and pays tribute to the men and women who bravely served our country. The Warriors and Warbirds Air Show began in 2007 and has become a huge success, drawing as many as 70,000 folks.

DECEMBER

CHRISTMASTOWN USA
McAdenville
(704) 824-3190
www.mcadenville-christmastown.com
Neighboring McAdenville is the site of this spectacular month-long Christmas light show. Drive through town each evening and view 750,000 holiday lights. Started by Pharr Yarns for the folks in this mill village and now overseen by the town of McAdenville. Christmastown USA has been featured on *Good Morning America* and other national shows. Free.

FIRST NIGHT CHARLOTTE
Uptown
(704) 332-2227
www.firstnightcharlotte.com

Ring in the new year with this alcohol-free celebration in Uptown each year on Dec. 31. A kids' celebration takes place from 3 to 7 p.m. and includes music, dance, theater, history, and science. Next up is the First Night People's Procession, a parade for the people, by the people. The evening program includes art, dancing, and live music leading up to a countdown to midnight. Free.

KWANZAA
Harvey B. Gantt Center for African-American Arts + Culture Center
(704) 374-1565
www.ganttcenter.org
This annual religious and cultural celebration focuses on African heritage and the family.

MEINEKE CAR CARE BOWL
Bank of America Stadium, Uptown
(800) 618-8149
www.meinekecarcarebowl.com
Introduced in 2002, this late December college football bowl game pits an Atlantic Coast Conference team against a team from the Big East Conference. Other festivities include an Uptown street festival and pep rally.

THE NUTCRACKER
North Carolina Blumenthal Performing Arts Center
(704) 372-1000
www.ncdance.org
www.blumenthalcenter.org
Presented annually by the North Carolina Dance Theatre, *The Nutcracker* ballet features more than 100 artists and tells the time-honored story of Clara and her trip to the land of the sugar plum fairies. Admission is $15 to $51.

SINGING CHRISTMAS TREE
Ovens Auditorium
(704) 377-9124
www.carolinavoices.org

More than 100 members of the Carolina Voices celebrate Christmas in song at this 50-year Charlotte tradition. Singers stand on huge platforms that arrange the group in the shape of a tree. Admission is $12 to $22, half price for children.

THUNDER ROAD MARATHON
Uptown Charlotte
(704) 358-0713
www.runcharlotte.com

Formerly the *Charlotte Observer* Run for Peace Marathon, the Thunder Road Marathon was moved from January to December. Individuals and three-person teams can participate in the 26-mile race, a qualifier for the Boston Marathon. The event also includes a 10K and 5K run/walk and a health and running expo. Cost ranges from $17 to $85.

DAY TRIPS

One of the most popular things about the Queen City is its proximity to both the mountains and the coast. If here long enough, you're guaranteed to hear somebody say: "I love Charlotte because it is only two hours to the mountains and three hours to the beach." While it is actually three and a half hours to the nearest beach—Myrtle Beach—just accept the fact that everybody says three hours. And the overall sentiment is correct.

In fact, no matter how deep into the mountains you travel or how far out you go along North Carolina's eastward stretching coastline, you're always within a half day's drive to the whispy sand dunes of the Atlantic Ocean and the highest mountains east of the Mississippi River.

In the regions closer to home, there's an abundance of historical sites, state parks, gardens, wineries, natural attractions, kids' entertainment, museums and other interesting places.

North Carolina and South Carolina tourism offices and interstate Welcome Centers provide catalogs and brochures on various regions and special events. For more details, go online to www.VisitNC.com or www.DiscoverSouthCarolina.com.

Entries in this chapter are arranged geographically within each area: beaches, the Piedmont, and mountains.

SOUTH CAROLINA BEACHES AND PORTS

Myrtle Beach

Charlotteans have long favored Myrtle Beach for its family focus, affordability, and variety of fun and exciting activities. Less than four hours away, the "Grand Strand" boasts 60 miles of wide sandy beaches for sun worshipping by day, and theaters, clubs, bars, dance halls, and entertainment pavilions for celebrating by night. On rainy days aquariums, shows, and shops await. Golfers flock to Myrtle for a cornucopia of 100 golf courses.

At one time the beach was pretty much a late-spring and summer draw for families with young children. Now it attracts teenagers and college kids celebrating spring break and post-graduation, golfers on outings with the guys, women on shopping excursions, snowbirds fleeing harsh northern winters, bikers on Harleys, businesspeople at conventions, arts patrons who love live theater, baby boomers who shag to '60s

beach tunes, and families with young children. There's something for every interest here. And, as long as you don't mind traffic and crowds, this unusual mix makes for great people watching.

Walk the beach at sunrise and watch hunky lifeguards prepare umbrellas and chairs for the day; curl up with a trashy paperback; pack a picnic lunch, stroll the new boardwalk that opened in April of 2010, and soak up the sunset. But don't miss the other things Myrtle Beach has to offer.

Broadway at the Beach, a $250-million shopping and entertainment center, includes more than 100 specialty shops, 20 restaurants, an IMAX theater with a six-story movie screen, minor-league baseball games, miniature golf, a water park and interactive fountain, rides, and a Build-A-Bear Workshop. The 350-acre complex also draws big crowds with souped-up go-kart racing at NASCAR SpeedPark and the world's longest underwater tunnel filled with sharks and colorful fish at Ripley's Aquarium. Many families make a day of it and eat dinner at the NASCAR Cafe, Planet Hollywood, Key West Grill, Johnny Rockets, Hard

Rock Cafe, or several other themed restaurants. For late-night fun, there are dance clubs, beer pubs, surf bars, dueling pianos, and daiquiri huts. There are even three chain hotels where you can stay-and-play. Located on US 17 Bypass at 21st Avenue North adjacent to the Myrtle Beach Convention Center. For details, call (800) 386-4662 or visit www .broadwayatthebeach.com.

Not far from Broadway at the Beach is the **Children's Museum of South Carolina,** an interactive museum with educational exhibits about science, health, art, and nature. For details, call (843) 946- 9469 or visit www.cmsckids.org.

Barefoot Landing, in North Myrtle Beach, is another popular entertainment area, with more than 100 retail and outlet shops, restaurants, and nightclubs. Kids can shimmy up a rock-climbing wall, find thrills in a motion simulator, take a river cruise along the Intracoastal Waterway, and learn about reptiles and exotic birds at Alligator Adventure. Located on US 17. Call (800) 272-2320 or visit www.bflanding.com for details.

The glitz of Las Vegas, the lights of Broadway, and the crooners of Branson have made Myrtle Beach one of the South's year-round entertainment capitals. With nine theaters and nearly 11,500 seats, Myrtle Beach venues present concerts by national acts, from country to alternative rock; variety shows; superstar impersonators; jousting knights and sword fighters; trick riders and prancing ponies; Broadway hits; international dance troupes; and local ghost stories. For details on shows and theater locations, see the Close-up in this chapter.

If you go south or north of Myrtle Beach, you'll find less crowded, less touristy conditions. To the north, just below the state line, families and golfers enjoy the slower pace of Cherry Grove and Little River. To the south, Murrells Inlet is known for its great family-owned seafood restaurants, while Pawley's Island is the place to go for handmade hammocks. At Pawley's be sure to see **Brookgreen Gardens,** the oldest and largest sculpture garden in the country. Opened in 1931 in a 91,00-acre nature preserve, the gardens include more than 550 pieces of American sculpture, centuries-old live oaks, and many native plants. Call (800) 849-1931 or visit www.brookgreen.org.

To learn more about the Grand Strand, call the **Myrtle Beach Area Convention & Visitors Bureau** at (800) 356-3016, visit www.myrtlebeach info.com, or pick up a copy of *Insiders' Guide to Myrtle Beach and the Grand Strand.*

It is quite common to be visiting Myrtle Beach and run into somebody you know from Charlotte.

Georgetown

The rice capital of the United States in the 1800s, Georgetown attracts visitors who appreciate its historic buildings and sites, bed-and-breakfast inns, and charming waterfront lined with quaint shops and restaurants. Georgetown bills itself as "the real South," and there are over 40 sites you can visit in the historic district. Some of the more popular sites are the **Rice Museum, the Kaminski House** (a seafarer's house dating to 1760), the **Man-Doyle House** (a rice planter's town house dating to 1775), the **Prince George Winyah Episcopal Church** (erected in 1747), and two rice plantations located south of town **(Hampton Plantation State Park and the Hopsewee Plantation).** Visitors to Georgetown also enjoy climbing to the top of the 85-foot-tall white-washed brick lighthouse that dates to 1812 and learning about the area's African-American history and heritage through Gullah tours. Call the **Georgetown Chamber of Commerce** at (800) 777-7705, or go to www.visitgeorgetowncountysc.com for more details.

Charleston

Although only three hours from Charlotte, Charleston should be enjoyed over at least a weekend. Since its founding in 1670, this aristocratic colonial port has been steeped in history. As a city it has endured fires, earthquakes, pirates, a Civil War, and hurricanes, yet it still retains grace, charm, and beauty. Charlestown boasts more than 70 pre-Revolutionary buildings, 136 from the late 18th century, and more than 600 structures built prior to the 1840s. The

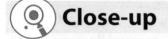

Close-up

Sun, Surf, and Shows

Myrtle Beach theaters offer a show to suit every interest and age, whether you seek country crooners, jousting knights, dancing highlanders, rock legends, or Broadway show tunes. Here's a look at the lineup:

- **Alabama Theatre**—The musical variety show One and national entertainers such as George Jones, Charlie Daniels, Loretta Lynn, Tanya Tucker, and theater namesake Alabama perform in this plush 2,000-seat theater with Broadway-style stage, costumes, and production numbers. Comedians such as Jeff Foxworthy and Carrot Top, Elvis impersonator Eddie Miles, and musicians from other genres, including the Temptations and the Glenn Miller Orchestra, also perform occasionally. US 17 in Barefoot Landing, North Myrtle Beach, (843) 272-1111 or (800) 342-2262, www.alabama-theatre.com.

- **The Carolina Opry**—Often considered the best in Myrtle Beach, the Opry also is the Grand Strand's original live musical variety show. High-energy production numbers, dancing, comedy, and music from show tunes and gospel anthems to country classics and '50s favorites make up the show, which is the No. 1 attended in the Southeast. The theater includes 2,200 seats with a main floor and auditorium seating, a $1-million sound and lighting system, a movable stage, and large video screens. Inside the lobby look for grand marble floors, gilded columns, sweeping staircases, and glittering chandeliers. 8901 US 17 North, Myrtle Beach, (800) 843-6779, www.thecarolinaopry.com.

- **Dolly Parton's Dixie Stampede**—This popular, family-friendly show is full of horse riding, comedy skits, live music, elaborate costumes, and a patriotic finale. Tiered benches overlook the 35,000-square-foot dirt-floor arena, where acts perform while patrons eat a four-course Southern supper of rotisserie chicken, barbecues, vegetables, homemade biscuits, and dessert. Junction of US 17 and US 17 Bypass, Myrtle Beach, (800) 433-4401, www.dixiestampede.com.

- **Ghosts & Legends of The Grand Strand**—Four ghosts tell local tales of lost love, pirates, Gullah hags, and an apparition who warns of natural disasters to come. Designed to look

historic structures, cobblestone streets, antiques shops, boutiques, quaint bed-and-breakfasts, and world-class restaurants make Charleston a "must see" destination for any newcomer. Some of the many historic homes open to the public for tours include the **Aiken-Rhett House, Edmondston-Alston House, Nathaniel Russell House, Heyward-Washington House,** and **Joseph Manigault House.** There are so many historic churches in Charleston that it is often called "The Holy City."

Newer attractions in Charleston include the South Carolina Aquarium, IMAX Theatre, Waterfront Park, and a museum dedicated to the Hunley, a recently recovered Confederate submarine. Other old favorites remain popular—Patriots Point Naval & Maritime Museum, Battery Park,

Rainbow Row, and White Point Gardens, which offer lovely views of the harbor and distant Fort Sumter, where the first shots of the Civil War were fired.

Charles Towne Landing is the site of the first permanent English settlement in South Carolina and offers guided tram tours of the original 1670 fortification as well as beautiful English gardens. If you loved *Gone With the Wind*, try to see some of the beautiful plantations located close by: Boone Hall, Drayton Hall and the adjoining Magnolia Plantation and Gardens, and Middleton Place.

Charleston also hosts many unique events, including the long-running **Festival of Houses & Gardens** in March and April, the Cooper River Bridge Run in May, and the 17-day Spoleto Festi-

like a Southern plantation parlor, this 60-seat theater features moving lights, surround sound, and smoke effects with the action just a few feet away from the audience. US 17 in Barefoot Landing, North Myrtle Beach, (843) 361-2700, www.ghostshows.com.

- **House of Blues**—The only House of Blues in the Carolinas, this rockin' two-story concert hall is modeled after an old Southern Delta juke joint and covered in funky folk art. Up to 2,000 people attend shows by performers such as Grammy-winner Norah Jones, country singer Travis Tritt, '80s heartthrob Rick Springfield, and beach music masters Chairmen of the Board. Don't miss the toe-tapping gospel brunch on Sundays. Teen Dance Night also is popular. US 17 in Barefoot Landing, North Myrtle Beach, (843) 272-3000, www.hob.com.

- **Legends in Concert**—A tribute show with uncanny look-alike, sound-alike performers impersonating 50 different superstars from Elvis Presley to Prince, Garth Brooks to the Blues Brothers, and Marilyn Monroe to Madonna. The lineup changes every few months, and each performer puts on a show with live musicians, back-up singers, dancers, and special effects. 301 Business Highway 17 South, Surfside Beach, (800) 960-7469, www .legendsin concertsc.com.

- **Medieval Times**—Voted Best of the Beach by readers of the *Sun News,* this live show features jousting knights on horseback, performing Andalusian stallions, hand-to-hand combat, and a classic knight-wins-the-princess love story. Guests enjoy a four-course feast while cheering the battling knights as they compete to become the kingdom's new champion. Fantasy Harbour, Myrtle Beach, (888) WE-JOUST, www.medievaltimes.com.

- **The Palace Theatre**—This majestic $20-million theater with Palladian windows, a towering dome, and 2,700 seats features Le Grande Cirque, an award-winning show described as "the greatest show ever to appear" in Myrtle Beach, playing to packed houses. Fans of gospel, country, rock, and opera enjoy Carolina Jamboree, a morning variety show that serves breakfast. 21st Avenue North and US 17 Bypass at Broadway at the Beach, Myrtle Beach, (800) 905-4228, www.palacetheatremyrtlebeach.com.

val USA performing and visual arts series in June. After all the touring, take a day of downtime at Charleston's beaches, just across the bridge to Isle of Palms, Sullivan's Island, Folly Beach, Kiawah Island, and Seabrook Island.

Call the **Charleston Area Convention and Visitors Bureau** at (800) 774-0006, go to www .charlestoncvb.com, or stop by the center at 375 Meeting St. To learn more about this area, pick up a copy of *Insiders' Guide to Charleston*.

Hilton Head Island

One of the most popular resort areas in eastern America, Hilton Head has come a long way since its discoverer William Hilton advertised for settlers in 17th-century London papers. Not connected to the mainland until 1956, the island boomed when the bridge was built and now features 12 miles of broad beaches, championship tennis, and golf. Another major reason for coming to Hilton Head is shopping, with choices spanning outlet stores to specialty shops. Accommodations range from oceanfront camping to world-class resorts. Call the **Hilton Head Island Visitor & Convention Bureau** at (800) 523-3373, or go to www.hiltonheadisland.org.

NORTH CAROLINA BEACHES AND PORTS

North Carolina has some of the finest beaches on the East Coast. More and more Charlotteans are opting for the North Carolina coast as bigger roads have made traveling there easier and crowds at South Carolina beaches have increased. The areas known as the Southern Coast, Crystal Coast, and the Outer Banks are beautiful and definitely worth a visit. The port cities of Wilmington, Morehead City, Beaufort, Southport, and New Bern offer a unique blend of history and modern-day commerce. The beaches near Wilmington make for good weekend trips. Others, especially along the Outer Banks, require a six- to seven-hour drive from Charlotte and are usually better for longer getaways.

The Southern Coast

Some of the more popular southern beaches of North Carolina include Wrightsville, Carolina, Kure, Holden, Ocean Isle, and Sunset. Though intimidating to early European explorers who named the area **Cape Fear,** today's traveler will enjoy the rugged beauty of the coast, its waters, and the gracious hospitality of its people. The small fishing village of Calabash is known far and wide for its distinct style of battered and deep-fried seafood. From Charlotte, Wilmington is a four-hour drive down US 74. To learn more about this area, contact the **Cape Fear Coast Convention & Visitors Bureau** at (877) 406-2356, visit www.cape-fear.nc.us, or pick up a copy of *Insiders' Guide to North Carolina's Southern Coast and Wilmington.*

Wilmington

Wilmington, the state's largest port city, is on the Cape Fear River and really worth more than a day trip. This historical city is becoming well-known for its film industry. Carriage and trolley tour guides can point out locations used in the many films shot in Wilmington, and movie buffs enjoy tours of EUE Screen Gem Studios, the largest TV and movie production studio outside of California. Television shows filmed in Wilmington include *Matlock, Dawson's Creek,* and *One Tree Hill.* The recent blockbuster movie *Nights in Rodanthe* was also filmed there.

Wilmington is the permanent home of the **USS North Carolina,** a 35,000-ton battleship memorial to the men and women who served in World War II. Downtown features a tour of historic homes and Chandler's Wharf, which shows the city as it was in the 1800s. The restored Cotton Exchange building is home to a variety of unique shops and restaurants near the Hilton Hotel.

Fort Fisher is located at **Kure Beach,** site of one of the country's largest land-sea battles in 1865, and houses a museum of items from Confederate blockade runners. The North Carolina Aquarium is less than 2 miles away. Here you can view live marine life and participate in special aquatic programs. Kids will also enjoy the amusement park atmosphere of Carolina Beach, a short drive down US 421 South.

Orton Plantation near Wilmington (910-371-6851, www.ortongardens.com) is one of North Carolina's best-known Southern plantations and rivals those of Virginia. It was an 18th-century rice plantation, and the gardens are now open to the public. The best time to visit is in the spring when the plantation's dazzling azaleas are in full bloom.

> Calabash is noted for its tasty fried seafood, and probably no place in this tiny North Carolina coastal hamlet has received more notoriety than Ella's. Legendary radio funnyman Jimmy Durante ate there once and was so smitten with Miss Ella and her food that for years he closed his radio show with the now-famous line, "Good night, Miss Calabash, wherever you are." Ella's is located at 1148 River Rd. in Calabash. A photo of the late Miss Ella hangs in the entrance.

Wrightsville Beach

Wrightsville Beach, just 15 minutes over the bridge from Wilmington, is on the barrier islands, which protect the state's Atlantic coast. This is an upscale community with miles of beautiful sandy beaches perfect for long walks, swimming, surf fishing, or most any water sport you enjoy. **The Wrightsville Beach Museum of History** (910-256-2569, www.wbmuseum.com), housed in a turn-of-the-20th-century cottage, showcases the early days of the island, when visitors arrived by trolley, swam by day, and danced by night under the lights of the Lumina Pavilion. Wrightsville's hurricane history also makes for an interesting rainy-day adventure for kids and weather buffs.

Brunswick Islands

The beaches along the jagged coast of Brunswick County are known as the Brunwick Isles. Many Charlotteans have been coming to these quiet, non-commercialized beaches for decades. The list includes Holden Beach, Yuppon Beach, Oak Island (formerly Long Beach), Ocean Isle Beach, and Sunset Beach. Families load up on groceries and supplies in the mid-sized town of **Shallotte** and settle into beach houses for weekly rentals. At least one visit to the seafood houses in Calabash is customary. Southport is a historic port city nestled on a point where the Cape Fear River reaches the Atlantic Ocean. For information on Brunwick County beaches, call (910) 755-5517 or go to **www.ncbrunswick.com.**

The Crystal Coast

The 85-mile **Crystal Coast** stretches from the southernmost portion of the Outer Banks to Emerald Isle, and includes the area around Beaufort, Morehead City, and the beaches of Bogue Banks. Visitors can choose among the historic preservation area of Beaufort, Morehead City's famous seafood boardwalk, golf courses, shopping, or any of the public beaches. From Charlotte, the Crystal Coast is a five-hour drive. To learn more about this area, call (877) 206-0929, visit www.crystalcoastnc.com, or pick up a copy of *Insiders' Guide to North Carolina's Central Coast and New Bern.*

Beaufort

This quaint seaport of 4,000 residents dates to 1713 and is the state's third-oldest town. The well-restored colonial village full of Southern charm takes visitors back in time to an early American fishing community with many historic homes and a historic site that includes a courthouse, jail, and apothecary. Beaufort's **Front Street** winds along Taylor's Creek near the Rachel

Carson Estuarine Reserve, Shackleford Banks, and the Atlantic Ocean. Visitors also enjoy walking the quiet streets lined with beautiful trees and Victorian homes. Be sure to look for the privately owned **Hammock House,** which was built in 1698 and regularly welcomed the fierce pirate Blackbeard when it was an inn. Beaufort's oldest standing home also was used for housing by the Union Army during the Civil War. History buffs can wander through the **Old Burying Ground** on Ann Street, where many of the town's notable residents were laid to rest. Beaufort also is home to the impressive **North Carolina Maritime Museum and Watercraft Center,** where visitors can watch master boatbuilders at work, go on nature excursions at Cape Lookout, and see artifacts from Blackbeard's sunken ship, the *Queen Anne's Revenge.*

Bogue Banks

Bogue Banks (Atlantic Beach, Pine Knoll Shores, Salter Path, Emerald Isle) is the southernmost of 23 barrier islands off the North Carolina coast. Unlike most of the Outer Banks, the 27-mile-long Bogue Banks runs from east to west. The Atlantic Ocean drums its southern shore while Bogue Sound laps its beaches to the north. This unusual orientation leads to one of the island's unique features: the sun both rises and sets over the water.

Atlantic Beach is the most highly developed of the Bogue Banks beaches. Its surf is mild, the beach is very wide, and the sun-warmed shallow water is the most enjoyable of the state's beaches.

The North Carolina Aquarium at Pine Knoll Shores is one of the three nationally accredited aquariums on the North Carolina coast. Visitors see sharks, river otters, stingray, and shipwrecks in this recently renovated facility five miles west of Atlantic Beach. For info, call (866) 294-3477 or visit www.ncaquariums.com.

Salter Path is a residential community making the transition to a tourist community. West of Salter Path is **Emerald Isle,** which was incorporated as a resort town in the mid-'50s and has been attracting North Carolina's sun lovers ever since. Emerald Isle features houses for rent—

beachfront, soundside, modern, rustic, casual, elegant, and in every price range. The annual Beach Music Festival is a popular event held in mid-May and features top beach music groups.

Morehead City

Morehead City ("Morehead" to everyone at the coast) is an easy town to like. Fill the town with internationally renowned sportfishing fleets and scuba diving charters that explore the "Graveyard of the Atlantic," and even then you only have half the story.

Unlike most coastal waterfronts, the **Morehead Wharf** is not devoted entirely to tourism. Commercial fishing, sportfishing, preparing fish, and eating fish keep the area bustling. The Sanitary Fish Market, at 501 Evans St. on the Morehead waterfront, is one of the coast's oldest and best-known restaurants. In addition, the waterfront offers scuba-diving charters (Olympus Dive Shop is world famous), sportfishing charters, boat rentals, sailboat excursions, party boat tours, and seafood sold fresh off the boats.

Day trips via ferry or private tour are available to **Cape Lookout National Seashore,** the famous Atlantic headland that extends over 55 miles of barrier islands. The seashore is a protected loggerhead turtle breeding ground and a great spot for shell hunting and fishing. Don't miss the black-and-white diamond-patterned Cape Lookout Lighthouse built in 1859.

New Bern

This historic little town of lacy crape myrtle trees is a four-and-a-half hour drive from Charlotte. Located at the confluence of the Neuse and Trent Rivers, New Bern buzzes with activity along the waterfront and around **Union Point Park,** where these two rivers meet. It was New Bern's linkage to Pamlico Sound and the Atlantic Ocean that made this an ideal port. The town was founded in 1710 and named for Baron Christopher DeGraffenried's home of Bern, Switzerland. It became the first colonial capital of North Carolina.

When Royal Governor William Tryon began building his residence/government capitol offices, they took on the appearance of a palace more than a modest government home with offices. The original palace burned in 1798, but it was completely rebuilt and restored to its former splendor. The restoration includes Tryon Palace, the John Wright Stanly House, the Dixon-Stevenson House that was occupied by Union troops during the Civil War, and the Academy Museum.

In the spring the **Royal English Gardens** are abloom with tulips. During the summer costumed guided tours bring history alive. Actors portray Governor Tryon, his wife, and their servants talking about the everyday happenings in the 1700s. By early December the palace is decorated much as it was during the holidays in 1770 for the Tryon Palace Christmas Celebration, a must-see holiday event.

For a good overview of the town, New Bern Tours offers 90-minute **trolley rides** that cover three centuries of history and architectural beauty. Other attractions include the Birthplace of Pepsi, a re-created soda fountain where pharmacist Caleb Bradham invented the soft drink in 1898, and the Fireman's Museum, with an extensive collection of early fire-fighting equipment, rare photographs, and Civil War relics.

For more details, contact the Craven **County Convention and Visitors Center** at (800) 437-5767 or visit www.visitnewbern.com.

Outer Banks

The Outer Banks are a six- to seven-hour drive from Charlotte and would be difficult to really enjoy in just a weekend. These barrier islands are marked with the names of American history and still include the longest stretch of undeveloped beach in the country. The Southern Banks include Ocracoke, a quaint village only reachable by ferry; Hatteras, home of the fabled **Cape Hatteras Lighthouse**, the tallest lighthouse in America; Bodie, home of the Bodie Island Lighthouse; and Roanoke Island, where history is reenacted in the outdoor drama *The Lost Colony*. Before show time, visitors can stroll through the authentic **Elizabethan Gardens.** Other worthwhile Roanoke tours include a visit to Fort Raleigh, site of the first English settlement; the *Elizabeth II*, a 16th-century English ship; and the North Carolina Aquarium.

In his 2007 survey of the best beaches in America, Stephen P. Leatherman, better known as "Dr. Beach," named Ocracoke Beach the top beach in the United States. Leatherman cited its undeveloped coast, golden sand, and charming village. "It is the perfect escape for someone looking to swim or relax," said Dr. Beach.

The Northern Banks include Nags Head, Kitty Hawk, Kill Devil Hills, Duck, Corolla, and Southern Shores. Famous throughout the world as the birthplace of aviation, **Kill Devil Hills** celebrated the 100th anniversary of the Wright Brothers' first flight in 2003. Today visitors can go to the Wright Brothers Memorial or try to fly themselves on hang gliders perched atop sand dunes several stories high.

Progress has altered the Outer Banks during the past 20 years, with miles of open beach becoming more populated. And you are now more likely to encounter resorts, restaurants, and an occasional strip mall. Still, the Outer Banks remain a respite for anyone wanting to enjoy beautiful, remote beaches. To learn more about the Outer Banks, pick up a copy of *Insiders' Guide to North Carolina's Outer Banks,* contact the **Outer Banks Visitors Bureau** at (877) OBX-4FUN (629–4386), or visit www.outer-banks .com.

i When traveling among the Outer Banks, take advantage of the free ferry that runs from Cape Hatteras to Ocracoke every half hour. Reservations are required and highly recommended for the ferry from Ocracoke to Cedar Island or to Swan Quarter. Both take just over two hours and cost $1 for pedestrians; $3 for bike riders; $10 for motorcycles; and $15 for cars under 20 feet, $30 for vehicles up to 40 feet, and $45 for vehicles up to 55 feet. For details call (800) BY-FERRY (293-3779).

THE PIEDMONT

The region located between the coastal areas and the mountains is known as the Piedmont and includes the Charlotte area. To make it easier to understand, we have subdivided the Piedmont further into Central Piedmont, the Triad, and the Triangle areas.

Central Piedmont
Bentonville Battleground

Located in Newton Grove, off I-95, a three-and-a-half-hour drive from Charlotte, this historic site is popular with American history buffs. The Battle of Bentonville was the last full-scale action in the Civil War, fought over three days, from March 19 through March 21, 1865. There were over 4,000 casualties in the armies fighting under Union General William T. Sherman and Confederate General Joseph E. Johnston, who surrendered on April 26 at Bennett Place near Durham.

The **Harper House,** where a field hospital was established, still stands and is outfitted as it might have appeared during the battle. The battleground maintains a picnic area and visitor center. Maps inside the center and a film presentation tell the history of the battle, the largest ever fought in North Carolina. On occasion the battle's anniversary is observed by reenactments. Call (910) 594-0789 for more information.

Pinehurst

Insiders know that Pinehurst is not just a golf destination. The lovely village in the Sandhills, about two hours east of Charlotte, is a charming getaway for couples and families. Equestrians love the many stables and horse-related activities, while history buffs can tour historic mansions, farms, and the **North Carolina Literary Hall of Fame.** It's easy to spend a day strolling Pinehurst's New England–style village shrouded in longleaf pines, and sampling the many fine restaurants located there. The opulent Spa at Pinehurst is a real escape. For area info, call (800) 346-5362 or go to **www.homeofgolf.com.**

Seagrove Pottery

Just north of Pinehurst, in the northern section of Moore County, is Seagrove, known for its large concentration of pottery studios. Here you'll find pottery being made from native clays, just as it was in the 1700s. In fact, some of the local potters belong to the same families that were shaping this native clay two centuries ago. Stop first at the **North Carolina Pottery Center** (336-873-8430), in Seagrove along Highway 220. Here you'll see samples of the area's world-famous pottery from the earliest days to the present. At the museum, which is open Tues through Sat 10 a.m. to 4 p.m., you can also pick up a map to the shops of some 75 local potters. Popular shops are Phil Morgan's Pottery, Jugtown, and Westmoore Pottery. Pottery Center admission is $2 adults, $1 students grades nine through twelve, and free to younger students. For details, visit **www.ncpotterycenter.com.**

North Carolina Zoo

Located 15 minutes south of Greensboro in Asheboro, the North Carolina Zoo gives visitors the chance to observe animals roaming in areas similar to their native habitats. It is the largest walk-through natural-habitat zoo in the country, with 1,000 wild animals and birds amid 10,000 exotic plants, making it a perfect outing for the whole family. Divided into 15 different habitats, the zoo showcases bison, black and grizzly bears, wolves, and elk in the **Prairie exhibit;** seals, polar bears, and sea lions in the **Rocky Coast;** and chimpanzees, crocodiles, gorillas, lynx, monkeys, and meerkats in the **African Pavilion.** Elephants, white rhinos, zebras, lions, tigers, giraffes, gazelles, and ostriches are some of the other more unusual species living at the zoo.

You won't want to miss the **R. J. Reynolds Forest Aviary,** the only one of its kind. A 55-foot-high glass dome houses exotic plants and birds from all over the world. Walking through the aviary is like exploring a tropical forest, complete with all the sights and sounds.

Located off of Highway 220, south of Asheboro, the zoo is open daily, except Christmas Day, from 9 a.m. to 5 p.m. Apr through Oct, and 9 a.m. to 4 p.m. Nov through Mar. Admission is $10 adults, $8 seniors, and $6 for ages 2 to 12. For details, call (800) 488-0444 or visit www.nczoo.org.

Snow Camp

About an hour northeast of Asheboro off Highway 49 is Snow Camp, a historical site dating to the mid-1700s. The name derives from Pennsylvania hunters who camped here and cut trees level with the 2 to 3 feet of snow blanketing the camp. When they returned, they recognized their earlier campsite from the tall stumps! The village contains a number of historic buildings and a restaurant. Today Snow Camp is the site of two popular **outdoor dramas.** A cast of up to 75 presents the shows on alternate days at 8 p.m. Thurs through Sat from late June to mid-Aug. *Sword of Peace* portrays the conflict experienced by peace-loving Quakers confronted by events of the American Revolution at Alamance and Guilford Courthouse, and *Pathway to Freedom* is the story of how antislavery North Carolinians and freed African Americans helped hundreds of escaped slaves to flee to the north prior to the Civil War. A museum is open on show days. Shows are $15 adults, $13 seniors, $7 children under 12. Information on both shows is available at (800) 726-5115 or www.snowcampdrama.com.

Uwharrie National Forest

Spanning parts of three counties, Uwharrie National Forest contains over 47,000 acres of scenic landscapes, nature trails, campgrounds, and picnic areas. Three rivers, the Uwharrie, Yadkin, and Pee Dee, cross through the forest. Town Creek Indian Mound (910-439-6802) is located near Mount Gilead in the Uwharrie Mountains. This state historic site commemorates the life of the Indians who inhabited the area hundreds of years ago. The reconstruction is based on archaeological excavations. Guided tours are available. Just across Badin Lake on the Pee Dee River is Morrow Mountain State Park, (704) 982-4402. The park has 4,600 acres for hiking, camping, boating, and swimming.

Yadkin Valley Wine Region

North Carolina's flourishing wine industry is only about an hour and a half north-northeast of Charlotte. The Yadkin Valley has been designated an American Viticultural Area (AVA) and is home to more than 30 wineries, with additional wineries on the way. The bucolic rolling hills of the Yadkin Valley have excellent soil and good weather conditions for growing grapes. In general, North Carolina now ranks eighth in the nation in wine production and is ninth in grape production.

It's easy to spend a day (or two) touring North Carolina's wine country. Two excellent wineries to see are **Shelton Vineyards** (336-366-4724; www.sheltonvineyards.com) in Dobson, and **RagApple Lassie Vineyards** (336-367-6000; www.ragapplelassie.com) in Boonville. Also worth a visit is the first certified organic winery in the state, **Carolina Heritage Vineyards** (336-366-3301; www.carolinaheritagevineyards.com) in Elkin. Owners Clyde and Patricia Colwell graduated from the Viticultural program at nearby Surry Community College and have established this certified organic winery on 35 acres of rolling land.

While in the Yadkin Valley region, there's a treat for fans of the *Andy Griffith Show* waiting in nearby **Mount Airy.** Griffith grew up in Mount Airy and patterned the television show's town of Mayberry after his beloved Mount Airy. In Mount Airy, you can visit the Andy Griffith Museum (336-786-7998), which houses the world's largest collection of Griffith memorabilia, including many neat items from the show. You can also take a squad car tour (336-789-6743) of Mount Airy to see the sights, including Andy's boyhood home, and taste the famous fried porkchop sandwiches at Snappy Lunch on Main Street. Snappy Lunch was mentioned several times on the show.

The Yadkin Valley and Mount Airy are part of a nine-county region called the Cascade Highlands, which includes four counties in Virginia. A good resource for this area is www.thecascade highlands.com.

The Triad

The Triad refers to the cities of Greensboro, High Point, and Winston-Salem.

Greensboro

The Guilford Courthouse National Military Park (336-288-1776) in Greensboro is the site of the Revolutionary War battle that pitted General Nathanael Greene against British General Lord Cornwallis. Nearly 30 monuments and a visitor center are spread across 200 acres. Admission is free. In mid-March each year, a reenactment and mock battle is staged by Redcoats and soldiers of the Revolution. Living-history exhibits and demonstrations are held at the national military park and adjacent **Tannenbaum Historic Park** (336-545-5315), while the city's **Country Park** (336-545-5343) hosts the battle reenactment, a living history military camp, and a merchants' area. Country Park also is home to the city's only off-leash "bark park" for dogs.

Next door to Country Park is Greensboro's **Natural Science Center,** a hands-on museum for children with dinosaur skeleton reproductions, rock and mineral exhibits, fish and reptiles, a small petting zoo, a planetarium show, two small lakes, and nature trails. Call (336) 288-3769 or visit www.natsci.org for details.

In the downtown area, plan to visit **Blandwood Mansion and Carriage House,** the 19th-century home of Governor John Motley Morehead, which is on the National Register of Historic Places. Call (336) 272-5003 for details. Also downtown is the Greensboro Children's Museum (336-574-2898, www.gcmuseum.com), with hands-on educational and entertaining displays in the areas of the environment, health and medicine, and transportation. *Child* magazine ranked the facility among its top 50 children's museums in the United States. Two downtown sites appeal to history buffs. The **Greensboro Historical Museum** (336-373-2043, www.greensborohistory.org), founded in 1924, showcases the city's military history, its early settlement, and its famous natives, from Dolley Madison to O. Henry. Within walking distance is the International Civil Rights Center & Museum (336-274-9199, www.sitinmovement.org).The museum is located in the former Woolworth store where four students from nearby North Carolina A&T State University were refused service at the lunch counter Feb. 1, 1960. This launched the sit-movement that integrated Woolworth lunch counter and other eating places across the South. The $23-million museum opened in February 2010 with 30,000 square feet of exhibit space and portions of the historic Woolworth's lunch counter.

The luxurious **Proximity Hotel** (336-379-8200, www.proximityhotel.com) in Greensboro is also the "greenest" hotel in America. It has been certified LEED platinum and received worldwide acclaim.

High Point

High Point is best known for its furniture manufacturers and the International Home Furnishings Market, which draws hundreds of thousands of industry visitors to buy and sell furniture twice a year. The "furniture market," as it's known to locals, is open to the trade only, but the city has many retail furniture outlets where visitors can shop year-round, often at bargain prices. A fun, drive-by oddity related to High Point's furniture industry is the **World's Largest Chest of Drawers,** a four-story bureau-shaped building at 508 North Hamilton St.

Other attractions include the newly expanded and renovated **High Point Museum and Historical Park** (336-885-1859; www.highpointmuseum.org) and the **Angela Peterson Doll and Miniature Museum** (336-885-3655) with more than 2,500 dolls, miniature displays, dollhouses, and unusual artifacts collected by one woman.

For more information, contact the **High Point Convention & Visitors Bureau** at (800) 720-5255 or visit www.highpoint.org.

Winston-Salem

About 90 minutes northeast of Charlotte, Winston-Salem is home to Old Salem, a restored 18th-century Moravian town with nearly 100 historic buildings, four museums, and living-history demonstrations. Tours of the town are taken at your leisure, but costumed docents at several buildings share information on the history and way of life in early America. Some buildings are private homes, but around a dozen are open, including the Old Salem Tavern, the Single Brothers' and Sisters' Houses, and Winkler Bakery, where visitors can buy delicious Moravian sugar cakes. MESDA, the **Museum of Early Southern Decorative Arts,** showcases furniture and decorative arts of the South. The Old Salem Toy Museum highlights historic and modern toys from around the world, and the **Old Salem Children's Museum** has interactive historical exhibits for youngsters. Old Salem also hosts special events at Christmas, Easter, and Independence Day. Tickets are $21 adults, and $10 ages 6 through 16 for all four museums. For details, call (336) 721-7350 or visit www.oldsalem.org.

Also in Winston-Salem, **Reynolda House** (336-758-5150; www.reynoldahouse.org), the former home of tobacco baron R.J. Reynolds, is now a museum of American art. The collection features paintings by diverse artists ranging from 19th-century landscape painter Frederic Church to Thomas Eakins and Mary Cassatt. The house contains many of its original furnishings and is fascinating in its own right. Open Tues through Sun. Tickets are $10 adults, $9 seniors and AAA members, and free for students and children. Just down the road from Reynolda House is the Southeastern Center for Contemporary Art (SECCA; 336-725-1904; www.secca.org). SECCA is well worth a visit. It is a complex of galleries with rotating exhibits by contemporary Southern artists. It is located on the former estate of the Hanes family, and many of the galleries are in the Hanes home. It is open Tues through Sun. Admission is free.

A trip to Winston-Salem wouldn't be complete without making a stop at **SciWorks** (336-767-6730; www.sciworks.org). This interactive "touch me" museum offers children and adults a variety of exhibits and displays utilizing nature, science, and technology. Before scheduling a trip, call first for planetarium show times. The 50-foot tilted dome has a Spitz star machine that produces eye-boggling laser effects. The museum also has a room for toddlers and preschool children to play. Open Mon through Sat. Tickets are $10 adults, $7 seniors and youths, $5 ages 2 through 5.

Southwest of Winston-Salem is **Tanglewood Park** (336-778-6300; www.tanglewoodpark.org), located in Clemmons. Tanglewood's hardwood forest was so tangled with gnarled overgrowth back in the 1900s that it looked like a mythical place from Hawthorne's *Tanglewood Tales*. The idyllic lake, now called Mallard Lake, completed this fantasy setting for Margaret Griffith, who gave the park its name. In the early '50s, Tanglewood was left to the people of Forsyth County to use as a park. Tanglewood's brambling undergrowth has been cut back to provide for horseback-riding trails, a swimming pool, tennis courts, a fenced area for deer, a steeplechase course, nature trails, a rose garden, a lake filled with canoes and paddleboats, and campgrounds. Two championship golf courses and a driving range also run along the forest.

The park hosts a variety of events from a Spring Steeplechase to the Festival of Lights display during the holidays. Camping is available, or you may stay at the historic **Manor House Bed and Breakfast Inn.** Tanglewood Park is open year-round from dawn to dusk. Park admission is $2 per car, $8 per bus. There are additional fees charged for golf, tennis, and horseback riding.

The Triangle

The Triangle refers to the area that includes Raleigh, Durham, and Chapel Hill. Historical sites, major universities, museums, and government buildings make the Triangle well worth the visit.

Raleigh

Raleigh is the state's capital and offers a variety of interesting sites and events. For an overview of attractions, contact the Raleigh Convention & Visitors Bureau at (800) 849-8499 or visit www.raleighcvb.org. When you arrive, be sure to visit the Capital Area Visitors Center, 301 North Blount St., (919) 807-7950, to get area information.

Top attractions include the **North Carolina Executive Mansion,** 200 North Blount St., (919) 807-7950. Home to state governors since 1891, the mansion is a classic example of Queen Anne cottage–style Victorian architecture, also known as the gingerbread style. The 40,000-square-foot building was completed in 1891, using mostly native materials, and is filled with antiques. Tours take about 30 minutes and are open to the public in the fall and spring. The **State Legislative Building** at 16 West Jones St. (919-807-7950) is the only state building in the country devoted exclusively to the legislative branch. Watch history in the making as house representatives and state senators discuss and debate law. The desks and chairs in the building were built by Raleigh cabinetmaker William Thompson in 1840 and are in mint condition today. Free tours are given daily. The **North Carolina State Capitol** (919-807-7950), built in 1840, is one of the best-preserved examples of Greek Revival architecture in the country. The Capitol is still in use. Free tours may be scheduled.

The **North Carolina Museum of History,** 5 East Edenton St. (919-807-7900, www.ncmuseumofhistory.org), opened in 1994 and contains grand short-term and permanent exhibits on North Carolina history. Across the plaza at 11 West Jones St. is the North Carolina Museum of Natural Sciences (919-733-7450; www.naturalsciences.org). This museum covers four floors of exhibits, including great whales, dinosaur replicas, and displays that incorporate live animals.

Mordecai Historic Park (919-857-4364; www.raleighnc.gov) was once part of a vast plantation that grew corn, wheat, cotton, and other crops. The city's oldest home, the Joel Lane House, was built in 1785. President Andrew Johnson was born in a small dwelling on the park's village street, in a residence behind a historic inn where his father cared for travelers' horses. At nearby Historic Oakwood (www.historicoakwood.org), visitors can stroll or drive 20 blocks full of restored Victorian homes built between 1870 and 1912. Adjacent to the neighborhood is the 1869 Oakwood Cemetery, the resting place of 2,800 Confederate soldiers, 5 Civil War generals, 7 governors, and numerous U.S. senators.

City Market is also located close to downtown, adjacent to Moore Square. The circa-1914 buildings, originally a farmers' market, and the cobblestone streets are home to a variety of shops, restaurants, and art galleries. Along Hillsborough Street, visitors can stroll the campus of North Carolina State University. The North Carolina State Fairgrounds at Hillsborough Street and Blue Ridge Road (919-821-7400; www.ncstatefair.org) is the site for the State Fair, which lasts 10 days starting the third Fri of Oct. The fair highlights agriculture and features top-name entertainment, rides, food, horticulture, crafts, and fireworks. Close by, the **North Carolina Museum of Art** moved into a new 127,000-square-foot building in April 2010. This premier art museum (919-839-6262; www.ncartmuseum.org) has become one of North Carolina's treasure houses for the visual arts. European paintings by Italian, Dutch, and Flemish artists are considered the museum's finest.

Other family-friendly attractions include **Exploris,** a state-of-the-art interactive learning center with hands-on exhibits about different cultures of the world. The museum also has a seven-story-screen IMAX theater (919-834-4040, www.exploris.org). For a fun time, head to Pullen Park (919-831-6468) with its 1911 carousel, train rides, boat rentals, ball fields, tennis courts, playgrounds, and theater-in-the park program. Visitors and locals alike love Carolina Mudcats baseball games at **Five County Stadium** in nearby Zebulon (919-269-2287; www.gomudcats .com).

Durham and Chapel Hill

Many cities in the Southeast have specialty museums and educational centers for children, but none have the special element of Durham's **Museum of Life and Science** (919-220-5429; www.ncmls.org). More than 50 varieties of live butterflies from around the world float, dance, and play in a three-story glass conservatory filled with tropical vegetation and stream gardens. The butterflies, which arrive in a chrysalis and hatch for a two- to four-week life cycle, are replenished weekly. In addition, the museum has hands-on exhibits about insects, Carolina wildlife, farmyard animals, weather, aerospace, geology, and basic science concepts. Outside, kids can ride the Ellerbe Creek Railway or play at Loblolly Park.

One of the more notable historical sites in Durham is **Bennett Place** (919-383-4345). In April 1865 two battle-fatigued adversaries—Generals Joseph E. Johnston and William T. Sherman— met on the farm of James and Nancy Bennett to work out a peaceful settlement to the Battle of Bentonville fought nearby. Johnston surrendered, resulting in the largest troop surrender of the Civil War and ending the fighting in the Carolinas, Georgia, and Florida. The present buildings were reconstructed in the 1960s from Civil War sketches and early photographs. While in Durham, be sure to also visit **Duke Chapel** (919-681-1704), the **Duke Homestead and Tobacco Museum** (919-477-5498), and the **Sarah P. Duke Gardens at Duke University** (919-684-3698).

Chapel Hill is home to the University of North Carolina. The **North Carolina Botanical Garden** is also a part of UNC, located on 330 acres off US 15–501 (919-962-0522; http://ncbg.unc.edu). As the largest natural botanical garden in the Southeast, it features native plants arranged by habitat, plus more than 2 miles of wooded trails. Although established for research and conservation of plants native to the southeastern United States, the garden is open to the public. A trip to Chapel Hill would not be complete without a visit to the **Morehead Planetarium and Science Center** at 250 East Franklin St. (919-962-1236; www.moreheadplanetarium.org). The 68-foot dome and Star Theater draw 100,000 visitors a year; more recent additions are science exhibits and an 86-seat surround-sound digital theater.

> **i** Chapel Hill is a great place to spend a fall afternoon strolling around campus and the shops on Franklin Street, cheering for the Tar Heels, and meeting friends for postgame parties. Locals-in-the-know head to the Ramshead Rathskeller—everyone calls it "the Rat"—for pizza, lasagna, and sizzling steaks called gamblers. It's in an alley off Franklin Street.

MOUNTAINS

About an hour and a half west of Charlotte you begin an ascent into the third distinct region of North Carolina: the Mountains. This region itself is divided into three areas: Northern Mountains, Central Mountains, and Southern Mountains. Each area demands at least a weekend to explore. For further reading on this area, pick up a copy of *Insiders' Guide to North Carolina's Mountains.*

Northern Mountains
Blowing Rock

Blowing Rock is a resort town featuring a charming main street lined with pyramid-shaped planters spilling over with pink and white begonias. Since the days when the historic Green Park Inn was built atop the Eastern Continental Divide, the town has taken on an aristocratic appeal.

Window shopping on **Main Street** is a favorite pursuit with lots of antiques, boutiques, and home furnishings shops. Famous North Carolina artist Bob Timberlake maintains a gallery showcase of his landscape paintings and high-end line of furniture. The park on Main Street is a gathering place for tennis, people watching, and monthly Art in the Park craft shows spring through fall. The town also hosts many special events such as Independence Day parades with everything from trikes to trucks. Christmastime is an especially good time to visit. The town is aglow in beautiful lights and Mother Nature often cooperates with a fresh coat of snow. Chetola Resort on the edge of downtown hosts an impressive festival of lights throughout December and January.

The **Blue Ridge Parkway** skirts Blowing Rock and folks enjoy horseback riding and hiking along miles of carriage trails at the **Moses H. Cone Manor** along the Parkway (828-295-7938). Blowing Rock is also home to the Blue Ridge Wine Festival, a popular April event that brings together many of the top North Carolina wineries.

Children in North Carolina grow up on trips to **Tweetsie Railroad** on US 321/221 near Blowing Rock (800-526-5740; www.tweetsie.com). The drawing card is a 3-mile adventurous ride on an original mountain train, complete with Wild West gunfights and settler rescues. The attraction has amusement rides, live entertainment, crafts, shops, and a small zoo. Tweetsie is open from May through October. Another neat attraction is The Blowing Rock, for which the town is named. The **Blowing Rock** is the oldest visitor attraction in North Carolina. Since 1933, folks have visited this magnificent rock that provides some of the best views in the High Country. Contact the **Blowing Rock Tourism Development Author-**ity at (877) 750-4636 or www.blowingrock.com for more information.

Boone

Located 10 minutes from Blowing Rock, Boone is bigger, more touristy, and more diverse with the beautiful campus of Appalachian State University. During the summer (mid-June to mid- Aug), make reservations for the famous outdoor drama *Horn in the West,* held since 1952. The musical drama takes place in the **Daniel Boone Amphitheater** and highlights the life of early families in this region, particularly those "Regulators" who fled into the mountains to escape British tyranny. Daniel Boone is not the hero of the drama, but is an important figure. The show runs nightly, except Mon, and starts at 8 p.m. Tickets are $18 adults and $9 children. For reservations call (828) 264-2120 or go to www.horninthewest.com. On the grounds of the complex, you'll find Hickory Ridge Homestead, which is an interesting tour of five representative homesites of the 1800s, and the eight-acre Daniel Boone Native Gardens.

A great arts festival each July since 1984 is **An Appalachian Summer** (www.appsummer .org), which brings a diverse mix of theater, dance, music, and visual arts to venues on and around the ASU campus. Musical performances over the years have included the North Carolina Symphony, Arlo Guthrie, Emmylou Harris, Doc Watson, Mary Chapin Carpenter, and Pinchas Zukerman.

For information on the many things to see and do in Boone, call (800) 852-9506 or go to www.visitboonenc.com. Another good resource is www.exploreboonearea.com.

Grandfather Mountain

This famed 5,946-foot mountain can be seen for miles and gets its name from the way the mountain's top resembles the profile of a sleeping grandfather. One of North Carolina's top outdoor attractions, Grandfather is known for beautiful mountain scenery, a mile-high swinging bridge, native wildlife, a natural museum, alpine hiking trails, and family picnics. You'll want to visit the natural habitats for native black bear, white-tailed deer, cougar, otters, and bald and golden eagles. Stop in at the nature museum that offers state-of-the-art displays along with entertaining movies on native wildlife (especially the film on the red-tailed hawk). For those brave enough to cross it, the Mile High Swinging Bridge rewards you with a spectacular view as it connects the gift shop area with the jagged Linville Peak. The museum's restaurant is a great place for lunch. You can also picnic on the mountain.

Grandfather Mountain is open year-round, weather permitting. Admission is $15 adults, $13 seniors, and $7 ages 4 through 12. Call (800) 468-7325 or visit www.grandfather.com for information.

An exciting Grandfather Mountain experience is the annual Highland Games the second weekend in July. You don't have to be Scottish to enjoy the bagpipes, dancing, caber-toss, and watching border collies return lost sheep to the flock, as well as other games of skill. Another popular yearly event that comes the fourth Sun in June is Singing on the Mountain, a free all-day gospel sing and Grandfather tradition for nearly 90 years.

Linville Falls, Linville Caverns, and Old Hampton Store

At Linville Falls and Gorge there are three hiking trail options, from easy to rugged, depending on your energy and time. The gorge is the deepest slash in the earth's crust east of the Grand Canyon. As it tumbles into the gorge, the Linville River creates a 90-foot waterfall. To reach the falls, you'll walk through a half-mile tunnel of towering trees so dense that spatters of sunlight are rare. Waterfalls—some dramatic, others serene—draw visitors to watch their grand displays. This is not a picnic area, but restrooms are available, and the park is open year-round, depending on weather.

There are interesting caves all through the mountains. Linville Caverns, like others, was discovered accidentally in 1822 when curious fishermen followed trout disappearing into the side of a mountain. Trout in this 20-million-year-old limestone cave are blind due to the lack of a light source. The caverns, on three levels, are an interesting and enjoyable half-hour experience. It's open year-round at a constant temperature of 52 degrees, but check times, (828) 756-4171 or www.linvillecaverns.com. Admission is $7 adults, $5.50 seniors, $5 for children ages 5 through 12.

The **Old Hampton Store** (828-733-5213) sits just outside the town of Linville. This neat 1921 general store, restaurant, and gristmill offers a wide assortment of notions that you need and some that you probably don't—such as horse hoof medication. Churns and washtubs hang from the ceiling, and the back screened door is perpetually in motion. Out back the stone gristmill grinds cornmeal and grits nearly every afternoon. These products are sold along with apple butter, local jams, and old-fashioned tin cookware. Best of all is lunch. The store serves the leanest and most delicious barbecue around, and its root beer is excellent. Top this off with a slice of terrific carrot cake.

i If you're touring Linville Caverns, you may want to bring along a jacket. Temperatures in the centuries-old caves hover around 52 degrees year-round and the caverns often drip with water.

Ski Country

During winter North Carolina provides some of the best snow skiing in the South. Each year thousands of Charlotte skiers monitor the weather reports in anticipation of mountain snow. And when it comes, you'll see packed cars bearing ski racks heading for one of the three High Country ski resorts.

Appalachian Ski Mountain (800-322-2373; www.appskimtn.com), home of the French-Swiss Ski College, is located near Blowing Rock, not far from Boone. App has one of the best teaching schools for beginners. The resort has 11 slopes, including three terrain parks, and a peak elevation of 4,000 feet. About 40 minutes away in Banner Elk is **Sugar Mountain Resort** (800-784-2768; www.skisugar.com). Sugar is the largest ski resort in North Carolina, with 115 skiable acres. It has 20 slopes and the only double black diamond slope in North Carolina. Sugar's peak elevation is 5,300. Just a few minutes north of Sugar Mountain, via an ascent up Beech Mountain, is **Beech Mountain Resort** (800-438-2093, www.skibeech .com). Also known as Ski Beech, this resort has 15 slopes, including two terrain parks, and is the highest ski area in the East with a peak elevation of 5,506 feet. The resort has a charming alpine village featuring an outdoor ice skating rink encircled with shops and restaurants. **Hawksnest** (800-822-4295; www.hawksnest-resort.com) converted from skiing to a tubing park in the winter of 2008–09. It is the largest snow tubing operation on the East Coast and also offers zip line tours, even in the snow.

A good catch-all site for skiing info, including webcams, is www.skithehighcountry.com.

i The annual Woolly Worm Festival, held the third weekend in October in Banner Elk draws thousands for crafts, food, artwork, and live entertainment. The fuzzy caterpillars for which the festival is named are raced, with the winning worm's 13 black and brown bands predicting the severity of the weather during the 13 weeks of winter. For details on the festival, call (800) 972-2183 or go to www.woollyworm .com.

Valle Crucis

Valle Crucis is a historic farming community that received its unusual name in the 1840s when an Episcopalian bishop looked down upon the valley and saw streams forming the shape of a cross. He called it *Valle Crucis,* which is Latin for "Vale of the Cross." Though the streams no longer intersect because of a 1940 flood, the valley remains practically the same as it did years ago. Folks still farm the land and gather 'round the pot-bellied stove at Mast General Store. And there's still an indelible Episcopalian presence with the Valle Crucis Conference Center, housed in the old Episcopal mission.

Valle Crucis (www.vallecrucis.com) became North Carolina's first rural historic district in 1990.

It's so unique that the entire community is listed on the National Register of Historic Places. Historic buildings abound, with many like The Baird House (1790), Mast Farm Inn (1812), Old Episcopal Mission (1842), and Mast General Store (1883) restored to their initial splendor while still serving the area today.

Located about five miles east of Boone, Valle Crucis is a "can't miss" stop in the North Carolina mountains. The general store is the genuine article, and horseback riding is available at Dutch Creek Trails, where they also have a certified cowboy poet.

Valle Crucis is one of many great places that make up the North Carolina High Country. For year-round tourism info on the region, contact High Country Host at (800) 438-7500 or www .mountainsofnc.com.

Central Mountains
Asheville

Nicknamed the "Land of the Sky," this mountain city where wealthy vacationers once came for summer heat relief still draws plenty of visitors. However, today's visitors come for a more diverse experience and artsy vibe. Asheville has been a media darling in recent years, picking up honors like "Top 10 Southern Destination," "America's Top 25 Arts Destination," and "Top 100 Adventure Towns."

For more details, visit **www.exploreashe ville.com** or call (888) 247-9811. The centerpiece of the downtown historic district is Pack Place Education, Arts, and Science Center. This bustling complex contains four museums, a performing arts theater, courtyards, permanent exhibitions, a gift shop, restaurant, and lobby galleries. Tickets are required for admission to theater events and to each of the four museums: the Asheville Art Museum, the Colburn Gem and Mineral Museum, the Health Adventure, and the YMI Cultural Center. You may buy a one-day pass that is good for all four, or you can buy single tickets. No admission charge is required for visitors to enter Pack Place and view the historic exhibit *Here Is the Square,* visit the Craft Gallery that spotlights regional crafts, or shop in the Museum Gift Store. The fourth Fri of each month is Free Day, when you may visit all of the museums with no charge for admission. Call (828) 257-4500 for further ticket information and hours.

A landmark in itself, **Pack Place** also serves as the logical starting point for a number of walking tours of downtown Asheville featuring buildings of architectural and historic significance, including the home of Thomas Wolfe. A popular retreat into the past, this is the Dixieland Boarding House readers will remember from Wolfe's novel *Look Homeward, Angel.*

i Dillsboro is a neat, walk-about village of shops, studios, restaurants, and inns located 45 minutes west of Asheville. This quaint railway town comprises historic houses and buildings, many dating to the late 1800s. People come from all over to eat the famous Southern cookin' at the Jarrett House Inn, and to have a slice of vinegar pie for dessert. While any time is good to visit, we recommend the Western North Carolina Pottery Festival, held the first Sat in Nov, and the Dillsboro Lights & Luminaries Festival, held the first two weekends of Dec. For more information, visit www .visitdillsboro.org.

Biltmore Estate and Winery

One of the best day trip excursions is to the **Biltmore Estate, Gardens, and Winery,** which is still the largest private residence in the United States. Between 1888 and 1890 George Washington Vanderbilt, grandson of the railroad promoter Cornelius Vanderbilt, purchased a total of 125,000 acres of land for the estate he planned to build. The architectural style was designed by Richard Morris Hunt to resemble a château in France's Loire Valley, and it rivals the grandest palaces abroad. The castle–like house contains 255 rooms, which took 1,000 artisans five years to build for the six residents and their guests (not including the 100 servants). You can tour the main house with its beautiful antique furnishings, priceless paintings, and ceiling frescoes that are

kept in excellent condition. The servant's quarters, where even the butler had his own servant, are also interesting.

A favorite time is the Christmas season, when the house is resplendent with thousands of poinsettias and Christmas trees trimmed with many original ornaments. Musical concerts fill the magnificent halls. The estate is open from 9 a.m. to 4 p.m. Jan through Mar, 8:30 a.m. until 5 p.m. Apr through Dec; closed Thanksgiving, Christmas Day, and New Year's. For more information, call (800) 411-3812 or log on to www .biltmore.com.

Another enjoyable—as well as tasty—tour is that of the estate's winery, which was converted from an old dairy barn. The winery started producing wine in 1978. The tour offers a video presentation and interactive displays explaining the wine-making process. The Tasting Room offers samples of more than 20 varieties available for purchase.

The open-air restaurant, aptly named Deerpark (you may see herds of deer roaming the land), serves an assortment of entrees. Afterward stop at **Biltmore Village,** where the original construction worker's houses have been converted into shops and restaurants. Now guests can stay overnight too at the luxurious Inn on Biltmore Estate, (800) 624-1575.

Blue Ridge Parkway and Mount Mitchell

The scenic Blue Ridge Parkway meanders uninterrupted for 469 miles through two states. The Parkway, known as America's Favorite Drive, was a public works project created by FDR during the Depression. It started in 1935, but took many years to be completed. The last link was the Linn Cove Viaduct over Grandfather Mountain. It is the most visited unit of the National Park system. Frequent overlooks afford breathtaking panoramas of high peaks, waterfalls, and lakes tucked into verdant valleys. Late spring is alive with color as mountain laurel and red rhododendron bloom in awesome abundance, and fall brings its own spectacular display in a blaze of color with crimson, rust, and gold leaves.

An interesting side trip off Highway 80 in Yancey County is **Clear Creek Guest Ranch.** City slickers can spend a night or two at this upscale ranch, riding horses, hiking, fishing, swimming, and eating three full meals of chow a day in the lodge. Clear Creek is great for families, because there are tons of activities to entertain the kids. This area of Yancey County is also a haven for pottery studios.

Not far away is **Mount Mitchell State Park** at Milepost 355. Mount Mitchell, elevation 6,684 feet, is the highest peak east of the Mississippi River, and you can hike the park's many nature trails and enjoy great views from a handicap-accessible observation tower built in 2009. Call (828) 675-4611 to reserve one of the nine campsites. In Little Switzerland at Milepost 334, you'll find the North Carolina Mining Museum at Emerald Village, (828) 765-6463. The museum offers an underground tour of the mine and panning the flume for gems. The **Mitchell County Chamber of Commerce** at (800) 227-3912 or www.mitchell-county.com can provide you with more information.

Southern Mountains
Brevard
Surrounded by the Pisgah National Forest, Brevard offers a variety of activities from rugged outdoor adventures to communing quietly with nature to delving into the magical mountain lore through music, drama, or local crafts.

You can spend the day locating a few of the 250 **waterfalls** in Transylvania County and Brevard. The best way to see them is to take the scenic 79-mile drive that loops through the Pisgah National Forest. You can also hike along the designated trails or explore on horseback.

Check out the annual summer **Brevard Music Festival** that features many well-known musicians. The seven-week festival is held at the Brevard Music Center (888-384-8682; www.brevardmusic.org). If you're a bluegrass fan, go to **Silvermont** on East Main Street for original mountain music and bluegrass. Drive back down US 64 to Flat Rock and take in a play at the

Flat Rock Playhouse (828-693-0731, www.flatrockplayhouse.org), the state theater of North Carolina. Flat Rock is also the site of Connemara, the summer home of poet laureate Carl Sandburg.

Throughout the mountains you'll find handmade quilts, mountain furniture, and toys. Insiders like the Curb Market (farmers' market) in nearby Hendersonville on Tues and Sat mornings for its handmade articles, jellies, fresh vegetables and fruit, and the like. Call the Brevard Chamber of Commerce at (800) 648-4523 or log on to www.visitwaterfalls.com.

Cashiers and Highlands
Beautiful Cashiers, high in the Blue Ridge Mountains, is a resort town famous for its many waterfalls, including the beautiful Silver Run Falls and the spectacular Whitewater Falls, which at 411 feet is the highest waterfall in the eastern United States. For more information, contact the Cashiers Chamber of Commerce at (828) 743-5941 or log on to www.cashiers-nc.com.

Just a 10-minute drive from Cashiers is **Highlands,** an upscale mountaintop town full of historic inns and quaint B&Bs, unique boutiques, and designer shops. Known as a wealthy second-home community, Highlands also has a reputation as a culinary paradise with four *Wine Spectator* award-winning restaurants. Call the visitor center at (828) 526-2114 or go to **www.highlandschamber.org for details.**

Cherokee
The history of the Eastern Band of the Cherokee Indians and the 58,000-acre reservation can be explored by a stop at the Museum of the Cherokee Indian on Drama Road (828-497-3481, www.cherokeemuseum.org). This is a modern museum displaying artifacts over 10,000 years old with explanatory audiovisual programs that chronicle the events of the Cherokee.

The not-to-be-missed **Oconaluftee Indian Village** (800-438-1601; www.cherokee-nc.com) is a reproduction of how the Eastern Band of the Cherokees lived 200 years ago. The **Qualla Arts and Crafts Mutual** in the village is a shop that looks more like a museum. This shop of artisans' works is responsible for keeping alive the authentic arts and crafts of the Cherokee. It is also the only place that you'll find these distinct crafts.

No trip to Cherokee would be complete without attending *Unto These Hills* at the **Mountainside Theatre** (828-497-7777). The outdoor drama unfolds the tragic story of how the proud Cherokees were driven west on the Trail of Tears from their Smoky Mountain homeland. Tickets are $8 to $18.

Cherokee is also the home of **Harrah's Cherokee Casino** (828-497-7777; www.harrahs.com), which opened on the Cherokee Indian Reservation in the late 1990s. It is the only legal gambling casino in North Carolina. Open to ages 21 and older, the casino features an array of video gaming, including poker, blackjack, slots, and craps. The casino also has a luxury hotel, three restaurants, and a 1,500-seat theater with national acts.

Before leaving the area, drive north half a mile on US 441 to the entrance of the **Great Smoky Mountains National Park.** Just inside is Pioneer Homestead, a series of 15 buildings needed by settlers to survive in the mountain wilderness. Additional information on this area can be obtained from **Smoky Mountain Host of North Carolina** at (800) 432-4678 or www.visitsmokies.org.

SOUTH CAROLINA
OLDE ENGLISH DISTRICT

Many of the Palmetto State's undiscovered treasures lie hidden in the Olde English District, a seven-county area due south of Charlotte that includes Chester, Chesterfield, Fairfield, Kershaw, Lancaster, Union, and York.

The **Olde English District** offers a variety of accommodations—from luxury hotels and motels to bed-and-breakfast inns. The Wade-Beckham House in Lancaster (dating back to the 1800s) offers three guest rooms. Cheraw has two bed-and-breakfast inns in the historic district—314 Market Street Bed & Breakfast at 314 Market St. and the Spears Guest House, 228 Huger St. Cabins are available at Cheraw State Park. Camden has several options, including the

Greenleaf Inn. The Inn at Merridun in Union is a destination in itself, offering dinner by reservation and a four-course breakfast. Built in 1855, it has five bedrooms, each with a private bath. A good place to hang your hat in Rock Hill is the Book and the Spindle across from Winthrop University. Camping is offered at Paramount's Carowinds and in a number of the state parks.

For more information, contact the **Olde English District Visitor Center** at (800) 968-5909 or www.sctravel.net.

Camden

Steeplechase fans know this town well. It's the scene of the Carolina Cup Race in the spring and the Colonial Cup in the fall, as well as the National Steeplechase Museum, open September through April. Horses aside, Camden is an interesting place to visit any time of the year. The Camden Historic District, which is on the National Register of Historic Places, covers 3 square miles and features beautiful historical homes and estates dating to the 18th and 19th centuries. Many of the buildings are open to the public, and others can be visited during home and garden tours during the year.

The **Fine Arts Center of Kershaw County** (803-425-7676) holds exhibits and special performances featuring nationally renowned artists throughout the year. A permanent gallery features the work of equine artist Carroll K. Bassett. Researchers enjoy the collections at Camden Archives and Museum (803-968-4037). A restored 18th-century grain mill and a general store are on Boykin Mill Pond, located about 8 miles south of Camden on Highway 261.

For further information on Camden, go to www.camden-sc.org.

Cheraw

Picturesque Cheraw, located on US 1 in the northeastern corner of the Olde English District, is home to **Old St. David's Church,** the last Anglican church to be established under King George III in 1772. Buried within its shadows are the town's most prominent citizens, including a steamboat captain or two. General Sherman's troops found Cheraw to be "a pleasant town and an old one with southern aristocratic bearing" and left it intact. In 1880 Cheraw was the setting for the last legal duel in South Carolina, which took place between Col. E. B. C. Cash and Col. William M. Shannon.

For details on visiting Cheraw, go to www .cheraw.com.

Chester

South on US 321 is Chester, a lovely historic district with three **Revolutionary War battlefields** and a state park centered around the old Landsford Canal, built in 1832. Another park ideal for fishing and picnicking is **Chester State Park,** 2 miles west of town on Highway 72. East of Chester on the same highway, you'll find **Cruse Vineyards and Winery,** which offers free wine tastings on Fri and Sat afternoons. For more information, visit www .chestersc.org.

Chesterfield

Located on Highway 102, Chesterfield serves as the county seat of Chesterfield County. Tour brochures are available at the Hospice Building on Main Street. Chesterfield claims to be the site of the first secession meeting in South Carolina (November 19, 1860), but it also boasts a courthouse designed by Robert Mills and several historic homes. The **John Craig House,** built in 1798, is where Sherman spent one night while passing through the state.

Fort Mill

Just south of Charlotte across the state line, Fort Mill in York County is home to the Charlotte Knights minor-league baseball stadium and portions of Paramount's Carowinds and Lake Wylie. The **Anne Springs Close Greenway** draws many visitors with its 2,000 acres of lakes, pastures, and oak, hickory, and dogwood forests with hiking and biking trails and picnic areas.

Lancaster

Lancaster is known for its Robert Mills Courthouse (built in 1828) and the Andrew Jackson Birthplace Site, now a state park on US 521. A small museum is housed in the visitor center, and a one-room schoolhouse, similar to one that was here in the mid-1700s, has been reconstructed. Call (803) 285-3344. **The Lancaster County Council of the Arts** holds an annual spring festival here. Also in Lancaster County, near Taxahaw, is the Flat Creek Heritage Preserve and Forty-Acre Rock, a 1,325-acre natural preserve of rare and endangered plants, including the pool sprite, which grows in water reserves trapped on the huge rock surface. The preserve is open during daylight hours only.

Rock Hill

The Gateway to the City and the Civitas sculptures, which incorporate pillars from the old Masonic Temple in Charlotte, can be seen in Rock Hill. Also worth your time is Glencairn Gardens, (803) 329-5620, where the **Come-See-Me festival** is staged each spring. At the **Museum of York County** (803-329-2121), you can see Catawba Indian pottery, illustrations by Vernon Grant (who originated Kellogg's Snap, Crackle, and Pop), the Settlemyre Planetarium, and the Stans African Hall.

South of Rock Hill off US 321 is **Historic Brattonsville** (803-684-2327), a restored village of 18th- and 19th-century structures. The Revolutionary War battle that occurred here in 1780—the Battle of Huck's Defeat—was the first defeat of the British in South Carolina after the fall of Charleston. For more details, visit www .yorkcounty.gov.

Union

South on Highway 49, the Federal-style home of Secession Governor William Henry Gist is located at **Rose Hill Plantation State Historic Site.** Built between 1828 and 1832, it once overlooked thousands of acres of cotton. Call (864) 427-5966 for details.

Winnsboro

Off I-77 and south of Chester off US 321 in Fairfield County, Winnsboro has a Robert Mills courthouse (built in 1823) and the Ebenezer Associate Reformed Presbyterian Church dating to 1788. Winnsboro is best known for its town clock, which has run continuously since 1833. The **Fairfield County Museum** (803-635-9811) is outstanding, and genealogy buffs delight in its collections. At the News & Herald Tavern, housed in the old newspaper office, you can catch up on all the local happenings and enjoy some of the best food in the Olde English District.

York

Northwest of Rock Hill on Highway 5 is York. Often called the "Charleston of the Upcountry," it has historic structures dating to the 1700s. The Yorkville Historical Society has developed a walking tour of the area. Their brochure is available at the McCelvey Center, a center for arts and history, on East Jefferson at College. For more information, call the **York County Convention & Visitors Bureau** at (800) 866-5200 or log on to www.visityorkcounty.com.

LIVING HERE

In this section we feature specific information for residents or those planning to relocate here. Topics include real estate, education, health care, and much more.

RELOCATION

Welcome to Charlotte, a city with a thriving business community, family-friendly neighborhoods, a vibrant arts community, exciting sports teams and an interesting blend of natives and newcomers.

If you've decided to make the move, you're not alone. In recent years, the Queen City was named the most popular place to move by the American Moving & Storage Association. Thanks to our high concentration of financial institutions and other white-collar industries, Charlotte also has seen one of the biggest population increases in the country among young professionals under age 40.

Like many up-and-coming cities across the United States, Charlotte experienced its longest economic growth period without a downturn in the 1990s. NationsBank took over BankAmerica, renamed the company Bank of America, and helped Charlotte become the No. 2 banking center in the country with more than a trillion dollars in bank resources. In 2001 Wachovia merged with First Union, creating another banking giant that was eventually purchased by Wells Fargo.

In addition to banking, Charlotte offers a broad mix of employment opportunities, including information technology, retail and wholesale trade, insurance, real estate, construction, manufacturing, transportation, and agriculture. The city's diverse manufacturing base—local companies make everything from tires to computer parts to snack foods— has traditionally helped the economy stay healthier than in other large cities.

Sitting in the middle of the Piedmont crescent, an area from Raleigh to Greenville, South Carolina, at the junction of I-85 and I-77 has catapulted Charlotte into the sixth-largest wholesale center in the country. The Charlotte Chamber of Commerce takes an active role in recruiting, and in the past decade an Uptown economic development group called Charlotte Center City Partners has taken major steps to boost the economy and promote the area. Charlotte's variety of industry draws more than 100,000 commuters from 10 surrounding counties every day, and its business-minded outlook and can-do attitude continue to bring new companies to town.

Charlotte offers a wide variety of housing options for every age and lifestyle. You'll find lovely restored Victorians and condo high-rises in busy Uptown, finely crafted bungalows and mansions on winding tree-lined streets in early suburbs such as Dilworth and Myers Park, new neighborhoods overlooking golf courses and lakes on the edge of the city, and quiet country homes in surrounding counties.

The Charlotte Observer's Saturday Real Estate section should be your first stop for up-to-the-minute market offerings. There are several local publications that can be helpful if you are buying, building, or selling a home. These free guides are available at many newspaper and magazine racks or at local grocery stores such as Harris Teeter.

The Charlotte Chamber of Commerce (330 South Tryon St., 704-378-1300, www.charlotte chamber.org) provides information on the city to residents and potential residents. Listings in this chapter are alphabetical; neighborhoods are geographic.

REAL ESTATE

The Multiple Listing Service (MLS) divides Charlotte real estate into nine areas, which branch out from Uptown in pie-shaped wedges. The following areas start in the north and go clockwise. Uptown is considered Area 99; Areas 10 to 17 cover surrounding counties such as Union, Cabarrus, Iredell, Lincoln, Gaston, and York. Lake Norman falls under Area 13; Lake Wylie is in Area 88.

Area 99, Uptown Charlotte

Area 99 includes the Center City within the I-277 inner belt. I-277 comprises the Brookshire Freeway, the John Belk Freeway, and I-77. Many years ago Uptown became a ghost town when its 50,000 workers went home for the day, and streets weren't considered safe. But then a few brave souls began fixing up turn-of-the-century Victorians in Fourth Ward in the 1970s and 1980s. In the mid to late '90s, developers pounced on the center city as an untapped market for upscale condominiums. Today, Uptown is a vibrant, thriving community, only slightly dazed by the Great Recession of 2008-2009. Many Uptown residents are young professionals who work there and embrace the urban lifestyle of parking the car and walking to the office, to dinner, and to sophisticated clubs and neighborhood taverns.

All the conveniences you need have finally come back to Uptown, too, providing residents with a full-service grocery store, gourmet food shops, great restaurants, retail locations, cultural attractions, professional sports, and many service businesses catering to folks who live here.

In its earliest days Charlotte was divided into four political districts, or wards. Starting at the northeast quadrant of The Square at Trade and Tryon and moving clockwise, Uptown includes First Ward, Second Ward, Third Ward, and Fourth Ward.

First Ward

First Ward is home to the Bank of America Corporate Center, the North Carolina Blumenthal Performing Arts Center, the Museum of the New South, and the Charlotte-Mecklenburg Public Library. First Ward Place is a unique, fairly new community of apartments, condos, and single-family homes in which a portion of the population receives housing assistance. A true mixed-income community, public assistance residents live beside those who pay full market rates.

Second Ward

Often called the government district, Second Ward includes the county courthouse, county office buildings, school administration buildings, the law enforcement center, the Federal Reserve building, the convention center, NASCAR Hall of Fame, hotels, and Marshall Park. Second Ward has not had significant residential housing options in many years.

Third Ward

Third Ward is Uptown's most diverse district, with Bank of America Stadium and the Carolina Panthers practice fields, the new Johnson & Wales University campus, the federal courthouse, Frazier Park, the Carillon office tower, the Greyhound bus terminal, and Gateway Village, a community of offices, shops, restaurants, and 500 residential units. Many design firms also are located in Third Ward, along Cedar Street.

Fourth Ward

One of Charlotte's most affluent neighborhoods, Fourth Ward was renovated in the mid-'70s, when the area was full of dilapidated homes, drugs, crime, and prostitution. Today Fourth Ward is a mixture of restored century-old Victorian homes and new, expensive condominiums. Just a few blocks from The Square in the heart of Uptown, Fourth Ward combines the charm of a small town with the convenience of a big city. Residents can easily walk to the city's arts, culture, and entertainment hub.

Uptown Condominiums

In the past several years, pricey new condominium high-rises have been climbing to the clouds along Tryon and Church Streets within walking distance of restaurants, offices, and cultural attractions.

The Ratcliffe overlooking a park called The Green is among Uptown's most elite addresses. Other popular Uptown condo buildings are 230 South Tryon, TradeMark, The Ave, Courtside, The Trust, and Fifth & Poplar.

The Vue, a 40-plus story condo tower in Fourth Ward, is scheduled to open in 2011.

Need Help? Here's the Number

Have a question or need to report a problem to local officials? Wading through more than 40 customer contact numbers for 100 different government services can be confusing.

But Charlotte and Mecklenburg County have a set of three-digit numbers designed to make reaching the right person easier. Citizens can call 311 to reach a one-stop complaint center for everything from water bills to barking dogs and potholes to garbage pickup.

Planned or in-place numbers include the following:

- 211   Social services (Mecklenburg, Cabarrus, and Union Counties)
- 311   City and county services
- 411   Directory assistance
- 511   Traffic assistance (statewide)
- 611   Often used by phone companies for customer service
- 711   Connecting line for speech- or hearing-impaired
- 911   Emergencies

Area 1, North Mecklenburg

Extending north from the Center City between I-77 and US 29/49 to the Mecklenburg County line, this area contains many University City neighborhoods popular with young families, as well as upscale golf course communities in Huntersville and Davidson.

University City

A planned development built near UNC Charlotte, this area contains a bustling commercial district with hotels, restaurants, movie theaters, and retail shops off W. T. Harris Boulevard. University Hospital and the business complexes of University Research Park and University Executive Park are also located here.

Popular neighborhoods in this area include Highland Creek, one of the largest communities in Charlotte, with two 18-hole public golf courses, three swimming pools, six tennis courts, a clubhouse, and more than 4,000 homes. Other neighborhoods in this area include Devongate, Eastfield, Eastfield Village, Glenview, and Prosperity. On the eastern edge of Area One you'll find upscale neighborhoods such as Lexington, Fountaingrove, and Claybrook.

Area 2, Northeast Mecklenburg

Bordered by US 29 and Central Avenue/Albemarle Road, this area includes the southern part of University City and many older, established neighborhoods.

UNC Charlotte is located in this part of University City, along with retail and office developments on University City Boulevard. Housing options vary from townhomes to single-family homes.

North Davidson (NoDa)

Often called NoDa for the main street of North Davidson, this area a few miles from Uptown was originally a mill village where workers in local textile mills and their families rented affordable housing from their employers. In the 1990s a few artists moved into the area and began opening galleries and shops while renovating the mill houses into hidden gems. Now developers have discovered the secret, and NoDa is being transformed into a community of new condos, coffeehouses, and trendy retailers. But the funky, colorful area known for hosting gallery crawls hasn't lost its soul yet.

Plaza-Midwood

Located in midtown Charlotte between the Plaza and Central Avenue, this is one of Charlotte's most popular older areas. Renovated bungalows full of character line the narrow tree-lined streets, and neighbors can walk to some cool hangouts such as Thomas Street Tavern and Fuel Pizza. Redevelopment along Central Avenue has spruced up the commercial district, and city officials recently enacted a plan to create more pedestrian-friendly projects with on-street parking, crosswalks, trees, and benches.

Neighborhoods in this area offer a full range of choices and prices from fixer-uppers to homes already refurbished to new homes being built on old lots.

Other neighborhoods in Area Two include expensive homes around Charlotte Country Club, which dates to 1910; the Hickory Grove Road and W. T. Harris Boulevard area; and Newell, which mixes suburban homes with a rural feel.

Area 3, East Mecklenburg

One of the busiest commercial districts in Charlotte, this section is bordered by Central Avenue/Albemarle Road and Independence Boulevard. Homes here are conveniently located close to department stores, supermarkets, drugstores, specialty shops, and a wide selection of restaurants. Along Independence Boulevard you'll also find a large concentration of automobile showrooms, home-supply stores, and membership-only warehouses.

Close to Uptown, along Independence Boulevard, are Chantilly and Commonwealth. These popular, older neighborhoods offer reasonable prices to first-time home owners who may be looking for a small place or a fixer-upper.

Area 4, Southeast Mecklenburg

Extending from the outskirts of Uptown to Matthews, Area Four is bordered by Independence Boulevard and Providence Road. This area is known for its concentration of hospitals and medical centers. Central Piedmont Community College is also headquartered here.

Cotswold

Located close to Uptown, Cotswold is a 1950s-style neighborhood with a mixture of older ranches, semi-contemporary homes, newer houses, and apartment complexes.

Eastover

This older neighborhood of mostly grand and expansive homes on large lots has one of the city's highest price tags. Small cottages and bungalows also are located here, but expect to pay for location and proximity to specialty shops, restaurants, and the Mint Museum.

Elizabeth

Located on the east side of Randolph Road across from Myers Park, Elizabeth is another older, pricey neighborhood with many attractive renovated homes.

Providence Plantation

Located near Matthews, this is a close-knit community with monthly socials, barbecues, and several women's clubs.

Rama-Sardis

This is an established neighborhood with large lots and higher-priced homes. The neighborhoods of Olde Stonehaven, McClintock Woods, and Medearis have active community groups.

Area 5, South Mecklenburg

One of Mecklenburg County's most expensive districts, Area Five is bordered by Providence Road to the east and Park Road to the west. The area stretches from close-in neighborhoods such as Myers Park, the city's first suburb, all the way down to the county line near Ballantyne, an upscale and fast-growing community. Newer homes, especially the many town houses and city homes on small lots a few minutes from Uptown, are mixed in with stately mansions, renovated bungalows, and smaller mill houses. Known for its tree-lined streets, nice parks, and clusters of shops and restaurants, Area Five also is home to Carolinas Medical Center and Park Road Shopping Center.

Ballantyne

Located just off the I-485 outer belt, Ballantyne popped up in the 1990s with an extensive office park, shops and restaurants, a country club, a resort hotel, and two golf courses. The prestigious HomeArama, in which the city's best builders and designers showcase their work in about 12 new homes each spring, chose Ballantyne Country Club a few years ago.

Dilworth

Developed in 1891 by Edward Dilworth Latta, Charlotte's early suburb had an electric streetcar extending from the city to entice people to live there. Today Dilworth is a trendy location, anchored by a thriving commercial district on East Boulevard. Older homes still sell for a high price.

Myers Park

Although only a few minutes' drive from Uptown, Myers Park's gracefully curving streets and soaring shade trees provide a parklike setting for its expensive, classic houses. This area is home to Queen's University at Charlotte, Wing Haven Garden & Bird Sanctuary, and Freedom Park. The preferred spot for old-money Charlotteans.

Providence Country Club

Located south of the city on 600 acres of trees, lakes, and open spaces, this upscale golf community is still growing. A family-oriented neighborhood, it has tennis courts, a pool, and an 18-hole golf course highlighted by an elegant clubhouse. Homesites are available for custom homes.

Quail Hollow

Located between Park Road and Sharon Road, this area contains Seven Eagles, a private community, and Quail Hollow Country Club, which hosts Charlotte's PGA tournament. Spacious

newer subdivisions and several apartment and condominium complexes offer residents a variety of housing options. Homes in Seven Eagles are among the city's most expensive.

Raintree

Many of the homes in this community, established in the 1970s, are contemporary in design and clustered around two golf courses. This large neighborhood is located near the Arboretum shopping center.

Southpark

With more than 30,000 workers, numerous office buildings, trendy restaurants, and upscale shopping, this area has become a "mini city." Communities such as Foxcroft, Morrocroft, Mountainbrook, Olde Providence, Beverly Woods, Sharon Woods, Candlewyck, and Barclay Downs are clustered around SouthPark Mall, which recently underwent a massive renovation. Morrocroft, a gated community, has some of Charlotte's largest and most expensive homes.

Area 6, Southwest Mecklenburg

Extending to the South Carolina border, Area Six is a narrow strip of land bordered by Park Road to the east and Nations Ford Road to the west. South Boulevard, the main thoroughfare running through the center of this area, offers a variety of businesses and shopping centers, including a growing number of international retail establishments. Area Six is served by the Lynx light rail line, which runs trains from I-485 to Uptown.

The area's bustling South End Historic District contains a cluster of former textile mills that has been converted into shops, galleries, and restaurants. One example is Atherton Mill, which now contains a variety of eating establishments, interior design stores, and live-work spaces.

Less than a mile from the Center City, South End is a good choice for young professionals who want to be close to Uptown but within walking distance of restaurants, shops, and parks along East Boulevard. Factory South, built in the old Lance cracker factory, has lofts with high ceilings, exposed brick walls, hardwood floors, and huge windows. The Arlington, also on South Boulevard just outside the I-277 loop, is the 25-story residential tower made of Pepto-pink glass.

Between Park Road and South Boulevard you'll find city neighborhoods, older ranch and split-level homes, and new developments. New subdivisions are farther south, along US 521.

Area 7, West Mecklenburg

Area Seven begins at Nations Ford Road and extends west to the Catawba River, south to the South Carolina state line, and north to Wilkinson Boulevard. Charlotte/Douglas International Airport, the Charlotte Coliseum, and the Charlotte Regional Farmers Market are located here. Arrowood, an industrial and business complex, and LakePoint, an office park with Microsoft Corp., AT&T, Belk Stores Services, Kemper Insurance, and other large companies, are also located here.

Lake Wylie and Paramount's Carowinds are located on the North Carolina–South Carolina border. Both facilities offer a wide variety of recreational activities.

Steele Creek

Settled by the Scots-Irish in the mid-1700s, this community is one of the oldest in the Charlotte area. Lakeside cottages and starter homes help maintain its rustic charm, while new developments bring Steele Creek into the 21st century. Neighborhoods include Sullivans Trace, McDowell Meadows, Oak Hill Village, and Yorkmont Park.

Wilmore

This older neighborhood with cottage-style homes from the early 1900s once contained two of Mecklenburg's largest gold mines. Wilmore was neglected for years, but is undergoing a renaissance as people desire to live closer to the center city. Older bungalows are being remodeled and sold at significant prices, although less-than-desirable houses still exist.

Area 8, West Mecklenburg

Area Eight extends from Uptown to the Catawba River, with Wilkinson Boulevard as its southern boundary and Bellhaven Boulevard as its

northern boundary. The U.S. National Whitewater Center is located here. Area Eight offers inner-city neighborhoods, new developments, and working-class country living.

Area 9, Northwest Mecklenburg

Extending west from Statesville Road to the Catawba River, with Bellhaven Boulevard to the south and Lake Norman as its northern border, Area Nine is one of the hottest areas for new-home communities.

Birkdale

Birkdale, in the Lake Norman town of Huntersville, is one of the city's most popular neighborhoods, with apartments, Cape Cod–style starter homes, and more upscale brick houses set around an 18-hole golf course. Across the street is a village of retail shops, movie theaters, restaurants, and apartments.

Overlook

Located just off Highway 16 at Mountain Island Lake, Overlook also mixes a wide range of housing levels in one community.

Other popular neighborhoods in Area Nine are Wynfield, Claiborne Woods, Towne Meadows, and Cedarfield.

Area 10, Union County

Located southeast of Mecklenburg, Union County is one of the fastest growing counties in the nation. In the 1990s Union's population jumped 47 percent and that growth continued into the new millennium. Many folks are drawn to the county's suburban-rural feel, quaint downtowns, and Main Street way-of-life. Traditional values, less traffic, lower taxes, and real estate deals also bring people here. One of the most popular areas is Weddington, whose population in the last decade grew 35 percent to 9,467. Weddington is located just across the county line and within a 10-minute drive of the I-485 outer belt.

Area 11, Cabarrus County

Cabarrus County, located east of Mecklenburg, is feeling the pressure to become Charlotte's next bedroom community as University City has grown and the I-485 belt in this area has opened. About 20,000 Cabarrus citizens work outside the county, many of them in Mecklenburg, but lower taxes and highly regarded schools keep them crossing the line to come back home.

Area 12, Iredell County

North of Mecklenburg, Iredell includes the Lake Norman town of Mooresville as well as the county seat, Statesville. One of the fastest-growing counties in the region, Iredell is a mix of suburbs around the lake, shopping centers clustered on I-77, and some remaining rural farms producing cattle, chicken, and hay. Mooresville is especially known for having more NASCAR teams than any other place in the country.

Area 13, Lake Norman

Created by Duke Power Company to generate hydroelectric power, Lake Norman offers 520 miles of meandering shoreline where huge stucco, stone, and brick mansions overlook sparkling water. Popular areas include the Peninsula, a sprawling neighborhood off West Catawba Avenue in Cornelius where NASCAR owner and former Super Bowl coach Joe Gibbs lives. A private club, waterfront golf course, and yacht club are part of the Peninsula, which also has many shops and restaurants just outside its entrance. River Run in Davidson is a private country club with an 18-hole golf course. Another neighborhood of special note is The Point, an upscale area of Lake Norman with Cape Cod architecture and a private 18-hole golf course designed by Greg Norman.

Area 14, Lincoln County

Still somewhat rural and full of country charm, Lincoln County is beginning to grow as Mecklenburg spills across its border. The fastest-growing area is in eastern Lincoln County on the western shores of Lake Norman. Denver, the main township here, recently built a new community center and library branch. Verdict Ridge, a fairly new golf course community, is one of the most popular neighborhoods.

Area 16, Gaston County

Located west of Mecklenburg, Gaston County has maintained a slower 9 percent growth rate while others around Charlotte have been as high as 47 percent. But development is coming this way, especially with the completion of the I-485 outer belt near Belmont.

Area 17, York County

Southwest of Mecklenburg across the South Carolina line, York County includes Rock Hill, the state's fourth-largest city, and much of Lake Wylie's shoreline.

Area 88, Lake Wylie

Smaller and less crowded than Lake Norman, Lake Wylie has both North Carolina and South Carolina shores. Riverpointe is an upscale neighborhood that was once home to the owner and several players from Charlotte's first NBA team. River Hills is an older community with contemporary homes and a golf course just across the South Carolina line. On the Gaston County side of the lake, Misty Waters, Woodland Bay, and a few other new developments are under way.

PUBLICATIONS

The Charlotte market has many newcomer publications to help you find an apartment, town house, or single-family home. Most are available free at grocery stores.

APARTMENT FINDER
(800) 222-3651
www.livingchoices.com
Quarterly full-size magazine with color photos of 250 apartment communities.

CHARLOTTE NEW HOME GUIDE
(704) 540-9550
www.newhomeguide.com
Thick, full-size quarterly with overall and area-specific maps, detailed listings, and a mail-in card for free information on advertised services and products.

GREATER CHARLOTTE APARTMENT GUIDE
(704) 523-0900
www.apartmentguide.com
Free monthly guide with over 300 shop-and-compare listings with maps, photos, features, and prices.

HOMES & LAND OF METRO CHARLOTTE
Estates & Homes of Metro Charlotte
(704) 527-6553, (800) 277-7800
www.homesandland.com
Around 200 pages of home ads with photos and detailed information. Separate magazines are available for Union and Anson Counties, as well as Concord, Kannapolis, and Harrisburg.

REAL ESTATE BOOK
(800) 841-3401
www.realestatebook.com
A monthly publication chock-full of color ads for existing homes and new communities in the metro area.

CORPORATE TEMPORARY HOUSING

A PLUS ACCOMMODATIONS AND RELOCATION
462 Crompton St.
(704) 587-0012, (888) 306-6048
www.aplusaccommodations.com
Fully furnished and accessorized one-, two-, and three-bedroom corporate apartments are offered with flexible short-term leases, starting with a minimum of 30 days. Unfurnished apartments are also available.

BRIDGESTREET CORPORATE HOUSING
8809 Lenox Pointe Dr., Ste. F
(704) 676-4886, (800) 278-7338
www.bridgestreet.com
BridgeStreet offers furnished corporate apartments for as short as seven days or as long-term as needed. There are one-, two-, and three-bedroom apartments located throughout Charlotte, as well as some privately owned condos Uptown.

CANDLEWOOD SUITES
16530 Northcross Dr.
Huntersville
(704) 895-3434

8812 University East Dr.
(704) 598-9863
Airport

5840 Westpark Dr.
(704) 529-7500
(800) 226-3539
www.candlewoodsuites.com
Billed as "Our Place, Your Space," this extended-stay hotel features a lot of perks: a free video and CD library, 25-cent soft drinks from the hotel cupboard, free local phone calls, free washer and dryer usage, two phone lines, a full kitchen, and a fitness center.

EQUITY CORPORATE HOUSING
(704) 364-6114, (877) 875-2584
www.equitycorporatehousing.com
One-, two-, and three-bedroom apartments and townhomes are available for stays of at least 30 days and then on an "as-needed" basis. The apartments are fully furnished, and maid service is available. Local phone, utilities, cable TV, washer/dryers, and high-speed Internet are included in the monthly fee.

EXECUSTAY BY MARRIOTT
3301 Woodpark Blvd.
(704) 599-1575, (800) 789-7829

1025 Yorkmont Ridge Lane
(704) 426–5656

2714 Mill Valley Court
(704) 536-0250
www.marriottexecustay.com
For stays of 30 days or longer, ExecuStay offers fully furnished one-, two-, and three-bedroom apartments. Relocating families with young children, infants, or pets can select their accommodations based on their preferences. Basic telephone service, cable, and utilities are included on one monthly invoice. Maid service is available by request.

HOMESTEAD STUDIO SUITES
710 Yorkmont Rd.
(704) 676-0083, (888) 782-9473
www.homesteadhotels.com
Part of the Extended Stay chain, Homestead Studio Suites provide rooms for extended-stay lodging with affordable nightly, weekly, and monthly rates. The large studio-style rooms feature king- and queen-size beds, a work station, a fully equipped kitchen, and satellite TV. Guests can make free local calls, buy supplies from the lobby pantry, and work out at a nearby gym.

OAKWOOD CORPORATE HOUSING
2401 Whitehall Park Dr.
(704) 588-4668
www.oakwood.com
Oakwood Corporate Housing provides temporary housing throughout the greater Charlotte area and in more than 400 cities nationwide for stays of one month or longer. Fully furnished apartments are supplied with linens, housewares, cable TV, telephone, and maid service. Everything is billed on one convenient monthly invoice. Oakwood caters to clients on extended business travel, in training, relocating, or between homes for one month or longer.

STAYBRIDGE SUITES BY HOLIDAY INN
Ballantyne, 15735 John J. Delaney Dr.
(704) 248-5000

Arrowood, 7924 Forest Pine Dr.
(704) 527-6767
www.staybridgesuites.com

Charlotte
www.ichotelsgroup.com
A residential feel with the amenities of an office is the allure of this extended-stay chain. There are studios through two-bedrooms with full kitchens, high-speed Internet access, 24/7 business center, indoor pool, fitness center, and library. Guests can enjoy a complimentary breakfast buffet, evening receptions, and golf privileges at the nearby Ballantyne Resort. The Arrowood location is close to the airport.

SUBURBAN LODGE
8615 Hankins Rd.
(704) 598-5033

10225 Feld Farm Rd.
Pineville
(704) 544-3993

9211 East Independence Blvd., Matthews
(704) 845-2001

W. T. Harris Blvd.
(704) 598-5445
(800) 951-STAY (7829)
www.suburbanlodge.com
Suburban Lodges provide homelike amenities for extended-stay guests, including fully equipped kitchens, on-site laundry facilities, and housekeeping services. Free local calls and cable TV with HBO, CNN, and ESPN are also included.

REAL ESTATE AGENTS

There are thousands of licensed real estate agents in the Charlotte area. Membership in the Multiple Listing Service allows real estate agents to access information on homes located throughout the region. The companies listed below provide a popular sampling, but are not the only ones to consider. For a complete list, go to www.mls.com.

THE ALLEN TATE COMPANY
Relocation Center and SouthPark office
6700 Fairview Rd.
(704) 365-6910, (800) 277-6901
www.allentate.com

7824 Pineville-Matthews Rd.
Carmel
(704) 542-4300

13526 Johnston Rd.
Ballantyne
(704) 541-6200

218 North College St.
Center City
(704) 331-2122

716 East Blvd., Dilworth
(704) 348-1446

7212 Albemarle Rd.
East Charlotte
(704) 563-6000

10851 Providence Rd. (I-485)
(704) 849–8300

145 West W. T. Harris Blvd.
University
(704) 547-8900

605 South New Hope Rd.
Gastonia
(704) 868-4188

19460 Old Jetton Rd.
Cornelius
Lake Norman
(704) 896-8283

165 South Trade St.
Matthews
(704) 847-6400
www.allentate.com

Charlotte's largest locally owned independent real estate company was founded in 1957 by Allen Tate and currently has more than 1,600 agents in offices throughout the Carolinas. The company's Relocation Center is extensive, offering a personalized newcomer kit, a video presentation, home-finding tours, and special information for families with children. A referral service and mortgage financing are also available. Additional offices in Belmont, Concord, Fort Mill, Lancaster, Monroe, Mountain Island Lake, and Rock Hill.

CENTURY 21
756 Tyvola Rd.
(704) 527-2910

2905 Queen City Dr.
(704) 940-1724, (888) 627-5891

8401 University Executive Park Dr.
(704) 547-0210, (800) 521-2206

8400F Belhaven Blvd.
(704) 399-4848, (866) 727-4945

10801 Johnston Rd., Ballantyne
(704) 541-6306, (800) 868-6306

19300 Statesville Rd., Cornelius
(704) 892-6556, (800) 274-7721
www.century21.com

All of the above are independently owned affiliates of the nationwide company.

COLDWELL BANKER
Relocation Center
(800) 325-0986

7907 Providence Rd.
Arboretum
(704) 541-6100

3440 Torington Way
Ballantyne
(704) 541-5111

6633 Fairview Rd.
SouthPark
(704) 364-3300

1001 W. T. Harris Blvd.
University
(704) 547-8490

311 Williamson Rd.
Mooresville
(704) 664-5253

Union County
(704) 821-6647

Serving North and South Carolina, Coldwell Banker also offers a nationwide relocation service.

COTTINGHAM-CHALK/BISSELL-HAYES REALTORS
Main Offices
6846 Morrison Blvd.
(704) 364-1700

122 Cherokee Rd.
Myers Park/Eastover
(704) 887-0540
www.ccbhrealtors.com

This company was created in 2009 with the merger of longtime Charlotte firms Bisell-Hayes and Cottingham-Chalk. CCBH specializes in properties in high-demand areas such as Myers Park, Eastover, Ballantyne, Foxcroft, Piper Glen, and SouthPark. Relocation and referral services are available.

i The Home Builders Association of Charlotte sponsors the annual Luxury Lifestyle Home Tour and the Parade of Homes, Charlotte's largest open house. It can also help with information on the building and financing process, building codes, and more. For details, call (704) 376-8524 or go to www.hbacharlotte.com.

DICKENS-MITCHENER & ASSOCIATES
2330 Randolph Rd., Eastover
2719 Coltsgate Rd.

Relocation Division
2316 Randolph Rd.
(704) 342-1000
www.dickensmitchener.com
Founded in 1991, Dickens-Mitchener is home to dedicated agents known for their extensive knowledge of the area and great customer service. The firm's easy-to-use Web site lets customers search by area, look at exterior and interior shots, and even take a virtual 360-degree tour. Dickens-Mitchener also has a full-time relocation department.

FIRST CHARLOTTE PROPERTIES
232 Cottage Place
(704) 377-9000
www.1stcharlotte.com
First Charlotte Properties has been active in the Charlotte market since 1979 and has more than 30 agents.

FIRST PROPERTIES OF THE CAROLINAS
2222 Gold Hill Rd., Fort Mill
(877) 751-0131

1 Executive Court, Lake Wylie
(800) 545-3342

11040 South Tryon St.
(800) 943-7682
www.firstproptc.com
Established in 1980, First Properties is a key player in the real estate market in Lake Wylie, Tega Cay, and Fort Mill. The firm has more than 30 agents and offers a relocation and referral service.

Important Phone Numbers

Animal Care
Animal Control/Pet Licenses
(704) 336-3786
Emergency Veterinary Clinic
(704) 844-6440
Spay-Neuter Clinic
(704) 333-4130

Cable
Time Warner Cable, (704) 377-9600

Driver's License
(704) 527-2562, (704) 392-3266
(704) 547-5786, (704) 531-5563

Electricity
Duke Energy, (704) 382–8000

Gas
Piedmont Natural Gas,
(704) 364-3120
Suburban Propane
(704) 375-1721

Trash
Charlotte Department of Sanitation
(704) 336-2673
General Recycling Information
(704) 336-6087

Water and Sewer
Charlotte-Mecklenburg Utilities
(704) 336-7600

HELEN ADAMS REALTY
2301 Randolph Rd., Eastover
(704) 375-8598

15235 John J. Delaney Dr., Ballantyne
(704) 341-0279

Relocation Office
(800) 851-5253

8600 Sam Furr Rd., Huntersville
(704) 439-3300
www.helenadamsrealty.com
This company, with more than 100 agents, specializes in exclusive listings and new developments in the greater Charlotte metro area. The Ballantyne location is a one-stop information center for south Charlotte, with details on local builders, mortgage lenders, and real estate attorneys.

HENDRIX-MITCHENER PROPERTIES
4725 Piedmont Row Dr.
(704) 552-9292
www.hmproperties.com
A newer firm in the Charlotte market, formed by the partnership of successful sellers Patty Hendrix and Valerie Mitchener, Hendrix-Mitchener specializes in luxury, exclusive properties and has 50 agents.

KELLER WILLIAMS REALTY
3430 Toringdon Way
Ballantyne
(704) 887-6600

520 Collins Aikman Dr.
University City
(704) 409-4700

2115 Rexford Park Rd.
SouthPark
(704) 602-0400

1700 East Independence Blvd.
Indian Trail
(704) 684-1000
www.kw.com
Keller Williams has four offices in the busiest parts of the region, with a strong presence south and southeast of the city.

LAKE NORMAN REALTY
Relocation Services
20117 West Catawba Ave., Cornelius
(704) 892-9673, (800) 315-3655

522 River Hwy., Mooresville
(704) 663-3655

135 Cross Center Rd., Denver
(704) 827-7890
www.lakenormanrealty.com
Lake Norman Realty was founded in 1978 and with 50 agents has grown to meet the new development needs of the area. Relocation and referral services are also offered.

THE MCDEVITT AGENCY
237 South Tryon St.
(704) 333-2475
www.themcdevittagency.com
The McDevitt Agency is a boutique firm of 13 agents who focus on properties in Uptown Charlotte and surrounding neighborhoods.

PRUDENTIAL CAROLINAS REALTY
2901 Coltsgate Rd.
Relocation Service Center
(704) 366-5545

3420 Toringdon Way
Ballantyne
(704) 542-1100

7930 West Kenton Circle
Huntersville
(704) 892-1424

7505 Hwy. 73
Denver
(704) 489-1471
www.prudentialcarolinas.com
This firm is one of the largest independently owned and operated real estate companies in the Southeast, with 18 offices in North and South Carolina. The company offers in-house mortgage services, corporate relocation, title insurance, and concierge service.

WANDA SMITH & ASSOCIATES
Relocation
(800) 755-3261

4920 Monroe Rd.
(704) 366-6667
www.wandasmith.com
Founded in 1987, the Wanda Smith agency has 22 agents, specializes in home resales, and serves

as the exclusive sales agency for many of Charlotte's top home builders.

LOCAL GOVERNMENT

As Charlotte's population becomes larger and more diverse, its ability to reach a consensus is challenged. Some favor progressive growth, while many longtime residents prefer that the city remain more like a big small town.

The City Council includes the mayor and 11 members—7 from districts and 4 at large—elected every odd-numbered year in partisan elections. Meetings on the second and fourth Mon of the month are general business sessions beginning at 6:30 p.m. On the third Mon at 6 p.m., the council deals only with matters related to zoning. All are held at the Charlotte-Mecklenburg Government Center, 600 East Fourth St. General meetings are broadcast live on Cable Channel 16. For information on the agenda or to speak at a meeting, call the City Clerk at (704) 336-2247.

Mecklenburg's nine-member Board of County Commissioners is elected in partisan elections held in even-numbered years. Six members are elected from single-member districts, with three at-large members. The board holds three meetings each month on Tues at the Charlotte-Mecklenberg Government Center. First and third Tuesdays are general business sessions that begin at 6 p.m. On the second Tues the board holds a zoning meeting. The board also holds a luncheon meeting on the Thurs preceding the first Tues of each month. Sessions are broadcast live on Cable Channel 16 and rebroadcast during the week in which the meeting was held. For information on the board's meeting agenda or to speak at a commission meeting, contact the clerk to the board at (704) 336-2247.

Charlotte-Mecklenburg is served by the city-county form of government. Generally, the city provides urban services, such as water, sewer, trash disposal, and recycling, while the county provides human services such as health, education, welfare, mental health, and the environment. The other towns in Mecklenburg County—Pineville, Matthews, Mint Hill, Davidson, Huntersville, and Cornelius—each have their own city government.

If you have a question or need information regarding city or county government, call Charlotte-Mecklenburg Customer Service & Information at (704) 336-2040 or visit www.ci.charlotte.nc.us.

CHILD CARE

Charlotte has hundreds of day-care and child-care programs at churches and schools, in homes, and at nurseries. A good starting point and reference for any parent is Child Care Resources (704-376-6697, www.childcareresourcesinc.org). This non-profit organization is tied into all child-care and preschool education opportunities in the community. See the Education and Child Care chapter for more details on child care in Charlotte.

REGISTERING TO VOTE

If you have been a resident for 30 days, you are eligible to register to vote. You can register at the Board of Elections, 741 Kenilworth Ave., Suite 202; at any branch of the Charlotte-Mecklenburg Public Library; at the town halls of Cornelius, Matthews, and Pineville; or at the Department of Motor Vehicles Drivers License Offices. Call (704) 336-2133 for details.

EDUCATION AND CHILD CARE

One of the most important decisions in choosing a place to live is the quality of schools. If you're moving to Mecklenburg County, much of the decision of where your child will attend school is up to you.

The Charlotte-Mecklenburg School System (CMS) uses a Choice Assignment Plan that allows families to have a voice in school selection. Started with the 2002–2003 school year, the plan allows families to choose a school close to their home, a magnet school, or a school elsewhere in the county. Students are guaranteed a spot at their home school, but must apply for a spot at others. Around 76 percent of students receive their first choice.

But the road to the Choice Assignment Plan was quite bumpy for CMS. While the issue of school assignment has been a hot topic in the last 10 years, the issue actually dates back more than five decades. Three years after the U.S. Supreme Court ruled separate schools are not equal in the 1954 case *Brown v. The Board of Education of Topeka, Kansas,* four black students began integration of Charlotte schools. But in 1965 a black couple sued after their son was denied enrollment at the school closest to their home, a primarily white school. In 1969, a judge ordered CMS to use all known ways of desegregation, including busing. The landmark case set a precedent for school desegregation across the nation, and the U.S. Supreme Court upheld the ruling in 1971.

The tables were turned in September 1997 after a white parent sued CMS claiming his daughter was denied enrollment in a magnet school holding spaces for minority students. Six more parents joined the suit in 1998 to contest all the district's race-based policies. After a two-month trial, a federal judge issued a landmark ruling ending Charlotte-Mecklenburg's use of race in student assignment. The school board rushed to design a race-neutral plan, then scrapped it when a federal appeals court overturned the first ruling. However, under further review, the federal court reversed the first appeal and affirmed the earlier ruling, saying CMS had achieved unitary status and that the district should operate without regard to desegregation no later than 2002–2003. Appeals continued until the U.S. Supreme Court refused to hear the case.

CMS moved forward with its Choice Assignment Plan. Since then, critics say the choice plan has increased crowding at some schools and boosted concentrations of poverty at others. Some schools, especially in high-growth suburban areas, were forced to take many more students than they were designed to hold. Other new schools in less desirable areas were left with empty seats as families in those neighborhoods chose alternatives.

Despite the challenges and ongoing controversy, more than 130,000 students attend Charlotte-Mecklenburg public schools. CMS, led by Dr. Peter Gorman, is the largest school system in North Carolina and the 19th largest in the nation. The district employs 18,862 faculty, staff, and support personnel. In recent years CMS has been honored nationally for award-winning programs, closing the achievement gap, raising test scores across the board and making rigorous courses accessible to all students.

The CMS Web site at www.cms.k12.nc.us is an excellent tool for learning about CMS, its Choice Assignment Plan, and the most up-to-the-moment news in the district. Parents and students can also tune into CMS-TV3 (Cable Channel 3) for updated news and information.

Entries in this chapter are arranged alphabetically by type of program. Listings are located in Charlotte unless otherwise noted.

EDUCATION ABCS

Board of Education

CMS is governed by a nine-member Board of Education elected on a countywide basis to serve rotating four-year terms. One of their duties is to appoint the superintendent.

The Board of Education holds regular meetings on the second and fourth Tues of each month in the boardroom on the fourth floor of the Education Center. These meetings are open to the public, and an agenda is available in the boardroom prior to the meeting. Board meetings are broadcast live on CMS-TV (Cable Channel 3).

Registering Your Child

To register your child with CMS, call (980) 343-5335 or visit the Family Application Center at 700 Marsh Rd. Parents also can pick up an enrollment form at local schools or from the CMS Web site at www.cms.k12.nc.us. School offices remain open through the summer.

Children entering kindergarten must be five years old on or before August 31 of the year they are enrolled. To register, a new student must bring a birth certificate or other acceptable proof of age and an immunization record signed by a physician. This immunization record must include five DTP/Dtaps, four oral polio vaccines, one MMR, and one mumps/rubella vaccine. Health assessments are required for all new kindergarten students and include a medical history and physical examination with screening for vision and hearing. Parents must also provide the school with three proofs of residency in Mecklenburg County to register their child. A power bill, lease or purchase agreement, bank/credit card statement, and property tax statement are among items considered proof of residency.

North Carolina law requires all children from ages 7 to 16 to attend school. State law requires a minimum of 180 school days per year for grades kindergarten through 12. Each high school offers assistance to students who are preparing for the Scholastic Aptitude Test. In addition, 10th-graders take the Preliminary Scholastic Aptitude Test at no charge.

i Third- through eighth-graders take math and reading tests; fourth- and seventh-graders also take writing exams. High school students take about a dozen tests, ranging from algebra to English to biology. Students in the third, fifth, and eighth grades who do not pass their tests could be held back a year. Summer school is offered to students who fail the exams. In a few years, high school seniors will be required to pass an exit exam.

How the Choice System Works

Mecklenburg County has 176 home (neighborhood) schools—103 elementaries, 33 middle schools, and 31 high schools. Students are guaranteed a seat at either their home school, at the magnet school in which they are currently enrolled, or at a school where they have a sibling. Families who do not file an application for the home school, or who request an alternative and are denied, are generally assigned to their home school as well.

To find out about home schooling for any address, contact the student placement office at (980) 343-5335 or via e-mail at student.placement@cms.k12.nc.us.

Students who are new to CMS or who are moving up to middle or high school must file an application listing up to three desired schools. Current students seeking a new school also apply. The forms are due in late January. Students who are entering the system at other times can call (980) 343-5335 or visit the Family Application Center at 700 Marsh Rd.

Students who wish to attend a school other than their home school are placed in an assignment lottery. Each person receives a randomly assigned number. After students with guaranteed seats are assigned, the district determines the number of available seats by grade level. The odds are steep at crowded schools where students with guaranteed seats claim all or most of the seats. Students who do not get their first choice are placed on a waiting list. Families also can appeal to the CMS staff or to the Board of Education.

Transportation

The school system has 1,155 buses traveling an average of 129,000 miles a day. Four large "choice zones" make up the county. Transportation is provided to schools within each student's choice zone. If students attend a school outside their choice zone, they generally cannot ride the bus.

i The Charlotte-Mecklenburg School System is among the 20 largest school districts in the United States, with 176 schools and more than 130,000 students. About 18,000 students attend the district's magnet schools. The average SAT score among students in the top 10 percent of their class is 1782. The district has 18,862 employees, including 8,965 full-time teachers.

MAGNET SCHOOLS

Magnet schools offer all core curriculum—math, science, and language arts—as well as special programs. Themes include accelerated learning, leadership and global economics, performing arts, International Baccalaureate, language immersion, learning immersion and talent development, math, science, environmental studies, Montessori, Paideia, technology, and traditional.

Some schools are full magnets, with all students enrolled in the program. Others are partial magnets with only a portion of students in magnet programs.

For the 2010–2011 year, the district will offer 11 magnet themes in 40 schools. Magnet schools offer numerous opportunities for parents to cultivate interests and strengths in their children and provide school locations all over the county.

For more information about the magnet school program, call (980) 343-5030.

PRESCHOOL AND DAY CARE PROGRAMS

There are hundreds of day-care programs in Mecklenburg County, including child-care centers, family child-care homes, and part-day nursery programs. Many churches also offer facilities and programs. Nationwide child-care centers such as La Petite and KinderCare are popular options, and many parents who work for large corporations such as Bank of America and Wachovia/Wells Fargo have child-care options through the workplace. You may also want to ask a friend or neighbor about a specific care provider.

Child Care Resources, Inc. (704-376-6697, www.childcareresourcesinc.org) at 4601 Park Rd., a private nonprofit organization, is a marvelous resource and a great starting point for any parent looking for child-care options. Funded by the United Way, it's tied into all child-care and preschool education opportunities in and around the community.

A comprehensive listing of child-care centers and services is provided in the Charlotte Yellow Pages.

PRIVATE SCHOOLS

Mecklenburg County has nearly 70 independent and special schools with more than 17,000 students enrolled in prekindergarten through grade 12. These schools employ nearly 2,200 teachers. Following are the county's larger and longer established private schools.

ANAMI MONTESSORI SCHOOL
2901 Archdale Dr.
(704) 556-0042
www.anamimontessori.org
The Anami Montessori School was founded in 1986 as a fully accredited AMI (Association Montessori Internationale) institution. Programs are offered to meet the needs of children ages 3 to 12 years. The school places emphasis on encouragement, respect for the individual, choice, and personal responsibility. Anami Montessori has dedicated, caring teachers and small classes

where children often work to the sounds of classical music. The spacious facilities on Archdale Drive back up to the 120-acre Park Road Park.

BARBARA AND JERRY LEVIN MIDDLE SCHOOL
5007 Providence Rd.
(704) 366-4558
www.jewishcharlotte.org

Opened in fall 2002, the Barbara and Jerry Levin Middle School is affiliated with Charlotte Jewish Day School and is housed in the same building at Shalom Park. About 20 students in grades 6 through 8 attend.

BIBLE BAPTIST CHRISTIAN SCHOOL
2724 Margaret Wallace Rd.
(704) 535-1694
www.bbcscolts.com

This school enrolls students in preschool through grade 12, with extended before- and after-school care as well. Offering a traditional curriculum, the school is college preparatory in mission.

BRISBANE ACADEMY
5901 Statesville Rd.
(704) 598-5208
www.brisbaneacademy.org

This math and science preparatory academy is an accredited, state-licensed independent school with more than 10 years in Charlotte. About 90 students attend prekindergarten through grade 12, learning principles such as organization, discipline, self-motivation, and accepting educational challenges. Brisbane also offers after-school enrichment, a tutoring center, and summer camps.

BRITISH AMERICAN SCHOOL OF CHARLOTTE
7000 Endhaven Lane
(866) 341-3236
www.britishschool.org/charlotte

Opened in September 2004, this private school for elementary and middle school students of all nationalities is led by administrators and teachers from the United Kingdom and international

schools worldwide. Charlotte is the school's fifth location, following Houston, Boston, Chicago, and Washington, D.C. Ages 3 through 11 attend classes with a maximum enrollment of 20 students in each class. Following a U.K. curriculum, students learn core subjects but focus on skill level rather than grade level. Nursery students learn to read before kindergarten, and students throughout the school take classes in art and world studies. In addition to a rigorous curriculum, the school stresses a quiet and courteous atmosphere. British sports such as cricket, soccer, and rounders also are played at the school.

CARMEL CHRISTIAN SCHOOL
1145 Pineville-Matthews Rd., Matthews
(704) 849-9723
www.carmelchristian.org

Carmel Baptist Church founded Carmel Christian in 1992 to aid Christian families seeking a traditional academic approach to education. More than 300 students attend the K–8 Southern Baptist–affiliated school, which is accredited by the Southern Association of Colleges and Schools and the Association of Christian Schools International. Carmel Christian aims to develop all aspects of a child—physical, mental, emotional, and spiritual. Its curriculum integrates academic growth, character development, and biblical truths. The school has an arrangement with Covenant Day School whereby Carmel Christian students continue their high school education at Covenant Day.

CHARLOTTE CATHOLIC HIGH SCHOOL
7702 Pineville-Matthews Rd.
(704) 543-1127
www.gocougars.org

Coeducational and college preparatory, Charlotte Catholic began as part of St. Mary's Seminary, which dates to 1877. Five elementary schools and one Catholic middle school feed into Charlotte Catholic, which serves nearly 1,400 students in grades 9 through 12. Non-Catholics may attend. The student-faculty ratio is 15 to 1, and the school offers several Advanced Placement classes, drama, band, dance, theater, and chorus.

A member of the public-school North Carolina Athletic Association, the school has 31 athletic teams in 14 sports. Charlotte Catholic is accredited by the Southern Association of Colleges and Schools, the North Carolina State Department of Public Instruction, the North Carolina Association of Independent Schools, and the Diocese of Charlotte.

CHARLOTTE CHRISTIAN SCHOOL
7301 Sardis Rd.
(704) 366-5657
www.charlottechristian.com

Charlotte Christian is an interdenominational, independent day school. Founded in 1950, it provides college-preparatory education for more than 1,000 students in prekindergarten through grade 12. Students come from 750 families representing 130 different churches. In addition to its excellent academic program, the school offers 31 athletic teams, art, theater, band, and choir. Charlotte Christian is a member of the Association of Christian Schools International, the North Carolina Association of Independent Schools, and the Southern Association of Colleges and Schools.

CHARLOTTE COUNTRY DAY SCHOOL
1440 Carmel Rd.
(704) 943-4500
www.charlottecountryday.org

Founded in 1941, Charlotte Country Day is the oldest independent school in the area. The school provides a liberal education for its 1,600 students—one that develops the intellect, body, spirit, and character. Three divisions make up the school: Lower School (junior kindergarten through grade 4), Middle School (grades 5 through 8), and Upper School (grades 9 through 12). There is an International Baccalaureate program, as well as an extensive international exchange program. Since 1992 more than 700 students have participated in study-abroad programs, and over 450 school families have hosted a foreign student. Around 100 students from 30 different countries are enrolled in classes on the south Charlotte campus. The school is technologically advanced, with 700 computers in use

and high-speed Internet access in all classrooms, computer labs, and libraries. Country Day also has an outstanding arts program, encompassing music, dance, drama, chorus, and the visual arts. Athletic programs via 64 sports teams draw an approximately 90 percent participation rate in organized athletics. Service projects are also a part of school life. Small classes, dedicated teachers, and individualized instruction in all classes allow every child to experience success. An independent, nonsectarian, coeducational school, Charlotte Country Day welcomes students regardless of race, color, national or ethnic origin, or religion.

CHARLOTTE ISLAMIC ACADEMY
4301 Shamrock Dr.
(704) 537-1772

Students follow the standard curriculum required by the state Board of Education, but also take classes on Arabic language and Islamic teachings based upon the Quran.

CHARLOTTE ISLAMIC SCHOOL
1615 Fifth St.
(704) 333-4160
www.charlotteislamicschool.org

One of two Islamic schools in the city, the school offers classes from prekindergarten through eighth grade. Students follow the curriculum required by the state Board of Education, but also take classes on Arabic language and Islamic teachings based upon the Quran and Sunnah.

CHARLOTTE JEWISH DAY SCHOOL
5007 Providence Rd.
(704) 366-4558
www.cjdschool.org

This school has students in kindergarten through grade 5. The school's Jewish culture and environment helps the students develop a sense of security in their roots and a pride in who they are. They are given a multifaceted education based on academic performance, social growth, and feelings of self-worth. Classes are small enough to ensure that each student receives individual attention, but large enough to develop vital friendships that enhance social skills. Music, art, physical education, Hebrew, and Spanish are also offered, along with computer labs.

CHARLOTTE LATIN SCHOOL
9502 Providence Rd.
(704) 846-1100
www.charlottelatin.org

Charlotte Latin School, founded in 1970, is a coeducational day school with more than 1,300 students in transitional kindergarten through grade 12. Located on 122 wooded acres, Charlotte Latin is one of the city's finest in terms of academic quality and diversity. The school is divided into the Lower School (transitional kindergarten through grade 5), Middle School (grades 6 through 8), and Upper School (grades 9 through 12). Latin's curriculum is college preparatory, with 17 Advanced Placement programs. Latin students routinely score more than 200 points above the national average on the SAT, and 100 percent four-year college placement is the norm.

Charlotte Latin encourages individual development and civility in its students by inspiring them to learn, encouraging them to serve others, and offering them many growth-promoting opportunities. Latin was the first school in the country with a senior class who funded and built a Habitat for Humanity home; in the past 12 years, students have completed four Habitat houses. In addition to its well-rounded academic and community service program, more than 65 Charlotte Latin School teams annually compete in 17 different sports. Around 90 percent of Latin students play at least one sport. The school also offers extensive programs in fine arts, leadership, and international studies. Its facilities rival those of a small college, with 14 major buildings, 10 science labs, 13 computer labs, an engineering room, 5 art studios, 5 music studios, a 740-seat auditorium, a 17,630-square-foot media center, a 13,275-square-foot dining room, 3 gyms, a fitness center, 6 tennis courts, a 22-lane pool, and a 1,400-seat stadium.

Charlotte Latin has been named an Exemplary School by the U.S. Department of Educa-tion. On three occasions it has also received the U.S. Department of Education Blue Ribbon Award for leadership, school environment, parent and community support, and documented success.

CHARLOTTE MONTESSORI SCHOOL
219 East Blvd.
(704) 332-7733
www.charlottemontessori.com

The oldest Montessori school in Charlotte and one of the oldest in the Southeast, Charlotte Montessori was chartered in 1971. In 1995 the school relocated to Dilworth, a convenient location for parents who work Uptown. The school is affiliated with the American Montessori Society and is approved by the North Carolina State Department of Public Instruction. Following the philosophy of Italian doctor and physician Dr. Maria Montessori (1870–1952), the school regards children as individuals with a unique learning pace and range of talents. The school offers children a unique environment that develops self-discipline, independence, and an enthusiasm for learning. Programs are available for children age 18 months through kindergarten.

CHARLOTTE PREPARATORY SCHOOL
212 Boyce Rd.
(704) 366-5994
www.charlotteprep.com

A sister school to Charlotte Montessori, Charlotte Prep includes preschool through grade 8. After a transitional kindergarten program, students learn through a core knowledge curriculum. The school, which has around 350 students, has earned dual accreditation from the Southern Association of Colleges and Schools and the Southern Association of Independent Schools. Charlotte Prep added a gymnasium, performance hall, and classroom facility in 2004.

CHRISTIAN MONTESSORI SCHOOL AT LAKE NORMAN
14101 Stumptown Rd., Huntersville
(704) 875-1801
www.lakenormandayschool.com

In the growing Lake Norman area north of Charlotte, this independent college-preparatory day school is set on 20 rural acres. The school offers a Montessori environment for children age 15 months through sixth grade.

COUNTRYSIDE MONTESSORI SCHOOL
4755 Prosperity Church Rd.
(704) 503-6000

9026 Mallard Creek Rd.
(704) 549-4253

4125 Johnston Oehler Rd.
(704) 936-5580
www.countrysidemontessorischools.org
Chartered in 1975 and affiliated with the American Montessori Society, Countryside offers preschool for children ages two to five at the Prosperity location, elementary programs for first through sixth grade at the Mallard Creek site, and middle and high school programs at the Johnston Oehler campus.

COVENANT DAY SCHOOL
800 Fullwood Lane, Matthews
(704) 847-2385
www.covenantday.org
Covenant Day School, a ministry of Christ Covenant Church, is a coeducational Christian day school for kindergarten through grade 9. The school serves over 640 students and offers academic excellence in a nurturing Christian environment. Beginning with kindergarten, the school offers a superior reading program. Instruction in French and Latin is combined with modern computer technology to provide a comprehensive academic program. At selected grade levels, students receive laptops for around-the-clock computer access, with the ability to e-mail work to teachers, participate in online learning projects, and to obtain Internet-related research.

Extracurricular programs include art, music, journalism, yearbook, and band. A varied sports program is also offered. Covenant Day has built another campus on Christ Covenant Lane and partnered with Carmel Christian School to start a high school.

DAVIDSON DAY SCHOOL
412 Armour St., Davidson
(704) 896-3585
www.davidsonday.com
A private school in the quaint town surrounding Davidson College, Davidson Day was founded in 1999. The school with prekindergarten through grade 9 stresses academic and personal success through small classes, cutting-edge instructional methods, and individual learning plans. In 2004 the school completed a new library, soccer field, playground, high school expansion, and environmental studies path to Lake Davidson. Davidson Day also has a technology center. Students may participate in soccer, basketball, baseball, swimming, golf, and tennis, as well as dance, theater, drama, art, and music. All students from prekindergarten and up take foreign language classes. After-school programs are varied and interesting, with activities such as horseback riding.

DORE ACADEMY
1727 Providence Rd.
(704) 365-5490
www.doreacademy.org
Charlotte's oldest college-preparatory school for students with learning disabilities and attention disorders, Dore Academy serves 130 students in grades 1 through 12. Maximum class size is 10, with only 5 students in each reading class. The school's student-teacher ratio is 7 to 1. Students typically attend Dore Academy for three to five years before returning to mainstream classrooms. The school also offers computer labs, writing labs, a multipurpose room with stage, a basketball court, two playing fields, a wooded picnic area, and a playground for younger children. Dore is a member of the North Carolina Association of Independent Schools, International Dyslexia Society, Council for Exceptional Children, Learning Disabilities Association, and CHADD (Children and Adults with Attention-Deficit/Hyperactivity Disorder).

HICKORY GROVE BAPTIST CHRISTIAN SCHOOL
6050 Hickory Grove Rd.
(704) 531-4008
www.hgbcs.org

Started in 1995 by Hickory Grove Baptist Church, this Christian school near UNC Charlotte now has nearly 1,100 students in transitional kindergarten through grade 12. The student-teacher ratio is 15 to 1, and high school students may enroll in three Advanced Placement and five honors courses, as well as foreign language, music, and art. Hickory Grove also has a full sports program.

NORTHSIDE CHRISTIAN ACADEMY
333 Jeremiah Blvd.
(704) 596-4074
www.ncaknights.com
Founded in 1961, Northside Christian serves 875 students, kindergarten through grade 12, and also includes a preschool. One of the many ministries of Northside Baptist, the school shares facilities with the church. Northside Christian requires uniforms and has behavior guidelines. The college-preparatory coeducational school also has a full sports program, fine-arts program, computer labs, science labs, and many student clubs. Church members and families with more than one child in the school receive a discount.

OMNI MONTESSORI SCHOOL
9536 Blakeney-Heath Rd.
(704) 541-1326
www.omni-montessori.org
An AMI-affiliated Montessori school, this center near the growing Ballantyne area opened in 1985. Up to 100 students ages 3 through 12 are taught in classes with an average size of 24 children. The school's eight-acre campus includes six classrooms, a library, garden, playground, and recreational field.

PROVIDENCE CHRISTIAN SCHOOL
4906 Providence Rd.
(704) 364-0824
www.providencechristschool.org
An outreach mission of Providence Road Church of Christ, this school provides a well-rounded curriculum for students in kindergarten through grade 5. In addition to basic courses, classes in Bible, computers, physical education, art, and

music are offered. Classes are small with a student-teacher ratio of 16 to 1. Extended care is available from 7 to 7:30 a.m. and after school until 6 p.m. In 2004 Providence Christian was nominated a Blue Ribbon School by the Council for American Private Education.

PROVIDENCE DAY SCHOOL
5800 Sardis Rd.
(704) 887-7041
www.providenceday.org
Providence Day School has been cited for excellence by the U.S. Department of Education, the National Council of Teachers of English, and the College Board Advanced Placement Program. The coeducational school was founded in 1970 and is located on a 45-acre campus in southeast Charlotte. It serves 1,500 students in transitional kindergarten through grade 12 and offers a traditional college-preparatory education. Providence Day does not use a class rank system and does not require community service as several other prominent private schools in Charlotte do. Approximately 75 percent of students participate in athletics or extracurricular activities.

SOUTHLAKE CHRISTIAN ACADEMY
13901 Hager's Ferry Rd., Huntersville
(704) 949-2200
www.southlakechristian.org
Affiliated with Southlake Presbyterian Church, this school is located on 14 acres in the growing Lake Norman area north of Charlotte. Nearly 850 students attend elementary through high school, and classes have an 14-to-1 student-teacher ratio. The school promotes rigorous academics and extracurricular activities in a nurturing environment. Accredited by the North Carolina Department of Non-Public Instruction, Southlake also is up for accreditation by the Association of Christian Schools International. Students routinely perform 40 percent higher than the national average on standardized tests. A full sports program with football, soccer, volleyball, basketball, golf, wrestling, baseball, and cheerleading is available.

Charter Schools

A growing number of parents are sending their children to charter schools, which are smaller, often parent-organized alternatives to public schools. Charter schools receive tax dollars and do not charge tuition, but are run privately by nonprofit, nonreligious groups.

In North Carolina, local school boards have no jurisdiction over charter schools. The state school board reviews every charter application before the school is formed. The state also monitors charter school performance, but does not control daily operations.

For more information on charter schools, contact the North Carolina Department of Public Instruction at (919) 807-3300 or www.dpi.state.nc.us.

These charter schools operate in the Charlotte region:

Cabarrus
Carolina International School
8810 Hickory Ridge Rd., Harrisburg
(704) 455-7247
www.carolinainternationalschool.org

Gaston
Piedmont Community Charter School
119 East Second Ave., Gastonia
(704) 853-2428
www.pccharter.org

Iredell
American Renaissance Charter School
111 Cooper St., Statesville
(704) 924-8870
www.amerren-charterschool.org

American Renaissance Middle School
217 South Center St., Statesville
(704) 878-6009
www.armsnc.org

Success Institute
1424 Rickert St., Statesville
(704) 881-1441

Lincoln
Lincoln Charter School
133 Eagles Nest Rd., Lincolnton
(704) 736-9888
www.lincolncharter.org

Mecklenburg
Community Charter School
926 Elizabeth Ave.
(704) 377-3180
www.commcharter.org

Crossroads Charter High
5500 North Tryon St.
(704) 597-5100
www.crossroadscharter.org

Lake Norman Charter School
12820 South Church St., Huntersville
(704) 948-8600
www.lncs.org

Metrolina Regional Scholars' Academy
7000 Endhaven Lane
(704) 503-1112
www.scholarsacademy.org

Queen's Grant Community School
6400 Matthews-Mint Hill Rd., Mint Hill
(704) 573-6611
www.heritageacademies.com

Sugar Creek Charter School
4101 North Tryon St.
(704) 509-5470
www.thesugarcreek.org

Union
Union Academy
3828 Old Charlotte Hwy., Monroe
(704) 283-5678
www.unionacademy.org

LIVING HERE

TRINITY EPISCOPAL SCHOOL
750 East Ninth St.
(704) 358-8101
www.tescharlotte.org
While most area students take a bus to Uptown field trips, the students who attend this private Episcopal school simply walk a few blocks to events at Spirit Square, the Public Library, and the Uptown YMCA. The K-8 school was opened in August 2000 by several Episcopal parishes and stresses a strong academic program with lessons beyond the classroom. Students are encouraged to explore their creativity, enhance critical thinking, and sharpen their curiosity and individual leadership. Afternoon care is available, with programs including band, art, cooking, gardening, and computers.

UNITED FAITH CHRISTIAN ACADEMY
8617 Providence Rd.
(704) 541-1742
www.ufca.org
A ministry of United Faith Assembly of God, this prekindergarten through grade 12 Christian school was founded in 1985. Nearly 300 students attend small classes. Students also can participate in art, music, band, chorus, and drama, as well as a full sports program with volleyball, girls' and boys' soccer and basketball, baseball, softball, coed golf and cross-country, and cheerleading. Students from more than 70 churches attend the academy.

SPECIAL PROGRAMS

CMS offers a variety of special programs for students. For complete listings and more detailed information, contact the Public Information Office at (980) 343-7450 or visit www.cms.k12.nc .us/cmsdepartments.

ADVANCED PLACEMENT (AP) COURSES
(980) 343-6955
College-level courses are offered in more than 30 subjects, from calculus to statistics, biology to physics, art history to U.S. history, and English language to Latin literature. Students earn college credit through scores on end-of-semester AP exams. CMS offers more AP courses than any independent or private school in the region, and was one of the first school systems in the country to award an AP diploma. Nearly 11,800 CMS students were enrolled in AP courses in 2006–2007.

ADVANCEMENT VIA INDIVIDUAL
DETERMINATION (AVID)
(980) 343-6955
This program targets middle school students not previously enrolled on a college-preparatory path for eligibility and success in a four-year college or university. Students are encouraged to enroll in advanced courses by high school and are made better aware of college opportunities and requirements.

AFTER SCHOOL ENRICHMENT PROGRAM
(980) 343-5567
This program provides after-school supervised care for children of working parents in kindergarten through sixth grade. After-school care is available at all elementary schools and in several middle schools. Before-school programs are also available at schools with bell times prior to 8:30 a.m.

The registration fee is $25. Weekly fees range from $46 to $56 a week for after-school care and $18 to $25 for before-school care. Programs include activities such as art and music, drama and dance, computers, homework sessions, science experiments, cooking projects, games and sports, nature, literacy, and math centers. There is also a summer enrichment day camp for eight weekly sessions at several elementary schools around the county.

BRIGHT BEGINNINGS
(980) 343-5950
This award-winning prekindergarten provides a literacy-focused curriculum to ensure all children in Mecklenburg County enter kindergarten ready to learn. The full-day program for 4-year-olds serves 3,000 children at 5 centers and 14 elementary schools, along with another 300 students at 16 community sites. End-of-grade test scores in literacy and math have shown significant benefits among Bright Beginnings students.

CMS-TV3
(980) 343-5194

CMS broadcasts a mix of news and information, original local productions, and national programs on Channel 3. Locally produced shows include Board of Education meetings; *Math Extra,* a live call-in show for students to get help from CMS math teachers; *Sportsbeat,* featuring student athletes; *Upfront!,* with Superintendent Peter Gorman; *CMS Magazine,* with news, features, and human-interest stories; and *Diversity Matters,* which explores diversity in CMS. High school students can intern at the station.

CHARLOTTE-MECKLENBURG PUBLIC SCHOOLS FOUNDATION
(980) 343-6265

With county funds tight, CMS started this independent, nonprofit organization in 2004. Nineteen of the area's top business and community leaders work to raise and manage funds to support programs that improve student achievement and enhance teaching excellence.

A CHILD'S PLACE
P.O. Box 33302, Charlotte 28233
(704) 343-3790
www.achildsplace.org

This nonprofit organization works in conjunction with Charlotte-Mecklenburg Schools to provide transitional placement for homeless children. Students receive a stable education and support services such as food, clothing, personal hygiene products, school supplies, medical and dental treatments, and mentoring from volunteers.

DOLLY TATE TEENAGE PARENT SERVICES
1817 Central Ave., Midwood Center
(704) 343-5460
www.charmeck.org

A cooperative effort of the Mecklenburg County Department of Social Services, Carolinas Medical Center, Mecklenburg County Health Department, and Charlotte-Mecklenburg Board of Education, this organization provides education and comprehensive health services to pregnant middle and high school girls. Child-care services are provided to students to enable them to complete the academic year in which their child is born.

DRIVER'S EDUCATION
(980) 343-6159

All area students in public, private, charter, or home schools are eligible for free driver education through CMS. The course includes 30 hours of classroom instruction and 6 hours behind the wheel, and is intended as a base for continued parental instruction. North Carolina uses a graduated license program. Students under 18 must complete driver education, pass 70 percent of academic courses, stay enrolled in school, and have a valid learner's permit with no violations for one year before obtaining an unrestricted driver's license.

ENGLISH AS A SECOND LANGUAGE
(980) 343-0432

This program provides intensive instruction in English to students whose native tongue is another language.

EXCEPTIONAL CHILDREN'S DEPARTMENT
700 East Stonewall St.
(980) 343-6960

This program serves special-needs children from preschool to age 21 and promotes community efforts to ensure all children enter school ready to learn. Free screenings and evaluations are available. Programs are offered for children who are autistic, hearing impaired, visually impaired, mentally disabled, multi-handicapped, orthopedically impaired, behaviorally/emotionally disabled, speech/language impaired, or who have traumatic brain injuries.

INTERNATIONAL BACCALAUREATE (IB)
(980) 343-6955

The most challenging curriculum offered in the United States, the International Baccalaureate program requires a minimum of college-level English, math, and foreign language courses. Some IB students enter college as sophomores. CMS was the first district in the state to offer IB courses, and now has approximately 1,900 students enrolled in IB programs at five high schools and four middle schools.

JUNIOR ACHIEVEMENT OF THE CENTRAL CAROLINAS
201 South Tryon St., Suite LL100
(704) 536-9668
www.jacarolinas.org
Devoted to teaching children about America's economic system and its private enterprise sector, Junior Achievement of Charlotte is the 12th largest in the nation. It involves volunteers from the business community and currently provides both private and public schools with programs that range from kindergarten through grade 12.

METRO SCHOOL
405 South Davidson St.
(980) 343-5450
This is a self-contained school for nearly 200 mentally and physically handicapped students with academics based on grade-appropriate standards following the North Carolina Extended

Content Standards' Curriculum, as well as in music, art, media skills, community-based instruction, horticulture, consumer science, prevocational and vocational skill instruction, and adapted physical education.

TALENT DEVELOPMENT AND ADVANCED STUDIES PROGRAM
(980) 343-6955
This is a state-mandated program providing advanced content, higher-level thinking, and developmental courses for those students who need academic challenges beyond those regularly found in the advanced classes. Students must meet CMS program eligibility requirements.

TUTORING SERVICES

Many tutoring services in Charlotte can help students with basic skills, advanced classes, and testing, often eliminating frustration and boosting confidence. See Tutoring in the Yellow Pages, or ask your child's teacher to recommend a tutoring service.

HIGHER EDUCATION

Whether you are interested in earning a degree or simply taking a class on computer programming or music, Charlotte's colleges and universities can accommodate you. The greater Charlotte region is home to 11 universities, 9 private liberal arts colleges, 10 public community colleges, and 7 professional schools. Ten have master's or doctoral programs. Many junior colleges, community colleges, and technical institutes offer two-year associate's degrees.

Around 150,000 students are enrolled in area universities, colleges, community colleges, and professional schools, with nearly as many attending business, industrial, and continuing education classes.

Here is an overview of the many educational opportunities that exist in the Charlotte area.

FOUR-YEAR INSTITUTIONS

BELMONT ABBEY COLLEGE
100 Belmont–Mt. Holly Rd., Belmont
(888) 222-0110
www.belmontabbeycollege.edu
Founded in 1876 by Benedictine monks, Belmont Abbey College provides an education rooted in the 1,500-year-old tradition of value-based teaching. Approximately 1,000 students from 25 states and 15 foreign countries attend "The Abbey," located 15 minutes west of Charlotte across the Gaston County line.

Numerous undergraduate and preprofessional programs prepare students for graduate school and a variety of careers. Belmont Abbey also offers Post-Baccalaureate Certificate Programs. Students ages 22 and older who are pursuing a bachelor's degree can enroll in the Adult Degree Program with weeknight, weekend, and day classes designed to work around job and family schedules.

In an area of the South known for its abundance of Presbyterians, Baptists, and other Protestant denominations, the private school is proud of its rich Roman Catholic heritage. The picturesque 650-acre Belmont campus, once used for farming and forestry, is now on the National Register of Historic Places. Highlights include the Abbey Basilica, a striking German Gothic Revival cathedral erected in 1892–1893 by the monks, and its intricately painted and heat-fused windows that resemble stained glass.

DAVIDSON COLLEGE
Davidson
(704) 892-2000
www.davidson.edu
Davidson College is a private, coeducational liberal arts college located 20 miles north of Charlotte. Founded by the Presbyterian Church in 1837, the college is intentionally small, with an enrollment of approximately 1,700 men and women, and is governed by an honor code that stresses honesty and integrity.

U.S. News & World Report consistently ranks Davidson among the Top 10 Best Liberal Arts Colleges in the nation. Admission is highly selective, and students come from 45 states and 28 countries. The school offers 20 majors, 10 minors, and 10 concentrations, with a total course offering of more than 850 classes a year. Seventy percent of Davidson students study abroad, and a high percentage compete in the school's 21 NCAA Division I sports or intramural teams. The college also has produced 23 Rhodes Scholars.

Davidson's 167 professors conduct classes with an average size of 15 to 20 students. Several faculty members have been honored with silver and gold medals by the Council for the Advancement and Support of Education; one was named national professor of the year, and three were deemed state professors of the year.

Davidson alumni are known for their community service, responsible leadership, and passion for lifelong learning. Among the college's 18,000 alumni are many doctors, attorneys, ministers, U.S. congressmen, and North Carolina governors.

The 450-acre campus includes several buildings on the National Register of Historic Places: Oak and Elm Rows were dorms for the college's original 56 young men; at the neoclassical mid-1800s Eumenean and Philanthropic Halls, students debated points of the day from facing balconies; and the 1860 Chambers Building is now a massive classroom facility with a beautiful dome and columns.

JOHNSON & WALES UNIVERSITY
801 West Trade St.
(980) 598-1000
www.johnsonandwales.edu
Johnson & Wales is Charlotte's newest member in the higher education community and a fresh presence in Uptown, with its developing campus in Third Ward's Gateway Village. The school—which also has campuses in Providence, Rhode Island; North Miami, Florida; and Denver, Colorado—is known for combining career-focused educational programs with a full university experience from athletics to Greek life.

In Charlotte the school offers associate's and bachelor's degree programs with its three colleges—Business, Culinary Arts, and Hospitality. Classes began in fall 2004 with 825 students; nearly 2,600 are currently enrolled. New residence and academic facilities, including culinary arts instruction labs, classrooms, and administrative offices, have been built, along with practicum facilities to offer hands-on training in areas from retail store management to hospitality to food service. The university has purchased the Doubletree Hotel in Uptown as a practicum site.

JOHNSON C. SMITH UNIVERSITY
100 Beatties Ford Rd.
(704) 378-1000
www.jcsu.edu

Johnson C. Smith University is a premier institution of higher learning and one of the nation's oldest historically black colleges. The private, coeducational liberal arts institution was founded in 1867 under the auspices of the Presbyterian Church. Its 100-acre inner-city campus offers 33 areas of study leading to bachelor's degrees. Admission is open to all qualified people regardless of race.

Nearly 1,500 students attend Johnson C. Smith, which has a 17-to-1 student-faculty ratio. The only historically black college to become an IBM Thinkpad University, the school distributes an IBM laptop with wireless capabilities to each student. Other programs include study abroad, service learning, and career development with a wide range of internships.

Among comprehensive colleges in the South, Johnson C. Smith has been named to the top tier of Best Colleges and the second Best Value by *U.S. News & World Report*. In 2003 the school received the *USA Today*/NCAA Academic Achievement Award. *Black Issues* magazine also credits Johnson C. Smith as one of the Top 50 Best Colleges in the country.

MONTREAT COLLEGE
5200 Seventy-seven Center Dr.
(800) 436-2777
www.montreat.edu
A private Christian college whose main campus is in a valley of the Blue Ridge Mountains, Montreat is affiliated with the Presbyterian church and dates to 1916. About 575 students attend the School of Professional and Adult Studies. The school offers associate's degrees in business and education, a bachelor's degree completion program in business administration, and an MBA. Hallmarks of the college are small classes, real-world relevance, and instructors who are academically credentialed business professionals.

PFEIFFER UNIVERSITY AT CHARLOTTE
4701 Park Rd.
(704) 521-9116
www.pfeiffer.edu
Pfeiffer's main campus of 900 students is located 45 minutes northeast of the city in Misenheimer,

but the Charlotte college in SouthPark caters to more than 1,000 nontraditional adult students pursuing undergraduate and graduate degrees.

Students can take degree-completion courses in business administration, criminal justice, health-care management, liberal arts, and information systems. These evening programs are designed to suit the schedules of working adults, making it possible for a student with a two-year degree to complete his or her bachelor's degree by attending classes two nights a week for two years. Pfeiffer also offers master's degrees in business administration, organizational change and leadership, Christian education, health administration, and elementary education, and dual MBA/MHA and MBA/MSL degrees.

QUEENS UNIVERSITY OF CHARLOTTE
1900 Selwyn Ave.
(704) 337-2200, (800) 849-0202
www.queens.edu

Queens University of Charlotte, located in historic Myers Park, is a private school with close ties to the Presbyterian Church. Since its founding in 1857, Queens has evolved into a diversified institution of higher education serving a variety of students. More than 1,700 degree-seeking men and women of all ages are enrolled in Queens' three colleges. The College of Arts and Sciences is a coed undergraduate program that emphasizes the traditional liberal arts. The Pauline Lewis Hayworth College is a program for working men and women earning undergraduate and graduate degrees through evening or Sat classes. The Graduate School offers mostly evening and Sat courses leading to a master's degree in business, education, organizational communication, teacher licensure, fine arts/creative writing, or the Executive MBA program. The Hugh McColl Jr. School of Business serves business students in all three units of the university.

Of all the elements that combine to make Queens' undergraduate program distinctive, two deserve special mention: the award-winning required core curriculum in the liberal arts, which emphasizes the interconnection of all knowledge, and the John Belk International Program, which guarantees every full-time student an opportunity for travel abroad at no extra cost. In addition, Queens offers internships, both professional and exploratory, that allow students to learn more about the world of work. Queens also provides lifelong learning opportunities through several continuing education programs.

The university enjoys unusually close ties with the Charlotte community. The Learning Society of Queens College sponsors a top-notch public speakers series. Belk Chapel at Queens is a popular place for weddings, and the Charlotte Civic Orchestra, the Charlotte Symphony Youth Orchestra, and the Charlotte Youth Oratorio Singers perform periodically in Dana Auditorium.

UNC CHARLOTTE
9201 University City Blvd.
(704) 687-2000
www.uncc.edu

Now a doctoral/research-intensive university with more than 21,000 students, UNC Charlotte was founded in 1946 as Charlotte College to serve the educational needs of returning World War II veterans. In 1961 the college moved from Uptown to 270 acres of undeveloped farmland located eight miles to the northeast on Highway 49. By 1964 the college had expanded to 910 acres and, a year later, was renamed UNC Charlotte. In 2000 UNC Charlotte was designated a doctoral research institution and today is the fourth largest of the 16 campuses within the University of North Carolina system. It has been listed in Barron's Best Buys in College Education and cited for quality and value in *U.S. News & World Report* and *Money* magazines.

The UNC Charlotte student population includes residents from throughout the United States and 80 foreign countries. Minorities represent 27 percent of the student body, which enjoys a 15-to-1 student-faculty ratio.

UNC Charlotte is composed of the College of Arts and Sciences and seven professional colleges: Architecture, Arts and Sciences, Business Administration, Education, Engineering, Health and Human Services, and Information Technology. The university's Honors College serves about

400 undergraduates in university and business honors, as well as the teaching fellow and merit scholarship programs. Programs leading to bachelor's, master's, and doctoral degrees are available.

The university's first emphasis is on teaching, followed by research and public service. Its contract research amounts to $18 million a year, and its service outreach extends into each of the 14 counties in the surrounding metropolitan region. The university is committed to serving its community through a variety of outreach programs, including the Urban Institute, Cameron Center for Applied Research, Ben Craig Center (a business incubator), Center for International Studies, Office of Continuing Education and Extension, Center for Engineering Research and Industrial Development, Charlotte Institute for Technology Innovation, and University Research Park, the sixth largest of its kind in the nation.

UNC Charlotte visitors can tour outstanding botanical gardens, including the VanLandingham Glen, a collection of hybrid and native rhododendrons and wildflowers; the Susie Harwood Gardens, with an oriental motif that features ornamental plants from around the world; and the McMillan Greenhouse, which features collections of orchids, cacti, and carnivorous plants and a simulated tropical rain forest.

The campus features modern architecture surrounded by beautifully landscaped walks and trails and includes a panoramic view of northeast Charlotte from the university's regional library, which has more than 1.5 million volumes. It also offers an outdoor sculpture garden and several art galleries and theaters.

WINGATE UNIVERSITY
315 East Wilson St., Wingate
(800)755-5550
www.wingate.edu
Founded in 1896 as an independent institution, Wingate is coeducational and offers bachelor's degrees in 40 majors and graduate degrees in business, education, and physician assistant studies. Students can also earn a Doctor of Pharmacy degree and a Doctor of Education degree, At the

school's satellite campus in Matthews, students earn undergraduate degrees in business, communication, and human services, or graduate degrees in business administration and education.

Wingate has 2,159 students with a student-to-faculty ratio of 13 to 1 and all classes are taught by professors. The school's pioneering international study/travel program has made it possible for thousands of students to travel and study abroad. Another outstanding program, the University and Community Assistance Network, has been recognized nationally for its student volunteer record.

WINTHROP UNIVERSITY
701 Oakland Ave., Rock Hill, SC
(803) 323-2211
www.winthrop.edu
Winthrop was founded in 1886 as a women's college. It became coeducational in 1974 and is now a national-caliber, comprehensive teaching university. Its 6,300 undergraduate and graduate students may choose among 82 undergraduate and 45 graduate programs of study in the arts and sciences, business administration, education, and visual and performing arts. The university also offers the New Start Program for undergraduate students age 25 and older, as well as nationally accredited Executive MBA and traditional MBA programs.

In 2004 Winthrop was named one of the South's Top 10 Public Universities by *U.S. News & World Report,* the 12th consecutive year the school received the honor. The *Princeton Review* also named Winthrop to its first Best Southeastern Colleges list.

TWO-YEAR INSTITUTIONS

CENTRAL PIEDMONT COMMUNITY COLLEGE
1201 Elizabeth Ave. at Kings Drive
(704) 330-2722
www.cpcc.edu
Central Piedmont Community College (CPCC) is an innovative and comprehensive two-year school and the largest of the state's 58 community colleges. Open to the public, CPCC is working to

become a national leader in workforce development and to strengthen the economic, social, and cultural life of the Charlotte area. CPCC provides high-quality, flexible educational programs and services at six convenient campuses across Mecklenburg County: Central Campus (Center City), North Campus (Huntersville), Northeast Campus (near UNC Charlotte), Levine Campus (Matthews), Southwest Campus (Hebron and Nations Ford Road), and West Campus (near Charlotte/Douglas International Airport). Online courses are offered through the school's Virtual Campus.

The school was founded in 1963 when Mecklenburg College and the Central Industrial Education Center merged. CPCC began with just a dozen vocational programs, some liberal arts courses, and a mere 2,000 students. Today CPCC offers thousands of courses to nearly 70,000 students annually. It has 1,000 full-time faculty and staff, and 1,500 part-time faculty and staff.

In 2001 CPCC was honored for its outstanding workforce development by the U.S. government and the Ford Foundation. More recently the school was named Community College of the Year by the National Alliance of Business.

Locally CPCC provides custom-designed, job-specific training for businesses and industries in addition to a comprehensive program for small-business owners. Training is offered at the CPCC Corporate Training Center, at other college facilities, at job sites, and online. The school offers extensive computer training, as well as technical programs that incorporate CAD/CAM workstations, robotics, and automation. Students also can apply for apprenticeships and cooperative education classes that offer practical learning.

High school students may take courses for college credit, and adults can take precollege courses such as Adult Basic Education, Adult High School, GED, and Limited English Proficiency. College students also may apply credit for CPCC classes toward a bachelor's degree at UNC Charlotte. The school offers more than 100 specialties, from business to health and community service to technology. Many other students take classes for personal enrichment, for professional advancement, or to upgrade their job skills.

An open-door institution, CPCC provides academic assessment and counseling, program advisement, and financial aid and career guidance, in addition to a variety of student clubs and organizations.

GASTON COLLEGE
201 Hwy. 321 South, Dallas
(704) 922-6200
www.gaston.edu
With two campuses in Gaston County and a third in Lincoln County, Gaston College is one of the state's larger community colleges, enrolling more than 20,000 people each year. Approximately 5,000 students enroll each quarter in curriculum programs, with another 16,000 students annually in continuing education programs. More than 90 areas of study are offered for a diploma, certificate, or associate's degree. Gaston offers day and evening courses, as well as online classes. One of the most distinctive features of the school is WSGE 91.7 FM, the college's 24-hour radio station, which plays adult alternative music, Carolina beach and shag tunes, and an eclectic mix of talk radio and special programming.

YORK TECHNICAL COLLEGE
452 South Anderson Rd., Rock Hill, SC
(803) 327-8008
www.yorktech.com
Just south of Charlotte in Rock Hill, York Technical College offers technical training in business, health, computers, and industrial and engineering technologies, in addition to associate's degrees in the arts and sciences.

MBA PROGRAMS

MONTREAT COLLEGE
520 Seventy-seven Center Dr.
(800) 436-2777
www.montreat.edu

PFEIFFER UNIVERSITY AT CHARLOTTE
4701 Park Rd.
(704) 521-9116
www.pfeiffer.edu

QUEENS UNIVERSITY OF CHARLOTTE
MCCOLL SCHOOL OF BUSINESS
1900 Selwyn Ave.
(704) 337-2224
www.mccollschool.edu

STRAYER UNIVERSITY
South Campus: 2430 Whitehall Park Dr.
(704) 587-5360

North Campus: 8335 IBM Dr.
(888) 378-7293
www.strayer.edu

UNC CHARLOTTE
BELK COLLEGE OF BUSINESS
9201 University City Blvd.
(704) 687-2165
www.belkcollege.uncc.edu

WAKE FOREST UNIVERSITY
BABCOCK GRADUATE SCHOOL OF
MANAGEMENT
6805 Morrison Blvd., Ste. 150
(704) 365-1717
www.mba.wfu.edu

WINGATE UNIVERSITY GRADUATE CENTER
110 Matthews Station St., Ste. 2A, Matthews
(704) 233-8148
www.wingate.edu

WINTHROP UNIVERSITY
701 Oakland Ave., Rock Hill, SC
(803) 323-2211
www.winthrop.edu

PROFESSIONAL SCHOOLS

ART INSTITUTE OF CHARLOTTE
Three LakePointe Plaza
2110 Water Ridge Parkway
(704) 357-8020
www.artinstitutes.edu/charlotte
Founded in 1973, this college offers training in fashion marketing, interior design, graphic design, multimedia and Web design, and culinary arts. Opportunities and benefits include small classes, internships, and financial and employment assistance. Courses of study are available days or evenings and take 18 to 21 months to complete. The college, located in west Charlotte, boasts an excellent graduation and placement rate. It is also approved for veteran's benefits and vocational rehabilitation.

BROOKSTONE COLLEGE OF BUSINESS
8307 University Executive Park Dr.
(704) 547-8600
www.brookstone.edu
This accredited business college specializes in network technology, computer software and technology, accounting, medical health, and office technology with hands-on experience. About 70 percent of the school's 200 students are employed full- or part-time. Financial aid, job placement assistance, and federal grants are available.

CAROLINAS COLLEGE OF HEALTH SCIENCES
1200 Blythe Blvd.
(704) 355-5043
www.carolinas.org/education/cchs
Part of the Carolinas HealthCare System, which operates the region's largest hospital, Carolinas Medical Center, CCHS educates health-care providers. Students are recent high school graduates, college graduates, and adults in career transition. Study areas include nursing, life support, emergency medical sciences, phlebotomy, medical tech, radiologic tech, and surgical tech.

ECPI COLLEGE OF TECHNOLOGY
4800 Airport Center Parkway
(704) 399-1010

124 Floyd Smith Dr., Concord
(704) 971-5050
www.ecpi.edu
A technical college located near the airport, ECPI offers flexible scheduling, small classes, and quick degree completion for professionals. Programs of study include business system administration, medical administration, medical assisting,

practical nursing, computer network technology, IT/Web design, and IT/networking and security management. About 475 students attend classes in Charlotte.

KING'S COLLEGE
332 Lamar Ave.
(704) 372-0266
www.kingscollegecharlotte.edu
King's College was founded in 1901, making it the oldest business college in the Carolinas. King's offers a full-time job placement service with contacts throughout the business and professional community. Courses of study include administrative assistant, accounting, computer programming, computer specialist, graphic design, legal secretary, medical-office assistant, paralegal, and travel and hospitality. Associate's degrees, diplomas, and certificates are available. Some programs offer on-the-job training.

NASCAR TECHNICAL INSTITUTE
220 Byers Creek Rd., Mooresville
(704) 658-1950
www.uticorp.com
If you want to work behind the scenes in the stock-car racing industry, the NASCAR Technical Institute is the first technical training school to combine automotive technical training with NASCAR-specific courses. What's more, its location just north of Charlotte is where more than three-fourths of Sprint Cup, Nationwide Series, and Camping World Truck Series series race teams are based. NTI opened its doors in May 2002 with a $12-million 146,000-square-foot facility on 19 acres. The trade school has more than 45 classrooms and several different hands-on labs. Students choose from 57-week or 69-week programs, which include hands-on experience in engine repair, fuel and ignition systems, chassis fabrication, transmissions, brakes, electronics, diagnostic equipment, and NASCAR technology.

STRAYER UNIVERSITY
South Campus: 9101 Kings Parade Blvd.
(704) 499-9200

North Campus: 335 IBM Dr.
(704) 717-4000

Huntersville Campus: 13620 Reese Blvd.
(704) 379-6800
www.strayer.edu
Strayer University offers higher education programs for working adults in information technology, accounting, and business. Students can earn an associate's degree, bachelor's degree, MBA, master of science, or executive graduate certificate. Originally Strayer's Business College in Baltimore, the university now has more than 50 campuses, including three in Charlotte. On-campus and online courses are available seven days a week. Strayer's is accredited by the Middle States Commission on Higher Education and in 2002 was approved by the University of North Carolina Board of Governors to offer classes in Charlotte and Raleigh.

HEALTH CARE

Charlotte's hospitals offer the latest in medical techniques as well as some of the most qualified specialists. With health-care costs slightly below the national average, medical services are another financial positive of life in the Charlotte area.

Medical facilities are expanding at a rapid rate throughout the city and region, so wherever you live in the area, you probably won't have to drive far to find the services you need. The city is nationally and internationally known as a center for cardiac care and research. Hospitals in two systems, the Carolinas HealthCare System and Presbyterian Healthcare, regularly perform open-heart surgery, as well as other highly specialized medical services. Both hospitals are also known for their cancer centers.

Most Charlotteans find the medical care they need in their own backyard; those who need more specialized procedures are generally less than 45 minutes away. Over the past decade, hospitals have expanded with surgery centers, medical complexes, and new general hospital facilities in the growing suburbs in south and north Mecklenburg County. Carolinas HealthCare System is now the largest employer in Charlotte with 31,000 employees, while Presbyterian Healthcare is fifth largest with 13,323.

Meanwhile, regional hospitals in surrounding counties are also adding more beds, treatment areas, and advanced equipment to meet the rising demand.

Charlotte health-care facilities are listed in this chapter alphabetically by type of service offered. Listings are in Charlotte unless otherwise noted.

HOSPITALS

General Hospitals

CAROLINAS MEDICAL CENTER
1000 Blythe Blvd.
(704) 355-2000
www.carolinashealthcare.org
Carolinas Medical Center (CMC), which opened in 1940, is the flagship facility of the Carolinas HealthCare System. This system operates Charlotte-area hospitals in Elizabeth, Pineville, University, Union County, and Lincoln County, plus elsewhere in the Carolinas. With 874 beds, the medical center is the second-largest hospital in North Carolina. In addition, CMC treats a significant number of patients from South Carolina and all over the southeastern United States.

The medical center has eight specialized intensive care units, serves as a regional referral center for high-risk pregnancies, and operates the area's only hospital-based air ambulance service with helicopters and fixed-wing aircraft.

A Level I trauma center and one of only five academic medical-center teaching hospitals in North Carolina, Carolinas Medical Center offers 11 medical and dental residency programs. The hospital also is an off-campus teaching facility for the University of North Carolina School of Medicine.

The Carolinas Heart Institute is the major center for heart transplantation in the Carolinas, performing more than 15,500 cardiac surgeries and catheterizations per year. CMC also offers liver, pancreas, and kidney transplants.

The 20,000-square-foot Blumenthal Cancer Center has been designated as a Teaching Hospital Cancer Program, the second-highest designation available from the American College of Surgeons' Commission on Cancer. There are more than 100 cancer specialists involved in patient care. Unique services include Novalis Shaped Beam technology, allowing precise radiation treatment of tumors without harm to surrounding tissue, and the use of PET technology to diagnose tumors and follow the progress of treatment.

Other centers within CMC include the Carolinas Neuroscience and Spine Institute with its Neuromuscular ALS Center, the MS Center, the Women's Institute, the Orthopaedics Institute, and the James G. Cannon Research Center.

The Charlotte Institute of Rehabilitation, Behavioral Health Center, Carolinas College of Heath Sciences, medical complexes, primary and specialty physician practices, and extended care facilities also fall under the CMC umbrella.

CAROLINAS MEDICAL CENTER–MERCY
2001 Vail Ave.
(704) 304-5000
www.carolinashealthcare.org
Established in 1906 by the Sisters of Mercy as the first Catholic hospital in North Carolina, CMC–Mercy (formerly Mercy Hospital) moved under the Carolinas HealthCare System umbrella in 1995. The 185-bed hospital is located in the heart of the Elizabeth district, not far from the main Carolinas Medical Center in Myers Park.

CMC–Mercy is an adult acute care facility, best known for its specialty services and personal approach to patient care. Mercy's specialized departments include the Lung Center for patients suffering from pulmonary disease; Southeast Pain Center, with more than 100 years of combined experience in relieving chronic pain; and the Heart Center, with complete cardiac services including stress tests, echocardiograms, exercise echocardiograms, bypass, angioplasty, valve replacement, and implants of pacemakers and cardiac defibrillators.

Mercy's Behavioral Health Center's Horizons program is a short-stay inpatient medical detoxification program for alcohol- and drug-dependent adults. CMC– Mercy also has a dialysis unit, home health-care unit, and nursing school.

CAROLINAS MEDICAL CENTER–PINEVILLE
10628 Park Rd., Highway 51 and Park Road Extension
(704) 667-1000
www.carolinashealthcare.org
Formerly known as Mercy Hospital South, CMC–Pineville opened in 1987 and today is the hub of a growing medical community in south Charlotte. The full-service hospital has 109 beds and is in the midst of a $174-million expansion project that will add 285,000 new square feet and approximately 100 beds by 2013. These enhancements will transform CMC-Pineville into a leading tertiary care center, building on a comprehensive selection of services that includes an open heart surgery program, comprehensive surgical services, and one of the community's busiest obstetrical units.

Also available are a 24-hour emergency department; three intensive care units for premature newborns, adult, and those who need specialized cardiac care; a sleep center; a diagnostic center; cardiopulmonary services; and physical therapy. The maternity center was the first in the area to offer homelike labor/delivery/recovery suites. Today the center has expanded to 22 suites with whirlpool tubs, a Web nursery, and the neonatal ICU. The hospital's imaging center has state-of-the-art equipment. CMC–Pineville has won national Top Performer awards for patient satisfaction in quality of care.

CAROLINAS MEDICAL CENTER–UNIVERSITY
8800 North Tryon St.
(704) 863-6000
www.carolinashealthcare.org
CMC–University opened in 1985 to serve the rapidly growing region of northeast Mecklenburg County and northwest Cabarrus County. The 130 private rooms are configured in the "snowflake" design, with every patient just a few feet from a nurses' station yet isolated from much of the traffic in the traditional corridor arrangement.

The hospital offers a wide range of health-care services, and its sleep services program was the first in the Charlotte area to be fully accredited by the American Sleep Disorders Association.

A major expansion of the Maternity Center, emergency department, and outpatient services has bolstered the hospital's offerings. The Maternity Center works with more than 2,000 families each year, providing personalized support and education throughout the pregnancy, delivery, and recovery. There are special perinatal and neonatal services for high-risk pregnancies and deliveries, and the Level III Neonatal Nursery is prepared for newborns needing extra care.

There is also an intensive coronary care unit, a telemetry unit for patients requiring closer supervision, and a surgery department with operating rooms and space dedicated to cystoscopy and urological procedures. The emergency department, Charlotte's second-busiest, averages nearly 70,000 patient visits per year. It is staffed 24 hours a day and is equipped to handle minor and life-threatening emergencies. CMC–University features a fixed MRI and a cardiac catheterization facility. It also offers diagnostic radiology and mammography services along with a respiratory diagnostic center and full-service laboratory for inpatients and outpatients.

Adjoining the hospital is University Medical Park, a growing home for physician groups and satellite offices.

LEVINE CHILDREN'S HOSPITAL
1000 Blythe Blvd.
(704) 381-2000
www.levinechildrenshospital.org
The newest addition to the CMC system, the Levine Children's Hospital opened in late 2007 on the campus of Carolinas Medical Center. The 240,000-square-foot facility is the largest children's hospital between Washington, D.C., and Atlanta. The hospital features 234 beds and was built at a cost of $85 million.

The hospital offers more than 30 specialized pediatric services including kidney, liver, and heart transplants; blood and marrow transplant; cardiac and cancer care; neurosurgery; rehabilitation service; and the highest designated level of neonatal intensive care.

The hospital caters to the needs of families. There are hotel-like rooms, complete with showers, for parents to stay overnight, as well as resource centers and family lounges throughout the facility. There's a playroom on every floor, a rooftop terrace, and a teen room for occupying brothers and sisters of patients.

PRESBYTERIAN HOSPITAL
200 Hawthorne Lane
(704) 3844000
www.presbyterian.org
Established in 1903, Presbyterian is a 581-bed regional referral, tertiary care medical center serving Charlotte-Mecklenburg and surrounding counties. It is the flagship hospital for Presbyterian Healthcare, an integrated health-care system with four hospitals, outpatient facilities, more than 90 primary care physicians, some 200 specialists, and more than 1,200 physicians with admitting privileges.

Presbyterian Hospital, located just east of Uptown, offers a wide range of specialized diagnostic and therapeutic services. The Cardiovascular Institute offers advanced care, including an accredited chest pain center, heart catheterization services, open-heart surgery, and a Stroke Center. Presbyterian Cancer Center, the first in North Carolina designated as a Community Hospital Comprehensive Cancer Center, treats more cancer patients than any other center in the region. Presbyterian Orthopaedic Hospital is the region's premiere hospital for orthopedic care and has received national recognition for its outstanding work. Presbyterian also participates in national clinical research trials in cardiology, cancer, and orthopaedics, which offer patients the latest in treatment options in these areas.

A new Women's Center opened in late 2004 to serve the medical needs of women and newborns. The center includes 16 new birthing suites, 35 postpartum suites, and 14 high-risk antepartum suites. There also is a Level III neonatal intensive care nursery for critically ill or premature newborns. Other services include lactation consultants, osteoporosis programs, and general education programs on women's health topics.

Presbyterian Hemby Children's Hospital, which opened in 1993, is dedicated to family-centered care and meeting all the needs of children from the time they are admitted to the time they go home. Full-time pediatric physicians provide additional care in the pediatric intensive care unit.

The hospital also offers a full range of in-home services, including adult home care, hospice, and the Lifeline personal emergency response system.

PRESBYTERIAN HOSPITAL HUNTERSVILLE
10030 Gilead Rd., Huntersville
(704) 316-4000
www.presbyterian.org
Presbyterian Hospital Huntersville opened in November 2004 at exit 23 off I-77. Huntersville is a boomtown of about 40,000 residents north of the city near Lake Norman. The town's original hospital was converted to a nursing home more than two decades ago.

The 50-bed hospital offers a wide range of medical services, including emergency, maternity, critical care, surgery, and endoscopy. Attached to the hospital is a medical complex housing outpatient services and doctors' offices.

Presbyterian Hospital Huntersville serves the communities of Huntersville, Cornelius, Davidson, and Mooresville and other areas of northern Mecklenburg and southern Iredell Counties.

i Many hospitals now offer Web nurseries in their maternity centers. New parents are issued a 10-digit security code to give to faraway family and friends who can log on to the Internet to see pictures of the newborn babies.

PRESBYTERIAN HOSPITAL MATTHEWS
1500 Matthews Township Parkway Matthews
(704) 384-6500
www.presbyterian.org
Presbyterian Hospital Matthews was designed to be both efficient and user-friendly for patients, their families, and visitors. Located in Matthews, this 102-bed hospital offers a full range of diagnostic and treatment services, including emergency, surgery (inpatient and outpatient), and maternity.

All but the most specialized kinds of surgery are performed at Presbyterian Hospital Matthews.

Features include large maternity rooms with Jacuzzi tubs, TVs, DVD players, refrigerators, and daybeds for dads to spend the night. All rooms in the hospital have similar features, including a daybed. With physician approval, even the critical care rooms encourage overnight visitors.

The 24-hour emergency department has separate entrances for drive-in and ambulance patients. The hospital's emergency department also houses a Chest Pain Center for early diagnosis and treatment of heart attack patients.

Meals at the hospital are delivered to each patient at the time he or she specifies. The two inpatient wings each have a family medical resource center and a large family kitchen.

The hospital, which is part of Presbyterian Healthcare, serves the Matthews–Mint Hill–Pineville and Ballantyne communities, as well as other areas of southern and eastern Mecklenburg and western Union Counties.

Regional Hospitals

Residents of counties surrounding Mecklenburg often find quality health care and major medical services at regional hospitals in their own areas. Gaston, Lincoln, Iredell, Cabarrus, York, and Union Counties all have their own hospitals.

CAROLINAS MEDICAL CENTER—LINCOLN
200 Gamble Dr., Lincolnton
(704) 735-3071
www.lincolnmedical.org
Lincoln Medical Center, part of the Carolinas HealthCare System network, is the primary inpatient health-care provider in Lincoln County with 101 beds, more than 70 physicians, and 170 nurses. Opened in 1969, the hospital has four operating rooms, an emergency department that serves more than 28,000 people annually, a sleep center, the Chronic Pain Management Program, and an obstetrics/birthing center that delivers more than 500 babies a year. Lincoln Medical also offers extensive cardiopulmonary services such as stress tests and EKGs, and radiology services including CT scans, ultrasound, and mobile MRI.

CAROLINAS MEDICAL CENTER—NORTHEAST
920 Church St. North, Concord
(704) 403-3000
www.northeastmedical.org
A comprehensive medical center for folks in Concord and the surrounding region, NorthEast has 457 beds. Billed as "miles ahead, not miles away," the hospital offers trauma and emergency care; comprehensive cardiology services; private labor, delivery, and recovery rooms in the Hayes Family Center; the only accredited community cancer center in north Charlotte; a surgery center; and a pediatric ICU. In 2003 a new outpatient surgery and imaging center was completed. Health-Grades, a health-care information company, rated the Cannon Heart Center as having the best overall cardiology care in Charlotte, Hickory, Concord, and Gastonia. The maternity center also earned the group's top five-star rating.

CAROLINAS MEDICAL CENTER—UNION
600 Hospital Dr., Monroe
(704) 283-3100
www.unionregional.org
Union County, southeast of Charlotte, is one of the fastest-growing counties in the state. This 223-bed facility is meeting the growth demand with a $47-million expansion that has brought advanced equipment, more outpatient services, and a chance to treat local patients in their own backyard. In April 2002 the hospital unveiled a new observation unit and chest pain center to reduce hospital time and make room for patients with more serious ailments. The hospital's 64,000-square-foot outpatient and cancer care center, unveiled in late 2002, is both functional and aesthetically pleasing.

GASTON MEMORIAL HOSPITAL
2525 Court Dr., Gastonia
(704) 333-9033
www.GastonHealthCare.org
Twenty-five minutes to the west in Gaston County, Gaston Memorial Hospital operates 435 beds in private rooms. Other services include the Comprehensive Cancer Center, Radiation Oncology Center, Cardiac Rehabilitation Center, and Caro-Mont Heart Center. Recent expansions have doubled the size of the emergency department and added more space for surgery, radiology, laboratories, and support services. The Birthplace, which opened in fall 2004, includes 52 labor/delivery/recovery suites, each with a full-size sofa bed, refrigerator, Internet access, TV, VCR, DVD and CD players, and whirlpool bath. Reflecting pools, flowing water, art, and sculptures create a soothing environment. Parents' families appreciate the media room, dining room, and kids' play room. Gaston Memorial also has a neonatal ICU and electronic security in its nursery.

LAKE NORMAN REGIONAL MEDICAL CENTER
171 Fairview Rd., Mooresville
(704) 660-4000
www.lnrmc.com
North of Charlotte in Iredell County, Lake Norman Regional Medical Center has 117 beds and a medical campus offering complete health-care services. Opened in June 1999, the $41-million hospital complex features a fully equipped emergency room, the Stork's Landing Maternity Center with homelike suites, and the state-of-the-art Diagnostic Imaging Center with advanced radiological services. Other services include cancer care; outpatient surgery; cardiopulmonary and sleep labs; home health care; neurosurgery; orthopedic and spine services; pediatric care; a joint replacement center; gastroenterology; a rehabilitation center; and physical, occupational, and speech therapy.

PIEDMONT MEDICAL CENTER
222 South Herlong Ave., Rock Hill, SC
(803) 327-4664
www.PiedmontMedicalCenter.com
Piedmont Medical, part of the national Tenet Healthcare Corp., is the primary general hospital for York, Chester, and Lancaster Counties just across the South Carolina line from Charlotte. The 288-bed hospital offers 24-hour emergency care; critical, cardiac, and cancer care; a sleep disorders center; pediatric, surgery, and rehabilitation services; extensive imaging and diagnostics; and a digestive disease center. The hospital

has a PET scanner to pinpoint and treat cancer more accurately, and women undergoing cancer treatment can receive appearance enhancement help with free wigs, scarves, and turbans. The $34-million, four-story Women's Center features private rooms, Jacuzzi suites, sleeping sofas, and Internet access. The 95,000-square-foot center also includes the Community Health Education and Resource Center. Patients at Piedmont Medical Center can set up secure Web pages to keep friends and family posted.

Specialty Hospitals and Centers

In addition to major hospitals located throughout the region, Charlotte has a number of specialty medical centers focusing on chemical dependency, mental illness, traumatic injuries, orthopedics, occupational therapy, and issues affecting older adults.

CAROLINAS HEALTHCARE SYSTEM
BEHAVIORAL HEALTH CENTERS
24-hour information and assistance
(704) 444-2400
www.carolinashealthcare.org

CHARLOTTE INSTITUTE OF REHABILITATION
1100 Blythe Blvd.
(704) 355-4300
www.carolinasrehabilitation.org

MCLEOD ADDICTIVE DISEASE CENTER
145 Remount Rd.
(704) 332-9001
www.mcleodcenter.com

MERCY REHABILITATION CENTER
2001 Vail Ave.
(704) 304-5248
www.carolinashealthcare.org

PRESBYTERIAN HEMBY
CHILDREN'S HOSPITAL
200 Hawthorne Lane
(704) 384-4021
www.presbyterian.org

PRESBYTERIAN ORTHOPAEDIC HOSPITAL
1901 Randolph Rd.
(704) 316-2000
www.presbyterian.org

THE REHAB CENTER
2610 East Seventh St.
(704) 375-8900
www.TheRehabCenter.com

MEDICAL CARE

A variety of physicians and specialists are located throughout Charlotte. And, as the city has grown, so has its community. Doctors' offices and clinics are no longer clustered near hospitals, and they now offer satellite offices and new clinics throughout the Charlotte area. So unless you're looking for someone in an extremely specialized field, you will probably find a doctor you like located near your home or office.

If you are visiting or if you need medical help and haven't found a physician, there are numerous urgent-care centers around town providing minor medical emergency services and walk-in health care. You don't need an appointment, and most have extended hours.

As with anything else, word-of-mouth is usually a good way to find a physician. Your neighbors, friends, and coworkers can give you advice on the doctor's personality, how well the staff treats its patients, and/or how long you can expect to wait. Charlotte also has formal services that can refer you to physicians and other healthcare professionals. These referral services can be a great help if you are new to the area.

Referral Services

MECKLENBURG COUNTY MEDICAL SOCIETY
1112 Harding Place, Ste. 200
(704) 376-3688
www.meckmed.org
This is a nonprofit society of about 1,400 physicians in the Charlotte region. It provides physician referrals for family practitioners, internists, and specialists by phone, 9 a.m. to 1 p.m. Mon through Fri, or anytime via the Web site. It will usually give you three names.

PRESBYTERIAN CARE CONNECTION
(704) 384-4111
This community service, available 24/7, gives physician referrals not only by specialty, but also by geographic location and type of insurance accepted. Care Connection also has information on various hospital programs. For maternity information, call (704) 384-4949.

PRESBYTERIAN WOMEN'S HEALTHLINE
(704) 384-4966
A free service of Presbyterian Healthcare, this resource line offers information on women's services at Presbyterian Healthcare, support group and class information, and answers to general health questions.

UNITED WAY 211 HOTLINE
Mecklenburg County, (704) 377-1100
Cabarrus County, (704) 788-1156
Union County, (704) 283-1537
211 from home phone
www.uwcentralcarolinas.org
A United Way service, this call line is open from 8 a.m. until midnight seven days a week and is staffed by referral specialists who can answer questions or provide referrals on anything regarding human services in Mecklenburg, Cabarrus, or Union Counties.

SPECIAL SERVICES AND PROGRAMS

The Charlotte area also has several facilities and agencies focusing on special assistance for physical, emotional, or mental disabilities. Here are a few:

ALEXANDER CHILDREN'S CENTER
6220 Thermal Rd.
(704) 366-8712
www.alexanderyouthnetwork.org
This is a nonprofit agency offering intensive treatment for emotionally troubled children, stable home environments for graduates of the treatment center, emergency care for abused or neglected children, after-school care, day programs, and summer camps.

i Need help choosing a physician or specialist? The North Carolina Medical Board (800-253-9653, www.ncmedboard.org) and the South Carolina Board of Medical Examiners (803-896-4500, www.llr.state.sc.us/pol.asp) provide information on licensed medical doctors and physician assistants, including education background and disciplinary actions. The North Carolina State Board of Dental Examiners (919-678-8223, www.ncdentalboard.org) offers similar information on dentists.

BELK UNITED CEREBRAL PALSY DEVELOPMENTAL CENTER
716 Marsh Rd.
(704) 522-9912
A branch of United Cerebral Palsy of North Carolina, this center provides education and therapy for children ages one through five with cerebral palsy or similar disorders, as well as training for parents in Mecklenburg and surrounding counties. Tuition is based on a sliding-fee scale.

CATHOLIC SOCIAL SERVICES
1123 South Church St.
(704) 370-3228
www.cssnc.org
This organization offers many services, including individual, family, adoption, marital, and substance abuse counseling, and pregnancy support. Fees are based on a sliding scale.

CHARLOTTE SPEECH AND HEARING CENTER
210 East Woodlawn Rd., Ste. 150
(704) 523-8027
www.charlottespeechhearing.com
This nonprofit center offers screening, evaluation, consultation, education, and therapy to anyone with a speech, language, or hearing problem. Free and sliding-fee-scale programs.

CHILD AND FAMILY DEVELOPMENT, INC.
4012 Park Rd., Ste. 200
(704) 332-4834

10508 Park Rd., Ste. 130
(704) 541-9080
www.childandfamilydevelopment.com

This is a private evaluation/treatment clinic for children from birth through high school. Professional therapists specialize in ADHD, learning disabilities, cerebral palsy, motor disabilities, speech and language disorders, and emotional/social difficulties.

COMMUNITY HEALTH SERVICES
601 East Fifth St., Ste. 140
(704) 375-0172
www.chs-nc.org
This multi-service United Way agency offers affordable—sometimes free—health screenings and educational programs in five areas: diabetes services, occupational health, senior health services, Parkinson's disease support groups, and children's medicine. Immunizations and flu vaccines are also available.

FLETCHER SCHOOL
8500 Sardis Rd.
(704) 365-4658
www.thefletcherschool.org
This special school for learning-disabled children and children with attention deficit disorders provides a structured, individualized academic program that prepares them to return to the regular classroom environment whenever possible.

HOLY ANGELS
6600 Wilkinson Blvd., Belmont
(704) 825-4161
www.holyangelsnc.org
A ministry of the Sisters of Mercy of North Carolina, this nonprofit facility 20 minutes away in Belmont is a full-time residence for 70 children and adults with multiple and severe mental disabilities. Other services include education; nursing; physical therapy; and vocational, horticulture, and arts programs. Many residents work nearby at Holy Angels' small business, Cherubs Cafe & Candy Bouquets, in downtown Belmont.

HOSPICE & PALLIATIVE CARE CHARLOTTE REGION
1420 East Seventh St.
(704) 375-0100
www.hospiceatcharlotte.org

A dedicated team of professionals and volunteers provides health care to terminally ill patients and support to the patient's family during the course of the illness. Care includes medical direction, nursing, social services, volunteer support, in-home aides, bereavement support, spiritual care, and art therapy. There are multiple offices throughout the region.

> **i** By the end of 2010, Charlotte will no longer be the largest city in the nation without a Ronald McDonald House. Construction began in the first quarter of 2010 on a 28-room Ronald McDonald House on East Morehead Street. The facility will provide a place to stay for families of children being treated in Charlotte for life-threatening illnesses. The location will be convenient to both major hospitals, as well as the new Levine's Children Hospital. Ray Evernham, a former NASCAR team owner, donated a quarter million dollars in early 2010 to ensure the project would remain on schedule.

LIFESPAN
200 Clanton Rd.
(704) 944-5100
www.lifespanservices.org
Established in 1973, this center offers programs to Mecklenburg County residents with severe or profound mental disabilities or who are at high risk for a severe disability. Services include preschool, special education, and summer school programs for children; and sheltered workshops, developmental activities, and supported employment for adults. In 1993 the Circle School was developed to assist in mainstreaming special-needs children with other children.

MCLEOD ADDICTIVE DISEASE CENTER
145 Remount Rd.
(704) 332-9001
www.mcleodcenter.com
This community agency provides counseling and support groups for chemically dependent young people and adults and their families.

MECKLENBURG COUNTY
HEALTH DEPARTMENT
2845 Beatties Ford Rd.
(704) 336-4700

249 Billingsley Rd.
(704) 336-6400 main office
www.charmeck.org
The health department provides health education; maternity, family planning, and well-child clinics; home and school health services; employee health and safety programs; nursing services for new mothers and their infants; environmental services; and communicable and chronic disease control.

NEVINS CENTER, INC.
3523 Nevin Rd.
(704) 596-1372
www.nevinsinc.org
This Adult Developmental Activity Program provides vocational training, supported employment, and training in a sheltered workshop for developmentally disabled adults.

THE RELATIVES CRISIS SHELTER
1100 East Blvd.
(704) 377-0602
www.therelatives.org
This family-oriented crisis-mediation center provides emergency shelter (1 to 14 days) with round-the-clock admittance for young people ages 7 to 17. Free and confidential services include individual and family mediation, community referral, follow-up, and 24-hour assistance by hotline or walk-in visit. Services are available to both parents and children.

THOMPSON CHILD & FAMILY FOCUS
2200 East Seventh St.
(704) 376-7180

1645 Clanton Rd.
(704) 333-5382

6800 Saint Peter's Lane, Matthews
(704) 536-0375
www.thompsoncff.org
What began as an Episcopal Orphanage in 1886 has evolved into a multifaceted agency that assists at-risk children and families through healing, teaching, worship, and play. Thompson merged with The Family Center in 2008 to provide a higher level of service.

UNITED FAMILY SERVICES
601 East Fifth St., Ste. 400
(704) 332-9034
www.unitedfamilyservices.org
A United Way agency, United Family Services offers counseling and education, crisis intervention, domestic violence services, and economic independence assistance. Family counseling is available. Fees vary and are based on a sliding scale; however, no one is turned down because of an inability to pay. The Big Brothers/Big Sisters division (704-377-3963) provides adult friendship and guidance to children ages 7 to 15 living in single-parent families in the Mecklenburg County area.

RETIREMENT

Charlotte, along with the rest of the United States, is experiencing a "boom" in the senior population and has become a popular retirement destination during the past decade. As part of the Sunbelt, Charlotte steadily attracts older citizens tired of rigorous winters. Parents are also following their children and retiring within visiting distance of grandchildren.

Older newcomers settle in Charlotte for the same reasons as younger people: good climate, vibrant cultural life, safe neighborhoods, excellent medical care, and an international airport. As the senior population has grown, so have the number and level of services provided.

There has been a substantial increase in retirement communities in Charlotte and Mecklenburg County offering residents independent living, assisted living, and nursing care. These continuing-care communities are ideal because the level of care adapts to the needs of the resident.

In independent-care communities, active seniors give up the hassle of taking care of a big house for the convenience and activities of a retirement community. Residents live in single detached homes, patio homes, condominiums, or apartments. When needed, residents move into assisted living or the higher-need nursing-care division. Some communities require seniors to enter as independent-living residents first.

Assisted-living communities provide help with the activities of daily living, such as preparing food, taking daily medications, local transportation, and housekeeping. Residents typically live in their own room or share one. Meals are taken in a community dining room, and residents often go on planned excursions to shop, visit tourist sites, or go out for ice cream. These communities allow seniors to stay in their home as long as possible, then move to assisted living when needed.

Nursing-care communities offer full-time, around-the-clock, long-term health care. While many nursing-care tenants can do things for themselves, they often need assistance, either medically or physically. Such care is for those who are too ill or impaired to be ambulatory but do not need hospitalization.

Other seniors choose home health-care providers who can act as a companion, assist with daily living needs, or administer medications.

RETIREMENT COMMUNITIES

Here is a sampling of a few of Charlotte's better-known retirement communities.

ALDERSGATE
3800 Shamrock Dr.
(704) 532-7000
www.aldersgateccrc.com
A United Methodist retirement community formerly known as the Methodist Home, Aldersgate is located on a 232-acre campus in northeast Charlotte. Two facilities provide quality retirement living and top-rated health care. Epworth Place has new cottages and apartments for active older adults with assisted-living service available. Asbury Care Center offers assisted-living facilities and an award-winning memory support service for seniors with Alzheimer's and dementia. Amenities include 24-hour security, fine dining, weekly housekeeping, diverse social opportunities, and on-campus health-care services.

ATRIA MERRYWOOD
3600 Park Rd.
(704) 523-4949
www.atriaseniorliving.com
This beautiful wooded site blends well with the history and Southern charm of the Park Road and Dilworth neighborhoods that surround it. Close to shopping, next door to the YWCA, and just minutes away from Uptown and hospitals, Merrywood is a 174-unit rental apartment community offering active independent living, personal care, and assisted living for senior adults. Studio and one- and two-bedroom balcony apartments are available. Amenities include a washer/dryer, walk-in closets, an elegant dining room, a private dining room for special occasions, a barber/beauty shop, a library, and a card room.

CARMEL HILLS RETIREMENT COMMUNITY
2801 Carmel Rd.
(704) 364-8302
www.carmelhills.org
This 94-unit continuing-care retirement community with a Christian focus provides one daily meal, biweekly housekeeping, linen service, security, laundry, recreation, and transportation. A private one-acre lake is part of the grounds.

> **i** The Centralina Area Agency on Aging has information on services and activities in Mecklenburg and eight surrounding counties at (704) 372-2416 or www.centralina.org. SupportWorks can share information on support groups and agencies in the area at (704) 331-9500 or www.supportworks.org. For information and Web site links on a wide variety of senior-related issues, visit www.seniorlivinghelp.com.

CARMEL PLACE RETIREMENT COMMUNITY
5512 Carmel Rd.
(704) 930-0760
www.carmelplace.net
A rental independent-living community, CarMel Place offers a nice south Charlotte location with a terrific amenities package, including housekeeping services, three meals daily, a barber and beauty salon, 24-hour security, transportation, planned activities, a big-screen TV lounge, library, billiard room, exercise room, and craft room. Studio, one-bedroom, and two-bedroom apartments with full kitchen are available. Linens and all utilities except phone service are included.

CARRIAGE CLUB OF CHARLOTTE
5700 Old Providence Rd.
(704) 366-4960, (877) 225-2831
www.BrookdaleLiving.com
Located on 44 acres in prestigious south Charlotte, the Carriage Club is a top-notch rental retirement community with independent living and higher levels of care, if needed. It offers apartments and villas and a variety of amenities, including a pool, exercise room, washer/dryer units in all apartments, housekeeping, and meals. Transportation is provided to medical appointments and worship services, as well as a wide range of social activities. Divided into separate centers, the Carriage Club offers 274 independent-living units, the Coach House offers 54 personalized assisted-living units, and the Carriage House provides 42 skilled nursing-care units. Carriage Club also has Alzheimer's and dementia care, and skilled nursing care options for seniors.

THE COTTAGES AT CAROLINA PLACE
9916 Bishops Gate Blvd., Pineville
(704) 544-8889
www.thecottagescharlotte.com
Choose from several floor plans in this community of senior-owned patio homes near Carolina Place Mall in south Charlotte. Amenities include two-car garages; maintenance-free lawns; gated entry; security cameras; on-call handyman, a clubhouse with pool, fitness center, and putting green; walking trails; and on-campus staff at all times. Meals and activities are available next door at the Dorchester, a retiree apartment community. The Manor condominium homes were added in 2007.

The Charlotte-Mecklenburg Senior Games holds an annual competition in a variety of sports and other activities. For details on how you can participate as an athlete or a volunteer at the games, call (704) 332-4020 or visit www.charmeck.org.

COVENANT VILLAGE
1351 Robinwood Rd., Gastonia
(704) 867-2319
Located in neighboring Gastonia, Covenant Village offers apartments and cottages for independent and assisted living, as well as a nursing-care center. Amenities at the upscale retirement community include three daily meals, linen service, a fitness center, weekly housekeeping, transportation, security, recreation, and private dining rooms. A library, bank, craft center, and store are located on the grounds.

THE CYPRESS OF CHARLOTTE
3442 Cypress Club Dr.
(704) 714-5500, (800) 643-1665
www.thecypress.com
Built in 1999, the Cypress is one of Charlotte's most upscale retirement communities. The Cypress includes villas and individual cottages for independent living, an elegant 40,000-square-foot clubhouse, and an on-site health center providing assisted living and Alzheimer's and skilled nursing care. Members may purchase homes from 17 different floor plans from 800 to 3,100 square feet. Garages and covered parking are available. The Cypress clubhouse features lakefront fine dining, casual dining on the veranda, an indoor pool with water aerobics classes, fitness center, library, art studio, bank, and hair salon. Other amenities on the 60-acre grounds include home-delivered meals, housekeeping, home maintenance, transportation, security, and valet service. Located in SouthPark, the Cypress was named the Best Seniors Housing Community in the United States by the National Association of Homebuilders.

There is generally a waiting list to get into the Cypress.

HUNTERSVILLE OAKS
13001 Old Statesville Rd., Huntersville
(704) 875-7400
The largest long-term care facility affiliated with Carolinas HealthCare System, Huntersville Oaks has 417 beds in a country setting near Lake Norman. Skilled nursing is available during rehabilitation or long-term care. Twenty-four-hour professional nursing supervision and physician coverage, 24-hour security, and dental, ophthalmological, psychiatric, and pharmacy services are provided, along with a wide range of group activities.

LAWYERS GLEN RETIREMENT LIVING CENTER
10830 Lawyers Glen Dr.
(704) 545-9555
www.lawyersglen.com
Opened in early 1997, this locally owned retirement center provides assisted-living units overlooking Rebecca Lake on the outskirts of Charlotte. Residents can design their own healthcare plan, with options for assistance with bathing, dressing, medications, and getting to and from the dining room. Activities include tours, bridge clubs, porch parties, fitness classes, gardening, and arts and crafts.

MORNINGSIDE ASSISTED LIVING
500 Penny Lane Northeast, Concord
(704) 795-1200

2755 Union Rd., Gastonia
(704) 810-0111
www.morningsideassistedliving.com
Part of the Five Star Quality Care chain operating in 27 states, these assisted-living communities also include wings for patients with Alzheimer's and other memory-loss diseases. Weekly housekeeping, laundry and linen service, inviting common areas, gardens, sunrooms, and wellness programs make Morningside an upscale choice.

THE PINES AT DAVIDSON
400 Avinger Lane, Davidson
(704) 896-1100
www.thepinesatdavidson.org

This nonprofit retirement community offers detached cottages and apartments for independent living, assisted-living apartments, and nursing-care rooms in a quaint college community at Lake Norman. Amenities include a central and private dining room, game room, billiards, laundry facilities, library, chapel, beauty parlor and barber shop, resident storage, a bank branch, a post office, and a wellness clinic with an exercise room, whirlpool, and warm therapy pool. Residents are close to Davidson College, allowing them to audit classes and attend a multitude of cultural events. Residents also receive membership at nearby River Run Country Club.

THE PLACE AT SOUTHPARK
2101 Runnymede Lane
(704) 525-5508

Amenities at this upscale assisted-living community include licensed staff 24 hours a day, transportation to medical appointments, short-term respite care, and a program for memory-impaired residents called Life Connections.

PLANTATION ESTATES
733 Plantation Estates, Matthews
(704) 847-4800
www.acts-retirement.org

If you enjoy fine dining and super recreational facilities, check out the spacious Colonial Williamsburg–style apartment homes here. Plantation Estates offers its residents all levels of care from independent living to nursing care, with a special unit for Alzheimer's and dementia patients. Residents enjoy an indoor pool, arts and crafts, cards, fishing, gardening, and guest apartments.

SHARON TOWERS
The Presbyterian Home at Charlotte
5100 Sharon Rd.
(704) 553-1670
www.sharontowers.com

Located in the popular SouthPark neighborhood, Sharon Towers is one of the oldest and most established retirement communities in the area, providing more than 200 apartments and cot-

tages for independent living and long-term care. It offers on-site recreational facilities, a library, and a bank.

SOUTHMINSTER INC.
8919 Park Rd.
(704) 551-6800
www.southminster.org

Founded in 1987 by two local churches, Southminster's independent-living area contains apartments and cottages equipped with emergency call systems and such options as housekeeping and maintenance. A full-service dining room, barber and beauty salon, general store, bank, wellness clinic, scheduled activities, and transportation are also available. The Health Center offers four levels of care—independent living, assisted living, skilled nursing care, and dementia care.

SUNRISE ASSISTED LIVING
Brighton Gardens of Charlotte
6000 Park South Dr.
(704) 643-1400

Sunrise on Providence, 5114 Providence Rd.
(704) 900-0126
www.sunriseassistedliving.com

Sunrise Assisted Living has served seniors in the Charlotte area for more than 25 years.

Charlotte offers a range of helpful services for seniors and their families. Just 1 Call is a service of Mecklenburg County government and has information and referrals about government, nonprofit, and private services for aging and disabled adults. The service also is available in Spanish. For details, call (704) 432-1111 or go to www.just1call.org.

WESTMINSTER TOWERS
1330 India Hook Rd., Rock Hill, SC
(803) 328-5000, (800) 345-6026

Opened in 1989 and since remodeled, Westminster Towers is a not-for-profit community of Westminster Presbyterian Church. It was the first retirement community in South Carolina to earn accreditation through the Continuing Care Accreditation Commission. Retirees can choose a studio, one-bedroom, or two-bedroom apartment in the independent-living community, or move to the assisted-living manor or nursing-care facility, if needed. Amenities include housekeeping, prepared meals, an indoor heated swimming pool, a fitness facility, and planned outings and events.

WILORA LAKE HEALTH CARE CENTER
6001 Wilora Lake Rd.
(704) 563-2922
Located on a 14-acre campus off Albemarle Road, the Wilora Lake Health Care Center is a 120-bed nursing center offering all levels of care, including a post–acute care unit and a specialized dementia unit with 20 beds. Open since October 1995, Wilora Lake offers its residents a full continuum of care.

WILORA LAKE LODGE
6053 Wilora Lake Rd.
(704) 537-8848
www.arclp.com
Developed by Crosland Properties in 1987 and now operated by American Retirement Corporation, Wilora Lake offers 136 private apartments for independent retirement living. Catering to active seniors, it provides amenities such as housekeeping, dining, 24-hour security, and transportation. Access to coordinated health care is available. Assisted-living services are available at the Cove at Wilora Lake on-site.

The Senior Grapevine is an e-mail bulletin reporting on senior-related activities and events in the Charlotte area. Developed by the Better Business Bureau Consumer Foundation, the Carriage Club, and Home Instead Senior Care, the electronic newsletter is free by signing up at www.seniorgrapevine.org.

SENIOR CENTERS AND SERVICES

To satisfy this rapidly growing age group, the Charlotte area offers a variety of services and publications.

CHARLOTTE-MECKLENBURG SENIOR CENTERS INC.
Tyvola Senior Center
2225 Tyvola Rd.
(704) 522-6222

NORTH MECKLENBURG SENIOR CENTER
18731 West Catawba Ave., Cornelius
(704) 892-4041

WEST SIDE SENIOR SERVICES
Bette Rae Thomas Center
2921 Tuckaseegee Rd.
(704) 393-7333

SHAMROCK CENTER
3925 Willow Farrow Rd.
(704) 531-6900
www.cmseniorcenters.org
With four locations, Charlotte-Mecklenburg Senior Centers Inc. provides a broad range of services and programs for all adults age 55 and older. Seniors can sign up for programs in computers, dance, art, foreign language, and fitness, and go on trips, play bridge, find a job, volunteer, and take educational seminars. The centers also can arrange for nutritious low-cost meals to be delivered daily, for visits to the homebound elderly, and for assistance in caring for grandchildren. The Shamrock Center in northeast Charlotte tailors its programs to that area's growing ethnic and multicultural population.

COUNCIL ON AGING
1609 East Fifth St.
(704) 527-8807
Funded by the county and the United Way, the Council on Aging acts as a resource center,

Senior Services—Phone Index

Adult Care and Share Center	(704) 567-2700
Centralina Area Agency on Aging	(704) 372-2416
Community Care Service Center	(704) 384-7460
Council on Aging	(704) 527-8807
CPCC Continuing Education	(704) 330-4223
Family Outreach Adult Day Care	(704) 333-2033
Friendship Trays	(704) 333-9229
Health Department	(704) 336-4700
Mecklenburg Co. Tax Administrator:	
Property tax exemption for the elderly	(704) 336-2813
Mental Health Services	(704) 358-2700
Programs for Accessible Living	(704) 537-0550
Special Transportation Services:	
Handicapped	(704) 336-2637
Transportation assistance (county)	(704) 336-4547

clearinghouse, and advocacy group for seniors. The council offers workshops, conferences, and educational programs for and about seniors.

LONG-TERM OMBUDSMAN PROGRAM
1300 Baxter St.
(704) 372-2416
www.centralina.org
This program is made up of regional ombudsmen and volunteer advocates from nine counties who work to protect the rights of those living in nursing homes, rest homes, and family-care homes. They are also available to answer any questions about long-term care and provide information on the options available.

MECKLENBURG COUNTY SENIOR CITIZEN NUTRITION PROGRAM
301 Billingsley Rd.
(704) 336-4877
www.charmeck.org
This program offers on-site meals as well as social interaction and activities in 20 different locations.

It also provides home-delivered meals and transportation services.

i Want to further your education? The Senior Scholars is a nonprofit group that offers weekly programs designed to stimulate intellectual, cultural, and spiritual growth. The group meets at 10 a.m. Tues at Myers Park Baptist Church. For information, call (704) 376-4201 or visit www.seniorscholars.net.

RETIRED SENIOR VOLUNTEER PROGRAM (RSVP)
2225 Tyvola Rd.
(704) 522-6222
www.cmseniorcenters.org
This special program is geared toward placing volunteers aged 60 and over in meaningful positions in nonprofit and public organizations. Volunteer positions are available all over the county in local hospitals, the American Red Cross, and libraries and museums. RSVP is unique in that it

reimburses its volunteers for mileage and meals and offers liability and accident insurance.

RETIREMENT LIFESTYLES
(888) 742-7362
www.retiresouth.net
Whether you already live in the Carolinas or you're thinking of moving here, *Retirement Lifestyles* highlights the best places in the south for active older adults. The free quarterly magazine based in Charlotte also publishes articles on senior lifestyles and interests.

SHEPHERD'S CENTER OF CHARLOTTE, INC.
P.O. Box 6052, Charlotte 28207
(704) 365-1995
www.shepherdscharlotte.org

With offices at Myers Park Baptist Church, the Shepherd's Center is an interfaith organization sponsored by churches and synagogues that serves older persons with or without religious affiliation. It promotes the concept of able people of retirement age learning and enjoying life and assisting their peers who need help to stay in their own homes. Services include small home repairs, medical transportation, grocery shopping, travel, seminars, and computer loans.

THE VOLUNTEER CENTER
301 South Brevard St.
(704) 371-6251
www.uwcentralcarolinas.org
Call the Volunteer Center to learn more about the wide variety of opportunities for seniors to become involved in the community.

MEDIA

Charlotte's traditional media landscape, once dotted with intriguing outlets and colorful characters, has become a bit homogenized in the new millennium. Long gone are favorites like weekly newspaper The Leader, and AM radio station Big Ways, both owned by renegade Stan Kaplan, who once buried a large cache of money in town and had thousands following his cryptic clues to its whereabouts and digging holes all over the Queen City.

Change has certainly come to the 25th-largest media market in the United States with 2.6 million people, and much of that is being driven by the electronic age. Our daily newspaper, *The Charlotte Observer,* is shrinking and putting more resources into its online efforts, while our primary cable system provides a 24-hour local and regional news channel. Local television news devotes copious amounts of time to the weather, while once-robust sports departments are relegated to a minute or two to attempt to cover a growing major-league sports market. Once popular publications like the *Lake Norman Times, Ballantyne Magazine, Charlotte Taste,* and the right-leaning *Rhinoceros Times* have gone under.

Alternatively, a wide range of niche media have surfaced, speaking to targeted audiences in new and creative ways. The Internet and wireless technology continue to alter how we access media, and that will no doubt continue. Of course some people, like yourself, will still turn to time-honored avenues like this printed guidebook to receive information.

Entries in this chapter are alphabetical by media type. Listings are located in Charlotte unless otherwise noted.

DAILY NEWSPAPERS

CHARLOTTE OBSERVER
600 South Tryon St.
(704) 358-5000
www.charlotteobserver.com
Founded in 1886, the Charlotte Observer is the largest daily newspaper in the Carolinas and 46th largest in the country with a paid circulation of 167,546 daily and 226,030 on Sun. The *Observer* is a Pulitzer Prize–winning paper that was sold as part of the Knight-Ridder chain in 2006 to the McClatchy Company.

Generally speaking, the *Observer* leans slightly left. It is criticized by the region's large number of conservatives for what they consider to be an overly liberal bias, while proponents argue the paper is fair and provides accurate coverage and hard-hitting investigations of community issues. There's no question the *Observer* has focused

attention on worthwhile causes over the years, from substandard workplace conditions in the poultry industry to government corruption to safety issues in NASCAR.

The strength of the Big O has forever been its ability to convey "what Charlotte is" to readers. There's always been a sense of place in the newsroom. You see that today in the words of columnists like Tommy Tomlinson, Dannye Powell, and Tom Sorensen, and the features of talented writers like David Perlmutt, Karen Garloch, Ron Green Jr., Stella Hopkins, and Bruce Henderson. Jim Morrill is excellent on the political beat, as is Mark Washburn, who covers the media and writes humorously biting columns. Olivia Fortson ably covers Charlotte's social circles, while veteran Joe Depriest brings a tear to the eye or a warmth to the heart when he captures the everyday tales of our fellow citizens in the western Piedmont. On Sun, John Bordsen produces a superb travel section focused heavily on the Carolinas and surrounding destinations. Photojournalism remains a strength as well.

Visitors and locals alike find Friday's CLT section handy with coverage of weekend movies, art, theater, concerts, restaurants, and family activities. Regional sections cover the Lake Norman area, Cabarrus County, Gaston County, Union County, and York County, S.C.

Like all newspapers, the *Observer* is losing circulation and ad revenue. The Great Recession accelerated both. Several rounds of McClatchy-mandated layoffs have taken their toll on the newsroom, as well as the advertising, printing, and circulation departments. Some media insiders are concerned the newsroom is becoming top-heavy by jettisoning reporters and news-gatherers while retaining many editors and upper management. Others say the newspaper is faring as well as can be expected in trying times. A lot of time and resources are being invested in the paper's Web site, www.charlotteobserver.com, as the *Observer* looks to the future in an uncertain media landscape.

For now, newsstand price is 75 cents daily and $1.50 Sun. Annual subscriptions are $171.

NONDAILY NEWSPAPERS

CAROLINA WEEKLY NEWSPAPERS
South office: 1421-C Orchard Lake Dr.
(704) 849-2261

North office: 501 S. Old Statesville Rd.
(704) 766-2100
www.carolinaweeklynewspapers.com
A growing force on the Charlotte media scene, Carolina Weekly Newspapers started in 2002 by publishing a free, tabloid-sized paper called *South Charlotte Weekly*, which evolved into the *Charlotte Weekly*. As that community-focused paper grew, the company launched free weeklies in other parts of the city, and also purchased existing weeklies like the *Huntersville Herald* and the *Mountain Island Monitor*.

Today, Carolina Weekly is a conglomerate of six papers serving South Charlotte, Huntersville/

Lake Norman, Union County, Matthews-Mint Hill, Mountain Island, and University City. The company is led by two managing editors: Regan White, a feisty Yale graduate in her late 20s known for her weekly column, "Regan's Rant," and Frank DeLoache, a respected industry veteran who's held upper-level positions at the *Charlotte Observer* and *Salisbury Post*. DeLoache oversees the three northern publications, while White handles the three southern publications.

In general, the papers provide local news and features, with sections on schools, restaurants, faith, arts and entertainment, sports, community announcements, event listings, and classifieds. Free at area racks.

CATHOLIC NEWS AND HERALD
1123 Church St.
(704) 370-3333
www.charlottediocese.org
Some 50,000 Charlotte-area Catholic parishioners receive this weekly newspaper published 44 times yearly. The *News and Herald* reprints articles and features from an online Catholic news service and covers regional stories concerning Catholic issues and interests in western North Carolina. Cost of the direct-mail newspaper is assessed through the church.

CHARLOTTE BUSINESS JOURNAL
1100 South Tryon St., Ste. 100
(704) 973-1100
www.bizjournals.com/charlotte
Part of the Charlotte-based American City Business Journals empire, the *Charlotte Business Journal* arrived in 1986. Publisher Kevin Pitts leads a hard-hitting news staff that provides the business community with the latest business news and interesting in-depth articles. Anything business or economy related is covered in this tabloid-sized journal, mailed weekly to 12,767 subscribers. You'll also find regular columns by local business people on their area of expertise. Issues are available for $1.50 at racks; annual subscriptions are $94 and include the popular *Book of Lists*.

CHARLOTTE JEWISH NEWS
5007 Providence Rd.
(704) 944-6765
This monthly newspaper reaches 4,000 readers through local synagogues and temples. Founded in 1979, it covers issues, events, and announcements in the Jewish community.

CHARLOTTE POST
1531 Camden Rd.
(704) 376-0496
www.thecharlottepost.com
Considered the "Voice of the Black Community," the *Charlotte Post* is a weekly newspaper that has serviced an African-American readership since 1878. The *Post* is published every Thurs and has expanded to cover a 50-mile radius around Charlotte. It has a solid reputation in the community and reaches about 89,700 readers. Cost is $1 on newsstands, or $40 for an annual subscription, or $60 for a two-year subscription.

CREATIVE LOAFING
1000 Seaboard St., Ste. C-2
(704) 522-8334
www.charlotte.creativeloafing.com
Creative Loafing is a weekly publication with a circulation of 58,000. Available every Wed, it is free and distributed through boxes located throughout the area. Although primarily an entertainment newspaper, it carries on the tradition of alternative papers with a different perspective on politics, business, and the arts scene. *Creative Loafing*'s personals are always a hot topic of conversation.

EL PROGRESO HISPANO
756 Tyvola Rd., Ste. 102
(704) 529-6624
www.elprogresohispano.com
The first Spanish-language newspaper in the Carolinas, this 16-year-old newspaper publishes every two weeks. With 32,000 readers, *El Progreso Hispano* covers international, national, and local news, with features on religion, restaurants, and entertainment. Free; available on racks in Charlotte and surrounding counties.

LA NOTICIA
5936 Monroe Rd.
(704) 568-6966
www.lanoticia.com
The most widely read Spanish language newspaper in the Carolinas, *La Noticia* reaches 88,000 readers each Wed. The 13-year-old publication covers local, state, national, and international news, and provides information about immigration, family events, business, and entertainment. *Ventana Magica*, a children's magazine, also is included with the paper. Free on newsstands; $78 annual subscription.

LAKE WYLIE PILOT
8 Executive Court, Lake Wylie, SC
(803) 831-8166
www.lakewyliepilot.com
Owned by the McClatchy Company, this weekly community newspaper delivers news to the Lake Wylie region every Tues. The *Pilot* is mailed directly to some local neighborhoods, including River Hills, Lake Wylie Woods, River Pointe, Royal Oaks, and The Palisades. Copies of the *Pilot* are 50 cents and in racks located throughout Steele Creek, Tega Cay, Belmont, and Lake Wylie. A subscription to the paper is $25 per year. The newspaper was founded in 1984 as *Lake Wylie Magazine* and has a circulation of 7,000.

MATTHEWS RECORD
130 Library Lane
(704) 443-0017
www.matthewsrecord.com
This weekly paper, published on Thurs, covers all the local happenings of Matthews such as town council meetings, sports, and human interest stories. The newspaper is independently owned and has a circulation of about 18,000. Free in Matthews.

MECKLENBURG TIMES
1611 East Seventh St.
(704) 377-6221
www.mecktimes.com
For many decades, the *Mecklenburg Times* was a court and business publication that gave pub-

lic information on topics such as real estate transactions, residential and commercial building permits, new corporations, foreclosure notices, bankruptcies, and tax liens. In recent years, it has expanded to feature news articles and feature articles on issues affecting the business climate of Charlotte.

Published every Tues and Fri, a typical issue has about 10 pages of news and editorial content, followed by 40-50 pages of public notices. The *Mecklenburg Times* is available for $1 on newsstands and $81.19 for a 12-month subscription.

Q-NOTES
P.O. Box 221841, Charlotte, 28222
(704) 531-9988
www.goqnotes.com
Q-Notes is a lesbian, gay, bisexual, and transgendered (LGBT) newspaper that has been serving Charlotte and the Carolinas since 1986 with news, features, entertainment, lifestyle and political reporting, and advertising. The newspaper is free at dozens of locations in Charlotte and throughout the Carolinas. Published every two weeks, *Q-Notes* has a circulation of 10,000.

MAGAZINES

BUSINESS NORTH CAROLINA
5605 Seventy-seven Center Dr., Ste. 101
(704) 523-6987
www.businessnc.com
Similar to a statewide *Forbes* or *Fortune,* this business monthly provides a good overview of North Carolina's business trends. Corporate executives and deep-pocketed bosses are most often featured, but small-business owners are also covered, especially if they bring something quirky or unique to the marketplace. *Business North Carolina* is not afraid to take on controversial topics, often with in-depth cover stories. Some say the magazine tends to focus on what's wrong with commerce in the Old North State. Independently owned, the magazine distributes 30,000 copies. *Business North Carolina* has won more than 40 reporting and design awards from the Associa-

tion of Area Business Publications. Cost is $3.95 per issue or $30 for an annual subscription.

CAROLINA BRIDE
600 South Tryon St.
(704) 358-5910
www.carolinabride.com
Now a division of the *Charlotte Observer,* this quarterly publication founded in 1991 gives brides-to-be resource information in a seven-county area. Weddings of local celebrity couples and everyday Joes and Janes are also featured. Free at more than 400 locations, including bridal salons, jewelers, and select retailers; $3.95 at local bookstores and Harris Teeter supermarkets.

CHARLOTTE MAGAZINE
309 East Morehead St., Ste. 50
(704) 335-7181
www.charlottemagazine.com
This magazine is more in-depth and "newsy" than a typical city lifestyle publication. Articles examine politicians and business leaders, delving into both the good and bad of what transpires in the Queen City.

That's not to say it doesn't have plenty of what makes a city magazine a city magazine. Readers find concise and accurate information on how to get the most out of living in Charlotte. Restaurant reviews and the dining guide are first-rate, and there's great stuff on shopping, fashion, and travel. Circulation is 40,000 a month; the magazine also publishes *Charlotte Home & Garden*. Price is $3.95 on newsstands; $19.95 annual subscription.

CHARLOTTE PARENT
2125 Southend Dr., Ste. 253
(704) 344-1980
www.charlotteparent.com
Founded in 1987, this complimentary parent- and child-oriented publication offers information essential for parents raising children. Published monthly, it features articles written for and by parents, as well as a calendar of family-friendly events. *Charlotte Parent,* which also holds free summer camps and activity fairs, has a circula-

tion of 55,475. It is available in area supermarkets, schools, libraries, specialty shops, bookstores, and medical offices.

CHARLOTTE LIVING
2010 South Tryon St.
(704) 375-3286
www.charlottelivingmagazine.com
Formerly a quarterly magazine called *Charlotte Place,* this publication has evolved into *Charlotte Living,* an upscale lifestyle glossy published six times per year. It focuses on people, events, fashion, food, shopping, architecture, regional travel, and history. Heidi Billotto, a well-known local food writer, headlines the culinary coverage. Circulation is 80,000 per issue.

Price is $5.95 on newsstands and $19.95 for a one-year subscription.

ELEVATE MAGAZINE
201 West Morehead St., Ste. 100
(704) 716-2005
www.elevatecharlotte.com
Contemporary and cutting-edge, this pocket-sized monthly magazine is geared toward the 20-something to 30-something set.

Elevate covers culture, fashion, entertainment, and lifestyle, and bills itself as the source for everything cool in Charlotte. *Elevate* is a great resource to find out what's happening in Charlotte nightlife and to check out photos of pretty people from various destinations out on the town. Free on racks.

LAKE NORMAN CURRENTS
P.O. Box 1676, Cornelius
(704) 749-8788
www.lncurrents.com
Lake Norman Currents, a glossy, full-color publication, debuted in 2008 and is a monthly magazine devoted to the upscale lifestyle along the banks of Charlotte's largest lake. It features an excellent wine column by Trevor Burton of Mooresville.

Circulation is 30,000 and is available for free at area businesses, or for $25 for an annual subscription.

LAKE NORMAN MAGAZINE
20916 Torrence Chapel Rd., Cornelius
(704) 892-7936
www.surfthelake.com
A full-color, glossy monthly owned by the *Charlotte Observer,* this publication covers all the action on the lake from regattas to real estate. The free, 40,000-circulation magazine is filled with informative, interesting articles and great photography. Distributed free in the four-county area surrounding Lake Norman. Annual subscriptions also available for $20.

LITTLE ONES
P.O. Box 49586, Charlotte 28277
(704) 236-4490
www.littleonesmagazine.com
The brainchild of two local moms, *Little Ones* is a quarterly glossy published in February, May, August, and November. Written for parents, from expecting to experienced, the attractive magazine covers fashion, books, wellness, organization, child care and schools, parties and playtime, and informative features on topics such as playgroups, local excursions, and road trips. The magazine also is a good resource for local kid-friendly businesses. Free on racks, $12 mailed subscription.

MI GENTE MAGAZINE
4801 Independence Blvd., Ste. 604
(704) 531-6633
www.migenteweb.com
Published every Mon, this newsprint magazine founded in 2002 has a circulation of 25,000. The Spanish-language *Mi Gente*—My People—covers local, regional, and national news for Latin Americans, as well as features on culture, restaurants, art, and education. Free on racks.

PIEDMONT LAKES PILOT
801 East Morehead St.
(704) 372-3131
www.pilotmedia.us
Boaters, fishermen, and outdoor enthusiasts look to this informative guide for reference maps, feature stories, restaurant reviews, and insight on

waterfront communities on Lake Norman, Lake Wylie, and Mountain Island Lake among others. Published six times a year. Free at grocery and convenience stores, marine service centers, and restaurants; $15 subscription for six issues per year.

PRIDE MAGAZINE
312 West Trade St., Ste. 702
(704) 375-9553
www.pridemagazine.net
This high-end, bimonthly publication focuses on African-American social issues, economic concerns, and topics concerning home, health, and the arts. The magazine also sponsors the annual black-tie Pride Awards and the Sunset Jazz Festival. Free on racks, $13.25 mailed subscription.

RETIREMENT LIFESTYLES
P.O. Box 11968, Charlotte 28220
(888) 742-7362
www.retiresouth.net
Retirement Lifestyles highlights great locations in North and South Carolina for folks considering retirement. Its 40,000 readers learn more about small towns and big cities, educational and recreation activities for seniors, and communities that cater to active older adults. Free at visitor centers, chambers of commerce, and welcome centers; $24 subscription for four issues per year.

SKIRT! MAGAZINE
1700 Camden Rd., Ste. 101
(704) 334-4100
www.charlotte.skirt.com
Started in Charleston and Columbia, South Carolina, in 1994, *Skirt!* now publishes in about 30 cities nationwide, including Charlotte. This newsprint monthly celebrates the variety and diversity of women's lives and interests through unconventional and unpredictable personal essays. Topics include work, play, family, creativity, style, health, wealth, body, and soul. Free on racks.

SOUTHPARK MAGAZINE
600 South Tryon St.
(704) 358-5936
www.southparkmagazine.com

Published monthly under the guidance of editor Leigh Dyer, this upscale glossy magazine offers a look into fine living, with profiles of Charlotte's movers and shakers, luxury travel pieces, features on exclusive homes, and pictorials. There are also columns on entertaining, art, restaurants, cooking, and books, plus *Swirl*, a monthly guide to Charlotte's best galas provided by *Charlotte Observer* social writer Olivia Fortson. *SouthPark* is owned by the *Observer* and has a circulation of 40,000. It is available free of charge at SouthPark Mall and racks in the area. Subscription is $14.95 annually.

TODAY'S CHARLOTTE WOMAN
5200 Park Rd., Ste. 111
(704) 521-6872
www.todayscharlottewoman.com
Published 12 times per year, this business and lifestyle magazine for Charlotte-area women features successful women, listings of professional and social meetings, how-to business articles, and sections on home and garden, books, fashion, travel, art and entertainment, and humor. The magazine as a distribution of 34,000; free at area grocery stores and other retailers and $20 for an annual subscription.

UPTOWN MAGAZINE
111 Central Ave., Ste. 310
(704) 944-0550
www.uptownclt.com
Uptown Magazine was started by Todd Trimakas after he tired of working in Charlotte's buttoned-down corporate world and wanted to do something more meaningful and vibrant. With no writing or publishing experience, most thought *Uptown Magazine* wouldn't last very long. That was 2005.

Uptown has found its niche with the trendy residents of the center city, and with those who march to the beat of a slightly different drummer. It's hip and edgy, and if you want to know who wrote the story you are reading, look around for a little box that says "words by . . ."

Trimakas has found his voice with a monthly column, particularly with an insightful piece in

2009 about the notion that print is dead. "I first heard this sort of thing three years ago when the representative of an online video firm . . . told us that our medium would be dead in a couple of years," Trimakas wrote. "Unfortunately, they are no longer in business."

The magazine also has essays and fashion shoots.

The magazine is mailed to about 10,000 Uptown residents; another 18,000 copies can be found on racks in Uptown, South End, NoDa, and Plaza-Midwood.

RADIO

Children's

WGFY 1480 AM
(704) 377-2223
Radio Disney affiliate playing high-energy pop music from the likes of the Jonas Brothers, Hilary Duff, Miley Cyrus, and Aly & AJ.

Christian, Gospel

WBZK 980 AM
(803) 325-1533
www.wbzk.com
This Rock Hill–based station has converted from Hispanic format to contemporary praise and worship music.

WHVN 1240 AM
(704) 596-12400
Christian talk and Spoken Word programs. Simultaneous broadcasts are on WAVO 1150 AM and WCGC 1270 AM.

WRCM 91.9 FM
(704) 821-9293
www.newlife91.com
Adult contemporary Christian with no commericals.

Classical

WDAV 89.9 FM
(704) 894-8900
www.wdav.org

Twenty-four-hour classical station sponsored by Davidson College. NPR newscasts are broadcast at 8 a.m., noon, and 4 p.m.

Contemporary

WBAV 101.9 FM
(704) 342-2644
www.v1019.com
Adult contemporary and oldies geared to African-American listeners.

WKQC 104.7 FM
(704) 570-1047
www.star1047.com
Billed as Charlotte's cool music station, K104.7 plays hits from Sheryl Crow to Elton John. Continuous Christmas music November and December.

WLNK 107.9 FM
(704) 374-3500
www.1079thelink.com
Tune into syndicated morning team Bob & Sheri for hilarious chat rooms, celebrity interviews, and lots of laughs. Matt & Ramona spice up the afternoon drive with wacky tales, listener tirades, and many interesting guests.

WLYT 102.9 FM
(704) 570-1029
www.wlyt.com
Continuous "lite" adult contemporary—the kind of make-everybody-happy music many offices play.

Country

WKKT 96.9 FM
(704) 570-9690
www.wkktfm.com
All-American country with Paul Schadt on the morning drive.

WSOC 103.7 FM
(704) 570-9762
www.wsocfm.com
Charlotte's top-rated country station with NASCAR coverage and 24-in-a-row tunes. Rob Tanner

in the morning has emerged as the top country morning show host in the market.

Foreign Language

WGSP 1310 AM
(704) 442-7277
Mexican regional.

WNOW 1030 AM
(704) 665-9355
www.wnow.com
Catering to Charlotte's growing Latino community, this station carries Mexican regional talk and music and draws many listeners from age 18 to 30.

Modern Rock/Alternative

WEND 106.5 FM
(704) 570-1065
www.1065.com
Cutting-edge contemporary rock station, live concert sponsor, and staunch supporter of local bands. The comedy-based Bob & Tom show from 6 to 10 a.m. has been syndicated out of Indianapolis since 1995. Local listeners can join the Freeloader Club for area details. Retro new wave 80s on Sun mornings with The Wiz.

News/Talk

WBT 1110AM/99.3 FM
(704) 570-1110
www.wbt.com
In 1922, WBT became the first commercial radio station licensed in the Southeast with a strength of 100 watts. It now operates at 50,000 watts and can be heard at night up and down the East Coast. The format has varied over the years but is now news talk with a right-leaning lineup of: Rush Limbaugh, Neal Boortz, and well-regarded local personalities such as Keith Larson, John Hancock, Pete Kaliner, and Tara Servatius. The station currently has the rights to broadcast Carolina Panthers games in Charlotte.

Public Radio

WFAE 90.7 FM
(704) 549-9323
www.wfae.org
National Public Radio station featuring Morning Edition, the Diane Rehm Show, Fresh Air with Terry Gross, Garrison Keillor, and Charlotte Talks, a one-hour, locally produced talk show discussing politics, growth, culture, the arts, social issues, and human interest.

R & B

WBIT 96.1 FM
(704) 338-9600
www.charlottesbeat.com
Billed as Charlotte's party station, 96.1 The Beat plays hip-hop, rap, Top 40, and urban contemporary. Also features the A. M. Mayhem morning show led by Brotha' Fred.

WPEG 97.9 FM
(704) 342-2644
www.power98fm.com
Longtime urban contemporary station is No. 1 for blazin' hip-hop and R & B.

WQNC 92.7 FM
(704) 358-0211
A classic R & B station; features Tom Joyner's nationally syndicated morning show.

Rock

WRFX 99.7 FM
(704) 570-9739
www.wrfx.com
Classic rock station with a Southern tilt, and home to the nationally syndicated morning team of good old boys John Boy & Billy.

WXRC 95.7 FM
(704) 527-0957
www.957theride.com
Independent rock radio that focuses mostly on classic rock. The Ride will play deep cuts in addition to hits, and has a regular selection of live recordings from various artists.

Sports

WFNZ 610 AM/1660 AM
(704) 570-9610
www.wfnz.com
Charlotte's top sports talk station featuring Prime-time with the Packman, Charlotte 49ers and Wake Forest games, and an afternoon show with former Panthers Frank Garcia and Brentson Buckner. Also airs syndicated sports shows and national game broadcasts.

Top 40

WNKS 95.1 FM
(704) 570-9595
www.kiss951.com
Popular Top 40 station with Ace & TJ in the morning. Plays range of music, from Akon and Beyoncé to the Black Eyed Peas and John Mayer. Other artists you will hear regularly are Pink, Taylor Swift, Kanye West, and Lady Gaga.

TELEVISION

NEWS 14 CAROLINA
316 East Morehead St.
(704) 973-5800
www.news14charlotte.com
The city's only 24-hour news station, News 14 Carolina is available on channel 14 to Time Warner Cable customers. Viewers get local, statewide, and national news, with a splash of international happenings. Also, weather forecasts six times an hour on the 1s, traffic updates, and lifestyle features. There are brief sports updates throughout the day, with a 30-minute sports show at 10 p.m. nightly. News 14 debuted in June 2002 and had separate operations in Greensboro and Raleigh. The three entities have now merged, with some programming locally generated in Charlotte, and some statewide programming originating from the other bureaus.

WAXN-64, INDEPENDENT
1901 North Tryon St.
(704) 338-9999
www.wsoctv.com/waxntv

WAXN (cable channel 10) features movies, sitcom reruns, talk shows, kids' programs, sports events, and Action News at 10 p.m. produced by sister station WSOC.

WBTV-3, CBS
One Julian Price Place
(704) 374-3500
www.wbtv.com
Started in 1949, WBTV (cable channel 2) is the oldest TV station in the Carolinas and one of the oldest CBS affiliates in the country. WBTV also is home to ACC football and basketball, as well as strong hometown sports coverage. The station is the only one in Charlotte with an Uptown studio.

WCCB-18, FOX
One Television Place
(704) 372-1800
www.foxcharlotte.com
WCCB (cable channel 11) features the Fox network's hit programs, talk shows, sitcom reruns, and Carolina Panthers NFL games. Local news broadcasts stand apart with a fast-paced, fun style geared toward a younger demographic. The station has a morning show, *Fox News Rising,* and an evening show called *The Edge* that is irreverent and sometimes controversial.

WCNC-36, NBC
1001 Wood Ridge Center Dr.
(704) 329-3636
www.nbc6.com
This NBC affiliate (cable channel 6) carries a full lineup of network programming, along with nightly local newscasts that are critically acclaimed but often trail in the ratings. WCNC produces hard-hitting investigative reports and is known for revealing poor sanitation ratings of local restaurants in a feature called "Eat, Drink and Be Wary." WCNC has developed a news partnership with the *Charlotte Observer* newspaper in which the two share content.

WJZY-46, THE CW
3501 Performance Rd.
(704) 398-0046
www.wjzy.com

Morning Show Mecca

Did you know Charlotte is a mecca of popular radio shows? Each weekday, millions of Americans can listen to syndicated shows originating right here in the Queen City.

Charlotte's morning kings are John Boy & Billy. These two wise-cracking—but lovable—good old boys started in the early 1980s on what was then WBCY 108 FM (now 107.9 The Link). After a brief split in the mid '80s, they reunited, caught fire, and jumped to WRFX 99.7 FM. They began syndicating in the 1990s, aided by the growing popularity of NASCAR. Today, they're on more than 75 radio stations across 21 states. You can hear John Boy & Billy from Myrtle Beach to Macon, from Tallahassee to Texarkana, and from Tupelo to Atlantic City.

Bob & Sheri are another in-demand duo who broadcast from Charlotte. Their morning show features Sheri as the savvy, urbane, and sarcastic female, while Bob is the likable, but bumbling, guy who's often the butt of Sheri's jokes. Since forming at 107.9 The Link in 1992, the Bob & Sheri Show has grown via syndication to more than 50 radio stations coast to coast, from Bangor, Maine, to Yuma, Arizona.

Ace & TJ on Kiss 95.1 are newer to the game. This funny, and often irreverent, odd couple started in 1998 and are syndicated to eight markets in seven states. This morning show is well-received along the Gulf Coast, which makes sense because both are Louisiana natives.

The Matt & Romona Show is an afternoon broadcast that also originates from 107.9 The Link. Geared toward the 25-44 female audience, the show focuses on current issues, male-female relationships, and interesting callers. Ramona usually has the last word, and it is syndicated to six stations scattered far and wide, from Minnesota to Vermont to Florida to Kansas.

Formerly a UPN station, WJZY (cable channel 8) became part of the CW in September 2006. Top shows include *One Tree Hill, America's Next Top Model, Gossip Girl, Smallville, Everybody Hates Chris,* and the new *Melrose Place.* Reruns of *Two and a Half Men* are also popular.

WMYT-55, MY NETWORK TV
3501 Performance Rd.
(704) 398-0046
www.wmyt12.com
Formerly the WB, WMYT (cable channel 12) is a newer network that features such primetime shows as *Are You Smarter Than a Fifth Grader? Deal or No Deal, The Unit,* and *WWE Smackdown.*

WSOC-9, ABC
1901 North Tryon St.
(704) 338-9999
www.wsoctv.com
WSOC (cable channel 4), is typically Charlotte's top-rated news station. This ABC affiliate ascended to the top of the local news ratings in the late 1980s and has stayed there pretty much ever since. Popular regular segments are "Action 9," a consumer advocate report, and "Whistle-Blower 9," which investigates government waste and wrongdoing. In recent years, WSOC has lost three of Charlotte's all-time most popular anchors—Debbie Faubion, Bill Walker, and Harold Johnson—to retirement, which could lead to shake-ups in the ratings.

i Retired Charlotte sportscaster Harold Johnson has thrown his hat into the political ring. Johnson was known as "the Big Guy" during three decades covering Charlotte sports, mostly for WSOC Channel 9, and hopes to use that name recognition to win the race for the 8th Congressional District's seat in the U.S. House of Representatives. If Johnson can advance out of the Republican primary, he will challenge incumbent Larry Kissell, a Democrat, in the fall of 2010.

WTVI-42, PBS
3242 Commonwealth Ave.
(704) 372-2442
www.wtvi.org

WTVI is one of three PBS stations in the Carolinas. Shown on cable channel 5, it regularly broadcasts meetings of the Mecklenburg Board of County Commissioners and the Charlotte-Mecklenburg School Board, plus it produces *Final Edition*, a weekly half-hour program that features a lively discussion of local events by area news- and businesspeople. The station also has a weekly business update program called *Carolina Business Review*.

Two other PBS stations, WUNG-58 (Cable Channel 13) and WNSC-30 (Cable Channel 15), also reach the Charlotte market.

INDEX

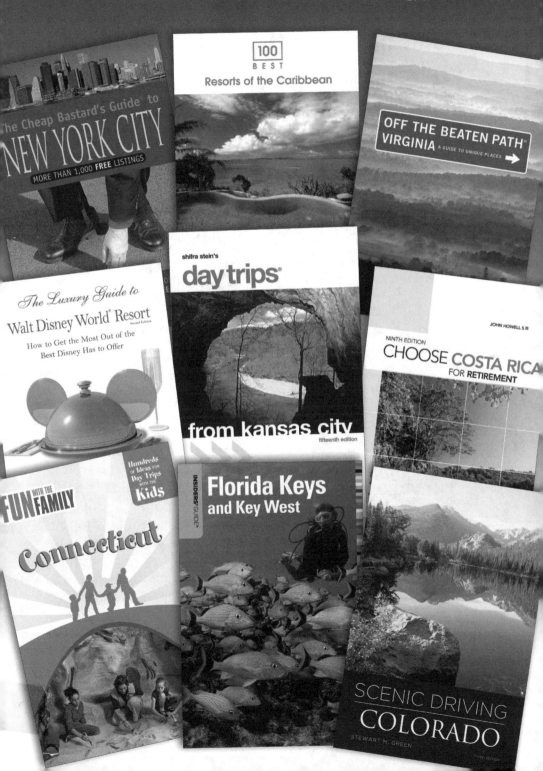